# FOUNDATIONS
# POST-KEYNES
# ECONOMIC ANAL

NEW DIRECTIONS IN MODERN ECONOMICS
Series Editor: Malcolm C. Sawyer, Professor of Economics,
University of Leeds

**New Directions in Modern Economics** presents a challenge to orthodox economic thinking. It focuses on new ideas emanating from radical traditions including post-Keynesian, Kaleckian, neo-Ricardian and Marxian. The books in the series do not adhere rigidly to any single school of thought but share an attempt to present a positive alternative to the conventional wisdom.

Post Keynesian Monetary Economics
New Approaches to Financial Modelling
*Edited by Philip Arestis*

Keynes's Principle of Effective Demand
*Edward J. Amadeo*

New Directions in Post-Keynesian Economics
*Edited by John Pheby*

Theory and Policy in Political Economy
Essays in Pricing. Distribution and Growth
*Edited by Philip Arestis and Yiannis Kitromilides*

Keynes's Third Alternative?
The Neo-Ricardian Keynesians and the Post Keynesians
*Amitava Krishna Dutt and Edward J. Amadeo*

Wages and Profits in the Capitalist Economy
The Impact of Monopolistic Power on Macroeconomic Performance in the USA and UK
*Andrew Henley*

Prices, Profits and Financial Structures
A Post-Keynesian Approach to Competition
*Gokhan Capoglu*

International Perspectives on Profitability and Accumulation
*Edited by Fred Moseley and Edward N. Wolff*

Mr Keynes and the Post Keynesians
Principles of Macroeconomics for a Monetary Production Economy
*Fernando J. Cardim de Carvalho*

The Economic Surplus in Advanced Economies
*John B. Davis*

Foundations of Post-Keynesian Economic Analysis
*Marc Lavoie*

The Post-Keynesian Approach to Economics
An Alternative Analysis of Economic Theory and Policy
*Philip Arestis*

# FOUNDATIONS OF POST-KEYNESIAN ECONOMIC ANALYSIS

**MARC LAVOIE**
*ASSOCIATE PROFESSOR*
*DEPARTMENT OF ECONOMICS*
*UNIVERSITY OF OTTAWA*

Edward Elgar

© Marc Lavoie 1992

All rights reserved. No part of this publication may be reproduced, stored in a retrieval system, or transmited in any form or by any means, electronic, mechanical, photocopying, recording, or otherwise without the prior permission of the publisher.

Published by
Edward Elgar Publishing Limited
Gower House
Croft Road
Aldershot
Hants GU11 3HR
England

Edward Elgar Publishing Company
Old Post Road
Brookfield
Vermont 05036
USA

A CIP catalogue record for this book is available from the British Library

A CIP catalogue record for this book is available from the US Library of Congress

Printed and bound in Great Britain by
Hartnolls Ltd, Bodmin, Cornwall

ISBN 1 85278 322 2
    1 85278 816 X (Paperback)

# Contents

*Preface* vii

1 The Need for an Alternative 1
  1.1 Objectives of the book 1
  1.2 Research programmes and all that 4
  1.3 Presuppositions of the neoclassical and post-classical paradigms 6
  1.4 The dominance of neoclassical economics 14
  1.5 Empirical studies and neoclassical economics 20
  1.6 The limits of neoclassical theory 26

2 Theory of Choice 42
  2.1 The distinction between risk and uncertainty 42
  2.2 Procedural rationality: rules and norms 50
  2.3 A theory of household choice 61
  2.4 An overview of the alternative 92

3 Theory of the Firm 94
  3.1 Features and domain of validity of the post-Keynesian firm 94
  3.2 The objectives of the firm 99
  3.3 The constraints on growth 105
  3.4 Cost curves and excess capacity 118
  3.5 Pricing theory 129
  3.6 Cost-plus prices and production prices 144

4 Credit and Money 149
  4.1 The monetary circuit 151
  4.2 The endogenous money supply 169
  4.3 Interest rates and liquidity preference 192
  4.4 The structural view of endogenous money 203
  4.5 Consequences 215

5  Effective Demand and Employment                                       217
   5.1  Characteristics of the post-Keynesian labour market              217
   5.2  The utilization function                                         225
   5.3  The simple macroeconomics of employment                          230
   5.4  Pricing, rates of utilization and profits                        255
   5.5  Two-sector models                                                275

6  Accumulation and Capacity                                             282
   6.1  Historical versus logical time                                   282
   6.2  The neo-Keynesian growth model: the inflationist version         284
   6.3  The Kaleckian growth model: the stagnationist version            297
   6.4  Doctrinal issues around the Kaleckian model                      327
   6.5  Finance and accumulation                                         347

7  Inflation                                                             372
   7.1  A typology of inflation                                          372
   7.2  Inductive reasons for inflation                                  379
   7.3  Permissive reasons for inflation                                 385
   7.4  A simple conflicting-claims model of inflation                   391
   7.5  Variants of the conflicting-claims model of inflation            405

8  Concluding Remarks                                                    422

*References*                                                             424
*Name Index*                                                             449
*Subject Index*                                                          455

# Preface

This book is designed for all those who would like to study post-Keynesian economics but do not know from where to start. In contrast to the mainstream, post-Keynesian economists have put little effort over the past 20 years into offering a condensed but comprehensive picture of their theories. It is sometimes difficult for neophytes to get a clear idea of what post-Keynesian economics is now all about. In my case, I remember finding extremely useful the survey of Alfred Eichner and Jan Kregel. Their article came out soon after I had been introduced to the work of Robinson, Kaldor and Pasinetti in the seminar for honours' students given by T.K. Rymes at Carleton University.

For close to ten years I have taught a course in post-Keynesian economics entitled 'Money and effective demand'. The material presented in the course constitutes the core of the present book. For this reason, it is mainly intended for readers who are finishing their undergraduate studies or who are in the midst of their graduate training. I hope that, along with others such as Alfred Eichner and Peter Reynolds who have proposed a synthesis, I have helped in filling a void and convinced many young minds that post-Keynesian economics is an avenue full of promises.

I am afraid that my post-Keynesian friends and colleagues will find little new in the book. The novelty mainly lies in clearing up matters and in linking together ideas that otherwise are scattered in very diverse fields. Still, I hope that many of these colleagues will read the book, and discover that their own work is part of a larger and coherent tradition, as I have attempted to demonstrate in the following chapters. Largely because of the constraint of space, but also because a simplified presentation was not possible, I have not been able to deal with the consequences of an open economy, except in the chapter on money. I believe this to be the main drawback of the book.

The idea of the volume first came to me following discussions with Alfred Eichner. After his death, I put the idea aside for a while until I saw an invitation by Edward Elgar to submit outlines of manuscripts. I originally submitted two proposals. I am now very grateful that he would only accept one! I cannot imagine myself being compelled to write a second book right away, having spent a whole sabbatical glued to a word processor.

The various menial tasks involved in writing the book were alleviated by a research grant from the Social Sciences and Humanities Research Council of Canada, which also provided travel support. As will be abundantly clear from the references, the works of a large number of economists have inspired my view of economics. Special thanks go to more senior colleagues who have visited my department over the past 12 years, providing encouragement and intellectual stimulation to myself and Mario Seccareccia, with whom I have had countless discussions about economics in general and my manuscript in particular.

Various people have read parts of the book, or have provided answers to my questions. These colleagues are in no way responsible for the errors that may remain. I wish to thank Mario Seccareccia (chapters 1, 2, 3, 7, 8), Sheila Dow (chapter 1), Lex Hoodguin (first half of chapter 2), Peter Earl (second half of chapter 2), Basil Moore (chapter 4), Nancy Wulwick (the part on Okun's law in chapter 5), Amitava Dutt (chapter 6), and Anwar Shaikh and John McCombie (the part on Verdoon's law in chapter 6). I am also very grateful to the editorial staff of Edward Elgar for their extensive and minute revision of the manuscript.

Finally I wish to thank my spouse, Camille. While the Research Council provided the money, Camille supplied time, the only truly scarce commodity according to my *regretté* colleague, Jacques Henry. She kept away my two- and three-year-old children when I was sitting in front of the computer screen, and she made sure that she would not deliver our third son before the last chapter had been finished.

MARC LAVOIE

# 1. The Need for an Alternative

## 1.1 OBJECTIVES OF THE BOOK

The major objective of the book is to provide a convenient synthesis of post-Keynesian economics, by showing that it constitutes a coherent set of theories that can provide an alternative to the dominant neoclassical paradigm. It is my belief that post-Keynesian economics can be presented within a framework that is just as coherent as the neoclassical framework, and that as a consequence it can offer a viable alternative to those who are disenchanted with orthodox economics. To that effect, it will be shown that microeconomic foundations can be associated with post-Keynesian economics, and that these are consistent with its macroeconomics. My purpose is thus identical to that of Eichner (1986a, p. 3), who wanted to present post-Keynesian theory 'as an integral whole, thereby demonstrating that it is just as comprehensive and coherent as the neoclassical synthesis'.

It must be recognized from the outset that the term *post-Keynesian* itself is rather vague and has been used to define different sorts of economics and economists. As a first approximation, I shall define as post-Keynesians those economists who are extending and generalizing the seminal ideas of the unorthodox Cambridge economists of the 1950s, most notably the ideas of Joan Robinson, Richard Kahn and Nicholas Kaldor. Of course, there were other famous non-orthodox economists in Cambridge in those days, such as Maurice Dobb and Piero Sraffa. They will be considered, however, only to the extent that they influenced the economics of the above-named authors, or to the extent that their economics can be meshed with those of the post-Keynesians. Furthermore it is also clear that these Cambridge authors were influenced by other contemporary or earlier economists. In particular the economics of Keynes was the obvious inspiration of Kaldor and Robinson.

It has now become evident, however, that, if the economics of Kalecki was not initially recognized to be of the same paramount influence, it was in the end identified as a preferable foundation for an alternative to neoclassical theory. This is, for instance, the opinion of Bhaduri (1986, p. ix), who believes that the radical content of Keynesianism must be learned from Kalecki. Similarly, Dostaler (1988, p. 134) maintains that 'Kalecki can be considered the real founder of post-Keynesian theory'. Even those who contributed to the development of the Keynesian revolution have passed similar judgements. Kaldor has noted that 'Kalecki's original model of unemployment equilibrium, which takes monopolistic competition as its starting point, is clearly superior to Keynes's' (1983a, p. 15). When Kaldor (1983b, p. 2) describes the principle of effective demand in his later assessments, he is using a presentation akin to Keynes's *Treatise on Money*, which resembles that of Kalecki, rather than that of the *General Theory*. It can be said that, over time, both Kaldor and Robinson turned away from Keynes and towards Kalecki. Robinson has argued that, because 'Kalecki was free from the remnants of old-fashioned theory which Keynes had failed to throw off', he was better able 'to weave the analysis of imperfect competition and of effective demand together and it was this that opened up the way for what goes under the name of post-Keynesian theory' (1977, pp. 14–15). The economics of Kalecki are not, as Keynes (1973, xii, p. 831) once thought, 'esoteric abracadabra'.

We shall later understand the reasons for these judgements on the importance of Kalecki, as we shall become better equipped to pinpoint how post-Keynesian economics should be defined. We shall see that several streams of non-orthodox economics can be regrouped under the same umbrella, notably the post-Keynesians, the neo-Ricardians, the (Marxist) Radicals and the Institutionalists. Whereas Sawyer (1989) refers to the combination of those same four schools of thought as radical political economy, I shall call the common elements of these four approaches the post-classical research programme, a term used by others in the same context (Henry, 1982; Eichner 1986a, p. 3).

As has been pointed out by Pasinetti (1990, p. 16), those Cambridge economists who attempted to revolutionize economics did not spend much time trying to build bridges between themselves. Each one of them was too jealous of his or her intellectual independence. This, however, should not deter us from trying to link together contributions which were substantially different but that were made in the same spirit. It is our task to generalize them and find extensions. One of the objectives of this book is to show that a synthesis of the various streams of post-classical economics as well as of the various contributions to post-Keynesian economics is possible. It is acknowledged that some of the contributions cannot be easily integrated, or that some of the authors may make strange bedfellows. Rather than following the idiosyncrasies of one or the other, the task which I have assigned myself is to present the views of a sort of representative post-Keynesian. Although none of the concerns of the neo-Ricardians for multi-sector analysis will be dealt with here, I believe that the theoretical framework of the representative post-Keynesian should be strongly influenced by many of the insights brought forth by the neo-Ricardian school.

The position adopted here, then, differs from that of Hamouda and Harcourt (1988) who believe that a search for a coherent vision is a futile endeavour. My position is closer to that of Eichner and Kregel (1975) who called for the adoption of a new paradigm unifying the main neo-Ricardian and post-Keynesian concepts. Like Kregel (1973, p. xv), I believe that it is possible to reconstruct political economy by linking Keynes's theory of effective demand, set in the short run and in a monetary economy, to that of the classical authors, who were concerned with income distribution and accumulation in the long period. Note that this was also the belief of Robinson, who, even after she had denied the importance of the capital controversies, argued that the task of post-Keynesians was to reconcile Keynes and Sraffa and claimed that post-Keynesian theory had 'a general framework of long- and short-period analysis' which made it possible 'to bring the insights of Marx, Keynes, and Kalecki into coherent form' (1978, pp. 14, 18). This, after all, may be the appropriate definition of what post-Keynesianism is. Such a position may, however, require relinquishing the most extreme views which cannot be entertained within the synthesis, however fundamental these views seem to be from the point of view of their proponents.

One example is Keynes's treatment of price theory which, as already noted, is deemed to be too closely associated with neoclassical views to be kept within the synthesis. Indeed the endless debates about the appropriate representation of Keynes's aggregate supply function, as well as the recursive and inconclusive debates about Keynes's classical postulates regarding the determination of employment, demonstrate that the adoption of neoclassical core assumptions within post-Keynesian economics only leads to sterile controversies, even if these assumptions are turned on their head. As Kaldor (1983a, p. 10) harshly put it, 'so long as one sticks to neoclassical microeconomics, Keynesian macro-economics amounts to very little'. The same drawbacks appear in some parts of Keynes's monetary theory, at least as it is presented in the *General Theory*, which is a modification rather than the abandonment of the Quantity Theory. Keynes is too monetarist for post-Keynesians, as noted both by Kaldor (1982a, p. 21) and the recanted Hicks (1982, p. 264). We could even conclude that 'the real author of the so-called "neo-classical synthesis" was not Paul Samuelson, it was Keynes himself' (Kaldor, 1983a, p. 47). Keynes may have had good strategic reasons for presenting his analysis the way he did. These reasons are no longer valid. In that sense, the term 'post-Keynesian' may not be wholly appropriate, but it is a term established by tradition.

I myself believe that the economics derived from Kaldor and Kalecki, and, because of the latter, from Robinson, are the better bridge between the classical and the post-Keynesian analyses. One could thus say that the intent of this book is to present a mix of Kaldorian and Kaleckian economics.

## 1.2 RESEARCH PROGRAMMES AND ALL THAT

At this stage, the reader may be rather weary of these various schools of thought being thrown around, be they neoclassical, post-classical, post-Keynesian or neo-Ricardian. The object of this section and of the following one is to clear up any misunderstanding about these various terms. My view of the science of economics is that it is composed of two major research programmes. If one does not like the Lakatos framework, call them paradigms (*à la* Kuhn), or research traditions (*à la* Laudan). They are the neoclassical and the post-classical research programmes. It is not any easier to define the former than the latter. Both research programmes extend through all fields and domains of economics; within each field, each of these research programmes encompasses several theories or schools of thought; each theory entertains several models.

It is thus a difficult task to delineate neoclassical economics. There is an almost infinite number of models dealing with a vast amount of questions, from various viewpoints. It has been argued by various methodologists that the Lakatosian concepts of hard core and protective belt cannot be appropriately applied to economics, because they have been designed to deal with formal models. There are formal models in neoclassical economics, but they tackle too diversified a set of topics for cores to be of any practical use. It has thus been suggested that each field should have its own core, or what Remenyi (1979) has called 'demi-core'. Macroeconomics would thus have its own demi-core, while general equilibrium theory would have another.

My perception of neoclassical economics is similar to that of E. R. Weintraub (1985, pp. 134–5). General equilibrium theories provide scientific rigour for macroeconomic theories, partial equilibrium theories or other microeconomic applied work. As a consequence I would argue that the core of neoclassical economics is defined by the core of Walrasian economics. And since very little of practical benefit can be achieved within Walrasian general equilibrium theories, less rigorous works and applied economics can be considered to be within the protective belt of Walrasian economics. To justify their approach, neoclassical practitioners will indeed refer to general equilibrium results, while general equilibrium theorists will refer to empirical work being done in the protective belt to justify the worth of their highly abstract theories. The demi-cores of Remenyi are thus the cores of the neoclassical theories which are lower in the hierarchy; that is, which are less rigorous (according to neo-Walrasian standards) and more applied. The common elements of these demi-cores can be brought together into one set, which I call the protective core. The latter basically delineates partial equilibrium neoclassical theories as well as aggregate neoclassical theories.

The core and the heuristics of neoclassical economics are thus the rules which neo-Walrasians inflict upon themselves, while what I call the protective demi-core brings together the standard textbook assumptions (diminishing returns, substitution, utility maximization, prices equating demand and supply, and so on). The heuristics of that demi-core basically formalize the hierarchic link between vulgar and highbrow theory, and the way the latter is used as a scientific warranty of the validity of the former. For instance, it could be assumed that aggregate production functions are a proper simplification and that the uniqueness and stability of equilibrium have been demonstrated.

It would be possible at this stage to outline the various elements of the neo-Walrasian demi-core or those of the protective demi-core (Lavoie, 1991). Such an exercise would, however, leave in the dark the fundamentals of the neoclassical research programme. It would leave aside what Leijonhufvud has called the presuppositions of neoclassical economics; that is, the set of commonly held metaphysical beliefs, which cannot be put in a formal form, and which are anterior to the constitution of the hard cores. These are the essentials of the research programme. They are 'grand generalities somewhat in the nature of cosmological beliefs' (Leijonhufvud, 1976, p. 72). These are the kind of essentials that I would rather define.

Before we do that, we still need to address the question of the definition of the post-classical research programme. As in the neoclassical case, the post-classical paradigm contains a vast array of schools of thought and theories which are stretched over several fields. In my view, the post-classical programme groups together a vast number of non-orthodox economic theories. Marxists, Radicals, Institutionalists, Structuralists, Evolutionarists, Socioeconomists, the French circuit and regulation schools, neo-Ricardians and post-Keynesians (with or without the hyphen) all belong to the post-classical research programme. Although they may have substantially different opinions on various topics, such as the theory of value or the relevance of long-period analysis, I believe they hold the same metaphysical beliefs prior to the elements constituting the hard core of their respective theories. These post-classical economists are thus linked by something more than their dislike for neoclassical economics. If they dislike neoclassical theory it is precisely because neoclassical economics exudes presuppositions which are contrary to the metaphysical beliefs held by these non-orthodox economists. This is why they have become non-orthodox. Otherwise, since some versions of neoclassical economics, such as that of the New Keynesians, can lead to the recommendation of many of the economic policies advocated by non-orthodox economists, it would be irrational not to be part of the dominant paradigm.

Showing that post-classical economics has suppositions, that is fundamental beliefs, which are different from those entertained in the mainstream will help to answer the main objection to the conception of an alternative to neoclassical economics. Mainstream economists rarely understand why any economist would work outside the framework of neoclassical economics. It is often believed that neoclassical theory offers the only viable approach to economic problems. Those who are not within the mainstream are said not to be exactly within the realm of science. What is argued here is that there are two research traditions in economics, each with its own presuppositions, and that one cannot be called more scientific than the other.

In the next section I shall discuss the essentials which characterize and give unity to the post-classical research programme. To exemplify these essentials, as in the rest of the book, I rely mostly on elements from neo-Ricardian and post-Keynesian theories.

## 1.3 PRESUPPOSITIONS OF THE NEOCLASSICAL AND POST-CLASSICAL PARADIGMS

I have come to associate four presuppositions with neoclassical economics. Two of them are at a methodological level; the other two are more of a technical matter. These presuppositions are instrumentalism and individualism, on the one hand, substantive rationality and exchange on the other. Of course, others might find my choice unsatisfactory and propose some other presupposition or essential. Note, however, that some recent descriptions of the essentials of the neoclassical programme come close to those presented here. For instance, Heijdra and Lowenberg (1988, p. 275), in their plea for a unified definition of the neoclassical programme, also underline methodological individualism and individual rationality.

Table 1.1  *Presuppositions of the neoclassical and the post-classical research programmes*

|                   | Paradigm                |                        |
| Presupposition    | Neoclassical theory     | Post-classical theory  |
| ---               | ---                     | ---                    |
| Epistemology      | Instrumentalism         | Realism                |
| Ontology          | Individualism           | Organicism             |
| Rationality       | Substantive rationality | Procedural rationality |
| Focus of analysis | Exchange                | Production             |

Similarly, when comparing the methodology and the scope of neoclassical and post-classical economics, Sawyer (1989, pp. 18–28) underlines the issues of rationality, unrealism, and exchange versus production.

Realism, organicism, procedural rationality and production (Table 1.1) are, then, the corresponding four presuppositions of post-classical analysis (Lavoie, 1992a). There is much coherence between those divisions and those suggested by Baranzini and Scazzieri (1986, pp. 30–47). They suggest two long-lasting lines of research, the exchange and the production programmes. Their frameworks are respectively scarcity, linear production, an individualistic vision, feasibility and simultaneity on the one hand; and producibility, circular production, a social-class vision, viability and causality on the other. Since causality can be associated to a large extent with realism, Baranzini and Scazzieri's essentials are identical to those to be defined here. The proposed essentials thus have some foundations: they are not arbitrary; they have a significance of their own. We now proceed to a discussion of each of the four sets of presuppositions.

**Instrumentalism versus Realism**

Instrumentalism is the dominant epistemology in neoclassical economics. Although there have been endless debates about Milton Friedman's essay on methodology (1953), I take it that there are now two consensuses about it. First, Friedman was basically taking a sophisticated instrumentalist stance; second, Friedman's position has now been widely endorsed by his fellow neoclassical economists. The second point, if the first is correct, is not difficult to understand. In neoclassical economics, the empirical work done in the more 'vulgar' parts of the theory is the predictions of the more abstract neo-Walrasian programme. Yet we know, because its proponents have not attempted to deny it, that neo-Walrasian theory is not descriptive. There is no effort to put forth hypotheses that are realistic. Axioms are chosen, not for their likelihood, but for their ability to allow the existence of an equilibrium or its uniqueness. Neo-Walrasians describe the world as it should be rather than as it is. Since the more 'vulgar' neoclassical economists rely on general equilibrium theory for their scientific security, they are forced to start from unrealistic and non-descriptive hypotheses. This methodology extends to partial equilibrium studies. For instance, when Walters (1963, p. 40) assesses the possibility of constant marginal cost curves, he complains that its proponents have not shown that it is 'a necessary consequence of some set of fundamental and self-evident postulates'. We must thus conclude that the neoclassical programme is based on methodological unrealism tainted with instrumentalism.

In his contribution on post-Keynesian methodology, Caldwell (1989, p. 55) seems to have been struck by the fact that the major criticism of post-Keynesians against neoclassical theory is that it lacks realism. He then recommends to post-Keynesians the development of an epistemological position based on realism. This is, in my view, a correct descriptive and prescriptive assessment (cf. Eichner and Kregel, 1975, p. 1309; Lawson, 1989; Rogers, 1989, pp. 189–92; Dow, 1990). For post-classicals, a theory cannot be correct unless it incorporates realist hypotheses. The necessity of abstraction for any successful theorizing does not relieve one of the need to be somewhat descriptive. Whereas neoclassical analysis can be realistic only in its auxiliary hypotheses, post-classicals require realism at the level of their initial and essential hypotheses. This would explain the fond interest of post-classicals in *stylized facts* (fixed coefficients of production, cost-plus or mark-up procedures, constant marginal costs, endogenous money, involuntary unemployment, and so on).

Now one should point out that several realistic characteristics are framed within a multitude of neoclassical models. Great efforts have been made in that direction. But these are auxiliary hypotheses, of secondary importance. When, in applied work, neoclassical authors make attempts at verification or falsification, the basic hypotheses (for instance, decreasing returns or profit maximization) are never the subject of falsification. Neoclassical authors dress up their unrealistic basic model with realistic auxiliary hypotheses, prediction serving as the means to rank the validity of the auxiliary hypotheses. The question, then, is whether it is possible to arrive at a model adequately describing the real world by adding auxiliary realistic characteristics. Kaldor (1966, p. 310), for one, thought it was not possible: in an attempt to relieve the programme of its unrealistic foundations, the whole edifice would crumble. Neoclassical economists claim that their basic unrealistic hypotheses are required for simplification purposes, as a first approximation; but when these assumptions are relaxed, even more unrealistic assumptions are required for the previously obtained results to hold.

The adoption of realism as an explicit or implicit methodology has several important consequences. Obviously, standard assumptions become subject to much more empirical scrutiny than the evaluation of predictions. Furthermore a story has to be told. This, I suspect, is what Joan Robinson meant with historical time. It has also been pinpointed by Caldwell (1989, p. 58): 'Post Keynesians value explanation in economics more than they do predictions.' It is precisely the approach underlined by philosophers of science who support realism as a serious and legitimate methodology (Sayer, 1984, ch. 3). What is emphasized is the capacity of a theory to explain the generation of events or structures and to understand the mechanisms at work (Lawson, 1989, p. 63). In a somewhat discursive manner, Blaug (1980b, p. 16) has attributed this 'storytelling' method to the Institutionalists, which he has linked to their call for more realism. Certainly the same could be said of post-Keynesians. Now, for a proper story to be told, some causal mechanism must be presented, some causal process must be reconstructed. To say that supply or demand has shifted is not enough (Simon, 1986, p. 20). A natural consequence of this realist approach is that causality becomes a major concern. Several neoclassical economists avoid the concept altogether or associate causality with temporal ordering, as in some modern empirical assessments of it. On the other hand, post-Keynesians have been particularly careful to safeguard causal and asymmetric relationships, as in recursive models.

While it may seem obvious that post-classicals of the post-Keynesian strand have repeatedly called for more realism in economics, some may doubt that there is any link between realism and neo-Ricardians. This is not so. For instance, Milgate (1982, p. 11) defines the neo-Ricardian method as the 'abstract characterization of the actual economy ... to capture the systematic, regular and persistent forces at work in the system'. This search for the persistent elements of the system may be associated with the post-Keynesian focus on the most essential rather than the most general elements of the economy. Furthermore some neo-Ricardians describe the pure Sraffian model as a snapshot, a photograph, of the existing economic system. Consequently few hypotheses are superimposed upon the observed technological facts. Technical coefficients are what are being observed. They are not necessarily the result of a maximizing procedure. Indeed the standard hypothetical neoclassical demand and supply curves are criticized by neo-Ricardians in part because they cannot be observed (Roncaglia, 1978, p. 104). They are counterfactuals (Dutt, 1990a, p. 136). There is a strong belief among neo-Ricardians in requiring theoretical elements to be observable and objective, rather than metaphysical and subjective. This we can interpret as a desire for realism.

**Individualism versus Organicism**

The second object of opposition is the distinction between the individualistic and the holistic approaches. In neoclassical economics, the analysis starts with the behaviour of individual agents (Boland, 1982, ch. 12). The individual is at the heart of neoclassical economics. This is where ideology might set in. The wants and the preferences of individuals are sacred. They must therefore be in the forefront of the theory, as they are in neo-Walrasian economics. Institutions, firms and banks are a front for the preferences of individuals. Individuals, although they are different because of their distinctive preferences, are all equal as to their impact on the economy. There are no classes of individuals. This philosophical view has an impact on the neoclassical theory of value. Since the preferences of individuals are sacred, they should have an effect on prices, as we know they do in neoclassical theory. This fascination with the rights of individuals can be found in its extreme form among the neo-Austrians. It is no surprise that subjectivism appears so strongly there.

The obsessive concern of neoclassical theorists for individualism explains why they have little interest in macroeconomic distribution issues. Since the behaviour of individuals is related to their personal characteristics, rather than to their social environment, the social class distribution of income is not a determinant of economic activity, but rather an unessential aggregation resulting from technical conditions and prior individual endowments. By contrast, in all post-classical approaches, the distribution of income is a crucial determinant of economic activity, as well as a centre of conflicting claims subject to bargaining and demonstrations of economic power based on class interests.

In post-classical economics, although individual choices are not necessarily denied, they are severely constrained by the existing institutions, socioeconomic classes, social norms and social pressures, and even macroeconomic events. Individual behaviour is interdependent. The social context plays an important role in the manner beliefs are formed. Institutions embody values to which an individual is habituated. Individuals can influence and are influenced by their social environment. Every entity is 'the outcome of its relation with other entities' (Winslow, 1989, p. 1173). Some may speak of a form of holistic approach or of organicism.

In all post-classical models there are social classes, workers, capitalists, entrepreneurs and rentiers. The consideration of these classes, for income distribution purposes or for the theory of effective demand for instance, arises from the presupposition that the definition of individual preferences is not sufficient to allow us to understand society. The consideration of individuals as social beings rather than atomistic ones allows not only for the explicit introduction of dominant institutions and imperfect markets, but also for the appearance of macroeconomic paradoxes (Dow, 1988, p. 9). All sorts of paradoxes, conflicting micro- and macroeconomic logic, arise in the post-classical framework, among them the famous effective demand principle with its paradox of thrift. The relaxation of individualism allows one to further abandon individual optimizing procedures since there are superior macroeconomic constraints.

To abandon the individualistic approach allows post-classicals to focus upon the institutional forms of competition rather than the atomistic neoclassical one. Although there is no infinite multitude of agents or producers, competition exists in post-classical analysis. Whereas the mainstream views institutions as imperfections preventing perfect competition, post-classical authors see them as providing some stability (Hodgson, 1989, p. 116). This is particularly important in a world of uncertainty, where rational responses will develop along the lines of organic interdependence, and where stability will generally be provided by social conventions, until these break, as we shall see in the coming subsection.

**Substantive versus Procedural Rationality**

Caldwell (1989, p. 59) has recently pointed out that the principle of rationality is a very powerful device if not an absolute requirement for any theory in the social sciences. What should be made clear, however, is that the neoclassical programme is not founded on just any sort of rationality principle. Neoclassical economics is based upon substantive rationality, a very peculiar type of rationality. The main characteristic of substantive rationality is that it is loaded with computational facilities and information. The rational economic man of neoclassical economics might be able to predict all future events, or make use of a probability distribution tracing all possible alternatives, or form expectations integrating all available knowledge. The environment assumed to be surrounding the economic agent will be such that this substantive rationality can always be put to use.

Some limits may be imposed upon the available information when some realism or some economic policy results warrant such tampering; but the basic principle of substantive rationality is preserved. It can be argued that, when neoclassical authors model more realistic decision problems, they do so by upgrading the computational and knowledge requirements of economic agents, thus moving away from observed behaviour. Substantive rationality is quite compatible with instrumentalism. For its advocates it appears legitimate to assume that all possible events are known and that their consequences can be assessed, even if this sounds perfectly unrealistic, provided some predictions can be made.

On the other hand, post-classical authors entertain a form of cognitive realism, that of procedural rationality, as defined by Simon (1976). Procedural rationality is bounded rationality, with limited capacities to acquire information, to treat information, to compute outcomes. Individuals are not omniscient; they must rely on group behaviour, numbers bringing confidence. Bounded rationality is compatible with organicism because, as a consequence of these real-life deficiencies in the logistics of choice making, procedures and rules of thumb have to be followed (Winslow, 1989, p. 1180). These rules are common to a whole range of individuals, firms or banks. They set norms and conventions which have to be followed and which have effects upon the real economy. Blaug (1980b, p. 15) has conjectured that Institutionalists could be viewed as favouring the idea of 'group behaviour under the influence of custom and habit'. This certainly applies to post-Keynesians as well.

The environment in which bounded rationality can be put to use is quite different from the one warranted by substantive rationality. There is no need to know the probability distribution of all possible future events. True uncertainty, of the Knight/Keynes/Shackle variety, can be entertained. Neither individuals nor firms are assumed to optimize. It is enough to know that they follow the rules established by the various subgroups of society as best as they can. Expectations need not be of the neoclassical rational type. Conventions dominate. In fact, it is shown by O'Donnell (1989) that, in both of his major works on probability and economics, Keynes attempted to demonstrate that true uncertainty necessarily led to the adoption of a different kind of rationality, which we now call procedural rationality.

Some might argue that neo-Ricardians have often expressed aversion for the concept of uncertainty. Taking up the principle of bounded rationality first, one should note that it is implicit in the snapshot idea of Sraffian models: there is no presumption that the optimal technique has indeed been chosen; the technical coefficients are what they are: they are not necessarily the optimal ones (Nell, 1967a, p. 22). As to uncertainty, Eatwell (1983a, p. 127) points out that it is 'an element, together with "convention", of the general environment in which the systematic processes of production and accumulation must operate'. Roncaglia (1978, p. 24) makes a similar claim. Indeed one could argue that the regularities and permanent features of the economy that the neo-Ricardians are so keen on are provided precisely by the existence of fundamental uncertainty and the consequent rule-governed behaviour (Heiner, 1983). Neo-Ricardians play down the role of expectations and uncertainty because they are afraid that these could be considered as imperfections in their critique of neoclassical economics. However, once the negative part of the job is done, neo-Ricardians and post-Keynesians alike recognize that theories must be built within an uncertain world, with procedural rationality (Milgate and Eatwell, 1983, p. 273).

**Exchange and Production**

We now come to the last distinctive essential, that of exchange versus production, as authors of various horizons have put it (Hicks, 1976a, p. 213; Henry and Seccareccia, 1982, p. 6; Baranzini and Scazzieri, 1986) and which we could call the scarcity versus production presupposition.

As early as the first class of principles, the student of economics is confronted with the basic definition of the neoclassical research programme, which is wrongly attributed to economics as a whole (that is, to all schools of thought in economics). Textbooks use Lionel Robbins's definition of economics, calling it the science of the (optimal) allocation of scarce means (1932, p. 16). The concept of scarcity is in my view the fourth essential of the neoclassical programme. Scarcity is the fulcrum of neoclassical economics. Various conditions will be set to preserve it outside the standard conditions of exchange economies: full employment, a fixed and given stock of money, and so on. Scarcity justifies the supply and demand analysis. It gives prices their crucial role. It governs the behaviour of the economy. It explains why neoclassical economists attach such importance to the allocation of resources or why so many of them define the techniques of constrained optimization as the epitome of neoclassical economics. When all resources are scarce, they are fully employed, and therefore all questions revolve around the proper use of existing resources, rather than about the creation of new commodities.

Scarcity is particularly obvious in pure exchange models. The supplementary hypotheses that can be found in the various sophisticated neoclassical production models are, however, being introduced precisely to safeguard all the main conditions and results of the pure exchange model (Walsh and Gram, 1980, p. 171; Rogers, 1983). Production in neoclassical economics is a form of indirect exchange, between individual consumer agents who own resources which transit through the same individual agents, then christened producers. These producers are nothing other than arbitragers who are attempting to benefit from existing scarcities.

In the post-classical research programme, the notion of scarcity is put aside, while that of reproducibility is brought to the forefront (Roncaglia,

1978, p. 5). With their emphasis on production, post-classical economists embark on the tradition of the classical economists, with their concern with the causes of progress and accumulation. In his review of the Cambridgian critique, Rymes (1971, p. 2) makes it clear that the neo-Ricardian concern for reproducibility is in the lineage of the economic thought of Robinson, Kaldor and even Harrod. It is no surprise that Pasinetti (1981, p. 24) and Rymes, who have carefully studied economics with growing output per head as a result of technical progress, have put so much emphasis on the notion of reproducibility.

In post-Keynesian models, where output is not disaggregated, the emphasis on production appears through the assumption that in general neither capital goods nor labour are fully employed. In this sense, resources are not scarce. The major problem is not how to allocate them but how to increase production or the rate of growth. The principle of scarcity is put aside, as it is generally possible to increase the rate of utilization of capacity, and as there are reserves of labour. The principle of scarcity is replaced by the principle of effective demand. The true constraint is not supply but effective demand. As Kaldor (1983b, p. 6) says, 'For production to be demand-determined, excess capacity must exist as well as unemployed labour'.

Therefore, although neo-Ricardians have put much emphasis on the trade-off between the real wage rate and the profit rate, I would be prepared to argue that, if neoclassical economics is the research programme of a world of scarcity, post-classical economics is the research programme of a world of abundance. Of course some goods, even produced goods, may become scarce. But as pointed out by Pasinetti (1981, p. 7), classical authors, in particular Ricardo, focused on the permanent feature of reproducibility, considering that produced goods could be multiplied without limits, and thus judging that, besides land, scarcity conditions could only be of a temporary nature. This is where the neo-Ricardians and the post-Keynesians join forces, since Hayek, when rejecting Keynes's economics in 1940, is precisely invoking the basic importance of scarcity (Parguez, 1988, p. 144). Scarcity is the essence of neoclassical economics. To proclaim the existence of an economy of plenty is to negate the foundations of orthodoxy.

## 1.4 THE DOMINANCE OF NEOCLASSICAL ECONOMICS

Now that we know that there are at least two lines of research in economics, each with its own set of presuppositions, each set being presumably just as potentially appealing as the other, the student of non-orthodox economics may wonder why neoclassical economics has been apparently so dominant over the past years. One obvious answer would be that the neoclassical research programme is progressive, in the Lakatosian sense, whereas the post-classical programme, in its various incarnations, would be degenerative. No doubt this would be the answer offered by most neoclassical practitioners. It would be argued that, over the past 100 years, the neoclassical framework has allowed a remarkable amount of relevant facts and theories to be gathered, a feat unparalleled by other research programmes. Notwithstanding these great achievements of neoclassical theory, there are other reasons which explain how neoclassical economics came to dominate political economy, as it was formerly called, and why it still dominates now.

To explain why neoclassical economics dominates the field of economics, now that it is entrenched as the dominant paradigm, is a rather simple task. Several studies have underlined the sociological underpinnings of the economic profession, or of the scientific community in general (Canterbery and Burkhardt, 1983; Earl, 1983b; Eichner, 1983, pp. 225–35; Katouzian, 1980, ch. 5). However, one does not have to be a keen sociologist to understand what is going on in our institutions of knowledge. Pressures to conform to the orthodox canons are exerted from the very start, with the imposition of the well-known and voluminous first-year university textbooks. The multiplicity of compulsory microeconomic and macroeconomic courses, where the same contents are invariably repeated from the intermediate to the PhD levels, only with increasing mathematical sophistication, ensures that all students believe that the neoclassical approach is the only scientific one, or at least the only one worthy of their study time. To get their degrees, students of economics must pass these courses, and pass comprehensive examinations which test their ability to comprehend or memorize the most futile of newest neoclassical theoretical developments. What becomes important, as shown by the interviews of graduate students conducted by Klamer and Colander (1990), is not so much the knowledge of the economy or of the overall economic literature, as the ability to learn mathematical techniques of constrained optimization, a panacea linked to the neoclassical presupposition of universal scarcity.

In the end, students have a 'vested interest' in thinking these tricks important, as 'they will devote their lives to teaching them to new generations. So the system perpetuates itself' (Robinson, 1973, p. 127). If a student has shown enough moral strength to go through these examinations without believing that the subject matter is highly relevant, he or she is then subjected to the examination of a dissertation, where only standard neoclassical hypotheses can be entertained without risk, since the jury is usually composed of a majority of economists opposed to non-orthodox views. At this stage, most students whose presuppositions do not conform to those of the neoclassical paradigm have usually given up, either by failing to complete a dissertation which they know has little chance of being accepted, or by switching to some more tolerant department – political science for instance.

Those who managed to hide their true opinions by letting themselves be 'socialized' into the mainstream groove, or those who were lucky enough to be groomed in more eclectic departments, now face the difficult task of finding an employer. The same vicious circle will arise if the chosen market is that of academia. Initial hiring depends on the subject of dissertation and the opinions of jury members. Tenure is granted if publications are made in the proper journals of the profession. As we know, these journals are under the editorship of economists from the mainstream. Young scholars are thus faced with a dilemma: they can either attempt to publish neoclassical papers, in which case their chances of getting tenure are increased, especially since their previous technical training has usually been channelled in that direction, but then running the risk of acquiring such an expertise in neoclassical theory that the cost of surrendering that human capital to non-orthodox economics might become too large; or they can attempt to publish outside the mainstream, which usually means outside the prestigious journals, in which case the probability of being granted tenure is much less, at least within the better known universities. The same dilemma applies for future promotions.

The fact that, perhaps in opposition to what could have been done some years back, it is not possible, or almost impossible, to publish an article dealing with some post-classical questions in a major mainstream journal does not necessarily have to do with overt discrimination against non-orthodox economists. As Earl (1983b, p. 110) reminds us, editors and referees of journals tend to respond favourably to methods and theoretical orientations which correspond to those in which they have been themselves trained, or in which they train their own students. Non-orthodox work is not published in mainstream journals because the language is different, being based on divergent presuppositions, and because the theoretical questions being tackled by these non-orthodox economists are not fashionable. Neoclassical economists who do not belong to the major departments face a similar problem, since prestigious journals are under the control of a handful of departments. The most renowned members of these departments decide on the fads and set the trends of economic literacy. The less fortunate neoclassical members of the profession thus have to know what the rules of the game currently are – what are the hot topics, the fashionable pursuits, the trendy puzzles. 'Models are chosen on the basis of whether they will lead to a publishable article, not on the basis of how illuminating they are' (Colander, 1990, p. 192).

The rules of the game, however, do not only apply to publishing in journals. They are also ruthlessly implemented in the attribution of research funds. Some of us do not need much financial help to conduct research: access to a library, a pen and some paper is all there is required. Research can, however, be highly time-consuming without the help of assistants, and obtaining pertinent data may be quite expensive. Money thus constitutes the sinews of war, if the 'publish or perish' constraint can be considered some sort of warfare. The financial issue in research brings to the forefront the question of ideology. Publicly-funded research councils are usually under the sway of the invisible college, that is the most prestigious members of the neoclassical community. Getting funds from this source is thus usually difficult. Getting funds from the private sector is just as intricate, for even if the opinion of the members of the invisible college is not solicited, the ideas and theories of the non-orthodox researcher will not correspond to conventional wisdom. Furthermore the interests of the private sector may often collide with those of the non-orthodox researcher. Concretely, a lot of non-orthodox work could only be supported by labour unions and other popular organizations. These institutions, however, do not deal with the highly abstract questions which fill the pages of the learned journals. Also their financial resources are much smaller than those of private firms, or those of employers' associations, who can set up private research institutes, which neoclassical economists can then tap for funds and research contracts with an overflow on their theoretical work.

These links between neoclassical economics and the dominant economic powers within a nation help to explain how the neoclassical research programme came to overcome the classical school in the last century. As we have seen in the previous section, neoclassical economics is exclusively concerned with the individual, whereas the post-classical programme, following the classics, is concerned with socioeconomic classes. In the midst of the various revolutionary waves that were hitting Europe in the second half of the nineteenth century, the simultaneous appearance of marginalist works, breaking away from several of the classical concerns and concepts, provided a breath of fresh air to the threatened political and economic establishment. Furthermore marginalism, as it was then called, offered an alternative to Marx's extension of the classical school (De Vroey, 1975; Pasinetti, 1981, pp. 11–14). Because Marx's premises were similar to those of the classicals on so many points, it was difficult to reject his analysis and his conclusions altogether. Getting rid of the classical theory of value and of the classical explanation of the origin of profit by embarking on the path of marginalism was the answer of the European bourgeoisie. The economists also climbed on the bandwagon, so that by the 1900s marginalism had swept over economics. There was a convergence in those days, perhaps still today, between the presuppositions and agenda of neoclassical economics and the interests of the political and industrial establishment. While various versions of marginalism had been expounded before the 1870s, Cournot's being the most famous, economists did not seem to see in it any hint of superiority. But with the advent of Marx it became imperative for the establishment, long annoyed with some of the conclusions drawn from classical economics, to find a less class-conscious and more apologetic alternative.

This does not mean that ideology is the crucial element separating the neoclassical programme from the post-classical one, as some believe (Marglin, 1984a, p. 481). As claimed before, neoclassical theory is flexible enough with the introduction of auxiliary hypotheses (externalities, imperfections) to allow for just about any sort of economic policy. This explains why many graduate students with left-wing inclinations do not object to being drilled in neoclassical economics. However I would be prepared to argue that some subprogrammes within each of the two major neoclassical and post-classical research programmes may be led by ideology (monetarism, neo-Marxians) and that ideology played a major role in the successful development of the marginal revolution.

Of course other reasons did militate in favour of the then emerging research programme. In particular, the proponents of marginalism brought with them a mathematical apparatus which helped to persuade that the new economics was more scientific than the old classical one, since obvious analogies could be made between the impersonal laws of the market and the newly discovered natural laws of physics (Mirowski, 1990). Calculus, differentials and integrals were being imported into the subject of economics. On the other hand, Marx's transformation problem and Ricardo's problem of the invariable measure of value seemed intractable. While some economists, both inside and outside the neoclassical school, claimed that mathematics in marginalism discredited the latter, ultimately marginalism triumphed because of the presence of mathematics. Today there are still some remnants of this early belief in the superiority of mathematical economics held by the early exponents of marginalism: as Leijonhufvud (1973, p. 329) recalls, the priestly caste of mathematical economists occupies the highest caste-ranking. Their skills are looked at in awe by their colleagues. In journals, especially the more prestigious ones, a great deal of attention is paid to mathematical techniques, imaginary puzzles being solved provided they require some technical virtuosity. Whereas at some junctures of the history of economics the introduction of mathematics allowed some rigour to prevail, mathematics now play a paradigm-preserving role. They force the focus of attention away from the larger issues and towards minute details. Such is their importance that the graduate students of the departments run by the invisible college now consider that being good at problem solving and excellence in mathematics are more important for a successful academic career than a knowledge of the economy and of the overall economics literature (Klamer and Colander, 1990, p. 18).

The reader might wonder whether the statements made above are indictments of formalized economics. Not at all. Formal models are a requirement of all schools of economics, as they bring a form of rigour and may illuminate comprehension. All of the non-neoclassical schools of economics carry mathematically trained economists. Non-orthodox economists have led the way in some research areas, such as non-linear dynamics. Mathematical formalism should not, however, be an end in itself. The contents should not be lost for the sake of the form. Highly sophisticated techniques should not produce ultimately meaningless results. It is true that a lot of non-orthodox economists are reluctant to use mathematics or to do econometric work when they are involved in empirical research. This is not surprising. There is a higher propensity to reject neoclassical economics among those who are more interested in the concepts than in the models. Rejecting models usually leads to the construction of other models within the same paradigm; rejecting concepts leads to the search for new or different concepts, in some cases to different presuppositions. Those who do so join the ranks of the non-orthodox.

This may help to explain why post-classical economists seem to be unduly busy with criticizing each other or the mainstream, or even dead authors, rather than making constructive contributions to their fields. To some extent, it is in the nature of non-orthodox scientists to be critical rather than constructive. Furthermore the post-classical research programme was to some extent put in limbo with the successful marginal revolution, so that, whereas a multitude of minds assisted in defining the neoclassical research programme over the past decades, with its cores, its rules, its conventions, only a relative handful of economists have contributed to the development of post-classical economics. Neoclassical economics thus benefits from a mass of textbooks, which offer at least pedagogical coherence, and a multitude of empirical studies, which offer the illusion of a well verified programme. These, unfortunately, are claims that post-classical economists cannot yet make.

## 1.5 EMPIRICAL STUDIES AND NEOCLASSICAL ECONOMICS

The multitude of research studies which supposedly demonstrate the validity of this or that neoclassical theory in various fields of economics is one of the most puzzling aspects encountered by students dissatisfied with the mainstream approach. Whereas they confusedly perceive that several of the hypotheses that underlie the tested neoclassical models lack substance or realism, students are being swamped with successful tests of these models. It seems as if the real world behaves according to these absurd hypotheses. Puzzlement is reinforced when, in courses dealing with the capital controversies, students are being told that the neoclassical aggregate production function does not hold water. Under these circumstances how can econometricians find such high $R^2$s and such good $t$ statistics? Some of the answers are given in their econometrics course, but somewhat implicitly. The critical student is left perplexed. With all its lack of realism, it would seem that neoclassical economics is better than other schools of thought since most neoclassical theories have been demonstrated to be verified one way or another, a feat which rival research programmes cannot claim. This is further reinforced by the fact that many non-orthodox economists are so much aware of the methodological difficulties encountered in empirical research that they hesitate to engage in it.

The belief in the verdict of econometrics has usually been reinforced from day one in the economics department when, in the first pages of the introductory textbook, the student reads that 'a theory is tested by confronting its predictions with evidence', and that 'the scientific approach to any basic issue consists in setting up a theory that will explain it and then seeing if that theory can be refuted by evidence' (Lipsey, *et al.*, 1988, p. 23). It is in those two textbook statements that are found the seeds of instrumentalism, which is the dominant epistemology of the neoclassical research programme, as I have already claimed, and those of falsificationism, the methodology that the mainstream often claims to practice, or which is exhorted in replacement of verificationism (Blaug, 1980a). The naive student is thus left with the conviction that mainstream economists engaged in empirical research relentlessly try to falsify theories proposed by themselves or by their mentors; or the student is brainwashed into believing that realist hypotheses are unimportant provided the model can make successful predictions. Indeed the student is often told that the more unrealistic the hypotheses the better, since the model is then more general.

It should be clear, however, as is recognized even by those who advocate falsificationism (Blaug, 1980a, p. 128), that neoclassical economists practice at best an innocuous version of falsificationism. More likely, they are still engaged in verificationism, that is the attempt to find confirming evidence of their theories. In their review of over 500 empirical articles published in the major orthodox journals, Canterbery and Burkhardt (1983, p. 31) find that only three articles actually try to falsify anything. This is one of the reasons why instrumentalism is so popular among the majority of mainstream economists, whatever their degree of interest in methodological questions. Instrumentalism justifies the combination of highly unrealistic hypotheses, inherent to the neo-Walrasian hard core of the neoclassical programme, with the desire to be associated with a positivistic view of science, whereby what is scientific must necessarily be testable. That a theory can be empirically confirmed under some circumstances seems to be satisfying enough.

Philosophers of science have given many reasons for which the verification of a theory is insufficient to give support to that theory. There has also been substantial criticism of the possibility of falsification, given the *realpolitik* of research programmes (Caldwell, 1982, ch. 5 and 12). These methodological criticisms notwithstanding, why do neoclassical theories always seem to be supported by some empirical evidence? Those who have dealt with empirical data know that it is not always easy to obtain a satisfying econometric relation. Some students present dissertations where $R^2$s verge on zero. Why then do empirical facts in orthodox economic journals always appear to verify orthodox theory?

The first thing to notice is that journals usually do not publish inconclusive results, except when they provide a scapegoat which can then be used to highlight the rival pet theory of their editors. As a consequence, authors do not bother submitting results which are inconclusive. Only a biased sample of the empirical work that is going on is thus published. Most of the unsuccessful attempts at verification go unnoticed, and a lot of the unsuccessful attempts at replicating published empirical models do not end up in the learned journals.

The second cause of this proliferation of fortunate empirical studies is the manner in which empirical research is being conducted. This applies to neoclassical researchers as well as to researchers of other persuasions. The typical economist draws a theory, outlines a simplified functional form which could be empirically tested, and adds a few secondary variables which could be of significance. With the help of the computer and some arbitrary algorithms, the analyst then searches for the best equation. Several rounds might be needed to find regressions that offer any fit, and on the way several variables and several specifications will have been tested and discarded, bringing as well a revision of the theory. Furthermore the data might be divided into subperiods, part of the data might be discarded, dummy variables might be introduced, and so on. In the end the theory claimed to be tested may have only a remote relationship with the one originally posited. This is the so-called interaction between data and theory. Some prefer to speak of 'data mining', 'data fishing' or 'data massaging'.

The end result of this iterative interaction, however, is that the standard statistical tests are worthless; that is, 'they give misleading estimates of the confidence that one can place in econometric relations' (Thurow, 1983, p. 107). The reason, basically, is that the number of degrees of freedom, which helps to decide whether the testable form of the theory is significant or not, is essentially diminished as tentative regressions are run and new specifications are adopted, since the number of degrees of freedom is equal to the number of observations minus the number of explanatory variables used. The analyst should decide the final form of the equation to be tested before regressions are run. Other critics of standard econometric practices prefer to speak of information filtering (Denton, 1988) or of pre-test bias (Darnell and Evans, 1990, ch. 4). Whatever the point of view taken, the consequences are identical. There are no readily available theoretical solutions to this problem, apart from caution when interpreting results. Equations which appear to be validated or confirmed according to the standard statistical tests could not be so if one were to follow the canons of classical statistics. It should be no surprise, especially with the high-speed computers now available to all, that through trial and error some specification of the proposed theory should be eventually confirmed, even if the theory is wrong. The *a priori* theoretical opinions of the majority, that is the neoclassical school, will thus appear as the most confirmed view.

Data massaging or 'equation massaging' are not the only cause of excessively successful testing. Macroeconomics makes extensive use of time series. It has been shown repeatedly that series of random walks which are absolutely independent of each other may exhibit high correlation coefficients. Granger and Newbold (1974), for instance, have shown that on average an $R^2$ of 0.59 could be obtained when regressing such a random walk over five variables also exhibiting a random walk. In 37 per cent of the simulations, the coefficient of determination exceeded 0.7! This shows that spurious correlations may easily be obtained in the case of time series. Variables which have nothing to do with each other may appear to have some economic relationship.

Another good historical illustration of the above is the use and misuse of the Durbin–Watson test, now available on all regression computer programs, despite the existence of much more powerful tests. This test helps to pick up spurious correlations under certain conditions and when only first-degree residuals are autocorrelated. One should remember that the famous empirical debates of the 1960s between the neoclassical Keynesians and the Monetarists, that later filled the pages of macroeconomic textbooks, were conducted with time series and without any use of this now elementary test (Desai, 1981, p. 125). One should also remember that the Durbin–Watson test is biased towards the acceptance of the hypothesis of no autocorrelation in circumstances in which mainstream economists have often tested their models, more specifically when a lagged value of the dependent variable is included among the regressors. This is especially the case when mathematical manipulations are required to transform the equation to be tested into an equation that can be more easily estimated, and where we end up with endogenous lagged variables. Examples include adaptive expectations, the Koyck distributed lag model, which allows for the introduction of an infinity of complex lags, and the estimation of a desired variable, for instance the desired level of capital stock in several neoclassical investment theories. Since neoclassical authors are often searching for some stationary state, the desired level of some key variable is a crucial component of their model building. All these uses bring with them the further possibility that the found correlations would be spurious, and possibly a lot of past successful studies relying on desired levels, lags or adaptive expectations were indeed spurious.

There are now numerous more sophisticated econometric tests which help to avoid these fake correlations. However editors of learned journals rarely require these less elementary tests, and as a consequence few researchers bother to use or provide them. There is thus no indication of how the successful estimation was arrived at. One might suspect that, if there were an attempt to do so, several results just could not be published even today. Hendry (1980) shows that he could put forward a sound theory of inflation by relating the price index $P$ in Great Britain to an exogenous variable $C$, which is closely monitored by the entire population and whose data are quickly released by the government. With the help of a few hypotheses on the specification of the relation between $P$ and $C$, he is able to find a perfect fit, with no obvious residual autocorrelation. Furthermore the model predicts well when applied to further years. It seems that $C$, being the exogenous variable, is indeed the cause of inflation that everyone has been searching for. But it turns out that $C$ is cumulative rainfall in Great Britain. The regression would not have survived a couple of more sophisticated specification tests. One shudders at the thought of all these less obvious spurious results that were hailed as great empirical laws resulting from neoclassical theory. The lesson to be drawn, with time series especially, is that when a theory is confirmed there is some probability that the results are spurious: the more so when sophisticated econometric or mathematical manipulations are carried out to arrive at the successful specification; and the less so when some powerful tests are being conducted.

Econometricians and most applied economists are of course aware of all the previously mentioned drawbacks and limitations of econometric testing, not to mention all others. Some ways out have been suggested. Economists have been urged to report the search process that finally led to the successful specification. Some procedures have been suggested as conforming to a falsification strategy rather than a verification one (Darnell and Evans, 1990, chs 4–6). The most popular solutions, however, seem to be those which abandon all pretence at mixing econometrics and economic theory. These newer methods, VAR models and cointegration techniques associated with Sims and Granger, of which the now famous and widely used causality tests are a part, try to mimic time series and are atheoretical. They are in the purest sense instrumentalist. They solve the difficult problem of mixing economic theory with facts by doing away with economic theory. Furthermore, as has been pointed out by Rowley and Renuka (1986) in the case of the Granger–Sims so-called causality tests, some of these newer methods are soft econometrics, in the sense that again the validity of the conclusions reached (here the presence or absence of temporal causality and its direction) depends on the procedures actually followed by the researcher, in particular the filters used. Since there is a wide variety of possible filters, the reported results may reflect the theoretical opinions of the researcher.

Even if one were to accept some of the relations uncovered by some of these newer techniques, it remains to be explained how these relations came about. For this we need an economic theory, for which the new econometric techniques are useless, since several sorts of economic theory could underlie the data. For instance, it is practically impossible to distinguish the random shocks of business cycle theories *à la* Lucas from the chaotic behaviour (which is not random) of non-linear difference equations (Kelsey, 1988, p. 20). The fact that most models are tested *vis-à-vis* the null hypothesis, rather than compared one with another, also helps to explain why neoclassical models always appear to be validated: the partisans of free-market competition rarely practise it in their scientific research. They do not test competing theories. To find means of actually differentiating alternative theories is of course an old and difficult problem. It constitutes another reason for which the non-orthodox student should not be disturbed by the apparently huge amount of confirming evidence in favour of mainstream theory.

There are many instances of this methodological mistake, especially in the field of human capital theory and in macroeconomics. A typical example is Friedman's permanent income hypothesis, which has been hailed as a major neoclassical contribution and one that has come through the test of confirmation with flying colours. The problem with such an assessment is that, when Friedman's theory is actually tested, no attempt is made to differentiate it from a more simple and more intuitive habit persistence theory (Green, 1984) and, when such an attempt is made, it appears that the latter rather than Friedman's hypothesis (or for that matter Modigliani's life-cycle hypothesis) is substantiated (Marglin, 1984a, ch. 18). The problem here is that neoclassical authors claim to test theory $A$ but are actually testing theory $B$. In this case, Friedman's and Modigliani's hypotheses should rely on future income, but they are tested with a proxy, some combination of past income. The doubts on the validity of such tests are further compounded when one realizes that this combination of past incomes can have just about any structure of lags. There is an infinity of possibilities. It is thus no surprise that these theories have been substantiated. As pointed out by Pesek (1979, p. 66), with the use of modern computers it is impossible *not* to verify the permanent income hypothesis and the theory of the demand for money based on it, or some variants thereof.

This brings to the forefront the fact that the objective of a lot of applied work is the econometric estimation of the parameters of the chosen model, rather than the attempt to falsify the theory upon which the model is built. Of course estimation is also worthy of interest, for policy simulations for instance, but one should make sure beforehand that the underlying theory is valid. One should thus be aware that a substantial amount of empirical work, dealing with production functions for instance, is simply exercises in estimating parameters. In these cases, the data cannot prove or disprove the underlying theory, unless there is some theoretical restriction on the values that the parameters could possibly take. The data cannot be inconsistent with the theory. This is what Pencavel (1986, p. 5) has ironically called 'measurement without testing', applying the expression to the many studies dealing with the supply of labour. Measurement without testing has been appropriately denounced by Kaldor:

In economics, observations which contradict the basis hypotheses of prevailing theory are generally ignored ... And where empirical material is brought into conjunction with a theoretical model, as in econometrics, the role of empirical estimation is to 'illustrate' or to 'decorate' the theory, not to provide support to the basic hypothesis (as for example, in the case of numerous studies purporting to estimate the coefficients of production functions). (Kaldor, 1972, p. 1239)

Still baffled by the wealth of these illustrating estimations, the non-orthodox student might ask: if aggregate neoclassical production functions make so little sense, and if the capital controversies, to be discussed next, have any impact on the real world, why is it that most studies seem to demonstrate that the actual labour share is indeed the exponent of the labour factor in the fitted Cobb–Douglas function; and why do the sum of the labour and capital shares add up to one, implying that the function is nearly homogeneous of the first degree? If the neoclassical production function did not have any empirical validity, the coefficients found through the estimation of the production functions would not be consistent with the actual shares of capital and labour obtained from national accounts. This is certainly puzzling for the non-orthodox, drilled in his compulsory classes with countless fits of Cobb–Douglas functions having these properties and high degrees of determination. It is now time to tackle the limits of neoclassical economics.

## 1.6   THE LIMITS OF NEOCLASSICAL THEORY

Over the past 20 years, neoclassical theory has faced two major setbacks. The first one has been well publicized in non-orthodox circles: it has mainly to do with production theory in aggregate models and is known under the name of the Cambridge controversies in the theory of capital (Harcourt, 1972; Birner, 1990; Ahmad, 1991). The second is lesser known, specially among non-orthodox authors (with exceptions, such as Eatwell and Milgate, 1983b, p. 2 and Schefold, 1985, p. 112), because non-orthodox economists were not involved in its denouement, and also because the results are so destructive that few orthodox authors have dared to draw the appropriate conclusions. That second setback has to do with the stability of general equilibrium theory and is known as the Sonnenschein–Mantel–Debreu theorem. We shall also call it the impossibility theorem.

**The Cambridge Controversies**

Since the details of the Cambridge controversies are generally well known (see Harris, 1978 and Moss, 1980 for pedagogical presentations), their consequences will be mainly discussed here. Whereas the mainstream usually views the capital controversies as some aggregation problem, it is not the point of view of the post-classical economists, although we shall concentrate our attention upon aggregate models of production. Robinson (1975, p. vi), for instance, has clearly indicated that 'the real dispute is not about the *measurement* of capital but about the *meaning* of capital'. In all of her contributions to the debates, in particular in her opening and closing ones, she has underlined the fact that the neoclassical production function with factor substitution is set in a timeless world (Robinson, 1953–4, 1975a). When labour is substituted for capital, it is assumed that the new machines, corresponding to the new technology, can be installed instantaneously and without cost. Although it is usually believed that Kaldor had no interest whatsoever in the capital controversies, it should be pointed out that he was making a very similar point when arguing that the distinction between the movement along a production function and the shift in the production function is entirely arbitrary (1957, p. 595). The artificial character of this distinction becomes clear when one considers capital as a produced commodity rather than as a given endowment.

The reproducibility of capital in opposition to capital as a primary input is, I believe, the message that the economists from Cambridge, England, were trying to carry across. Of course, neoclassical authors have long been aware of the necessity to distinguish capital from land or natural resources (cf. Malinvaud, 1953), but in practice the distinction has been ignored. The fact that capital is reproducible is more obvious in situations of growth and technical progress than in stationary states. This might explain why post-Keynesians were so much aware of capital reproducibility, since post-Keynesians focused their attention on growth. Harrod, Robinson, Kaldor and Pasinetti (and of course Sraffa) all had the same vision of commodity capital. One can even add to this group the name of Kalecki. It turns out, indeed, that the proper measurement of technical progress with reproducible capital proposed by Rymes (1971) was inspired by the work of a colleague (Lawrence Read, from the department of religion!) who himself got suggestions from Kalecki when working at the United Nations. There is thus an homogeneous conception of the nature of production and of that of capital among post-Keynesians and neo-Ricardians. The Cambridge controversies are just one outlet, among many, which highlight this common vision. As pointed out by Rymes (1971, p. 180), 'aggregation problems and non-smooth production surfaces are matters for secondary complaint. The oft-found suggestion in the literature that consistent aggregation would blunt the attacks on the neoclassical structure clearly misses the main point.' We shall nevertheless focus our attention on the consequences of the Cambridge controversies for the aggregate version of the neoclassical model.

One should perhaps recall that the *coup d'envoi*, from the neoclassical side, was provided by Samuelson's (1962) attempt to demonstrate that Solow's empirical manipulations of the Cobb–Douglas production function were perfectly legitimate. Samuelson was also trying to respond to Joan Robinson, following her visit to MIT. One may suspect that this rare opportunity of exchange between rival research programmes was provided by the fact that both Robinson and Samuelson were dealing with linear production models, so that mainstream economists could grasp to some extent what the non-orthodox economists were up to. Samuelson claimed that the macroeconomics of aggregate production functions were 'the stylized version of a certain quasi-realistic MIT model of diverse heterogeneous capital goods' processes' (1962, p. 201–2).

The controversies finally resolved, among other things, that the main properties of aggregate production functions could not be derived from a multi-sector model with heterogeneous capital, nor for that matter even from a two-sector model with one machine but several available techniques. More specifically, it could not be said that, economy-wide, the rate of profit was equal to the marginal productivity of capital. Nor could it be said that there existed an inverse relationship between the capital/labour ratio and the ratio of the profit rate to the real wage rate at the level of the whole economy. In Figure 1.1,(a) and (b) illustrate respectively the assumed neoclassical relation and the one which may generally arise.

For our purposes, the response of the mainstream was basically twofold. Many orthodox authors took the view that disaggregated neo-Walrasian theory was safe from the neo-Ricardian critique, and that therefore the core of the neoclassical programme (general equilibrium theory) had been left intact. Some of them recognized that the aggregate version of the neoclassical programme was in jeopardy. The others thought that the consequences were not very profound. This latter reaction may be linked to the second major neoclassical response, which was to deny the empirical relevance of the Cambridge critique, by claiming that the neoclassical model 'worked'. With the first response, one may mainly associate Frank Hahn (1982), who appears to have changed his mind as to the consequences of his response, initially being quite critical of aggregate theory, later to become a partisan of the pragmatic view.

When the aggregated version of the [neoclassical] theory is used simplicity is obtained at the cost of logical coherence, and in general such theories give wrong answers ... The view that nonetheless it 'may work in practice' sounds a little bogus and in any case the onus of proof is on those who maintain this. (Hahn, 1972, p. 8)

I doubt that they [the Sraffians] are correct in their view that the simple (essentially one capital good) models are useless ... We use simple models (e.g. macroeconomics) to gain insights of a certain kind. Simplification is never without cost and the cost is sometimes loss of rigour. It remains to be shown that the cost is too high in this instance, i.e., that in actual problem application the chance of large mistakes is great. I know no Sraffian who has shown this. (Hahn, 1982, p. 370)

While in 1972 the onus of the proof that the Cambridge controversies have profound consequences on the aggregate neoclassical version lay on the shoulders of mainstream economists, in 1982 the burden of the proof has been switched over to the neo-Ricardians! This may be owing to the

*Figure 1.1 Relationship between capital per unit of labour and the profit rate/real wage ratio: (a) in the 'vulgar' neoclassical view; (b) in the neo-Ricardian view*

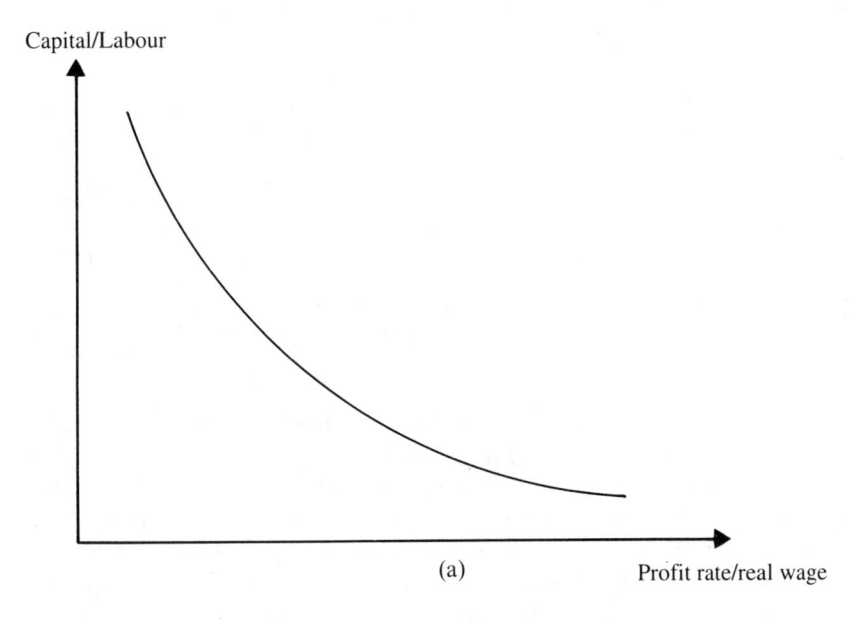

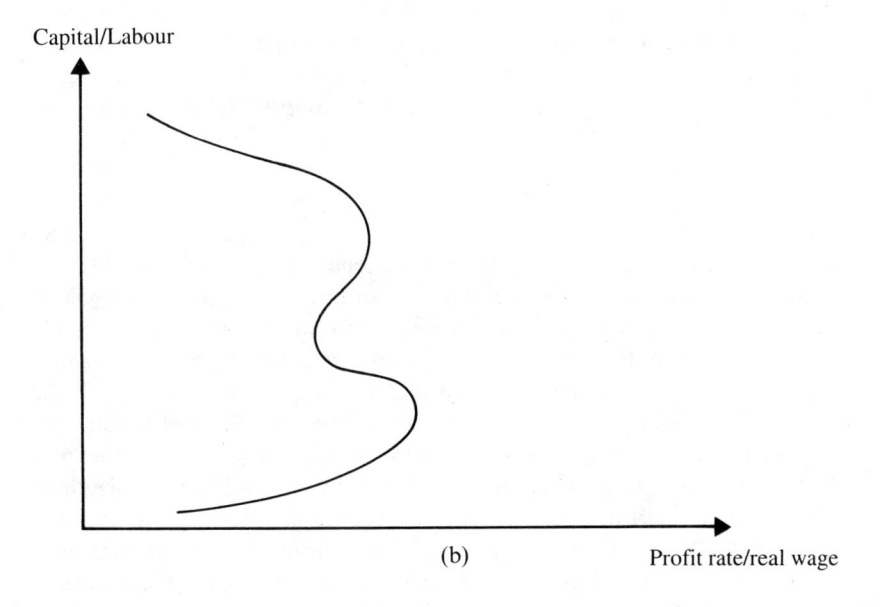

fact that by 1982 the damaging consequences of the controversies for neoclassical theory had been better spelled out. Since the neoclassical theories of value and output are interdependent by definition, any flaw in the theory of value must be of consequence for the theory of output. 'The theory of value, based on demand and supply, is one and the same thing as the theory of output' (Eatwell and Milgate, 1983b, p. 2). Standard macroeconomics, which deals with the theory of output by relying on the discredited aggregate neoclassical theory of value, is thus in jeopardy. The argument has been neatly summarized:

The well-known deficiencies of orthodox capital theory ensure that there is no logical foundation to the idea of a demand curve for labour elastic with respect to the real wage, nor a demand curve for capital, nor indeed demand curves for individual commodities. Hence the adjustment of demand to capacity in consumption and production as a function of relative prices is deprived of theoretical credence. (Eatwell, 1983b, p. 280)

These consequences for neoclassical economics had been understood by Garegnani as early as 1964, but his work was not translated into English until much later (Garegnani, 1978). Since then, several authors have emphasized the deficiencies of the aggregate neoclassical model in its various incarnations, because of the impossibility of finding an inverse relation between the capital/labour ratio and the profit rate/wage rate ratio. Economists are generally aware that the value of capital is usually not an inverse and continuous function of the rate of profit, as was made clear during the controversies. However many other standard assumptions fall with the demise of the neoclassical aggregate theory of value. In the labour market, for instance, one cannot suppose that the demand for labour is inversely related to the real wage rate (Roncaglia, 1988a). In neoclassical models with money and financial assets, one cannot presume the existence of a natural rate of interest. These monetary models, like the real ones, fall to the Cambridge critique (Rogers, 1989). Nor can we presume the existence of the standard efficiency schedule of capital (Petri, 1992). This results from the fact that the continuous negative relationship between investment demand and the real rate of money interest ultimately relies on the belief that lower real rental rates entail investments in technologies that are more capital-intensive, leading to a lowering of the marginal physical product of capital until it equates the real rental rate. The reader can only compare these discredited relationships with those actually hypothesized in standard macroeconomic models to realize how little should be left of neoclassical macroeconomics. The case of employment in the labour market is illustrated by Figure 1.2, with (a) representing the assumed standard case while (b) is a possible case. One may note

*Figure 1.2 Demand for labour curve: (a) assumed neoclassical relation; (b) possible neo-Ricardian relation*

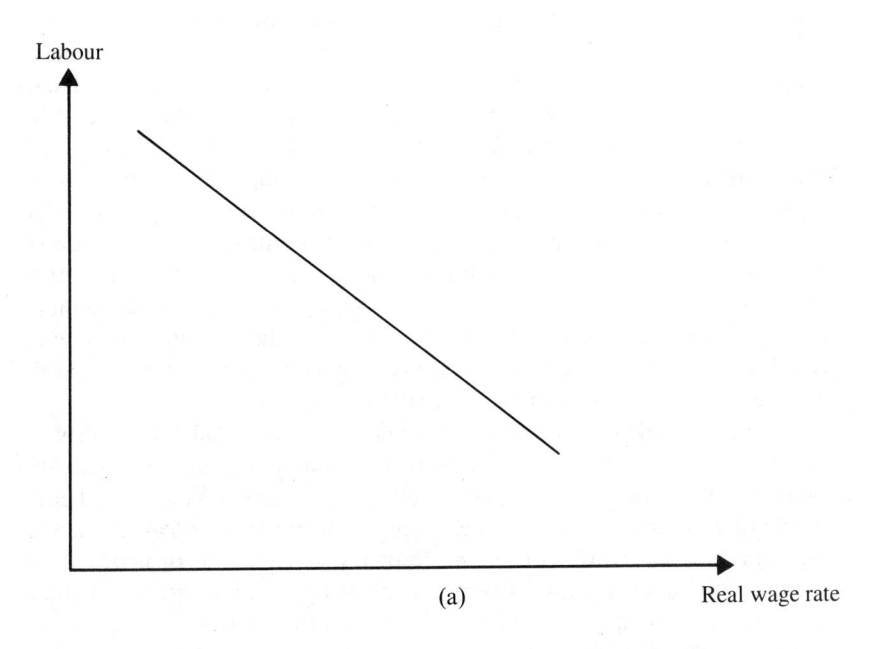

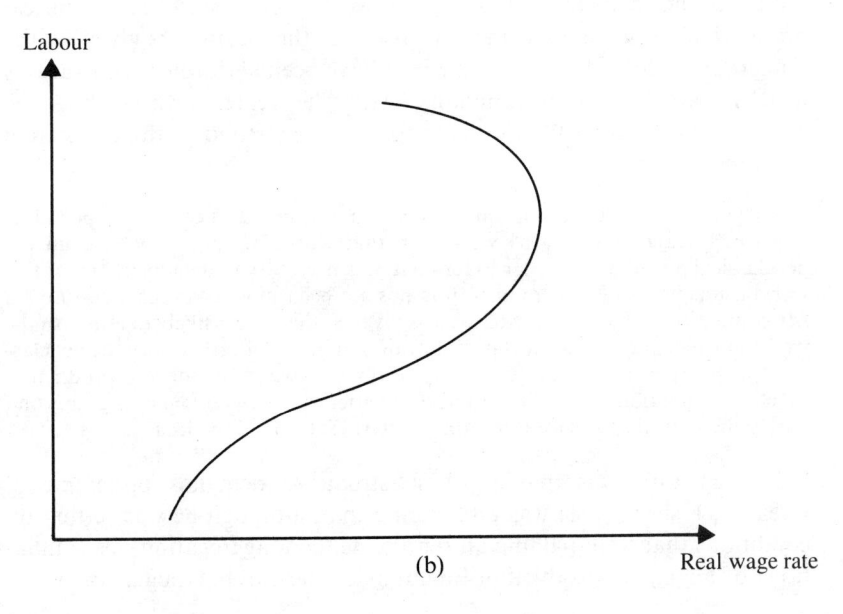

that a fall in the real wage rate does not necessarily imply a higher demand for labour.

Furthermore the above 'paradoxical' relationships are not limited to economy-wide effects. Steedman (1985, 1988) shows that one does not necessarily find a downward-sloping demand curve for any input, even at the direct industry level, when all adjustments are considered. These findings are crucial because they show that the paradoxes identified at the economy-wide level for the relationship between the value of capital and the profit rate apply just as well at the level of industries and to other inputs. For instance, in an industry, higher labour/output ratios may be associated with a higher real wage rate. Thus not much is left of macroeconomics, nor of mesoeconomics. Furthermore standard partial equilibrium analysis is shown to be just that, very partial and without proper foundations. Neoclassical economists are thus left with the two lines of defence that I have previously outlined: general equilibrium theory and the empirical avenue. Let us now consider the latter.

Several orthodox economists have taken the view that the validity of neoclassical theory was an empirical question, not a logical one. One presumes that the stance implicitly taken is that neo-Walrasian theory does not have much to offer when it comes to more practical issues and that one then has to rely on the more pedestrian versions of neoclassical theory to be able to make any practical recommendations. What these authors then argue is that the Cambridgian critique is right in a formal sense, but they deny that it has any real-world consequence. The empirical proof which is usually advanced to back up this position is given by the numerous successful regressions which have been performed with various neoclassical production functions, with the regressions yielding the expected coefficients. We are back to where we stood at the end of the previous section.

It is argued that there is a not-too-small world in which the neoclassical postulate is perfectly valid. As long as we live in that world, we need not give up the neoclassical postulate. In order to refute it, it is necessary to demonstrate that this world is imaginary. This demonstration has not been supplied in the literature ... My contention is that the state of the arts given at this time is likely to establish the world in which the neoclassical postulate dominates ... Furthermore the neoclassical postulate itself is in principle empirically testable in the form of production function estimation of the CES and other varieties. This can make us go beyond purely theoretical speculations on this matter. (Sato, 1974, p. 383)

Just as Sato was making these strenuous demands on empirical research, Fisher (1971) was discovering that, although he was setting up conditions that were baffling all requirements of aggregation, his simulations of aggregate production functions of the Cobb–Douglas or of the

CES type were successful. This led Fisher to conclude with the following oft-quoted remarks:

> The suggestion is clear, however, that labour's share is not roughly constant because the diverse technical relationships of modern economics are truly representable by an aggregate Cobb–Douglas but rather that such relationships appear to be representable by an aggregate Cobb–Douglas because labor's share happens to be roughly constant ... If one rejects the Cobb–Douglas form in favor of an alternative aggregate production function, the suggestion ... remains that the apparent success of such a function in explaining wages occurs not because such functions really represent the true state of technology but rather because their implications as to the stylized facts of wage behavior agree with what happens to be going on anyway. The development of the CES, for example, began with the observation that wages are an increasing function of output per man and that the function involved can be approximated by one linear in the logarithms. The present results suggest ... that the explanation of that wage-output per-man relationship may not be in the existence of an aggregate CES but rather that the apparent existence of an aggregate CES may be explained by that relationship. (Fisher, 1971, p. 325)

By now the reader should have lost all faith in the ability of neoclassical theory to redeem itself through empirical verifications and confirmations. A final proof should, however, be inflicted upon the incredulous reader. Start out with the dynamic Cobb–Douglas function, with constant returns to scale, $q$, $K$ and $L$ being as usual the output, the capital and the labour force, while $t$ and $\mu$ are the indices of time and technical progress:

$$q_t = e^{\mu t} K^\alpha L^{1-\alpha} \tag{1.1}$$

We know that, if the rental rates of capital and labour are equal to their marginal physical products, the coefficient $\alpha$ is the share of profits and the coefficient $(1-\alpha)$ is the share of labour in the national product. What is disconcerting about estimations of Cobb–Douglas functions is that the estimated coefficient $\alpha$ is usually equal to the actual share of profits in national accounts. But this should disconcert us no more, as was shown by Shaikh (1974, 1980). Rewriting the above Cobb–Douglas as output per unit of labour, that is dividing (1.1) by $L$, we get:

$$y_t = e^{\mu t} k^\alpha \tag{1.2}$$

with $y$ and $k$ being output per head and capital per head. Taking the logarithmic derivative of (1.2) one gets the standard form under which dynamic Cobb–Douglas production functions are empirically estimated, with $\hat{y}$ and $\hat{k}$ the rates of growth of output per head and capital per head:

$$\hat{y} = \mu + \alpha \hat{k} \tag{1.3}$$

A very similar result can however be obtained from the national accounting identities. With ω the real wage rate and $r$ the rate of profit, national income is:

$$Y = \omega L + rK \tag{1.4}$$

Output per head is then:

$$y = \omega + rk \tag{1.5}$$

Taking the derivative of equation (1.5) with respect to time yields:

$$dy/dt = d\omega/dt + k.dr/dt + r.dk/dt$$

This can be rewritten as:

$$dy/dt = \omega(d\omega/dt)/\omega + kr(dr/dt)/r + rk(dk/dt)/k$$

We now divide this whole expression by $y$. Recalling that $(dy/dt)/y$ is the rate of growth of output per head, which we denote by $\hat{y}$, the sign ^ generally indicating the rate of growth of a variable, we get the following equation:

$$\hat{y} = (\omega/y)\hat{\omega} + (rk/y)\hat{r} + (rk/y)\hat{k} \tag{1.6}$$

This can be rewritten as:

$$\hat{y} = \tau + \pi\hat{k} \tag{1.7}$$

with the actual share of profits $\pi$ equal to:

$$\pi = rk/y \tag{1.8}$$

and:

$$\tau = (1-\pi)\hat{\omega} + \pi\hat{r}$$

Equations (1.3) and (1.7) are thus similar, with both the parameters $\alpha$ and $\pi$ representing the profit share. But the first equation is derived from the peculiar Cobb–Douglas production function and its complicated assumptions, while the second is just a dynamic expansion of the national accounts. It is thus no surprise when income shares are more or less constant through time (time series data) or through sectors (cross-section data) that the Cobb–Douglas would give a good fit: it can be derived from income identities. But the same remarks can be addressed to the users of the popular CES function, as shown by Herbert Simon (1979). Ironically Simon did not mention Shaikh's 1974 piece, despite his acknowledgement of Solow's comments. Solow had been one of the original proponents of the CES function and had published a tentative rebuttal to Shaikh's arguments. One must therefore conclude that Solow did not bring Simon's attention to Shaikh's paper which had previously covered similar ground. Simon argues that the proponents of CES production functions are basically estimating the following function:

$$\log(y) = \log(a) + b \log(\omega) \tag{1.9}$$

Going back to equation (1.6) of the national accounts, and remembering from (1.8) that $rk$ can be written as $\pi y$, we have:

$$y = \omega + \pi y$$
$$y(1 - \pi) = \omega$$

Taking logarithms, the national accounts become:

$$\log(y) = -\log(1 - \pi) + \log(\omega) \tag{1.10}$$

We thus find again that equation (1.9), derived from neoclassical aggregate production functions, and equation (1.10), derived from national accounts, are nearly identical. The two equations are identical when the share of profits is a constant (or nearly so in statistical terms) and when the coefficient $b$ in equation (1.9) is equal to one. The first condition is similar to the one that we found for the Cobb–Douglas function to conform to accounting identities. Recall that it was also under these conditions that Fisher's simulations gave good results. With respect to $b$, it is recalled by Simon (1979, p. 467) that, when good statistical methodology is used, the best fits obtained with the CES function are those where the elasticity of substitution is close to one. This means that the CES function is in fact of the Cobb–Douglas type, and that the coefficient $b$ is equal to one.

Similarly, more complex forms of production functions yield Cobb–Douglas results under certain conditions. The reason for which the parameters of those more general production functions always seem to correspond to those yielding simple Cobb–Douglas functions with constant returns to scale is that a host of sophisticated mathematical manipulations in the end produce nothing more than modified accounting relations.

Well-known neoclassical economists still believe that 'the estimated elasticities that seem to confirm the central prediction of the theory of labor demand are not entirely an artifact' and they marvel at the empirical discovery that the Cobb–Douglas function with constant returns to scale 'is not a very severe departure from reality in describing production relations' (Hamermesh, 1986, pp. 454, 467). They should not. As shown by Shaikh and Simon, production data with sufficient constancy in the share of labour can always be approximated by a functional form that is mathematically identical to a Cobb–Douglas production function with the proper marginal products, whether the data come from a time series or from a cross-section. When the share of labour is not constant, the fit is not so good, and more sophisticated production functions must be called to the rescue. Still, only accounting identities are being verified, even in that case (McCombie and Dixon, 1991).

We can therefore conclude that the estimation of CES or other production functions has in no way tested the empirical validity of the neoclassical postulate, as Sato and others would like us to believe. On the contrary, it has simply verified accounting identities which have no link to aggregate neoclassical theory. Whereas the Cambridge controversies showed that neoclassical macroeconomics were left without theoretical foundations, the review of the above empirical aspects reveals that, if we are to believe the Frank Hahn of 1972, neoclassical macroeconomics is also left without any empirical foundations.

**The Stability Nightmare**

The consequences of the Cambridge controversies which have been described above have also sometimes been perceived as a stability problem that would mar the results of an aggregate production economy. The neo-Ricardians themselves have given rise to this interpretation with some of their statements. For instance, Garegnani argues that the Cambridge controversies 'deny plausibility to the traditional argument about a *long-period* tendency towards the full employment of labour' (1983, p. 73). Rogers (1989, p. 33) speaks of the 'problematic stability' of the long-period equilibrium solution. Nevertheless the neo-Ricardians themselves have generally preferred to emphasize the fact that, if the overall employment curve for labour looks the way it does in Figure 1.2(b), then one cannot really talk of a demand for labour as such (Garegnani, 1983, p. 73). A claim is then made that demand and supply conditions, based on the flexibility of prices, cannot explain the prevailing wage rate nor the level of employment (Mongiovi, 1991, p. 28). Some other explanation, not based on these functions of prices, must then be the pertinent one, perhaps to do with norms, conventions or notions of fairness. Another way to present this is to say that, since the neo-Ricardians have shown that there can be unstable equilibria, looking at it from the point of view of standard supply and demand analysis, and since we observe no such blatant instability in the real world, the mechanisms at work must be something other than the standard supply and demand price theory.

The pedestrian neoclassical answer is to argue that, since instability is rarely observed, either the system is always in equilibrium despite instability (because of rational expectations) or that only stable equilibria actually occur, thus dismissing the practical relevance of the neo-Ricardian critique. The more sophisticated answer is again to revert to the neo-Walrasian model, arguing that the full neoclassical general equilibrium model does not require aggregation and does not necessarily deal with long-run positions. The instability problem uncovered by the neo-Ricardians is thus of little interest to the neo-Walrasians since it concerns aggregated economies and assumes normal supply prices. What would be of more importance would be the proof that in general the neo-Walrasian model lacks stability results. This is the position taken by Hahn in the 1970s:

The neo-Ricardians ... have demonstrated that capital aggregation is theoretically unsound. Fine ... The result has no bearing on the mainstream of neoclassical theory simply because it does not use aggregates. It has a bearing on the vulgar theories of textbooks ... Results most damaging to neoclassical theory have recently been proved by Debreu, Sonnenschein and Mas-Collel. (Hahn, 1975, p. 363)

The damaging result proved by Sonnenschein and others is the following (cf. Kirman, 1989; Guerrien, 1989). Starting from the usual maximizing behaviour of individuals, resulting from the assumptions required for the demonstration of the existence of a general equilibrium of the Arrow–Debreu type, it is shown that the excess demand functions satisfying Walras's law in an exchange economy can take almost any form. This is damaging to neoclassical theory because one would have hoped that the excess demand functions would always be downward-sloping. This would ensure that, when the price of a good is too low, and consequently the excess demand positive, the *tâtonnement* process leads to a decrease in the excess demand as a result of the *commissaire-priseur* calling higher prices. This is illustrated by Figure 1.3(a), which in a sense corresponds to the well-behaved employment function of Figure 1.2(a). What the so-called Sonnenschein–Mantel–Debreu theorem, or impossibility theorem, demonstrates is that nothing in the standard hypotheses of individual choice behaviour precludes the excess demand functions from looking like Figure 1.3(b), which again can be related to the possible neo-Ricardian

*Figure 1.3 Excess demand curves in general equilibrium theory: (a) desired neoclassical relation; (b) possible relation arising from the impossibility theorem*

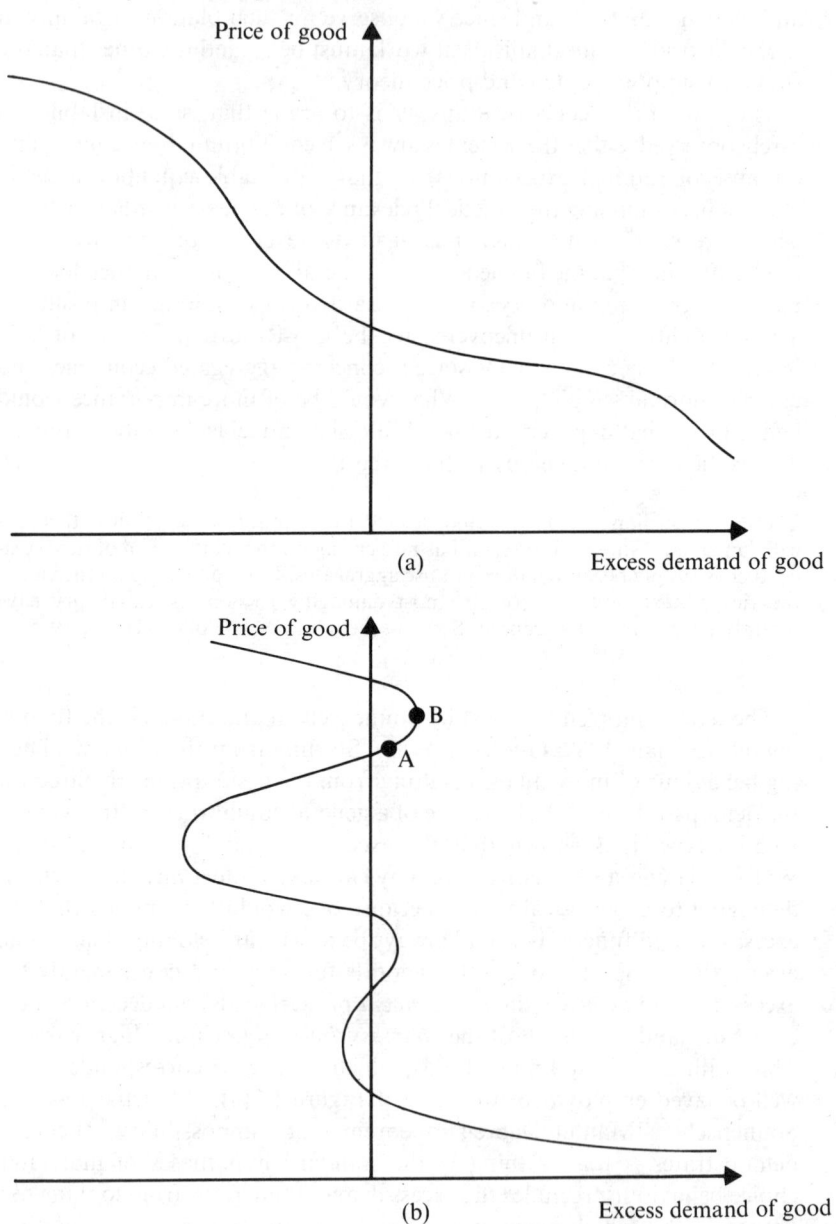

long-period employment function illustrated in Figure 1.2(b). As can be seen, there are several equilibria, and increasing the price when at point *A* would initially increase excess demand to point *B*. The only constraints on the shape of the function is that, for some high price, excess demand should be negative, and as price approaches zero the curve should tend towards infinity.

The impossibility theorem can of course be linked to the following well-known general equilibrium result: the decrease in the stock of a given resource may induce a fall (rather than a rise) in the rental rate of the resource. This is because the owners of the resource, as a consequence of the fall in their initial endowments, may decide to reduce their demand for products requiring the intensive use of this resource. The decrease in the demand for the resource could overcome the initial decrease in its supply. This type of paradoxical result, due to the existence of income effects overcoming substitution ones, despite the powerful and extensively used axiom of gross substitutability (often a target of Davidson's critique of general equilibrium theory (1980a)), was annoying to neoclassical theorists since they could not predict the sign of price changes resulting from an increase in the quantity of a single endowment, while all other endowments were assumed to be constant. Prices thus could not be considered as simple indices of scarcity, measured from the supply side. However scarcity analysis was preserved, since higher prices resulted from the presence of excess demand. The impossibility theorem denies that such prices are always stable or that they are unique. Small changes in the value of the data may lead to large changes in prices, precisely what the Cambridge controversies had underscored in the context of long-period positions of aggregate production economies.

Neo-Walrasians may thus be able to prove the existence of an equilibrium, but they are unable to prove its uniqueness and its stability even in the simple case of an exchange economy without production. The same problem plagues the intertemporal model *à la* Arrow–Debreu and the temporary equilibrium models, where expectations of future prices add a further arbitrary dimension (Polemarchakis, 1983). All these results are like a 'nightmare' for neo-Walrasian economists (Ingrao and Israel, 1990, p. 317). They mean that all comparative results are useless. They also imply that the invisible hand, even if prices are perfectly flexible, may be of no help to attain an equilibrium, not to speak of the optimum one. The neoclassical programme is thus in danger, since the major questions which are incorporated in the heuristics of the programme cannot be ascertained. Furthermore, and perhaps more damaging, the only way out of these negative results on stability seems to entail relinquishing at least one of the four presuppositions on which the whole research programme is built, that of methodological individualism.

Several attempts have been made to get out of this impasse, as the reader may have guessed. It has been suggested that models incorporating production, rather than being limited to exchange, might help to get rid of the arbitrariness of excess demand curves. There may be grounds for these hopes, but it should be realized that, even if a production sector is superimposed upon an exchange economy in which the arbitrariness of excess demand functions had been eliminated by assumption, by the introduction of the axiom of gross substitutability in demand, several equilibria could arise.

Other attempts were made from within the exchange model. However these attempts, when successful, only highlight the arbitrariness of the assumptions required to arrive at the desired result. For instance, unless there is an *infinite* number of consumers, excess demand functions can take any form, despite all agents having the same preference maps and their initial endowments being equal up to a constant multiplicative factor. Under these conditions, the Sonnenschein–Mantel–Debreu theorem falls only if all agents have identical preferences and equal income. This means that the structure of consumption would not depend on income, a not very realistic and promising simplification. One is back to the single representative agent, so much in use in neoclassical macroeconomics. It implies, furthermore, that the realms of microeconomics be left and that the methodology of building the foundations of economics from independent individuals be abandoned. The consequences have been well summarized by a participant to these negative theorems:

The independence of individuals' behaviour plays an essential role in the construction of economies generating arbitrary excess demand functions. As soon as it is removed the class of functions that can be generated is limited ... If we are to progress further we may well be forced to theorise in terms of groups who have collectively coherent behaviour. The idea that we should start at the level of the isolated individual is one which we may well have to abandon. (Kirman, 1989, p. 138)

The same conclusion is reached by another critical observer of these neo-Walrasian controversies:

Throughout the book, we have adopted a neoclassical viewpoint, trying to show that even the most fervent adepts of 'flexibility' cannot back their statements within their own models. A consequence of our study has been to show the limits of methodological individualism: the axiomatic construction of society, starting from agents and the maximizing principle, leads to inextricable situations, which take away from the model any predictive (or even explanatory) content. (Translation of Guerrien, 1989, p. 290)

The consequences of the Cambridge controversies were a setback for the neoclassical research programme, but they only applied to the aggregate versions of neoclassical theory. They dealt with production economies in fully adjusted positions. The impossibility theorems which have been demonstrated by Sonnenschein and others are a major setback for the neoclassical programme. They apply with equal force to the two major branches of the core theory, the intertemporal and the temporary versions of general equilibrium theory, even in the simplest case of exchange economies. The stability of the neoclassical model, whatever its degree of sophistication, the highbrow version or the vulgar one, thus cannot be demonstrated. This implies that comparative analysis cannot be performed within the standard neoclassical framework of supply and demand responding to market forces, at whatever level of aggregation. Furthermore the standard assumptions made in macroeconomics or in partial equilibrium microeconomics have no justification whatsoever. Barring imperfections of all sorts, the flexibility of prices will not guarantee the attainment of the optimal Walrasian equilibrium. The problem is not one of imperfections, it is one of structure. Moreover many of the restrictions which are imposed on the sign of parameters in econometric verifications are left without foundations. We have already seen that Cobb–Douglas production functions in these models are without scientific support. We now know that the Cobb–Douglas utility functions in exchange models are no better justified, since their object is to ensure the axiom of gross substitutability and avoid counter-intuitive excess demand functions.

There is no doubt that a number of neoclassical economists are now groping for an alternative programme, and that several more will do the same when the consequences of the above impossibility theorems become fully understood. There is thus a need for an alternative research programme. The object of the following chapters is to show that, to a large extent, such a coherent alternative research programme already exists. Such a programme does not rely on principles of substitution based on relative prices, or on the market forces of supply and demand. The major explaining force will be the income effects that so much jeopardize the neoclassical framework.

# 2. Theory of Choice

The object of this chapter is to present the way in which economic agents take their decisions in a post-Keynesian world. Since most of these decisions are set within a world of uncertainty, a concept which post-Keynesians have been keen to underline, the notion of uncertainty will be defined with care. Furthermore, although post-Keynesians have an organic view of the world, we shall pay much attention to the rationality which underlies the actions of economic agents, in particular within a world of uncertainty. Finally we shall deal with the much neglected issue of consumer choice, about which we shall discover that post-Keynesians have, surprisingly, a common view.

## 2.1 THE DISTINCTION BETWEEN RISK AND UNCERTAINTY

Before embarking on the study of the way agents take decisions, it is necessary, as a preliminary step, to describe the environment in which these decisions are usually taken. Post-Keynesian economists, in particular those which Coddington (1976) has called the fundamentalist Keynesians, are known for their insistence on the importance of fundamental uncertainty. American post-Keynesians, in particular Hyman Minsky (1976, chs 3 and 6) and Paul Davidson (1972, ch. 2), have stressed the role played by uncertainty, especially in conjunction with money and monetary economies. In this section I will make no claims regarding the possible links between the presence of uncertainty and that of money (Hoogduin, 1991). Rather the aim of this section is to distinguish clearly between situations of risk, which are those usually described by neoclassical authors, and situations of uncertainty, which are those faced by agents in a Post-Keynesian world. My intent is to clear up the confusion that the term 'uncertainty' has generated. This will allow us to tackle the question of procedural rationality with a clearer mind, although it should be pointed out right away that procedural rationality, rather than substantive or global rationality, does not require the presence of uncertainty to be exercised. However, whenever there is uncertainty, procedural rationality must of necessity prevail.

**A Definition of Uncertainty**

The relevance of fundamental uncertainty, despite the post-Keynesian exhortations to include it in economic analysis, has not been taken very seriously by most mainstream economists. In fact, mainstream economists are often annoyed at being told that they do not deal with uncertainty. They point to the mainstream journals, the pages of which are filled with papers entitled 'the economics of uncertainty of this or of that', which deal with asymmetric or incomplete information, stochastic elements of some sort, probability densities, and so on. For a neoclassical economist, what is not certain is uncertain. There is thus a semantic confusion arising from the fact that the word 'uncertainty' is being used by both post-Keynesian economists and mainstream economists, but with different meanings. What should really be said is that these mainstream papers are set in an environment of risk, or one of certainty equivalence. Annoyed mainstream economists thus do not recognize the distinction between risk and uncertainty.

Besides the neo-Austrians (Lachmann, 1977) or economists who have close links with them (Shackle, 1971, 1972; Loasby, 1976), there are also some orthodox economists who have acknowledged the importance of the distinction between risk and fundamental uncertainty. For instance, E. R. Weintraub, no doubt influenced on that matter by his father, Sidney Weintraub, while taking note that general equilibrium theory had not dealt with fundamental uncertainty, has written that Keynes's treatment of uncertainty is 'an innovation of sublime importance ignored for almost thirty years by most economists and still ignored by many' (1975, p. 530). He adds that 'there is no way uncertainty problems can be reduced to problems involving risk' (p. 532). Thus even those who make little use of the distinction recognize its significance and its importance. We shall deal later with the question as to why enlightened neoclassical writers still leave aside situations of fundamental uncertainty.

Let us now see how uncertainty should be defined within a three-way typology (Lavoie, 1985a):

1. There is *certainty* when each choice invariably leads to a specific outcome, the value of which is known.
2. There is *risk*, or certainty equivalence, when each choice leads to a set of possible specific outcomes, the value of which is known, each outcome being associated with a specific probability.

3. There is *uncertainty* when the probability of an outcome is unknown, when the value of an outcome is unknown, when the outcomes that can possibly result from a choice are unknown, or when the spectrum of possible choices is unknown.

There would thus be three types of uncertainty. The first one, the uncertainty of probability, is most often discussed in the economic literature. The question revolves around how one can get proper estimates of these probabilities. This is not considered to be a true problem by the mainstream. Estimates of probabilities can always be made, from a logical or subjective point of view. The uncertainty of value, when one ignores the values (presumably the monetary ones) attached to the different outcomes, can be easily brought back to a situation of risk, by making use of sensitivity analysis. There is finally what one could call fundamental uncertainty, where the individual is ignorant of the available courses of action or of the extent of future states of the world. Such a form of uncertainty leads to unknown probabilities, or to what Keynes and others call non-measurable probabilities. This is the type of uncertainty which is the least likely to be subsumed within standard analysis. This is what post-Keynesians mean when they speak of fundamental or true uncertainty, or of Knightian or Keynesian uncertainty.

The concept of uncertainty is an extension of the presupposition of realism, as pointed out by Lawson (1988). It is not difficult to think of situations where the essence of the problem is to find the options which are available, and where all future prospects cannot be listed. Technological advancement would be a good example of fundamental uncertainty, involving as it does the impossibility of knowing what the novelty will be, when it will appear, and how large its impact on society will be. Keynes and Knight underline fundamental uncertainty because they believe that it is a crucial element of our economic environment. When agents make their decisions, they act according to this uncertain knowledge, rather than *as if* risky situations prevailed. Thus both Keynes and Knight were convinced that a radical distinction between situations of risk and situations of uncertainty had to be made, and that economic analysis had to take this distinction into consideration.

> The calculus of probability . . . was supposed to be capable of reducing uncertainty to the same calculable status as that of certainty itself . . . This false rationalisation follows the lines of the Benthamite calculus. The hypothesis of a calculable future leads to a wrong interpretation of the principles of behaviour which the need for action compels us to adopt. (Keynes, 1973, xiv, pp. 112, 122)

I still find a fundamental significance in the analysis of uncertainty in the essay, and am puzzled at the insistence of many writers on treating the uncertainty of result in choice as if it were a gamble on a known mathematical chance. (Knight, 1940, p. xiv)

## The Weight of an Argument or the Credibility of Information

There have recently been many assessments of Keynes's philosophical views and their impact on his notions of probability and uncertainty, as well as their evolution through time (Carabelli, 1988; O'Donnell, 1989, 1990). Furthermore several authors have attempted to underline the differences in Keynes's and Knight's accounts of uncertainty (Hoogduin, 1987). None of these topics will be dealt with in what follows. On the contrary I shall concentrate on the aspects that are consistent within each author, and focus on the common points in the analyses of these two authors. My view, again like that of Lawson (1988) I believe, is that fundamentally Keynes and Knight are in agreement. To highlight their minor differences would be like looking at the trees without seeing the forest.

Knight and Keynes both recognize that, for some experiences or decisions, the orthodox calculus of risk is the appropriate one, in particular in situations of scientific experimentations. Standard deviations can be computed and for point estimates we can even obtain a confidence interval, based upon the set probability of error. This can be linked to what Knight (1940, p. 226) calls the 'probability of error', and which Keynes (1973, viii, p. 82) names the 'probable error'. Both agree that in repetitive situations these probable errors are useful.

On the other hand, both Keynes and Knight would argue that, generally, decisions have to be taken under conditions where standard errors and probabilities are meaningless, even though they might be estimated and computed. This is certainly the case of most long-term business decisions. To clarify this matter, in his *Treatise on Probability*, Keynes defines a new concept, which he calls the 'weight of an argument'. The weight represents the relative amount of information which is available when a decision must be taken. It represents our relevant knowledge relative to our relevant ignorance (Keynes, 1973, viii, p. 77) or the degree of completeness of our knowledge (Keynes, 1973, viii, p. 345). Georgescu-Roegen (1966, p. 266) calls it the 'credibility' attached to a set of probabilistic expectations. Others refer to its quality or to its epistemic reliability (Anand, 1991, p. 200).

In some cases, the standard error of statisticians and the weight of an argument may be closely related. Where the law of large numbers applies, an increase in relative knowledge tends to decrease the standard error, without the probabilities of the various outcomes being modified. This is why in these cases one can associate the standard error with the weight of an argument. The credibility of the probability statement augments with the size of the sample. There is a practical connection between the two. It may be, however, that additional evidence leads to an increase in standard deviation, as Keynes shows (1973, viii, p. 82). In general the evolution of the weight and that of the standard deviation or standard error might thus diverge. Keynes believes that the former rather than the latter is then of significance. When probabilities are purely subjective, the standard deviation is without meaning, since it only reflects whether or not the agent has given high probabilities to the outcomes the value of which are around the most likely value. An argument of high weight is not one in which the standard deviation is small.

The more relevant factor is the quality of information or the relative quantity of information which has led to the estimates of outcomes and probabilities. Keynes himself believed that the weight always increases with further information (1973, viii, p. 84). We need not follow him in this regard. In truly uncertain situations, further information might reduce the degree of confidence without necessarily changing the assessed probabilities, in the case of political crises, for instance (Minsky, 1976, p. 65). There is new information, but this information has destroyed part of the past accumulated knowledge, or it has uncovered new aspects of unsuspected ignorance. The stock of relevant information relative to ignorance has decreased. Weight may decrease with the acquisition of new evidence and can thus be defined as 'the balance of the absolute amounts of relevant knowledge and relevant ignorance, on which a probability is based' (Runde, 1990, p. 290).

Keynes's conclusion is that 'in deciding on a course of action, it seems plausible to suppose that we ought to take account of the weight as well as the probability of different expectations' (Keynes, 1973, viii, p. 83). This is how actions between risky and uncertain situations become distinguished. When standard errors are relevant, the probability density function is not independent of the measure of risk. In the case of fundamental uncertainty, probabilities and the weight of the argument are independent properties. Knight comes to the same conclusion. He also emphasizes the independent character of the weight of an argument and the probability distribution in situations of uncertainty. He is simply using words that will be later adopted by Keynes in the *General Theory* and after.

The business man himself not merely forms the best estimate he can of the outcome of his actions, but he is likely also to estimate the probability that his estimate is correct. The 'degree' of certainty or of confidence felt in the conclusion after it is reached cannot be ignored, for it is of the greatest practical significance.

## Theory of Choice

The action which follows upon an opinion depends as much upon the amount of confidence in that opinion as it does upon the favorableness of the opinion itself ... Fidelity to the actual psychology of the situation requires, we must insist, recognition of these two separate exercises of judgment, the formation of an estimate and the estimation of its value. (Knight, 1940, p. 227)

We thus see that the weight of an argument is here called by Knight the degree of certainty or the degree of confidence, or the worthiness of a probability estimate. As is well known, when in the *General Theory* Keynes refers to uncertain factors, or to uncertainty, he quotes the chapter dealing with weights of arguments of his previous *Treatise on Probability*. The weight of an argument is then translated by the 'state of confidence' or by the 'animal spirits' of the entrepreneurs. The following quotation shows clearly that Knight and Keynes are fundamentally making the same distinction.

The state of long-term expectations, upon which our decisions are based, does not solely depend, therefore, on the most probable forecast we can make. It also depends on the *confidence* with which we make this forecast – on how highly we rate the likelihood of our best forecast turning out quite wrong. (Keynes, 1973, vii, p. 148)

The upshot of the matter is that situations of uncertainty cannot come down to situations of risk. When taking a decision in an uncertain world, a rational agent cannot only rely on the probability distribution which arises from past similar events or from subjective introspection. The credibility or the reliability of the acquired information, the degree of confidence in the assessed probabilities, must also be considered. It is also claimed by Georgescu-Roegen (1966, p. 267) that the lack of weight of an argument cannot be compensated by the high probability attached to the main outcome (although Keynes, 1973, viii, p. 348, is not so clear about this). Otherwise probabilities and weight could be summarized under one index, and we would be back to a revised form of expected utility theory. But if such a distinction between situations of risk and situations of fundamental uncertainty can indeed be established, why is it that neoclassical authors have generally ignored the distinction, and have reasoned or modelled problems as if the distinction did not exist?

### Objections to Fundamental Uncertainty

The neoclassical arguments against the use of fundamental uncertainty can be organized in three stages. First there are those economists who argue that economic events are recurrent. This is a view of probability based on observed frequencies. It is believed by those economists that past distributions of outcomes are a good indicator of future ones. As a consequence, probabilistic expectations of the future can be based on past distributions (Lucas, 1981, p. 223–4). But such an argument, Davidson (1982–3, 1988a) claims, is based on an ergodic view of the world. Ergodic processes ensure that 'the probability distribution of the relevant variables calculated from any past realisation tends to converge with the probability function governing the current events *and* with the probability function that will govern future economic outcomes' (Davidson, 1988a, p. 331). When historical processes are non-ergodic, such convergence does not exist and we cannot rely on statistical distributions of the past to provide reliable data to estimate present or future distributions. Uncertainty then prevails. Non-stationary stochastic processes with structural breaks or crises, or even some stationary stochastic processes such as limit-cycles, are examples of non-ergodic processes. Uncertainty prevails in the real world because economic processes are not usually ergodic. The observed frequencies of the past cannot be a guide for the future. This sort of argument against the neoclassical frequentist viewpoint is usually attributed to Knight and Shackle. They both contend that most long-term business decisions have a unique character and hence cannot rely on past empirical measures, previous decisions having changed the economic environment.

At this stage, neoclassical authors come up with their second line of opposing arguments against the consideration of fundamental uncertainty. They argue that probability estimates are mainly of a purely subjective sort. The fact that historical processes are ergodic or not is irrelevant. In the less extreme subjectivist views, an agent may rely on past experience to establish probabilities, but basically probabilities are indices of the subjective belief in outcomes. Probabilities thus constitute a code of coherence to apprehend a world without certainty, and as such have given rise to axiomatic formulations. All situations can be described with the help of these subjective probability distributions, with means and standard deviations. At the limit, if future outcomes or possible choices are unknown, as they would in the case of fundamental uncertainty, risk analysis or expected utility theory can still be safeguarded by relying on the principle of insufficient reason which imputes an equal probability to all uncertain states. With this principle, a given probability distribution corresponds to every situation. When further pressed, neoclassical authors observe that, if compelled to, any person will quote a betting quotient on any outcome.

We now understand why Knight and Keynes insist so much on the distinction between risk and uncertainty; they both reject the principle of insufficient reason on the grounds that it will not lead to rational decisions in an uncertain world (Knight, 1940, p. 222). As Blatt says (1982, p. 267): 'This is a possible rule. But it is a fool's rule.' Keynes is pretty clear about this, both in the *Treatise on Probability* and in the *General Theory*. When future outcomes or choices are unknown, that is when the set of known alternatives is not exhaustive, the principle of insufficient reason cannot be applied and therefore situations of uncertainty cannot be reduced to ones of risk.

The recognition of the fact, that not all probabilities are numerical, limits the scope of the principle of indifference [insufficient reason]. It has always been agreed that a numerical measure can actually be obtained in those cases only in which a reduction to a set of exclusive and exhaustive *equiprobable* alternatives is practicable ... A rule can be given for numerical measurement when the conclusion is one of a number of equiprobable, exclusive and exhaustive alternatives, but not otherwise. (Keynes, 1973, viii, pp. 70, 122)

Nor can we rationalize our behaviour by arguing that to a man in a state of ignorance errors in either direction are equally probable ... For it can easily be shown that the assumption of arithmetically equal probabilities based on a state of ignorance leads to absurdities. (Keynes, 1973, vii, p. 152)

Keynes's position when probabilities are non-numerical in the above sense is that decisions must take into consideration both the credibility of the information (the weight of an argument) and the assumed probability distribution. In Chapter 12 of the *General Theory*, Keynes focuses on the predominant importance of the state of confidence or that of the weight of information, represented by the strength of animal spirits. There he goes so far as to say that decisions 'cannot depend on strict mathematical expectations, since the basis for making such calculations does not exist' (Keynes, 1973, vii, p. 163). Mainstream analyses either precisely assume the existence of an exhaustive description of the possible actions and the possible states of the world, or they omit the question of credibility and behave as if the credibility of information was not an issue, as in search theory, for instance (High, 1983–4).

Their reasons for doing so, assuming they accept Keynes's critique of the principle of insufficient reason, must be linked to the third line of defence of the neoclassical refusal to consider fundamental uncertainty. Neoclassical authors argue that the framework of expected utility, or that of portfolio theory, since under some conditions it can be shown to be equivalent to expected utility theory (Sinn, 1983, p. 96), is simple and allows one to obtain unambiguous results (Arrow, 1951, p. 411). If one were to discuss situations of fundamental uncertainty, rather than ones of risk, either several results would be possible (as in game theory, with no possible definition of what rational behaviour could be) or economics would be following a nihilistic path. 'In cases of uncertainty, economic reasoning would be of no value' (Lucas 1981, p. 224). It is thus argued that fundamental uncertainty unnecessarily adds complexities. Neoclassical authors continue to assume that knowledge of the future is perfect, or that all uncertain situations can be reduced to ones of risk. They behave as if there was no fundamental uncertainty in the real world and as if agents could assign probabilities to every conceivable event and act upon these. They prefer to follow 'a passage more fertile in analytical results – rather than ... be content with making smaller, yet more relevant, strides' (Georgescu-Roegen, 1966, p. 242); or, in harsher terms, they 'prefer to be precisely wrong rather than roughly right or accurate' (Davidson, 1984, p. 572). This analytical position arises from the presuppositions of the neoclassical research programme, more precisely its instrumentalist epistemology.

In the case of uncertainty, the neoclassical justification for such an instrumentalist position would be that the adoption of a realistic concept of uncertainty leads nowhere. One must admit that some defenders of the notion of fundamental uncertainty, most notably Shackle (1984, p. 391), have left their readers with the impression that uncertainty only allows nihilistic conclusions. But this is not the position of the majority of post-Keynesians, and certainly not the position taken in this book. The impact of uncertainty on economic analysis and on economic results depends on 'how individuals are supposed to respond to the fact of uncertainty' (Coddington, 1982, p. 482). Neoclassical analysis relies on a very special sort of rationality, that of substantive rationality. This is why it cannot make sense of situations of fundamental uncertainty. The argument of the following section will be that, once procedural rationality is introduced into the behaviour of agents, the presence of uncertainty does not necessarily generate chaotic behaviour or prevent economic modelling.

## 2.2 PROCEDURAL RATIONALITY: RULES AND NORMS

Let us now recapitulate some of the lessons drawn from the previous section. When the economic environment is certain or is equivalent to certainty, that is, when situations of risk are encountered, the standard optimizing procedures, or some revised version thereof, might be rational. When fundamental uncertainty prevails, decisions have to take into consideration the credibility of the acquired knowledge. The standard optimizing procedures will not mimic the behaviour of economic agents. Decisions will depend as much on the degree of confidence attached to the forecasts made as on whether the forecasts are favourable or not. If we forsake optimizing procedures, what are we going to replace them with?

**Definitions of Rationality**

At this stage we have to introduce more clearly the distinction between substantive rationality, upon which neoclassical economics is based, and procedural rationality (also called bounded rationality), which characterizes post-Keynesian economics. Simon defines substantive rationality and procedural rationality in the following way:

> Behavior is substantively rational when it is appropriate to the achievement of goals within the limits imposed by given conditions and constraints ... Given these goals, the rational behavior is determined entirely by the characteristics of the environment in which it takes place ... Behavior is procedurally rational when it is the outcome of appropriate deliberation. Its procedural rationality depends on the process that generated it. (Simon, 1976, pp. 130–1)

The definition of substantive rationality is consistent with the view that most neoclassical economists have of their research programme: they see it as a science of constrained optimization. The goals of substantive rationality are usually some form of utility or profit maximization. The conditions and the constraints are the existing and possible states of nature, that is the external characteristics of the economic environment. Now, for the conditions and the constraints to be given, they must be known or probabilistically known, or as in game theory the description of the various outcomes must be exhaustive. Otherwise substantive rationality loses much of its strength.

Procedural rationality only requires appropriate reasoning. Behaviour is rational if there are good reasons underlying the observed behaviour (Lawson, 1985, p. 918). Bounded rationality focuses on the fact that there are other constraints on the agent taking decisions besides the external ones. These are the constraints on the capabilities of the agent in processing information. There are internal constraints which are not taken into consideration by neoclassical theory. Thus whether available information is complete or not, in all but the simplest of problems, is accessory. It will not be possible for the agent taking decisions to proceed with standard optimizing procedures. The computational and classifying requirements are too great, or the necessary information is just not available. March (1978, p. 590) says that agents develop procedures which are *sensible* given the decisional constraints, although they could look unreasonable if the constraints were removed. In a similar spirit, Cyert and Simon have offered the following extensive definition of procedural rationality:

> The rationality of the business firm is a rationality that takes account of the limits

on its knowledge, on its information, on its capacity for computation, and on its understanding of theory. It is a rationality that makes extensive use of rules of thumb where a more exact application of theory is impossible whether because the theory is not understood, because the data needed for estimating its parameters is not available, or because the decision must be made under conditions of uncertainty. (Cyert and Simon, 1983, p. 104)

In standard neoclassical models the individual must gather information on all possible actions, all possible states of nature, and therefore on all possible outcomes induced by the previous two sets. Probabilities, often complex conditional probabilities, must be ascertained for each outcome, and each outcome must be assigned numerical (monetary) values. We have already discussed the complexity of this part of substantive rationality. But on top of that, through a system of preferences, with or without utility measures, with or without desired features such as transitivity, the agent must choose the most preferred action, the one that will optimize the situation. The agent must thus consider all of the various final outcomes, with their numerical counterparts, go back to find out what possible results each initial action generates, and then compare these to find the action generating the optimal set of possible outcomes. Optimality necessitates recourse to a backward induction reasoning which requires a substantial number of computations (Hey, 1983). The same huge computational capabilities are required in situations of certainty, when consumers make choices with respect to different goods, for instance. The stress put on human capabilities is not only limited to probabilistic or uncertain situations. It affects most situations of certainty as well. In a way, this is a more destructive critique than the notion of uncertainty since it does not rely on the scarcity of information but rather on its overabundance (Hodgson, 1988, p. 83).

Let me give an anecdotal instance of an overload of information in the case of a consumer choice in a world of certainty. A few years back, Professor Sergio Parrinello (1982) gave a talk at the University of Ottawa on a possible extension of the theory of consumer choice, basically arguing that the larger the range of choices the happier the consumer would be. We then took Professor Parrinello to a Chinese restaurant. Upon looking at the menu, which, like most Chinese menus, had a wide selection of more than one hundred dishes, our colleague asked somehow distressfully if there was not some set course of dishes that would allow him to avoid the pains of making choices among these too numerous alternatives. We told him that we had chosen a Chinese restaurant precisely in the light of the theory he had so convincingly presented to us in the afternoon. It turned out, given the state of fatigue of Professor Parrinello's computing abilities after his long trip, that the possibility of a wider choice had led to confusion rather than to satisfaction. Substantive rationality needs to be replaced by procedural rationality.

We are thus left with the conclusion that substantive rationality is not possible either when there is a lack of information or when information is too extensive to be processed. In both of these cases, substantial rationality is of little use to describe what economic agents actually do and to prescribe what they should be doing. Information processing, whether the gathered information is complete or not, is costly and time-consuming. As a consequence agents do not optimize, nor should they, according to the logic of marginalism itself, since presumably the marginal costs of optimizing computational procedures always surpass the marginal returns from optimizing. There is no point in relying on substantive rationality if no procedure can be devised that will make the amount of required computations reasonable. By abandoning optimizing rules, and adopting satisficing ones, we recognize the limits of the human mind, even when helped, as they are now, by computers. To some extent, the presupposition of procedural rationality is thus one of realism.

It should be noted that neoclassical theory, by relying on substantive rationality, gets further away from realism every time it tries to introduce some realistic component to its theoretical edifice. When they are being accused of not dealing with situations of uncertainty, neoclassical authors respond with models of risk, in which agents know all possible events and their accompanying probabilities. Similarly, some neoclassical authors have interpreted search theory as a response to the criticisms of Simon. It is felt that procedural rationality and its accompanying rule of satisficing means optimization under the costly constraint of information gathering. But the computations and the information required for the optimal resolution of this search are even more intricate. It may have taken months for the theorist to find the optimal solution of the model, without even having had to find concrete data. Furthermore the optimizing approach leads to a problem of infinite regress. To know whether or not the information search has been optimized, agents need to know beforehand the value of the information to be gathered. To argue that agents have a probabilistic view of the information to be gathered makes even more unlikely the practical possibility of such optimizing computations.

Whereas neoclassical authors claim that their new models make it possible to get away from the assumptions of perfect knowledge, they are in fact moving the neoclassical programme further away from realism. 'The reason is that in order to apply the traditional optimizing concepts, the competence of the agent has been implicitly upgraded to handle the extra complexity resulting from an unpredictable future' (Heiner, 1983, p. 571). What neoclassical theorists basically do when they construct models is to match the computational capabilities and information-gathering abilities of the agents to the requirements of finding an equilibrium, preferably a unique one. The extent of substantive rationality is thus defined in accordance with the goals being pursued by the modeller. Agents are assumed to be able to gather the necessary information and to process it fully.

On the other hand, the presupposition of procedural rationality, or what is also called bounded rationality or sometimes weak rationality, presumes that, in all but the simplest problems, there exists a gap between the relevant amount of information and the information that can be effectively processed. The relevant information might not be processed either because it is not known – this is the case that we have examined in our discussion of uncertainty – or because the computational and intellectual limitations of the agent prevent part of the available information being dealt with. To the extent that we might consider available information that is not processed as unknown information, it could be argued that the gap between processed information and relevant information is a measure of the extent of uncertainty, or the reciprocal of what Keynes called the weight of an argument. This is precisely what Heiner (1983, p. 562) does: he calls this gap the C–D uncertainty gap, or the gap between the agent's competence and the difficulty of the problem to be solved. Under those terms, uncertainty will thus be the higher the more complex the problem to be solved and the more feeble the perceived competence of the decision maker.

Under this revised definition of uncertainty, complex risk situations, or even ones of the certain type, would be classified under the category of uncertain situations since the computational requirements would be too great. This might explain in part why it has repeatedly been shown that, even in simple risk situations, individuals do not respond accordingly to the expected utility theory. Furthermore, with this revised definition of uncertainty, the concepts of uncertainty and procedural rationality become intertwined. All situations of uncertainty require procedural rationality, as we have previously argued, and decisions made on the basis of procedural rationality would be by definition related to situations of uncertainty. I believe, however, that it is more profitable to distinguish between certain, risky and uncertain situations in accordance with the definitions of the previous section, bearing in mind that even risky or perfectly certain situations may not permit the use of substantive rationality.

## Rules of Procedural Rationality

Having shown that fundamental uncertainty precludes the existence of a best solution, and that the limited computational abilities of the human mind preclude the search for the best solution, we are thus left with the notion that procedural rationality is the process that leads to finding good solutions. This is where the idea of satisficing, rather than optimizing, comes about, without denying that some maximizing procedures may be used within procedural rationality. Agents may maximize, but within a very constrained framework, bounded either by the set of information which they have decided to process or by the rules and conventions which they have imposed upon themselves. The solutions sought, whether or not they are the result of some internal highly constrained maximizing procedure, are good or satisfying solutions.

Procedural rationality, in cases of uncertainty or of insufficient capabilities to process existing information, thus consists of means to avoid complex calculations and considerations, and of procedures enabling decisions to be taken despite inaccurate information. Some of these procedures are conscious – we may then speak of rules – while others are unconscious – we may refer to them as habits (Hodgson, 1988, p. 106). For instance, a large part of our spending as consumers is based on habits. Furthermore shortcuts are used to arrive at quick decisions. Some forms of lexicographic ordering are used to process alternatives. For instance, in the Economics Department of the University of Ottawa, only Canadian (by law) and bilingual (by choice) candidates are seriously taken into consideration for recruitment, unless otherwise exceptional. This allows the recruiting committee to focus its attention on 15 rather than 100 candidates. Similarly, banks do not try to compute an interest rate that would compensate for a too high risk of default on the part of the borrower: they simply do not lend.

Because these procedures do not rely on optimizing behaviour, they are usually considered as instances of market failure and are called, sometimes disdainfully, rules of thumb. However, in a world of ignorance and of complexity, these rules of thumb are rational, because 'they are modes of behavior that the firm (or individual) develops as guides for making decisions in a complex environment with uncertainty and incomplete information' (Cyert and Simon, 1983, p. 105). There are many examples of rules of thumb in the real world: pay-back periods for investment decisions; mark-up pricing or full-cost pricing for firms or retailers; the normal rate of utilization of capacity; financial ratios of all sorts, leverage ratios, cash ratios, liquidity ratios for firms; ratios of interest payments to gross income for households wanting to take a mortgage; all bureaucratic rules. The examples could be almost infinite. Rules allow individuals or institutions to take decisions without having to consider or reconsider all of the available information.

That agents follow rules of thumb cannot be doubted, in situations of uncertainty and, more surprisingly, in situations of risk as well. Hey (1982) has given many examples of the type of rules of thumb employed by agents when searching at a cost for an acceptable price to buy: accept an offer if the quote is larger than the previous quote less the search cost, and so on. Furthermore there have been numerous studies showing the deficiencies of the standard expected utility theory in risk situations. Even when agents face relatively simple problems, with the knowledge of the appropriate possible outcomes, their values and their probabilities being known, it has been discovered that the axioms of substantive rational behaviour (transitivity and the like) are not verified. Although several complex variants of expected utility theory have been proposed, such as regret theory, none can explain all the violations of axioms which have been recurrently observed (Machina, 1987, p. 149). After observing that choices depend heavily on the manner in which the problem is being put, Tversky *et al.* (1990, p. 275) conclude that, even in the simplest situations of choice, those of risk, one cannot assume that agents respond with any optimizing procedure of the traditional sort. One must therefore conclude that, in the more likely uncertain environment, agents will have recourse to satisficing rules.

On a more general plane, various procedures have been suggested by Keynes and Simon to handle the complexities of decision making, especially in situations of true uncertainty. These are:

1. When a satisfactory solution has been reached, stop searching.
2. Take the present and the recent past as guides for the future.
3. Assume that the present evaluation of the future is correct.
4. Follow the opinion of the majority.
5. Look for alternative actions when existing ones are too uncertain.
6. Take actions that reduce the amount of uncertainty.
7. When uncertainty is too large, postpone the decision.

The first rule is in fact the core of procedural rationality. It presumes that the decision maker sets aspiration levels which make it possible to distinguish between what is acceptable and what is not. However the problem of ranking all of the possibilities is avoided since the agent is looking for one solution within the acceptable range, rather than the best among all solutions. All alternatives do not have to be considered in detail. The next three rules have been proposed by Keynes (1973, xiv, p.

114) to deal with uncertainty. Rules (2) and (3) are somewhat reminiscent of an economic forecast with adaptive expectations, onto which the latest news would have been grafted. This is precisely what forecasting agencies generally have to offer and what firms are looking for.

The fourth rule, that of relying on the opinion of the majority, is perhaps the rule the implications of which are the most important. When the available information is not very reliable or too complex to be processed, it seems that a rational reaction is to rely on the opinions of others, which are either better informed or which represent the majority view, that is the view that should prevail on the markets. The rationale here is that there are less chances of getting burned when one is following the crowd. For instance, unless one is a speculator with a better informed opinion, it is rational for businessmen to launch a new product when other businessmen are optimistic, that is when one can expect effective demand to be strong (Barrère, 1981, p. 153). The less confident we are in our own views, the more we should rely on the judgement of others. Furthermore, as Keynes said (1973, ix, p. 156), a banker who has been ruined is a sound banker provided he has followed all the rules and traditions of the profession and has gone under with a few of his colleagues. 'Worldly wisdom teaches that it is better for reputation to fail conventionally than to succeed unconventionally' (Keynes, 1973, vii, p. 158). The illusion of strong rationality in very uncertain situations will thus be safeguarded by mimicking others (Orléan, 1987).

This type of imitative behaviour has strong consequences. The rules that we have mentioned, financial ratios and the like, will be normalized through imitation. Not only do they constitute helpful guidance to decisions, but they also become norms and conventions which have to be respected. These norms are usually not the average of the aggregated opinion of all individuals, since the opinion of some is judged to be of more weight than that of others. As a consequence these norms represent focal points, determined in great part by the opinions of some powerful and respected group. We have already seen that procedural rationality is linked to the presupposition of realism. Now we see that procedural rationality is consistent with the presupposition of organicism (Lawson, 1985; Winslow, 1989). When they take decisions, or even when they set their preferences, entrepreneurs and households rely on habits, customs, conventions and norms. This means that, to a large extent, when proceeding to analyse the overall economy, we can dispense with going into the intricate details of individual behaviour and content ourselves with the study of the interaction between the various groups and classes of society based on the received conventions. There is thus consistency between the presupposition of methodological organicism and that of procedural rationality. When the limitations of information processing are taken into consideration, the limits of individualism are even more striking.

Having established that conventions are the main response to uncertainty and excess information, it remains to discover when these conventions change. Rule (5) implies that when the old routines cannot provide a satisfactory answer they have to be replaced. In particular when the old routines imply too high a level of uncertainty, then some new information must be gathered and some new channels of thought must be found. Outlets for action that generate more confidence must be devised. For instance, when there are political or economic crises, uncertainty often rises, with the result that what before appeared as reasonable routines must now be discarded. This of course is the difficulty of post-Keynesian analysis: having established the importance of rules and conventions, when are these rules changed, when are the customs replaced? There must be some mechanism explaining the evolution of the customs, but apart from external shock factors and some reference to endogenous innovation, post-Keynesians still have little to offer by way of an explanation (Bianchi, 1990). This, of course, should be the contribution of the Institutionalists and their Veblenian evolutionary economics.

Finally rules (6) and (7) provide the ultimate responses to uncertainty and insufficient capabilities. In general, agents try to avoid having to take decisions involving a substantial amount of uncertainty. As is the case of stuntmen, who do their best to eliminate imponderables (uncertainty) while knowing that they cannot eradicate all risks, firms attempt to reduce the extent of uncertainty by signing contracts and extending their domain of control. I would argue that the power of a firm is a measure of its command over uncertainty. In the end, when doubts are too large, it is always possible to delay a decision (Pasinetti, 1981, p. 234). This is rule (7). It explains to some extent the fluctuations of the economy. Investment requires a conscious decision to increase or replace the existing stock of capital. Furthermore, when consumers are in doubt as to the products upon which they should spend their income increases, they can always postpone their decisions by saving their incomes. This is consistent with theories of aggregate consumption based on habits (Marglin, 1984a, chs 17–18; Green 1991). If a decision must be taken in any case, the strategy of decision making may change if the level of uncertainty increases. For instance, in classical decision theory, it is often assumed that risk-averse agents follow a maximin strategy; that is, they choose the action which minimizes the possible maximum losses, rather than pursuing a strategy that maximizes the minimum gains. I would argue that the choice of these strategies has nothing to do with the psychological character of the individual, but rather that the more risky strategy appears more appealing when

## Implications for Theoretical Analysis

the relative level of available pertinent information is sufficiently high. When uncertainty is greater, the more prudent strategy will usually be followed.

It is now time to evaluate the theoretical implications for economic modelling of accepting, on the one hand, the Keynesian/Knightian view of uncertainty, and on the other hand the concept of procedural rationality *à la* Simon. We have seen in the previous section that mainstream economists ultimately reject the adoption of fundamental uncertainty because they dread the nihilistic consequences for economic theorizing. Not only are they afraid that the standard optimizing tools of the *homo œconomicus* could not be utilized, but also they are fearful that introducing uncertainty would destroy any pretence at establishing laws and regularities. Furthermore, for neoclassical economists, models not based on microeconomic foundations of the constrained optimization sort are not scientific for they do not rely on individual rationality. The rest of this section demonstrates that these fears are not substantiated.

Let us first tackle the question of the nihilistic component of fundamental uncertainty. As already pointed out, it must be admitted that those authors who have emphasized the importance of uncertainty have generally overestimated its destructive consequences for economic analysis. Two destructive paths have been pursued: one underlying the presumed irrationality of the agents, and the other the instability of the economic capitalist system. The reader should be convinced by now that uncertainty does not of necessity breed irrational behaviour. In fact, it can be argued on the contrary that, in both the *Treatise on Probability* and the *General Theory*, Keynes is striving to define a realistic and practical theory of procedural rationality based on the limitations of human knowledge and capabilities. When deprived of knowledge, reason cannot be based on simple probabilities and must turn to alternative strategies based on conventions and other procedures. In this context, 'Keynes may be viewed as basing the whole of economic theory on a single, broad, non-Neoclassical conception of agent rationality' (O'Donnell, 1989, p. 272).

The second path towards nihilistic conclusions follows some of Keynes's arguments. It has been assumed that uncertainty leads to instability since long-term decisions hinge on flimsy foundations, subject to sudden changes (1973, xiv, p. 114). This has meant to some that a proper theory set in historical time, where these violent changes in opinions would have to be recorded, is beyond the reach of economics. Sticking to Keynes for the moment, it is well known that he also considered uncertainty to be a stabilizing influence on the economy, since a variety of opinions and of the confidence with which they are held ensures mitigated aggregate reactions to news (Keynes, 1973, vii, p. 172). The position taken here is that the presence of fundamental uncertainty, combined with a rationality based on procedures, generates regular patterns, except in exceptional crises (bifurcations and the like).

The basic argument is that the rules and conventions of procedural rationality spare the economic agents from reacting to every perturbation in the economic environment. Since agents are not assumed to be maximizing some objective function, they do not have to react to every little change in the parameters of the function, whether these changes can objectively be ascertained or whether they are assessed from a hysterical subjective perspective. Provided that the new information leaves the agents in the satisfactory range, the existing procedures continue to be followed. As was said before, what counts with regards to the stable or unstable influence of uncertainty is how agents react to it. Uncertainty *per se* is no more a destabilizing force than it could be a stabilizing one. Only in situations of crises, when all rules or conventions seem to go by the board, could uncertainty be a destabilizing force. In normal circumstances, uncertainty is a source of regularities, as shown by Heiner. He concludes that 'greater uncertainty will cause rule-governed behavior to exhibit increasingly predictable regularities, so that uncertainty becomes the basic source of predictable behavior' (1983, p. 570). This is a conclusion reached independently by other post-Keynesians: 'In the real world economic systems function coherently, insofar as they do, *because* of the bounds produced by imperfections of knowledge rather than, as in conventional theory, *despite* them' (Earl, 1983a, p. 7).

Heiner's conclusions basically rest on the proposition that the greater the amount of uncertainty, the greater is the risk of taking the wrong decision; that is, deciding to change the procedures when this leads to losses, or deciding not to change procedures when a move would have produced a gain. If the world was known with certainty, one would always recognize the proper time to make a move. However, when there is uncertainty and incomplete knowledge, many false signals are received and, as a consequence, changes to existing behaviour seem worthwhile only when there are substantial expected gains; that is, when the gains (or the net gains compared to the no-change situation) and their probability are high. The argument of Heiner is thus based on some sort of compensatory calculus between the probability of an event and the weight of an argument, in the spirit of what Keynes seemed to have suggested in his *Treatise on Probability*, when he said that, to make decisions, 'we ought to take account of the weight as well as the probability of different expectations' (1973, viii, p. 83).

The implications of all this are that models based on rules of thumb, such as mark-ups, target return pricing, normal financial ratios, standard rates of utilization, propensities to consume, lexicographic rules and so on, are perfectly legitimate since they rely on a type of rationality which is appropriate for the usual economic environment. In a world of uncertainty and of limited computational abilities, the economic agent cannot but adopt, except in the simplest of problems, a rationality which is of the procedural type. The models built on rules of thumb are not *ad hoc* constructions. Rather they reflect the rationality of reasonable agents. As such they have microeconomic foundations which are just as solid, if not more from a realist point of view, as those of the standard mainstream models. There is thus no need to demonstrate that such or such element results from some maximizing procedure. Optimizing conditions may have some legitimacy when the problems to be solved are simple, but they describe neither the means nor the results of rational economic behaviour under the more realistic conditions of uncertainty or of limited information processing.

## 2.3 A THEORY OF HOUSEHOLD CHOICE

We have not yet tackled the issue of household choice. The object of neoclassical household choice is to make sure that the axiomatic conditions ruling household preferences are such that the existence of an equilibrium, preferably unique, can be demonstrated. In the more vulgar versions of neoclassical theory, this objective is reinforced by the requirements that the theory be amenable to mathematical manipulations. These objectives, which have little to commend them by way of realism, have been criticized from the very beginning. It is striking to see that the criticisms that could be levelled against marginal utility theory, or revealed preferences theory even before its inception, are still relevant today. Here are some extracts from such an 80-year-old critique.

Marginal-utility theory has usually been formulated in hedonistic terms . . . Hedonism is hopelessly discredited by modern psychology . . . Deliberation, reasoned choice plays but a minor part in the affairs of men. Habit, not calculation, governs the greater part of all our acts . . . The habits of thought which count for most in shaping choice are not the result of prevision, but are of the nature of conventions uncritically accepted by virtue of membership in a particular group . . . Calculation is difficult work. It is much easier to act on a suggestion than to weight alternatives . . .

Adherents of the marginal-utility school . . . deny that the marginal-utility doctrines stand or fall with hedonism . . . [They] assert that economics is concerned only with the fact of choice between goods or between alternative activities, and not with the basis of choice . . .

If the marginal utility theory be interpreted hedonistically it is psychologically invalid. If the theory be deprived of its hedonistic content it is reduced to the unobjectionable statements: that men will not buy a thing unless they want it; that a commodity cannot be sold for more than somebody is willing to pay for it . . . (Downey, 1987, pp. 48, 49, 51, 53)

Thus we see that the criticisms of mainstream theory, and the alternatives which are suggested, have not changed over time. Downey argues that marginal utility theory is based upon a deficient view of human conduct. He rejects substantive rationality, because it ignores habits and the difficulties of comparing choices. He emphasizes the role of social conventions. He recognizes that mainstream choice theory does not need the concept of utility or hedonism, that is some unique measure of pain and satisfaction; but then he suggests that, deprived of it, the neoclassical theory of choice is almost a tautology. The post-Keynesian theory of household choice builds upon several of the intuitions mentioned by Downey: the substantial role played by habits and social conventions, procedural rationality and a more proper psychological foundation.

**An Overview of the Principles of Consumer Choice**

There have been little efforts made by post-Keynesians to explain how consumers make choices. Granted, there are several studies on the choices which entrepreneurs have to make when their firms face uncertain prospects, *à la* Shackle. Also neo-Ricardians are known for their analysis of the choice of technique in production. But, except for a few authors, such as Earl (1983a, 1986) and Baxter (1988b), post-Keynesians have been relatively silent about the microeconomics of household choice. Does that mean that post-Keynesians, or all post-classical economists for that matter, accept the neoclassical way of determining the composition of consumption output, that is the final demand for individual products? Would post-Keynesians endorse the axiomatic neoclassical presentation of consumer's choice?

The answer is no. Although there have been few contributions, or even few comments about consumer behaviour by post-Keynesian authors, there is a remarkable degree of coherence among these few contributions. The object of the present section is to outline the points upon which post-Keynesians seem to agree. I should point out from the outset that no axiomatic or formal model of choice behaviour will be offered to the reader. The concepts rather than the mathematics will be discussed. What will come out of all this is that substitution effects, relying mainly on changes in relative prices, will be of little importance compared to habits and income effects.

The common ground of post-Keynesian choice theory can be summarized in the form of six principles:

1. the principle of procedural rationality;
2. the principle of satiable wants;
3. the principle of non-independence;
4. the principle of the subordination of needs;
5. the principle of the irreducibility of needs;
6. the principle of the growth of needs.

We have already discussed at length the issue of procedural rationality. This more realist type of rationality will be applied to the question of consumer behaviour. The second principle, that of satiable wants, can be likened to the neoclassical principle of diminishing marginal utility. It says that eventually more of one good or more of a characteristic will bring less supplementary satisfaction, however that last term is defined. In neoclassical economics, satiation arises only if prices are null or if incomes are infinite. In post-Keynesian economics, satiation often arises with positive prices and finite income. The principle of non-independence focuses on the fact that decisions and preferences are not made independently of those of other agents, an assumption which runs in opposition to the standard neoclassical models of choice. The derived satisfaction also depends on existing social norms. Finally, the last three principles, identified by Georgescu-Roegen (1954, p. 515) and implicitly utilized by Roy (1943) in two brilliant contributions, have been picked up in various guises by post-Keynesians. The principle of subordinate needs can be related to notions of hierarchies, thresholds and dominance. The principle of irreducibility states that some needs cannot be substituted for others, and that, as a consequence, 'everything does not have a price'. The principle of the growth of needs asserts that the growth of real incomes will induce the creation of new needs.

To define these six principles, and to give some substance to them, it has been necessary to go beyond the writings of self-assessed post-Keynesian writers. As pointed out by Earl (1983a, p. 2), there is no chapter on consumer behaviour in the essays of the post-Keynesian study guide edited by Eichner (1979). This is no chance omission. There are, however, several pieces of work which fit, like a puzzle, the presuppositions of the post-classical research programme or major conceptions advanced in other fields of economics by post-Keynesian authors. Earl himself has found these links with the behaviouralists (Andrews, Richardson, Kay). I was myself put on the track by the humanistic economics of Lutz and Lux (1979).

At this stage the reader might think that he or she is being misled: that there is no more a post-Keynesian theory of consumer choice than there is a theory of frisbee flying; that perhaps one can talk of a behaviouralist consumer theory or a humanistic one, but not of a post-Keynesian consumer theory, since post-Keynesians have made no concerted effort to define such a theory. To this unbelieving reader, the following quotations from four well-known post-classical authors are offered.

There is a kind of competition in consumption, induced by the desire to impress the Joneses, which makes each family strive to keep up at least an appearance of being as well off as those that they mix with, so that outlay by one induces outlay by others ... Generally speaking, wants stand in a hierarchy (though with considerable overlaps at each level) and an increment in a family's real income is not devoted to buying a little more of everything at the same level but to stepping down the hierarchy. (Robinson, 1956, pp. 251, 354)

Although possibilities of substitution among commodities are of course relevant at any given level of real income, there exists a hierarchy of needs. More precisely, there exists a very definite *order of priority* in consumers' wants, and therefore among groups of goods and services, which manifests itself as real incomes increase. (Pasinetti, 1981, p. 73)

Post-Keynesians generally assume that, in an economy that is expanding over time, it is the income effect that will predominate over the relative price, or substitution, effects ... Substitution can take place only within fairly narrow subcategories. Consumer preferences are, in this sense, lexicographically ordered ... A household's consumption pattern, at any given point in time, thus reflects the lifestyle of the households that constitute its social reference group. (Eichner, 1986a, pp. 159–60)

There are hierarchies of needs from basic needs up to higher needs such as the need for self-fulfilment. The needs are taken as given in a given environment. There are segments in the population which correspond to income classes ... To different segments there correspond different patterns of consumption to satisfy the hierarchies of needs. (Schefold, 1985, p. 116)

All four quotations mention the principle of subordination of needs or of wants. By introducing lexicographic ordering, Eichner is opening the door for the principle of irreducibility. Note also that these authors refer to the principle of non-independence: there is a class structure or at least an income structure to the composition of consumption. Finally, Eichner and Pasinetti put emphasis on the predominance of income effects over the substitution effects, which is the principle of growth of needs. We thus have in these short quotes four of the five exclusive post-Keynesian principles of consumer choice which I have listed above. As I have claimed before, the fifth principle, the principle of procedural rationality, is part of the presuppositions of the post-classical programme, and thus it cannot be doubted to be part of a post-Keynesian theory of choice.

I thus hope to have shown that some coherent view of consumer's choice is emerging from post-Keynesian circles, although the latter have paid little attention to the question. Furthermore I hope to show that this post-Keynesian view of household's choice is perfectly compatible with the rest of the post-Keynesian research programme, and that in many ways it can be related to the views of the classical authors, thus reasserting the linkages between the neo-Ricardians and the post-Keynesians, and reaffirming the significance of the usage of the term 'post-classical'.

## The Distinction between Needs and Wants

In standard economics, as pointed out in the introduction of this section, everything can usually be brought under the heading of utility. This means that everything desired by an individual corresponds to a want. Every want can be compared to all the others, and in that sense all wants are equal. It is possible to rank the various wants, but this ranking solely depends on the ability of each want to create utility. This, however, was not the view of classical economists, nor initially that of the marginalist economists. It has been recalled by several specialists in consumer behaviour that both Karl Menger and Alfred Marshall considered a hierarchy of needs, that is groups of wants that could be distinguished from each other. Menger proposed a list of needs of differential importance: water, food, clothing, lodging, transportation and tobacco(!), from the essential to the less essential (Lutz and Lux, 1979, p. 18). Marshall also recognized that there existed a variety of wants, some being more basic than others. From his discussion, we can identify the following hierarchy of needs: biological needs (food, clothing, shelter, variety); health, education and security; friendship, affection, belonging, conformity with social customs; distinction; excellence; morality (Haines, 1982, p. 111).

The above lists look strikingly similar to the pyramid of needs suggested by Abraham Maslow and his humanistic school of psychology. This pyramid is said to be constituted by five sets of needs, from the more basic to the highest: physiological needs (air, water, food, sex, sleep); safety needs (health, education, shelter, stability, protection); social needs, subdivided into two sets: belongingness and love needs on the one hand, and self-respect and the esteem of others on the other; finally the moral needs, which Maslow called self-actualization; that is, the search for truth, justice, aesthetics, the meaning of life, achievement (Lutz and Lux, 1979, p. 11; Lea *et al.*, 1987, p. 499). Although there is little doubt that these lists were constituted independently, the needs that are identified appear in the same order. We may thus suspect that the proposed order is of significance. This does not mean that all individuals have the same ranking, or that there is no interpenetration of the needs. But we can certainly presume that every individual entertains a ranking of the above sort. In fact, later research seems to demonstrate that needs are clustered around two or three levels: the lower level, which is represented by Maslow's first two layers of needs, and the higher level dealing with love, esteem and self-actualization (Lea *et al.*, 1987, pp. 146, 501). These two layers broadly correspond to what we want to have and what we would like to be.

If we assume that individuals respond to differentiated needs, rather than to undifferentiated wants, it becomes easier to presume that the fulfilment of each of these needs cannot be compared. In neoclassical standard versions of consumer theory, diminishing marginal utility is explained by the variety of wants. A post-Keynesian view would focus on the hierarchy of needs, where some needs are more basic than others, which implies that they must be fulfilled as a priority. In that sense all needs are not equal. We should thus differentiate between needs and wants. Needs are susceptible to a hierarchic classification and are the motor of consumer behaviour, while wants evolve from needs and constitute 'the various preferences within a *common* category or level of need' (Lutz and Lux, 1979, p. 21).

At this stage it might be preferable to give a simple example of the above distinction between needs and wants, an example which will highlight the difference in emphasis between the neoclassical and the post-classical research programmes. Kagel *et al.* (1975) have reported an experiment made with rats, where these animals had to pay to obtain goods. More precisely, rats had to press on a lever a certain number of times to obtain drinks or solid food. What neoclassical authors have retained from this experiment is that, when the price of root beer goes up compared to that of some other soft drink (when the number of presses required to get one portion of root beer increases), rats shift their consumption of drinks away from root beer (McKenzie and Tullock, 1978, p. 59). This clearly represents a triumph for neoclassical theory, for it shows that price substitution effects are so universal that they adequately describe even the consumer behaviour of rats. If rats show economic rationality of the neoclassical sort, it must be presumed that the concept of the *homo œconomicus* cannot be so far-fetched for humans. Post-Keynesians, on the other hand, have focused their attention on another part of the experiment, the one showing that, although the price of food relative to water is being increased fourfold, the rats refuse to drink more and eat less (Lutz and Lux, 1979, p. 69). The income-compensated demand for food is a vertical. This shows that drinking and eating are two different physiological needs, which to a large extent cannot compensate for each other. They are in this sense incommensurable. On the other hand, the various types of drinks represent wants. They can be substituted one for another. You need to drink, but you want a beer.

The fact that needs lack commensurability puts in jeopardy a standard concept of neoclassical analysis, the notion of opportunity cost (Lutz and Lux, 1979, p. 21). It is clear that the concept of the opportunity cost can only apply to wants within a given category of need. When different levels of needs are considered, there is no clear-cut definition of the opportunity cost. When lower needs are being fulfilled, the satisfaction of higher needs is not being given up since those needs are not yet active. While wants may lend themselves to quantitative measurement, needs are of a qualitative nature. There is no unidimensional measure of the satisfaction that these irreducible needs can generate.

Neoclassical authors usually assume that all needs can be subsumed into wants, so that in the end one can always offer enough of a good to compensate for the loss of another. This is also called the principle of Archimedes. An extreme version of this principle, although it cannot be derived from the behaviour of individuals, is the axiom of gross substitutability, which we have already mentioned in Chapter 1 and which says that an increase in the price of any good induces an increase in the demand for each of the other goods. The emphasis for neoclassical theory in its various incarnations is clearly on price substitution. On the other hand post-Keynesians insist that needs at different stages of the pyramid of needs cannot be substituted for each other. Fulfilling the higher needs cannot be a substitute for the fulfilment of the lower ones. The Archimedes principle is invalid.

## Procedural Choice among the Wants

Let us assume that there exists a pyramid of needs. Within each need, say furniture, there is a wide variety of possibilities. How are rational households going to decide between these possibilities? We previously argued that economic agents follow rules of thumb to avoid time-consuming decisions. In the case of consumer behaviour, where a substantial amount of consumer expenditure is of the repetitive type, it can be presumed that a large portion of these expenditures occurs through routines. That is, they depend on past behaviour, the habits which have been incorporated in the consumer behaviour. These habits may come from past family behaviour, that is the behaviour of parents, or from cultural behaviour, or from the visible behaviour of friends, neighbours or colleagues at work. They may also have been acquired through persuasion, that of publicity and advertising.

There are also some expenditures, often on the semi-durable or the durable goods, which are not the result of routine decisions and which require a conscious choice. It may also be presumed that a lot of present routine expenditures are the consequences of past conscious decisions. How are these decisions taken? Post-Keynesians would argue that in general the main rule of thumb is some sort of non-compensatory choice. These rules of a lexicographic nature actually apply at three levels. First, we have already seen that needs could be ordered, some having priority over the others. Secondly, within a given category of need, there may be several types of sub-needs, for instance furniture within the need for lodging. One has to decide what kind of furniture has priority: beds, bedroom set, tables, dining set, kitchenware, libraries, sofas, paintings or various household appliances and gadgets. We may then speak of wants within sub-needs. At this level it has been demonstrated that households establish a pattern of consumption (Paroush, 1965; Clarke and Soutar, 1981–2). Some types of goods are acquired before others in a consistent manner.

Finally lexicographic ordering also plays a role in the actual choice of the good, once the preferred sort of want has been established. For instance, once the household has decided to add a compact disc (CD) player to its audio capabilities, it remains to choose the kind of CD player and its make. As we all know, unless we rely on the judgement of the seller at the audio shop, which is another possible rule of thumb, and assuming we had no difficulty in selecting the appropriate store, this can be a very agonizing decision, involving a large number of comparisons and the weighting of several different characteristics. At this stage, another decision rule of the lexicographic type may help us to take a quick decision: some characteristics will be considered to be incommensurable with others; that is, CD players without these characteristics will be excluded outright. This is what Earl (1986, p. 183) calls non-compensatory filtering procedures. A limit to the maximum price to be paid may be one of the required characteristics. In this fashion, the range of choices can be drastically reduced to some malleable number. Only at this stage might it be possible to employ compensating schemes of the sort favoured by mainstream authors, that is weighting the various characteristics of the remaining makes.

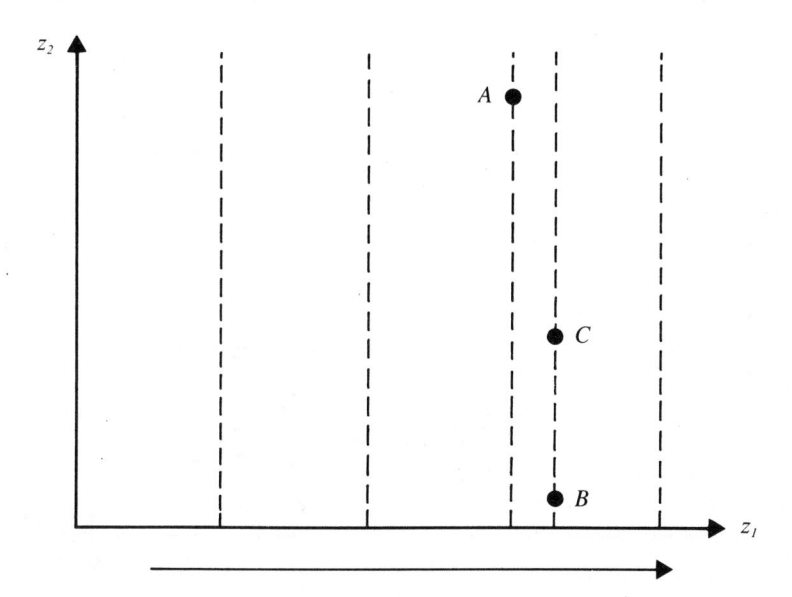

*Figure 2.1 Lexicographic ordering: the disjunctive rule*

Orderings of a lexicographic nature may take several forms. The most extreme form would be what Earl (1986, p. 233) calls the naive lexicographic rule, where choice is based on a single characteristic. The product which scores best with respect to this characteristic is the chosen one, regardless of the other characteristics, unless there is a tie, in which case the next characteristic in the priority list becomes the crucial one. This is illustrated in Figure 2.1, where point $B$ is preferred to point $A$, since characteristic (or need) $z_1$ has absolute priority over characteristic (or need) $z_2$, but where $C$ is preferred to $B$ since there is a tie with respect to $z_1$.

Many more non-compensatory filtering rules which appear more reasonable are nevertheless possible. They may be called behavioural lexicographic procedures. Figure 2.2 illustrates such a possibility, which relies on a saturation or satiation level $z_1^*$. It is assumed that satisfaction $S$ depends on characteristic $z_1$ only, up to the level $z_1^*$. Any higher level of $z_1$ is preferred to any level of $z_2$. On the graph, point $B$ is preferred to point $A$ on the grounds of that priority, but points $B$ and $C$ would be indifferent. We may thus write:

$$\text{If } z_1 < z_1^*, \quad S = S(z_1) \tag{2.1}$$

Turning now to the right-hand side of Figure 2.2, we suppose that the

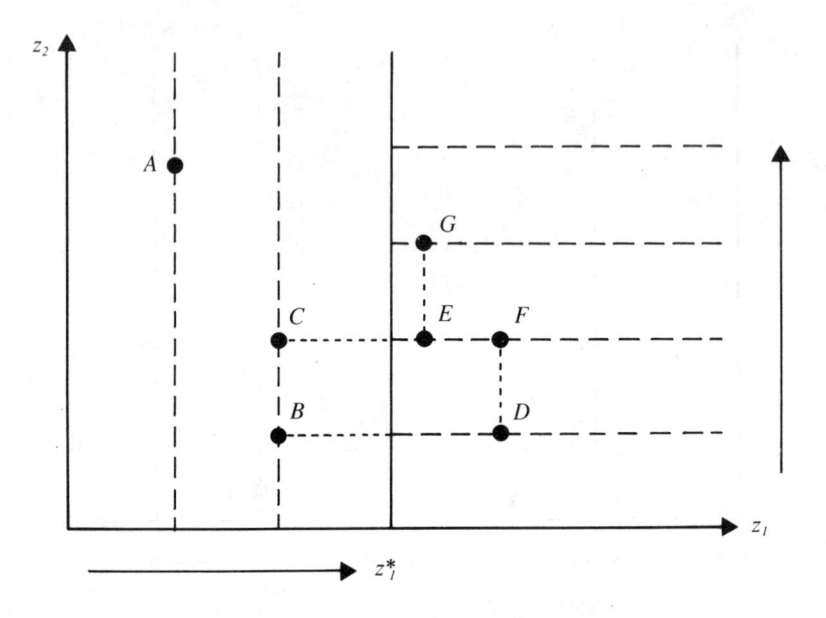

*Figure 2.2   Ordering of a lexicographic nature, with saturation point*

saturation level $z_1^*$ has been exceeded and that in this case satisfaction depends on the saturation level $z_1^*$ and on the second characteristic, $z_2$. The order of preference between the various combinations indicated is given by the following inequalities: $G>F = E>D>C$. Note that the consumer would be indifferent between combinations $F$ and $E$, since it is assumed that the characteristic $z_1$ does not matter once the saturation level $z_1^*$ has been overcome. The level of satisfaction is:

$$\text{If } z_1 \geq z_1^*, \quad S = S(z_1^*, z_2) \tag{2.2}$$

In Figure 2.3, we suppose that $z_1^*$ is not exactly a saturation level, but rather a threshold. This means that, although the consumer needs exceeds this threshold, resulting in characteristic $z_2$ becoming relevant, increases in $z_1$ provide supplementary satisfaction. Standard analysis could then apply beyond $z_1^*$, with the usual compensatory indifference curves. The following equalities or inequalities would hold: $F>D=E>C=B>A$. The level of satisfaction could be written as:

$$\begin{aligned}&\text{If } z_1 < z_1^*, \quad S = S(z_1) \\ &\text{and if } z_1 \geq z_1^*, \quad S = S(z_1, z_2)\end{aligned} \tag{2.3}$$

*Figure 2.3  Ordering of a lexicographic nature, with indifference curves beyond threshold*

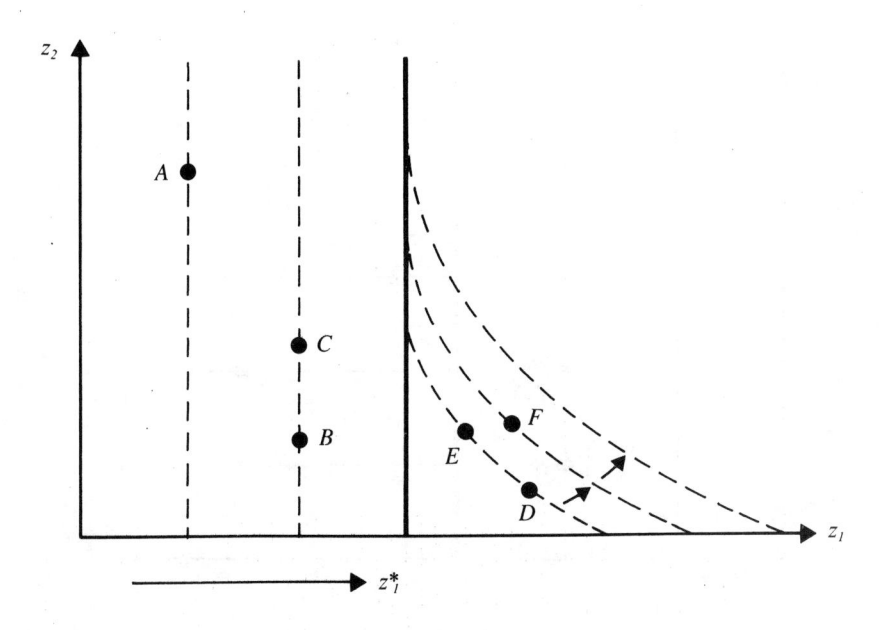

Finally, another kind of lexicographical ordering, suggested by Georgescu-Roegen (1954) and formalized by Encarnación (1964), could be imagined. It is illustrated by Figure 2.4, and it again corresponds to a threshold level rather than to a level of satiation. Below the threshold point of $z_1^*$ corresponding to the first priority, preferences are ordered according to the highest level of characteristic $z_1$. However, for a given $z_1$, the agent prefers to have more of characteristic $z_2$ than to have less of it. Beyond the threshold point $z_1^*$, the reverse occurs: preferences are ordered according to characteristic $z_2$, but for a given $z_2$ the agent prefers to have more of $z_1$ than less of it. The lines which are so constructed represent quasi-indifference curves. All points on each of these curves are now unambiguously ordered. Suppose there are two goods, $A$ and $B$, offering the characteristics $z_1$ and $z_2$. We can then write:

$$\text{When } z_1 < z_1^*, S(z_1^B, z_2^B) > S(z_1^A, z_2^A) \text{ if } z_1^B > z_1^A$$
$$\text{When } z_1 \geqslant z_1^*, S(z_1^B, z_2^B) > S(z_1^A, z_2^A) \text{ if } z_2^B > z_2^A \quad (2.4)$$

In the case of Figure 2.4, the following preferences hold: $G > F > E > D > C > B > A$. The standard utility analysis is now insufficient

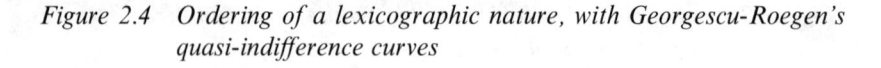

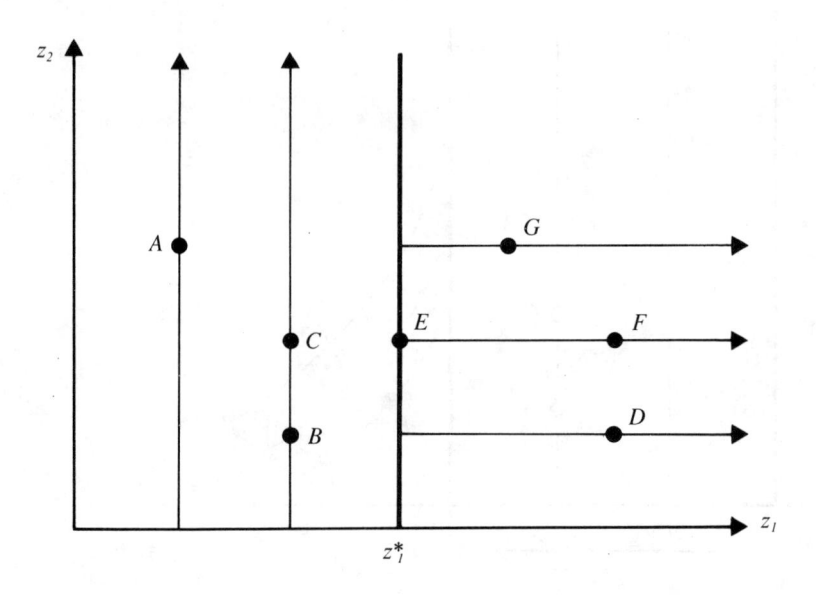

*Figure 2.4 Ordering of a lexicographic nature, with Georgescu-Roegen's quasi-indifference curves*

to represent this ordering. Satisfaction must be represented by a vector. From a mathematical point of view, this type of vectorial representation of preferences may appear more complex than the standard utility analysis, where all characteristics or goods may be substituted for each other. From a decisional point of view, however, things are much simpler. The individual does not have to assess a myriad of possibilities to take a decision, trying to compute whether or not the loss of a characteristic can be compensated by the gain of another. No compensation has to be performed. The individual simply has to assess whether the threshold has been attained or not.

The principles of subordination and of irreducibility thus rely on the structure of needs, which are the psychological pillars of the theory, and on the decision-making process of the individual consumer, basically rules of a lexicographic nature. It has also been emphasized that, when individuals are grouped within one household, or when an individual has several conflicting personalities, lexicographic choice may be the main rule which solves the inner conflicts and allows decisions to be taken (Earl, 1986, ch. 6; Steedman and Krause, 1986).

## Growths of Needs and Conventions

Having assumed that there indeed exists a hierarchy of needs, or of semi-needs, how do consumers move up the steps of the pyramid? The basic answer is that individuals move upwards in the hierarchy according to income effects. Of course, as has already been pointed out, different individuals have different scales, and it is likely that widely different income levels are needed to reach the upper grades of the hierarchy of needs. Different individuals have different threshold levels. However the principle remains. Unless there is some Freudian fixation with some type of need, that is a neurotic obsession with some set of goods, the needs of individuals will grow as their lower needs are gradually fulfilled.

This is the principle of the growth of needs. When a need has been fulfilled, or more precisely when a threshold level for that need has been attained, individuals start attending to the needs which are situated on a higher plane. There are always new needs to be fulfilled. The needs of the lower levels, however, require income to be satisfied. To go from one level of need to another dictates an increase in the real income level of the individual. The fulfilment of new needs and, therefore, the purchase of new goods or new services are thus related to income effects. This is the microeconomic counterpart of the post-Keynesian focus on effective demand, that is on macroeconomic income effects. What is being asserted is that income effects are much more important to explain the evolution of expenditures on goods than are substitution effects. The latter only play a minor role in a static analysis of consumer behaviour. Still, even within a static analysis, income and related effects, such as interdependence, may play the dominating role.

The emphasis of traditional theory on substitution effects has led to the neglect of the study of the hierarchy of consumption and of the income effects. Beyond the physiological needs, convention is the main reason for which it is believed that a hierarchy of needs or semi-needs will be more or less identical for all individuals of a similar culture. A household's pattern of consumption 'reflects the lifestyle of other households that constitute its social reference group' (Eichner, 1986a, p. 160), that is 'the consumption of each class will be guided by a conception of its appropriate lifestyle, given its place in the social pyramid' (Nell, 1992, p. 389). The consumption pattern of individual households is thus influenced by the demand structure of households with similar incomes or similar types of jobs, as it has been empirically shown (Alessie and Kapteyn, 1991).

The relationship between income levels and the quantities consumed of a given good is known as the Engel curve. Engel curves thus depend to a large extent, again beyond physiological needs, on the existence of

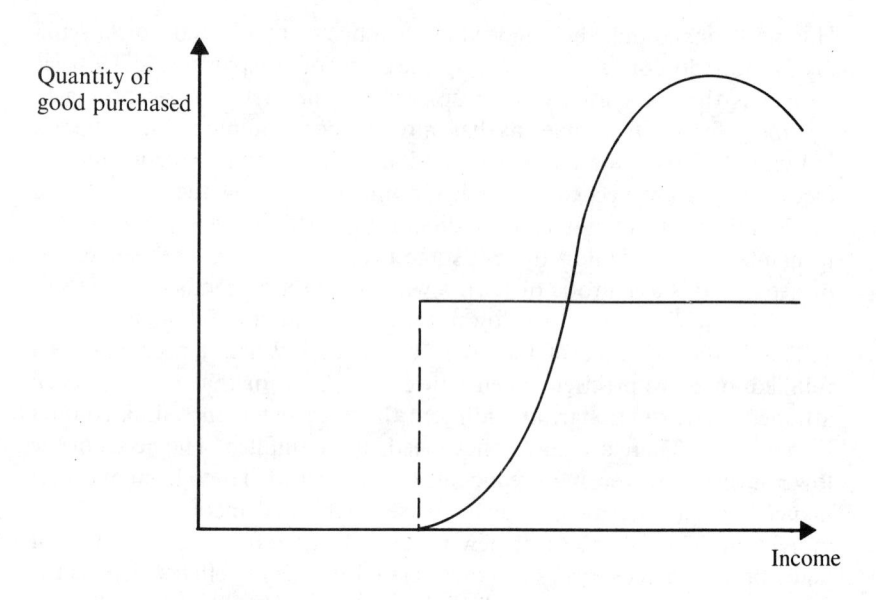

*Figure 2.5  Engel curves: importance of income effects*

customs and conventions. For a given individual or household, the Engel curve of a given good, or of a set of goods satisfying a given need, may appear as shown in Figure 2.5. When the revenues of the household are low, no amount of the good is being purchased, unless the good contains characteristics fulfilling the lowest of the needs. This is because the income of the household is insufficient to fulfil the needs which stand lower in the hierarchy. Goods which respond to higher needs will not be bought irrespective of their price. When the satiation or the threshold levels of these lower needs have been reached, as a result of income increases, the consumer may consider the purchase of goods of higher standing. The new good will be increasingly purchased, again until a threshold has been reached, at which point the quantities purchased might stay the same or decrease, as in the case of the so-called inferior good. The same graph may apply in a macroeconomic setting. Another possibility, associated with one-shot purchases such as travels abroad on summer vacations by an individual household, is illustrated by the kinked line (Eichner, 1987a, p. 642). The choice is then a binary one, whether to purchase or not at all. The upshot of all this is that changes in relative prices, unless they are so drastic that they change the ordering of needs or demi-needs, will have a very minute impact on the shape of the Engel curves or on the thresholds with which they are associated.

This ordering of needs and semi-needs is to some extent the result of innate preferences, especially again with respect to the lower physiological needs. It is clear, however, primarily with respect to the more social needs, that the publicity being exerted by the producing sector, as well as the acquired traditions, will have a substantial impact on the composition of consumption. This is where the principle of non-independence plays its part. What is being asserted is that the behaviour of the consumer, as well as the satisfaction which is derived fron consumption, is not independent of the behaviour of other consumers. Economists, who follow fads in their research, would be hard-pressed to deny this role of conventions.

The notion that consumers care about others, or about their relative position, is nothing new in the literature. Thornstein Veblen (1899) is known precisely for having emphasized these points. Furthermore even Pareto distinguished between the notions of ophelimity, which he reserved for the traditional notion of independently assessed satisfaction, and that of utility, which was supposed to take into account the consumption of other agents. That distinction was not retained by mainstream economists, except for Duesenberry's (1949) relative income hypothesis, for mathematical convenience one may suspect. The fact remains, however, that consumers care about each other. To the hierarchy of needs corresponds a hierarchy of consumers, of which marketing officers of large corporations take advantage, something which Galbraith (1962, ch. 11) calls the dependence effect.

Many sociological or psychological arguments can be advanced to explain why consumers want to go beyond their physiological and most basic material needs. They are usually based on some comparison with the situation of other consumers. In the semiological view of consumption, consumer goods are a sign which flashes to the outside world which rank of the consumers' hierarchy the agent occupies (Baudrillard, 1972). This leads to a desire for belongingness, or for normality. The consumer wants to demonstrate that he or she belongs to a certain class of society, to a certain group within the hierarchy of consumers. This brings comfort to the consumer. Households, or at least members of the household, will thus attempt to imitate the behaviour of other consumers. They will follow what appear to be the existing norms of consumption, to show that they belong to the appropriate rank of the hierarchy. This is what Harvey Leibenstein (1950) has called the bandwagon effect.

There are other reasons for which one should expect individual demands for a given product to be a positive function of the demand of society for that product. Consumers watch and copy other consumers because in so doing they learn how to spend their increased purchasing power. Consumers need to discover their preferences (Pasinetti, 1981, p.

75). They are not innate. They are acquired by experience and by imitation of the consumption pattern of friends or of people of higher ranks in the consumers' hierarchy. Purchases of specific products in chain reaction are thus explained by the informational content of consumption by neighbours, relatives, friends or acquaintances (Marris, 1964a, p. 146). The impact on purchases of socioeconomic contact reinforces the belief that the composition of demand depends on socioeconomic classes.

On the other hand, there will also exist a contradictory desire, that of differentiation, held by all consumers. Those of the higher ranks of the hierarchy attempt to distinguish themselves through their ostentatious consumption, while the consumers of the middle ranks try to transgress temporarily the limits of their rank. The norms set by the upper classes will in this case define the composition of this temporary consumption. In this spirit, Leibenstein has devised the snob effect, where individual demands for a product are an inverse function of the overall aggregate demand for that product, and the Veblen effect, where individual demand is an inverse function of the perceived price of the product.

René Girard's envy is the other sociological explanation of customized consumer behaviour which has recently been advanced. Girard's envy is very similar to Runciman's concept of relative deprivation. Individuals feel relatively deprived when they want a certain good that a reference group possesses, and when they believe that it is feasible to obtain the good (Baxter, 1988b, p. 52). Envy is defined as a desire to get what others have. It is thus distinct from jealousy, which is a desire to keep what one already has. The goal of publicity, besides the creation of purchasing habits, is to provoke envious feelings. Publicity makes one realize what the Joneses are up to, and indicates how to suppress the unhappy feeling of envy: the consumer need only buy the good which the Joneses have already incorporated into their structure of consumption (Dumouchel and Dupuy, 1979, p. 47). The norms of consumption are thus set either by imitation or by envy. Whatever the spring of action, the result is the same: the hierarchy of needs or semi-needs becomes the same for all, since all consumers try to emulate those which belong to the upper echelons of the hierarchy of society. These consumer elites set the trends. 'Emulation effects normally follow the social hierarchy; the consumption styles of the rich and famous set standards to which the rest aspire (or, sometimes, against which they react)' (Nell, 1992, p. 392).

Another consequence of this analysis based on envy or on relative income positions is that happiness is a function of the rank occupied in the consumers' hierarchy. This is a well known phenomenon. While individuals in a given industrialized country are not happier than those of the previous generation despite huge changes in standards of living, it appears

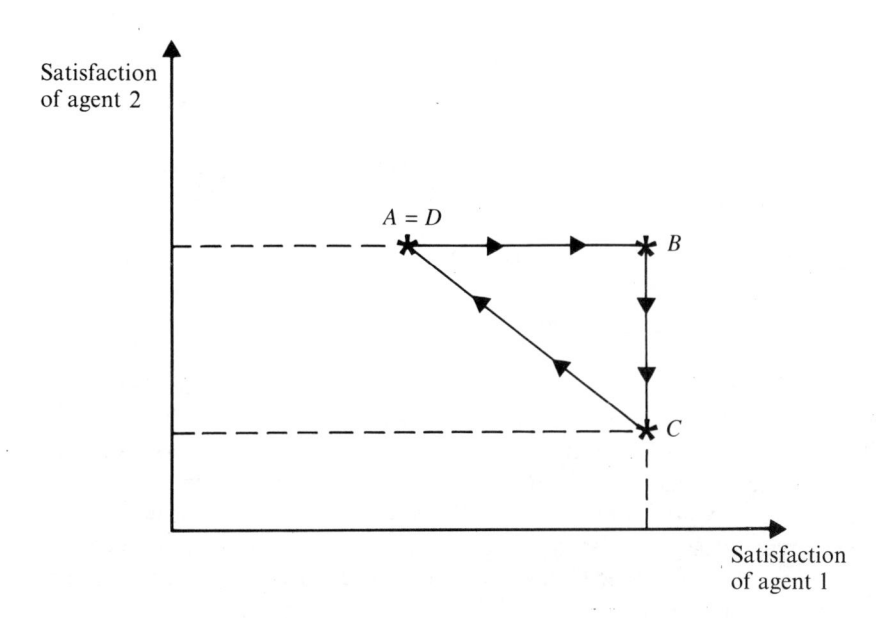

*Figure 2.6  The non-independence principle: the relativity of satisfaction*

that on average individuals in rich countries are happier than individuals from poor ones (Veenhoven, 1989). Similarly it has been discovered that within a country individuals belonging to the upper income echelons generally consider themselves happier than those with low income (Scitovsky, 1976, p. 136). Happiness or the satisfaction of needs is thus dependent on one's relative position, on the national or the global scale. Material needs only fulfil social needs to the extent that they allow an individual to move up the social hierarchy. Figure 2.6 illustrates this intuitive fact. Assume two individuals, each with their own level of satisfaction or happiness initially given by point $A$. Suppose individual 1 obtains an increase in wage income, leading to the fulfilment of higher needs. Point $B$ will now represent the new situation, until individual 2 discovers that his or her relative position has changed for the worse, at which stage point $C$ will represent the two levels of satisfaction. When individual 2 manages to overcome his or her envy by consuming more goods, the initial relative position of the two individuals in the hierarchy will be re-established, and very likely the final situation, $D$, will be identical to the initial one, $A$ (Attali and Guillaume, 1974, p. 142).

Some of the consequences of the principle of non-independence will become more obvious later. For instance, the notions of fairness and justice will play an important role in the analysis of the labour market and of inflation since the increase or the decrease in relative wages will allow consumers to satisfy their social needs, that is those needs related to the rank established within the hierarchy of consumers. For the moment it may be noted that the above comments help to justify the classical method of dividing households into two or three classes, the workers, the rentiers and the capitalists. It can be presumed that their consumption behaviour as households, including their propensity to save (or not to save), is similar within a class. This will apply with even greater force when these classes are subdivided into income classes.

**Characteristics and Hierarchy**

The question now is how to formalize, to some extent, the principles which have been developed in the previous subsections. Various formulations have been explicitly or implicitly suggested by various authors working outside the mainstream. In their presentation of humanistic economics, Lutz and Lux (1979) put together the Maslowian pyramid of needs and Georgescu-Roegen's plea to use lexicographic ordering or some form of lexicographic ordering. In his search for more adequate foundations of consumer behaviour, Arrous (1978) proposes to put together Georgescu-Roegen's lexicographic ordering and Lancaster's analysis of the characteristics of goods. This approach is also the one which dominates Earl's latest essay on consumer behaviour (1986, p. 234). Pasinetti (1981, p. 75) recommends making use of Lancaster's definition of a group of goods to identify a need, while Nell (1992, p. 390) observes that a lifestyle is specified by standards of characteristics. We will thus attempt to put together an analysis of needs that relies on an ordering of a lexicographic nature, where decisions are made on the basis of non-compensating priorities. The characteristics of the goods rather than the goods themselves will be the crucial distinctive elements, assuming, however, that goods can be joined together into groups.

It must be recognized that such a view is not totally novel, nor uniquely post-Keynesian. In their textbook of psychological economics, Lea et al. (1987, pp. 496–501) associate Lancaster's economics with Maslow's needs. In his own presentation, Lancaster (1971, pp. 146–56) recalls the importance of the hierarchy of needs (or of wants, as he calls them) as presented by certain earlier marginalists, relating these needs to sets of characteristics. Lancaster explains hierarchies by the possibility of satiation effects, when prices are positive and incomes finite. He establishes a link between the satiated needs of an individual and the income class to which that individual belongs, with the assumption that needs are partially ordered in a lexicographic way, which Lancaster calls dominance. Similarly, Ironmonger (1972) proceeds to an analysis based on Georgescu-Roegen's distinction between utility and needs, using a technique which is reminiscent of Lancaster's. In Ironmonger's book, goods fulfil wants (Lancaster's characteristics), the latter being lexicographically ordered, with various satiation levels and income levels. These non-orthodox views, however, have not been much disseminated among the mainstream, and as a result they can be considered as typically post-Keynesian.

Let us start by considering a consumption technology; that is, the relationship between goods and the characteristics that these goods provide. As a first approximation, one may think of these characteristics as being various wants. Let us suppose that there is a very simple consumption technology, with three characteristics, which we shall call $z_1$, $z_2$ and $z_3$, and four goods, which we shall call $x_1$, $x_2$, $x_3$ and $x_4$. The technology matrix is given by $\mathbf{T}$ and the $t_{ij}$'s indicate how many units of each characteristic are provided by one unit of each good. Prices are not considered at this stage. We thus have in matrix form:

$$\mathbf{z} = \mathbf{T}.\mathbf{x} \qquad (2.5)$$

More explicitly, this equation looks like the following:

$$\begin{bmatrix} z_1 \\ z_2 \\ z_3 \end{bmatrix} = \begin{bmatrix} t_{11} & t_{12} & t_{13} & t_{14} \\ t_{21} & t_{22} & t_{23} & t_{24} \\ t_{31} & t_{32} & t_{33} & t_{34} \end{bmatrix} \begin{bmatrix} x_1 \\ x_2 \\ x_3 \\ x_4 \end{bmatrix}$$

If all $t_{ij}$'s are positive, this means that each of the four goods contains all three characteristics. The four goods thus provide the same characteristics, but, unless the $t_{ij}$'s are proportional, the proportions in which these characteristics are being provided by each good are different. Note that here it has been assumed that the consumption technology is linear; that is, doubling the quantity of a good doubles the amount of characteristics provided. This assumption is a simplifying one and is not very important, unless one attempts to derive from it conclusions about the shapes of demand curves, based on the optimality and uniqueness of the chosen bundles of goods (Watts and Gaston, 1982–3).

Let us now suppose that each good cannot fulfil all characteristics. Let us suppose further that we can separate goods according to the set of characteristics they fulfil; that is, goods that fulfil a given set of characteristics cannot fulfil other characteristics. These goods thus constitute an intrinsic group; that is, they respond to very precise and limited wants.

The matrix of consumption technology is then said to be decomposable into submatrices. An example of such a decomposable matrix, with the previous notation, would be the following:

$$\begin{bmatrix} t_{11} & t_{12} & O & O \\ t_{21} & t_{22} & O & O \\ O & O & t_{33} & t_{34} \end{bmatrix}$$

Expanding the matrix, the relationship between the goods and the characteristics would then be the following:

$$z_1 = t_{11}.x_1 + t_{12}.x_2$$
$$z_2 = t_{21}.x_1 + t_{22}.x_2$$
$$z_3 = \phantom{t_{11}.x_1 + t_{12}.x_2} t_{33}.x_3 + t_{34}.x_4$$

In this example there are two distinct intrinsic groups. The first group is constituted by the goods $x_1$ and $x_2$, since they only cater to characteristics $z_1$ and $z_2$, while there are no other goods which can fulfil these two characteristics. We can also see that only goods $x_3$ and $x_4$ can provide characteristic $z_3$, and that these two goods provide no other characteristic. Therefore goods $x_3$ and $x_4$ also form a group, distinct from the first one. Lancaster's argument is, then, that one must distinguish between two types of substitution effects. Within a group, the increase in the price of a good might lead to its abandonment by all consumers since the other goods might eventually offer the same characteristics more efficiently, that is, for a lower price. This is called by Lancaster efficiency substitution. All consumers should act in a similar way within a group of goods. In the example above, in the second group, suppose that $t_{33}$ is larger than $t_{34}$. This means that the price of good $x_4$ must be proportionally smaller than that of $x_3$ if both goods are to be part of the consumption basket. Otherwise, characteristic $z_3$ can be obtained from good $x_3$ at a cheaper cost than from good $x_4$, and the latter will not be bought at all. Efficiency substitution effects are based purely on technological parameters. They are not related to the preferences of individuals. Personal preferences play a role when it comes to comparing characteristics within a group or sets of characteristics between groups. For instance, if the agent has a strong preference for characteristic $z_1$, while good $x_1$ provides that characteristic at a low price, good $x_1$ may be preferred to good $x_2$, although the latter good provides characteristic $z_2$ very efficiently.

We thus see that the combination of personal and efficiency substitution effects may provide the usual price substitution effects that mainstream theory relies upon. Notwithstanding the fact that substitution within a

*Figure 2.7   Subordination and irreducibility of needs: groups and subgroups of goods*

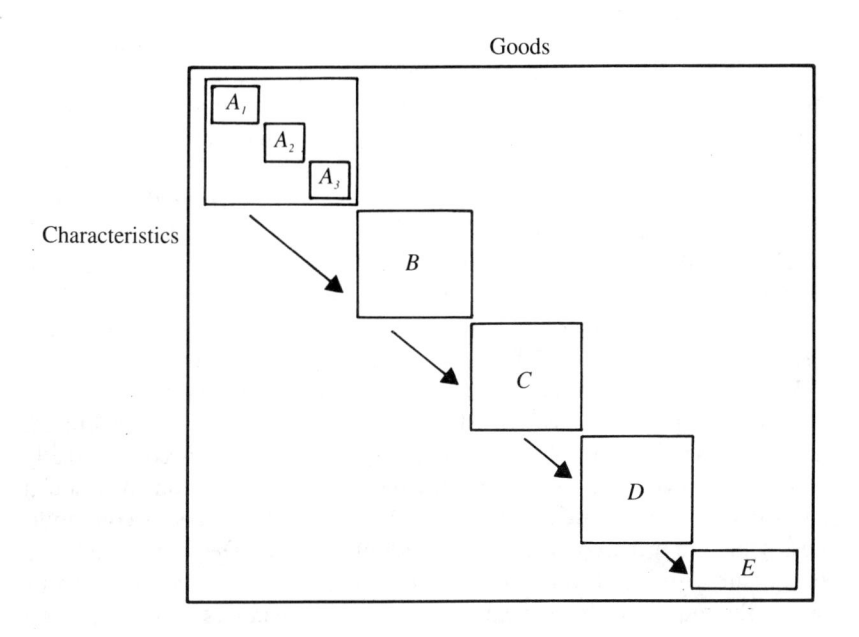

group can be questioned when the technology of consumption is not linear, as was pointed out above, the notion of group can be expanded in a direction that severely limits the extent of price substitution effects. Lancaster's analysis may be generalized to include the notion of needs and their irreducibility. Submatrices can in fact themselves be decomposed to form subgroups (Arrous, 1978, p. 259). We might thus suggest that efficiency substitution occurs only within subgroups. Each of these subgroups contains essentially identical goods, that is the same goods under various brands (manufactured by different producers). Personal preference substitution occurs only between subgroups of the same group, while neither type of substitution can arise between goods of different groups. Irreducible needs are thus formally represented as sets of group characteristics, these sets showing no commensurability. Such a vision of consumer theory drastically reduces the extent and the power of price substitution.

Figure 2.7 illustrates the decomposition of a matrix of consumption technology along the proposed lines. Within the technological matrix, the submatrices $A_1$, $A_2$ and $A_3$ of matrix $A$ represent three subgroups of goods between which there exists personal preference substitution. Within each of these submatrices, there can be efficiency and personal substitution.

However between the set of characteristics of $A_1$ and that of $A_2$ there can only be personal substitution. On the other hand, the matrices **A, B, C, D, E**, are in order of dominance as they would be in Maslow's hierarchy of needs; that is, the characteristics of matrix **A** fulfil lower needs than those of matrix **B**, while those of **B** fulfil lower needs than the characteristics of matrix **C**, and so on. The needs corresponding to matrix **A** must be fulfilled; that is, the various thresholds and satiation levels must be attained before the consumer can start to consider the goods which belong to the groups of matrix **B**. To each of the five matrices within the matrix of consumption technology one could attribute one of the five levels of needs ascribed to Maslow. We could thus say, following our earlier distinction in terminology, that the matrices **A, B** and so on represent needs, for which there exists a hierarchy, while the submatrices $A_1$, $A_2$ and so on represent the various wants, which can to a large extent be compensated.

We know that in reality things are not so simple. We have already seen that the hierarchy of needs of Maslow has not been well demonstrated, and that it seems that only two or possibly three levels of needs can really be distinguished: one corresponds to the material needs and their social spin-offs, from which we can perhaps isolate the most necessary commodities, while the other coincides with the higher moral needs, the two levels being truly irreducible and independent of each other. Forgetting for now about the moral needs, one can also think of consumers as setting threshold levels for various types of expenditures, such as transport, lodging, vacations, entertainment and so on, and then deciding on a lexicographic order within each of these categories, as does Eichner (1987a, p. 648) in his presentation of a decision tree. Let us call sub-needs these various types of consumption expenditures which are ordered in a hierarchy. Consumers rank their possible expenditures on these sub-needs in a lexicographic pattern, each sub-need corresponding to a set of characteristics. While it is understood that the order is not irreversible, only the closest sub-needs may be substituted for each other. Each increase in income brings a revision of the thresholds, and therefore each consumer goes over the same need on numerous occasions as income rises.

This type of behaviour is illustrated in Figure 2.8. Each of the three main matrices represents a category of expenditures, say food, lodging and entertainment. Each category of expenditures presents characteristics which are linked to each other. The various submatrices **A, B, C** ... represent the various sub-needs, each letter representing the rank of the sub-need. Consumers thus fulfil first their physiological needs, here food, then the other necessary ones, such as lodging. Entertainment is considered last, but then, when some low thresholds have been reached, the consumer revises the criteria serving to appraise whether or not the need is

*Figure 2.8  Subordination and overlap in needs: decision tree and sub-needs*

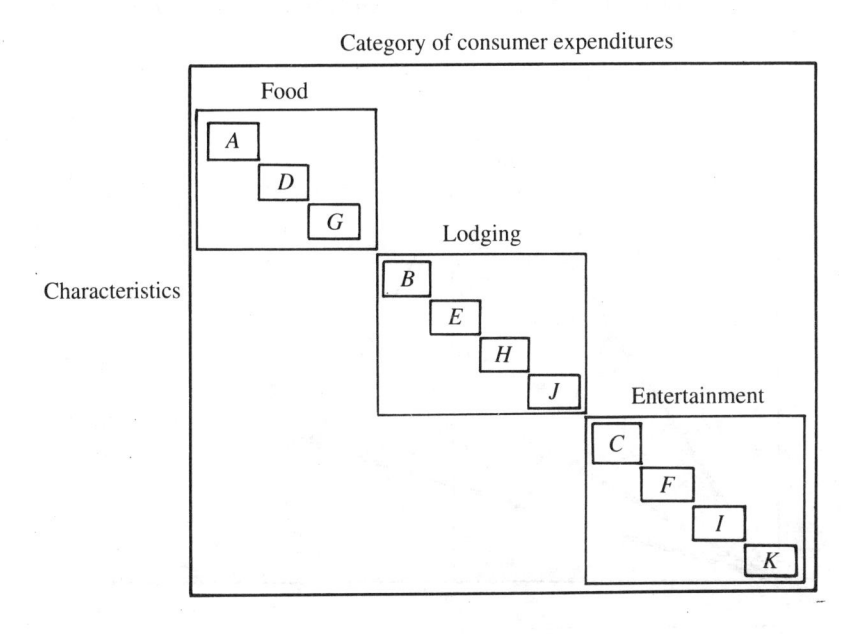

being fulfilled, and new characteristics are then considered. The consumer may start looking for more sophisticated characteristics of food (submatrix **D**), instead of only checking the caloric intake. As income continues to rise, the criteria of acceptable housing, for instance, may be revised upwards and the consumer may then start to look for some completely different type of housing, trying to fulfil the sub-need corresponding to submatrix **E**. All sub-needs are thus ordered in a lexicographic manner, but because of a considerable overlap between needs, as suggested by Joan Robinson in the passage quoted at the beginning of the section, consumers may visit each major need a considerable number of times. If the order is not perfectly lexicographic, as one would reasonably expect, one can imagine situations where sub-need **H** could be fulfilled before sub-need **G** but never before sub-need **F**. There would thus be some limited possibility of personal preference substitution between submatrices of adjoining rank, while efficiency substitution would be possible only within each submatrix.

The lack of importance of substitution effects and the importance attached to income effects by post-Keynesian authors is fully compatible with orderings of a lexicographic nature. This can easily be shown heuristically even if the matrices given by equation (2.5) are not fully decompos-

*Figure 2.9 Characteristics and ordering of a lexicographic nature: the importance of income effects and the irrelevance of substitution effects*

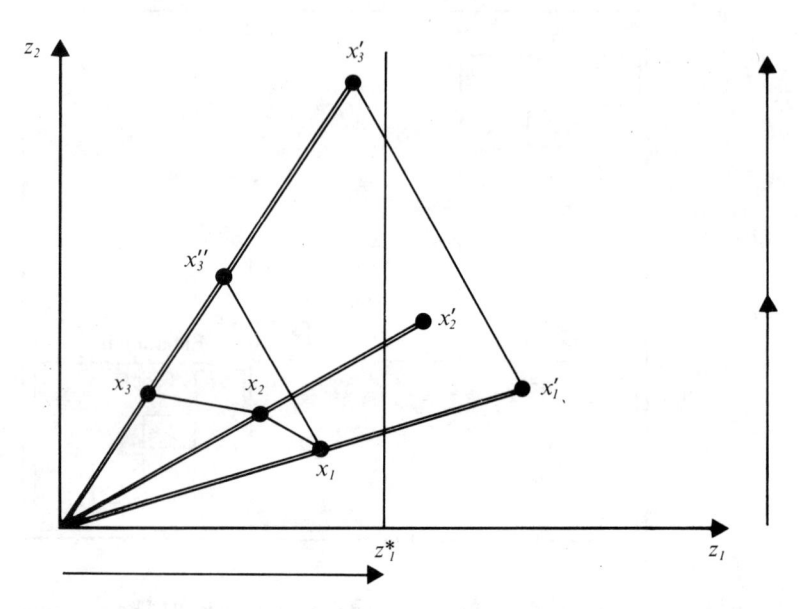

able. Let us suppose that consumers make choices according to Georgescu-Roegen's quasi-indifference curves, as represented by equation (2.4) and as illustrated by Figure 2.4. Consumers have a priority list of their needs, the $z_1$ characteristic representing the lower need and the $z_2$ characteristic representing the next need in the hierarchy. This order in priorities is upheld until a threshold level $z_1^*$ is reached. Beyond this threshold, the $z_2$ characteristic becomes the prime determinant of choice. Let us use Lancaster's representation of characteristics, here illustrated by Figure 2.9. It will be shown that, even if goods cannot be isolated into distinct groups, there are severe limitations to substitution effects when there are lexicographic filters.

Let us assume that there are three goods, $x_1$, $x_2$ and $x_3$, which fulfil the two needs represented by $z_1$ and $z_2$. The prices of these three goods being given, and his income being given, the consumer is constrained in the fulfilment of his needs. The constraint is usually represented by the efficiency frontier, illustrated in the initial situation by the kinked line $x_1 x_2 x_3$ of Figure 2.9. The maximum quantity of good $x_j$ which the consumer can buy is given by $Y/p_j$, with $Y$ being income and $p_j$ the price of the $x_j$ good. The level of characteristic $z_i$ which can be attained is thus $t_{ij} \cdot Y/p_j$.

With lexicographic ordering, consumers choose what neoclassical authors call a corner solution. Here only good $x_1$ is purchased. The consumer buys the good which allows him the highest fulfilment of characteristic $z_1$, because his income and the existing prices do not allow him to reach the threshold $z_1^*$.

Let us now suppose that the price of good $x_3$ is cut in half. The ray representing good $x_3$ doubles in length. The new efficiency frontier would be the straight line $x_1 x_3''$. Neoclassical authors would argue that the price change has induced efficiency substitution effects. All consumers who used to purchase good $x_2$ would abandon the product. In our example, the price change induces no change in the choice of all consumers whose threshold relative to income is $z_1^*$. They would all keep purchasing good $x_1$. There are no substitution effects here. Suppose now that real income doubles, all rays doubling in length to $x_1' x_2', x_3'$. For a neoclassical author this would not change the shape of the efficiency frontier; it would now be $x_1' x_3'$, consumers purchasing either good $x_1$ or good $x_3$. In a world of lexicographic ordering, however, consumers abandon good $x_1$ and purchase good $x_2$, since the combination offered by point $x_2'$ is the one that offers the highest level of characteristic $z_2$ while exceeding the threshold level $z_1^*$. Rational consumers may choose point $x_2'$, although it is not part of the efficiency frontier. This illustrates the secondary importance of substitution effects and the primary importance of income effects, while showing how inferior goods arise naturally from choices of a lexicographical nature.

To sum up, the impact of substitution is severely constrained. This is true in all cases: when the structure of consumption looks like the one illustrated by Figure 2.7, which corresponds precisely to the scheme of Maslow's hierarchy of needs; when the structure of consumption looks like the one shown in Figure 2.8, which reproduces Eichner's lexicographic ordering of sub-needs; or even if only lexicographic filters prevail.

**Consequences for Price Theory**

The emphasis of orthodox theory on static behaviour has led to an excessive amount of research on substitution effects. On the other hand, income effects have been either neglected or assumed away. (Whereas income effects used to be seriously considered, the famous Engel curves being a tribute to the interest generated by these dynamic effects, their importance in the eyes of most researchers has vanished.) Those who have attempted to estimate the importance of pure substitution effects on the general categories of consumption expenditures, having taken into consideration the income effects through time, have discovered that these substitution effects, own-price elasticities and cross-elasticities, are quite negligible (Deaton and Muellbauer, 1980, p. 71). While the own-price elasticities of food, fuel, drinks, travel, entertainment and other services turned out to be negative, as expected, the absolute value of these elasticities was found to be no greater than 0.05. The price elasticity of clothing and housing was not statistically different from zero. These findings seem to correspond to the picture of consumer behaviour which has been drawn in the preceding subsection. The cause of these small substitution effects, within the post-Keynesian framework, is that the large categories of consumer expenditures fulfil important needs which cannot compensate one for another. Variations in their relative prices induce no change in consumption behaviour, or very small ones. Only within each one of these large spending categories could one possibly observe more substantial substitution effects. One can thus presume that the more disaggregated the analysis is, the more likely we are to find high absolute values of price elasticities. However the findings of Houthakker and Taylor (1970) show that, even at a much more disaggregated level, that is with over 80 categories of consumer goods, consumption expenditures are mainly determined by habits and income effects, while price substitution effects play a fairly modest role.

The crucial issue here is that the fluctuations in the price of a good, unless they are really substantial, will not have much impact on the quantities sold. The major exception to this prediction would be new goods being introduced to consumers. Innovations on the consumer market either create new needs or fulfil existing needs which were previously poorly met. Besides these innovative commodities, the reason that fluctuations of relative prices would have little impact on demand is that all goods respond to a need (or to a set of needs). Provided that these needs, or sub-needs, are arranged in a preset order, the decrease in the price of a good will only make it more attractive to consumers who have already attained that part of the pyramid. All those who are still trying to attain their threshold levels with respect to lower needs will not be concerned by this price decrease. Furthermore, since a substantial amount of expenditure occurs on the basis of habits and customs, the decrease in prices may go unnoticed unless it is heavily publicized. The decrease in the price of a good will only have an impact to the extent that it can replace other goods fulfilling the same needs, or, more precisely, what we have called the same wants. This is the traditional substitution effect, limited however to the goods which have similar characteristics. In classical theory, these goods were for practical purposes treated as identical (Schefold, 1985, p. 112).

The symmetric consequences of the above is that changes in the prices of goods fulfilling needs of the higher levels of the hierarchy will have no impact whatsoever on the consumption of the goods of the lower levels of the hierarchy (Roy, 1943). The reason is that these goods are not part of the basket or of the hypothetical basket of consumption of all consumers which have not yet fulfilled the required thresholds of their lower needs. These poorer consumers just do not care about the prices of the goods which help to fulfil the higher needs since these goods cannot be acquired owing to their budget constraint. On the other hand, if there is an increase (or a decrease) in the relative price of the goods which help to fulfil the lower needs, this will have repercussions on the quantities sold of all goods belonging to the higher part of the hierarchy. A lower relative price will increase the real income of all households, leading to an increase in the consumption of all goods fulfilling the higher needs of the hierarchy.

What we have here is an asymmetric relation which is similar to the one established by the classical authors when they were discussing necessary and luxury goods (Roncaglia, 1978, p. 52). According to the classical classification, luxury goods were non-necessary goods that were not consumed by the workers. Only the rentiers and the capitalists could spend their income on luxury goods. Necessary goods, on the other hand, were consumed by both the workers and the upper classes. The consequence of this, according to Ricardo, was that changes in the production conditions of luxury goods or in their prices did not have repercussions on the overall rate of profit or on the cost of producing necessary goods. On the other hand, changes in the prices or the production conditions of necessary goods had repercussions on the overall rate of profit and on the cost of production of luxury goods. The neo-Ricardians have drawn similar conclusions from Sraffa's analysis of basic and non-basic commodities, the former playing the role of the necessary goods, so to speak, while the latter replaced the role played by luxury goods. Steedman (1980) has integrated the classical theory with the neo-Ricardian approach by showing that in a world of heterogeneous labour, the rate of profit does not depend on the overall average real wage rate. Rather only the real wage rate of workers producing goods consumed by workers is a determinant of the rate of profit.

There is thus a strong relationship between the classical and neo-Ricardian asymmetric conception of the economy and the post-Keynesian theory of consumer behaviour, based on a hierarchy of needs and hence presumably on a hierarchy of goods, from the more basic necessaries to the products of high luxury. Whereas the neo-Ricardian focus is on the consequences of this asymmetric relation for the determinants of relative prices, the impact of the asymmetry for the post-Keynesian theory is on the quantities consumed. Using the same conceptual framework which distinguishes between goods fulfilling lower needs and those responding to higher needs, the neo-Ricardians tell us how a change in the conditions of production or in the composition of demand by the workers could affect relative prices or the purchasing power of consumers through the cost side. On the other hand, the post-Keynesian theory shows how these changes in purchasing power are translated into increases in the quantities consumed of the various products, and how little substitution effects are induced by changes in relative prices, owing to the existence of hierarchical needs and sub-needs.

One may thus conclude that when changes in relative prices are small, the substitution effects that they induce can be ignored, either because they are negligible, as in the case of goods fulfilling different needs, or because they concern goods which for all practical purposes may be considered identical. On the other hand, substantial changes in the relative price of a good are usually associated with novel products, which create new needs. Pure substitution effects in this case do not arise, since this consumption innovation needs to be incorporated within the hierarchy of needs and wants. This picture of the lack of importance of the substitution effect in consumer behaviour is certainly compatible with the views of neo-Ricardian authors:

If the effect of the price on the quantity bought is not appreciable, then the effect can be ignored without great error. Alternatively, when the effect is important enough to need general consideration, it seems it will often be the case that the effect constitutes an *irreversible* change, which is incompatible with its treatment in terms of a demand function. That is the effect will entail a permanent change in the habits of consumers, which even marginalist authors would have to treat as a change in 'tastes' (Garegnani, 1990, p. 131)

If one accepts the principles which are the building blocks of the post-Keynesian theory of consumer theory, macroeconomic constructions which focus on classes and groups of agents appear more reliable. We have seen that stability of the neoclassical theory of the exchange economy depended in the end on assuming the existence of a representative agent, that is on the assumption that all agents had identical preferences and identical income. Post-Keynesian analysis leads to the belief that agents or households belonging to the same income class have a similar structure of consumption. We know, however, that agents do not have identical incomes. There is thus ample justification for utilizing income classes rather than the representative agent or a large number of differentiated individuals in macroeconomic studies. Furthermore, since income changes rather than price changes appear to be the main influence on changes in consumption, the importance of the study of income effects in macroeconomics is reasserted.

## Saving Decisions of Households

Little attention has been given so far to savings decisions. This is no accident. In traditional theory, savings and consumption are linked, since savings are time vehicles designed to smooth consumption through time. Savings are viewed as a decision to retard consumption and maximize intertemporal utility. Savings are the result of a rational choice by individuals, based on given preferences and expectations of future incomes.

In post-Keynesian theory, savings are mostly carried out by institutions or through institutional vehicles. Generally speaking, savings by households is not the result of rational choice, but rather the accidental effect of other decisions and events. Furthermore household savings are to a large extent determined by institutional rules. As is recalled by Green (1991, p. 107), both the Institutionalists (*à la* Veblen and Galbraith) and the post-Keynesians (such as Kaldor) see the bulk of savings as being controlled by the business sector. As we shall see in the next chapter, firms with some oligopolistic power set their prices on the basis of a target level of retained earnings. These retained earnings are the savings of the business sector.

Still, national accounts show that households save. Besides the fact that a large proportion of household savings must be attributed to unincorporated businesses which are included with individuals in the national accounts, one must recall that about half of the remaining household savings result from investment in owner-occupied housing. These savings are, so to speak, forced savings. They arise from the decision of households to acquire their own lodging and, in that sense, they arise as an afterthought rather than as a conscious decision to save. The other half of household savings is the acquisition of financial assets. Again a large part of these savings is carried out under the guise of private pension funds and is included in personal savings in national accounts. The amounts collected by private pension funds are often non-discretionary: the individual has no say in the decision to save; the exact amount is imposed by some formula worked out in the collective agreement. Furthermore these funds are under the control of the corporations which are offering pension plans to their employees. The individual has little or no say in its use. The same can be said of the amounts which are collected by government in the case of universal public pension plans: the sums are non-discretionary and no control can be exercised by the individual.

One must thus conclude, firstly, that a substantial part of the savings of an economy is not carried out by the household sector, but rather by the business sector; and secondly that a substantial part of the savings of the household sector is the result of institutional constraints or of the decision to invest in housing. Furthermore several post-classical authors believe that even a large part of the remaining household savings is not the result of a deliberate and discretionary decision to save. This position has been presented in particular by Marglin (1975). He argues that the remaining personal savings are largely accidental. They are a residual, the result of a temporary disequilibrium. For most households, 'the pressures to spend are supposed to be too great for the typical household to resist' (Marglin, 1984a, p. 144). We are in a Galbraithian world, where corporations hammer the consumer with their advertising, which arouses envy and imitative behaviour. 'Good resolutions to behave in a thrifty manner are hard to keep when they are constantly assaulted by advertising and the temptation of new commodities' (Robinson, 1956, p. 251). As a rule, households spend all of their incomes, sometimes even more, except when incomes are so large that they can hardly be spent on consumer goods and have to be invested in conspicuous durables, which are partly consumption goods and partly an alternative to financial intertemporal vehicles.

Most households, then, but assuredly not all, only save when there is an increase in their incomes. The reason for this saving behaviour is not to be found in the belief that the increase is temporary, but rather in the time that is required to learn how to spend the extra money. This view is consistent with the post-Keynesian approach to consumption decisions. Consumers are not viewed as having ordered preferences defined over all types of goods. On the contrary, consumers set themselves priorities over the types of goods that they are likely to consume. Income increases bring into consideration possibilities that had not been assessed before. Beyond near-subsistence levels, where urges rather than preferences rule, these possibilities have to be learned. The acquisition of habits prevails over instincts. When incomes are rising, learning prevails over habits. As Pasinetti (1981, p. 233) points out, when per capita income is increasing 'consumers themselves may be uncertain about the direction in which their demand is going to develop'. Households save while they learn how to spend their increased purchasing power.

The post-classical theory of savings is thus based on habit persistence and income effects, the same effects that had been emphasized to explain the structure of consumption and its evolution. It is ironic to note that, when the standard neoclassical savings theory, such as the permanent income and the life-cycle hypotheses, have been reformulated to make them amenable to empirical testing, they have been rendered almost indistinguishable from the post-Keynesian habit persistence savings theory (Green, 1984, p. 99). While the neoclassical theories assume that present wealth and future incomes determine present consumption, they are actually tested by making use of present and past incomes or consumption, precisely the variables that would enter a savings theory based on income and habits. The reason for which the neoclassical version, rather than its non-orthodox cousin, has been so popular is that it is based on substantive rationality, whereas the habit persistence theory is based on procedural rationality. Furthermore the apparent empirical success of the neoclassical savings hypotheses has justified the theoretical inclusion of wealth stocks in the consumption function, adding credibility to the Pigovian full employment argument based on real balance effects. Once we realize that neoclassical authors have instead tested a restricted version of the habit persistence theory, which does not rely on wealth stocks, the arguments based on the stabilizing effects of real money balances are greatly diminished.

The evidence available from the 1980s reinforces this post-Keynesian theory of incidental household savings. In nearly all industrial countries, rates of both saving and income growth have simultaneously been falling. An empirical study conducted by Bosworth *et al.* (1991) shows that there has been a decline in the savings propensities of a vast majority of households, whatever their income. Bosworth *et al.* conclude that the cause of this decline cannot be found at the microeconomic level. Rather, they believe that slower income growth is the most plausible cause for lower savings rate by households throughout the world. 'The problem is that the hypothesis is in direct conflict with popular theoretical models of consumers who base their decisions on forward-looking, rational expectations' (1991, p. 227). While this may be a problem for neoclassical authors such as Bosworth, it is not for post-classical authors. Post-Keynesians posit that households save 'when their incomes are rising faster than they can adjust their spending' (Marglin, 1975, p. 22). It follows that the rates of saving of households of all income classes and the rate of growth of real income are intimately connected in post-Keynesian theory. As Marglin (1975, p. 24) has put it, 'the direction of causality is opposite to that customarily assumed; household savings are not a cause of growth, but the result of it'. One would predict from this post-Keynesian theory of saving that the saving rate of households would decline with a slowdown of the growth rate of real income.

What are the consequences for post-Keynesian macroeconomic models? Post-classical economists of all allegiances usually follow the classical savings hypothesis in assuming that the propensity to save out of wages is equal to zero. *Workers spend what they get.* At the very least, the propensity to save out of profits is assumed to surpass the propensity to save out of wages. As was explained by Kaldor (1966, p. 310), this inequality is mainly due to the institutional framework. Corporations have large retained earnings. Unless shareholders spend more than what they get in the form of dividends, the propensity to save out of profit income is necessarily greater than that out of wage income. The habit persistence theory adds that, beyond institutional saving and owner-occupied housing, most households save by accident, when their real incomes increase. The great majority of households, those which may be called workers, thus have a propensity to save which is very close to zero once we exclude housing from productive investment. For all practical purposes, the propensity to save out of wage income may thus be considered equal to zero, especially in long run models. Indeed, in his initial presentation, Marglin (1975, p. 29) found an estimate of the long run propensity to consume which was equal to one.

The rest of the households, a small proportion of the population, may behave differently. They save a substantial proportion of their high incomes. A large portion of their revenues is not wages, however, but property income and salaries which can be assimilated to property income. As Kalecki (1971, p. 76) would have it, the salaries of higher business executives 'are rather akin to profits'. The savings of wealthy households may thus be seen as an addition to the savings from profits, rather than savings from wages. In a simplified mode, the propensity to save from profits will thus reflect a combination of the retention ratio on profits of the business sector, as well as the positive propensity to save of those wealthier households. In a slightly more complex mode, profits will have to be explicitly divided into retained earnings, on one hand, and distributed profits and interest payments, on the other. This will allow us to distinguish between the savings realized by the business sector and those of the household sector, still assuming that no savings arise out of wages. All these assumptions will be used in Chapters 5 and 6.

## 2.4 AN OVERVIEW OF THE ALTERNATIVE

In this chapter we have seen that situations of uncertainty are definitely different from those of certainty or of risk. Taking into account uncertainty does not forcefully convey nihilistic conclusions. Uncertainty does not necessarily lead to irrational behaviour or to global instability. In situations of uncertainty, rationality is of the procedural sort. Agents follow rules of behaviour that allow them to face a lack of knowledge and the lack of faith with which they can hold their expectations. The same type of bounded rationality is followed when agents face a problem symmetric to that of uncertainty; that is, when they are overloaded with information. In both cases there is a gap between the amount of information which would be required to take an optimal decision and the amount of information which is accessible, either because proper information just does not exist or because that information is too complex to be adequately processed.

Whereas mainstream authors have avoided discussing fundamental uncertainty because they feared its devastating consequences for theoretical analysis, post-Keynesians argue that on the contrary uncertainty and procedural rationality provide the regularities that we observe in the economic world. There is thus no excuse for not taking into consideration this fundamental fact of our environment. The use of cost-plus prices or normal ratios is thus the legitimate consequence of an analysis based on procedural rationality.

Similarly, the use of macroeconomic models based on the analysis of income classes and on income effects is the legitimate outgrowth of a post-Keynesian theory of the consumer where price-substitution effects are not important or are severely constrained to goods which respond to similar characteristics, and where increases or changes in demand are mostly determined by increases in real incomes or changes in consumer preferences. This post-Keynesian theory of consumption, based on the hierarchical nature of needs, is also reminiscent of the classical distinction between necessaries and luxury goods and of the neo-Ricardian division between basic and non-basic commodities. Under these circumstances, to ignore substitution effects, based on relative prices, appears to be much less disastrous than to ignore income effects and threshold levels.

From the empirical standpoint, the post-Keynesian theory of consumer choice points in the direction of studies that would try to identify the groups of goods that would respond to the various sub-needs, and that would trace the order of acquisition of these various groups of goods. Also, rather than trying to estimate imaginary demand curves, empirical studies should focus on estimates of income and price elasticities, taking into account preference interdependence and the imbedded and hierarchical nature of needs or groups of goods within categories of expenditures.

# 3. Theory of the Firm

## 3.1 FEATURES AND DOMAIN OF VALIDITY OF THE POST-KEYNESIAN FIRM

First-year students of economics are usually impressed by the symmetry of mainstream microeconomics. Firms maximize profits, just as households were assumed to maximize utility. Having mastered the shapes of the total utility curve and that of the indifference curves in the chapters covering consumer theory, students simply have to reproduce these curves to obtain the total product curve and the isoquants of production theory. The U-shaped cost functions are then derived. It is at this stage that the instructor has to be most vigilant, for many students who have had working experience will object to the implication that average total costs (when profits are non-negative) are increasing with sales. The law of decreasing returns has to be hammered in for order to be preserved. Further confusion sets in, however, when textbook authors attempt to demonstrate the practical usefulness of the rule equating marginal cost with marginal revenue by relying on instances of decreasing average costs and constant marginal costs which have nothing to do with marginal pricing rules (see Baumol *et al.*, 1988, p. 496; incidentally the example has disappeared from the latest edition). Nevertheless, when students enter intermediate microeconomics, these doubts about the coherence between reality and theory will be washed out by the necessity to handle the required mathematics and Lagrangians.

The object of the present chapter is to present a more realistic view of the firm and to show that this view of the typical firm is shared by all post-Keynesians. Five themes will be tackled: what are the objectives of the firm; what are the shapes of cost curves and why is there excess capacity; how are margins on costs set when pricing; what happens to prices when demand fluctuates; and is there any link with the Sraffian prices of production?

To answer these questions the contributions of authors from various non-orthodox schools will be considered. Although there is no necessary agreement on the details of the theory of the firm, these various authors share a common vision. Post-Keynesian authors, at least since the late 1960s conceive of the firm on similar grounds. The picture occasionally drawn by Kaldor and Robinson is consistent with that presented by Kalecki and the Kaleckians such as Steindl. There is also much consistency with the then contemporary views of Oxford specialists of the firm, such as Harrod, Andrews and Brunner. The same can be said of the views of American specialists of administered prices, such as Means and Lanzilotti, or even those of Galbraith and Baran and Sweezy. More recently the works of post-Keynesians, mainly Eichner and Lee, have highlighted the importance of non-neoclassical foundations of the theory of the firm, following the footsteps of Sylos Labini. We shall also see that the framework developed by all these economists is quite coherent with the notion of bounded rationality which we have presented in the previous chapter, and which is developed in the case of the firm in the so-called behavioural theories of Cyert and March. It is of course possible to find other, perhaps lesser-known, authors who have developed various aspects of the post-Keynesian theory of the firm. We do not wish to deal strictly with economic history, however, and shall stick to the ones already identified above.

I would argue that what characterizes all these authors is the recognition that prices set by firms in the short run are not market-clearing prices, and are not even intended to be so. According to Lee (1990, p. 685, 1984a, p. 156), this was the striking lesson to be drawn both from Means's administered prices and from the surveys conducted by Hall and Hitch (1939). The novel and radical feature of the classic article of the latter was that prices are not designed to clear markets. Prices are not such that they equate supply and demand schedules. In a context where supply is flexible, firms do not necessarily attempt to equate demand to the normal use of capacity when they set prices. This in my opinion is what distinguishes the markets in which firms of the post-Keynesian type operate and those in which the standard neoclassical firm still makes sense. The position taken here is that these non-clearing markets are the rule whereas the clearing ones are the exception.

To clarify matters, it might be appropriate at this stage to use Alfred Eichner's description of the four important characteristics of the relevant firm in the modern world, a firm which Eichner (1976) calls the megacorp. As its name indicates it is a large firm; management is separated from proprietorship; marginal costs are approximately constant; and the firm operates in at least one industry of the oligopolistic type. Our discussion of the characteristics of the post-Keynesian firm will thus evolve around these four characteristics.

The main point of contention, related to the non-clearing aspect of prices, is whether or not the typical firm that post-Keynesians describe is necessarily set within an oligopolistic industry. My opinion is that it need not be, recognizing, however, that to study the behaviour of the price leader in an oligopoly may lead to more satisfactory and more determinate results than if one studies the behaviour of a small firm operating in an industry where there is no dominant actor. Besides Eichner, several other post-Keynesians have noted that oligopolies constitute their representative post-Keynesian industry. Kaldor, for instance, has indicated on a number of occasions that the industrial model he is implicitly working with is 'a kind of oligopoly-cum-price-leadership theory' (1970a, p. 3); that is, a theory where one assumes 'the prevalence of imperfect markets and oligopolistic competition, where prices are set by the leading firms, based on costs' (1978a, p. xxi).

To argue that the post-Keynesian firm operates mainly in oligopolistic industries unnecessarily restricts the range of post-Keynesian theory. Means has denied that cost-plus pricing, or administered pricing as he called it, only applies to monopoly: 'Administered prices should not be confused with monopoly ... In general monopolised industries have administered prices, but so also do a great many vigorously competitive industries in which the number of competitors is small' (quoted in Clifton, 1983, p. 24). Similarly, we can deny that cost-plus pricing only applies to monopolies and oligopolies. It has been recognized by several economists that the phenomenon of mark-up pricing, one of the important features of post-Keynesian firms, is 'simply too pervasive across the United States economy to be attributable to oligopoly' (Okun, 1981, pp. 175-6). Rigid cost-plus pricing is observed not only in the car or the computer industries but also in retail trades in which large firms do not dominate. This was also one of the remarkable results of the survey by Hall and Hitch:

The answers also suggest that the distinction between monopoly and monopolistic competition on the one hand and monopolistic competition with an admixture of oligopoly elements on the other is not of very great importance ... It proved to be extremely difficult in practice to distinguish between oligopolistic firms and others. The distinction seems to be almost entirely one of degree, for all firms were conscious to some extent of the presence of competitors and the possibility of reactions to changes in their price and output policy ... Where this element of oligopoly is present, and in many cases where it is absent, there is a strong tendency among businessmen to fix prices directly at a level which they regard as their 'full cost'. (1939, pp. 30–1)

The view taken here is thus the converse of that advanced by the advocates of contestable markets (Baumol, 1982; see Davies and Lee, 1988, for a critique). All markets, with the exceptions soon to be elaborated upon, can be brought back under the umbrella of imperfect markets, where prices in the short run basically depend upon costs, according to some principle of mark-up or full cost pricing. Sylos Labini (1971) argues along the lines of this definition. For him, prices in the short run in competitive industries depend on both demand and supply, while in imperfect markets, which he calls oligopolies, these prices only depend on costs. Hicks (1976b, p. 417) has made the same distinction with the help of the dichotomy between flexprice and fixprice markets. The latter are associated with normal costs, to be found in manufacturing but also in the primary sector where oligopolies prevail. To these, Sylos Labini (1971, p. 245) adds the tertiary sector. All this is consistent with Kalecki's opinion, according to which the prices of agricultural products and raw materials are determined by the interaction of supply and demand, mainly because any increase in production requires long delays, but also because mining products being homogeneous they are subject to speculation on futures markets. On the other hand, finished goods and industrial products are cost-determined because there exist reserves of capacity which allow flexibility in responding to demand changes. Kalecki adds that in these markets there must be some form of imperfect competition for excess capacities to prevail in the long run (1971, pp. 43–5). While there is clearly an agreement as to whether the secondary and even the tertiary sectors fall under the domain of the imperfect market and therefore of the post-Keynesian firm, the case of the primary sector is less clear. As to mining products and even some agricultural goods (through marketing boards), competition does not always prevail and we should therefore expect prices to be fixed independently of demand. We could thus say that the representative post-Keynesian firm prevails everywhere, except in competitive industries of the primary sector or in auction markets.

One could also link this post-Keynesian firm to the notion of reproducible goods: where products are reproducible, we should expect marginal costs to be linear up to capacity; that is, we should observe inverted L-shaped average variable cost curves. Commodities which are not reproducible, as is the case of natural resources, or which require long delays to increase their production – the case of agricultural goods – correspond to the U-shaped marginal cost curves of the standard neoclassical firm. The ability to fix prices, what Means has called administered prices, relies on something more than monopolistic power. It relies on the shape of the costs inherent to the type of technology in use. This is a point made by Means (1936, p. 35) himself, when he links the presence of administered prices, in opposition to flexible prices, to the existence of modern technology. We can relate this to Kalecki's distinction between cost-determined and demand-determined sectors, where 'it is clear that these two types of price formation arise out of different conditions of supply' (Kalecki, 1971,

p. 43). According to Kalecki, there is a link between cost-determined prices or fixed prices, excess capacities, constant marginal costs and imperfect competition. On the other hand, prices flexible according to variations in demand are associated with rising marginal costs and homogeneous products, the latter being an element of traditional competition. The same link between administered pricing and the modern conditions of production of reproducible goods has been proposed by Kahn in his critique of Malinvaud's model of unemployment based on fixed prices. Kahn argues that administered prices which are insensitive to demand must be associated both with market imperfections and non-increasing costs.

Fixed or 'sticky' prices are found in manufacturing and distribution, where products are not homogeneous and labour costs are constant or decreasing up to the limits of capacity . . .
Flexible prices are found in those markets for a limited range of primary products where products are homogeneous, demand to the individual producer is almost perfectly elastic, and costs rise with output due to fixed natural resources . . .
The whole notion of sticky prices, based on the studies of the real manufacturing world . . . cannot be squeezed into the textbook notion of homogeneous products and rising cost curves. If on the other hand, one wishes to justify the assumption of sticky prices by returning to reality, then one must assume constant or falling variable costs. (Kahn, 1983, p. 224)

We may thus sum up the issue of the domain of validity of the post-Keynesian firm by saying that post-Keynesians assert that there are hardly any markets where prices are not administered by firms. Most industries are thus to some extent imperfect or monopolistic markets, even those that at first sight might appear to be competitive. This is a precise counterpoint to the contestable market doctrine. All sectors, however, are not of the cost-determined type, although they will be assumed to be so in the macroeconomic part of the book. Post-Keynesians believe that the secondary and the tertiary sectors are under an administered price regime, with cost-determined prices that are basically inflexible in the face of variations in short-run demand. Although by no means required, it is assumed that the typical firm operates in an industry where a few large firms account for the vast majority of sales, another stylized fact (Kaldor, 1985a, p. 58). It is thus understandable that Eichner would include among the four characteristics of the typical post-Keynesian firm the large size of the firm and the associated dichotomy between management and ownership. We shall see, however, that size and the possible divorce of control from ownership are only modulating factors, rather than determinants, of the objectives of the firm.

## 3.2 THE OBJECTIVES OF THE FIRM

**Power**

If one attempted to characterize briefly the received view of the objectives of the firm, one would draw the following picture: small firms operate in competitive markets and attempt to maximize profits, more specifically short-run profits; larger firms, because they operate in imperfect markets and because their management is divorced from ownership, generally pursue goals other than profit maximization. I shall argue here that the objectives of firms are the same, irrespective of their size and of their type of control, and that these objectives are not profit maximization. To the extent that profit motives have a substantial role to play, it will be argued that profits are means rather than ends.

The question of the objectives of the firm or those of their managers has generated a substantial amount of attention from economists. Various maximands such as sales, managers' utility and valuation ratios have been proposed, not to speak of goals of the satisficing type, such as normal rates of return or market shares. Faced with this debacle of objectives, the only rational response is to assume that firms have multi-purpose objectives. This, in fact, is the view that many empirical researchers adopt after admitting that the empirical evidence is unclear (Koutsoyiannis, 1975, p. 258). Indeed, in surveys of their objectives, entrepreneurs often indicate several of them rather than the standard profit maximization hypothesis (Shipley, 1981, p. 442). Among post-Keynesians, while John Kenneth Galbraith (1975, p. 124) has claimed that it would be a serious error 'to seek a single explanation of how firms behave', Joan Robinson (1977, p. 11) has argued that firms have motivations that are multi-dimensional and that, as a consequence, 'it will never be possible to get a knock-down answer'. Besides the obvious fact that there is no reason to presume that different firms will behave identically, or that the various constituents of the modern firm pursue identical goals, the main cause of these distressful results is that the ultimate objective of the firm can only be defined in very general terms. The consequence of this is that various intermediate goals that serve to fulfil that ultimate objective will be proposed, by either the theoreticians or the business world itself.

My opinion is that power is the ultimate objective of the firm: power over its environment, whether it be economic, social or political. 'Power is the ability of an individual or a group to impose its purpose on others' (Galbraith, 1975, p. 108). The firm wants power over its suppliers of materials, over its customers, over the government, over the kind of technology to be put in use. The firm, whether it be a megacorp or a small family firm, would like to have control over future events, its financial requirements, the quality of its labour force, the prices of the industry and the possibility of takeovers. 'The firm is viewed as being able to exercise a degree of control over its environment through R&D, market development, interfirm cooperation, entry deterrence' (Davies and Lee, 1988, p. 21). In a world without uncertainty, the notion of power dissolves and loses much of its importance. In such a world, for instance, firms always have access to all of the financial capital that they require provided their investment project is expected to be profitable. The source of financing is immaterial.

However, in a world where fundamental uncertainty prevails, firms must find means to guarantee access to financial capital, all of their material inputs, or critical information. Powerful relations allow corporations to have access to scarce information without which the firm would be immobilized. Furthermore the control over events constitutes the means by which firms can evade the inaction which pervades uncertain situations. Power allows firms to 'control the consequences of their own decisions in order to prevent their desires being thwarted by others' (Dixon, 1986, p. 588). All firms thus look for more power over their environment. At a more fundamental level perhaps, the search for power procures security for the individual owner or for the organization. Firms would like to insure their long-run survival, the permanence of their own institution. 'For any organization, as for any organism, the goal or the objective that has a natural assumption of preeminence is the organization's survival. This, plausibly, is true of the technostructure' (Galbraith, 1972, p. 170). A powerful control over events and human actors provides the conditions required for such long-run existential goals.

The notion of power, except when related to the case of the pure monopoly, has been systematically ignored in economics, with the exception of Institutionalists and Marxists. Among the former, Galbraith is the most well-known recent exponent of the importance of power in the economic sphere. As argued above, the power that firms attempt to obtain is not limited to the market sphere: it extends to the political and the social spheres. Besides the implementation of new processes, the differentiation of old commodities and the marketing of new products, firms try to escape the established market structures and to act on these structures through the lobbying of public authorities and the formation of social norms. It is amusing to note that these strategies were outlined by French economist Jean Marchal, in an article published in the *American Economic Review*, to which the referee objected that power struggles pertained to Europe but not to the United States, where 'we have the purest of pure competition' (Marchal, 1951). It is then easy to comprehend why Galbraith's vision of the American industrial state generated so much negative response from his fellow economists. Galbraith has emphasized the role of power for the megacorp along the lines suggested by Marchal. One should not forget, however, that this search for power is just as important for the small entrepreneurial firm which is trying to take off as it can be for the technostructure.

> The need to control environment – to exclude untoward events – encourages much greater size. The larger the firm, the larger it will be in its industry. The greater, accordingly, will be its influence in setting prices and costs. And the greater, in general, will be its influence on consumers, the community and the state – the greater, in short, will be its ability to influence, i.e., plan, its environment. More important, as organization develops and becomes more elaborate, the greater will be its freedom from external interference. (Galbraith, 1975, p. 56)

The quest for power and growth is also as valid at the level of the organization as it can be at the level of the individual working within the corporation. Whereas a successful quest for power will endow the firm with stability and permanence, it will simultaneously endow the individual with a successful career, the opportunity of promotions, the availability of higher social status and the respect of peers, all the items which comprise the upper echelons of Maslow's pyramid of needs. Here we can understand the numerous studies which have underlined the maximization of the satisfaction of the managers, the so-called managerial theories of the firm. The gains from a more powerful corporation are not limited to the managers, however; they apply to the whole technostructure. Galbraith's previous quote continues:

> As organization acquires power, it uses that power, not surprisingly, to serve the ends of those involved. These ends – job security, pay, promotion, prestige, company plane and private washroom, the charm of collectively exercised power – are all strongly served by the growth of the enterprise. So growth both enhances power over prices, costs, consumers, suppliers, the community and the state and also rewards in a very personal way those who bring it about. (1975, p. 56)

This brings to the forefront the question of the separation between management and ownership, famous since the publication of the classic study of Berle and Means (1933), and known to Institutionalists as the Veblenian *absentee ownership* (Leathers and Evans, 1973). Would the managers of a company still controlled by its owners behave any differently from those of a management-controlled one? Both Eichner and Galbraith imply that they would, insisting as much as they do on the consequences of the divorce between proprietorship and management. My opinion is that there is no need to emphasize that divorce. Whether the owners are still in control or not is irrelevant: those individuals taking decisions within the firm are in search of power; and their behaviour and motivations will reflect that fundamental fact. Incidentally, it is a bit ironic to note that, to sustain his thesis of the all-powerful technostructure, Galbraith (1972, p. 174) is led to cite a minority study which provides evidence of performance differentials between owner-controlled and management-controlled corporations. Most studies seem to show that there is no discrepancy with respect to growth, advertising, salaries, the variability of investment and dividends, and, most importantly, there is no differential with respect to profitability (Kania and McKean, 1976). An argument could then be made, similar to that supporting the contestable market hypothesis, that the forces of competition constrain management-controlled companies to behave as efficiently as firms controlled by their owners. It appears, however, that firms operating in concentrated industries and firms which are dominant in their markets do not exhibit any larger differentials than those operating under more competitive conditions, so that it must be concluded that *'competitive forces* are unlikely to be the *root* cause of similarity in owner-manager performance' (Kania and McKean, 1976, p. 288, emphasis in original).

The concept of the Galbraithian technostructure thus applies with equal force to both the managerial firm and the one still controlled by its owners. In the latter, owners can benefit from the power exerted by their corporation. They can also grab part of the corporate surplus, in the sense defined by Baran and Sweezy (1968), extracted by their technostructure. There is thus no reason to suppose in this case that their behaviour would be much different from that of the managers. Consequently, when owners truly control a corporation, they benefit from the gain of power, and should seek it as much as their managers. On the other hand, when owners still control the board of directors, but without being able to share in the benefits of corporate power, one may suspect that the complexity of the operations will be such that it will be quite difficult for the owners to have much impact on the performance of the firm. In particular, the large institutional shareholders rarely attempt to modify the behaviour of management. The position of this type of owners is no different from that of the major money lenders to the firm, as will be argued later. When unsatisfied, institutional owners would rather sell their shares than tamper with management practices. The repercussions of these sales for management are minute, unless those who buy back the shares intend to make a hostile takeover.

The view of the enterprise taken here is thus one of a going concern, where *the entrepreneur is the firm* (Strauss, 1944). As the Institutionalists would argue, the firm has a sort of collective will, defined by tradition, the working rules, the dividend policy and so on. This is not to deny the importance of individual leaders. True leaders succeed in instilling enthusiasm and good traditions within the technostructure. They may turn around the performance of a previously ill-managed firm. The positive contribution of these individual leaders, however, is not so much a function of the dividends garnered by the shareholders, but rather is assessed by its impact on the possibility of long-run survival of the institution. With perhaps the exception of the smallest of firms, the notion of permanence pervades the thinking of decision makers of these going concerns (Eichner, 1976, p. 22). Long-run considerations affect pricing or investment decisions, whoever controls the corporation.

**Growth**

Having been convinced of the universal validity of power as the ultimate objective of almost all types of firms, the reader may then wonder how that objective can be met. The answer is very simple: to become powerful, firms must be big; to become big, firms must grow. As a first approximation, it may then be said that, if firms attempt to maximize anything, they try to maximize their rate of growth. The compelling need to survive, says Galbraith (1972, p. 174), requires 'the greatest possible rate of corporate growth as measured in sales'. Thus he concludes, 'the primary affirmative purpose of the technostructure is the growth of the firm' (1975, p. 116). This is not surprising: the larger the firm is, the easier it is to overturn market forces, and 'the greater the scope for conscious planning of economic activity' (Penrose, 1959, p. 15). Besides Galbraith, and also historian Alfred Chandler (1977, pp. 8–10), several economists of the managerial school have emphasized the importance of growth as the major measurable objective of the firm, Marris (1964a) being the prime example.

Growth is also a recurrent theme of post-Keynesian economics. Post-Keynesians have consistently asserted that firms maximize the rate of growth, subject to various constraints, or that the main analytical objective of the firm is to grow. Survival and growth are often associated, in opposition to the neoclassical viewpoint. This is asserted at both the microeconomic and macroeconomic levels. For the latter, for instance, Robinson (1962, p. 38) indicates that 'the central mechanism of accumulation is the urge of firms to survive and to grow'. A similar view can be found in Kaldor (1978a, p. xvi), for whom 'the individual enterprise – for reasons first perceived by Marx – must go on expanding so as to keep its share in the market'. The reasons attributed to Marx, but also to Allyn Young, are the existence of increasing returns to scale, which give a cost advantage to firms holding large shares of the market. Increasing returns to scale preclude the neoclassical concept of the optimal firm size. It may be that the managerial coordination of activities becomes increasingly difficult as the firm gets bigger, but this is largely compensated by the increasing returns experienced on other inputs and through power. Growth, then, ensures economic power for those who already have it, no less than for those who strive for it. Indeed, as underlined both by Galbraith and by Eichner, growth simultaneously provides for the survival of the firm, the satisfaction of the managers and the hopes of the employees within the technostructure.

> But the growth of the firm also serves as does nothing else the direct pecuniary interest of the technostructure. In a firm that is static in size an individual's advancement awaits the death or retirement of those above him in the hierarchy ... In a growing firm, in contrast, new jobs are created by expansion. Promotion ceases to be a zero sum game in which what one wins, another loses. All can advance. All can succeed. (Galbraith, 1975, p. 116)

> For the executives who exercise effective control of the megacorp, the growth of the firm over time, because of the increase in power, prestige and remuneration which it brings in its wake, is the most important desideratum ...
> It turns out that those megacorps which are most likely to survive in the long run are the megacorps which have attempted to grow at the highest possible rate by continuously diversifying and expanding into newer, more rapidly growing industries. Thus it is the need to ensure survival that dictates maximum growth as the goal of the firm. Those firms which fail to expand apace with the economy are likely to find themselves at an increasing disadvantage on a number of fronts. (Eichner, 1987a, p. 360–1)

I have asserted before that the structure of control of the corporation would not have any noticeable impact on the behaviour or the goals of the firm. To acquire power, the ultimate objective, the decision makers of the modern megacorp try to expand as quickly as is reasonably possible. The objective of growth, rather than the consumption of profit, is predominant. This is true in the modern world, whatever the size of the firm and whoever controls the firm, despite the opposite view of Robin Marris (1964a). Adrian Wood, a post-Keynesian economist, has also emphasized the universality of the motive of growth, valid for the small as well as for the large firm, for the owner-controlled as well as for the management-controlled corporation:

> The basic goal of those in charge of the firm is to cause sales revenue to grow as rapidly as possible ... But I do not agree with Marris that this pattern of behaviour is caused by the separation of ownership from control. Instead, I believe it to reflect the fact that (in so far as the two conflict) the urge for power is stronger than the urge for money. As a result, growth maximisation is a phenomenon which is to be observed in (all except the smallest) unincorporated firms and in closely owned companies as well as in large quoted companies with widely dispersed ownership. (Wood, 1975, p. 8)

This type of behaviour is not something entirely new, however. 'At all stages of capitalism development the growth of the firm has been the requisite for survival among competing firms' (Clifton, 1977, pp. 147–8). The old tycoons, so well described by Veblen, also strove for power and growth; so did the builders of the railways of the last century; and we may even presume that growth was the main objective of the small family firm of yesterday, despite being the neoclassical ideal of competition and free market. Joan Robinson has admirably well summed up this point of view in a long paragraph, and this is why it is worth reproducing it in full to conclude this subsection.

Why do firms grow? Some contemporary writers are inclined to treat growth as a specially modern phenomenon arising from the divorce between control and property in the modern corporation, legally owned by a floating population of shareholders and operated by a cadre of salaried managers; they seem to suggest that there was a past period to which the textbook scheme applied. Yet obviously the successful family businesses of the early nineteenth century must have been just as keen on growth as any modern corporation. Anyone who is in business naturally wants to survive (particularly if his own heirs and successors are involved) and to survive it is necessary to grow. When a business is prosperous it is making profits; for that very reason it is threatened with competition; it would be feckless to distribute the whole net profit to the family for consumption; part must be ploughed back in increasing capacity so as to supply a growing market, to prevent others coming in, or to diversify production if the original market is not expanding. Any one, by growing, is threatening the position of others, who retaliate by expanding their own capacity, reducing production costs, changing the design of commodities, or introducing new devices of salesmanship. Thus each has to run to keep up with the rest. (Robinson, 1971, p. 101)

## 3.3 THE CONSTRAINTS ON GROWTH

Now that the primary objectives of the post-Keynesian firm have been established, these objectives being growth and the acquisition of power, what of the neoclassical concern with profit maximization? What is the role of profits in the post-Keynesian theory of the firm? What is the role, if any, of the shareholders?

### The Importance of Retained Earnings

The standard critique of the neoclassical theory of the firm is that profit maximization is not possible because of the lack of pertinent knowledge due to an uncertain environment. Profit maximization is then replaced by profit satisficing. Firms are assumed to set themselves threshold levels of profits; that is, minimum levels of profits or of rates of return. This view of the firm is certainly partially valid. In particular it reflects the need for the technostructure to provide a constant stream of dividends to the shareholders, in order to keep them quiet. This satisficing view of profits must, however, be reassessed in a context of growth. The consensus opinion among post-Keynesians is that profits are the means which allow firms to grow. By financial necessity, profits cannot be disconnected from investment and growth. The growth objectives set by the decision makers are constrained by the financial requirements of profitability, past and expected. There is thus some opposition to the neoclassical view of perfect capital markets, according to which only profits expected in the future matter for the financing of investment projects.

The post-Keynesian view, based on the concrete reality rather than an abstract idealized one, asserts that bankers only loan money to those who already have it. Outside the neoclassical world of certainty or certainty equivalence, the biblical principle 'unto every one that hath shall be given' generally applies, as pointed out by Kaldor (1978a, p. xvi). 'Finance raised externally – whether in the form of loans or of equity capital – is complementary to, not a substitute for, retained earnings' (Kaldor, ibid.). To be financed externally, firms must prove their capacity to generate profits. Banks and financial institutions are much more reluctant to finance developing firms than they are to finance well-established firms because the latter have already demonstrated their ability to run successful projects and to make profits. This is a typical example of procedural rationality. Bankers make use of one of the rules of thumb which we have identified in Chapter 2. The uncertainty about the future, as well as the lack of relevant knowledge about the competence of the managerial team and about the profitability of the project, forces bankers to rely on the performance record of the past, that is the profits generated in the past by the firm. As will be argued in the next chapter, this does not mean that investment is objectively constrained in the aggregate by a fund of savings which the firms would acquire through their retained earnings. Rather it means that corporations can safeguard their financial independence either by generating themselves the funds which are necessary for their expansion projects, or by staying within the borrowing norms which are set by the financial system. Put briefly, growth is the objective, and profits are the means to realize this objective.

The key strategic variable becomes the level of capital expenditures derived from the investment plans of firms, with competitive rivalry focused on relative growth rates and relative market shares. Rather than making short-run profit maximization an end in itself, firms see profits as a means to an end, that of enabling them to expand over time, preferably by increasing their market share. Post-Keynesian writers argue that the behavioral goal of the firms is to maximize the growth in sales revenue over time, subject to a minimum constraint (industrial economists have found, of course, that it is hard to distinguish empirically between growth measured in terms of sales revenue and growth measured in some other manner – for example, in terms of profits over time. But however measured, it is clearly growth that is the goal of the firm). (Kenyon, 1979, pp. 37–8)

The end of the quotation mentions the very obvious following problem: as soon as it is admitted that profits are a requirement to finance growth, either internally or through leverage, is there any practical difference between the post-Keynesian hypothesis of maximizing growth and the neoclassical hypothesis of profit maximization? The truth of the matter is that, in the long run, in part because imperfections and uncertainty will transform any maximizing behaviour into an *ex post* satisficing one, there will not be much practical difference between the consequences of maximizing profits and those of maximizing growth, nor will it be possible empirically to distinguish between the two kinds of maximand. This has been readily admitted by several post-Keynesian and Institutionalist writers (Eichner, 1976, p. 24; Sylos Labini, 1971, p. 251; Harcourt and Kenyon, 1976, p. 451; Galbraith, 1975, p. 132). Indeed some post-Keynesians have even adopted the hypothesis of long-run profit maximization as a simplification (Skott, 1989). The reader may then wonder why so much emphasis had been put on the motives animating the firm. The reason is that, while *long-run* maximization of profit may not end up terribly different from growth maximization, there will be substantial differences in behaviour between a growth maximizer and the *short-run* profit maximizer that the neoclassical theory of the firm has accustomed us to. These differences will reflect themselves in dividend and investment policies, and particularly in the price-setting behaviour, as we shall see in the coming section. Notwithstanding the differences in short-term or medium-term strategies, even in the so-called long run, one can find analytical differences in the consequences of maximizing growth or the rate of profit. These reasons, plus those that are linked to methodological realism make imperative, in my opinion, the study of the firm on the basis of growth maximization.

It may be preferable at this stage to present a simple model illustrating the theses that have been put forward in this section. To be able to do so, we must first deal with the question of the dividends of the shareholders. In the Galbraithian and post-Keynesian firm, shareholders play a purely passive role. There are two major causes for this compliance, each more pertinent according to the size of the firm. With respect to the megacorp, the lack of information is certainly the most crucial element. Decision making in huge corporations relies on various committees, which spend days gathering the necessary knowledge. Shareholders or their elected directors just do not have the time to be impregnated with the necessary information that full-time staff take years to absorb. In the case of smaller firms, shareholders quickly come to understand that, without retained earnings, the expansion possibilities of the firm are severely limited, and that as a consequence the dividend pay-out must be an indicator of the wealth of the corporation rather than a truly significant revenue to the owner. The result of mingling these two causes is that dividend payments become not very different from interest payments on borrowed funds. Managers mitigate the fluctuations of dividends in the attempt to keep the shareholders happy and the stock market quiet. Managers usually keep constant the level of dividends or have them slowly increasing, assuming that shareholders do not object to the existing level of dividend payment or dividend ratio, since otherwise they would not have bought the shares in the first place (Wood, 1975, pp. 40–51). 'On this view, dividends would be looked on as a cost to be kept at a level no higher than necessary to keep investors happy' (Penrose, 1959, p. 28). The rate of dividends is a convention (Robinson, 1962, p. 38).

Shareholders, then, should be regarded as non-residual factor claimants against the enterprise, while dividends are its quasi-contractual obligation (Herendeen, 1975, p. 215). Both interest and dividend disbursements may thus be considered as fixed costs, the payment of which may be temporarily suspended in periods of crisis. Indeed, while interest and dividend recipients can both be considered as rentiers, the influence of the former on management may be paradoxically stronger than that of the latter (Eichner, 1976, p. 59). This is because the interest-debt holders are usually powerful banking or financial conglomerates, which have the resources to monitor the management of the firms in which they have invested. Whatever control the financial sector is able to exert over the industrial corporation (Berle, 1959), however, the fact remains that the payment of dividends is a *de facto* obligation of the firm, similar to its *de jure* obligation to make interest payments. This was recognized early on by Joan Robinson in her discussion of the rentiers, and, as seen in her previous quotation, it is clear that the argument applies equally to small unincorporated firms and to megacorps. When modelling the firm, the proper simplification may thus be to consider interest and dividend payments on the same footing; that is, to consider both type of costs as fixed costs.

An obligation to pay interest is a contractual agreement, while the amount of dividends and personal profits paid out is at the discretion of the entrepreneur; but neither the obligation nor the discretion is absolute in practice. When profits are so low that the payment of interest would lead to bankruptcy, creditors often find it preferable to compromise and keep alive a goose they hope will lay again in the future, so that, to some extent, interest payments fluctuate with earnings. On the other hand, dividends fluctuate less than earnings, for entrepreneurs are reluctant to reduce dividends... and they are reluctant to increase them... Thus interest to some extent behaves like dividends, and to an important extent dividends behave like interest. A similar argument applies to personal profits. (Robinson, 1956, pp. 247–8)

## The Finance Frontier

We are now in a position to analyse the relationship between profit goals and growth objectives in the post-Keynesian firm. This relationship, as previously outlined, is based on the hypothesis that firms will dare to borrow only to the extent that they have been accumulating their own means to finance investment, and, similarly, that banks and other financial institutions will grant loans or finance share and bond issues only to the extent that their corporate customers have been profitable in the past. The fact that a firm can or is willing to borrow only limited amounts, related to its previously accumulated internal funds, is known in post-Keynesian circles as Kalecki's *principle of increasing risk*. Several interpretations of this principle abound in the literature, and we shall stick to Kalecki's later version of it.

The principle of increasing risk is based on the intuitive notion that the higher the gearing or leverage ratio, that is the higher the proportion of outside funds financing investment, the larger the potential fluctuations of earnings net of interest payments. In general, the management of the firm will self-impose stricter limits, being more cautious in its borrowing than lenders about lending (Wood, 1975, p. 31). This means that firms will be free to borrow as much as they desire within the limits that they have themselves set, based presumably on some multiple of their retained earnings. In periods of crises the reverse may occur. In such cases it will be impossible for a firm to borrow as much as they would have liked to, constrained as they are by the leverage ratio judged acceptable by the banks. Corporate borrowers will be unsatisfied, whatever the expected profitability of their planned investments and whatever rate of interest companies are willing to pay for borrowed funds. In the orthodox literature, the problem facing the bank and its customer, or the capital markets at large, is called a moral hazard. In standard terms, the supply of finance is infinitely elastic up to some multiple of the retained earnings of the firm, at which point it becomes infinitely inelastic. More will be said on that topic when we discuss money and credit in the next chapter. For the moment note that, as early as 1937, Kalecki (1937) had made clear the presence of that moral hazard, while he later insisted upon the necessity of retained earnings and the innocuity of the interest rate as a market mechanism.

It would be impossible for a firm to borrow capital above a certain level determined by the amount of its entrepreneurial capital [that is the amount of capital owned by the firm]. If, for instance, a firm should attempt to float a bond issue which was too large in terms of its entrepreneurial capital, the issue would not be subscribed in full. Even if the firm should undertake to issue the bonds at a higher rate of interest than that prevailing, the sale of bonds might not be improved since the higher rate in itself might raise misgivings with regard to the future solvency of the firm . . . It follows from the above that the expansion of the firm depends on its accumulation of capital out of current profits. This will enable the firm to undertake new investments without encountering the obstacles of the limited capital markets or 'increasing risk'. Not only can savings out of current profits be directly invested in the business, but this increase in the firm's capital will make it possible to contract new loans. (Kalecki, 1971, pp. 105–6)

A very similar prescription is offered by Davidson:

In an uncertain world, firms must guard against illiquidity while creditors fear the inability of firms to meet long-term obligations. Thus both entrepreneurs and lenders are anxious to see that some portion of investment is funded internally. In an uncertain world, therefore, internal and external finance are complements rather than substitutes and a firm's access to the new issue market will normally be limited by institutional rules about gearing ratios. (Davidson, 1972, p. 348)

We can now formalize the relationship between the total funds available to finance expansion and the realized profits of the firm, along the lines suggested by Sylos Labini (1971). Let $\Pi$ be the gross earnings of the firm, before dividends and interests are paid out. Let us call $K_s$ the capital owned by the shareholders and $K_b$ the capital borrowed through loans or bond issues, while $i_s$ and $i_b$ are the rate of return on shares and the rate of interest on borrowed capital. The retained earnings of the firm, which are in fact additions to the capital owned by the shareholders, are then equal to:

$$\Delta K_s = \Pi - i_s K_s - i_b K_b \tag{3.1}$$

As a simplification, we may assume that the two rates of return are identical. This is not too unrealistic a simplification, as we have argued that the dividend pay-out is a quasi-contractual obligation of the firm. Dividend payments are a convention. It is safe for firms to adhere to the conventions, one of which surely must be the rate of interest on bonds. The enterprise must remunerate the shareholder according to the rules of the financial markets. One might thus expect market forces to keep the rate of return on shares on a par with the yield of fixed-income financial assets of a similar class (Herendeen, 1975, pp. 215–8). Under this assumption, equation (3.1) becomes:

$$\Delta K_s = \Pi - iK \tag{3.2}$$

Kalecki's principle of increasing risk then tells us that the maximum amount of capital that can be newly borrowed is a multiple of the current level of retained earnings:

$$\Delta K_b = \rho\,(\Pi - iK) \tag{3.3}$$

The multiple $\rho$ is an example of a conventional rule of thumb, as outlined in the previous chapter, the convention being determined by the interaction of the lender's risk as perceived by the banks and other financial actors and of the borrower's risk as perceived by the managers of the non-financial firms. We may assume, again for simplification, that all surplus funds gathered by the firm are used to finance investment expenditures. In that case, from the previous two equations, we get the relationship between investment ($I$) and profits, that is equation (3.4) below. Dividing this equation by $K$, we get its dynamic equivalent; that is, the relationship between the rate of growth ($g = I/K$) of the company and its rate of profit ($r = \Pi/K$).

$$\Delta K = I = (\Pi - iK) + \rho(\Pi - iK)$$

$$I/K = (1+\rho)(\Pi/K - i) \tag{3.4}$$

$$r = i + g/(1+\rho) \tag{3.5}$$

Equation (3.5) is known as the finance constraint of the firm, and a similar constraint may be found in Marris (1964a, p. 9). It tell us that, if the firm desires to grow at a faster rate, it must collect a higher rate of profit, given the average rate of interest payable on its capital and given the proxy $\rho$ of the leverage ratio which is admissible. Incidentally, one may note that a higher rate of interest will require a higher rate of profit for growth to keep up at the same rate, while a higher permissible leverage ratio (measured here by its proxy $\rho$, representing the ratio of the funds that can be borrowed to the retained earnings) will naturally allow for a lower minimum profit rate.

Figure 3.1 illustrates the meaning of this finance constraint. The hatched area under the financial constraint curve (here a straight line) is not accessible to firms. Companies which would happen to be in this zone for some time could not sustain their rate of growth since external financing would not be forthcoming any more. Firms which stretch their financial capabilities to the limit would lie on the financial constraint curve. In the long run, firms must therefore lie either on the financial constraint curve or above it, where there is some financial leeway.

The financial constraint is, however, better known in a slightly revised

*Figure 3.1  The finance frontier of the firm*

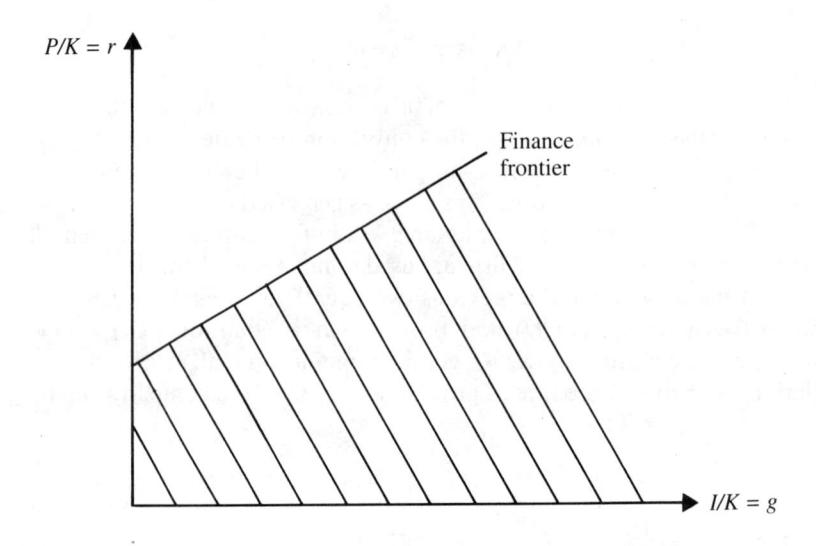

version, that presented by Wood (1975). In his formulation, the crucial parameter is the retention ratio $s_c$. The retention ratio is the ratio of retained earnings to gross profits, that is:

$$s_c = (\Pi - iK)/\Pi \tag{3.6}$$

Under this formulation, retained earnings are thus equal to:
$$\Delta K_s = s_c\Pi = \Pi - iK. \tag{3.7}$$

Assuming still that borrowed funds are a multiple of retained earnings, that is by combining equations (3.3) and (3.7), we get another form of the financial constraint:

$$I = (1+\rho)s_c\Pi$$
$$r = g/s_c(1+\rho) \tag{3.8}$$

Equation (3.8) closely resembles Wood's formulation of the finance frontier, one that can also be found in the macroeconomic models of Kaldor (1966) and Moss (1978). In these models it is assumed that firms decide or are allowed to finance a percentage $x$ of their investment from external sources, more precisely share issues in the Kaldor case. Investment expenditures are thus partly financed by retained earnings ($s_c\Pi$) and partly by borrowing ($xI$), such that:

$$I = s_c\Pi + xI$$

Dividing through by $K$ and rearranging yields the expression of Kaldor's famous neo-Pasinetti theorem, but here limited to the microeconomics of the firm, and Wood's formulation of the finance frontier:

$$r = g(1-x)/s_c \qquad (3.9)$$

Comparing equations (3.8) and (3.9), we see that the share of investment which is financed by inside sources, $1-x$, is equivalent to the ratio $1/(1+\rho)$, expressed in terms of the proportion of outside funds that can be matched to net retained earnings. Since equation (3.9) is strongly reminiscent of the standard Cambridge equation relating the macroeconomic rate of profit to the overall rate of growth, as we shall see in Chapter 6, it has usually been the preferred version of the financial frontier among post-Keynesian authors. A drawback of this formulation, however, is that the retention ratio $s_c$ is not entirely under the control of the firm since it depends to a large extent on the rate of interest, as can be seen from equations (3.1) and (3.6). The retention ratio cannot therefore be considered an appropriate exogenous variable that could explain the rate of profit. As a consequence, equation (3.5) should be preferred to equation (3.9) when formalizing the financial constraint of the firm, since the former explicitly takes into account the impact of the decisions of the monetary authorities.

Things can be slightly more complicated when the stock market and its valuation ratio are introduced into the picture; but even if stock market valuation ratios do constrain the behaviour of entrepreneurs, something that remains to be proved (Lavoie, 1990), the finance constraint remains the same for a given valuation ratio below which the firm must not fall (Marris, 1964a, p. 252). An alternative to the introduction of valuation ratios is to make a distinction in equation (3.5) between the rate of payment of dividends on the firm's own capital and the rate of interest on borrowed capital. Assuming that in the long run the average leverage ratio is equal to the marginal leverage ratio, we may suppose that $x$ is both the share of borrowed funds in new investment and the share of borrowed capital in the capital account of the firm. Equation (3.2) can thus be rewritten as:

$$\Delta K_s = \Pi - [i_s(1-x) + i_b x]$$

Assuming, as before, that a multiple ρ of these net retained earnings can be borrowed, and making use of the fact noted above that $(1-x)$ is equal to $1/(1+\rho)$, a novel expression of equation (3.5) can be derived, which takes into consideration the possible divergences between the rate of interest $i_b$ on borrowed capital and the rate of remuneration $i_s$ to shareholders. Equation (3.10) which follows shows that, when monetary policies are stringent and money interest rates are high, highly leveraged firms will require higher rates of profit to keep growing at the same rate as those which have borrowed little:

$$r = i_s(1-x) + i_b x + (1-x)g \qquad (3.10)$$

The finance constraint is not a far-fetched notion. Fazzari and Mott have shown in a cross-section study that firms with high internal finance (net of dividend payments) have high investment. They note that 'internal finance is quite important for explaining why different firms invest different amounts at any point in time' (1986–7, p. 184). They also show the importance of interest payments and capacity utilization for investment decisions.

**The Expansion Frontier**

We now turn to the other major constraint facing the firm. Looking at Figure 3.1 it would seem that there is no difference between the goal of maximizing the rate of profit and that of maximizing the rate of growth. The finance constraint is not, however, the only constraint facing the firm. Companies are further constrained by what Wood (1975, p. 63) calls the opportunity frontier, also named the efficient demand-growth curve by Marris (1964a, p. 250). We shall call it the *expansion frontier*. Whereas the finance frontier indicated the various profit rates that were required to sustain growth strategies, the expansion frontier associates with each growth strategy the profit rate that can optimally be realized. The shape of a typical expansion frontier is represented by Figure 3.2.

In a certain sense, the expansion frontier of the firm is a denial of the orthodox view of the firm. The latter considers that firms reach finite optimal sizes, as in the case of standard U-shaped long-run total average cost curves. The grounds for this shape are the limitations in the ability of the managerial factor of production to coordinate activities within large organizations. The proposition was denied very early on by various post-Keynesians: Kaldor (1934) and Kalecki (1971, p. 105), the latter in 1937,

*Figure 3.2   The expansion frontier of the firm*

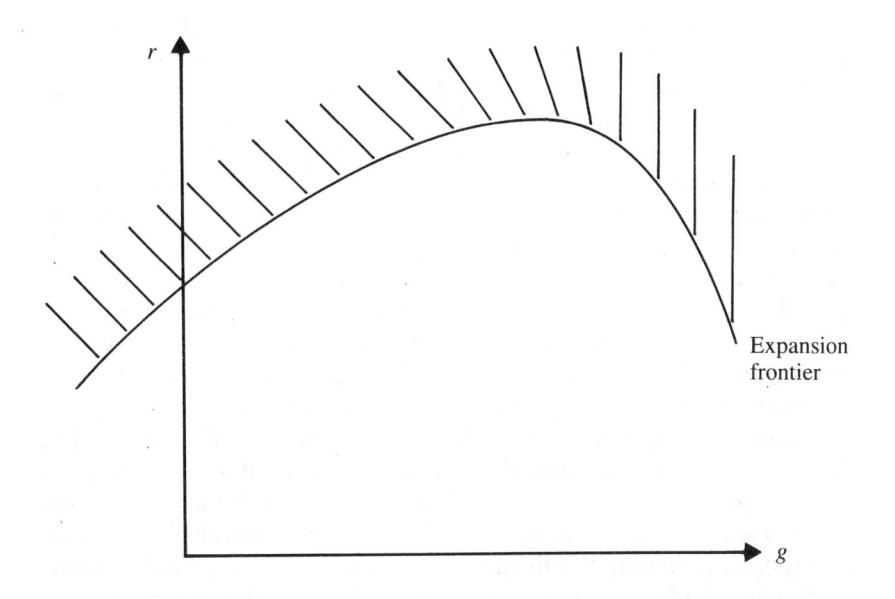

both argued that managerial coordination could be achieved by proper delegation of decision making and decentralization. Thus, although each plant may have a technologically defined optimal size, income distribution being given, the optimum size of a multi-plant firm is either indeterminate or infinite. Empirical evidence seems to show that there are no diseconomies of scale. In his summary of the evidence, Johnston (1960, p. 168) noted that the most notable element was 'the preponderance of the L-shaped pattern of long-run average cost that emerges so frequently from the various long-run analyses'. The limits of managerial coordination are therefore not to be found in the absolute size of the firm, but rather in its rate of expansion. There are no managerial diseconomies of scale, but there are increasing costs to growth. The negative segment of the expansion frontier as drawn on Figure 3.2 is thus due in part to the inherent difficulties of management in coping efficiently with change and expansion.

The negative relationship between the growth rate and the rate of profit is known as the Penrose effect, since Edith Penrose (1959) was the first clearly to illustrate the limitations of management in handling the speed of expansion, in contrast to the absolute size of an organization. Growing firms must integrate new managers within the organization and train them to handle the complexities of the business. This settling-in is time consuming, in particular for existing management, and consequently it is costly to the firm. There are also further reasons, partially related to these managerial limits. When firms expand, they may do it either internally or externally. In the latter case, the diversification into foreign markets and the diversification into other products are confined by the management's lack of knowledge about these new markets or products. Indeed many self-made millionaires have lost their shirts by venturing into markets about which they had little knowledge. When firms expand internally, attempting to increase the share of their main market, profit margins and hence profit rates may have to be cut back. More likely, non-pricing forms of competition will be used, with firms engaging into costly advertising, promotion, product innovation, and research and development (Wood, 1975, p. 66). These expenditures are then likely to increase unit costs as compared with rivals, and lead to lower profits per unit.

The reader may wonder what the ascending portion of the expansion frontier is due to. Three reasons may be advanced, all mainly related to internal growth. First, investment allows for the introduction of new and more efficient means of production. Growing firms will find it easier to incorporate technological advancements as they replace their old plants or as they build new ones. It will permit lower units costs as compared with those of more slowly growing rivals and will lead to higher profit rates. Secondly, in the oligopolistic environment with uncertainty which characterizes the real world, the profitability and survival of the firm and its control over events depend on sheer size. The control of the firm over events therefore depends on its share of the market. To grow slowly means to incur decreasing market shares, such that 'an individual firm's profit rate may also be negatively related to the rate of growth of its competitors' (Moore, 1973, p. 539). Thirdly, when firms expand through diversification, they may encounter novel products where temporary monopoly profits can be earned (Marris, 1964a, p. 251). These positive influences of the rate of growth on the rate of profit are exactly balanced by the Penrose effects at the top of the expansion frontier.

As before, the shaded area in Figure 3.2 represents the combinations of profit and growth rates which are not accessible to the individual firm. Those firms which are efficient, from the point of view of both selling and producing, will lie on the expansion frontier. Those which suffer from *X*-inefficiency, *à la* Leibenstein (1978), or which simply attempt to satisfice, *à la* Simon, will lie below the expansion frontier.

Assuming that firms do attempt to maximize their rate of accumulation, we can now see by combining the two frontiers that the hypothesis of growth maximization is not the same as that of profit maximization, even

*Figure 3.3  Maximum rate of profit and maximum rate of growth of the firm*

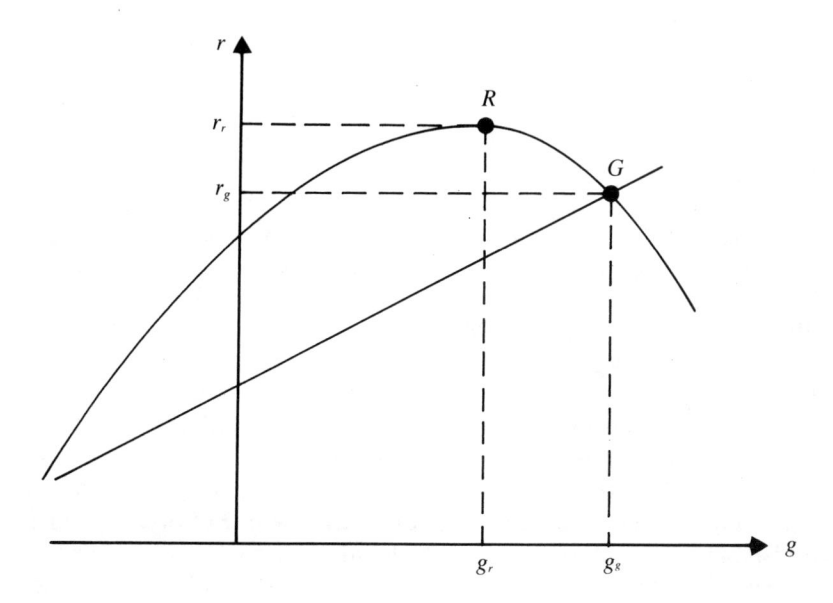

in the long run. Figure 3.3 combines the finance constraint with the opportunity constraint. Profit maximization would lead to point $R$ on the expansion curve, where the rate of profit is maximized at its rate $r_r$. At that point, the rate of growth, $g_r$, would be smaller than the possible maximum rate of growth, $g_g$, given by the intersection of the two finance and expansion frontiers at point $G$. We can see that the difference between the two types of firms, the one maximizing profit and the other maximizing the rate of growth, is that the former does not attempt to take advantage of all the borrowing leverage that is available to it, since it lies above its finance frontier. This means that the profit-maximizing firms avoid becoming engaged in investment or advertising expenditures that have low rates of return, although they could obtain the borrowed funds necessary to finance these expenditures. On the other hand, growth-maximizing firms engage in all expansion projects, provided these projects generate a rate of profit that is sufficient to provide the necessary internal and external finance. We see that, even though the profit rate plays an important constraining role both in the short run and the long run, it is still worthwhile analytically to define the firm as a growth-maximizing institution, attempting constantly to enlarge its power and control over its socioeconomic environment.

Furthermore, to conclude this section, the notion of a growth-maximizing firm provides us with some elements of a pricing theory. Although Figures 3.1, 3.2 and 3.3 have been expressed in terms of rates of profit, one could also label the vertical axis by using the margin of profit. It then becomes clear that the margin of profit set by the firm is the result of two conflicting pressures, both associated with growth maximization. On the one hand, businessmen would like to decrease their profit margin in order to steal customers from their competitors, mainly through advertising and the conception of new products. On the other hand, profit margins must be sufficiently high to generate enough retained earnings and sustain the ability of the firm to borrow from outside sources. The profit margin finally chosen must strike a balance between those two considerations (Wood, 1975, p. 86; Shapiro, 1981, p. 88).

In a world of uncertainty and of bargaining, the behaviour described above can, of course, only be approximated. To achieve their goals, firms will set targets, knowing that these targets will often not be reached and sometimes will be largely surpassed. Returning now to rates of profit, we can presume that, when setting prices, firms will use as an indicator of normal profits, that is as target rates of return, the rate of profit $r_g$ which corresponds to the maximum achievable rate of growth $g_g$ of Figure 3.3. More will be said about firms' pricing behaviour in the following section. Furthermore the relationships between accumulation, margins of profit, and realized and targeted rates of profit will be more fully developed in the chapters to follow. At this stage, what should be kept in mind is that there is no need to suppose that firms maximize profits, either in the short or in the long run.

## 3.4 COST CURVES AND EXCESS CAPACITY

### The Shape of Short-run Cost Curves

As mentioned in the introduction of the chapter, one of the facts most at odds with business intuition and experience is the neoclassical presumption, based on the standard U-shaped cost curves, that profitable firms face increasing average costs as they augment sales. In this section, I wish to point to three stylized facts of the post-Keynesian firm that will be of fundamental importance when we discuss macroeconomics. These three facts, naturally restricted to the domain of validity of the post-Keynesian firm which we have identified in section 1, are the following: short-run average costs are generally decreasing; average variable costs, also called direct or prime costs, are generally constant; firms generally produce at levels where there are reserves of capacity. Although those three stylized facts have been repeatedly observed – leading eclectic authors such as Koutsoyiannis (1975, p. 114) to refer to them as the modern theory of costs or modern microeconomics – they have not been incorporated in traditional economics.

As in orthodox theory, the shape of the cost curves essentially depends on the technology in use. In the traditional view, substitution between the various inputs is always possible, both in the short run and in the long run. In the short term, for instance, it is always possible to increase production by having more labour working on the same machine, thus decreasing the capital/labour ratio and therefore the marginal physical product of labour. In post-Keynesian theory, although some form of substitution can be contemplated in the long haul, through innovation and technical progress, no substitution is possible in the short run. Whether variable factors or fixed factors are considered, fixed technical coefficients prevail. As argued by Eichner (1976, pp. 28–30), plants, or more precisely segments of plants, are designed to operate with a given crew, using the most efficient quantity of raw materials. Even where machinery is so designed by engineers that variations in the number of operators may be considered, bureaucratic rules self-imposed by management will generally lead to a standard ratio of combined inputs. Once these standards are known and get the tacit approval of the workers involved, they become work rules, enforced by collective bargaining. Of course the enterprise may wish to experiment with new combinations, by trying to find more efficient ones. However this may have nothing to do with substitution effects as such, and it does not concern the short run.

Thus emerging from those fixed technical coefficients of production is a set of plant segments, each designed to operate at a most efficient level of output per unit of time. This most efficient level of output, which takes into consideration the necessary breaks in production to execute repairs and regular maintenance, is called the *engineer-rated capacity* (Eichner, 1976, p. 62) or the level of *practical capacity*. Steindl (1952, p. 7) defines practical capacity as 'the output achieved with normal length of working time, with sufficient shut-downs to allow for repairs and maintenance, and without disturbance in the smooth running of the production process'. This practical capacity must be distinguished from *theoretical capacity*, which is the highest degree of production which could be attained if regular maintenance and its accompanying shut-downs did not hinder production and if no breakdown occurred while the plant or its segment was operated at a rate higher than the one designed for. While any level of output below practical capacity corresponds to marginal costs which are relatively easy to ascertain and which are constant as a result of the fixed coefficients, levels of output in between practical and theoretical capacities are associated with the traditional increasing marginal costs. These rising costs are due to overtime payments, the damage to machines arising from the speed-up of operations, and the disproportionate reduction in the useful life of equipment as a consequence of its lack of repairs (Steindl, 1952, p. 7). The exact rise in marginal cost is fairly difficult to estimate, because the entrepreneur generally has no experience of production at those high rates of production, and he cannot measure in advance the costs induced by the intensified use of machinery and the supplementary faulty work, breakdowns or accidents that will occur as a result of this overworking (Harrod, 1952, p. 154).

A firm, unless it is of the small entrepreneurial family type, will thus be composed of several plants, each plant having a number of segments with its own practical capacity. The practical capacity of a plant will thus be the sum of the practical capacities of its segments; and the *full capacity* of a firm will be the sum of the practical capacities of its plants. Whereas there is no flexibility in the use of plant segment, unless one is prepared to go beyond practical capacity or unless one closes the segment on some days of the week or some weeks of the month, there is a substantial amount of flexibility at the level of the plant and at that of the firm. The reason is that management can increase or decrease production by reopening or closing plant segments or entire plants.

Figure 3.4 illustrates the relationship between marginal costs (or for that matter variable or direct costs) and the level of output of the firm, given the levels of practical capacity of its various plants or plant segments, and given the fixed technological conditions prevailing at each plant. The full capacity of the firm, $FC$, is the sum of the engineer-rated capacities of each segment, represented by $PC_i$. The marginal cost curve here is represented as a step function, under the assumption that various plants will not necessarily be of the same vintage, having been built at different points in time. Unless there is no technological progress, or unless technical improvements can be simultaneously embodied within the older plants, such a step function will necessarily prevail (Eichner, 1976, p. 34; Rowthorn, 1981, p. 37). However the differentials in efficiency from one plant to another might not be important, since some of the technical improvements are diffused to older plants. For this reason, and for simplification purposes, we shall assume away the upward drift of the marginal cost function and set the marginal cost as a constant in the rest of the book. The relevance of this simplification will be further discussed at the end of the section.

We are now in a position to represent the shape of the cost curves of the typical post-Keynesian firm. Assuming that marginal costs are constant

*Figure 3.4   Upward drift of the constant marginal cost segments of the firm*

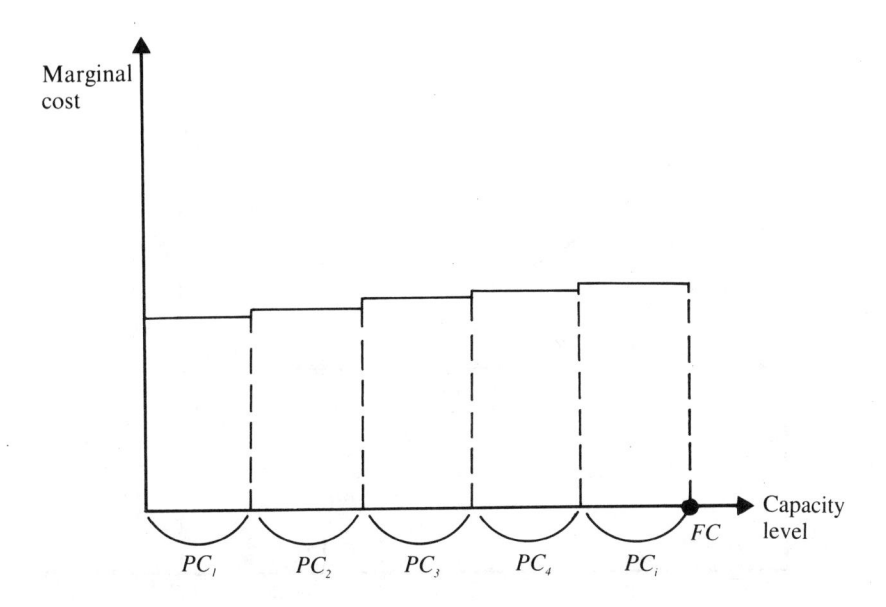

up to full capacity, it follows that average total costs in the short run are necessarily decreasing up to full capacity. Only beyond that point may marginal costs and average costs increase in the traditional manner. Figure 3.5 illustrates the cost curves of the typical post-Keynesian firm. Beyond full capacity, *FC* on the graph, more output can be achieved only by over-utilizing the machinery of the various plants above practical capacity. This can be done until theoretical full capacity, identified by $FC_{th}$ on Figure 3.5, is reached. There is a discontinuity in the marginal cost curve because, as noted above, it is assumed that the over-extensive use of machines will drastically inflate replacement costs and because workers will most likely have to be paid overtime. Whether there is a discontinuity or not is, of course, not fundamental. What is more essential is that firms will generally not be producing at levels of output where the marginal cost – and therefore also the average total cost – is increasing. The rising portions of the marginal and the average cost curves, so fundamental to orthodox microeconomics, are for all practical purposes irrelevant to the analysis of the post-Keynesian firm, since the enterprise will avoid by all possible means winding up in this region. In general, the firm will be operating at output levels where marginal costs are constant and where unit costs UC, are decreasing; that is, below full capacity as we have

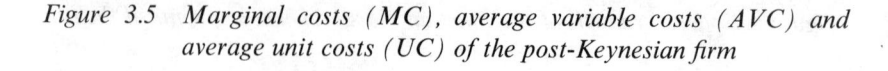

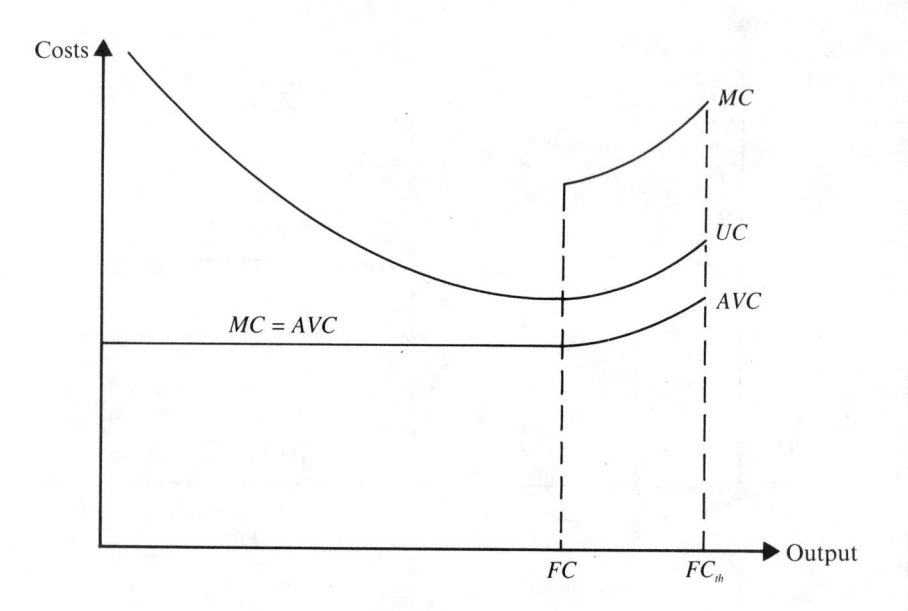

Figure 3.5  Marginal costs (MC), average variable costs (AVC) and average unit costs (UC) of the post-Keynesian firm

defined it. This means that the firm generally operates with reserves of capacity. Companies, such as General Motors, plan the presence of excess capacity, operating at rates of utilization of practical capacity which oscillate between 65 and 95 per cent, and aiming for normal rates of utilization in the 80–90 per cent range (Eichner, 1976, p. 37; Koutsoyiannis, 1975, p. 273). The normal rate of utilization of capacity is also called the load factor on the capacity or the standard operating ratio. It is defined as the percentage of total practical capacity at which the firm can expect to operate on the average over the business cycle (Eichner, 1976, p. 62). The rate of utilization at which the firm is planning to function in the coming period is the expected rate.

As mentioned above, there has been for a long time a vast empirical literature, both in the UK and in the USA, covering statistical and econometric studies as well as case studies based on questionnaires, which demonstrates the irrelevance of the neoclassical U-shaped assumption of cost curves while supporting the L-shaped long-run total average cost curve and the constant average variable cost curve (see, among many others, the surveys of Johnston, 1960, Walters, 1963 and Lee, 1986). Typical conclusions of these surveys or of original studies are that 'an absolute majority of the answers supported the view that the variable costs are proportional to output [while] quite a number held the belief that variable costs were moderately regressive, at least until close to capacity' (Fog, 1956, p. 46). Johnston (1960, p. 168) is of the firm opinion that 'the various studies more often than not indicate constant marginal costs and declining average costs as the pattern that best seems to describe the data'.

Less sanguine authors prefer to conclude, in defence of neoclassical economics, that, while the data on cost curves are not generally supportive of the U-shape curves, 'the evidence in favour of constant marginal cost is not overwhelming' (Walters, 1963, p. 51). As is reported by Cyert and Simon (1983), this does not stop famous neoclassical economists, such as Jorgenson, from asserting that the evidence is 'overwhelmingly favorable' to the neoclassical theory of the firm, citing the same prudent Walters to buttress their claim! Similarly, in the various editions of his well-known textbook of microeconomics, Mansfield (1991, p. 204) has been faithfully reporting the evidence in favour of constant marginal costs, without the evidence having any effect on his graphical representation of cost curves. If neoclassical economists were to recognize the irrelevance of the U-shaped cost curves, they would be at a loss, left without any determinate output, devoid as they would be of their required diminishing returns and second-order conditions.

These requirements do not concern post-Keynesian authors, and as a consequence they have been quite keen to accept and disseminate the empirical findings on the shape of cost curves. Graphical representations of the 'modern' theory of costs can thus be found in the works of Davidson (1972, p. 37), Eichner (1976), Harris (1974), Kregel (1973, p. 139), and Robinson and Eatwell (1973, p. 168). Keynes himself, after writing the *General Theory*, started to doubt the validity of the standard shape of the marginal cost curve (1973, vii, p. 405). The most famous proponent of the cost curves presented in Figure 3.5 is, however, Kalecki (1969, p. 51), who as early as the 1930s proposed a macroeconomic theory built upon the microeconomic foundations of a constant marginal cost with excess capacity. Kalecki's colleagues at Oxford also came to adopt the hypothesis of constant marginal or direct costs, as can be seen in the work of Harrod (1952, p. 154) and in that of Andrews (1949, p. 102) and his associate Brunner (1967, p. 42). With Kalecki, Kaldor is the other post-Keynesian who, from very early on, has attempted to rebuild macroeconomics on the basis of modern microeconomic foundations. Drawing a graph similar to Figure 3.5, Kaldor assumes that 'average and marginal prime costs are constant up to the point where the optimum utilization of capacity is reached' (1961, p. 197).

## Causes of Planned Excess Capacity

While Kaldor has long been explicit in his recognition of constant direct costs below full capacity output, he has also been quite explicit about the need for firms to keep reserves of capacity under all circumstances. It is not enough to show that marginal costs can be constant for some scale of production: one must show that firms stay below the point of full capacity, in the region where marginal costs are constant.

> The motives which cause firms, in a world of imperfect competition, to maintain capacity ahead of output – the motive of being in a position to exploit any chance increase in selling power – operate just as powerfully in times of full employment as at other times ... It is perfectly consistent to assume that, in long-term equilibrium, both output and output capacity should grow at the same rate, without implying that the one is equal to the other. (Kaldor, 1970a, p. 4)

> The manufacturing sector is the archetypal case of fix-price market ... In markets of this type uncertainties concerning the future growth of demand mainly affect the degree of utilization of capacity; it pays the manufacturers to maintain capacity in excess of demand and keep the growth of capacity in line with the growth of demand. (Kaldor, 1986, p. 193)

Besides the chance to exploit increases in selling power, due to random variations or to seasonal fluctuations, various reasons have been advanced to justify the continuous existence of reserves of capacity. For Sylos Labini (1971, p. 247), not surprisingly, excess capacity is a deterrent to entry by new or outside firms. It is part of the defensive strategy to limit entry into the industry, since any potential producer knows that the existing firms have the ability to increase output and cut prices without necessarily incurring losses. Thus Joan Robinson (1969, p. 261) connects the presence of imperfect competition with the existence of excess capacity, and the latter with a market which 'is not exactly foreseeable for the individual seller'.

Steindl (1952, p. 2) has linked the presence of reserves of capacity with the existence of uncertainty. Whereas households have cash holdings to satisfy their liquidity preference, firms hold excess capacities to face an uncertain future. The presence of excess capacities evidently allows firms to respond quickly to a boom in the demand for their product; but it also allows them to continue production of the standard good, while modifying idle plants when the evolution of consumer demand requires minor alterations to the style of the product being sold. Reserves of capacity thus provide flexibility in the face of the uncertainty about the exact composition of forthcoming demand. 'Demand is distributed between diverse types and qualities of output which require separate facilities, and this distribution of demand between types cannot be correctly foreseen. Therefore a reserve of capacity is necessary to take care of possible shifts in the pattern of demand' (Steindl, 1952, p. 8). As pointed out by Pasinetti (1981, p. 233), the future composition of demand is uncertain, not only because it may be difficult for managers to foresee the preferences of the consumers, but also because the consumers themselves, when their incomes are increasing, may be uncertain about what they want to purchase next. In this sense, excess capacity is truly analogous to precautionary demand for liquidity.

There are further reasons explaining the prevalence of excess capacity. They have to do with the technological aspects. There is some indivisibility of plants and equipment. The most efficient plant or plant segment may require a minimum level of practical capacity, because of economies of scale up to this minimum level. The installation of a new plant may thus temporarily bring an excess of capacity over demand, which should then be eliminated through the secular increase in demand; but, for the reasons outlined above, the temporary reserve will in effect be a permanent one, the firm consistently making sure that its capacity is ahead of demand in order to avoid the risk of losing its customers to more provident producers. The fact that producers carry excess capacity is also related to the technological fact that production takes time: plants cannot be built instantaneously; machinery cannot be stacked in inventories, since machines are often specific to the task at hand, and are therefore made on order. As a consequence, capacity cannot be increased overnight. The irreversibility of time lies in production, not in demand. A desired volume of unused capacity quiets the managers' concern with the possibility of losing the goodwill of their customers as a consequence of the overdelayed delivery of promised goods.

One could argue that firms could always take advantage of the excess of the theoretical capacities over the practical capacities, and aim at operating at the least costly level of production, that is at point *FC* on Figure 3.5. Aside from excesses in capacity due to indivisibilities, firms would thus generally attempt to operate at full capacity, where they could reap maximum profits. If demand randomly increases beyond full capacity, this increase in demand could usually be taken care of by the excess of theoretical capacity over practical capacity, along the rising portion of the marginal cost curve. Besides Sylos Labini's objections to such a short-run strategy, there are practical technical reasons which explain why such a strategy will not be pursued.

First, collective bargaining may have prohibited the extensive use of overtime work, or the possibility of night shifts. As Marris (1964b, p. 22) notes, 'in practice, most societies do collectively decide ... to live with a fairly low rate of capital utilisation, and thus ensure that shift-work is a minority experience'. Secondly, when capacity is overworked, machines are more likely to break down for lack of regular maintenance and accidents are more likely to occur. There is thus a danger for the firm, because of disruptions in the production process, of being incapable of responding to demand and thus, once more, of losing its share of the market and the goodwill of its customers. Furthermore, even if such disruptions were not feared, increased production could only be achieved at higher unit costs and, unless prices were increased, with generally diminishing profits. The financial capacity of the firm to expand its output potential would thus be curtailed precisely when funds would be most required for expansion. A firm without reserves of capacity would thus be at a cost disadvantage *vis-à-vis* its competitors, and the alternative solution of raising prices would again carry the risk of losing the goodwill of its customers, who could find elsewhere the same product at a non-increasing price.

All this has led various authors to associate rational behaviour, including long-term profit maximization, with excess capacity (Skott, 1989, p. 53). Kaldor (1961, p. 207) himself, in contrast to the quotation cited above, has at one point argued that 'under conditions of imperfect competition it is perfectly compatible with "profit-maximizing behaviour" to suppose that the representative firm will maintain a considerable amount of spare capacity'.

To conclude on the issue of excess capacity, we may say that there are good theoretical and practical reasons, as well as good strategic and technical reasons, that explain why corporations generally aim at operating much below their full capacity, in the range of constant marginal costs. Whatever one may think of the rationality of such behaviour, one must recognize, as the post-Keynesians do, that firms consistently function with large reserves of capacity, and that any analysis of the firm must take that fact into account.

**Constant Marginal Costs: a Myth or a Stylized Fact?**

Before closing this section on the costs of firms, we should tidy up an issue which, in previous discussion, has been left out in the open. More specifically, I would like to come back to the issue of the step function representing the marginal cost curve of the firm, as illustrated by Figure 3.4. As argued then, the steps from one segment of the curve to the other are due to the differentials in efficiency of the various plants owned by the firm, these differentials being caused by the various vintages of the plants. It has been recently argued by Lee (1986, 1988) that it is an error to assume away these differentials. Lee adds that case studies have shown in many instances that direct or marginal costs could be either decreasing or increasing at the level of the individual plant. As a consequence, to describe the overall marginal cost of the firm as a constant up to full capacity would be as misleading as using the traditional U-shaped curve.

I do not agree with this negative assessment. With respect to the individual plant, it has been answered by Yordon (1987) that the evidence in favour of increasing marginal costs was rather tenuous. As to the case of decreasing marginal costs, a pre-eminent case if judged by the results obtained by Fog (1956) and mentioned above, Yordon explains how they can in fact be reconciled with constant marginal costs. When post-Keynesians claim that marginal costs, prime costs, direct costs or average variable costs are constant up to full capacity, they exclude from these costs the labour overhead costs. These include the managerial staff but also the supervisors and foremen who are assigned to the various segments of plant. There is a certain ambiguity with respect to overhead labour costs. These salaries are not exactly fixed costs, since they could be cut substantially if the firm were to close, but neither are they variable costs since, once the plant has been started up, they 'remain roughly stable as output varies' (Kalecki, 1971, p. 44). As shown by Steindl (1952, p. 8), the salaries of overhead labour represent a substantial portion of labour's earned income, and as such they should not be ignored.

We shall see later that the distinction between direct and indirect labour, an underrated distinction according to Brunner (1967, p. 48), plays a very important role in the macroeconomics of income distribution. In empirical work, however, as well as for accountants, it is often very difficult to disentangle the salaries paid to overhead staff from the wages paid to labour directly involved with production. Since overhead staff does not increase with production, but rather with capacity, the practical impossibility of differentiating between direct labour and some overhead labour will lead to apparently slightly diminishing average variable costs, although pure direct costs are indeed constant. Some authors speak of paying-out fixed costs (Brunner, 1967, p. 48). Others speak of start-up costs, saying that prime costs consist of both marginal costs and overhead start-up costs. As Robinson (1969, p. 261) says, 'There is always an element of quasi-fixed cost which must be incurred when a plant is kept in running order. Thus average prime cost falls with output up to full capacity' (cf. Asimakopulos, 1970, p. 172; Kaldor, 1964b, p. xvi). On the basis of this proper distinction between true variable costs and start-up costs, we may thus conclude that, at the level of the plant, there is strong evidence to suggest that marginal or pure direct costs are constant.

Now what about the differentials in productivity between plants? Kaldor (1961, p. 198) argued a long time ago that the increased productivity of labour, due to the existence of overhead labour, precisely compensates for the diminishing productivity of equipment brought about by various vintages. Such an answer to Lee's objections to a constant marginal cost is not acceptable, however, if we want to continue to differentiate between direct and indirect labour, as we shall. Eichner's reply (1986b) to Lee's critique was to argue that without technical progress the overall marginal cost curve would be horizontal up to capacity, and that it is useful to assume it so. Lee's anticipated answer (1986, p. 409) to that reply was that instrumentalism could not be part of a post-Keynesian theory of the firm.

There is, however, a much more valid reply to Lee's criticism. Yordon (1987, p. 596) notes that, when they reduce production, firms do not necessarily close down the least efficient plants. Mainly because of transportation costs, a general reduction in the demand for the products of a firm will be met by closing down segments of all plants, rather than closing down all segments of the least efficient plant. The step-wise representation of marginal costs given by Figure 3.4 is thus an abstract one. The more concrete representation of marginal costs, its depiction in historical time, is the one offered by Figure 3.5, since it corresponds to the actual sequential behaviour of marginal and unit costs when firms increase or decrease their level of output.

A similar objection, and also a similar answer, can be made at the industry level. As Davidson (1960, p. 53) recalls, even if all firms do have constant marginal costs, this does not imply that the industry supply curve is horizontal, as post-Keynesians in the Kaleckian tradition would have it, since there may be low-cost as well as high-cost firms. In the next chapters, we shall assume nonetheless that the industry supply curve is a horizontal cost curve, because we shall presume that firms operate in parallel fashion, sharing in the variations of total output. For instance, when demand falls, the reduction in output is spread more or less proportionately over all firms. The least efficient firms do not bear the brunt of the reduction in activity, unless they are forced to go under. Inefficiency is reflected in profits per unit, rather than in prices. Symmetrically, when demand expands, unit costs for each firm go down, and hence 'productivity rises because the rise in output following the rise in demand is shared among *all* firms, not concentrated among the marginal firms' (Kaldor, 1985a, p. 47). It is the existence of excess capacity which allows such behaviour, as well as the irrelevance of the marginal pricing rule.

This brings to the forefront the question of pricing, which we must now tackle.

## 3.5 PRICING THEORY

**Variants of Pricing Procedures**

Whereas neoclassical pricing theory relies on the equality of marginal cost and marginal revenue, cost-plus pricing is a major characteristic of the post-Keynesian theory of the firm. Cost-plus pricing, or what Okun (1981, p. 153) calls cost-oriented pricing, includes three variants: mark-up pricing, full-cost pricing and target-return pricing. I shall argue that there is no fundamental difference between these three variants, and that as a consequence it can be said that post-Keynesians have a consistent theory of pricing.

The mark-up variant assumes that a gross profit margin is applied to unit direct costs or average variable costs. The pricing equation is then:

$$p = (1+\theta)AVC \qquad (3.11)$$

The price variable is $p$; $AVC$ represents the average variable costs, mainly labour wages and the cost of raw materials, while the percentage mark-up on direct costs is $\theta$. The relationship between the mark-up and the gross profit margin is simple. The share of gross profits, or the degree of monopoly in Kalecki's terminology, is equal to:

$$m = \theta/(1+\theta) \qquad (3.12)$$

The mark-up $\theta$ can be considered to be a proxy of the gross margin of profit $m$, since the former can be written as a function of the latter:

$$\theta = m/(1-m) \qquad (3.13)$$

Since marginal costs are assumed to be constant, as in Figure 3.5, it is immaterial whether one uses average variable costs or marginal costs as the multiplicand. For the same reason, there is no need to be more specific about the output level at which the average variable cost is being computed, since it will be the same provided the firm operates below full capacity. Figure 3.6(a) illustrates the mark-up procedure of equation (3.11). The full-cost variant assumes that a net margin of profit is applied to unit costs, which are the sum of average variable costs and average fixed costs (direct and overhead costs). This is illustrated by Figure 3.6(b). The overhead costs do not include interest costs and as a consequence equation (3.14) is consistent with the use of equation (3.11). The pricing equation of the full cost variant is:

Figure 3.6 (a) Mark-up pricing and gross profit margin; (b) full-cost pricing and net profit margin

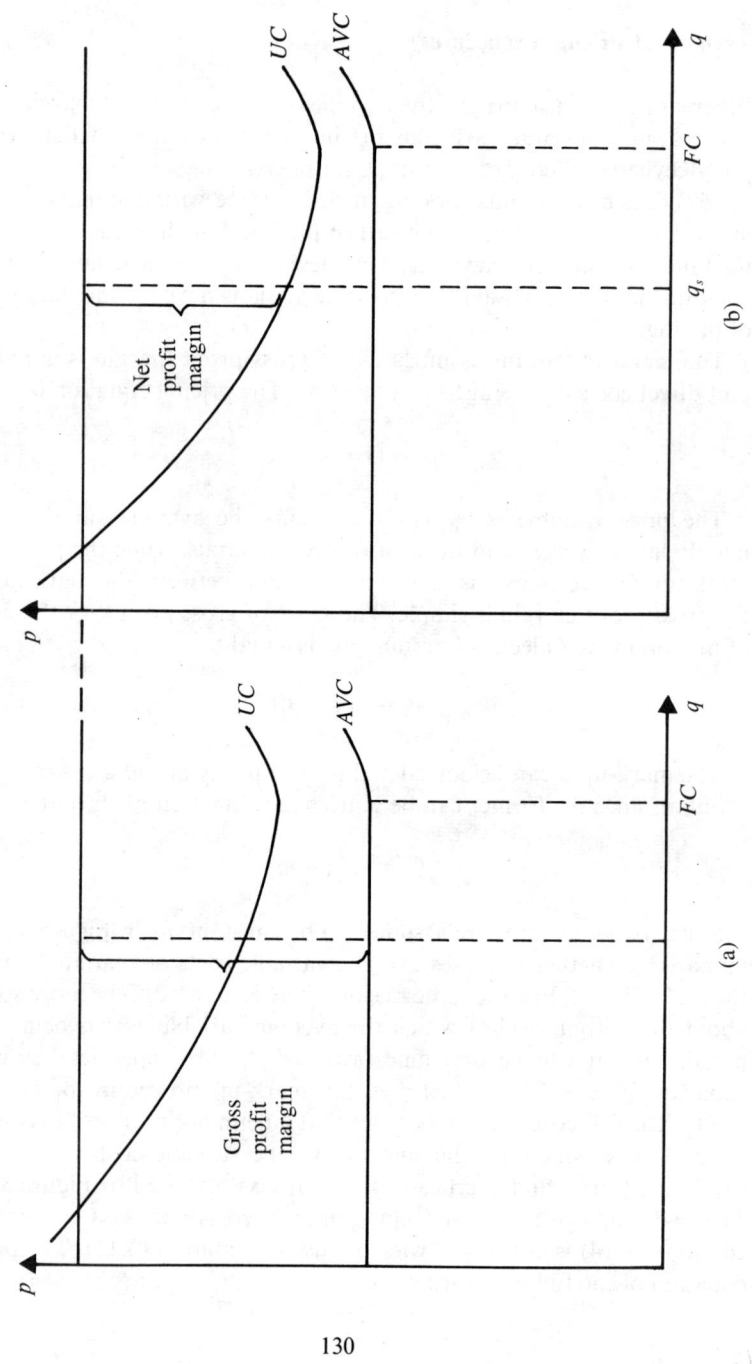

$$p = (1+\theta')UC \qquad (3.14)$$

It can again be said that the mark-up factor $\theta'$ is a proxy of the margin of profit – in this case the net profit margin – so that equations (3.12) and (3.13) still hold. Unit costs are, however, varying with output, so that the full-cost formula is incomplete unless one specifies at what level of output unit costs are measured. Four such levels of output have been suggested: the actual level, the expected level, full-capacity output and the standard level of output. When presenting the full-cost principle, Hall and Hitch (1939, p. 20) indicated that half of the firms were using the actual or the expected levels of output. This has led to the belief, held by many, that full-cost prices ought to change with variations in the expected or more recent level of output sales, as a result of the constancy of the net mark-up factor $\theta'$ and the variability of unit costs. Robinson (1977, p. 11) recalls that 'the old full cost doctrine ... appeared to hold that prices of manufactures ... fall when demand increases because overheads are spread over a larger output'.

It turns out, however, that most authors who have supported the principle of full-cost pricing have based the unit cost variable in equation (3.14) on a standard level of output, consistent with what we have called above the standard operating ratio or the normal degree of utilization of capacity (Brunner, 1967, p. 44; Sylos Labini, 1971, p. 247; Harrod, 1972, p. 398; Wood, 1975, p. 61; Lee, 1985, p. 206). As Harrod (1952, p. 165) remarks, this is a 'modification of the full cost principle *stricto sensu*'; but this is how full-cost pricing must now be understood: as a net margin of profit on standard unit costs. This is indeed how we shall define full cost from now on, noting that some authors prefer to use the expression 'normal cost pricing' (Rowthorn, 1981, p. 5; Bhaduri, 1986, p. 76). There is thus little difference between full-cost and mark-up pricing: both methods assume that the margin of profit and the price do not vary with reasonable fluctuations in output; both methods assume that prices will respond to fluctuations in standard or normal costs. The only difference between the two methods would appear to be that mark-up pricing does not take modifications of normal overhead costs into account, whereas full-cost pricing does.

The third variant of cost-plus pricing is target-return pricing. Target-return pricing may be considered more as a specification of full-cost or normal-cost pricing than as a variant of cost-plus pricing. Target-return pricing gives an explanation of the margin of profit. It says that 'margins added to standard costs are designed to produce the target profit rate on investment, assuming standard volume to be the long-run average rate of plant utilization' (Lanzilotti, 1958, p. 923). This pricing method seems the most prevalent. It was shown to be used both by large and small American firms (Lanzilotti, 1958; Haynes, 1964). A more recent survey of the British manufacturing industry has reinforced previous findings: most respondents indicate that a rate of return on their capital employed is an element of their pricing objectives, while for two-thirds of the sample it is the main element (Shipley, 1981, p. 430). A well-known example of target-return pricing is General Motors, here given by Scherer as one of two instances of the full-cost pricing rule:

> GM begins its pricing analysis with an objective of earnings, on the average over the years, a return of approximately 15 per cent after taxes on total invested capital. Since it does not know how many autos will be sold in a forthcoming year, and hence what the average cost per unit (including prorated overhead) will be, it calculates costs on the assumption of *standard volume* – that is, operation at 80 per cent of conservatively rated capacity. A *standard price* is next calculated by adding to average cost per unit at standard volume a sufficient profit margin to yield the desired 15 per cent after-tax return on capital. (Scherer, 1970, p. 174)

One can show that target-return pricing is a specification of full-cost pricing. Suppose that the standard target rate of profit is $r_s$ and the value of the stock of capital $pK$. Required profits for the period are then $r_s pK$. Let us assume a capital/output ratio $(K/q_{fc})$ of $v$, that ratio being valid at full capacity and for given prices of inputs. Variable $v$ is thus a capital to capacity ratio. If the standard rate of utilization of capacity is $u_s$, corresponding in the period to a level of output of $q_s$, the required profits for the period must be equal to $r_s v p q_s / u_s$. This must be equated to the total profits that are to be obtained by marking up unit costs at the standard rate of utilization of capacity: $\theta'(UC)(q_s)$. Doing so, we find that the previously identified mark-up $\theta'$ of equation (3.14) must be equal to:

$$\theta' = (r_s v / u_s)(p / UC).$$

Looking again at equation (3.14), we see that it can be rewritten as:

$$UC = p/(1+\theta').$$

Substituting this value of UC into the previous equation yields the equality:

$$\theta' = (r_s v / u_s)[p(1+\theta')/p]$$

Solving for $\theta'$, we obtain:

$$\theta' = r_s v / (u_s - r_s v). \tag{3.15}$$

We have now found the relationship between the proxy $\theta'$ for the margin of profit and target-return pricing. The full-cost equation in its target-return specification, it being understood that unit costs $UC$ are set at the standard rate of utilization of capacity, is thus equal to:

$$p = \left(1 + \frac{r_s v}{u_s - r_s v}\right) UC \tag{3.16}$$

Equation (3.16) is similar to the pricing model developed by Eichner (1987a, p. 357) in his explanation of the pricing behaviour of growing corporations. The only differences are that Eichner implicitly supposes full use of capacity, while he considers the rate of growth rather than the rate of profit to be the target of pricing procedures. It is obvious from Figure 3.6(b) and equation (3.16) that, if a higher rate of utilization is taken as the standard, prices should be lower because both unit costs at the standard rate of utilization and the mark-up $\theta'$ would be lower, everything else being equal. As one would expect, a higher standard rate of return, or a higher capital/capacity ratio, induces an increase in the mark-up $\theta'$, and hence in the price level when unit costs are fixed. If we take the first derivative of equation (3.15) with respect to $r_s$, we indeed get a positive expression:

$$d\theta'/dr_s = \frac{v u_s}{(u_s - r_s v)^2} > 0 \tag{3.17}$$

The presentation of these three variants of pricing helps to clarify a statement that was made at the beginning of the chapter. Prices set in the short run are not market-clearing prices. They are prices set on costs. They are not intended to equate supply and demand, whatever that means in a system with excess capacity, nor are they intended to equate demand to supply at the standard rate of utilization of capacity. Furthermore, firms know that the required rate of return employed in the full-cost formula may not be the realized one, even in the long run. Scherer (1970, pp. 174–5) reports that General Motors, for instance, has exceeded its normal rate of utilization of capacity in most years, and that as a consequence 'the realized return on invested capital has averaged well over the 15 per cent target rate'. Of course, when companies such as General Motors set their prices, they make adjustments to the standard prices of equations (3.10) or (3.14), taking into account business conditions, strategic goals and so on. Similarly retail firms may offer discounts on products the prices of which were fixed by a mark-up on the purchasing cost. These adjustments may be considered as frictions. They do not call the cost-plus principles back into question.

### Rituals and Cost Accounting

Cost-plus pricing is prevalent among firms because it constitutes a convenient rule of thumb in making what would otherwise be complex and difficult decisions in a world of uncertainty. This is particularly clear in the case of retailers who, without their customary margins, would be forced to take thousands of decisions (Galbraith, 1952, p. 18). The neoclassical theory of the firm assumes that entrepreneurs have knowledge of things which the entrepreneurs themselves claim to be ignorant of (marginal revenue, rising marginal cost schedules). Post-Keynesians, instead, base their theory of pricing on the knowledge that managers of firms are likely to be able to gather in an uncertain and complex environment. As is the case for consumers when they make their choices, there is a strong element of convention in the price decisions of firms. Pricing by custom is 'an indispensable simplification of what otherwise would be an inordinately complex task' (Galbraith, 1952, p. 18).

Besides the use of mark-up pricing, custom is linked to the conservation of goodwill; that is, convincing current customers that there is no need to try other suppliers. Goodwill, or brand loyalty, is the rule of thumb of the customer which says that there is no need to try other suppliers as long as the current price appears to be fair and the product satisfying. Firms must avoid giving the impression that they are overcharging (Okun, 1981, p. 178; Kaldor, 1985a, p. 48). To retain fair prices, firms seek price similarity with their rivals or they try to stabilize prices with respect to unit costs, thus keeping the margin of profit constant. To set fair prices, firms rely on fair or reasonable target rates of return on investment (Lanzilotti, 1958, p. 931; Shipley, 1981, p. 432). Presumably price leaders base the price setting on target rates of return, while other firms follow up the decisions of the price leader, imitating its price. Whatever the case, a simple rule of thumb approach predominates, based on feasible and practical procedures. These routines are called 'rituals' by Harrod (1952, p. 164). They reflect the fact that, in an interdependent world, where firms want to avoid price wars within their industry, some ritualistic pricing mechanisms must be known to all.

The rituals include known fair target rates of return, as well as industry standards for cost accounting and information on costs of individual product lines (Haynes, 1964, p. 317). The exact pricing variant which is enforced thus depends on the accounting procedures and cost information which are available to decision makers. The fact that various cost-plus pricing rules, such as mark-up, full-cost and target-return pricing, have been used through time or are still being used, is related to the availability of data on cost and to the proper accounting conventions to distribute overhead costs to the appropriate lines of product. When seen in this light, it is even more obvious that these three pricing formulae are variants of the same general procedure, and that 'the differences between them is explainable entirely in terms of the cost accounting procedures used in their formulation' (Lee, 1985, p. 206). Where, for instance, only data on direct costs are accessible or reliable – the less advanced accounting situation – one would expect mark-up pricing rather than full-cost pricing to be prevalent.

Various post-Keynesians or other eclectic authors have used one or the other formulation of cost-plus pricing. Mark-up pricing is mainly associated with the names of Kalecki, S. Weintraub (1958) and Okun (1981). More recently there have been many macroeconomic models of growth built around the notion of a fixed mark-up over direct wage costs (Dutt, 1990a; Taylor, 1985). It has been argued by Lee (1985, p. 207) that those who are only using mark-up pricing are showing a lack of understanding of actual pricing practices, since firms now make use of more sophisticated accounting procedures incorporating overhead costs, and since there has been undeniable evidence that firms mostly rely on full-cost or target-return pricing. Should all simple mark-up models be forsaken?

One should note again that the difference between mark-up and full-cost models has been greatly exaggerated. For instance, when Kalecki himself (1971, p. 51) attempts to differentiate his mark-up model from the full-cost one, he indicates that in his mark-up model the price of a firm is influenced by the prices of other firms and that it may (not that it must) be influenced by a change in its overhead costs. To that effect, he even mentions that there is a tendency for the mark-up to rise during a slump. This is what the French call wanting to split hairs. Once the possible influence of overhead costs has been recognized, there is no divergence between mark-up pricing and full-cost pricing, when the latter is appropriately understood to be normal cost pricing. A good example of this convergence of thought is Rowthorn's demonstration (1981, p. 36) that a mark-up pricing equation can always be derived from a full-cost pricing model. Another example is Asimakopulos's presentation of his Kaleckian model. Asimakopulos (1975, p. 319) sets up a Kaleckian mark-up on direct costs, but his explanation of the value taken by the mark-up relies on a target-return pricing procedure: 'These mark-ups are designed to cover, over time, both overhead costs and profits. Their values would thus be dependent on the standard rates of utilization of productive capacity used to calculate standard costs as well as on some expected rate of return.'

What is important to remember when using straightforward mark-up models is that the mark-up depends on overhead elements, such as overhead labour salaries, and on fixed or quasi-fixed interest costs. Despite their over-simplistic cost accounting underpinnings, mark-up models of pricing behaviour should not be abandoned. Their simplicity allows complex macroeconomic modelling to remain amenable to calculations. In this sense they may be said to be more useful than the full-cost model (Brunner, 1967, p. 45).

**Determinants of the Margin of Profit**

We have not yet discussed the determinants of the profit margin, with the exception of the target rate of return. The major criticism of cost-plus pricing, seen from the neoclassical side, is that it really is nothing more than profit maximization in disguise. The claim was made from very early on, in the 1940s, when the so-called marginalist controversies were raging (see Lee, 1984b, and Mongin, 1986). Kalecki (1939–40) himself, at some point, adopted the method of profit maximization, although he later dismissed it explicitly (Kalecki, 1971, p. 44). Even today, some post-Keynesians (Moore, 1988a, p. 213), as well as eclectic economists who show some sympathy for cost-plus pricing (Koutsoyiannis, 1975, p. 281; Tarshis, 1980, p. 11), conclude that it is a routine version of long-run profit maximization. Others argue that, since Kalecki has always denied the importance of overhead costs for pricing, he must have assumed at all times short-run profit maximization (Carson, 1990). One of the drawbacks of cost-plus pricing is that its earlier proponents have generally been silent about the determinants of the mark-up. This silence led Kaldor (1956, pp. 92–3) initially to reject cost-plus pricing, and it has helped neoclassical critics to reduce cost-plus pricing to marginalism. We shall now see how that can be done, and later discuss possible alternative determinants of the mark-up.

The proof of the equivalence of marginalist pricing and mark-up pricing is very simple. Profit maximization requires the equality of marginal revenue with marginal cost.

$$MR = MC$$

As is well known, marginal revenue can also be expressed as a function of the price charged and of the elasticity of demand, $e$.

$$MR = p(e-1)/e$$

Since cost-plus proponents usually assume constant marginal costs, average variable costs and marginal costs are equal, so that the profit-maximizing condition may be rewritten:

$$p(e-1)/e = AVC$$

The profit-maximizing price can thus be rewritten as:

$$p = [e/(e-1)]AVC = (1+\theta)AVC$$

We are back to the mark-up variant of cost-plus pricing, given by equation (3.11), with the mark-up $\theta$ equal to $1/(e-1)$. Marginalists argue that the lower the price elasticity of demand, that is the less sensitive is demand to price variations, the higher is the profit-maximizing mark-up which firms will eventually adopt through trial and error. Neoclassical authors thus claim to have shown that, while managers report that they are using cost-plus procedures, they are in fact maximizing profits in the orthodox marginalist manner without knowing it. This neoclassical interpretation of cost-plus pricing is illustrated at price level $p_r$ and output level $q_r$ in Figure 3.7. Marginal cost and marginal revenue are there equated at the appropriate gross profit margin.

The major weakness of this proof of the equivalence of mark-up and marginalist pricing is that, for it to make sense, the price elasticity of demand has to be above unity. Otherwise marginal revenue is negative and cannot be equated to the necessarily positive marginal cost. It turns out precisely that in many oligopolistic industries the price elasticity of demand $e$ is below unity. If we assume that there is a price leader in these industries, and that other firms follow the leader, thus keeping market shares constant, the price elasticity measured for these industries is exactly equal to the price elasticity of demand faced by the individual price leader. We may thus conclude that the marginal revenue – near actual prices – of the price leader is negative, and that as a consequence profit maximization as an hypothesis cannot be entertained (Steindl, 1952, pp. 15–17; Eichner, 1976, p. 48). Firms do not maximize profits. They set prices according to costs at a standard level of utilization of capacity. The price and output levels corresponding to this more likely case are labelled $p_s$ and $q_s$ in Figure 3.7.

The crucial question then becomes: how do firms decide on the value of the margin of profit over direct cost or unit costs? Various answers can be put forward, some more formal than others. The dominant view remains the one seeing a cost-plus price as a 'reproductive price and a growth price' (Lee, 1985, p. 209). Pricing is linked with investment decision. This view has been developed in the models of Eichner (1976), Wood (1975), Harcourt and Kenyon (1976) and Shapiro (1981). All these authors present a variant of the model of the firm that was suggested at the end of section 2, where the growth of the firm is restricted by the intersection of the finance

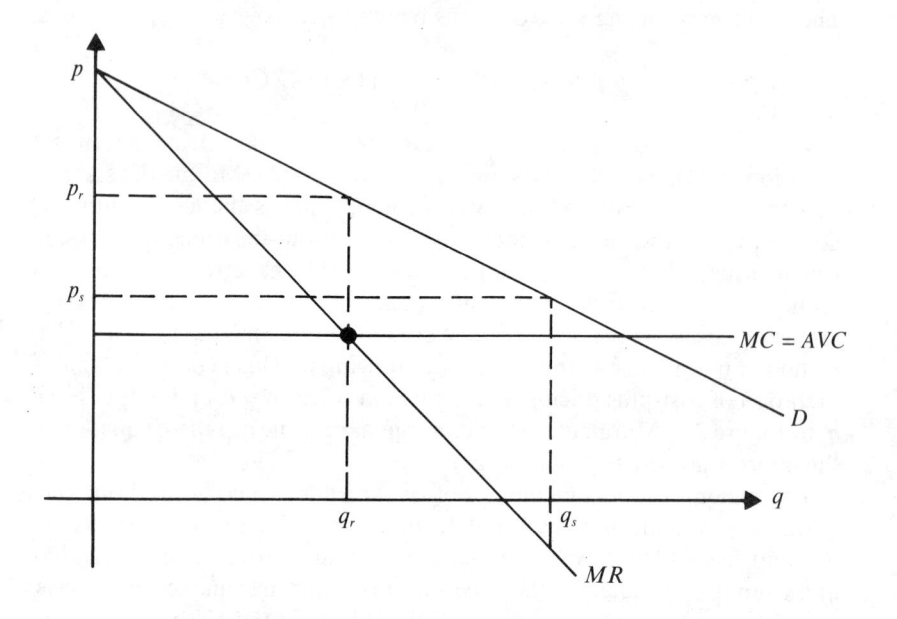

*Figure 3.7  Profit maximization, demand elasticity and cost-plus pricing*

frontier with the expansion frontier. This view of pricing did not impress Robinson, who argued that 'such theories can never be quite convincing for motivation in business is multi-dimensional and cannot be squeezed into a simple formula' (1977, p. 11), a point of view consistent with her previous claim that the profit margin 'depends very much upon historical accident or upon conventional views among business men as to what is reasonable' (1966, p. 78). Kaldor, however, endorsed an account of the mark-up based on the finance and expansion frontiers.

This objective – maximizing the attainable rate of growth – can mean several things. First, it means aiming at a price that will maintain, and, if possible, improve on their *share* of the market. This consideration would suggest that they should choose a price and hence a markup that is as *low* as they can make it.
Second, they must choose a markup that allows them to increase their *own* capital, by means of ploughed-back profits as much as possible ... Their main motive in all this is to prevent a situation where they become restricted in their expansion by a financial constraint ... This second consideration taken by itself suggests making the markup as high as possible, since the higher the markup, the higher the rate at which their own capital accumulates at any given plough-back ratio ... So these opposing considerations should determine the firm's judgment as to what the optimum markup should be. (Kaldor, 1985a, pp. 50–2)

We now have all the elements which allow us to integrate theoretical views on the behaviour of the firm (the use of the finance and expansion frontiers), empirical evidence (the use of target-return pricing), the determination of the margin of profit, and the systemic view of prices present in neo-Ricardian models, although the last element will only be discussed later. We saw earlier that target-return pricing could be considered a specification, rather than a variant, of full-cost pricing. Target-return pricing yielded a determination of the margin of profit $\theta'$ as a function of the target rate of return $r_s$. We may now ask: what determines the target or required rate of return? The answer lies at the intersection of the finance and expansion frontiers. In the very abstract, as the firm attempts to maximize its rate of growth, its managers perceive that, with the existing constraints (finance, but also competition, technology, knowledge, labour unions), there is a certain rate of profit that can and that has to be realized for all the constraints to be met. This corresponds to the rate of profit $r_g$ in Figure 3.3. This constrained rate of profit is the standard rate of return of the pricing formula.

Of course firms never know exactly the shape of their finance and expansion frontiers, and hence the exact value of their constrained optimal rate of profit $r_g$. Furthermore it can be presumed that the strength of the constraints frequently change, thus modifying in Figure 3.3 the shape and the slope of the frontiers. The target rate of return which results from these considerations is thus a conventional rate of profit, the equality of which with the realized rate of profit cannot be presumed, neither in the short run nor in the long run. This is why, in the words of Joan Robinson, the profit margins of full-cost pricing procedures 'are set at a level calculated to yield a satisfactory return on some normal or standard average level of utilization of capacity' (1971, p. 94) or 'settle at the level that yields the expected rate of profit (the best attainable in the given conditions) at an average degree of utilization of plant' (1969, p. 260). The firm can only know what the past rates of return have been; it cannot know what the present or what the future rates of profit will be. It must thus rely on some conventional measure of the rate of return that will fully recover part of both past and future expansion costs.

When Lanzilotti (1958, pp. 938–40) presented the results of his survey on the price behaviour of firms, he concluded by linking pricing to the planned profits required for investment and growth. The relationship between target-return pricing and the constrained rate of profit derived from our growth-maximizing model of the firm cannot be more obvious. Ironically it should be mentioned that, while present post-Keynesian authors believe that target-return pricing as here redefined applies mostly to oligopolistic industries and their price leaders, earlier exponents of target-return pricing thought that it applied with more force to competitive manufacturing industries. When discussing an industry with plenty of small producers, Steindl (1952, p. 51) resolves that competitive pressures are such that the margin of profit is just sufficient to cover the financial costs of expansion, given the acceptable gearing ratio. In the case of oligopolies, Steindl believes that, since firms possess some monopoly power, they are able to remain beyond their finance frontier, maximizing neither profits nor growth.

This brings us to the other post-Keynesian views about the determination of the mark-up on direct or unit costs. Steindl's theory of pricing, which he tried to substantiate in his book, was basically that higher margins of profit could be associated with higher industrial concentration ratios (1952, pp. 70–1). This, of course, is a development of Kalecki's degree of monopoly, that is 'the semi-monopolistic influences . . . resulting from imperfect competition or oligopoly' (1971, p. 160). The extent of the mark-up in each industry depends on the monopoly power of its firms, measured by the industrial concentration ratio or a proxy thereof. This view, now known as the monopoly power model (Dutt, 1987b, p. 65) or the monopoly capital model (Baran and Sweezy, 1968) relies in its microeconomic incarnation on the empirical evidence showing a positive relation between mark-ups and concentration ratios (Weiss, 1980).

There is no need to consider the monopoly power view as a rival of the full-cost reproductive price. The monopoly view can be incorporated into the model of the firm illustrated by Figure 3.3. A higher degree of monopoly can be interpreted as a shifting outwards of the expansion frontier. To higher concentration ratios would thus correspond higher possible profit rates. This would lead to higher target rates of return, and hence to higher mark-ups. A consequence of all this is that we should expect profit rates to differ from industry to industry.

A variant of the monopoly power view of the determination of mark-ups, also derived from Kalecki (1971, pp. 51, 156–64) and the work of neo-radical authors, can be similarly integrated. In this variant, monopoly power is not associated with concentration ratios, but with the corporate power of the firm over the whole economy (Dutt, 1987b, p. 71). As noted by Jossa (1989, p. 156), in his later writings Kalecki has associated the degree of monopoly not only with the struggle between competing firms, but also with the intensity of the struggle between social classes. The size of the mark-up on direct costs is in inverse relation to the bargaining power of the trade unions. Reciprocally the more successful the class struggle from the point of view of the workers, the higher the real wage rate and the lower the mark-up (Dutt, 1987a). This can easily be seen from the mark-up version of cost-plus pricing, as shown in equation (3.11). If average variable costs there are assumed to consist only of wages (the wage rate multiplied by the number of workers), a higher wage rate at fixed prices necessarily entails a lower mark-up. Again, from the point of view of the individual firm, this class bargaining variant of the monopoly power view can be interpreted as shifts of the expansion frontier of Figure 3.3. When trade unions have more bargaining power, firms perceive the expansion frontier as shifting inwards. This leads to a lower possible profit rate, and hence to a lower target rate of return and a smaller mark-up. This approach will be taken up in more detail when inflation is discussed in Chapter 7.

The upshot of all this is that, depending on the problem at hand, one might wish to consider a constant margin of profit or a flexible one. As in the case of mark-up pricing versus full-cost pricing, the degree of complexity of the analysis being pursued may favour one or the other hypothesis. It should be clear, however, that all the various variants which post-Keynesian authors are employing can be reduced to a canonical model, based on target-return pricing.

**Prices and Variations of Demand**

We have seen how prices are normally set. What happens when economic conditions are such that firms consistently produce below either the expected rate of utilization of capacity or the standard rate? What if the actual rate of utilization of capacity is above the standard rate? In other words, what happens to prices and the margins of profit during the business cycle? What would the post-Keynesian model of pricing predict? It all depends on the variant which is being used. The answer may also change according to whether the variables being looked at are prices or mark-ups.

Let us first assume that variations in the sales of firms of an industry have no impact on its direct unit costs; that is, the price of raw materials and the nominal wage rate are not influenced by these variations in output. Any change in the industry price would thus be a consequence of a change in the mark-up or in average indirect cost. Let us consider the case of a downturn. Four models of pricing may be considered. In the mark-up model, since the gross margin of profit is over prime costs only, variations of output should have no impact on prices, unless the mark-up is changed. In the full-cost model *stricto sensu*, that is in its old version, since fixed costs are spread on a smaller output, unit costs increase in the downturn. With a given net margin of profit, we should thus expect prices to go up in a recession. In the full-cost model as we have understood it, also called normal cost pricing, that is with the net profit margin calculated over *standard* unit costs, a downturn accompanied by a constant mark-up should lead to constant prices. This is because standard unit costs are independent of variations of output by definition. The same could be said of target-return pricing if the downturn has no impact on the conventional rate of return and the conventional rate of utilization which determine the mark-up. The net margin of profit, however, may change if the downturn is perceived as a secular decline in the rate of growth of the economy or of the industry. This is the effect emphasized by Eichner in particular, who conjectures that a fall in the perceived secular rate of growth of sales leads to a lower mark-up, presumably through the downward adjustment of the target rate of return. This effect on the pricing formula may nevertheless be compensated by a simultaneous fall in what is considered to be the normal rate of utilization of capacity.

All three possible effects of output variations on prices can thus be entertained within the various post-Keynesian variants of pricing. The main view that emerges from this quick assessment is that cost-plus pricing generally leads to the belief that output fluctuations have no effect on margins of profit. If prices fall in a recession, this may be the result only of a fall in direct costs, that is wages and raw materials, the latter fact having been noted by Kalecki (1969, p. 53). In the full cost model *stricto sensu*, however, an increase of the margin of profit will occur in recession times, while, in the Eichnerian variant of target-return pricing, a decrease in the margin of profit might occur in the downturn. This latter effect is naturally what orthodox theory would predict.

Various empirical studies seem to demonstrate that in actual fact all three possible effects of output variations on margins of profit are being observed. The empirical studies performed by Coutts, Godley and Nordhaus (1978), by Sawyer, Aaronovitch and Samson (1982) and by Domowitz, Hubbard and Petersen (1986) all highlight the fact that margins of profit can stay constant, increase or decrease in recessions. The same diversity of behaviour occurs in expansion. These studies conclude, nonetheless, that the impact of demand on prices or margins is small and that, overall, the number of cases where prices decrease in a recession compensate for the number of cases where prices increase. The response to changes in demand is predominantly a quantity response, not a price one. The conclusions reached by Coutts *et al.* are in clear support of the full-cost pricing procedure in its standard costs version, or any other similar procedure based on standard costs.

> The central tendency of these estimates, as well as the absolute size of even the most extreme estimates, indicate that there is no general or economically significant tendency for prices to change relative to normal costs over the course of the business cycle . . . The evidence did not support the view that demand affects prices

relative to normal unit costs: the effect of demand on the mark up was both statistically and economically insignificant. (Coutts *et al.*, 1978, pp. 72, 139)

The lesson to be drawn from all this is that it is a good approximation to assume that firms fix prices by adding a constant mark-up to their normal unit costs, calculated at a conventional rate of utilization of capacity and with a target rate of return in mind. The cause of this is that prices are not designed to be market-clearing prices; rather they are reproductive prices. If in a recession firms were to cut profit margins and engage in price wars, they would destroy the reproductive properties of cost-plus pricing procedures (Lee, 1985, p. 210). When it happens in an industry, observers usually refer to cut-throat competition or to destructive competition, thus highlighting its undesirable characteristics. Implicit collusion behaviour is upheld by price leaders and industry-wide customs and conventions. They guarantee that margins of profit will stay at a reasonable level, at least for the efficient or the average firms, and that enough profits will be generated through the cycle to finance the required investments. When firms keep their margins of profit constant through the business cycle, their flow of profit varies in proportion to their immediate needs. When capacity is strained to the limit, total profits and the share of profits are high; when production is below standard capacity, total profits and the share of profits are low. Total profits and retained earnings thus move procyclically although prices and margins of profit may stay constant as demand varies. This is because of the constant direct costs and the spread of fixed costs over a larger output.

Figure 3.8 illustrates this direct relationship between output and profits or the share of profits in the value of sales when the mark-up is constant. At the standard level of output, $q_s$, unit direct costs are equal to $OD$, fixed unit costs are $DF$, and unit costs are $OF$. The gross margin of profit, or what Kalecki called the degree of monopoly as reflected in equation (3.12), is thus the ratio $Dp/Op$. This ratio naturally does not change as output varies. The net margin of profit at standard unit costs is $Fp/Op$. If sales turn out to be equal to standard output, the share of profits out of the value of sales is precisely equal to that of the net margin of profit, $Fp/Op$. The value of profits is then equal to the shaded rectangle areas. However, when actual sales do not correspond to standard output, the net margin of profit and the share of profits do not correspond. Figure 3.8. illustrates the case of a recession, when the output level of the firm falls to $q_r$. The share of direct costs and unit direct costs stays the same; but unit fixed costs increase to $DR$ and the share of indirect costs in the value of output increases to $DR/Op$. As a consequence, profits per unit of output fall to $Rp$. The realized share of profits in the value of output decreases to

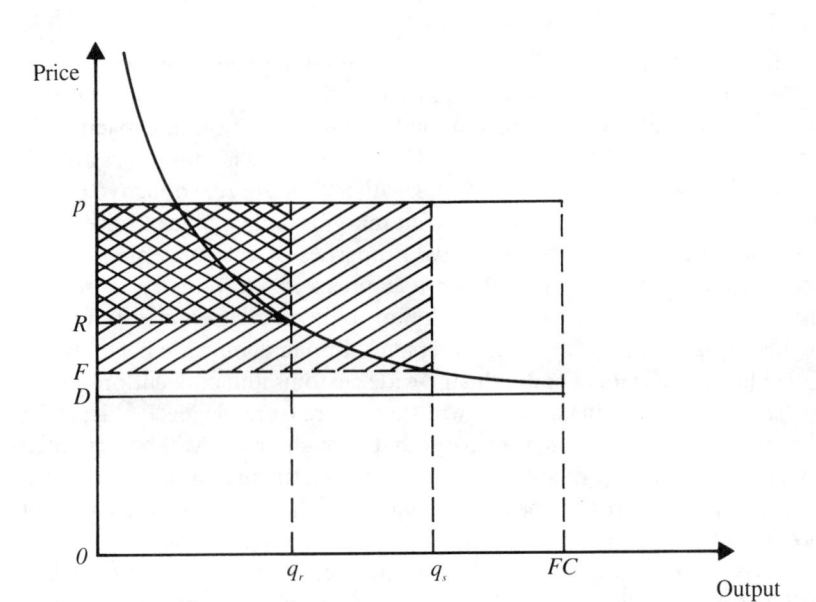

*Figure 3.8   Procyclical variations in profits with cost-plus pricing*

$Rp/Op$, and total profits shrink to the cross-hatched area in the diagram. The converse happens when output increases. In contrast to orthodox theory, profits necessarily increase when the output of the firm increases, provided the firm stays beneath full capacity. These effects of variations in the rate of utilization of capacity will be further analysed in Chapter 5, with the help of a simple algebraic form.

## 3.6   COST-PLUS PRICES AND PRODUCTION PRICES

It was argued in the introductory chapter that there exists a coherent set of presuppositions within post-classical economics and that various non-orthodox theories do have many common elements. The intent of this subsection is to show that the post-Keynesian theories of cost-plus pricing contain substantial elements which are similar to the neo-Ricardian production prices. This view, of course, is not original, as many authors have made the same claim in the past, either in general (Earl, 1983a, ch.2; Levine 1988) or with respect to the particular Kaleckian model (Mainwaring, 1977). Indeed some authors have even formally attempted to construct matrix-form mark-up models that incorproate the interdependent production prices with the mark-up behaviour of the firm (Semmler, 1984; Eichner, 1987b). We shall not do so here, as we shall focus on the common concepts, rather than on the technical details, assuming that the reader has some knowledge of prices of production (see Pasinetti, 1977).

There are basically four points of contact between cost-plus prices and production prices: (1) both visions of prices are cost-oriented; (2) they are reproductive prices; (3) they are based on normal conditions; and (4) market clearance is not at issue.

First, and very obviously, neither of these types of prices equates marginal costs with marginal revenues. In cost-plus prices as well as prices of production, the centre of attention is the cost of production. As Wiles (1973, p. 386) says, 'the main function of prices is not to be resource-allocators but cost-coverers'. The post-Keynesian and the neo-Ricardian prices are not indices of temporary scarcity, in opposition to neoclassical prices. As is clear in the model of Pasinetti (1981), prices of production are correctly weighted indices of labour costs. Demand plays no role, except in peculiar circumstances such as joint production, or the role of demand is an indirect one. For instance, the rate of growth of demand may have an impact on the target rate of return or the uniform rate of profit, something that can be interpreted as the need for more hyper-indirect labour.

Secondly, there is the reproductive quality of cost-of-production prices and cost-plus prices. We have already seen that cost-plus prices could not be associated with short-run profit maximization. The horizon of the firm, when it sets its prices, is more the long run than the short one. We have underlined in particular the importance of the expansion and the financial constraints on the mark-up decision of the firm. Prices must allow growth. In neo-Ricardian models, reproduction is also the crucial element (Walsh and Gram, 1980, p. 397). The existing situation and decisions must be repeatable in the future. Prices reflect long-period considerations, rather than short-run ones. In some variants the growth requirements are also underlined. Reproducibility enters through the explicit interdependent connections between the various products: the reproduction of commodities by means of commodities so central to neo-Ricardian analysis. The technological matrix, the input–output matrix, takes care of this interdependence. Some outputs are the inputs of other products, and therefore the variations in prices of these commodities have feedback effects. In cost-plus pricing, the interdependence is only made implicit: each firm is assumed to fix its prices according to its costs: that is, according to the prices of its inputs; but the prices of these inputs are themselves the result of a mark-up procedure.

The similarities between the cost-plus prices and prices of production are most obvious in the target-return pricing approach (Reynolds, 1987a, p. 179). In the canonical version of prices of production there is a uniform rate of profit on capital, output being assumed to be at its normal level. The rate of profit is thus the normal rate of profit, and output corresponds to the normal rate of utilization of capacity, each plant or segment of plant being operated at its optimal engineer-rated capacity. This is quite similar to the target-return view: standard or normal output, that is the normal rate of utilization, helps to determine unit costs and the mark-up; the latter also depends on the normal rate of profit that corporations wish to obtain in the long run on their investments and capital. The target rate of return thus plays a similar role to that of the uniform rate of profit in production prices.

We know that cost-plus prices are non-clearing prices. As such, they are not market prices, but administered ones. Cost-plus prices are not influenced by short-run variations in demand. Furthermore they certainly do not ensure that in the short run demand will equate the standard rate of utilization of capacity; but, as the case of General Motors did illustrate, the same can be said even in the long run: the average actual rate of utilization of capacity is not necessarily the standard rate. A similar claim has been made for neo-Ricardian prices. When they are interpreted as a photograph at a given moment of time, with given levels of output, 'there is no reason to suppose that prices of production should equate the quantity demanded with the quantity supplied for any commodity in the long period' (Roncaglia, 1978, p. 16). Generalizing General Motors' case to all firms and industries we may say that, even over the long period, the actual average rate of utilization of capacity is not equal to the normal rate. Symmetrically, we may presume that the actual rate of profit in the long period is generally different from what is considered to be the normal rate of profit (the target rate of return). Under that interpretation, prices of production based on normal rates of profit and normal rates of utilization of capacity would also turn out to be non-clearing prices.

The contention that, even over the long period, the actual rate of profit is different from the normal rate of profit is of course highly disputed by many neo-Ricardians, as we shall see in Chapter 6. The fact remains that the canonical neo-Ricardian model of prices of production assumes a normal and uniform rate of profit and normal rates of utilization of capacity. Unless we are convinced that there exists some mechanism ensuring the uniformity of the rate of profit and the normal use of capacity, we may interpret this neo-Ricardian model as being the notional version of the more realist cost-plus prices (Hodgson, 1989, p. 114). Prices of production are ideal prices, which would be exactly realized if all possible frictions of a true economy could be eliminated; incorrect information, past disequilibria, non-unique prices, debt structures, abnormal rates of utilization of capacity, differentiated profit rates, and so on.

Various levels of abstraction can be entertained. Several authors deal with prices of production models that do not assume the uniformity of the rate of profit or the uniformity of the industry rates of growth, based in particular on the notion of vertically integrated sectors (Pasinetti, 1981; Eichner, 1987b). Indeed, from the very beginning, various authors have asserted that the uniformity of the rate of profit is only a convenient hypothesis to make, and that differentiated rates of profit due to oligopolistic conditions and barriers to entry are perfectly compatible with the Sraffian model (Sylos Labini, 1971, p. 270; Roncaglia, 1978, p. 29).

Still, some claim that these models are inconsistent with the historical approach advocated by post-Keynesians and with their cost-plus pricing procedures. The main objection is that, in the real world, as reflected by cost-plus pricing models, the cost of materials and inputs is ascertained on the basis of historical cost. The same applies to depreciation of capital assets. The price of the commodity purchased yesterday as circulating capital to produce today is different from the price of the same commodity produced today. Standard input–output analysis and vertically integrated systems assume that these two prices are the same (Deprez, 1988, 1990). Similarly with fixed capital goods, neo-Ricardians must assume one of two things: either firms have perfect expectations about technical progress and the evolution of future prices of machines; or firms set depreciation allowances as if they were terminal ventures about to sell their machines (Lee, 1985, p. 214). While the objection relating to circulating capital may be countered by noting that accountants now rely more on replacement cost and less on historical cost, the question of perfect expectations and fixed capital prices remains.

What must be acknowledged is that, to be able to make any sort of progress when dealing with complex issues such as relative prices and the measure of technical progress with produced commodities, some convenient simplifications must be made. For the reasons outlined above, production prices and cost-plus prices are part of the same framework. They are part of the same vision. Production prices, or their multiple variants of the input–output sort, allow for the mathematical treatment of difficult issues and the achievement of practical computations, despite the complexities of interdependence, and without having to resort to aggregation. Statements to the effect that all variants of production prices are useless unless they incorporate historical prices, or claims that cost-plus theories have no theoretical content because they are not general, are not respectful of the fact that different levels of problems must be tackled with different tools and different levels of abstraction.

A more fundamental criticism of some interpretations of prices of production is tied to the classical notion of gravitation. Some authors confuse market prices with actual prices, and claim that market prices gravitate or may gravitate around long-period production prices, called the natural prices (Duménil and Lévy, 1987). The invisible hand of Adam Smith is invoked, with excess demand in an industry inducing price increases and profit increases which encourage capitalists to pour their financial capital into these industries. The consequent increase in supply would eventually get prices down, back to their natural level, while the rate of profit in that industry would return to its normal level. On the other hand, the fact that discrepancies between supply and demand in other industries may lead to momentary increases in the costs of production is generally not taken into account. The problem with this characterization is that it does not correspond to the real-world inflexibility of administered prices, while it closely resembles the neoclassical framework of partial demand and supply analysis. This notion of gravitation undermines its own foundations by resurrecting the orthodox market forces.

These confusing views on prices of production cannot arise once the relationship between prices of production and cost-plus prices is clearly established. Actual prices are not market prices which would clear out excess demand at each period (Arena, 1987, p. 105). Actual prices are set on the basis of costs, while supply adjusts to demand through changes in the use of capacity. 'Actual prices are therefore equal to prices of production but utilization fluctuates around a normal level' (Schefold, 1984, p. 4). The prices which oligopolistic firms set on markets *are* a variant of prices of production, price leaders fixing these prices by taking into account the various technical coefficients of production at the normal rate of utilization of capacity. If a manufacturer feels the need for lower prices, the usual response will be to redesign the product so that its costs of production are smaller. If the cost of inputs increases, because their normal price has increased, this will be incorporated in the administered price. Of course, in the real world, the administered prices are not exactly equal to prices of production. But the fact that they are not equal has to do with the various frictions noted above (monopoly, imperfect expectations, time) rather than the discrepancy between supply and demand. Actual prices are imperfect – but realistic – prices of production. They are administered by firms according to standard costs; they are not ruled by supply and demand. If one avoids the so-called process of gravitation, it then becomes clear that production prices and cost-plus prices are identical concepts, set at different levels of abstraction.

# 4. Credit and Money

We now enter macroeconomics. It may seem bizarre to start off by dealing with the topic of money and credit. Students are used to tackling money as an afterthought, once all the real phenomena have been taken care of. The ordering of topics which is proposed here is nonetheless perfectly legitimate. Any production, in a modern economy, requires access to credit. This, as we shall see, is a macroeconomic law. Indeed, in the previous chapter, we already had to touch upon the borrowing possibilities of the firm in its attempt to expand. Although one firm may conceivably be able to avoid borrowing, we shall see that, from a macroeconomic point of view, firms overall must get into debt for expansion to proceed.

Going over the post-Keynesian view of money and credit will give us, once more, the opportunity to take note of the internal coherence of post-classical theory. We shall see that the various strands of post-Keynesian economics hold views on money which have a common core, whether they reflect the French circuit approach, the Horizontalists, or the so-called structuralist endogenous view. The elements which appear to fit the least are in fact remnants of the orthodox supply and demand approach, remnants which have no room in a coherent synthesis. As such, they will be bypassed.

The main characteristics of the post-Keynesian theory of money are presented in Table 4.1 under the guise of the post-classical research programme. There are two reasons for this. Firstly, all post-classical authors, be they Radicals or neo-Ricardians, agree on these fundamental characteristics (Lavoie, 1992b). Secondly, those characteristics have a long tradition. Sylos Labini (1949, p. 240) argued, more than 40 years ago, that money has been endogenous for over 200 years. The post-Keynesian theory of money can be related to Thomas Tooke and the Banking School (Arnon, 1991; Wray, 1990, ch. 4), as well as to the non-orthodox monetary side of authors such as Marx, Wicksell and Schumpeter. Furthermore post-Keynesians theorize a monetary system which has been developed by the bankers for centuries, that based on scriptural means of payment, but which has been neglected by the mainstream as a result of its obsession with commodity money. Indeed some economic historians argue that

Table 4.1  *Characteristics of money in the neoclassical and post-classical research programmes*

| Characteristics | Neoclassical theory | Post-classical theory |
| --- | --- | --- |
| Money enters | in exchange | in production |
| Money is | an individual requirement | a social convention |
| Money | is a given endowment | as efflux/reflux |
| Money is | exogenous | endogenous |
| Interest rates are | endogenous | exogenous |
| Interest rates are | the market price of money | a distributive value |
| Focus of analysis is | substitution and portfolio effects | on income effects and liabilities |

scriptural credit money preceded fiat money and even coins (Courbis *et al.*, 1991; Heinsohn and Steiger, 1983). The proof of the above is that most of the so-called modern financial innovations, based on scriptural manipulations, were known since antiquity and were in practice during the Renaissance. 'Except for electronic technology, if an experienced banker from medieval Venice or Genova came to life again, he could understand the operations of a modern bank in a matter of days' (Niehans, 1983, p. 538). As a result, the neoclassical view cannot even be considered a correct account of past economic systems; nor can it be considered a correct account of non-capitalist monetary systems (Gedeon, 1985–6).

The neoclassical approach to money arises from the fundamental presuppositions which underlie the whole neoclassical research programme. In particular the neoclassical treatment of money is based on the general neoclassical concern for exchange and the individual. Furthermore money is seen as a given endowment, and therefore as an exogenous variable, as is any input in orthodox general equilibrium theory. Money behaves as if it were identical to any other commodity. Money is thus compatible with the neoclassical view of the world based on scarcity: everything worthy is scarce, including money. The price of money, the rate of interest, is thus market-determined, by a supply and demand mechanism, as are all goods in a neoclassical system. Finally substitution effects within portfolio assets are the focus of the monetary analysis in neoclassical theory: these are static considerations, which one would expect in a world of given and scarce endowments.

The characteristics outlined for the post-classical vision of money will become more obvious as we proceed. We shall see that money is integrated within the economy through production rather than exchange; that the creation of money arises as a result of the creation of new liabilities within the process of income expansion; that money is a social convention and that the interest rate is one of the conventions; that money must be understood as a flow, rather than as stock; and that, as a consequence, money is fundamentally an endogenous variable which can be created and destroyed.

## 4.1 THE MONETARY CIRCUIT

Post-Keynesians are well known for their claims that a proper theory must study a monetized production economy. Unfortunately, apart from references to monetary contracts, historical money costs, or liquidity preference, it is not always clear what these claims really mean in practice. The confusion is reinforced by two facts. First, the post-Keynesian models of growth and distribution that were developed mainly in Cambridge in the 1950s and the 1960s deal neither with money nor with interest rates. Second, the simple models presented by most of the partisans of the analysis of monetary production economies leave no role for the rate of interest, besides its standard effect on the investment function. Interest rates have no explicit impact in these models, neither in the determination of relative or absolute price levels nor in that of aggregate propensities to save. We have already seen in the previous chapter that the interest rate may have a role to play in the determination of the mark-up, via its impact on the finance frontier and the target rate of return. More will be said in the following chapters about the impact of the rate of interest on the level of effective demand and the distribution of income. Before modelling such impact, however, we should understand how money is introduced, and integrated into a production economy. This will allow us to better understand the causal relationships assumed in the following chapters, in particular the famous causal impact of investment upon savings.

The model of the monetary circuit that is presented below has been mainly developed by the economists of the French circuit school (Schmitt, 1966; Parguez, 1980; Lavoie, 1984b). There are, however, striking similarities with several non-orthodox works that were independently developed, mainly in Italy and in Germany. The concepts of the monetary circuit can also be found in similar forms among some post-Keynesian authors such as Graziani (1990), Wray (1990, ch. 9), Messori (1991) and Nell (1967b, 1986). The analysis presented by Godley and Cripps (1983) also conveys several similarities. The crucial element of all these formulations is that credit money is integrated into production and considered as a financial variable just as much as a monetary one. When money is being created or destroyed, there is a corresponding change in the stock of financial assets or liabilities.

**The Circuit without a Central Bank**

Let us first consider a monetary economy with only three groups of agents: the firms, the households and the banks. The firms produce goods for consumption and investment, according to their production plan and to their expectations. They distribute wages, dividends and interests to households, sometimes indirectly through the intermediation of the banks. Households provide their workforce. They receive revenues, which they either save, when acquiring financial assets, or spend, when buying consumption goods. Banks provide advances to the firms, to allow them to start production and remunerate labour and past debt. Banks also fulfil the role of financial intermediaries when households decide to keep part of their savings under the guise of bank deposits.

Let us imagine a production circuit whereby all firms plan production at the same time. As production starts, firms will have to remunerate their workers and eventually pay dividends and interest on past accumulated debt. To be able to do so, firms may have to ask for advances from banks. This is the beginning of the period of the circuit. At the end of the circuit, households will buy their consumption goods and new financial assets. The revenues that had initially flowed into the hands of the households will thus flow back into the pockets of the firms which will be able to reimburse the advances initially obtained from banks. The production circuit thus deals with the production of 1991 (the effective demand of 1991), tracing out what has happened with the incomes generated by that production (aggregate demand), even if they are spent in 1992. Keynes himself also came to realize that the links between effective demand and income could only be formally analysed in this way (Keynes, 1973, xiv, pp. 179–80). For those who feel uncomfortable with the monetary production circuit, one can imagine an agricultural economy where each spring farmers must borrow in order to pay advanced wages and the cost of raw materials, and where these advances can be reimbursed at the end of the summer when the products are sold. Indeed Le Bourva (1962, p. 38) points out that these phenomena are precisely observed in the case of agricultural crops in Africa.

In our macroeconomic model, production is assumed to be integrated. There are two sectors: some firms produce consumption goods, while the others produce investment goods. At the beginning of the circuit, firms of the two sectors distribute revenues $R_c$ and $R_i$ to households. These revenues include wages as well as the dividends and interests on past accumu-

*Table 4.2*

| Assets | Commercial banks | Liabilities |
|---|---|---|
| New loans to firms $R_c + R_i$ | | New deposits of firms $R_c + R_i$ |

lated debt. For simplification, one may assume that interests paid to the banking sector are fully redistributed to households, either as wages or as interests on deposits, as does Robinson (1956, p. 249). The firms could distribute these revenues either by reducing the liquidities they have accumulated in the past, or by asking for new bank loans. Let us assume, for reasons that will soon be obvious, that firms in the aggregate have no liquid assets; that is, they have no circulating financial capital that would allow them to finance production. In our simple model, firms do not hold bank deposits. They are forced to borrow the entire cost of production. At the beginning of the monetary circuit there will thus be a creation of money, arising from the needs of firms to obtain bank credit.

Let us be careful to distinguish money from credit. Credit is basically the loans that banks grant to firms, and eventually to households. These loans appear on the asset side of the balance sheet of banks. From the point of view of the banks, these credits to firms are financial assets. Money appears on the liability side of the balance sheet of banks. The liabilities of the banks are the deposits owned and held there by households or firms. Besides bank deposits, money also includes bank-notes. Table 4.2. indicates the changes in the balance sheet of the commercial banks. The latter have granted new loans to firms, and these same firms hold the equivalent deposits. A flow of credit money has been created *ex nihilo*, at a simple stroke of the pen. This flow of money is endogenous; it is the result of the credit needs of firms, consequent to their production plans. This is what Keynes (1973, xiv, p. 220) has called the finance motive, considering it to be the coping-stone of his monetary theory. Davidson (1972, p. 226) speaks of an income-generating finance process. Note that the finance motive is not limited to the provision of investment goods. It is equally relevant to the consumption goods, a fact underlined by Keynes: 'The production of consumption goods requires the prior provision of funds just as much as does the production of capital goods' (1973, xiv, p. 282). Credit money and production are integrated because they are both seen as a flow (Le Bourva, 1962, p. 38).

The situation shown by Table 4.2 can only be a very temporary one, since we have assumed that firms would not hold deposits unless they were

*Table 4.3*

| Assets | Commercial banks | Liabilities |
|---|---|---|
| New loans to firms $R_c + R_i$ | | New deposits of households $R_c + R_i$ |

*Table 4.4*

| Assets | Commercial banks | Liabilities |
|---|---|---|
| New loans to firms $R_c + R_i$ | | New deposits of firms $R_c + R_i - S_h$ <br> New deposits of households $S_h$ |

just about to use them. Indeed, if firms have to pay interest on their banking loans, they will borrow only when required to do so; that is, when they have to make payments, especially if the available rate of interest on deposits is much lower than that on loans. The finance motive helps us to understand the causal chain in the monetary circuit, but its temporal importance is minimal. The situation shown by Table 4.2 will soon vanish, to be replaced almost instantaneously by that seen in Table 4.3, where firms have drawn cheques on their banking account, to the benefit of the households.

Table 4.3 shows the more standard situation where those who hold money do not overlap with those who desire to be in debt (Keynes, 1973, xiv, p. 207). Still, this situation can only be temporary as well, since households will now make use of their newly acquired revenues. These can be either spent on consumption or saved. Let us suppose that, at a first stage, the money which is not spent is kept as banking deposits. If households save an amount $S_h$, their spending on consumption goods is then $R_c + R_i - S_h$. Households will write cheques to this amount, which will then flow back to the banking account of the firms of the consumption sector. After households have purchased their goods, the balance sheet of commercial banks will be as shown in Table 4.4.

Again this situation can only be a temporary one, since firms in the aggregate are now able to reimburse a fraction of their initial loans. The

Table 4.5

| Assets | Commercial banks | Liabilities |
|---|---|---|
| Loans to firms $S_h$ | | Deposits of households $S_h$ |

deposits held by firms, as a result of the consumer spending of households, will be used to reimburse the existing loans. Firms wind up with money that they do not wish to hold. They will use that money to get rid of their outstanding loans. Credit and money are being destroyed in the reimbursement process. As when money was being created, credit and money are being extinguished at the simple stroke of a pen. If we still assume that households keep all of their savings in the form of money deposits the balance sheet of commercial banks is as seen in Table 4.5.

The final step in this elementary analysis of the monetary circuit is to consider the fact that households do not keep all of their savings under the form of money deposits. Households buy some financial assets, either bonds or shares, which are issued by the non-financial corporations. The firms thus manage to directly get hold of a portion of the savings of households, which we may call $E_h$. The direct placements of households into firms will further allow the latter to reduce their borrowing from banks. In general, however, households will keep a portion of their savings as money deposits – call them $M_h$. At the end of the circuit, firms will thus be unable to reimburse part of their bank loan: the amount $M_h$. This amount will be the final increase in the stock of money, the amount that our national accountants will observe. What our analysis has shown is that this quantity of money is a residual. It has in itself no causal significance. As pointed out by Richard Kahn (1972, p. 80), it is simply 'the means by which the public hold that part of their wealth which is looked after by the banking system'. At this stage, the banking sector becomes a financial intermediary. The banks consolidate previously made loans to the firms, the amount of which is equal to the savings that the households do not wish to hold in non-liquid form. Table 4.6 illustrates this final stage.

The monetary circuit, from the point of view of the households, is now over. Firms also have to deal with their investment in capital goods. This, however, can be considered as a transaction taking place within the firms sector. We may consider that all firms wishing to buy investment goods benefit from an additional bank loan equal to the overall value of the purchased capital goods (Davidson, 1972, p. 270; Seccareccia, 1991c).

Table 4.6

| Assets | Commercial banks | Liabilities |
|---|---|---|
| Consolidated loans to firms $M_h$ | | Deposits of households $M_h = S_h - E_h$ |

When their capital goods are bought, the firms in the investment good sector receive cheques to an amount which exactly cancels the additional loan. This loan for capital expenditures is thus extinguished, and the situation described by Table 4.6 remains the same.

At the end of the circuit, households have thus increased their holdings of bonds and shares by the amount of $E_h$. They have decided to increase their holdings of money by the amount of $M_h$. The outstanding loans of the firms have thus increased by the same amount. In this model there is thus no difference between the outstanding amount of loans and the stock of money. The two quantities are necessarily equal, both at the beginning and at the end of the circuit. What should be clear, however, is that the additional amount of money held by households is largely a consequence of the new loans that were originally granted to the firms. The credits awarded to the firms have induced new deposits. Credits make deposits.

There has been no discussion of the question of the rate of interest, or that of the choice of the vehicle of household savings, but this is a subsidiary issue only. It is clear that differentials in the level of remuneration between private bonds and bank deposits will affect the distribution of household wealth between bonds and deposits, unless households require money solely for transaction purposes. These effects are not essential, in general, compared to the initial creation of credit money. At this stage of the analysis one should consider the rate of interest and its structure as an exogenous variable, a hypothesis that will not be changed substantially in later stages.

We may now draw the following lessons from our analysis of the circulation of money in the production circuit with three groups of agents. First, firms in the aggregate can never attract more money than they have distributed at the beginning of the circuit. If we assume that households generally increase their holdings of money through time, this means that firms can never entirely reimburse banks at the end of the circuit. The debt of firms *vis-à-vis* banks must increase from period to period, unless households decide to diminish their bank deposits. Firms are perpetually in debt.

Secondly, firms cannot build any circulating capital unless they decide to increase their debt towards banks at the end of the period, and unless banks accept that they do so. Any liquidities, that is bank deposits or certificate of deposits, that the firms hold overall correspond to increased unpaid loans. This justifies the assumption which was made initially, that firms do not hold any liquidities which they could deplete to finance production at the beginning of the circuit. In actual practice, when firms purchase real capital assets, they are not required to reimburse their loans immediately. This is how they acquire circulating financial capital. It should be clear, however, that what Keynes (1973, xiv, p. 219) has called the revolving fund of finance is in fact made up of unpaid debt. The revolving fund exists because banks roll over previously made loans. Even if there was no increase in the revenues distributed to households, firms would have to keep borrowing that revolving fund. This is underlined by Davidson (1987, p. 151) when he says that 'every repayment of the credit advanced by the authority must *immediately* be re-lent if activity is to be maintained'. He adds that each increase in activity 'must be *preceded* by additional bank credit creation'.

Thirdly, since firms cannot get back more revenues than they have thrown into the circuit, they cannot pay interest on their current loans. Firms can pay interest on past loans and past household savings if the banks initially lend the sums involved in these interest payments. This is why it was assumed that, at the beginning of the circuit, firms are paying dividends and interests due on the accumulated wealth of the previous period.

Of course, in historical time, the circuits of monetized production are interwoven. Firms do not all start producing at the very same moment, nor do households all spend their incomes at the same time. Firms are continuously entering new circuits of production. Loans are repaid, but immediately taken out again; that is, they are rolled over. In general the value of production is increased. As a consequence there is a continuous increase in finance requirements.

## The Determination of Profits

It may be helpful to provide a graphical representation of the monetary circuit. This will allow us to understand that there are close links between the monetary circuit and Kalecki's macroeconomic determination of profits. Indeed this is why Kalecki (1935, p. 297) has always claimed that investment expenditures are self-financing, a statement that was endorsed later by Keynes (1973, xiv, p. 222). Consider Figure 4.1. The rectangles $R_c$ and $R_i$ represent the revenues which are being distributed to the households at the beginning of the circuit by the firms operating in the consump-

*Figure 4.1 Profits in a two-sector model of the monetary circuit*

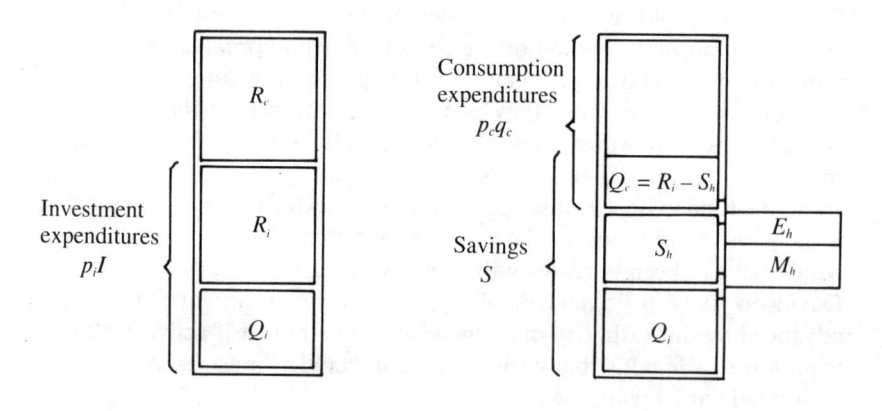

tion and the investment sectors. On the right-hand side, we can see what households do with their revenues. We know that they spend an amount $R_c + R_i - S_h$. The profits, or more precisely the retained earnings, realized by the firms operating in the consumption sector are thus equal to:

$$Q_c = (R_c + R_i - S_h) - R_c = R_i - S_h \tag{4.1}$$

These retained earnings, or internal profits, are simply equal to the difference between household consumption expenditures (usually labelled $p_c q_c$) and the revenues distributed by firms of the consumption sector. This turns out to be equal to the revenues distributed by the firms of the investment sector minus household savings. Similarly we can compute the internal profits realized by the firms of the investment sector. Again these are equal to the difference between the overall investment expenditures of firms in nominal terms (labelled $p_i I$) minus the revenues that were distributed by the firms of the investment sector:

$$Q_i = p_i I - R_i \tag{4.2}$$

The overall level of internal profits of firms is simply the sum of the above two expressions:

$$Q = Q_c + Q_i = p_i I - S_h \qquad (4.3)$$

Reduced internal profits are thus due either to firms refusing to engage in real capital expenditures or to households deciding to increase their savings with given revenues. Equation (4.3) makes it obvious that higher household savings can only reduce the level of retained earnings of firms. Higher household savings cannot reduce the final financial needs of firms. To insist on the virtue of households savings, as most neoclassical economists and businessmen representatives do, is absurd within a macroeconomic context. This was pointed out by Keynes in his famous banana parable. Following a successful thrift campaign, as households keep increasing their savings they will eventually surpass the value of investment. As equation (4.3) shows, firms taken as a whole will end up with negative retained earnings, or what Keynes called losses. If households do not want to buy bonds, because firms are making losses, their savings will be held as bank deposits, as is the case in Table 4.5. Keynes's comment to the Macmillan Committee on this issue, 'the public will provide the deposits and the whole of the deposits will be lent out to business men to make up their losses' (1973, xx, p. 77), is thus correct.

The realized internal profits can be smaller or larger depending on the extent to which the produced goods have been sold, and depending also on the price at which they have finally been sold. Profits can be smaller either because not all goods produced have been sold (the bananas have rotted), or because all goods produced have been sold at a discount. As Kalecki says, profits are invested before being created. 'Profits that are not invested cannot be retained because they are annihilated by the ensuing fall in production and prices' (1971, p. 29). This has nothing to do with the Keynesian multiplier having fully worked out its effects or not. Whether or not expectations are realized, investment expenditures of firms $p_i I$ are equal to overall savings. The total savings of the economy are equal to the savings of households $S_h$ plus the retained earnings of the firms $Q$. In this sense, investment expenditures are necessarily self-financing. This can be seen in Figure 4.1, and it is also obvious when rewriting equation (4.3):

$$p_i I = Q + S_h \qquad (4.4)$$

We can draw a further lesson from the above analysis of the circuit. One must carefully distinguish between initial finance and final finance (Graziani, 1984, 1990; Davidson, 1986). As we have seen, initial finance is of a temporary or short-term nature. It consists of advances made by the banking system at the beginning of the circuit. These advances concern the production of investment goods and that of consumption goods as well, as we pointed out when discussing Keynes's finance motive. These advances are to a large extent reimbursed at the end of the production circuit. From a logical point of view, bank advances are an absolute necessity for the production system. On the other hand, there is final finance, which concerns only the acquisition of capital goods. Figure 4.1 and equation (4.4) remind us that retained earnings and the savings of households are the means by which the final acquisition of capital goods is settled at the end of the circuit. In the aggregate, final finance is always forthcoming. Besides retained earnings, final finance is provided either directly by the sales of bonds or shares, or indirectly through the intermediation of banks, which lend to firms the savings that households wish to keep as banking deposits. In the aggregate, banks cannot dispose otherwise of these deposits. Problems may arise at the level of the individual firm only, if its level of retained earnings is too low or if it cannot attract any direct household savings. The issue of final finance is thus a subsidiary issue. What gets production going is initial finance; that is, the advances which banks grant to firms at the beginning of the circuit.

The above demonstrates that circuit theory is part of the conceptual frameworks of Keynesian and Kaleckian theories. The only difference, with Kalecki for instance, is that in the above no behavioural assumption has been introduced. There are no propensities to save on revenues, nor are there any implicit retention ratios. Equation (4.3) is thus both a version of Kalecki's explanation of profits, where gross profits are equal to investment plus capitalists' consumption expenditures, and of Keynes's fundamental equations of the *Treatise on Money* (see Lavoie, 1982; Graziani, 1990, p. 21). Keynes's banana parable, where a savings campaign leads to firms making losses, is a particularly striking example of the latter (Keynes, 1973, v, p. 158). Indeed equation (4.4), as well as the preceding ones, is a simple version of flow-of-funds analysis (Steindl, 1982). The analysis of the circulation of money highlights the causality running from investment to savings which post-Keynesians consider to be a crucial distinguishing feature of their theories by comparison with the neoclassical framework. Circuit theory demonstrates that savings play no role when production starts off at the beginning of the period, while sufficient savings are always forthcoming at the end of the period, without any necessary adjustment in interest rates. The causal elements are rather the production plans of firms and the bank loans which make these production plans possible and effective. Within this vision, the investment plans of firms are the causal element.

The fundamental difference between neoclassical economics and Keynesian economics thus remains the same, whatever the context of analysis – a short period model of fluctuations, or a long period growth model, an under-employment or a full employment model. In each case are implied suppositions concerning the chain of causation which are 'behind the equations' so to speak – in the neoclassical where the rate of interest is the main regulator, and where savings *govern* investment, and the Keynesian where investment *governs* savings, and where the share of profits in output is the main regulator. (Kaldor, 1962, p. 249, emphasis in original)

Thus the chain of causation 'behind the equations', in the long period as well as in the short period, relies upon the ability of the economic system 'to create monetary claims in advance of actual output' (Kregel, 1973, p. 159). This is the important role played by credit money, a role recently emphasized by all post-classical economists. Production can increase only if some agents agree to increase their indebtedness. To do so, credit money must be provided *ex nihilo* by the banks and there must be an increase in deficit spending (Eichner, 1987a, p. 838; Moore, 1988a, p. 313). 'Money does play an essential role for effective demand in that ... it allows the circle production–income–demand–production to break in the savings-investment link' (Garegnani, 1983, p. 78).

**The Circuit with a Central Bank**

The previous models were devoid of much institutional content: the profits of banks were not taken into consideration; there were no bank-notes, only bank deposits and cheques; there was neither a central bank nor a government. We were in a true credit economy, where commercial banks did not face any constraint set by the central bank. Let us now introduce some institutional elements, and demonstrate that the existence of these real-world factors does not modify the essential characteristics of the monetary circuit. In particular, the causal role of credit will remain.

Let us now suppose that there are monetary authorities, and that these authorities have decided to impose compulsory reserve requirements on banking deposits. Let the required reserve ratio be $t_d$, since many economists associate statutory reserves with a tax. In the situation shown in Table 4.6, banks would be forced to find the amount $t_d M_h$ of reserves. In the still simple world in which the model operates, there is no government, and as a consequence there are no Treasury bills. Banks cannot sell government securities in exchange for reserves, that is high-powered money. They cannot make use of their own banking deposits since these deposits constitute means of payments which the banks have themselves created. Still, banks are required by law to hold reserves. How are they going to get them? There is only one possibility: commercial banks must borrow these reserves from the central bank. Indeed this is what commercial banks do in many, perhaps in most, countries. In exchange for

Table 4.7

| Assets | Commercial banks | Liabilities |
|---|---|---|
| Consolidated loans to firms $M_h$ Reserves $t_d M_h$ | | Deposits of households $M_h$ Borrowing from the central bank $t_d M_h$ |

| Assets | Central bank | Liabilities |
|---|---|---|
| Loans to banks $t_d M_h$ | | Deposits of banks $t_d M_h$ |

commercial paper, which provides the collateral for the loans made to firms, central banks lend reserves to commercial banks. This is what Hicks (1974, p. 54) has called an overdraft economy. There are no liquid assets in existence. Firms must borrow from commercial banks and in turn commercial banks borrow from the central bank. Table 4.7 shows the balance sheets of the commercial banks and of the central bank when the latter has lent reserves to the former. The amount borrowed by commercial banks, $t_d M_h$, is exactly equal to the amount of reserves required. These borrowed reserves appear as deposits in the balance sheet of the central bank. This is a typical example of liability management. Commercial banks respond to the needs of their customers by supplying credit. They cannot respond to the reserve requirements by reshuffling their asset portfolio. They must do it by modifying their liability portfolio; that is, by borrowing high-powered funds from the central bank itself. It should be clear that the central bank has no control over the creation of high-powered money. The only solution for the central bank is to impose quantitative controls on new loans or to persuade commercial banks to restrain their credit activities (moral suasion). Once the loans have been granted to firms, deposits are created and the provision of reserves by the central bank becomes a lawful necessity. Commercial banks cannot obtain these reserves from any other source. They have to borrow them from the central bank. Since all of the lesser advanced financial systems and most of the more modern ones function in this way, the argument made by some authors (Chick, 1986; Niggle, 1991) that liability management would be a new phase in the development of financial systems does not seem to be correct. In overdraft economies, liability management is a perpetual necessity.

While the central bank normally has no control over the quantity of reserves, it clearly has control over the price at which it can provide the reserves. The central bank is the institution which sets the discount rate at which the reserves can be borrowed. The rate of interest which rules the economic system originates from the power of the central bank unilaterally to fix the discount rate. Commercial banks have no choice: they must get hold of the reserves, whatever their price. In this sense, the rate of interest is truly exogenous. It is fixed by the central bank, in accordance with its political or economic objectives, for instance the rate of unemployment, the distributive issue, or the external constraints on the balance of payments. The rate of interest on bank loans or on bank deposits is likely to adjust to the rate of discount set by the central bank. At the level of the individual bank, the constraints are similar. It may be that some banks have a structural imbalance between their deposits and their loans. The banks with excess deposits are then in a position to make loans to banks with a deficiency in deposits. The latter are again resorting to liability management to balance their activities. Borrowing or lending on the inter-bank market will be profitable as long as the rates of interest there are within the discount rate and the rate offered on deposits at the central bank. This inter-bank market, however, does not modify the overall reserve requirements. It simply allows some banks to move at their own pace, rather than being forced to 'keep in step' with the other banks.

The picture which arises from the above description of the laws of the monetary circuit is that of an economy endowed with endogenous credit money. Are things any different when we go beyond a pure credit economy and consider the possibility of households holding currency instead of bank deposits? Let us suppose that households desire to hold a proportion $t_{cb}$ of their money balances under the form of bank-notes issued by the monetary authorities. In the case which we have studied above, this means that, instead of holding the amount $M_h$ in bank deposits, households would only be holding the amount $(1-t_{cb})M_h$ in such deposits. They would want to hold the difference in the form of currency issued by the central bank. Households will thus go to the counters of their banks, asking tellers to withdraw $t_{cb}M_h$ from their accounts and give them that amount in cash. In distinction to what was going on before, banks cannot deal with such demands by simple scriptural manipulations. They must provide the public with actual bank-notes and coins. This is the so-called currency drain.

There is, however, some substantial similarity with the case of required reserves. Since commercial banks must provide these bank-notes, for fear of losing the confidence of the public, and since they dispose of no means of directly acquiring these bank-notes, they will have to borrow them from the central bank. Again the monetary authorities are constrained to

*Table 4.8*

| Assets | Commercial banks | Liabilities |
|---|---|---|
| Consolidated loans to firms $M_h$ | | Deposits of households $(1 - t_{cb})M_h$ |
| Reserves $t_d(1 - t_{cb})M_h$ | | Borrowing from the central bank $t_d(1 - t_{cb})M_h + t_{cb}M_h$ |

| Assets | Central bank | Liabilities |
|---|---|---|
| Loans to banks $t_d(1 - t_{cb})M_h + t_{cb}M_h$ | | Deposits of banks $t_d(1 - t_{cb})M_h$ |
| | | Notes outstanding $t_{cb}M_h$ |

provide this kind of high-powered money on demand; but the price at which the money issued by the central bank is being lent to the commercial banks is a discretionary decision of the monetary authorities (Whittaker and Theunissen, 1987). Table 4.8 illustrates the outlook of the balance sheets of commercial banks and of the central bank when the public desires currency. The reader may notice that, if commercial banks were themselves to hold bank-notes issued by the central bank, as precautionary balances to confront possible unexpected withdrawals, the size of the balance sheets would remain the same. The bank-notes in the vaults of the banks would be part of their reserves, and hence their overall borrowing from the central bank would not change. Only the composition of the liabilities of the central bank would be modified.

The comparison of Table 4.8 with Table 4.7 makes it clear that the demand from the public for bank-notes issued by the central bank plays a role similar to that of compulsory reserves. This is not surprising since both are part of what is usually called high-powered money, base money or central bank money. In both cases, commercial banks must borrow the necessary base money from the central bank. It should thus surprise no one that, in most countries where banks are indebted *vis-à-vis* the central bank and where a high proportion of money balances are detained under the form of cash currency, monetary authorities have felt little need to impose additional compulsory reserve requirements. Since commercial banks must borrow all of the required bank-notes from the central bank, at a rate of interest fixed by the monetary authorities, the latter have an appropriate control over the former despite the absence of formal reserve requirements. This was the situation of France in the 1950s and the early 1960s, since nearly half of the money stock was held in the form of banknotes (Le Bourva, 1962, p. 47).

We have proceeded to an extensive analysis of the so-called overdraft economies because they provide the clearest example of the impossibility for the central bank directly to control the quantity of money. In overdraft economies, the chain of causation clearly runs from the expectations of the firms and their demand for credit to the provision of money and high-powered money. The oustanding stock of money is a residual factor. It is a consequence of previous crucial decisions – the granting and the activation of lines of credit – and of subsidiary trivial portfolio decisions – the choice between holding one's wealth in bonds or in money. Inducing households to hold more bonds and less money has no meaningful consequence. Unless the central bank proceeds to direct credit controls, the monetary authorities have no means directly to control the supply of money or of base money. If the central bank does not supply the required amounts of base money, no one will! Unless the central bank is prepared to deny its citizens the right to have access to proper means of payments, that is currency, it is constrained to provide the appropriate amount of high-powered money, but it can do so at the price of its choice. By acting on the rate of interest, here the rate of discount, the central bank can induce firms and banks to modify their behaviour in a meaningful way. If central banks were to refuse the provision of currency, the convertibility of bank deposits would have to be suspended, and the central bank would have created a financial crisis of its own making.

One may wonder how these conclusions are changed in a model with a government and open market operations. This is what we must now tackle; and we shall see that the conclusions just reached are in no way modified.

**The Circuit with a Government**

Let us then introduce a fifth actor into our model. Let us suppose that there is a government empowered with spending and taxing authority. The Treasury of the government issues bonds when it is running a deficit. Note right away that, if the government were not running any deficit, and if it had not run any in the past, or if its debt was small relative to the outstanding stock of money and the flow of income, no monetary policy based on open market operations or the sale and purchase of Treasury bonds would be possible. The reason for which open market operations are so pre-eminent in North American financial systems is that central governments have been running huge deficits in the past, and that enormous amounts of government securities are available for trade. Without such deficits, banks could not hold any government securities in their asset portfolio. They would have none of the so-called secondary reserves which allow them to attain, by selling them when needed, the required compulsory reserves.

Note further that, in a financial system where only banks trade in government securities, a continuous expansion of the economy with a balanced government budget would necessarily entail a diminution of the proportion of government securities in the asset portfolio of the banks. Reciprocally there would be an increase in the proportion of private loans. Furthermore the proportion of government bonds held by the central bank compared to that held by the private banking system would necessarily increase. The reason for all this is that the amount of deposits held by the public for transaction purposes would necessarily grow with the absolute size of the economy; the level of required reserves would similarly grow, inducing sales of Treasury bills by the commercial banks to the central bank for the banks to fulfil their reserve obligations. In the aggregate, unless banks induce households to reduce the currency drain, more reserves can only be forthcoming by selling Treasury bills to the central bank. The theoretical consequences of the above are important: they show that the composition of asset portfolios of banks is not mainly a question of preferences. The trend in the composition of portfolios hardly depends on liquidity preference. It hangs on macroeconomic laws. These are obvious, but often forgotten, statements.

Let us now come back to our monetary circuit and study the impact of a government sector running a deficit. As a first approximation, let us assume that neither households nor firms hold government bonds. The deficit is thus entirely financed initially by the sale of Treasury bills to commercial banks. Provided the rate of return on government bonds is competitive compared to the rate of interest that is payable on loans to the private sector, banks will buy the bonds issued by the Treasury and add them to their asset portfolio. How will those bonds be paid? They will be paid in a manner identical to the way loans to the private sector are being paid. As they acquire the bonds, commercial banks create a deposit account in favour of the government with a simple stroke of the pen. The situation is identical to that shown in Table 4.2, except that the loans are now called Treasury bills or bonds, and that the deposits are held by the government. Soon, however, the deposits will be transferred into the hands of the households, so that, again, those who hold the deposits will be different from those who wish to be in debt, as in Table 4.3. At the end of the circuit, households will have spent all or a portion of the extra funds pumped into the economy by the government sector. Forgetting for the moment the possibility of central bank money, and calling the deficit run

*Table 4.9*

| Assets | Commercial banks | Liabilities |
|---|---|---|
| Loans to firms<br>$M_h - Def$<br>Treasury bills<br>$Def$ | | Deposits of households<br>$M_h$ |

by the government *Def*, the balance sheet of private banks will be as shown in Table 4.9.

Unless the deficit of the government has induced much larger transaction balances on the part of the households, the debt that firms are unable to repay to the banks will be smaller. In any case, when we introduce a government sector, there is a discrepancy between the stock of deposits and the credits granted to the private sector. The discrepancy is covered by the credits that have been granted to the public sector. It should be clear, however, that the credits awarded to the public sector do not constrain in any way the loans which banks grant to the firms. Granting loans to the public sector does not reduce the availability of credits to the private sector: in both instances, money is being created *ex nihilo*. There is no crowding out.

The irrelevance of crowding out also applies at the end of the circuit, when final finance is applicable rather than the advances of initial finance. We can see this by examining an expanded version of equation (4.3). When the government sector runs a deficit, households benefit from an additional source of income without the firms having to distribute more revenues. Suppose, as an example, that all government expenditures cover consumption goods, directly or indirectly. As above, call the value of the government deficit *Def*. The expenditures on consumption goods will thus be equal to the revenues distributed by both sectors of firms plus the additional revenues due to the deficit minus the savings of the households. The internal profits of the consumption sector, given by equation (4.1) when there was no government, are now equal to:

$$Q_c = (R_c + R_i + Def - S_h) - R_c = R_i + Def - S_h \qquad (4.5)$$

Unless households have increased their savings in proportion to the government deficit (Barro's Ricardian equivalence theorem), we see that the internal profits of the firms producing consumption goods are increased by the presence of a government deficit. The same applies to firms overall. Equation (4.3) becomes:

$$Q = p_i I + Def - S_h \qquad (4.6)$$

Equation (4.6) tells us that the deficit run by the government increases the internal profits of the enterprise sector. Government deficits do not reduce the funds available to private firms. On the contrary, government deficits generate additional internal funds for the private sector, helping firms to attain higher ratios of internal funds relative to their investment expenditures. Since government deficits help firms attain lower actual leverage ratios, one must conclude that government deficits relax the financial constraints that firms may be facing because of conventional rules. There is crowding in, not crowding out. That a sector (government) accepts getting into deficit spending allows the other sectors to increase their surpluses (savings).

After this aside, we may now see how banks deal with compulsory reserve requirements and currency in a world of government deficits. This time, banks hold secondary reserves which they can dispose of to acquire base money. They do not need to borrow any more from the central bank. Assuming similar currency drain and reserve ratios, the private banks will be selling an amount of $t_d(1-t_{cb})M_h + t_{cb}M_h$ worth of government bonds to the central bank, exactly the amount that they would have been forced to borrow under the overdraft system. This is illustrated by Table 4.10. The response to reserve requirements is now done through the asset side of the portfolio of banks. This is the only major change, compared to the situation described by Table 4.8 in the case of the overdraft economy.

Table 4.10

| Assets | Commercial banks | Liabilities |
|---|---|---|
| Consolidated loans to firms $M_h - Def$ Treasury bills $Def - [t_d(1-t_{cb})M_h + t_{cb}M_h]$ Reserves $t_d(1-t_{cb})M_h$ | | Deposits of households $(1-t_{cb})M_h$ |

| Assets | Central bank | Liabilities |
|---|---|---|
| Treasury bills $t_d(1-t_{cb})M_h + t_{cb}M_h$ | | Deposits of banks $t_d(1-t_{cb})M_h$ Notes outstanding $t_{cb}M_h$ |

Again it should be said that, if the central bank does not provide the required amounts of base money, the banks will have to borrow them through the discount window; and again, although the central bank has no direct control over the quantity of base money, it can still regulate the price at which the government bonds can be traded since commercial banks need to sell them, because of customs (currency requirements) and of law (reserve requirements). The causal scheme is still identical to the one prevailing in the pure overdraft economy, although the financial system is slightly more complicated. Things would be even more complex if true open-market operations were allowed, that is if the general public could buy and sell governments bonds. Nevertheless the additional effects encountered would be those related to portfolio decisions, which are subsequent to the causal decisions involving production and credit. They do not break the chain of causation which arises from the monetary circuit. It should also be clear that statutory reserve requirements are not a necessity. Indeed there have been no reserve requirements to speak of in Great Britain since 1971. Reserve requirements have been abolished in some countries: in Australia, New Zealand and Switzerland, for instance. Several central banks, among them the Bank of Canada, are now abolishing compulsory reserves. As long as the public desires bank-notes, which are under the monopoly of the central bank, banks face a cash drain and must obtain these bank-notes from the central bank. As a result, whatever the financial innovations that are going on, the monetary authorities keep control over the determination of interest rates since commercial banks are compulsory buyers of base money (Goodhart, 1984, p. 180).

The introduction of a sixth actor in our model of the monetary circuit, that is the external world, will await until the end of the next section.

## 4.2 THE ENDOGENOUS MONEY SUPPLY

### The Standard Post-Keynesian View

We are now in a position to recap the major elements emerging from a post-Keynesian theory of monetary production. The causal chain is the following. Firms make production plans according to their expectations; they demand advances from the banking system to implement these production plans. The demand for loans generates the creation of a flow of money identical to the flow of income. The portfolio decisions of the households lead to residual stocks of credit and of money. The central bank provides the required base money corresponding to the outstanding money stock, at the price of its choice. The supply of money is endogenous, in the sense that it is being determined by its demand, conditional on output, prices and interest rate levels. Such a view of causation is backed by recent and sophisticated empirical work (Moore, 1988a, ch. 7; Hendry and Ericsson, 1991).

Post-Keynesians are well known for their refusal to accept the standard neoclassical assumption of money exogeneity, so dear to Monetarists. The claim that the money supply is endogenous is now associated with the post-Keynesian school (Kaldor, 1970b, 1982; Moore, 1979, 1988a; Lavoie, 1984a, 1985b). This endogeneity can be seen at three levels. First, there is endogeneity at the junction between the firm and the private bank. When firms worthy of credit ask for a loan, banks create one. A flow of money is being created as soon as a new loan is being awarded to a firm. In this sense, we may say that the flow of money is credit-driven and demand-determined (Moore, 1988a, p. 19), or we may say that money has been generated by income flows (Davidson, 1972, p. 227). 'Money is *created* when banks make loans. The act of creation is also an act of expenditure and (therefore) of income creation' (Godley and Cripps, 1983, pp. 82–3). Secondly, there is endogeneity at the junction between the household and the bank. When households take a portfolio decision with respect to their wealth, the money which they desire to keep has already been created when banks made loans. This residual demand for money is necessarily accommodated by the commercial banks. The stock of money is thus demand-determined, and the main determinant of this demand is the finance motive, related to the income generated by the initial flow of loans. An accessory determinant is naturally the rate of interest and its structure, that is the portfolio decision. Thirdly, there is endogeneity at the juncture between the commercial bank and the central bank. The latter must provide the high-powered money that the former requires. Again, when reserve requirements come into effect, the loans inducing such requirements have already been made.

In a nutshell, the main post-Keynesian view of endogenous money can be presented as follows. Money is credit-driven; loans make deposits; deposits make reserves. The supply of and the demand for credit money are interdependent. The control instrument of the central bank is not a quantity but a price, the rate of interest. These views can be neatly summarized in one graph and one equation.

In orthodox monetary theory, the supply of new loans depends on the availability of free reserves. The stock of high-powered money set by the central bank determines the stock of money and ultimately the amount of outstanding loans through the standard money deposit multiplier. This can be represented by equation (4.7). Causality must be read from right to left, the independent and causal variable being the amount of base money or high-powered money $H$ under the control of the central bank, and the dependent variable being $M$. The multiplier $h_m$ is a function, presumably stable, of the proportions of money held under various forms, given their relevant reserve ratios.

$$M = h_m H \qquad (4.7)$$

As everyone knows, this standard neoclassical view can be represented by a graph in the interest rate and money space, where the supply of money is a vertical line, based on the presumed ability of the central bank to quantity constrain base money. This is shown in Figure 4.2. As many have argued, the orthodox assumption that, with proper management, the central bank would be able to set as it wishes the level of the money stock is a legacy of gold (Bootle, 1984). Money is seen as a commodity, the supply of which is given by existing stocks of gold. This is why the supply of money is assumed to be determined by the monetary authorities, independently of demand, itself assumed to be negatively related to the rate of interest. This relationship comes from portfolio analysis and substitution effects, since it is generally presumed that cash earns no interest and that deposits earn little more. As a result of the inelasticity of the money supply, any rightward shift in the demand for money function, for liquidity reasons or because of increased income levels, would necessarily lead to higher interest rates. As the traditional LM curve recalls, increases in income lead to increases in interest rates.

The post-Keynesian view assumes reverse causation. Banks first make loans and search later for the appropriate funds and reserves to cover the increase in their assets. This is illustrated in Figure 4.3. The demand for loans is the causal factor. It is assumed to be inversely related to the rate of interest because it is presumed that, eventually, higher rates will slow down the desire of some firms to go into deficit spending. The portfolio choices of households, between acquiring bonds issued by the private sector or keeping their wealth in bank deposits, will also have an impact on the outstanding amount of loans, as was shown in the first section. Following Le Bourva (1959, p. 720), we may represent the so-called money supply and supply of credit curves as horizontal lines, as illustrated in Figure 4.3 (cf. Kaldor, 1982a, p. 24, and Eichner, 1987a, p. 859). 'The supply of money is infinitely elastic – or rather it cannot be distinguished from the demand for money' (Kaldor, 1981, p. 21). An increase in income does not normally lead to an increase in interest rates. Hence the name *Horizontalists*, put forward by Moore to designate those holding the standard post-Keynesian view. Banks provide the necessary credit or the necessary deposits at a given price, while the central bank provides the amount of base money induced by the creation of money. The latter

172   *Foundations of Post-Keynesian Economic Analysis*

*Figure 4.2   Neoclassical view of exogenous high-powered money and endogenous interest rate*

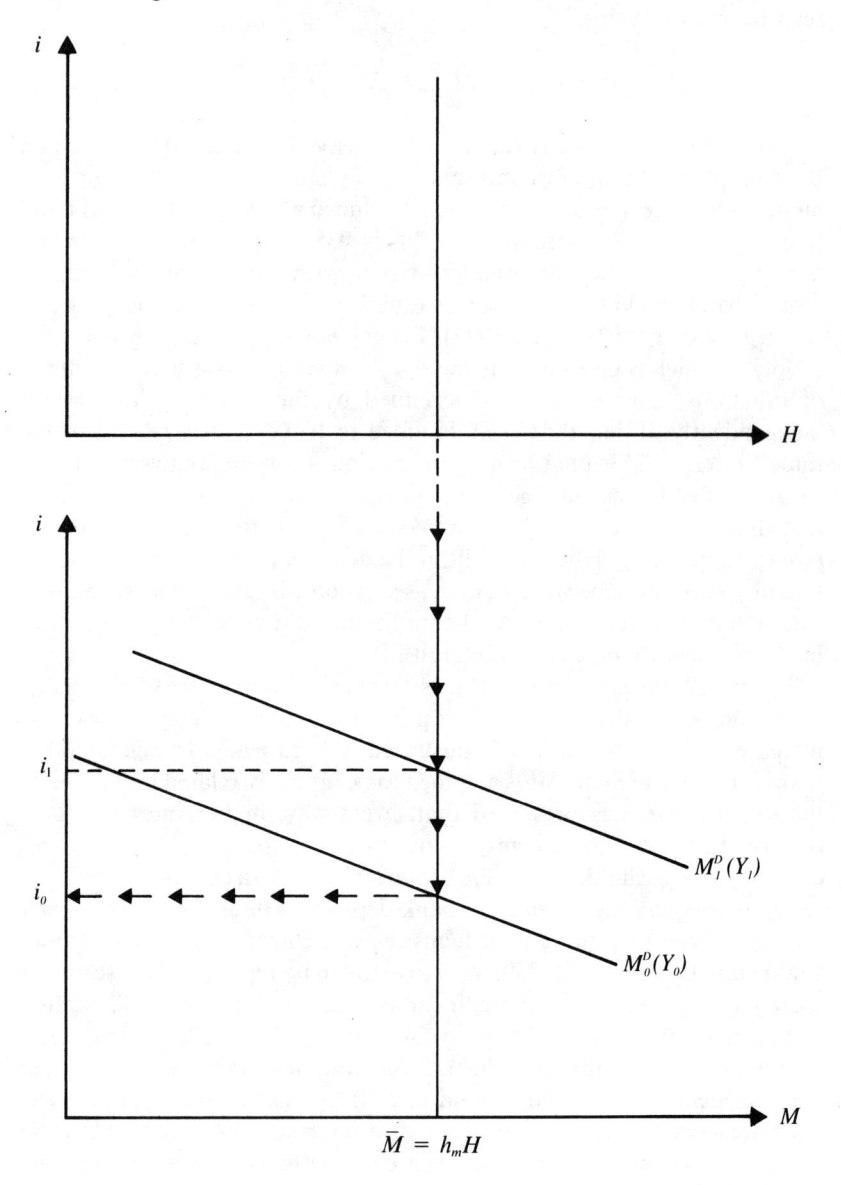

*Figure 4.3 Post-Keynesian view of exogenous interest rates and endogenous credit and money aggregates*

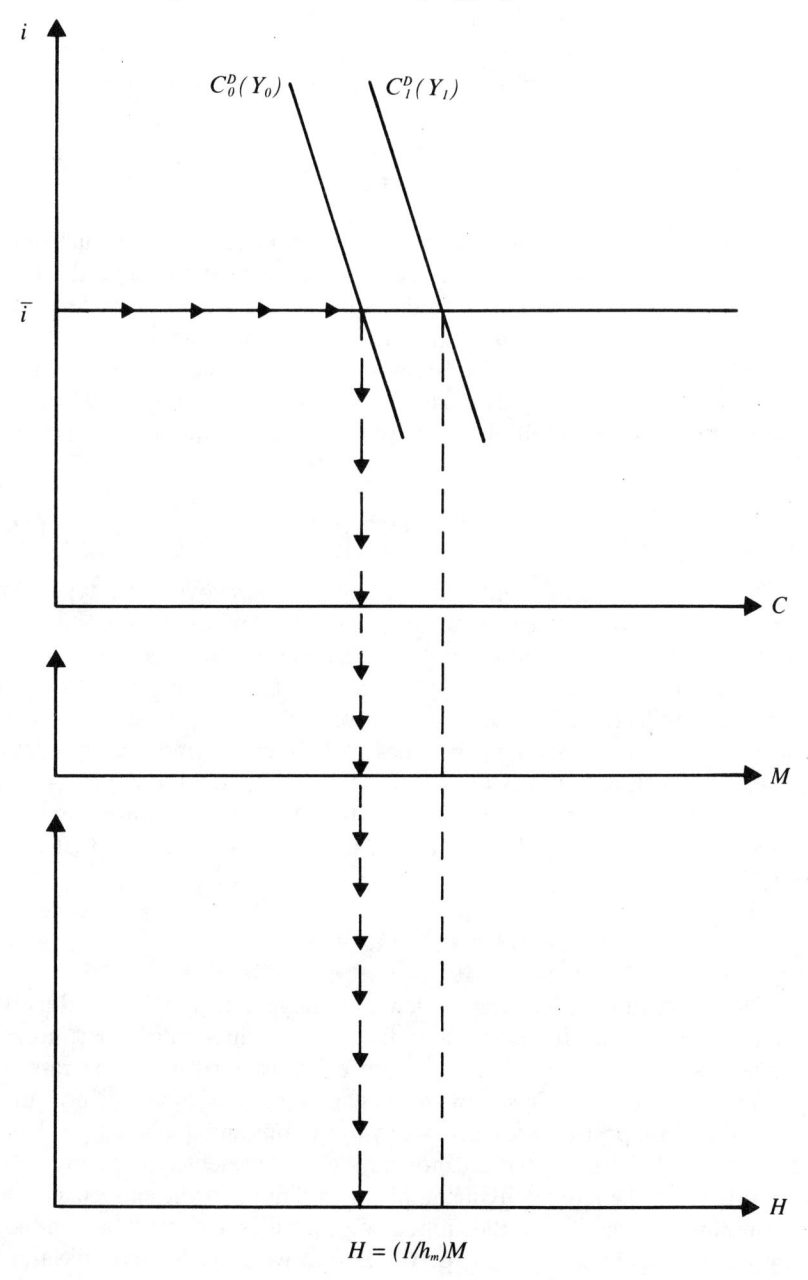

$H = (1/h_m)M$

relation may be represented by a credit *divisor*, which replaces the standard money deposit multiplier (Levy-Garboua and Levy-Garboua, 1972, p. 261). The credit divisor is represented by equation (4.8). Causality must be read again from right to left, the demand for loans, here called $C$, being the exogenous factor, while the quantity of base money is the dependent variable.

$$H = d_c C \tag{4.8}$$

Assuming away bank equity, when the financial system is such that commercial banks own no assets besides loans made to firms, the outstanding amount of loans is exactly equal to the stock of money, and therefore $M = C$. The reader can verify this equality by checking Table 4.8, which corresponds to the description of the monetary circuit without government debt. In that case, the credit divisor is exactly equal to the inverse of the money multiplier, and we may rewrite equation (4.8) as the following:

$$H = (1/h_m)C \tag{4.9}$$

In financial systems which are not of the pure overdraft type, the amount of loans to the private sector is not identical to the stock of money, as we saw in Table 4.10. As a consequence, the exact form of the credit divisor depends on the proportion of loans in the asset portfolio of the bank. Still, there is a definite relation between the stock of money demanded by the public and the stock of base money induced by it. We may then speak of a money divisor, which is again equal to the inverse of the money multiplier, as shown in equation 4.10, which can be found in Lavoie (1984a, p. 778), Rogers (1985, p. 243) and Arestis and Eichner (1988, p. 1009).

$$H = (1/h_m)M = d_m M \tag{4.10}$$

The standard post-Keynesian view of endogenous money can thus be summarized by the following four facts. Loans make deposits; money makes base money; the money supply curve is horizontal; the rate of interest is exogenous. This view of the endogeneity of money is not fully accepted by all post-Keynesians. Many objections and qualifications have been raised. It is hoped that the monetary circuit presented in the previous section will make more convincing Moore's claim that the endogeneity of money and the inability of the monetary authorities to control base money are a *logical necessity* (1988a, p. xi). Before we consider the objections advanced against the notion of endogenous money and its horizontal supply, objections which will allow us to understand better the real significance of the endogeneous thesis, let us appraise some of the arguments in favour of endogenous money.

**Bank Overdrafts of Firms**

It was said above that the endogeneity of money stood on three junctures. Since it is quite obvious that banks do not refuse the deposits demanded by the public, we shall focus our attention on the demand for banking credit by the firms, and the demand for central bank reserves by the commercial banks.

With respect to the former, it has been argued by Moore (1988a, p. 16) that banks are 'unable to increase or decrease their loan portfolios *directly* at their own initiative, but only *indirectly* by varying loan prices or selling expenses'. The volume of loans is thus 'a *nondiscretionary* variable from the point of view of an individual bank' (ibid. p. 25). The initiative belongs to the borrower, not to the lender. Of course, banks may attempt to sell loans by aggressive advertising, or by entering previously unexploited markets, but, in the end, the decision remains that of the borrower.

The main endogeneous factor at the juncture of the firm and of the bank nowadays is the extent of overdraft provision. Credit lines even exist for the banking accounts of households, notwithstanding their ability to use credit cards. As explained by Keynes (1973, v, p. 36), an overdraft is 'an arrangement with the bank that an account may be in debit at any time up to an amount not exceeding an agreed figure, interest being paid not on the agreed maximum debit, but on the actual average debit'. In countries based on overdraft financial systems, the use of overdrafts usually extends beyond the relation between the central bank and the banks. Firms also benefit from automatic borrowing facilities. The reason for this is simple. As we have shown in our model of the circuit, without large government deficits, firms cannot accumulate liquid funds unless they increase their outstanding debt. It is therefore rational for the entrepreneur to make payments by increasing his or her liabilities rather than by decreasing previously accumulated liquid assets. 'The entrepreneur, to save interest payments, as far as possible avoids borrowing in advance of actual outlays. He prefers to arrange for a "line of credit" (in the simplest case, overdraft facilities at a bank)' (Robinson, 1952, p. 81).

Where government deficits are large, and where open market operations are possible, firms may have accumulated net liquid assets which they can use to bridge outgoing and incoming payments. High interest rates, the fear of being constrained by temporary cash flow difficulties, and previous credit crunches will, however, eventually induce such firms to search for access to automatic credit-granting facilities. While it seems that American firms in the 1930s did not make use of the overdraft, in contrast to British firms (Keynes, 1973, v, p. 37), the situation has changed drastically. Most new loans to businesses in the United States are now made through pre-arranged credit facilities. Still, two-thirds of the commitments remain unused by the firms (Moore, 1988a, p. 25). This means that firms only use a portion of the agreed maximum loans to which they automatically have access. If firms want to borrow more, they can do so. The level of loans is demand-determined. The cost of the loan is the ruling prime rate, marked up according to the risk grade of the borrower.

Looking at the relationship between a firm and its bank, we may thus reassert that the supply of credit is a horizontal line. Firms usually have lines of credit which largely exceed their needs. Any decision on the part of the firm to draw on its credit line would be automatically made good, at the ruling prime rate of interest. Such loans are thus automatically created, without a discretionary decision on the part of the managers of the bank. The principle of increasing risk, as initially presented by Kalecki (1937), does not hold. Credit will not be granted to the individual firm at an increasing cost by the banking sector. The cost of borrowing is set in advance, according to the risk grade assigned to the firm, based mainly on the absolute size of its earning assets. A firm can draw as much as it wants on its agreed line of credit, at a fixed cost. If it needs more, the bank will have to take a decision. If the response of the bank is positive, the line of credit will be extended and the same interest rate will prevail. If the bank has no confidence in its customer, no increase in the rate of interest will compensate for the likelihood of failure. The bank will provide no further loan. Offering to pay higher interest rates on advances will not do. Several various authors have made this point, which appeals to common sense in a world of fundamental uncertainty. For Joan Robinson, 'It is of no use to try to attract finance by offering a rate of interest that no one believes the borrower will be able to honour' (1952, p. 83). Keynes (1973, vi, p. 228) writes that an entrepreneur who 'is unable to borrow from his bank, generally has no facilities ... for obtaining the funds he requires by bidding up the price of loans in the open market, even though he is quite willing to pay more than the market price'. Those are precisely the arguments offered by Kalecki (1971, p. 105) in the revision of his views on the principle of increasing risk when he wrote that, 'even if the firm should undertake to issue the bonds at a higher rate of interest than that prevailing, the sale of bonds might not be improved'. Either firms have access to credit at the ruling rate of interest, or they do not, whatever the rate of interest offered. The supply of credit is horizontal within the limits set by the norms of the financial system and the overdraft facilities. Beyond that the supply of credit vanishes.

The above comments may help to dismiss some confusion which arises in the discussion of the generality of the endogenous view of money. Some post-Keynesians object to Moore's *non-discretionary* lending behaviour of the banks and thus to the horizontal supply of credit curve. Some claim that banks have their own liquidity preference, a subject which we shall deal with later, when we discuss interest rates. Others claim that banks can and do constrain credit on occasion, especially in times of recession (Gedeon, 1985; Musella and Panico, 1992). This would imply that the utilization ratio of credit lines moves counter-cyclically. The claim, quite legitimate, that banks have some restrictions on their lending does not call into question the validity of the endogenous money view as presented in the preceding subsection. The theory of endogenous money is perfectly consistent with the fact that in times of recession banks are reluctant to lend, and may cut off credit lines. The reason for this is that the price of loans, the interest rate, is not a valid or sufficient exclusion mechanism. As indicated in previous chapters, because of uncertainty and the complexities of decision making, bank lending depends on whether or not the potential borrower fulfils various norms and customs. 'The amount of advances the banks can make is limited by the demand from good borrowers' (Robinson, 1952, p. 29). The norms establishing what a good borrower is change with the circumstances. Indeed the three most pre-eminent advocates of the endogenous money view have underlined the presence of these norms.

The banking system fixes a rate (or a set of rates) for the money market and then lends however much borrowers ask for provided that they can offer satisfactory collaterals. (Translation of Le Bourva, 1959, p. 719)

Commercial bank loan officers must ensure that loan requests meet the bank's income and asset collateral requirements. They must in general satisfy themselves as to the credit-worthiness of the project and the character of the borrower. It is precisely for these reasons that banks develop client relationships with their borrowers. (Moore, 1988a, p. 24)

At any one time the volume of bank lending or its rate of expansion is limited only by the availability of credit-worthy borrowers. When trade prospects are good or when the money value of borrowers' assets (collateral) rises as a result of a rise of prices, the demand for bank credit rises, but by the same token the credit-worthiness of potential borrowers also improves, so that the demand for and the supply of credit move simultaneously in the same direction. (Kaldor, 1981, p. 15)

The demand for credit which appears in Figure 4.3 is thus the effective demand for credit of firms (and eventually consumers), given the existing collateral and risk requirements for borrowing. When these requirements are modified, say relaxed, they shift upwards the effective demand curve for credit. The rules of thumb used as financial norms by the bank managers are thus shift variables which have nothing to do with the slopes of the demand for and supply of credit (Lavoie, 1985c, p. 845; Arestis and Eichner, 1988, p. 1010). In general, there will exist a *fringe of unsatisfied borrowers*, who cannot get bank advances although they consider their projected activities to be profitable at the market rate of interest. What matters, however, is the opinion of their banker. 'The fundamental banking activity is accepting, that is, guaranteeing that some party is credit worthy' (Minsky, 1986, p. 229). A banker may refuse to finance a firm for, basically, two reasons. First, he may not believe the projects of the firm to be profitable at the administered rate of interest on loans. The projects will thus not appear more profitable at a higher borrowing rate! Secondly, the potential customer may not fulfil the norms established for borrowing. In both of these cases the demand for loans is not effective. In contrast, if a firm is recognized as a credit-worthy borrower, the line of credit granted to the firm usually covers much more than its normal needs. Credit becomes demand-determined.

We shall discuss again the relationship between the borrower and the banks when we deal with the issue of liquidity preference. Meanwhile let us deepen our understanding of the relationship between the commercial banks and the central bank.

## Central Bank Money and the Commercial Banks

The crucial contention at the juncture between commercial banks and the central bank is that 'banks can always get the necessary reserves to support whatever level of liabilities they have incurred. The only influence that the central bank has on this process is to alter the price at which these reserves are obtained' (Rogers, 1985, p. 243). In the first section of this chapter we have seen why this must logically be so within a monetary production economy. We now provide statements from various participants to the monetary system which back up these claims.

As noted before, most monetary systems are under the overdraft regime. Some are perfectly so, the only assets of their commercial banks being loans to economic agents and reserves borrowed from the central bank. Many monetary systems are imperfect overdraft regimes: there may exist some sort of open market operations, but the banks are still forced to borrow funds from the monetary authorities. This may be done habitually or occasionally, directly or indirectly through dealers. The monetary market is then said to be 'in the Bank'. No one will be surprised to learn that the central bank of these countries behaves the way sketched in our description of the monetary circuit. Indeed, even the Governor of the Banque de France, when he examines the foundations of monetary policy, relies on a post-Keynesian analysis of money creation:

Recall that banks grant loans mainly to firms and borrow funds foremost from households. The . . . mechanism of money creation may then be summed up in the following manner: banks lend to firms money which they simultaneously create (money creation). The firms hand it over, for instance to their employees to pay wages, and the households keep it until they decide to spend it; then they return the money to the firms as they make purchases (money circulation). Finally the firms use the money received from the households to pay back the banking credits (monetary destruction). This scheme may be complicated but its essential structure cannot be changed. (Translation of De La Genière, 1981, p. 271)

Since the process of money creation starts with new credits to firms, the central bank must react to this creation, rather than initiate its own. As a consequence, the control of the central bank over quantities of base money is indirect, operating via the interest rates which they control. This is the clear message carried by both of the following extracts from the present Governor of the Bundesbank and a former advisor of the Bank of England.

The central bank must exploit its monopoly of central bank money, by setting the conditions – if necessary, harshly – on which it is prepared to satisfy the bank's demand for central bank money once it has arisen . . . In our opinion the bank's demand for central bank money is a given quantity in the short run; it cannot simply be 'reversed' in one month or two months. In the short run, all the Bundesbank can do is specify in which way and at what price it will satisfy this demand. (Schlesinger, 1979, p. 10)

Central bank practitioners, almost always, view themselves as unable to deny the banks the reserve base that the banking system requires, and see themselves as setting the level of interest rates, at which such reserves are met, with the quantity of money then simultaneously determined by the portfolio preferences of private sector banks and non-banks. (Goodhart, 1989b, p. 293)

Now one may be tempted to believe that the logic of the monetary circuit only applies to pure or impure overdraft monetary systems such as that of France, Germany, Italy, South Africa or even England. The contention made by post-Keynesians is that the logic of a monetary production economy is such that the consequences of an overdraft economy also apply to an economy with open market operations. That is, deposits make reserves, whatever the actual financial institutions. The American monetary system is subjected to the same constraints as are overdraft economies. This observation has been made by foreign observers of the US economy (see also Goodhart, as quoted in Moore, 1988a p. 91).

Free reserves of American banks are largely counterbalanced by borrowed reserves, which, in some months, may represent five or ten times the former. Hence, usually, the American banking system is indebted, overall, towards the Federal Reserve Banks, just like the French system towards the Banque de France ... It is totally erroneous to attribute the failure of the monetary policy of the Fed to its perpetual hesitation between *quantity* objectives over the issued amount of base money and objectives over *interest rates*. The truth is that the Fed only masters rates, and not quantities. It is through interest rates, and only them, that the Fed can hope to exert any action over the overall monetary creation of the system. (Translation of Thomas, 1981, p. 951)

One must come to realize that the American monetary system is also of the overdraft type, albeit of a very imperfect sort. We already know that firms in the United States make an extensive use of the bank overdraft. Furthermore, as in pure overdraft systems, the Federal Reserve System has a discount window, from which commercial banks can borrow base money when they have to. In contrast to French commercial banks, American private banks usually do not have to borrow from the central bank. Some of them even have free reserves. The amount of borrowed reserves nonetheless often exceeds the amount of free reserves, and hence the net free reserves of the overall banking system are negative, as pointed out by Thomas. Furthermore, as in the French case, not all banks are in the same situation. While the small country banks usually have free reserves, the large city banks run large reserve deficits. The latter, who are the loan-generating banks and the price leaders of their industry, are thus structurally indebted towards the financial system. Any change in interest cost induced by the central bank is thus passed on to the customers of all banks; but, as a counterpart, the Fed cannot avoid supplying the liquidity that the largest banks crave for. When the required reserves are not forthcoming on the open market, the Fed ends up providing them at the discount window.

As Schlesinger pointed out, the central bank cannot decide the total amount of reserves to be supplied, but it can choose in which way they will be provided. Two examples of the above can be given. One is the attempt of the Federal Reserve System to pursue quantitative objectives on monetary aggregates in October 1979. The Fed sold spectacular amounts of Treasury bills on the open market only to find its advances to commercial banks increase by a similar amount. 'The problem is that changes in borrowings at the discount window, a magnitude over which the System exerts only the most general influence, will offset the effects on total reserves of System actions taken to change nonborrowed reserves' (Davis,

1976, p. 454). A second example is that of the Bank of England, who syphoned base money out of the banking system by selling to the public government bonds the value of which was in excess of the government deficit. Commercial banks initially reacted by allowing their Treasury bills to mature, then by getting rid of their long-term public sector assets. When there were none left, the Bank of England was forced to provide huge amounts of base money by actually lending it to the banks. The quantitative restraints led to 'an almost farcical situation' (Goodhart, 1989b, p. 327).

The simple fact that the discount window has never been closed down, after so many years of monetarist domination over central bank policy, shows the impossibility for the banking system of forsaking its availability as a lender of last resort. All monetary systems must have an escape route: the central bank lends either directly, as is the case in France or in the United States, or it does so indirectly through dealers and discount houses, as in Canada and England. Of course monetary authorities can decide to tighten up the conditions under which the discount window can be used. The major impact of such a decision, however, would mainly be an increase of interest rates on money markets, such as the market for federal funds in the United States (Moore, 1988a, ch. 6). To a large extent, then, there is no difference between pure overdraft economies, where commercial banks are systematically indebted towards the central bank, and so-called market economies, where commercial banks can occasionally borrow from the central bank. If there is any distinction to be made between monetary systems of the French type and those of the North American sort, the distinction is of a legal rather than an economic nature. As was pointed out in the first section of this chapter, the possibility of open market operations complicates the analysis of the monetary circuit, but it does not modify its structure.

Still, many of those brought up in the conventional view, according to which monetary authorities can initiate increases or decreases in the money supply by buying or selling bonds on the open market and by moving around government deposits, have great difficulties considering the money supply process as fully endogenous. In fact, even some post-Keynesians have objected to the complete dismissal of the exogeneity thesis. We now turn to these objections.

**Initiatives of the Central Bank**

There are three main objections to the endogenous view of the money supply, when looking at the juncture between the central bank and the commercial banks. The first objection recalls the existence of open market operations and the traditional money creation process. The second objection is based on the concepts of accommodation and non-accommodation: only when central banks accommodate the demand for money is the supply of money really endogenous. The third objection is of a similar kind: if money is endogenous, how can monetarism be a scourge? These objections have led to the belief that the money supply is sometimes endogenous and sometimes exogenous (Chick, 1977, p. 89; S. Weintraub, 1978, p. 75). To assume that the money supply curve is horizontal would thus appear to be to adopt an extreme position, which any reasonable or eclectic economist, dealing with actual institutions, should not take. Here are two representative statements.

'Verticalists' notwithstanding, the money supply is *not* perfectly inelastic (exogenous), nor are the 'Horizontalists' right in arguing that it is perfectly elastic (fully endogenous). It is partly both. At any rate, the money supply is endogenous to a marked degree without being perfectly so. (Rousseas, 1989, p. 478)

An exogenous money system is only associated with the extreme case of a perfectly inelastic supply function. All endogenous money supply advocates have a less than perfectly inelastic supply function in mind when they argue that observed or measured changes in the quantity of money is normally an effect (of a change in the demand for money), rather than a cause. (Davidson, 1988b, pp. 158–9)

We may thus say that all post-Keynesians agree upon the statement that the money supply is largely endogenous. What they disagree upon is the ability of the central bank to directly affect the quantity of money or base money when monetary authorities decide not to accommodate demand, or when they decide to pursue offensive operations. Moore (1988a, p. 23) himself goes so far as to recognize that the central bank has the power exogenously to increase the money supply, a misleading concession, as we shall see. Traditionally economists view open market operations as the typical instrument of such active policy by the central bank. When the monetary authorities want to decrease the stock of money, they sell their government bonds to the banks or to the public; to increase the stock of money, they buy these bonds. The mechanism is well known. To induce the public to sell the bonds, for instance, the prices of these bonds are raised, allowing the sellers to realize a capital gain. The proceeds of the sale go into a banking account, to which correspond excess reserves. The money deposit multiplier process may then start off, with the bank making a new loan. The converse occurs when the public purchases bonds from the central bank: reserves fall off and loans must be called back, setting off the money deposit multiplier in reverse gear.

If we forget about the deposit multiplier and its impact on loans, this exogenous creation of money rests on a simple portfolio effect. Davidson

(1972, p. 227) calls it the 'portfolio-change process', in distinction from the 'income-generating finance process'. The public has decided to hold a larger portion of its wealth in the shape of bank deposits. This is the standard substitution effect. The price of bonds has gone up and hence interest rates on bonds and other assets are down. The public agrees to hold more money for precautionary motives. The increase in loans may be similarly understood. Loans may increase because the general fall in interest rates has induced an increase in borrowing: at the new interest rate, more projects are profitable. This has nothing to do with the deposit multiplier. It simply reasserts the orthodox interest sensitivity of investment expenditures. The interest rate has gone down as a result of the intervention of the central bank. The stock of money rises as a consequence of the increase in the demand for credit money.

My own view is that the standard monetarist argument based on excess reserves and the money deposit multiplier holds neither when the central bank tries to initiate increases in the money supply nor when it tries to constrain its growth. The only possible operative factors are the portfolio substitution effects and the interest elasticity effects on business expenditures which have been described in the above paragraph. Let us first deal with the possibility of exogenous increases in the money supply. Two sets of considerations make this possibility unlikely, the first related to large-scale operations, the other to attempts at changes on a more moderate scale. First, the historical record of the years of the Great Depression has shown that, when the central bank decides to flood commercial banks with high-powered money in an attempt to boost production, the available free reserves are not transformed into credit money (Temin, 1976; Kaldor, 1970b, p. 13). Banks wind up with excess reserves, being unable to find credit-worthy customers that would agree to borrow even at the lowest rates. In this extreme instance, the central bank is able to create new high-powered money, but the supply of money does not expand, since the value of the money deposit multiplier has decreased as a result of the increase in the actual reserves to deposits ratio.

The second reason for which central banks cannot directly create money through the money deposit multiplier has to do with the liability structure of commercial banks. In pure and many impure overdraft economies, commercial banks systematically owe money to the central bank. If monetary authorities decide to provide commercial banks with excess reserves, as they can do in imperfect overdraft systems through open market operations, these excesses will simply be used to reimburse outstanding borrowings at the central bank. This is of course underlined by French central bankers (Berger, 1975, p. 156). But the same applies to the Federal Reserve System in the United States. As we have seen, the largest

American banks are indebted towards the smaller ones, while the private banking system is structurally indebted overall towards the monetary authorities. Any undesired increase in the supply of high-powered money would be extinguished through the repayment of past debts. The decrease in the amounts of borrowed reserves would compensate for the increased amounts of non-borrowed reserves, a fact noted by officers at the Fed: 'If the Federal Reserve supplies nonborrowed reserves in excess of required reserves ... the result is likely to be mostly a paydown of outstanding borrowings and little if any buildup of excess reserves' (Davis, 1976, p. 454).

What we have here is an illustration of the efflux/reflux principle of Thomas Tooke. There can never be excess reserves as long as banks are indebted towards the central bank. This is the equivalent, at the bank level, of the claim made several times by Kaldor (1981, p. 20) that the supply of money can never be in excess of the amount which individuals desire to hold, since a firm or a household can always use excess balances for the repayment of bank loans. As Le Bourva (1962, p. 49) says, putting together themes that were later to be developed by Minsky and Kaldor, 'our monetary system is entirely based on the monetization of debts ... and on the fact that this monetization cannot exceed the needs of the public'. Indeed, firms often have automatic settlements of outstanding loans with the daily closing balance in their current accounts (Freedman, 1983, p. 103).

However central banks have recently attempted mainly to restrict, rather than to encourage, the creation of money. Again central banks can only indirectly restrict the growth of the money supply. Any extreme initiative they take with respect to base money is compensated for at the discount window in overdraft systems. In impure overdraft systems, commercial banks might let their stock of Treasury bills run off, forcing the central bank to supply government with its needed cash balances, which eventually end up as reserves in the banking system. As a consequence, there is very little connection in the short run between the open market operations of the central bank and the amount of reserves at the disposal of the commercial banks (Eichner, 1987a, p. 849; Moore, 1988a, p. 98). The causes of this chaotic relationship are the many technical factors which influence the level of reserves of banks, without any direct intervention of the central bank, notably changes in float and foreign reserves. Neither the central bank nor the commercial banks know if changes in free reserves are deliberate or stochastic. The upshot is that in the short run central banks must blindly provide the required reserves. Although they may have quantitative objectives with respect to the supply of money, base money, borrowed or non-borrowed reserves, central bankers rely on an estimate of the demand for money function to approximate their supply targets. Central bankers actually monitor interest rates, the only variable on which they have proper information and almost perfect control, even when they pursue monetarist policies (Poole, 1982, p. 578; Freedman, 1983, p. 103). This is true whether the reserve requirements are contemporaneous or lagged, as practitioners have acknowledged (Goodhart, 1984, p. 215; Meulendyke, 1988, p. 391).

It should nonetheless be stressed again that, if the central bank has no control over the quantity of base money, it can still have a monetary policy. There are mainly two channels for this policy: direct credit controls, about which more will be said later, and the level of interest rates. The inability of the central bank to set the level of bank reserves and its power to set interest rates have been clearly explained by Hicks. In the following quotation, he makes the extreme assumption that firms and households hold no precautionary cash balances; this will be so when interest rates are high. What is an open market operation under these conditions?

What happens, then, if the Bank attempts to draw cash from the market, by selling long-term bonds in the traditional manner? The only way it can do it, or appear to do it, is by itself, in some indirect manner, providing the cash which it is purporting to soak up. Borrowing at one door, it must be lending at another. It is nevertheless true that it is open to the Bank to choose the terms on which it will lend, so that the impotence of 'open-market policy' does not deprive the Bank of some power of controlling rates of interest. If the Bank tries to avoid coming to the rescue, interest rates will shoot up; still, at some point, it will have to come to the rescue. I think one can see that this is in fact what happens. (Hicks, 1982, p. 264)

Hicks concludes that the extreme case which he has described corresponds to the real world. In the orthodox view, higher interest rates on short-term bonds lead to a flight out of money. In modern economies, banking deposits earn interest rates which are competitive with the yields on bonds. Furthermore there are financial instruments the liquidity of which is competitive with that of banking deposits. As a result of these changes, higher interest rates on bonds do not induce a flight away from money, since they are accompanied by increases in interest rates on money deposits and other near monies. Consequently the negative relationship between interest rates and the (broad) money stock may not exist, as many empirical studies have recently shown (Lubrano, et al., 1986). The public has no particular reason to buy bonds instead of holding money deposits, unless relative interest rates change. Banks, however, can always increase interest rates and attract depositors, passing along the cost to their customers. Banks can also borrow the funds that have been attracted somewhere else.

Therefore even the portfolio-change process of exogenous money creation has been annihilated by recent financial and banking developments. The central bank never had the ability directly to control the quantity of base money. However it could do so indirectly through its capacity to vary the short-term rate of interest, and hence the rate of interest relative to that of money. This possibility is now foreclosed to a large extent because there are little differentials between the general rate of interest and the rate on money deposits. Any increase in interest rates would only change the composition of the money stock: agents would hold less of the bank-notes bearing no interest and more of the interest-carrying bank deposits. As a result, the negative relationship between general interest rates and the demand for money now depends on the interest sensitivity of economic activity and of demand for bank lending (Goodhart, 1984, p. 154). The slowdown in the growth of the money stock depends on the slowdown of incomes and their induced savings, of which money balances are a part (Kaldor, 1982a, p. 76). We have come back full circle: the money supply is determined by the demand for bank loans, even if the central bank does not accommodate.

**The Power of the Central Bank**

The lesson to be drawn from the above is that, whether the central bank is accommodating the demand for money or not, the supply of money is endogenous. It is thus incorrect to say that the supply of money is endogenous when the central bank is accommodating demand, while the supply is only partially endogenous when the central bank is not accommodating. The only difference between those two situations is the following: in the first case, the monetary authorities are pegging the rate of interest or are pushing it down; in the second case, they are pushing up interest rates. In terms of Figure 4.3, the supply curve of credit is staying put or shifting down in the accommodating case, and it is shifting up in the non-accommodating case. In a growing economy it is clear that the monetary authorities must always take a stance since new means of payments have to be provided (Cramp, 1971, p. 66). The central bank must decide on what terms they must be supplied. Monetary policy is represented, not by the level of reserves, over which the central bank has little control, but by the rate of interest (Kaldor, 1982a, p. 25).

The fact that the monetary authorities have an ineffective control over the money supply, or that the latter cannot be represented as a vertical or rising curve, does not mean, however, that they are powerless, as some critics of Kaldor have written (Harrington, 1983, p. 67). 'The meaning of monetary endogeneity is in no sense that central banks are impotent, or passive, or must necessarily accommodate, but rather simply that their control instrument is a price and not a quantity' (Moore, 1988b, p. 399). As the recent past can testify, the power of the central bank is substantial. Besides the use of direct credit controls, monetary authorities have the ability to hurt severely the real economy by their control over interest rates. High interest rates eventually will slow down the economy. Monetary policy is a potent tool when drastic measures are taken. This is a proposition that the post-Keynesian proponents of credit money theories have made time and time again. Indeed this is why Kaldor and others believe that monetarism has been a scourge throughout the world. The non-accommodating monetary policies pursued by central banks under the influence of monetarism have taken their toll on the economies of all countries. As a consequencce of these restrictive policies, interest rates have shot to previously unknown heights.

While small variations in interest rates have little impact on economic activity, large fluctuations in interest rates provoke large swings in production. 'Relatively moderate changes in interest rates may have no certain or predictable effect on either consumer expenditure or on business expenditure ... Only drastic and spectacular changes in interest rates can be counted on to exert a marked effect on capital expenditure' (Kaldor, 1964a, pp. 132, 134). The relationship between interest rates and bank lending, or between interest rates and investment, cannot be interpreted as a continuous one. Small increases in interest rates will generally not change the behaviour of firms or of households. Their behaviour will be resilient to quite an amount of variation. This is shown in Figure 4.4, when interest rates move between $i_0$ and $i_1$. This explains why empirical studies of the demand for bank credit based on data preceding the 1980s, with insufficient variations in rates, have found very small interest elasticities (Goodhart, 1984, pp. 139–45).

There always exists, however, a higher level of interest rates which will induce a bifurcation in the behaviour and the expectations of the entrepreneurs and of households. The exact point of bifurcation not being known to the monetary authorities, they have to make drastic changes in the level of interest rates to induce any noticeable slowdown in the level of productive activity. These discontinuities are shown in Figure 4.4 when the interest rate goes from $i_1$ to $i_2$. They illustrate that monetary control, or bank lending control, is a very uncertain business when conducted with the ordinary price mechanisms. Substantial increases in interest rates may have had no effect whatsoever on bank lending and production, but may suddenly plunge the economy into a recession. Rather than a stable step function, this phenomenon could also have been represented by a series of

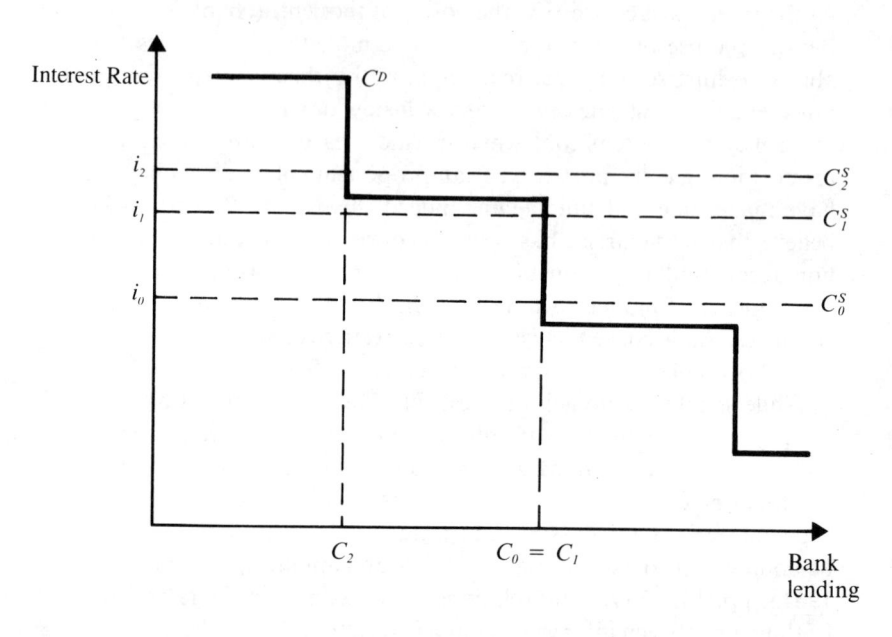

*Figure 4.4  Constancy and discontinuities in the demand for loans when interest rates are varying*

shifting demand for credit curves, representing the instability of the demand for loans function.

As noted above, the power of central banks is not restricted to the determination of interest rates. Central banks can also decide to follow a policy of direct controls over bank credit. Richard Kahn (1972, p. 128) wrote that a monetary policy is best expressed in terms of rates of interest and the amount of bank advances. Many countries, in particular those of the overdraft type, such as France, have long pursued policies of direct credit restrictions. In Great Britain these were known as the *corset*. This type of control is more rational, since it purports to restrain the growth of the causal factor, the loans which allow expenditures to proceed, rather than trying to constrain the residual consequences of these expenditures, the stock of money. Neoclassical economists are generally opposed to such controls, because they do not incorporate any market mechanism. It must be recognized that credit controls are not a panacea. Banks find ways to circumvent credit targets. This is the equivalent, at the credit level, of the financial innovations and increases in velocity which restraints may induce, and about which we shall say more in the next section. In the short run, however, credit controls can be extremely drastic and efficient, in part because they hit the economy where it hurts. As an observer remarked, 'the money stock – in contrast to oil or credit – is a meaningless abstraction' (Wojnilower, 1980, p. 324). This assessment applies as well to so-called market economies as it does to overdraft ones. The Fed found that out when, after some tampering with interest rates that led to little change in the rate of growth of monetary aggregates, it decided to introduce credit controls. These controls were in the form of ceilings on loan growth. They demonstrated their 'startling potency' (Wojnilower, 1980, p. 307).

To conclude, central banks can have a powerful impact on the economy, although they have no control over high-powered money. This impact, however, is felt either through drastic changes in the level of interest rates or through direct credit controls.

**The Compensation Thesis and Open Economies**

Before we deal more specifically with the issue of the determination of interest rates, a possible confusion in the meaning of endogenous money should be cleared. As is well known, standard neoclassical theory also argues that the money supply can be endogenous under certain circumstances. Monetarists, among others, claim that the supply of money is endogenous under a regime of pegged exchange rates. When firms get paid in foreign currency for their sales abroad, their banks draw additional reserves by exchanging these foreign currencies for domestic base money at the central bank foreign exchange counter. Countries which experience a balance of payment surplus, trade surplus or net capital inflow, will suffer from an increase in their supply of base money, with its perverse consequences for their rate of inflation. Similarly countries with a trade deficit face a reduction in their supply of money. This is the old gold-specie mechanism revived in a world without commodity money. It has led to the famous monetarist policy of flexible and market-determined exchange rates, which allow domestic monetary growth targets to be immune from being contaminated from abroad.

It should be clear to all that the endogeneity of money to which the neoclassical authors are referring in this international context is quite different from the endogeneity advocated by post-Keynesian authors. The latter point to a supply of money which is determined by demand. The former allude to a supply of money which is not under the control of the central bank but which is still independent of demand; money is still supply-determined. These two views cannot be reconciled. Furthermore the post-Keynesian view of money creation within an open economy precludes the notion that the supply of money be a function of the balance

*Table 4.11*

| Assets | Commercial banks | Liabilities |
|---|---|---|
| Consolidated loans to firms | | Deposits |
| Treasury bills | Borrowing from the central bank $CBL_b$ | |
| Reserves $R$ | | |

| Assets | Central bank | Liabilities |
|---|---|---|
| Credit to foreigners $CBL_f$ | | Notes outstanding |
| Domestic credit | | Deposits of banks $R$ |
|    Treasury bills $CBL_g$ | | |
|    Loans to banks $CBL_b$ | | |

of payment surplus (Le Bourva, 1962, p. 48). This is called by the French authors the *compensation* thesis (Berger, 1972).

The compensation thesis is a variation of the efflux/reflux principle. This principle plays a role at two levels, at the junction between the public and the banks, and at the junction between the banks and the central bank. With respect to the former level, when firms receive payments or capital inflows in foreign currency, they are generally transformed into domestic currency and deposited in bank accounts. The deposits may then be used to extinguish past loans contracted by the firms. This leads to a contraction of the money supply rather than its expansion. The efflux/reflux principle also intervenes at a later stage. When they receive foreign currency deposited by firms, banks get additional reserves as they exchange this foreign currency at the central bank. The additional base money can be used either to decrease their debt towards the central bank or to diminish their needs in new reserve requirements if their balance sheets are growing. The increase in the amount of base money obtained through foreign sources is compensated by a decrease in the amount of base money obtained through domestic sources. This is the origin of the expression 'compensation'. As Goodhart (1984, p. 192) says, there is 'some tendency towards negative covariation in these flows, i.e., they seem to interact in a way that produces some partial compensation'.

Table 4.11 helps us to understand the thesis of compensation. Suppose the commercial banks sell to the central bank the foreign currency which has been deposited at their counters by their customers. In a pure overdraft system this implies that the commercial banks are now in a position to extinguish part of their debt towards the central bank, denoted as $CBL_b$ in Table 4.11. Looking at the balance sheet of the central bank, we see an increase in its foreign assets resulting from the acquisition of foreign currency; that is, an increase in credits to foreigners, denoted as $CBL_f$. This increase in foreign assets is being compensated, however, by the decrease in its domestic assets, because of the decrease in its outstanding loans $CBL_b$ to commercial banks. The mechanism is similar to that outlined in a previous subsection (see p. 183), when the central bank attempts to create reserves that the commercial banks do not need: the free reserves are used to extinguish past debt rather than to create new monetary liquidities.

In an impure overdraft system, where banks hold government bonds and do not borrow from the monetary authorities, banks would try to get rid of their excess reserves by buying Treasury bills. Banks would not make new loans to previously unsatisfied customers since we have assumed that banks are 'loaned up'; that is, they have already lent to all of those who fulfil borrowing requirements (Le Bourva, 1962, p. 50). If the central bank responds to the downward pressures being exercised on the prices of government bonds it will sell the bonds that the commercial banks want to acquire. As in the pure overdraft case, the increase in the amount of foreign credit on the asset side of the balance sheet of the central bank is compensated by a decrease in domestic credit, here the domestic credit to government. The Treasury bills in the hands of the central bank, denoted by $CBL_g$, would decrease. The mechanism described here is similar to that called *sterilization*, except that the central bank does not have to initiate the sales of bonds. Sterilization is endogenous because of the compensation mechanism.

The theory of endogenous money and its compensation thesis in the case of an inflow of foreign currency may thus be summarized in the following manner: (1) the non-financial beneficiaries of foreign currency may use it to diminish their outstanding debt towards the commercial banks; (2) the banks may use this additional source of base money to diminish their debt towards the central bank, or (3) to diminish the rate of growth of their debt towards the central bank in a fast growing economy; (4) the banks may use the foreign source of base money to diminish their sales of Treasury bills to the central bank which are made in order to acquire compulsory reserves; or (5) if the economy is expanding slowly by comparison with the incoming flow of foreign currency, the banks may buy government bonds and accumulate secondary reserves.

If there is an outflow of foreign currency, the compensation principle and endogenous sterilization will play in reverse. Banks will increase the pace at which they borrow from the central bank and the central bank will have to increase the pace at which it provides liquidities to the banking system. All the issues and answers which have been discussed in the previous two subsections arise again. One should further note that, when foreign exchange flows are related to trade rather than to autonomous capital flows, there is an additional element of monetary endogeneity. Trade surpluses induce additional economic activity and therefore additional base money requirements, which are then provided without the central bank having to intervene directly. Reciprocally trade deficits slow down the economy and the needs for base money, which will be partly accommodated by the diminished foreign credits on the asset side of the balance sheet of the central bank.

Two major outcomes for fixed exchange rates emerge from this discussion of the compensation thesis. First, as pointed out by Arestis and Eichner (1988, p. 1015), 'so long as it is recognized that money supply is credit-driven and demand-determined, the exchange rate regime is of absolutely no consequence in the determination of money and credit'. Flexible exchange rates do not make monetary policy more independent from international disturbances than a fixed exchange rate regime. It also follows, even if one believes that excessive money growth is the source or the permissive factor of inflation, that countries running trade surpluses or capital inflows are not prone to future inflationary forces since there is no supply-led endogenous creation of money as the monetarists would have it. Monetary policy need not be perpetually restrictive, in the case of trade deficits to induce compensating capital flows, or in the case of trade surpluses for fear of inflation. This also puts in jeopardy the law of comparative advantage since there are no forces at work in countries accumulating trade surpluses to make prices likely to rise, while those of countries suffering from trade deficits are not likely to decrease.

## 4.3 INTEREST RATES AND LIQUIDITY PREFERENCE

**A Generalized Liquidity Preference**

Some post-Keynesians have lamented the fact that the emphasis on endogenous credit money has precluded much significance for liquidity theory (Dow and Dow, 1989, p. 147). In his review of Moore's book, Wray (1989, p. 1187) notes that 'there is no room for liquidity preference in the determination of interest rates'. These statements can be considered as both true and incorrect. It is true that in a theory of endogenous credit money, the role attributed to liquidity preference by the earlier neoclassical Keynesians loses its significance. The preference of the public for holding money does not play any role, either in the determination of the rate of interest or in that of the level of employment. In fact this was acknowledged favourably by Kaldor himself when he commented that 'liquidity preference turns out to have been a bit of a red herring' (1982a, p. 26) and also when he mentioned that 'if we regard money as an endogenous factor, liquidity preference and the assumption of interest-elasticity of the demand for money ceases to be of any importance' (1985b, p. 254). These statements seem to bring comfort to those neo-Ricardians who have always been reluctant to assign any role of importance to liquidity preference in the denial of full employment equilibrium (Garegnani, 1978; Eatwell and Milgate, 1983b, p. 7).

There is, nonetheless, a role for liquidity preference in a theory of endogenous credit money. To understand such a role, the meaning of liquidity preference has to be enlarged to all agents of the economy and to all financial instruments, as Keynes had it in his *Treatise on Money*, rather than being limited to households and money, as in the *General Theory* or the standard IS/LM model. Such a generalization has been proposed under various guises by several post-Keynesian authors (Kregel, 1984–5; Mott, 1985–6; Le Héron, 1986). Under those conditions, liquidity preference becomes a determinant of some interest rates, but its role is greatly diminished, limited as it is to temporary rather than permanent situations. This interpretation will allow us to show that the monetary views of the more fundamentalist of the post-Keynesians can be reconciled with those of the neo-Ricardians. The study of liquidity preference will also clear up further matters concerning the elasticity of the supply of money and the shape of its curve.

Up to now we have considered a single rate of interest, assumed to be determined by the monetary authorities. That rate of interest is exogenous. It is a purely monetary phenomenon. It does not depend in any stable way on economic variables, and certainly not on the marginal productivity of capital. The rate of interest is in fact a distributive variable based on monetary conventions. Eichner (1987a, p. 860) is quite clear about this when he writes that the basic rate of interest 'is a politically determined distributional variable rather than a market determined price'. Similarly, Rogers (1989, p. 253) claims that 'the interest rate reflects psychological, institutional, and other historical factors which cannot be specified *a priori*'; it is, in other words, an exogenous variable. This treatment is precisely what Moore (1988a) and Kaldor (1982a, p. 24) advocate, and also reflects Pasinetti's (1974, p. 44) view of how to interpret Keynes's liquidity preference theory. The economic model becomes causal-recursive with the rate of interest being exogenous; that is, influenced by the decisions of the monetary authorities and possibly by the sentiments of the public about liquidity.

By considering the rate of interest as an exogenous variable, post-Keynesians such as Moore and Kaldor are thus in complete agreement with neo-Ricardians. For instance, Pivetti (1988, p. 282) is of the opinion that 'interest rate determination is not subject to any general law ... The level of interest rates prevailing in any given situation appears clearly to be determined by the monetary authorities on the basis of policy objectives and constraints'. Similarly Panico (1988, p. 140) argues that Keynes's central point was the 'historical conventional character' of the determination of the rate of interest. This was precisely the view taken by Townshend in his response to Hicks's review of Keynes's *General Theory*. Anticipating the infamous IS/LM model, Townshend (1937, p. 157) contended that the rate of interest is 'an independent variable in the scheme of causation', and then went on underlining the importance of customs and conventions.

One may wonder if there are any limits to the value which this conventional rate of interest can take. There are limits which various authors have underlined, but these limits are rather indicative. On the one hand, the nominal rate of interest on bank loans should not be greatly below the rate at which the prices of reproducible commodities are increasing, otherwise anyone could make a gain by producing now and selling later (Eichner, 1987a, p. 860). On the other hand, the rate of interest cannot be above the rate of profit of the economy, otherwise all the surplus would go to the rentier and none to the entrepreneur. There is no *natural* rate of interest, as no rate of interest can ensure full employment. Since interest rates have an impact on income distribution, the consequences on output and employment of a lower rate of interest depend on the effect over effective demand, as we shall see in Chapter 6. Recalling that the rate of interest is fundamentally a distributive variable, the best that can be done is to define a *fair* rate. Such a fair rate is obtained when, *grosso modo*, the real rate of interest is equal to the rate of increase of labour productivity (Pasinetti, 1980–1). There is, then, no transfer of resources from the industrial to the rentier sector, or vice versa. This means that the rentiers are holding on to their purchasing power in terms of labour units. The fair rate of interest is equal to the rate at which the income of the representative person is growing (Harrod, 1976, p. 74). With inflation, the fair rate of interest would be equal to the rate of inflation plus the rate of growth of labour productivity. Under these conditions an amount of money equivalent to one hour of labour time, if lent at that fair rate of interest, will still be worth one hour of labour time when recovered with its interest returns.

The purchasing power of the rentiers increases only if the productivity of the overall economy and the purchasing power of workers have increased.

Two other distinctions, both made by Rogers (1989, p. 252), will help us to integrate a liquidity preference theory into an endogenous theory of money with conventional interest rates. We may first distinguish, in the traditional manner, short-term interest rates from long-term ones. This will allow us to introduce the liquidity preference of the households. We must also distinguish between transitory and permanent interest rate changes. An interest rate may be considered permanent when the public and the banks regard the current rate of interest set by the monetary authorities as the normal one; that is, the one that ought to prevail under existing conditions. When the rate of interest is at its permanent level, liquidity preference plays no role. By contrast, when the current rate of interest is considered as transitory, the liquidity preference of the public and of the banks will have a discernible impact on the rates of return of the various assets. In particular the rate of interest on short-term bills will be different from the rate of interest on long-term bonds.

In a revamped version of liquidity preference, the distinction between transitory and lasting changes in interest rates is crucial. Assuming that all agents of the economy show some preference for liquidity, we now have to consider three distinct rates of interest, rather than a single one. First, as we have previously emphasized, the monetary authorities determine the discount rate. This is the base rate, in analogy to base money, upon which all the other rates depend. In imperfect overdraft economies, where commercial banks rarely borrow from the central bank, the base rate may not be the discount rate, but a short-term money rate, such as the Federal funds rate or the Treasury bill rate, which is under the control of the central bank. Indeed in many monetary systems, in particular those where the money market 'is not in the Bank', the discount rate is automatically set just above such a money rate. The discount rate, or the rate on Treasury bills, may be considered as the expression of the liquidity preference of the central bank. Secondly, commercial banks express their liquidity preference by setting short-term lending rates (prime rates) at levels that are different from those offered or determined by the central bank, and by resisting changes in interest rates initiated by the central bank. The liquidity preference of banks may also be expressed by the norms required to be qualified as a credit-worthy borrower as well as the maximum amounts that may be borrowed on overdrafts. Thirdly, the long-term rate of interest, or more precisely the spread between the long-term and the short-term rates of interest, reflects the liquidity preference of households and non-banking financial institutions (Wells, 1983, p. 533). According to this view, the spread between long-term and short-term rates is determined by the preferences of the rentiers towards liquid or illiquid positions. The owners of financial capital or their representatives on financial markets thus decide on the spread between rates on short-term bills and rates on long-term bonds. Rates of interest, even when liquidity is introduced, are thus exogenous: they depend on preferences and tastes that cannot be explained.

We can sum up the above by saying that liquidity preference sets all other rates of interest around the level determined by the central bank. The central bank acts as a sort of price leader, which the banks follow more or less loosely. This means that liquidity preference sets the term structure of interest rates (Mott, 1985–6, p. 224). But it cannot set the base rate, upon which all the other rates depend. The base rate itself, that is the discount rate or the money rate set by the central bank, is the truly exogenous factor. It is a convention. Any change in interest rates orchestrated by the monetary authorities will be considered transitory as long as banks and rentiers have not adjusted to it. As the public and the banks come to believe that the current discount rate or base money rate is the normal rate of interest, it becomes the normal permanent rate. Then, imperfections excluded, the central bank discount rate, the lending rate and the long-term rate of interest will all be equal. In particular, when the public expects the current rate of interest to be no different in the future, there should be little differential between short and long rates.

This, in my view, is how the lack of importance attached to the liquidity preference theory of money by the neo-Ricardians can be reconciled with the post-Keynesian emphasis on that theory. Since neo-Ricardians are generally concerned with so-called permanent effects, rather than transitory ones, the above analysis shows that, in long period analysis, liquidity preference indeed has no particular role. What is of importance is the exogenous rate of interest; that is, the permanent rate, the effects of which will be discussed in Chapter 6. By contrast, in the short period, liquidity preference may play a causal role. This in fact is precisely how Kregel (1976, p. 219) recommends that the real world should be *tamed* when dealing with models of growth and capital accumulation. While some variables (such as capacity) become endogenous, others have to become given. Kregel regards liquidity preference and propensities to save as examples of the latter.

This view of liquidity preference gives much importance to the conventional base rate of interest established by the central bank. It should be clear that, to some extent, the convention adopted by the central bank depends on the conventions which rule in the private economy. At any moment of time, the behaviour of the monetary authorities may be influenced by what the most powerful groups in society, presumably the rentiers, think the normal rate of interest should be. The vagaries in the lobbying strength of the various groups within society may alter the convention held by the central bank and its monetary policy. The central bank may even relinquish its base rate policy, fearing a conflict with *market opinion*, in particular that of international financial markets, or being fearful of financial instability. As a consequence one may find that the interest rates under the control of the public and of the banks, such as the prime rate and long-term rates, have an influence upon the short-term money rates or even the discount rate set by the central bank (Pollin, 1991). This would mean that the managers of the central bank have yielded to the conventional opinion of the financial markets. Ultimately, however, the decision to determine the normal rate of interest rests on the shoulders of the monetary authorities. As noted by Pivetti (1985, p. 79), provided the monetary authorities are sufficiently persistent and consistent, they have the power to impose their own conventional view of what the rate of interest should be. 'If [the authorities] persist resolutely, a moment will come when the bears are convinced that the new low rate has come to stay' (Robinson, 1952, p. 30).

## A Rising Supply Curve of Money?

The view of liquidity preference which has been presented above superposes an exogenous opinion of what the interest rate should be upon an already exogenous base interest rate. The banks and the rentiers have a conventional view of the normal rate of interest, which may or may not conflict with the view of the monetary authorities. In the former case, the current rate of interest is of a temporary nature; in the latter case, the current rate is permanent. There is, however, another interpretation of the role of liquidity preference, according to which there are inescapable forces which, in a period of expansion, end up generating high interest rates. Graphically, as shown in Figure 4.5, it is represented by a supply curve of credit or of money which at some point becomes a rising curve. In this representation, an increase in output eventually leads to higher interest rates. We shall also deal with the case in which the inelasticity of the supply of credit is due to the restrictions imposed by the central bank. In both cases, I shall argue that it is a mistake to represent the supply function of credit as a rising curve.

The importance of liquidity theory for the rising supply curve of credit has mainly been emphasized by fundamentalist post-Keynesians or followers of Minsky. The major argument is that growth is conducive to more fragile financial structures. During a boom there is a tendency towards a more leveraged financial structure, both for firms and for banks

*Figure 4.5 Rising interest rates with increases in output and the rising supply curve of credit money*

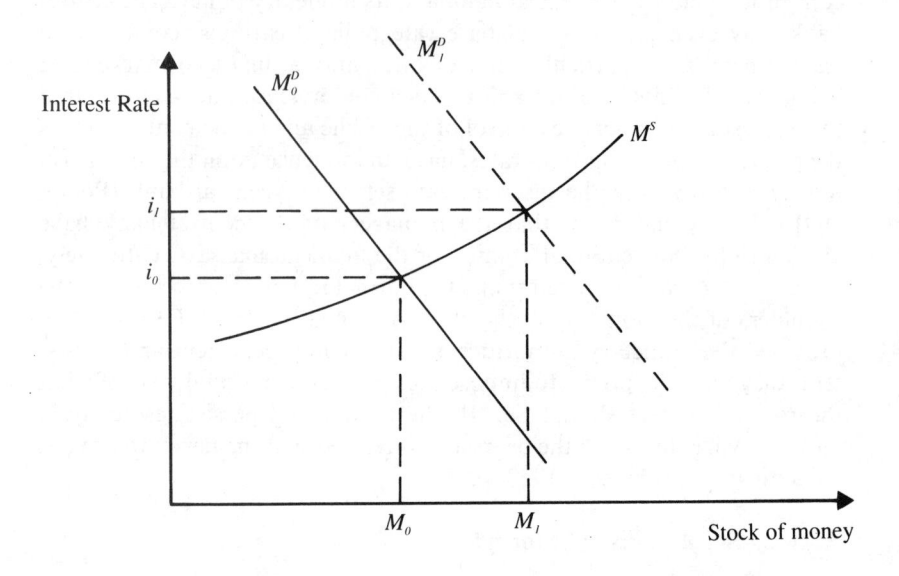

or other financial institutions. The gearing ratio of firms will become higher, while the ratio of banks' liquid assets will fall off. Both trends will induce the banks to increase lending interest rates, in order to compensate for the higher perceived risk, and also to reduce credit.

> Can liquidity preference or leverage ratios affect the size of the markup? That is, as banks balance sheets expand, do banks require rising interest rates to induce them to leverage equity and liquid assets? If so, then the money supply curve is upward-sloping rather than horizontal. (Wray, 1989, p. 1188)

> Up to some point, determined by conventions regarding acceptable balance sheets, banks will increase the money supply without raising interest rates on loans ... Beyond some point, banks will require higher interest rates, even for established customers, to compensate for greater perceived risk associated with further expansion of balance sheets. (Wray, 1991, p. 15)

The idea that more illiquid or more leveraged balance sheets induce higher interest rates surely appears to be a reasonable one. We must nevertheless ask two sets of questions. First: does the leverage ratio of industrial firms increase in expansion times? Do the banks care if it does? Secondly: do the balance sheets of banks become less liquid in expansion times? Do the banks care when it happens overall?

The first set of questions correspond to Minsky's financial fragility hypothesis. According to Minsky (1976, chs 5 and 6), as the boom develops, the acceptable leverage level may rise and hence firms will take more risks and more leveraged positions. Firms switch from conservative hedge finance to risky speculative finance, as the past historical record has shown (Minsky, 1980, p. 518). Minsky's financial hypothesis may, however, be challenged from both the historical and the theoretical point of view. With respect to history, Isenberg (1988) has shown that the debt ratios of manufacturing firms in the 1920s diminished rather than increased during the boom preceding the Great Recession. On the other hand, Niggle (1989) shows that debt ratios of non-financial corporations in the USA generally increase during the upswing, but that a substantial part of this increase is due to financial lending to customers at home and to financial investment abroad. Factual evidence, then, is only partially favourable to Minsky's thesis.

With respect to theory, the case of the representative firm developed by Minsky does not necessarily extend to the macroeconomic setting (Lavoie, 1986a). When investment increases, profits increase as well, unless other elements, such as a lower rate of savings by households or a deficient trade balance, induce reduced profits. Assuming away these external factors, the realized leverage ratio is more likely to fall, although entrepreneurs and their bankers are willing to increase the debt ratio. This is occasionally recognized by Minsky, for instance when he says that 'the improvement of realized profits partially frustrates the planned debt-financing of investments of firms' (1976, p. 114). The famous graphical representations of borrowing and lending risks popularized by Minsky (1976, p. 112) are thus another example of the fallacy of composition.

There are of course strong similarities between Minsky's arguments and those that are often attributed to Kalecki's earlier writings to justify a positive relationship between the level of income (or the rate of investment) and the rate of interest. One should be aware, however, that the macroeconomics of Kalecki's 1937 version of the principle of risk are such that expansion may lead to actual financial ratios that are less risky, a paradox noted some time ago by Robinson (1952, p. 23). This is not to deny that under some specific conditions expansion may lead to reduced profits, and hence to increased leverage. But even if this is the case, we cannot presume that interest rates will necessarily rise as a consequence of the increased leverage, for, as Minsky himself argues, in the expansion the acceptable degree of leverage increases, so much that banks encourage under-levered firms to go into debt and conform to the more relaxed emerging standards (Minsky, 1980, p. 517). Indeed, this may explain the previously mentioned findings of Niggle (1989): in a closed economy the overall leverage ratio does not increase in a boom, although each firm desires to take advantage of the more relaxed borrowing rules; firms can successfully increase their leverage ratio only by borrowing to invest abroad. On the other hand, when expansion ends and when more stringent borrowing standards are put in place by worried bankers, we should expect the number of credit-worthy borrowers to fall off. The banks may then judge that the rate of interest imposed by the central bank is too low and react accordingly.

We are thus left with the balance sheets of the banks to explain why there should be a positive relationship between the level of national income and interest rates. Those who take such a position can easily rely on the writings of Keynes, for it is Keynes (1973, xiv, p. 219) himself who sums up his liquidity preference theory by claiming that the rate of interest is determined by the interplay between the liquidity preference of the public and that of the banking system. He adds that the supply of money may be rising as it 'depends on the terms on which the banks are prepared to become more or less liquid' (p. 221). Keynes believed that an increased demand for initial finance could not be met without a rise in the rate of interest, unless the banks are ready to augment loans at the current rate of interest. 'But why shouldn't they?', asks Kaldor (1981, p. 21). According to Wray, when banks make loans they check their own level of liquidity, that is the ratio of loans to equity and the ratio of loans to safe assets such as government bonds and reserves. These ratios rise in boom times. 'Even where additional loans can be made which are no more risky than loans which have been made previously, banks may require higher interest rates to compensate for riskier leverage ratios' (Wray, 1990, p. 179). One may object that, if banks are making more profits on their loans than on their safe assets, the value of their equity should grow at a faster rate than their total assets, so that the rise in the loans to equity ratio during the expansion may be compensated by the fall in the total assets to equity ratio.

Several other objections can be raised against the analysis of the rising supply curve based on the liquidity ratios of banks. First it can be noted that Keynes (1973, xiv, p. 223) undercuts his own argument in the conclusion of his article on the liquidity of banks. He observes that banks pay no attention to the unused portion of their customers' overdraft facilities. Often their overall amount is even ignored. Since the unused portion of a credit line can be drawn at any time, inducing an increase in both the illiquid assets and the liabilities of the bank, one must conclude that banks do not really care whether or not the share of loans in their portfolio is increasing. If they did, the use of overdrafts would be curtailed. This brings to the forefront the fact that the business of banking is to create credit money. Banks make profits by lending to credit-worthy borrowers.

In that sense, they prefer illiquidity to liquidity (Sylos Labini, 1949, p. 240). As we have seen in the first section, commercial banks in pure overdraft economies own no liquid assets. They simply borrow the funds that they require. How is bank liquidity to be measured? Indeed, as pointed out by Moore (1988a, p. 33), there is little reliable yardstick to measure bank liquidity when banks count on liability management. This should come as no surprise, since overdraft systems are a pure instance of liability management.

Again one has to distinguish a microeconomic situation from the macroeconomic picture. If a single bank is pursuing aggressive lending policies, as it could in the present environment of generalized liability management, its credit-worthiness may become questionable and other financial institutions may refuse to lend to it. The main objective limit to the expansion of a bank is the rate of expansion of the other banks and the norms of prudent and acceptable behaviour self-imposed by the banking industry (Wray, 1990, p. 182). This is another application of Kalecki's theory of increasing risk. But if all banks 'move forward in step', they can safely create all the credit money which is required for production to increase (Keynes, 1973, xiv, p. 23). There is no theoretical limit to the amount of credit money which, overall, the banking system can create to satisfy the requirements of increased activity (Le Bourva, 1962, p. 46). The norms to follow are the average leverage and liquidity ratios of all the other banks of the same size. If all banks are expanding in step, all banks will experience similar transformations of their balance sheet. Indeed this is why norms slowly change in tranquil circumstances, when economic conditions are such that average structural coefficients cannot but alter. This is recognized in the end by Wray, who writes that 'an increase in money demanded to finance rising aggregate demand will not raise interest rates unless people believe it should' (1990, p. 188).

An upward-sloping supply curve of credit money, of the sort represented in Figure 4.5, cannot be justified on the grounds of bank liquidity preference. Those who support such a view of the endogeneity of money must ultimately rely on the non-accommodating behaviour of the central bank, and the fact that interest rates are not always pegged (Rousseas, 1986, p. 94; Niggle, 1991, p. 142). This is clearly the case of Seccareccia (1988, pp. 56-8), who argues that, as banks extend more credit in a non-accommodating situation, they are forced to attract deposits with lower reserve requirements. These deposits may be less liquid and therefore less attractive in the eyes of the public. Higher interest rates must thus be offered to depositors, to incite them to modify the structure of their deposit balances. The rising cost of funds on the liability side leads to increases in the lending rate of interest. According to Seccareccia, it is the changing structure of the liability side of the balance sheet of banks, rather than that of the asset side, which is responsible for the upward-sloping supply curve of credit. The composition of the stock of money changes as a result of the non-accommodating behaviour of the central bank. This goes to show that, while banks can avoid the quantitative consequences of tight money policy, they cannot fully avoid its interest rate consequences, despite the introduction of innovative liabilities, as we shall see further in the next section. If lending interest rates rise, it is because the central bank has so decided. It is not an endogenous feature of the system.

It is true that Kaldor (1939, p. 14) himself proposed a rising money supply schedule, but this was his initial reaction to the standard vertical supply curve, not a fully thought-out theory of endogenous credit money. Notwithstanding all the factual and logical reasons which have already been presented in the previous section to reject such a conceptualization of the supply of money, it should be remembered that central banks have *discretion* in setting interest rates. The decision to raise interest rates is a political decision which is not necessarily related to increases in the money supply as such. When the stock of money expands, rates do not have to rise; they may also decrease. Indeed, as Moore (1989, p. 486) points out, there is an inconsistency in a rising supply curve of money. When interest rates decrease, the reduction is said to be due to an exogenous shift in the monetary policy; when interest rates rise, they are said to be the result of normal endogenous forces. It must be granted that some central banks make use of an explicit rising marginal cost schedule, over which the borrowing costs for commercial banks rise in steps. The quantitative range of these steps is continuously revised upwards, however, so that the rising schedule is again a relevant microeconomic factor rather than a macroeconomic one.

It is therefore a mistake to represent the policy of the central bank as a rising supply curve in the interest rate and money space (Eichner, 1987a, p. 858). To portray the monetary stance of the central bank, or the liquidity preferences of banks, through an upward-sloping money supply is to reintroduce the standard LM curve of neoclassical analysis. Indeed Hicks (1937, p. 157) himself made no assumption of a vertical money supply curve to construct his infamous LM curve; he simply assumed a rising supply curve of money. This leads to the belief that there exist inexorable forces, those of neoclassical scarcity, that propel interest rates up whenever national income or money demand increases, as some post-Keynesians still portray it (Jarsulic, 1989, p. 43). To claim that a growing economy will eventually trigger rising (real) interest rates, presumably as a consequence of excess credit demand or lack of savings, is to reintroduce scarcity analysis through the back door. This would be the exact antithesis to the endogenous credit money theory.

Of course no one would deny that in output-accelerating situations central banks are tempted to raise nominal interest rates, either as a result of balance of payments constraints or because of possible inflationary pressures, exacerbated in the eyes of the central bank by the lobbying of those rentiers without indexation clauses. However central banks also push up interest rates when these pressures are absent, to counter what they perceive to be exchange rate misalignments, for instance. Taking a world view, there are no natural forces which inescapably push up interest rates (nominal or real). As Robinson (1952, p. 128) points out, 'when the boom is spread evenly over the world ... it is hard to see why finance should check the upswing'. If interest rates do rise, it is because central banks have consciously taken the political decision to raise them.

## 4.4  THE STRUCTURAL VIEW OF ENDOGENOUS MONEY

Some economists view the post-Keynesian proponents of endogenous money as being in two separate camps. On the one hand there would be those who believe that the central bank generally accommodates the base money needs of the banking system; on the other hand there are those who consider that some degree of non-accommodation by the monetary authorities is the norm (Pollin, 1991). According to this dichotomy, the authors from the second group would focus on the variability of the velocity of money and on financial innovation: endogeneity is structural. The intent of this section is to demonstrate that such a distinction may be helpful, but that it is an artificial one. The crucial aspect of the theory of endogenous money is the causation which runs from loans to deposits to high-powered money. Since all post-Keynesians agree that banks make loans first and search for the reserves later, the crucial direction of causality is not challenged by the possibility of unstable velocity. On the contrary, the presence of financial innovation and variable velocity reinforces the theory of endogenous money as it reveals how money can be endogenous in the long run despite the constraints imposed by the central bank.

**Financial Innovation and the Velocity of Money**

It was explained earlier that the logic of the monetary circuit is valid in all monetary systems. Causation is particularly clear when the monetary system is of the overdraft sort, with no restrictions on the borrowing of central bank money, or when the central bank is accommodating the needs of the commercial banks at a pegged rate of interest in the so-called market economies. Whereas the logic of the monetary circuit is valid under all historical cases, monetary authorities will decide to accommodate or not to accommodate depending on the political and economic circumstances. There may be periods in history where the central bank passively provides the required base money. One should then expect the velocity function of money or that of base money to be stable or slowly shifting, since there will be little incentive to introduce circumventing financial innovations. Indeed the earlier successful attempts by the monetarists to find correlations between money and income can be explained by the chiefly accommodating behaviour of central banks in that period.

In contrast, there are historical periods where monetary authorities have actively attempted to restrain the creation of credit money: one should expect wide swings along the velocity function as well as unpredictable shifts of that function. The decision over the past decades to pursue restrictive monetarist policies, with central banks throughout the world attempting to tamper with the stock of base money, have led to the wild shifts in velocity recently observed as well as to many financial innovations. These changes are long-run responses to the reluctance of central banks to provide base money. Indeed, in those European countries where banking systems are the closest to pure overdraft systems and hence where the use of a discount window prevails for structural reasons, it seems that the importance of financial innovations was greatly diminished.

In the theory of endogenous money which we have developed, the economy is immune, from a quantity point of view, from changes in the monetary policy of the central bank. This, however, is mostly relevant to the short run. In the longer run, banks and their customers may feel unjustifiably constrained by the actions or regulations of the central bank, and they will try to evade them. This is when banking innovation comes to the fore. Ironically the initial post-Keynesian opposition to the Friedmanian causal interpretation of the Quantity Theory of money relied primarily on the concept of banking innovation rather than on reverse causation. In his memorandum to the Radcliffe Committee, Kaldor (1964a, p. 130) emphasized the possibility of an infinitely increasing velocity of money, although he also recognized that money substitutes could be of some inconvenience. Minsky (1957) also claimed from very early on that the restriction of monetary aggregates was an almost impossible task because it would induce financial innovations that would mess up the measure of monetary aggregates. Rousseas (1986, ch. 5) has more recently reasserted the importance of the variability of velocity.

There is no inconsistency between these views and those based on the reverse causation of the money supply. Financial innovation should be considered as an integral part of the theory of endogenous money. If in the short run the economy can elude quantitative monetary restrictions, in the long run the monetary authorities have the upper hand. First, there may be substantial costs to the continuous use of the discount window. Second, the central bank could control the money supply and the economic activity through a proper knowledge of the demand for money function and by persistently setting the interest rate at its relevant level. What makes the theory of endogenous money pertinent even in the long run is that this demand for money function may shift unpredictably through time, and that the central bank can know by how much only after the fact.

To set long-run target rates of growth of monetary aggregates thus becomes a fruitless exercise for reasons which are not dissimilar from those that keep the central bank from setting short-run targets for base money. The futility of setting long-run targets in an environment of financial innovation has finally dawned on central bankers (Freedman, 1983). They have to identify an innovation, measure its past shifting incidence with a sufficient number of observations and, even worse, estimate its future impact. Each of these steps is a cause of time lags. Central banks may thus precisely control interest rates or even the monetary base in the long run; but they are impotent with respect to the money stock and the amount of bank loans. All stable relationships crumble with targets of monetary aggregates. No one should be surprised to learn that policy makers throughout the world have finally abandoned monetarism and its monetary targets (Goodhart, 1989b, p. 297).

Financial innovations have two major effects: they allow the public to economize on money balances and they allow the financial system to economize on reserve requirements (Podolski, 1986). When the central bank shows reluctance in accommodating, and interest rates rise, the public starts searching for new means to avoid this increasing opportunity cost, and the financial system innovates to accommodate this search. For the public, this means lower requirements for money balances, which in turn imply lesser requirements for official reserves. In Canada, for instance, while demand deposits with high reserve requirements continued to pay little or no interest, chartered banks started offering cheque facilities and daily interest at competitive rates on savings deposits with low reserve requirements. Part of the economizing is also done by escaping to fields that are left unregulated by the monetary authorities. Large firms act as financial institutions, lending directly their surplus funds to other companies. New savings vehicles, with low transaction and realization costs, replace standard money instruments. Economic agents who still hold standard money deposits may move these deposits out of regulated banks into unregulated financial institutions, near banks or eurobanks, where by definition deposits are not subjected to reserve requirements although they constitute means of payments. At the limit, with the proper electronic network and computer facilities, no deposits could be subjected to reserve requirements and currency would become a thing of the past. The theory of endogenous money would then have to be understood for what it really is: a theory of credit creation.

The structural view of endogenous money can be illustrated by a graph suggested by Minsky (1957), shown below as Figure 4.6. With small increases in interest rates, there are continuous increases in the velocity of money and base money as agents economize on cash and demand deposits within the existing financial environment. This corresponds to a move along the velocity curve. Eventually, as a result of persistently increasing interest rates or as a consequence of constraining quantitative or qualitative regulations, circumventing financial innovations takes place. This shifts the velocity function to the right, allowing a larger flow of income to be handled by a certain amount of money, or base money, at a given rate of interest. The velocity function is unstable. Furthermore exogenously determined technical progress in the financial sector also shifts the velocity

Figure 4.6  *Impact of high interest rates on the velocity of money and financial innovation*

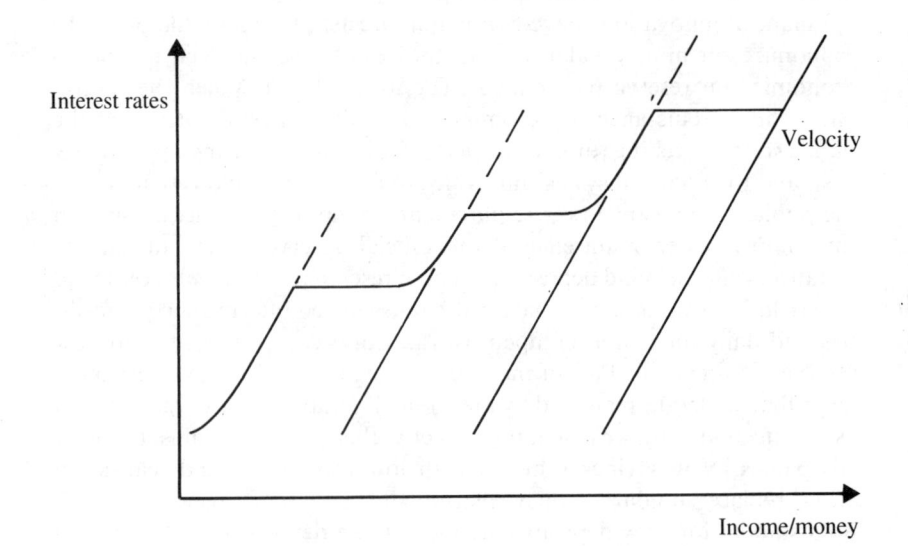

curve to the right, independently of what happens to interest rates. In practice, with the stupendous increases in interest rates that were imposed upon the economy in the 1980s, it has been very difficult for central bankers to decide whether the velocity curve had shifted or if the economy had simply moved up to previously unknown interest rates along the old velocity curve. Depending on the specification (log, semi-log), shifting appears or disappears (Freedman, 1983, p. 105).

**The Money Divisor Revisited**

The explicit determination of the money divisor may also contribute to the understanding of the links between the endogenous theory of money and the instability of velocity. Let us establish the value of the money divisor under some simple conditions.

Let $E$ be the *consolidated* deposits at near banks or at banks which are outside the regulating field of the monetary authorities. Let us assume that these near banks hold a fraction $t_e$ of their deposits as reserves. Since these financial institutions are not part of the regular banking system, they do not have to hold their reserves at the central bank. They will hold them instead under the form of deposits at commercial banks which are under the control of the central bank. These reserves deposited in commercial banks are then equal to:

$$R_e = t_e E \tag{4.11}$$

Let $D$ be the deposits held by the public at the standard commercial banks and let $B$ represent the cash balances, that is the bank-notes held by the public. We may now define three sorts of money supply. The broad money supply, which includes the deposits held at near banks, is equal to:

$$M_3 = B + D + E \tag{4.12}$$

A narrow definition of the money supply would exclude the deposits held by the public at near banks. Let us call it $M_1$.

$$M_1 = B + D \tag{4.13}$$

The third definition of money is that of high-powered money. To find out what it is, we must know more about the reserve requirements. Let us now assume that commercial banks must hold a fraction $t_d$ of *all* of their deposits as reserves. Compulsory reserves for the commercial banks are then:

$$R_d = r_d(D + R_e) \tag{4.14}$$

If there are no free reserves, the amount of high-powered money, denoted as before as $H$, is then equal to these required reserves plus the bank-notes held by the public:

$$H = B + R_d = B + t_d(D + t_e E) \tag{4.15}$$

Note that, alternatively, we may ignore near banks and consider $E$ to represent savings deposits (time deposits) at commercial banks, and assume that the required reserve ratio on these savings deposits is smaller than the one applying to demand deposits by a factor of $t_e$. Broad money would then include both demand and savings deposits. Let us now consider what the money divisor will be equal to when money is defined as broad money. From equations (4.12) and (4.15), the monetary base can be rewritten as a function of a money divisor, and one gets:

$$H = [(B/M_3) + t_d(D/M_3) + t_d t_e(E/M_3)]M_3 \tag{4.16}$$

The terms in brackets constitute the money divisor, which we previously denoted by $d_m$. Equation (4.16), which deals with broad money, may thus be written as:

$$H = d_3 M_3 \tag{4.17}$$

Similarly, we can define the money divisor in the case of the narrow measure of money. We then have:

$$H = [d_3(M_3/M_1)]M_1 = d_1 M_1 \tag{4.18}$$

We may also recall the definition of velocity. Calling $Y$ the nominal value of national income and $V$ the income velocity of money (either defined as base, narrow or broad), we have:

$$V = Y/M \tag{4.19}$$

In growth terms, with the symbol $\hat{}$ denoting a growth rate, we have:

$$\hat{V} = \hat{Y} - \hat{M} \tag{4.20}$$

Let us now attempt to assess the impact of a restrictive monetary policy with high interest rates on the above money divisors, and subsequently on the income velocity of money. Note first that, if market interest rates are high, while the interest rates on deposits are low, economic agents will attempt to economize on all sorts of deposits. In particular, companies will engage in cash management programmes: instead of holding money deposits, they will buy marketable securities and draw on their lines of credit only when payments are due, or they will use their daily closing money balances to pay back their overdrafts, and so on. For a given level of income, there is a decrease in the stock of all sorts of money, and hence an increase in the velocity of broad money. As illustrated by Figure 4.6, there are moves along the velocity curve as well as shifts of the velocity curve as new cash management techniques are gradually introduced to firms of all sizes.

Suppose now that the interest rates payable on deposits at near banks or on savings deposits at commercial banks are competitive with the yields on various bonds or marketable assets. This implies that the velocity curves of Figure 4.6 are nearly vertical: there is no incentive to avoid holding broad money, even at high interest rates. Indeed this is what the more recent studies on the demand for money seem to have observed: the interest elasticity of broad money is zero or nearly so. Agents hold more deposits of type $E$, and compensate by holding less bank-notes $B$ and less bank demand deposits $D$. The impact on the money divisor is obvious. The divisor $d_3$ becomes smaller, as can be seen from equation (4.16). For a given amount of broad money, less base money is required. A transfer of one unit of funds from cash to bank deposits reduces the requirements in base money by $(1-t_d)$ unit. Similarly a transfer of one unit of deposits from the banks to the near-banks (or from demand to time deposits) reduces the required amount of base money by $t_d(1-t_e)$ unit. If cash is transferred to deposits in near banks (or to time deposits at commercial banks) the reduction is $(1-t_e t_d)$. Putting together equations (4.17) and (4.20), with $\hat{d}_3$ a negative variable, the income velocity of high-powered money increases to:

$$\hat{V}_h = \hat{Y} - \hat{M}_3 - \hat{d}_3 \qquad (4.21)$$

Similarly, since the narrow definition of money $M_1$ is simply $M_3(M_1/M_3)$, and since the ratio $M_1/M_3$ is decreasing through time, the income velocity of narrow money increases to:

$$\hat{V}_1 = \hat{Y} - \hat{M}_3 - (\widehat{M_1/M_3}) \qquad (4.22)$$

The high interest rates and the non-accommodating monetary policy of the central bank induces portfolio shifts and financial innovations which tend to reduce the value of the broad money divisor and increase the income velocity of base money as well as that of narrowly defined money. While we have shown that in the short run the central bank ends up providing the amount of base money which the banks and the general public require, in the long run restrictive policies induce commercial banks to search for means to circumvent the required reserves. In the long run, monetary authorities succeed in restraining high-powered money either by slowing down the economy or by inducing the banking system to find ways to economize on required reserves. Unless they slow down the economy, through high interest rates or direct credit controls, the central banks cannot contain the rate of growth of broad money by restricting the rate of growth of base money, since the income velocity of base money is in fact endogenous in the long run. To a large extent, the flow of reserve-economizing financial innovations will be determined by the magnitude and the duration of the attempts by the central bank to impose restrictive policies.

The above allows us to better understand what Kaldor (1970b, p. 9) meant when he wrote that 'the Federal Reserve and the Bank of England are in a position of a constitutional monarch'. Central banks have large powers, but if they exercise them too frequently or too harshly, banks, other financial institutions and all non-financial institutions will look for means to avoid the stranglehold of the monetary authorities and circumvent their quantitative or legislative constraints. 'New forms of financial intermediaries and of transactions will appear which will cause the situation "to slip under the grip" of the authorities' (Kaldor, 1985b, p. 260). There will be wide swings in the different money or credit divisors as well as in the different income velocities of money. Moreover, as can be seen from equations (4.18) and (4.22), the evolution of the various money divisors and income velocities can be very different, rendering assessments of the monetary situation even more difficult. It becomes impossible for the monetary authorities to predict the consequences of their decisions, while the relationship between interest rates, money and national income grows unstable. Fine-tuning by the monetary authorities is only possible when they show moderation in the exercise of power. Otherwise, when restraint is a permanent policy, the various monetary aggregates become of no use to the operators of the central bank, who may wreck the economy without even knowing it. The only reliable index of monetary restraint is the rate of interest, either in nominal or in real terms, as central bankers have come to realize (Goodhart, 1989b, pp. 299, 333).

Some of the implications of unstable velocities of money are illustrated in Figure 4.7. Suppose that initially the restrictive monetary policy is such that to a rate of interest $i_0$ corresponds a demand for narrow money equal

*Figure 4.7   Possible reactions of central banks to financial innovations*

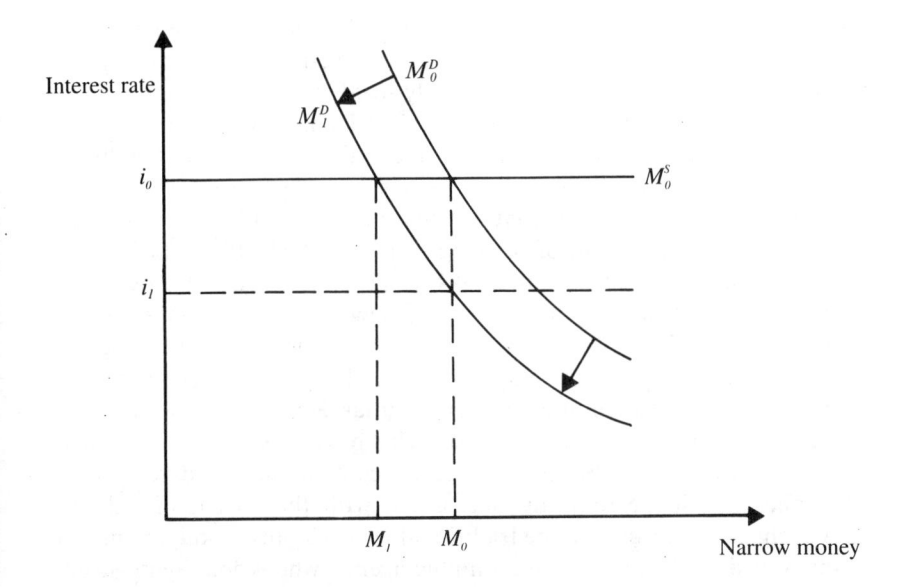

to $M_0$. Suppose that, as a result of this restrictive policy, financial innovations are induced and the velocity curve of narrowly defined money shifts out to the right, as indicated in Figure 4.6. Assuming no changes in the other economic variables, the demand curve for narrow money shifts to the left (and its slope may also change), as can be seen in Figure 4.7. If the monetary authorities were to hold on to their monetary target $M_0$, they would have to let the rate of interest fall to $i_1$. If indeed the central bank is pursuing a restrictive policy, this is not very likely. If the central bank decides to stick to its instrumental target, and pegs the rate of interest at $i_0$, the stock of narrowly defined money will fall to $M_1$, and so will the stock of base money. The actual income velocity of narrow money will increase. On the other hand, there will be no reduction in the quantity of broad money. In general one might expect the central bank to lose some confidence in the validity of its targeted monetary aggregates and in the appropriateness of the chosen instrumental interest rate. The horizontal supply of money will then lie somewhere between $i_0$ and $i_1$. The circumventing financial innovation will provide some temporary breathing space to the economy, until the authorities come to revise monetary targets or the definition of monetary aggregates, or until they push interest rates back up again.

## Liability Management

The concept of liability management having become so fashionable, no discussion of the implications of financial innovations could be complete without explicitly dealing with it. Broadly speaking, liability management refers to the ability of banks to increase their lending activity by borrowing funds which appear on the liability side of their balance sheet, without having to dispose of their marketable assets – mainly Treasury bills.

The traditional opinion is that liability management is a new stage in the historical development of banking systems (Chick, 1986). Before the advent of liability management, banks would passively wait for deposits, and only expand their lending activity if new depositors came forward. Banks would mainly manage their asset side, making sure that sufficient secondary reserves were available; that is, making sure they had enough marketable assets to sell in case of substantial deposit withdrawals or if more private loans needed to be made. This passive behaviour of banks, consistent with the causality and the concept of the standard money multiplier, would be radically overturned with the advent of liability management. According to the traditional view, liability management has transformed banks into active economic agents, who search aggressively for customers and adjust their liabilities later (Podolski, 1986, pp. 159–60). Some authors even go so far as to claim that, as a result of liability management by the banks, the expansion of monetary and credit aggregates is supply-led (Coghlan, 1978; Chick, 1986, pp. 117, 122). Commercial banks, rather than firms and households, would thus determine the rate of growth of credit money. In this extreme form, there is little difference between liability management and the monetarist story: in both cases there can be an excessive creation of money and hence inflation. In the first case it is the result of the greed of bankers, who lend beyond all reasonable limits; in the second case it is a consequence of the incompetence of the officials at the central bank.

The above traditional view of liability management is erroneous. Liability management is *not* an innovation that would have transformed the process of banking intermediation (Goodhart, 1989a, p. 30), as long as it is interpreted within the confines of a theory of endogenous money. Since money is credit-driven, liability management is a permanent phenomenon. Banks are perpetually engaged in passive liability management, as they must first consent to loans, and later search for funds to finance the deposits which are leaking out. If all banks are growing at approximately the same rate, leakages will be compensated by deposits coming in from rival institutions. Liabilities will thus automatically adjust to the autonomous growth of assets. This is not necessarily the case, however. In

Europe, and also in the United States, some large banks (the business banks) have systematically been indebted towards smaller institutions (the deposits banks). As a consequence they have been forced to enter into active liability management, borrowing funds from these institutions to compensate for the differential in the rates of growth of their loans and of their deposits.

Besides active liability management at the level of the individual bank, active liability management at the systemic level is nothing new. In fact, as was already pointed out in the first part of the chapter, all overdraft systems are compelled to practise liability management as a logical necessity. Most European banking systems, for instance France's, have structurally been indebted to the central bank. When banks of these systems increase their loan portfolio, they are required to augment their borrowings from the central bank. Any adjustment is done on the liability side, simply because no adjustment from the asset side is possible. In the case of North American systems, at least until recently, the dynamics were quite different since commercial banks held large amounts of government bonds that central banks were disposed to repurchase. In some circumstances, the central bank refused to do so, but, since this privilege was usually not abused, commercial banks complied. In the more recent past, however, banks have been subjected to systematic refusals from the central bank to accommodate. Furthermore the secondary reserves of Treasury bills and bonds, which were a vestige of the vast amounts of bonds accumulated during the Second World War, have been depleted, forcing banks to find other means to face unexpected deposit withdrawals without selling these precautionary assets or without calling back loans (Goodhart, 1989a, p. 32). Liability management has surged back. Indeed, as is recalled by Moore (1988a, pp. 27–8), active liability management was part of the American banking system in the 1920s, but it receded with the overabundance of primary and secondary asset reserves in the next two decades.

What makes the present situation so obvious is that liability management has been associated with a whole set of banking innovations in a financial environment dominated by the restrictive policies of the central bank. It should be clear, however, that financial management does not create reserves *per se* (Goodhart, 1984, p. 211). In a closed economy, base money is created either when banks borrow from the central bank or when the central bank buys bonds. Selling certificates of deposits or borrowing funds from other financial institutions does not in itself alleviate a lack of reserves. The impact on reserves is an indirect one. This can be seen by going back to our definition of the broad money divisor, in equation (4.16). If, for some reason, such as superior rates of return on near monies, the public can be induced to hold their balances in marketable certificates of deposits (CDs) instead of ordinary bank deposits, the share $D/M$ of the latter in the definition of broad money will fall. Furthermore, if financial institutions outside of the regulated sector directly lend their deposits to the regulated commercial banks, instead of depositing some of their funds as reserves, the coefficient $t_e$ in the definition of the money divisor will also fall off. The result of both of these effects is to decrease the amount of base money H which is necessary to support an amount $M$ of means of payments. In this sense, liability management may thus reduce the need for reserves and give some breathing space to the banking system.

**Eurobanks and Innovation**

Eurobanks are another example of banking innovation and liability management. The analysis of eurobanks and euromarkets is usually considered to be complex and within the reach of the initiated only. It should not be. Eurobanks, like domestic banks, play several roles. First, they create credit by lending to domestic or foreign corporations. Secondly, they are financial intermediaries, helping to transfer funds from countries with balance of payment surpluses to those with deficits and a lack of reserves in hard currencies. Thirdly, they operate on the forward exchange market, helping companies trading abroad to reduce their foreign exchange risks. These latter operations explain a large part of the balance sheets of the eurobanks and their seemingly enormous importance when aggregated. This is because a forward exchange transaction initiated by an exporting or importing firm must be decomposed, for the bank, into a spot exchange operation and a borrowing and lending operation in two different currencies. Since a large number of banks may be involved in a single transaction, with a eurobank lending right away to a second eurobank what it has just borrowed from a third eurobank, the balance sheets of eurobanks which are active in forward exchange markets are artificially swollen by this cascading effect.

For our purposes it is the first role of eurobanks which is of greatest interest; that is, the banking-specific role of eurobanks. Specialists now agree that eurobanks are similar to near banks (Niehans, 1984, p. 186). Like near banks, eurobanks hold some of their assets as deposits in the banks of the country which issues the currency in which these assets are denominated. Like near banks, eurobanks do not have access to the facilities of the issuing central bank. Unless they are so restricted, eurobanks can, however, borrow from the domestic commercial banks if they need to, as near banks would. There is, then, a three-stage banking system: the central bank; the domestic commercial banks, which hold their reserves at the central bank; and the eurobanks, which hold their reserves as deposits at their banking correspondents.

This three-tier system can be formalized by the same set of equations, (4.11) to (4.16), that was used to describe the impact of the near banks on the money divisor. The letter $E$ now represents the deposits in domestic currency which are held by households and firms at banks situated abroad; $D$ are the deposits held by the public in domestic banks; $R_e$ are the deposits held by the eurobanks at the domestic banks. As was the case for the near banks, it can be seen that a shift of deposits away from the domestic banks towards the eurobanks decreases the value of the credit divisor and hence diminishes the needs in base money of the economy. Restrictive measures by the monetary authorities should induce a transfer of the banking activities towards the foreign subsidiaries of the constrained domestic banks, to the extent that these activities can be transferred quickly and efficiently.

Hence eurobanks and euromarkets are one additional way for the financial system as a whole to economize on compulsory reserves. The rerouting of financial activities towards eurobanks is thus a form of liability management, based on technological and financial innovations. As was shown with equations (4.21) and (4.22) in the case of near banks, the velocities of base money and of narrowly defined money will increase with a shift of the banking activities towards eurobanks. This shift is an additional mean for the banks and their customers to avoid the constraints imposed by the monetary authorities. However this does not mean that a world with eurobanks is necessarily more prone to inflation. Eurobanks, like domestic commercial banks, cannot create any excessive money. It simply means that, if the central bank desires to slow the economy down, it will have to act more resolutely on the level of interest rates.

## 4.5 CONSEQUENCES

Some neoclassical economists have wondered why post-Keynesians attach so much importance to the endogeneity of money (Salant, 1985, p. 1179). This is rather surprising: it is clear that if monetarism could stand with exogenous money, it necessarily falls with demand-led endogenous money, as was recognized from the outset by Milton Friedman (1970). The intellectual casualties are not limited to monetarism, however. Nowadays all neoclassical macroeconomic theories rely on a framework the inspiration of which is monetarist. Today's neoclassical synthesis is constituted of variations centred around the old monetarist model. As noted by critics of Friedman and Schwartz, 'the exogeneity of prices and endogeneity of money are substantive issues' (Hendry and Ericsson, 1991, p. 30).

For our part, we have already noted some of the important consequences of a credit-led theory of endogenous money: it allows us to reassert the fundamental Keynesian causality running from investment to savings, as well as the fundamental opposition to the neoclassical concept of scarcity. There are other crucial implications. For instance, a theory of endogenous money implies that the government does not decide on the proportion of its deficit that it wishes to monetize. Insofar as the central bank sets the interest rate, it is the preferences and the needs of the public that determine the proportion of the deficit that will be transformed into high-powered money, as can be deduced from Table 4.10. Furthermore, since the stock of money is endogenous, all real balance effects or other similar Pigou or Patinkin effects are ruled out (Moore, 1988a, p. 384). This wipes out the main neoclassical justification for their downward sloping aggregate demand curve, as we shall see in the next chapter. The endogeneity of money and the exogeneity of the rate of interest provide post-Keynesian grounds to ignore real balance effects and focus instead on distributional issues in the analysis of effective demand, including the role of interest rates on the distribution of income.

The most obvious impact of an endogenous credit money theory is on the theory of inflation. Since the supply of money is not an exogenous variable, it cannot be held responsible for the general increase in prices. Inflation cannot be caused by an excessive rate of growth of the supply of money due to incompetent central bankers or to a favourable trade balance. Some other theory of inflation, different from the standard monetarist and now neoclassical view, must be provided. This will be attempted in Chapter 7.

# 5. Effective Demand and Employment

The focus of the chapter is the labour market and the employment of labour. The analysis will be pursued within the short-run framework, assuming given monetary conditions and a fixed level of investment. Long-run conditions will be studied in the next chapter.

## 5.1 CHARACTERISTICS OF THE POST-KEYNESIAN LABOUR MARKET

The major characteristics of the post-Keynesian labour market are the following: the labour market does not truly exist; the wage rate is not just another ordinary price: it has much influence on the overall economy; workers are not commodities: norms rule over supply and demand forces; the demand for and the supply of labour are not well-behaved (Appelbaum, 1979; Seccareccia, 1991a).

Ironically the major aspect of the post-Keynesian view of labour markets is that such markets do not really exist. Whereas one may admit that there is a market for peanuts or for bananas, with well-behaved supply and demand curves, the same hypothesis cannot be made in the case of labour. On the demand side, we have already seen in Chapter 3 that machines and labour are in fixed proportion in the short run. One cannot increase production by putting more workers on the same machine. No such substitution is possible. As to the longer run, we saw in Chapter 1 that the Cambridge controversies over capital have ramifications over all standard scarcity relationships, even at the industry level. *A fortiori*, at the aggregate level, one should not expect to find a continuous negative relationship between the demand for labour and the aggregate real wage, as was illustrated in Figure 1.2(b).

A further difference between the market for peanuts and the market for labour is that the former deals with things whereas the latter deals with human beings. This is why Eichner (1986a, ch. 4) calls the post-Keynesian approach an anthropogenic approach to labour. An essential distinction, emphasized by Eichner, between labour and commodities is that the former cannot be stored. If labour is not used in one period, because of cyclical unemployment, it is lost forever. Even worse, the skills and the productivity of the unemployed labour force depreciate through their lack of use, whereas they generally appreciate when they are being utilized, in obvious contrast to physical capital. Furthermore, in contrast to the view of neoclassical economics, work does not necessarily carry disutility; it also brings satisfactions. Work in itself can be rewarding.

The market for labour has to deal with labourers, which 'bring with them not only their labour-power but also their past history and norms of justice in the workplace' (Seccareccia, 1991a, p. 45). We mentioned in Chapter 3 that the notions of fairness and justice often permeate the determination of the prices of things, in particular the prices of manufactured goods. The question of justice and of norms is even more fundamental in the so-called market for labour. These norms enter all dimensions of labour: the real wage and also the relative wages to be paid, as was emphasized by Keynes (1973, vii, p. 14); the duration of the contract; the level of work effort or of productivity; the range of activities which can be assigned to the worker; the duration of the working week; the safety of the job, its security in the face of cyclical fluctuations, and so on. One could argue, using the terms proposed by Wood (1978), that in most markets anomic pressures overshadow normative ones, whereas in labour markets it is the reverse. In the market for labour, normative pressures, that is pressures linked to customs and equity, have much more importance than anomic pressures, that is pressures that lack organizational content such as market forces and conjunctural forces. In this chapter we shall deal with one aspect of these normative pressures, the impact of higher wages on the work effort of the workers, or what is known in the neoclassical literature as the efficiency wage hypothesis. The consequences of normative pressures for the determination of money wage rates, and hence the importance of relative wages, will be mainly discussed in Chapter 7, when the topic of inflation will be pursued.

A particular striking example of normative forces is those forces at work within the core economy of the now widely accepted dual labour market hypothesis. The labour market is assumed to be segmented into two submarkets, as has long been argued by institutional labour economists and also by neo-radical ones (Doeringer and Piore, 1971; Gimble, 1991). One of the submarkets corresponds to the core economy, where wages and productivity are relatively high, as are the requirements and the costs of labour training, as well as the costs of monitoring work. Within this economy there is a well structured wage or salary scale, where experience and seniority are given much prominence, and there is a high degree of unionization. Also each organization within the core economy tries to develop a sense of affiliation among its staff and workers. The other labour market is the peripheral one, where little training is required, where the monitoring of work is inexpensive, and where wages are systematically low. In the organizations of the peripheral economy, the turnover of employees is often encouraged.

To some extent the core economy corresponds to the sectors where prices are administered under oligopolistic control, and hence where sufficient profits can be generated to introduce more productive machinery, while the peripheral economy corresponds to products sold in competitive markets with few possibilities of introducing up-to-date technology, but this correspondence is imperfect (Reich, 1984). In particular, within the same industry, some jobs may be within the core economy while others are at the periphery. Large firms of the core economy may contract out work to non-unionized peripheral firms. Even within the same firm, some jobs may belong to the core and others to the periphery. In a university, for instance, professors who have tenure or who are on the tenure track are part of the core economy, temporarily for those who still do not have tenure. By contrast, many university teachers barely survive as lecturers, taking on a full teaching load at salaries which hardly exceed the minimum wage, either because they still do not have a PhD or because they did not happen to have graduated at the right time and at the right institution, or with the right sort of dissertation. Similar situations arise in all sectors, even in government services. It is of no use for those without a permanent job in the core sector to propose their services at a salary lower than the ruling one.

This bring us to the issues of the demand for and the supply of labour. In neoclassical analysis, the demand for labour is simply the marginal revenue product of the labour factor, while the supply of labour is the outcome of some choice between the consumption of leisure and the consumption of other goods. The greater part of this chapter will be devoted to the issue of the demand for labour. We already know that substitution effects, both at the sectoral and the aggregate levels, cannot predict increases in the product/labour ratio when the price of labour services increases as compared to the cost of other factors. Therefore substitution cannot explain variations in the demand for labour. Those who pretend the opposite, for instance Hamermesh (1986), carry on what we have called measurement without testing, postulating the existence of the traditional production functions to verify, rather than to refute, the standard substitution effects. In the following sections, the model of the firm that we have developed in Chapter 3, devoid of the standard marginal physical products and substitution effects, will be used to demonstrate the central importance of effective demand for the aggregate labour demand. The aggregate demand for labour is not the result of the aggregation of a multitude of marginal revenue products relying on price effects. Rather it depends on the principle of effective demand and hence on income effects. This is the major departure of the post-Keynesian approach to labour economics, as was pointed out by Appelbaum (1979).

Let us deal for the remainder of this section with the issue of the supply of labour. As Yellen (1980, p. 18) says, 'one thing notably absent from the Post-Keynesian model is a labor supply function'. We shall, however, attempt to provide one. Neoclassical macroeconomists generally assume that the supply of labour is well-behaved; that is, they assume that the supply of labour has a positive slope, the substitution effect overcoming the income effect. Leisure is assumed not to be too strongly an inferior good. This, combined with the standard assumptions ruling the demand for labour, produces the orthodox labour market, where the forces of supply and demand necessarily lead to an equilibrium wage rate. The equilibrium mechanism may only be impeded by various institutional imperfections, such as labour unions and imperfect information. Despite its human characterization, the labour market is still considered a market by neoclassical macroeconomists because, under ideal conditions, any chance increase in the actual real wage rate relative to the equilibrium one would generate market forces of demand and supply that would bring the price of labour services back to its equilibrium level. In the long run, if not in the short run, the labour market clears.

Neoclassical labour economists take a more prudent view about the shape of the supply of labour. Many empirical studies have shown that the income effect of a change in the real wage rate is more significant than the substitution effect. In particular, in the case of men, the wage elasticity of the number of hours worked is negative (Pencavel, 1986). When the real wage rate is decreased, for instance, hours worked increase. Although the lower price of leisure should induce people to work less or to stop working, they end up working more hours to compensate for the loss of income due to the lower hourly wage rate. The upshot of all this is that the supply curve of labour probably does not have the standard upward-sloping shape, nor the popular backward-bending one (Pencavel, 1986, p. 67). Rather the supply of labour, at least for men, would be a downward-sloping curve, as indicated in Figure 5.1.

Still, for a neoclassical economist, a downward-sloping supply curve of labour is not detrimental to the standard demand and supply analysis. The reason can be found by inspecting Figure 5.1. Provided that the absolute value of the slope of the supply curve is larger than that of the demand curve, any chance increase in the real wage rate above its equilibrium

*Figure 5.1 Downward-sloping supply of labour curve in a neoclassical labour market*

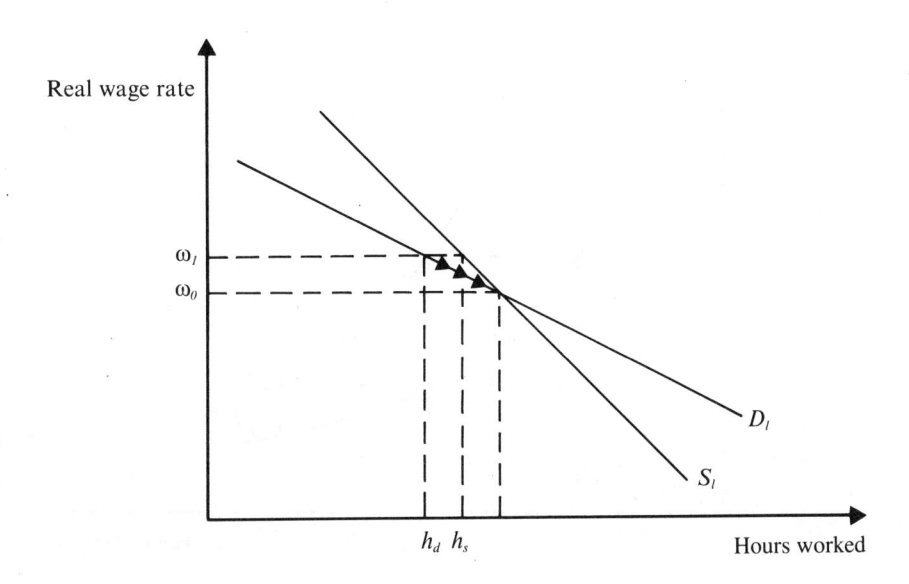

value, say from $\omega_0$, to $\omega_1$, will induce the appearance of an excess supply of labour and hence set in train forces that will bring the wage rate back to its equilibrium value. The precise shape of the supply curve of labour is not of fundamental importance. Even if the supply curve is backward-bending, a stable equilibrium exists. This may explain why the publication of controversial results is abundant on this topic. From the point of view of the non-orthodox economists, the results mentioned above provide substantial indications that neoclassical economists are in fact looking at behavioural responses which are of a relatively small order of magnitude when they focus on price effects in the labour market. Even when dealing with the supply of labour, income effects overcome price effects. We already know that price substitution effects are not reliable on the demand side of the labour market: a lower real wage rate may be associated with a lower labour/output ratio. A similar phenomenon may appear in the case of the supply curve of labour: many empirical studies imply that the income-compensated pure substitution effect has the wrong sign (Pencavel, 1986, p. 94). All of the above leads to the belief that the standard price effects must be left sideways. The focus of the attention must be the much neglected income effects.

222                Foundations of Post-Keynesian Economic Analysis

*Figure 5.2  Downward-sloping supply of labour curves at two different norms of living standards*

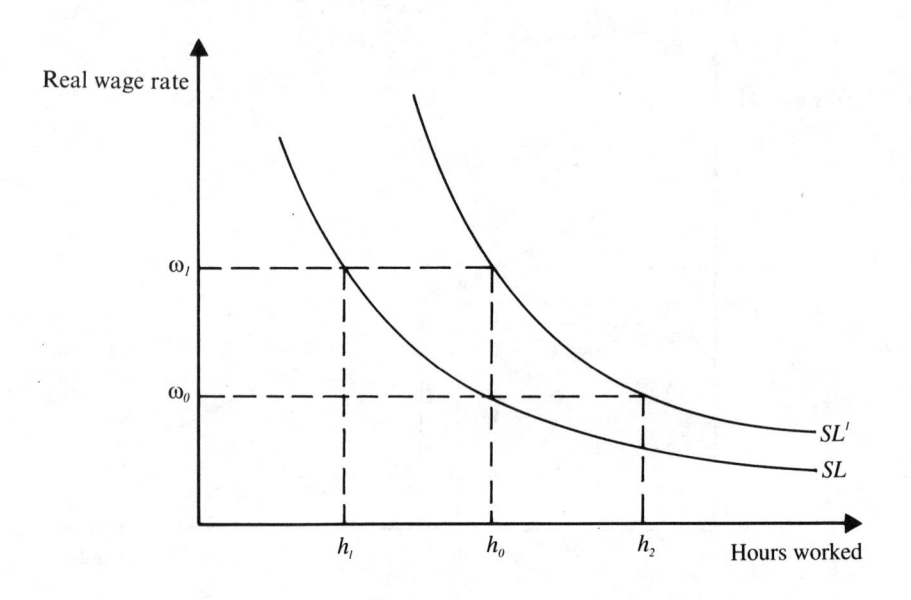

The outline of a post-Keynesian theory of the supply of labour could be presented along the following lines. Decisions to work and decisions to consume are not unrelated. The crucial objective of most individuals or of most households is to keep their position within the consumers' hierarchy, as we have explained in Chapter 2. As a consequence households feel an obligation to retain the levels of income to which they have been accustomed. Furthermore households, like firms, have contractual obligations (Rima, 1984a, p. 68; Appelbaum, 1979, p. 112). They have borrowed in the past to acquire housing, cars, electric appliances, furniture and other semi-durable consumption goods, perhaps even for their holidays. Households are thus compelled, for normative and cash flow reasons, to maintain customary income levels. The level of non-wage income being given, and the level of income of other households being given, the standard of living of an individual or of the household can be represented by a rectangular hyperbola in the plane described by the real wage rate and the number of hours worked, as shown in Figure 5.2 (Nell, 1988a, p. 123; Mongiovi, 1991, p. 39).

Any increase in the standard of living will be associated with another rectangular hyperbola, denoted $SL'$, above the previous one, called $SL$.

An increase in the real wage rate which is considered temporary, that is which does not change the customary standard of living, may then induce a worker to reduce the number of hours offered from $h_0$ to $h_1$, moving along the hyperbola. Only if the change in the real wage rate is considered to be a permanent one, that is if the worker feels that a higher rank of the consumers' hierarchy can be attained, will the desired number of hours of work stay the same, the individual shifting up to the $SL'$ curve. The main cause of this is that, when the household feels that a permanently higher level of income can be maintained, it will modify its borrowing behaviour accordingly, by increasing its liabilities and its cash flow requirements. A higher real wage rate associated with a higher standard of living and consumption norm will not modify the number of hours worked as the worker will conform to the existing social norm.

The supply of labour thus depends in large measure upon the normal standard of living of a household relative to that of other households. The supply of labour depends on the perceived mean income of the reference group against which a particular household is comparing itself, that is on the perceived mean wage rate and the perceived social norm regarding the number of hours worked per week (or per year). For instance, in Figure 5.2, if an individual believes that the mean income of the reference group has increased from $SL$ to $SL'$, while this individual feels that he should still belong to that reference group, he will attempt to increase the number of hours worked from $h_0$ to $h_2$ in order to remain at the same rank in the hierarchy of consumers. The supply of labour thus depends, both at the individual level and in the aggregate, on the perceived wage rate of the reference group and on the past standard of living. One would expect the amount of labour supplied to increase when a household is being subjected to a drop in the real wage rate and when a drop in standards of living relative to the reference group is being perceived. These two assumptions are the mainspring of the inflation theory to be developed in Chapter 7.

In brief, then, the supply of labour of an individual depends on his customary consumption level, as well as on his wage rate relative to that of other workers (Rima, 1984b, p. 541). The post-Keynesian view of the supply of labour is closely related to the post-Keynesian approach to consumption developed in Chapter 2: both underline the importance of peer groups and that of past income levels (Baxter, 1988b). What explains the social norm regarding the average number of weekly working hours may be harder to identify. One must certainly fall back on cultural explanations which have little to do with constrained individual behaviour. For instance, why is it that professors or businessmen now work more hours than they used to half a century ago (Scitovsky, 1976, pp. 100–

1)? This may have to do with the downfall of the leisure class and the reinforcement of the work ethic: all have to work, even those who do not need labour income.

The previous analysis of the labour supply is still quite idealistic. It assumes that individuals have a choice regarding the number of hours they can work. This may be true for independent professionals, businessmen, self-employed people or university professors, and also for those who work part-time. In general, however, employers offer full-time jobs with a fixed number of hours of work per week, and a fixed number of weeks of work per year (Eichner, 1987a, p. 883). The choice is simply between working the number of hours imposed by the institutional norm or to turn down the employment. As a result any change in the real wage rate is unlikely to lead to a different decision. Some flexibility may be added by searching for different employers, offering the optimal combination of wages and hours of work, although most companies of the core economy will tend to gravitate around the socially accepted norm. Flexibility in the number of hours worked may also be obtained by taking up part-time jobs with other employers, but the additional income, once additional income taxes and lost marginal benefits are taken into account, is usually much reduced compared to the real wage rate of a full-time job.

Part-time jobs are seldom offered in the core economy, which explains why so many women, who are constrained to search for part-time jobs when they rear young children, are found to work in the peripheral economy. This last point highlights a last possibility of flexible hours: within the household, one of the two main members of the household may choose to work part-time rather than full-time, or may choose not to work at all. Indeed it is well known that the supply of labour of married women increases in recession times, in an attempt to sustain the monetary standard of living of the household. On the other hand, the costs of entering the labour market are often significant for the second main member of the household, generally women. A high wage rate is more likely to induce participation. As a consequence researchers have often found a positive relationship between wages and the supply of labour in the case of women.

Once we realize that the aggregate supply curve of labour may take just about any shape, depending in part on the expectations regarding relative standards of living, and that to a large extent the exact shape of the supply curve of labour does not affect the analysis of the labour market, as could be seen in Figure 5.1 and as will be the case of the post-Keynesian view, we might as well simplify this part of the analysis and assume that the supply curve of labour is vertical in the short run. As a consequence, since we are to focus on the demand aspects of the market for labour in the sections which are to follow, we will make the simple assumption that the supply of labour is not a function of the real wage rate.

## 5.2 THE UTILIZATION FUNCTION

In the neoclassical approach, the demand for labour depends on the market wage rate and the exact form of the production function. In the post-Keynesian view, production functions do not have the expected form in the long run, where machines can be changed through investment in new capital, and they do not exist in the short run, during which the capital stock is assumed to be constant because new machines have yet to be installed. We have seen in Chapter 3 that the technical conditions, job definitions and management constraints are such that technical coefficients of production can be assumed to be fixed. Labour cannot be substituted for capital and vice versa. Still it is possible to modify the rate of employment in the short run, despite no possibilities of substitution, because various segments of plants can be closed down or opened up. With a given stock of capital, more labour can be employed because a larger portion of the machinery is being utilized. While there is no production function in the neoclassical sense, there is in post-Keynesian theory a *utilization function* relating output to employment (Robinson, 1964, p. 25). This short-period utilization function thus relates the level of employment to the rate of utilization of capacity (Nell, 1978, p. 7). In this section and the following, we will develop the algebraic implications of the cost theory of the firm that was presented in Chapter 3. This will allow us, in a later stage of this chapter, to develop a post-Keynesian theory of effective demand and aggregate employment.

Let us then begin with a single megacorp producing a single product. We assume away the existence of intermediate products and raw materials, since, in any case, these commodities disappear as we aggregate and proceed to vertical integration. The reader might want to imagine a representative firm which, when scaled up, represents the whole economy. Until we discuss the issues of aggregate demand, and until we address the peculiar issues of a two-sector model, we shall talk of this representative firm. The macroeconomics of the utilization function will be no different from the algebraic representation of its microeconomic underpinnings. The equations which follow may thus be understood as valid both for the individual firm and for the macroeconomic one-sector model about to be developed.

We start by adopting the important distinction between direct labour and overhead labour which has been underlined by Kalecki (1971, p. 44) and popularized by Asimakopulos (1970, 1975), Harris (1974) and Rowthorn (1981). The firm thus hires two kinds of labour. On the one hand, there are blue-collar workers, who are the variable factors of production, and who are directly linked to production. We shall denote them as $L_v$. On the other hand, there are white-collar workers, who are part of the overhead costs since their numbers depend on the level of full capacity, rather than on the level of production. These are the permanent staff, the administrative officers, the accountants, the lawyers of the firms and so on. In the short term, since the level of capacity is fixed, the salaries of white-collar workers are a fixed component of costs. We shall thus denote them as $L_f$. Calling $q$ the level of output and $q_{fc}$ the full capacity level of output, as we did in Chapter 3, and $L$ the overall level of employment of this firm, while $y_v$ and $y_f$ are constant labour coefficients which are indices of productivity, we have the following three equations:

$$L = L_v + L_f \tag{5.1}$$

$$L_v = q/y_v \tag{5.2}$$

$$L_f = q_{fc}/y_f \tag{5.3}$$

The utilization function is the relation linking total employment to production, the level of capacity being given. From the above equations, the utilization function may thus be written as:

$$q = [L - (q_{fc}/y_f)]y_v \tag{5.4}$$

In neoclassical terms, this would be a production function with a constant marginal physical product of labour. Taking the derivative of equation (5.4) with respect to labour would indeed yield a constant:

$$dq/dL = y_v \tag{5.5}$$

The peculiar production function of equation (5.4) is illustrated graphically in Figure 5.3. As long as the level of employment is below $L_f$, no output can be forthcoming. The relationship between output and employment is linear up to the level of full capacity $q_{fc}$, after which one may presume, as we did in Chapter 3, that the laws of diminishing returns take over. In the present chapter, however, as in the following ones, it will always be assumed that demand is such that production never exceeds what we have defined to be full capacity. Under this condition, the equations defined above always fully apply.

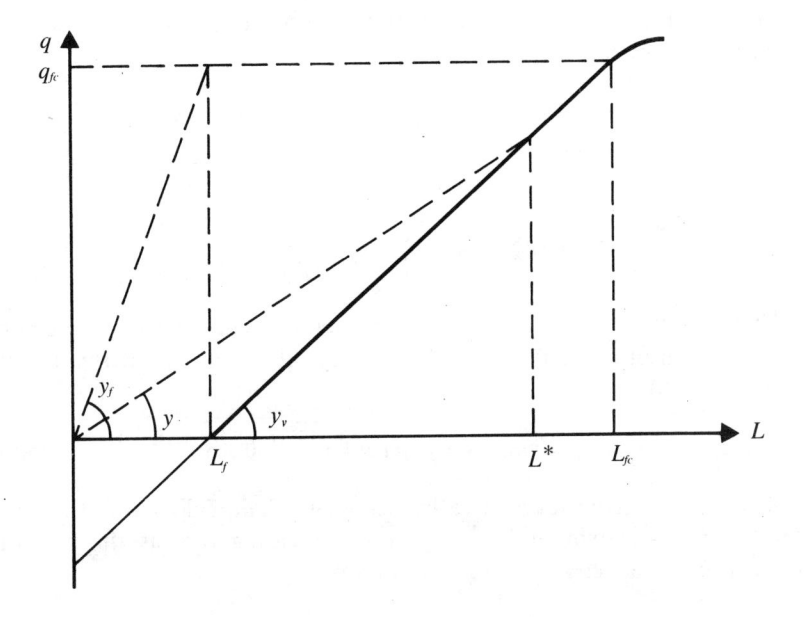

*Figure 5.3  Short-run post-Keynesian utilization function*

Equation (5.5) yields the marginal physical product of labour. This is represented in Figure 5.3 by the slope of the utilization function, as shown by the tangent of angle $y_v$. The tangent of angle $y_f$ represents the productivity of white-collar workers. If the angle were to increase, the amount of fixed labour required for a given level of capacity would decrease, and hence the productivity of overhead labour would rise. As a consequence, when the productivity of white-collar workers changes, the whole utilization function shifts; whereas when it is the productivity of blue-collar workers which changes, the slope of the utilization function changes.

A peculiar characteristic of the above production function is the evolution of the overall productivity per worker as the rate of utilization of capacity increases, shown by the tangent of angle $y$ on Figure 5.3 for a given level of employment $L^*$. Let us make use of the following two definitions. The overall productivity per worker is:

$$y = q/L \qquad (5.6)$$

And the rate of utilization of capacity is simply:

$$u = q/q_{fc} \qquad (5.7)$$

Making use of these definitions and of equations (5.1) to (5.3), the employment of overhead labour may be written: $L_f = q/(uy_f)$ and the overall productivity per worker $y$ may be written as a function of the rate of utilization of capacity.

$$y = \frac{L_v y_v}{L_v + \frac{L_v y_v}{uy_f}}$$

$$\frac{q}{L} = y = \frac{y_v}{1 + (y_v/y_f)/u} \tag{5.8}$$

The overall productivity per worker is an increasing function of the rate of utilization of capacity, as can be seen by taking the first derivative of equation (5.8):

$$dy/du = y_f y_v^2/(y_f u + y_v)^2 > 0 \tag{5.9}$$

Taking the second derivative by using the chain rule shows that the productivity per worker is rising at a decreasing rate as the rate of utilization of capacity increases up to unity.

$$d^2y/du^2 = -2y_v^2 y_f^2/(y_f u + y_v)^3 < 0 \tag{5.10}$$

Output and productivity are thus positively related in the short term. Figure 5.4 illustrates the labour productivity curve as a function of the rate of utilization of capacity. Visually this productivity curve is much like the standard production function of comparative statics. It appears to have the same look of diminishing returns. The variable on the vertical axis, the level of output per unit of labour, is also identical to the one that can be found in production functions. The variable on the horizontal axis, however, is different from the one to be found in production functions. In the traditional analysis, the capital/labour ratio would be the variable of the horizontal axis. Here we have the opposite: it is the level of employment, for a given stock of machinery, which is to be found on the horizontal axis. Although visually the productivity curve may seem like a neoclassical production function, the underlying relationship of the former curve is completely opposed to the one underlying traditional analysis. Whereas production functions usually rely on decreasing returns, we have here a sort of short run increasing returns to the use of labour. All these remarks could apply as much to the microeconomics of the firm as to the macroeconomics of the economy. We now turn more specifically to the latter.

*Figure 5.4* Average productivity of labour as a function of the rate of utilization of capacity

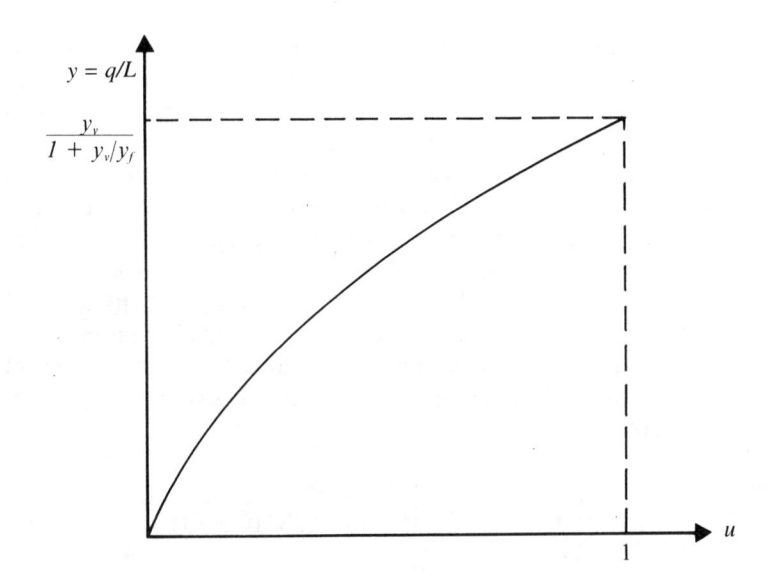

$$y = q/L$$
$$\frac{y_v}{1 + y_v/y_f}$$

Taken together, equation (5.8) and Figures 5.3 and 5.4 illustrate as well Okun's law, which asserts that a fall in the unemployment rate of 1 per cent is accompanied by a much greater percentage increase in output, in the range of 2 or 3 per cent, depending on the estimates. This means that, in the short run, an increase in employment is accompanied by a much faster increase in output; that is the output to labour ratio increases, as it does in equation (5.8) and Figure 5.4, when the rate of utilization of capacity rises. In post-Keynesian theory, Okun's law is a natural outcome of the theory, whereas in neoclassical economics *ad hoc* assumptions, severe restrictions, lags and extremely complex stories are necessary to integrate the well-verified empirical results of Okun to the standard decreasing returns (Wulwick, 1988). With the post-Keynesian utilization function, the presence of overhead labour, emphasized by Okun himself, combined with a constant marginal physical product of variable labour yields Okun's law without any additional assumption.

Indeed Okun's law reinforces the constructions which were proposed in Chapter 3, in particular the hypothesis that the marginal cost of multiplant firms may be considered constant despite plants or segments of plants of different vintage and productivity. The presumption made in

Chapter 3 was that firms, at the microeconomic level, do not necessarily close down their less efficient plants when the rate of utilization of capacity decreases. Similarly, at the macroeconomic level, firms of different efficiency share all increases in total output, as underlined by Asimakopulos (1975, p. 322) and also by Kaldor (1985a, p. 47) when he discusses the theoretical underpinnings of Okun's law. The cause of this sharing, except when prices fall so low relative to costs that the least efficient firms have to go under, is that in imperfect competition all firms adjust their prices to those set by the price leaders of the industry, with all firms operating with some excess capacity. This post-Keynesian view must be contrasted with the standard view, according to which reduced aggregate demand implies the disappearance of the least efficient firms or the unemployment of the least efficient workers, a view which Keynes (1973, vii, pp. 397ff) accepted until he was confronted with contrary evidence. In actual economies, the most efficient firms are not operating at full capacity; the least efficient firms do not operate only when the more efficient ones cannot respond to increased demand.

## 5.3 THE SIMPLE MACROECONOMICS OF EMPLOYMENT

**A Partial View**

Having settled the relationship between output and employment, we may now proceed to establish the determinants of the demand for labour. In the post-Keynesian tradition, income effects are the determinants of the demand for labour. Effective demand, rather then marginal revenue products, is the determinant of labour employment. Since post-Keynesians are particularly concerned with income distribution between classes, the distribution of income between wages and profits, as well as the respective propensity to save which can be associated with each class of income, will play a major role in the determination of employment. The issue of distribution will allow us to deal with the question of the relationship between the level of real wages and the demand for labour.

Let us start with a very simple model, which includes all the major simplifications which can be found in the literature. This will permit us to get down immediately to the essentials of the post-Keynesian theory of labour demand in the short period, without having to deal with many of its details. We shall release some of the simplifying assumptions later in the chapter.

The simplifying assumptions, most of which can be associated with

Kalecki and can be found in Asimakopulos (1975), are the following. There is only one type of good being produced, which serves both as a consumption and an investment good; that is, the model has only one sector; there is no depreciation of the capital stock; the price level is fixed and arbitrary; there is only one wage rate, although there are two kinds of workers; all wages which are distributed are spent: these are the non-discretionary expenditures; there is an amount of discretionary expenditures which is fixed in real terms: it includes investment or government expenditures (as well as trade surplus) and also autonomous consumption expenditures, such as those of rentiers. As a consequence the propensity to save on profits may be an endogenous variable and is not explicitly defined in this preliminary stage, but it is implicitly determined to be greater than zero, and hence superior to the propensity to save on wages. The fact that the propensity to save on wages is zero does not necessarily mean that individual workers do not save: it may be that the savings of some are exactly compensated by the dissavings of the others.

The treatment of investment is perhaps the most open to question. Mainly for this reason, no investment function will be discussed in the present chapter. In standard Keynesian models, the level of investment decreases with the real rate of interest. Although neo-Ricardians, for instance Pivetti (1985) and Petri (1992), deny the logical existence of an inverse relationship between the interest rate and investment, its validity is not contested by many well-known post-Keynesian authors. However, as McKenna and Zannoni (1990) show, the justification advanced by these authors for this inverse relationship ultimately depends on the assumption of diminishing returns. The only other post-Keynesian explanation relies on Kalecki's earlier version (1937) of the principle of increasing risk, a principle which Kalecki changed substantially in his later writings (1971), as we saw in Chapter 3. Indeed the changes are such that the later version of the principle of increasing risk cannot support the inverse relation between the rate of interest and investment. The impact of the rate of interest will have to await the next chapter, where we shall deal explicitly with the rate of profit and where various investment functions in a growth perspective will be discussed.

The position taken at this stage is that investment in the short run is based on past historical considerations as well as on 'animal spirits', neither of which can easily be modelled in a simple short-period model of effective demand. The historical aspects, in particular the link between past profits of firms and the funds which they are allowed to borrow to finance investment, have already been discussed in Chapter 3. The influence of expectations and entrepreneurs' animal spirits have been discussed by several post-Keynesian authors (Asimakopulos, 1971), but it does not lend itself easily to an algebraic treatment (however, see Dutt, 1991–2). The most effective description of the meaning of animal spirits seems to me to be the following.

> In the capitalist system, an entrepreneur with 'animal spirits' which are more optimistic than those of the group constituting the rest of the entrepreneurs is necessarily penalized. Whereas it would be in the interest of all entrepreneurs to have the highest possible 'animal spirits', it is in the interest of each entrepreneur not to be too optimistic, or at least, not more optimistic than the other entrepreneurs. (Translation of Grellet, 1976, p. 203)

When considering investment expenditures as autonomous, two possibilities may prevail. One is to suppose that investment expenditures are fixed in nominal terms: this is what Davidson (1962) and Kurz (1985) do. The other is to consider that investment expenditures are given in terms of increases in capacity, and hence that they are given in real terms. This is what Kalecki (1971) and Robinson (1962, p. 46) do, as well as several post-Keynesian authors of models of the type that is being presented here (Harcourt, 1972, p. 211; Harris, 1974). Consequently real investment expenditures will be assumed to be given.

With our previous notations, $wL$ is the amount of nominal wages paid and hence spent. We call $a$ the amount of autonomous expenditures which is given in real terms, and $A$ the same expenditures in nominal terms. With $p$ the price level, we may write aggregate demand $D$ to be equal to:

$$D = wL + A = wL + ap \tag{5.11}$$

The nominal value of aggregate supply $Y$ depends by definition on the price level $p$ and the real output $q$, $q$ being supplied according to the conditions of equation (5.4):

$$Y = pq \tag{5.12}$$

Since, as Keynes (1973, xiv, p. 181) pointed out, the principle of effective demand does not depend on whether or not expectations are realized, we might as well suppose for simplification that the short-run level of output expected by firms is indeed equal to actual sales. The condition of equilibrium is then:

$$D = Y \tag{5.13}$$

The very simple model including equations (5.1) to (5.3) and (5.11) to (5.13) can be represented in its partial equilibrium version by a graph

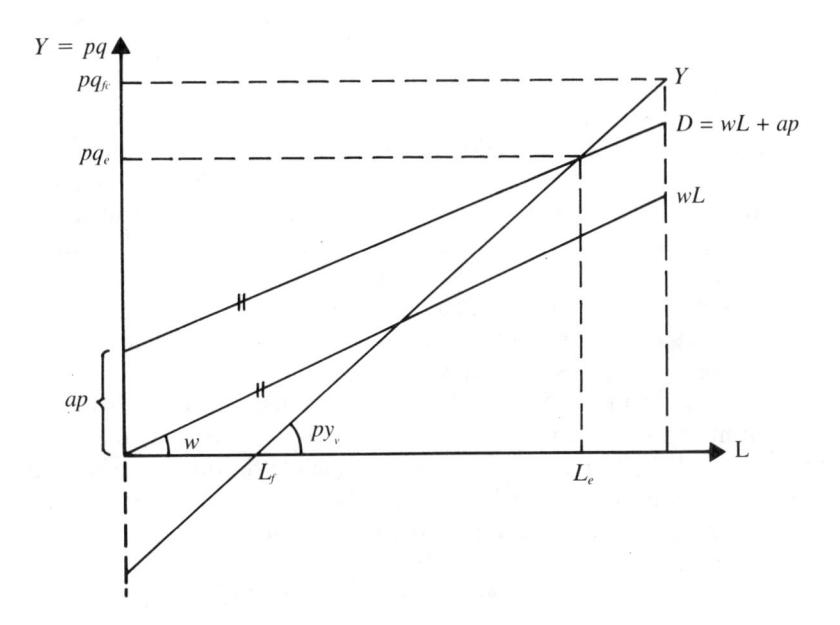

*Figure 5.5  Effective demand and employment in partial equilibrium*

relating effective demand to employment, as is done in Figure 5.5. This graph is an analogue to the old Keynesian fixed price representations of aggregate demand and supply. With given prices, any increase in the components of aggregate demand $D$, the wage rate or the autonomous expenditures (government expenditures, investment, consumption on distributed profits) raises the equilibrium level of employment $L_e$ and of real output $q_e$. When the wage rate rises the slope of the aggregate demand curve increases; when autonomous expenditures increase, the aggregate demand curve shifts up. There is thus a positive relationship between the real wage rate and the demand for labour, in contrast to the standard neoclassical assumptions.

On the graph, aggregate gross profits can be identified as the vertical difference between the $Y$ line and the $wL$ line, the latter representing wage costs. Obviously the level of profits is an increasing function of the level of output. The highest level of profit that firms overall could potentially attain, given the existing constraints on capacity, corresponds to full capacity output $q_{fc}$. It is there that the distance between the value of output and the costs of labour is the greatest. However, at such a level of output, the potential profits would not be realized. Demand would be insufficient to absorb all production, and there would be a substantial increase in stocks. A similar situation would arise for all levels of production beyond $q_e$. Only at the equilibrium level of output $q_e$, would the potential profits be exactly realized. The equilibrium level of output, according to the principle of effective demand, is thus the level of output where the amount of realized profits are maximized, given the autonomous demand conditions. If the real wage rate were to be reduced to slim down labour costs, there would be an equivalent reduction in aggregate demand. The level of the real wage rate is thus irrelevant to re-establishing the realization of potential profits. In the neoclassical story, labour demand is assumed to correspond to the point where potential profits are maximized because whatever is produced is supposed to be sold (Nell, 1978, p. 25). When neoclassical authors exclude mechanisms that automatically adapt aggregate demand to aggregate supply, they face the constraints of effective demand underlined by the post-Keynesians (Fujimoto and Leslie, 1983; Schefold, 1983).

In the case of the utilization function presented above, the standard tools of maximization are even more useless. In the vertically integrated firm, the level of potential profits is simply equal to the difference between the value of output and the labour cost. Making use of equation (5.4), total potential profits $p\Pi$ in nominal terms are thus:

$$p\Pi = pq - wL = p[L - (q_{fc}/y_f)]y_v - wL \qquad (5.14)$$

Taking the first derivative of this expression with respect to $L$, in an attempt to find the neoclassical demand for labour based on profit maximization, yields the following result:

$$d(p\Pi)/dL = py_v - w \qquad (5.15)$$

Setting this derivative equal to zero, we see that profits are optimized if the real wage rate $w/p$ is set equal to the marginal physical product of variable labour, $y_v$. To do so would, however, bring bankruptcy to the aggregate of firms since the overall productivity of labour, taking into account variable and fixed labour, is by definition inferior to the strict productivity of blue-collar workers. This can be seen by comparing the values of $y_v$ and $y$ in equation (5.8). Setting the real wage rate equal to the marginal product of variable labour would always bring the costs above the value of output! The firms would be making losses. In the context of the post-Keynesian utilization function, there is no real wage rate which corresponds to the standard maximizing conditions. This is one more argument in favour of the view according to which the real wage rate is truly a conventional phenomenon. It cannot be otherwise. The demand for labour thus cannot be explained by orthodox analysis, based on the maximization of potential profits. The demand for labour must be explained by the principle of effective demand.

Having now shown that the standard analysis of the demand for labour is deprived of any support within the context appropriate to an economy facing effective demand constraints and a linear utilization function, we examine the relationship between effective demand, the real wage rate and variations in the demand for labour.

**Real Wages and Labour Demand**

The algebraic relationship between the demand for labour and the real wage rate can be made explicit by solving the system of equations for the real wage rate. Using equations (5.1) and (5.2) and equations (5.11) to (5.13), one obtains:

$$\frac{w}{P} = \frac{(L-L_f)y_v}{L} - \frac{a}{L} \qquad (5.16)$$

Equation (5.16) represents all the combinations of employment levels and real wage rate levels which are compatible with the equality of aggregate demand $D$ and aggregate supply $Y$. This requires the equality of investment with savings, and as a consequence it is an algebraic representation of a variant of the IS curve (Yellen, 1980, p. 16). The graphical representation of this IS curve is shown in Figure 5.6. This curve is thus the demand for labour curve, or the employment curve. As we had seen within a partial framework, there is a general positive relationship between the demand for labour and the real wage rate, in contrast to the neoclassical view. The higher the real wage rate, the higher the level of employment which is offered by the firms since this level is compatible with all goods produced being sold.

The curve in Figure 5.6 thus illustrates both the demand for labour and the principle of effective demand. The level of equilibrium output or employment is not independent of the distribution of income, and in particular of the level of the real wage rate. That there is a positive relation between the real wage rate and the equilibrium level of employment can be seen by taking the first derivative of equation (5.16). One gets an expression which is always positive. On the other hand the second derivative is always negative, both derivatives justifying the shape of the curve which appears in Figure 5.6. This type of curve can also be found in the works of various post-Keynesian and neo-Ricardian authors, such as Schefold (1983, p. 244), Nell (1984, p. 149) and Mongiovi (1991, p. 38), the latter author having derived it from a multi-sector simulation exercise.

*Figure 5.6   Demand for labour curve, employment curve, or post-Keynesian IS curve*

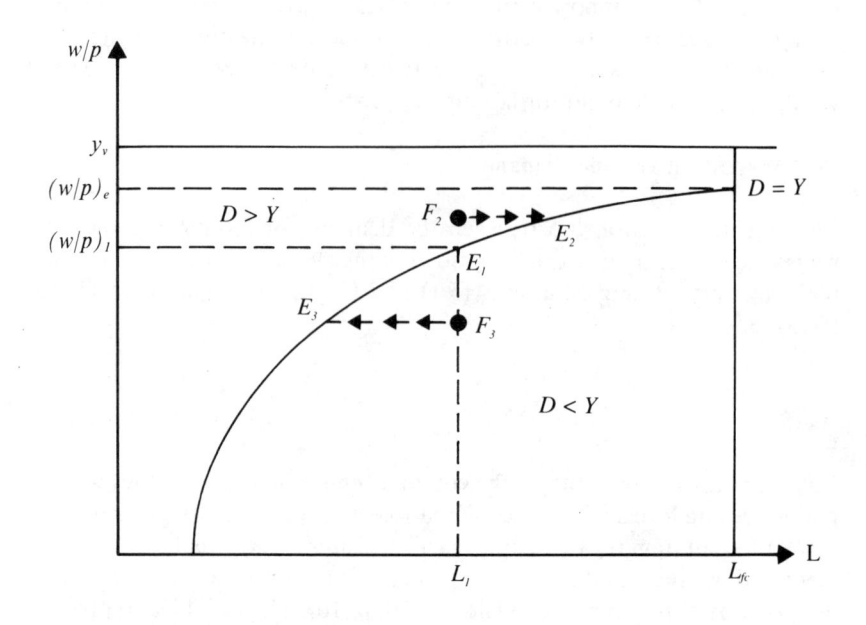

$$\frac{d(w/p)}{dL} = \frac{(y_v L_f + a)}{L^2} > 0$$

$$\frac{d^2(w/p)}{dL^2} = \frac{-2(y_v L_f + a)}{L^3} < 0 \qquad (5.17)$$

Coming back to Figure 5.6, the plane may be divided into three areas. On the curve, as already pointed out, aggregate demand and aggregate supply are always equal. This locus of equilibria has the shape of an asymptotic curve, the asymptote being given by the constant marginal physical product of variable labour, $y_v$. As was remarked above, the real wage rate can never exceed the productivity of blue-collar workers. Indeed, because employment is restricted by the number of workers which can be hired efficiently at full capacity output, denoted by $L_{fc}$ in Figure 5.6, the economy is not likely to approach the asymptote.

The other two areas of the plane shown on Figure 5.6 are determined by the curve representing equation (5.16). Above or to the left of the locus of equilibria, one would be in a situation of excess demand, aggregate demand for goods exceeding aggregate supply. Under and to the right of the curve, there is an excess supply of goods, aggregate demand being insufficient. This can be easily seen by imagining that the level of employment fixed by the firms in conformity with their expectations corresponds to $L_1$. The other conditions being given, there is only one real wage rate, $(w/p)_1$, which clears the market for goods. For instance, if the real wage rate were any higher, at a level corresponding to the point $F_2$ on the graph, aggregate demand would be higher than its equilibrium value, as can be seen from equation (5.11).

Looking at the relationship between the real wage rate and employment from the point of view of the goods market, we see that the model is stable since any excess demand in the market for goods should induce an increase in the supply of goods and hence in the demand for employment. As shown by the arrows in Figure 5.6, starting from the disequilibrium situation of point $F_2$, the economy would move to point $E_2$, where the overall supply of goods now equals aggregate demand, at a higher level of employment. Similarly, if prices were to respond in the conventional manner to the excess demand for goods, the real wage rate would drop until the economy reached point $E_1$. Reciprocally, if there were an excess supply of goods, caused here by an insufficiently high wage rate, as shown by point $F_3$, entrepreneurs would be induced to diminish production and the level of employment. The economy would move to point $E_3$, where the new equilibrium level of output and the new level of employment are smaller. Similarly, still ignoring for the moment the labour market, if prices were to respond in the conventional manner to an excess supply of goods, the real wage rate would go up and the economy would move from $F_3$ to $E_1$. Whatever the adjustment, of the conventional price sort or of the Keynesian quantity type, economic forces are such that the economy is always brought back onto the effective demand constraint curve.

Let us now look at the labour market *per se*, by contrast with the market for goods. Let us assume that the economy is continuously on the post-Keynesian IS curve, where the aggregate demand and aggregate supply of goods are equal. This curve is the demand for labour, since the profit-maximizing constraint is inoperative. Assume also that the supply curve of labour happens to correspond to the employment at full capacity, what we have denoted by $L_{fc}$. Let the real wage rate be given by $(w/p)_1$ and hence the current level of employment be given by $L_1$. The economy is then in a situation of unemployment, the amount of unemployed workers being equal to $L_{fc} - L_1$. According to neoclassical theory, the excess supply of labour should exert downward pressures on the wage rate, and an equilibrium in the labour market should be re-established. In the present case, however, a decrease in the real wage rate would only worsen the unemployment rate, since it would lead to a decline in effective demand and a lower level of employment. There is unemployment because of a deficiency in effective demand, not because real wages are too high, as in the neoclassical story. This is what Malinvaud (1977) and others call Keynesian unemployment. Whereas post-Keynesian models with standard production functions and decreasing returns can produce bouts of Keynesian and neoclassical unemployment (Lavoie, 1986b), only Keynesian unemployment may appear in a short-run model based on the typical post-Keynesian utilization function. The so-called market mechanisms are helpless in the case of Keynesian unemployment since the cure for unemployment is higher wages, not reduced ones. Looking again at Figure 5.6, we see that the real wage rate which ensures full employment is $(w/p)_e$. If for some reason the real wage rate were to fall below that level, an excess supply of labour would appear and a decrease of the real wage rate would get the economy away from full employment. Conversely, if the wage rate happened to be above $(w/p)_e$, the level of output would be constrained by the supply of workers and there would be both an excess demand for goods and an excess demand for labour. As Nell (1988a, p. 122) notes, in this case the excess demand for goods would be exactly proportional to the excess demand for labour, since the demand for labour results from the demand for goods. If the *prices* of both markets respond identically to demand pressures, there would be no change in the real wage rate. In the terms employed by neoclassical authors, the market for labour is not stable. Market forces do not bring back the real wage rate to its full employment value, even when there are no imperfections.

As Figure 5.7 shows, this lack of stability of the labour market is not modified, whatever the sort of labour supply curve which is postulated. In all cases, a real wage rate which is above the wage rate ensuring full employment leads to an excess demand of goods and of labour. When the real wage rate is below its full employment level, there is an excess supply of labour, that is unemployment. In this situation, to let the real wage rate fall in line with the hypothetical market forces, or to encourage a decrease in real wage rates would lead to perverse results, as the rate of unemployment would increase. The theory of labour demand which has just been presented reinforces Keynes's contention (1973, vii, ch. 19) that a flexible wage rate would be detrimental to employment, and cannot help to restore full employment.

The theory which has been expounded above gives rise to a simple explanation of the controversial positive relationship between output and employment on the one hand and real wages on the other, which has been empirically observed for most cycles in almost all countries (Schor, 1985).

*Effective Demand and Employment* 239

*Figure 5.7 Instability of the labour market: (a) with an upward-sloping supply of labour; (b) with a downward-sloping supply of labour*

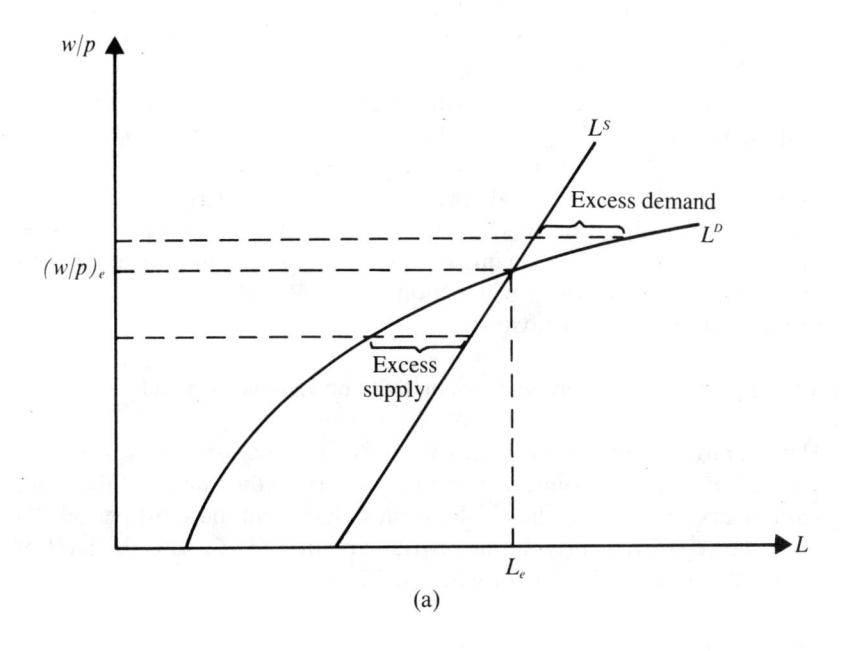

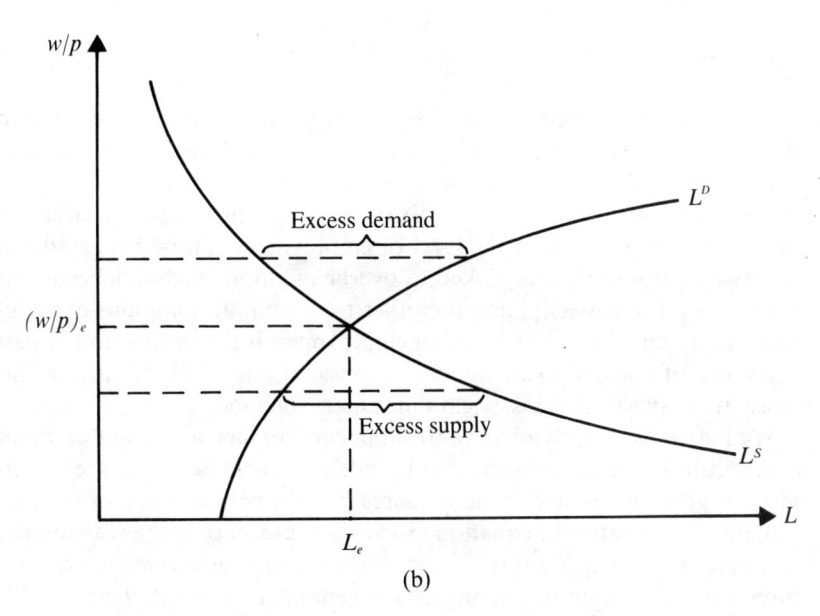

Although some authors deny that there is any significant cyclical pattern, none argue seriously that real wages are usually counter-cyclical, while many conclude that 'real wages are procyclical, rising during expansions and falling during recessions' (Tatom, 1980, p. 385). This pattern is even more obvious in the case of disaggregated data, since real wages of people with low incomes and employment opportunities rise particularly with output, an effect which aggregate studies cannot capture since these individuals are weighted according to their (low) income (Bils, 1985). The positive relation between real wages and employment is a direct consequence of the utilization function which has been proposed here. It does not require any convoluted construction or the use of lags, in contrast to models based on orthodox production functions and trying to reproduce procyclical real wage behaviour.

**The Impact of Investment and Productivity on Labour Demand**

Having now defined the peculiar role of the demand for labour in a post-Keynesian macroeconomic framework, we turn to the impact of the other parameters determining the employment of labour in the short period. To do so more conveniently, let us rewrite equation (5.16) with the level of employment as the dependent variable. We get:

$$L = \frac{a}{y_v - \frac{w}{p}} + \frac{L_f y_v}{y_v - \frac{w}{p}} \qquad (5.18)$$

Examining the denominator of equation (5.18) forces us to recall that the real wage rate must be inferior to the marginal physical product of variable labour for the model to make any sense; otherwise the level of employment is null or negative. Examining the numerator of equation (5.18), one may note that the level of employment can be broken down into two components: one linked to overhead labour $L_f$ and hence to the existing level of capacity, and the other to current autonomous expenditures, represented by $a$. The level of employment is thus a function of past decisions, of current spending and of expectations of the future. In this sense, we may say that historical time enters the model.

We may now directly observe the impact of an increase of autonomous expenditures on employment; that is, either an increase in private investment or government deficit, or an increase in the consumption of rentiers. Taking the derivative of equation (5.18) with respect to $a$, the real amount of autonomous expenditures (private investment, government expenditures, rentier consumption), one gets the employment multiplier:

*Figure 5.8 Impact on the employment function of an increase in autonomous expenditures or of a decrease in the productivity of white-collar workers*

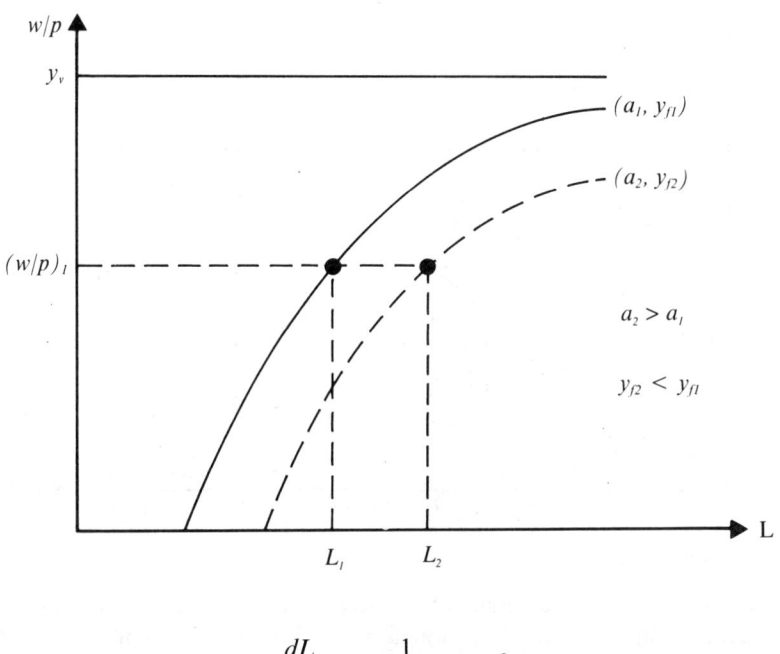

$$\frac{dL}{da} = \frac{1}{y_v - (w/p)} > 0 \tag{5.19}$$

As in orthodox Keynesian theory, the impact on employment of autonomous investment expenditures is always positive. The graphical interpretation of the partial derivative performed in equation (5.19) can be found in Figure 5.8. As autonomous expenditures rise from $a_1$ to $a_2$, the entire employment curve shifts down. The partial derivative just computed represents the impact on employment of an increase in autonomous expenditures, with all of the other variables being constant. The real wage rate, in particular, is thus assumed to be fixed. From the graph we can see that, at a constant wage rate, the level of employment increases from $L_1$ to $L_2$ following an increase in autonomous expenditures. From equation (5.19) we can also see that the value of this employment multiplier is greater the smaller the differential between the marginal product of blue-collar workers and the wage rate of workers. At a higher real wage rate, the multiplier effect of an increase in autonomous expenditures is more substantial than at low levels of the real wage rate.

*Figure 5.9 Impact on the employment function of an increase in the productivity of blue-collar workers*

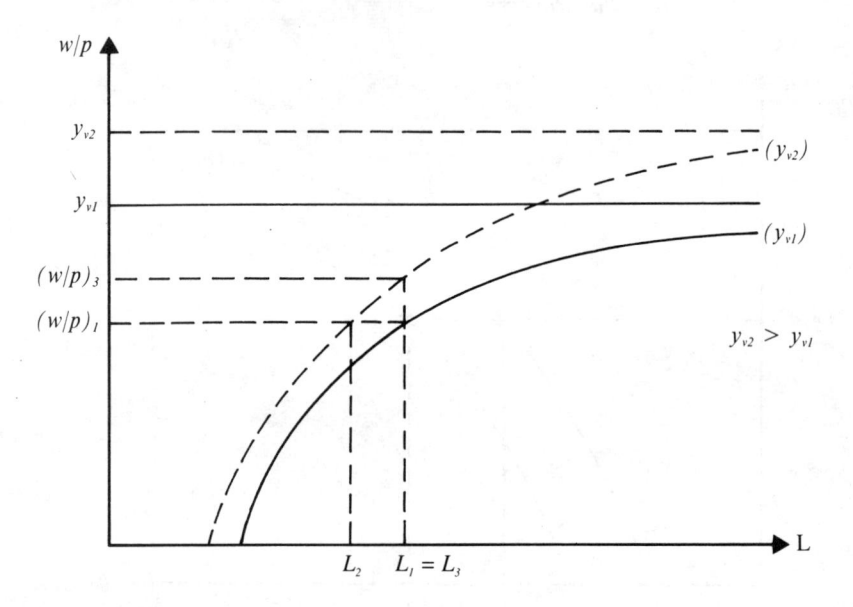

Let us now look at the impact of an increase in productivity. Let us first deal with an increase in the productivity of white-collar workers. It is obvious that such an increase would directly lead to a fall in fixed labour. There would also be additional negative effects on the overall level of employment, because of the employment multiplier. The employment curve would shift to the left in Figure 5.8, as productivity increases from $y_{f2}$ to $y_{f1}$. For a given wage rate, the level of employment would fall from $L_2$ to $L_1$. The same exercise could be repeated in the case of the productivity of blue-collar workers. Taking the first derivative of equation (5.18), this time with respect to $y_v$ one finds:

$$\frac{dL}{dy_v} = \frac{-a - L_f(w/p)}{(y_v - w/p)^2} < 0 \qquad (5.20)$$

Hence, as one would expect, an increase in the productivity of variable labour should lead to a decrease in employment, although fixed labour is kept constant. The case is illustrated in Figure 5.9, productivity increasing from $y_{v1}$ to $y_{v2}$ and employment falling from $L_1$ to $L_2$. The major difference from the preceding situation is that, when the productivity of variable labour rises, both the employment curve and its asymptote shift up.

It is often asserted that the real wage rate should increase in line with the productivity of labour. This is usually meant to imply that the rate of increase of real wages should equal the rate of increase of labour productivity. Such an economic policy, designed to preclude inflationary money wage increases, would nevertheless lead to a decrease in the level of employment in the short run (Nell, 1978, p. 20, 1988a, p. 124). This can be seen by examining equation (5.19) again. Assume there is no change in autonomous expenditures nor in the productivity of white-collar workers. For the level of employment to remain constant, any increase in the absolute value of the productivity level of blue-workers must be fully compensated by an equal increase in the absolute amount of real wages. When this is the case, the denominator of equation (5.19) determining the level of employment remains constant, in particular the expression $(y_v - w/p)$. As a consequence, and remembering that $y_v$ is necessarily greater than $w/p$, an equal *proportional* increase in productivity and in the real wage rate would imply a larger denominator in equation (5.19) and hence a decline of employment in the short run. In the short run, the simple rule of equating percentage increases in real wages to percentage increases in productivity will not keep employment constant. It must be reinforced by increased autonomous expenditures.

**Wealth Effects and Unemployment**

We have so far presented a theory of employment which is compatible with involuntary unemployment. Workers are out of work because firms are constrained in their sales by aggregate demand. In neoclassical theory, the flexibility of prices guarantees that such involuntary unemployment does not occur. In neoclassical models, a deficiency in the demand for commodities is made good by a fall in the general price level. Lower prices have a positive effect on aggregate demand through two possible channels, both linked to real money balances. On the one hand, lower prices accompanied by a constant level of the money supply generate lower interest rates and hence higher investment expenditures. This is the so-called Keynes effect. On the other hand, it is claimed that lower prices directly induce higher autonomous consumption expenditures since real wealth is higher. This is the Pigou effect. Despite these two similar mechanisms, there may be some reductions in employment below the point of full employment in neoclassical models, but these are the consequences of workers overestimating the consumer price index, as in new classical or new Keynesian theories. Unemployment in these neoclassical models is thus voluntary. Households choose to restrict their supply of labour as a result of erroneous expectations. Such hoarding of labour leads to a rise in the real wage rate, which induces firms to reduce their demand for labour and to reduce their output, on the basis of the principle of potential profit maximization.

We are now in a better position to compare the post-Keynesian macroeconomic model with the neoclassical one. In the latter, as shown in numerous orthodox intermediate textbooks, equilibrium output is at the intersection of an aggregate supply function and an aggregate demand function, both set in the price/quantity plane. In the post-Keynesian model there is no aggregate supply function to speak of. The aggregate supply function of neoclassical models is an outcome of firms attempting to maximize potential profits, according to the rule equating the real wage rate to the marginal product of labour. Such a function does not exist in the canonical post-Keynesian model, as we have seen in the previous subsections. The level of output offered by each post-Keynesian firm is determined by the demand for its products, and in the aggregate the supply of output is set by effective demand. There is no independent aggregate supply function. At best, the aggregate supply schedule may be interpreted as a horizontal curve, at the fixed price level. This is the major difference between the neoclassical model and the canonical post-Keynesian model.

By contrast, several post-Keynesian authors have criticized the textbook aggregate supply/aggregate demand neoclassical apparatus by questioning the downward slope of the aggregate demand curve, or by challenging its stability when prices change (Dutt, 1986–7; Fazzari and Caskey, 1989). We shall soon make use of some of these criticisms. For the moment it should be noted that, if we were to construct it, the aggregate demand function of the canonical post-Keynesian model presented above would have the same negative slope as that of the standard neoclassical model. This can be seen by rewriting equation (5.16), making use of the definition of output, given by equation (5.2). One then obtains an aggregate demand function à la neoclassical, with the price level $p$ as a function of output $q$:

$$p = w(L_f + q/y_v)/(q - a) \qquad (5.21)$$

Note that the parameters of this aggregate demand function are the nominal wage rate, overhead labour, the productivity of blue-collar workers and the level of autonomous expenditures. Taking the derivative of this function with respect to $q$, we find that the slope of the aggregate demand curve is always negative:

$$dp/dq = -w(L_f + a/y_v)/(q - a)^2 < 0 \qquad (5.22)$$

Naturally there is nothing surprising in such a result. The parameters of equation (5.21) and, in particular, the level of money wages being given, a decrease in the price level implies an increase in the real wage rate. We have found again the positive relationship between the real wage rate and effective demand as it was illustrated in Figure 5.6. The slopes of the aggregate demand functions in the neoclassical and post-Keynesian models thus have the same sign (Myatt, 1986, p. 453; Bhaduri, 1991). The slope of the aggregate demand function is therefore not the crucial issue. What is at stake is the existence of the aggregate supply function and the mechanisms which generate a negative slope for the aggregate demand curve. The justifications for the sign of this slope are quite different according to the chosen paradigm. In the neoclassical model, the negative slope results from the direct impact of real money balances on consumption and its indirect impact on investment, via interest rates. In the post-Keynesian model, it results from the redistributive impact of real wages on consumption through differentiated propensities to save. A higher level of output, and hence a higher level of employment, could be attained if prices could be brought down sufficiently to allow for a high enough real wage rate. Although the sign of the slope of the aggregate demand function is the same as in the neoclassical formulation, the mechanisms at work in the post-Keynesian theory and its economic logic are completely different.

A question that springs to mind is whether some features of the neoclassical model could not be integrated into the post-Keynesian model to create a hybrid improved model. Since the labour market mechanisms in the post-Keynesian model are helpless to bring back full employment, could we not introduce a real balance effect and arrive at full employment? If unemployment leads to decreases in money wages, as it should in a pure market economy, and hence to proportional decreases in prices as a fall-out of lower costs, could the resulting higher real wealth improve the employment situation as in the neoclassical model?

The answer is that in the abstract it could. Let us add a term to autonomous expenditures, one based on the existing stock of wealth. The condition of equality between aggregate expenditures and income, previously given by equation (51.11) becomes:

$$wL + a + \eta W = pq \qquad (5.23)$$

The nominal amount of wealth is $W$ and the proportion of it which is spent is $\eta$. Solving for the level of employment, as we did in the case of equation (5.19), one obtains:

$$L = \frac{a + (L_f y_v) + \eta(W/p)}{y_v - \frac{w}{p}} \qquad (5.24)$$

Obviously equation (5.24) shows that an increase in real wealth, other things being equal, would lead to an increase in the level of employment. Eventually, with a sufficient proportional fall in money wages and in prices, such that the real wage would not change, full employment could be achieved through this real wealth effect. Furthermore, even if the excess supply of labour combined with strong conventional market forces pushed down the real wage rate, the real wealth effect could still compensate for this negative effect on employment and bring back full employment with a large enough fall in nominal prices. The impact of the real wealth effect when prices have fallen is identical to that of an increase in autonomous expenditures. Graphically this corresponds to a downward shift of the employment curve in Figure 5.8.

One must thus rely on other non-orthodox arguments to refute the possibility of full employment through market forces and the real wealth effect. Here we must go back to the arguments that have been advanced by authors critical of the downward-sloping neoclassical aggregate demand curve. First, recall that one of the neoclassical explanations of this slope is the Keynes effect: if prices decrease, the real money supply rises, interest rates decline and hence investment expenditures rise, leading to a recovery at full employment output. The downward-sloping aggregate demand curve of neoclassical theory thus relies on the interest sensitivity of investment, the endogeneity of interest rates and the exogeneity of the money supply. In the simple post-Keynesian model presented so far, this Keynes effect could not be considered: there is no investment function; investment expenditures are purely autonomous. But even if investment were interest-sensitive, the post-Keynesian theory of credit money presented in Chapter 4 would preclude the functioning of the Keynes effect since the money supply is endogenous, while interest rates are the outcome of discretionary policy decisions, and hence exogenous.

Neoclassical authors must then go back to the Pigou effect which is underlined in equation (5.24) above. As was pointed out at the end of Chapter 2, the apparent econometric success of the permanent income and life-cycle hypotheses provided much-needed justification for the abstract Pigou effect. We know, however, that the empirical successes of these neoclassical constructions is an artefact of their empirical specification. We cannot presume that real wealth enters the consumption function. Furthermore neoclassical authors have themselves recognized that a substantial portion of wealth is set off by the debts held by the other agents of the economy. As a consequence, the real wealth effect was initially reduced to the real money balances effect, and the definition of money balances was restricted to outside money, that is to high-powered money, in contrast to bank deposits or inside money (Patinkin, 1965). High-powered money is said to be the only asset without debt as a counterpart. The practical impact of the real wealth effect is thus severely restricted since it relies on a small portion of money balances, as Kalecki (1944) was quick to note, even if one admits its conceptual validity.

Whatever is left of the wealth effect, however, is still open to criticism. Three such criticisms may be underlined. First, the small favourable effects on consumption due to increased real outside money balances could be completely swamped by the redistributive impact of decreasing prices on consumption. Lower prices redistribute real wealth from debtors to creditors. If the latter have a higher propensity to save, the redistribution of wealth will induce a fall in consumption expenditures (Tobin, 1975). Secondly, even if, despite these redistributive effects, the overall impact of price reductions is still favourable to consumption expenditures, one must not forget investment expenditures. Keynes (1973, vii, p. 264) objected to falling prices because he felt that they would increase the debt burden of the firms, decrease their cash flows, bring insolvency and lead to falling investment, all effects that have been more recently emphasized by Minsky (1976, p. 139). Kalecki (1944) also believed that the rising real value of debts would bring wholesale bankruptcy and a confidence crisis. As long as some contracts are made in nominal terms and extend through time, lower prices have a negative impact on the cash flow of the firm. Recalling the discussion of the finance requirements of the firm in Chapter 3, to the effect that past retained earnings are the multiplicand for future borrowing, reduced cash flows necessarily induce lower investment. This is where historical time enters the picture. While variable costs and some fixed costs are reduced in line with the reduced revenues of the firms, there are some fixed costs which depend on the higher prices of the preceding period. In particular the interest costs on borrowed capital are fixed, unless interest rates are reduced (Nell, 1978, pp. 26–7). But why would interest rates fall? We are back to the criticism of the Keynes effect: interest rates are a matter of monetary policy.

Finally one should recall that there is no theoretic presumption in favour of the real money balances effect. In a post-Keynesian theory of money, even high-powered money is endogenous. The amount of base money in the economy is determined by the needs of the banking system. If prices are to fall, the money supply will be proportionately reduced, and so will the amount of base money. This is particularly obvious in the case of pure overdraft economies. Agents which, as a result of the fall in prices, have too high cash balances, will reduce their amount of new borrowing or will pay back some of their loans with the excess cash. Similarly banks with excess base money will use it to diminish their debt towards the central bank. The initial increase in real money balances, caused by the lower prices, is dissipated without the excess cash balances having been spent on consumption goods. In a world with endogenous credit money, even outside base money cannot produce the Pigou effect that the neoclassical authors are looking for to preserve the neoclassical reliance on market forces.

We must thus conclude that the Keynes effect and the Pigou effect have no place in a post-Keynesian theory of aggregate demand. The very simple macroeconomic model that has been developed in the present chapter, based on the short-period utilization function and the existence of differentiated propensities to save, is sufficient to capture the essentials of employment and output determination. More complex versions of this model of effective demand may rightfully ignore the real balance effect.

## Efficiency Effects and Labour Demand

We now deal with some complications which can be entered within a short-period model of effective demand. We still remain within the confines of a one-sector model. We start with the possibility of variable productivity, an effect popularized under the expression of wage efficiency effects and which will be called the Webb effect.

In their search for a neoclassical theory of involuntary unemployment, new Keynesian authors such as Shapiro and Stiglitz (1984) have assumed the existence of a positive relationship between the productivity of workers and their real wage rate. Neoclassical authors have thus adopted the Marxian distinction between labour power and labour, the former corresponding to the potential number of hours of work, the potential work effort and the quality of work which is enclosed in the explicit or implicit labour contract, while the latter is the actual number of hours on the job and the actual work effort of the employee (Hodgson, 1982, p. 219). In the Marxian view, labour productivity is not given by the existing technology. The actual technical coefficients depend on various socioeconomic determinants, in particular the real wage rate. The difference between labour and labour power may also be explained by an inappropriate social organization of production (hierarchy instead of labour participation). The concept of actual efficient units of labour is linked to the dual market hypothesis: it purports to explain why workers with similar productivity characteristics are better paid in the core sector of the economy than in the periphery sector.

In both the neoclassical and the radical approaches, the crucial element explaining efficient labour units is the expected cost of job loss. This cost depends on the probability of being caught loafing and losing a job. It also depends on the differential between income earned on the job, on the one hand, and income earned on another job or while unemployed, on the other hand. The rate of unemployment or the average duration of unemployment, or sometimes the rate of increase of these two variables, the availability of social security benefits and the level of wage rates are thus important determinants of work effort (Schor, 1987). In the neoclassical version, utility functions are usually invoked to justify the shirking behaviour of workers and explain the *absolute* level of productivity per worker. The excessively high wage rate which is paid in the core economy induces workers to stop shirking, but it simultaneously creates unemployment, which increases the expected cost of shirking. In the radical version, class struggle and class conflict explain the resistance to innovations designed to enhance efficiency or work intensity, and hence the rate of growth of labour productivity. Strikes, slowdowns, sabotage and absenteeism are all reduced when there is a large reserve army of unemployed workers (Naples, 1987). Discipline is upheld by high unemployment rates and high wages or, in a dynamic world, by high increases in unemployment and in the cost of job losses.

The whole analysis is reminiscent of the standard distinction between labour and leisure. The typical individual of neoclassical analysis takes an all-or-nothing decision, deciding to withdraw from the labour force when the wage rate that he could get while working does not sufficiently exceed the income that he could receive as a leisurely unemployed person. Here the typical individual of efficient wage analysis reduces his amount of work intensity and increases his amount of leisure on the job when he judges that his wage rate is insufficient to cover the work effort for which he has been hired. Monetarist Michael Parkin, for instance, claims that, if the real wage rate of university professors was cut down, they would take more leisure and diminish either the quantity or quality of their teaching and research activities in an effort to maximize utility (Parkin and Bade, 1985, p. 658). There is thus some realization on the part of neoclassical authors that there are institutional difficulties in reducing the number of hours of work spent at the job, since they are often fixed by rules, but that a similar outcome can be achieved by reducing work intensity on the job.

On the whole the reasons presented above to justify the positive relationship between real wages and productivity seem to overemphasize the disutility of work. The positive impact of increased real wage rates on labour productivity may also be given other interpretations. Some authors, such as Akerlof (1982), have suggested social underpinnings which are more in line with the theory of the supply of labour which was presented in the first section of this chapter. Work can bring satisfaction. This satisfaction is to a large extent a function of the interpersonal relations among fellow employees, but also a function of the status of the job. Increased earnings, or increases in earnings relative to other groups of workers, boost the morale of employees. They reinforce the feeling of affiliation of the employee to the firm and enhance the satisfaction of work well done. Similarly, improved working conditions, which are part of the implicit wage rate, create a working environment which is more conducive to high productivity and satisfaction, since workers will not dread coming to work. Employees with a better morale are more likely to set for themselves higher work norms, and they require less monitoring. In a dynamic framework it is the rate of growth of earnings so defined which leads to increases in the rate of change of productivity, since satisfied workers cooperate better when faced with technical innovations (Weisskopf, Bowles and Gordon, 1983, p. 395). It has even been shown that there is a wage acceleration effect. Productivity growth depends not only on the rate of growth of real wages, but also on the acceleration or the slowdown of this rate of growth (Kohli, 1988). Within the statics of the short period, a higher real wage rate, compared to the previous one, would boost the morale of employees. Higher real wages are thus associated with higher effort intensity and a higher level of worker productivity. The static framework based on workers' morale is, however, harder to justify: if the wage increase occurs for all workers, no relative increase occurs; also, after a while, the spirit-boosting effect of the new salary should vanish.

It may thus be preferable to rely on a third group of reasons for which there would exist a variable productivity, positively related to the level of real wages. These reasons were particularly emphasized a long time ago by Sidney Webb (1912, p. 984) in discussions in favour of higher minimum wages. In a more technical sense, higher real wages may lead to the elimination of firms or of plants which have low productivity. Firms for which average costs rise above the price set by the price leader, because of general higher real wage rates, have to close down. On the average, the disappearance of firms whose productivity is low would lead to higher output to labour ratios, since demand would be redistributed towards firms which are more efficient. The technical coefficients of our utilization function would change. The positive relationship between higher real wages and labour productivity can thus be explained by low productivity firms being weeded out of the market (Nell, 1988a, p. 236). In the longer run, higher real wages also induce management to search for more efficient methods of production and to cut down on wasteful processes, in particular X-inefficiency (Leibenstein, 1978). As a result, the overall productivity rises. Because of his earlier appreciation of the positive impact of higher real wages on labour productivity, let us call 'the Webb effect' the relationship known to neoclassical authors as the wage efficiency effect.

Whatever cause of variable productivity one prefers to adopt, we may easily graft its effects onto our simple macroeconomic model. Among a few possibilities, let us assume that there is a positive feedback between the real wage rate and the productivity of blue-collar workers. Making use of a linear formulation, the product to variable labour ratio, which we previously assumed to be a constant, may now be written as:

$$y_v = y_{v0} + \varepsilon(w/p) \tag{5.25}$$

Replacing $y_v$ with its new definition in equation (5.19) yields a new employment function which incorporates the positive impact of higher wages on productivity. The employment function becomes:

$$L = \frac{a + L_f[y_{v0} + \varepsilon(w/p)]}{y_{v0} - (w/p)(1-\varepsilon)} \tag{5.26}$$

Again the marginal physical product of variable labour, $y_v$, as defined in equation (5.25), must be greater than the real wage rate for employment to be positive and the model to have any economic sense. We now take the first derivative of equation (5.26) with respect to real wages to find out under which conditions the positive relationship between real wages and employment holds. One gets:

$$\frac{dL}{d(w/p)} = \frac{a(1-\varepsilon) + y_{v0}L_f}{[y_{v0} - (w/p)(1-\varepsilon)]^2} \tag{5.27}$$

It is clear from equation (5.27) that a sufficient condition for the positive relationship between real wages and the level of employment to persist is that the reaction parameter $\varepsilon$ be smaller than unity. If this is the case, the employment function may still be described by a curve which is similar to the one previously drawn. Figure 5.10 illustrates the impact of the Webb effect when the reaction parameter is smaller than one. The employment function which incorporates the impact of higher real wages on labour productivity is denoted by *WE*, for Webb effect (or for wage efficiency effect). The curve is asymptotic to the straight line, $y_v$, which represents the now endogenous output to variable labour ratio resulting from changes in the real wage rate. Two partial equilibrium employment curves are also drawn. One assumes that the productivity of blue-collar workers stays at the level determined by a wage rate of $(w/p)_1$, whatever the actual real wage rate; similarly, the other partial equilibrium employment curve is based on the productivity set by a real wage of $(w/p)_2$. At the initial wage rate $(w/p)_1$, the level of employment is $L_1$. An increase to $(w/p)_2$ in the real wage rate would drive the employment level to $L'_2$ if there were no

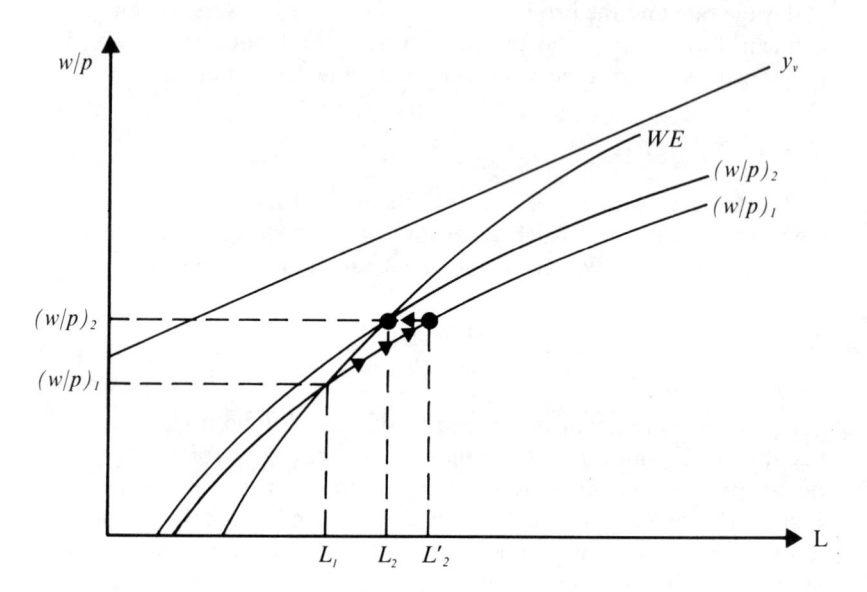

252   Foundations of Post-Keynesian Economic Analysis

*Figure 5.10   Employment curve when the parameter of the Webb effect is below unity*

efficiency effects. The increase in the wage rate, however, drives up the productivity of labour and consequently the partial equilibrium employment function shifts up, as we have seen in Figure 5.9. The global impact of the rise in the real wage rate is thus finally a smaller increase in the level of employment from $L_1$ to $L_2$. This is what the $WE$ curve incorporates.

Although the situation described by Figure 5.10 is the more likely case, it is not the only possible one. If increased wages induce a strong positive productivity effect; that is, if the reaction parameter $\varepsilon$ is so large that equation (5.27) has a negative sign, then the post-Keynesian employment curve takes on a downward slope. The description of Figure 5.11 is similar to that of Figure 5.10. This time, however, the negative impact on employment of the induced increase in labour productivity, $L'_2 - L_2$, overtakes the positive effect on employment of the raised real wage, $L'_2 - L_1$. The resulting change in the level of employment is then negative. As a result, the employment curve which incorporates efficiency effects, the $WE$ curve, has a downward slope. In such an economy, the demand for labour curve would have all the orthodox characteristics, since a decrease in the wage rate eventually would allow a return to full employment.

Seccareccia (1991b) has empirically tested a model for Canada which is

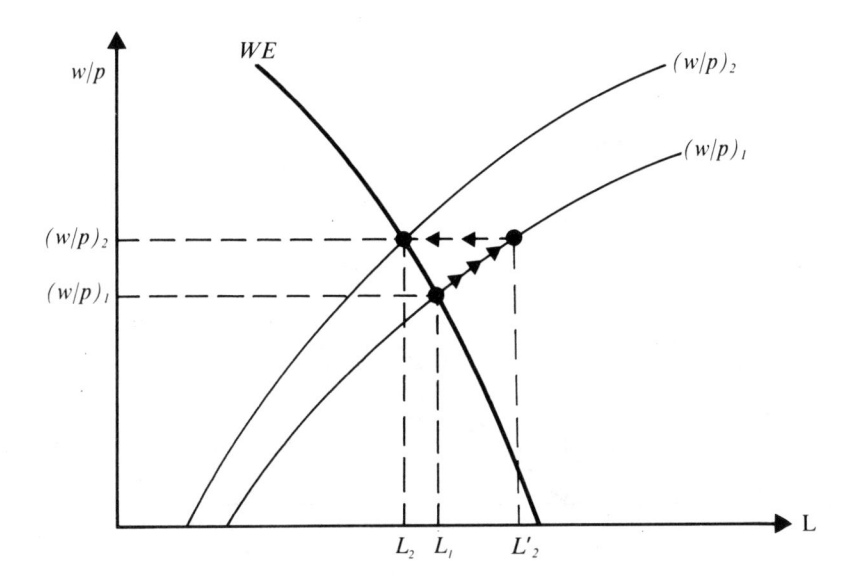

*Figure 5.11  Employment curve when the parameter of the Webb effect is above unity*

very similar to the one presented here. He finds a Webb effect, of which the value of the reaction parameter ε is equal to 0.34 in log-linear form. Seccareccia further demonstrates that the real wage rate has a positive and statistically significant impact on labour employment in the overall industrial sector. An increase of 10 per cent in the level of real wages leads to an increase of 1.3 per cent in the level of employment or the number of hours worked. Empirical data thus demonstrate the existence of an upward-sloping aggregate demand curve for labour, despite an important Webb effect. The employment curve *WE* of Figure 5.10 would seem to be the relevant one, not that of Figure 5.11.

Note that the introduction into our post-Keynesian model of the efficiency wage hypothesis in its strongest version has turned the neoclassical theory of involuntary unemployment upside down. The hypothesis was introduced in neoclassical models to allow for involuntary unemployment. With extreme productivity effects, the hypothesis destroys the possibility of involuntary unemployment in post-Keynesian models! Such a possibility is, however, highly unlikely. It would require highly dubious strong productivity effects in reaction to wage increases or decreases. We may thus continue to assume, when we introduce more complex elements

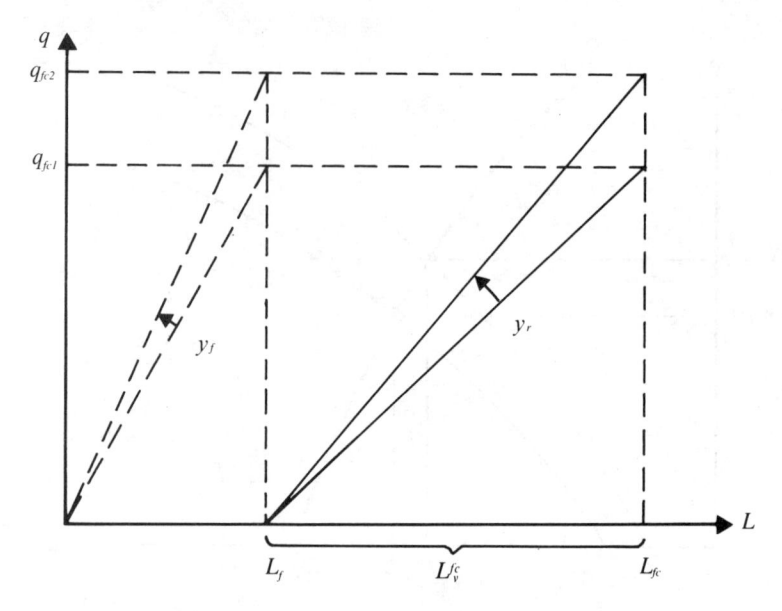

*Figure 5.12 Impact of a change in the productivity of the blue-collar workers on the productivity of the white-collar workers*

into our canonical post-Keynesian model, that the aggregate demand for labour is a direct function of the real wage rate.

We should close this section by noting that any increase in the $y_v$ coefficient of the blue-collar workers has automatic repercussions on the $y_f$ coefficient of white-collar workers. If an identical number of blue-collar workers, with the same equipment, can now produce a larger output, this implies that full-capacity output is now larger. If the same number of white-collar workers are required to supervise an equal number of blue-collar workers when the machinery is functioning at full capacity, this means that the ratio of full capacity output to white-collar workers has increased. The productivity of fixed labour has grown in the same proportions as the productivity of variable labour. This can be captured visually in Figure 5.12. The increase in the productivity of variable workers shifts the utilization function counter-clockwise. With the same number of operatives as before, if the plants were functioning at full capacity, the full capacity level of output would jump from $q_{fc1}$ to $q_{fc2}$. Assuming no change in the number of required white-collar workers $L_f$, the productivity of this fixed labour necessarily augments, as shown by the increase in the angle $y_f$. Algebraically, recalling the definitions of $y_v$ and $y_f$, given by equations (5.2) and (5.3), we may take note of the following relations:

$$f = \frac{y_v}{y_f} = \frac{q/L_v}{q_{fc}/L_f} = \frac{q_{fc}/L_v^{fc}}{q_{fc}/L_f} = \frac{L_f}{L_v^{fc}} \qquad (5.28)$$

The ratio $f$ is the ratio of the productivity of variable labour to the productivity of fixed labour. This ratio is also equal to the ratio of the number of overhead workers to the number of blue-collar workers when the firm or the economy is functioning at full capacity (Rowthorn, 1981, p. 4). As we can see on the graph, when this is the case, the number of workers $L_f$ and $L_v^{fc}$ do not change, regardless of the induced change in the marginal product of variable workers. We must thus conclude that any change originating from the productivity of variable labour induces a proportional change in the productivity of fixed labour. The ratio $f$ is a constant, regardless of the changes in the productivity of variable labour, unless there are other independent modifications in the number of permanent staff required to manage the existing capital stock. Looking again at equation (5.8), which defines the overall labour productivity ratio, we see that it can be further simplified by making use of the relationship noted above in (5.28).

$$\frac{q}{L} = y = \frac{y_v}{1 + f/u} \qquad (5.29)$$

Although we may look at $y_v$ as a variable which may vary because of the Webb effect, we may still regard the ratio $f = y_v/y_f$ as a constant which is independent of the variations of $y_v$ induced by the Webb effect or any other cause. We shall make use of this relationship in the next subsection and in Chapter 6.

## 5.4 PRICING, RATES OF UTILIZATION AND PROFITS

Up to now, the price level has been chosen arbitrarily. Let us, then, relate the price equations of the firm, which were discussed in section 5 of Chapter 3, to the utilization function of the present chapter. This will allow us to review the algebraic formulation of the various cost curves. We will then reassess the principle of effective demand by examining the influence of various variables in terms of the rate of utilization of capacity and by discussing the behaviour of the share of profits.

**Cost-plus Pricing Procedures Revisited**

We start by showing how the cost curves and the price behaviour of firms that were informally discussed in Chapter 3 are related to the post-Keynesian utilization function. The reader may recall that three variants of cost-plus pricing procedures were identified. These were mark-up pricing, normal or full cost pricing, and target-return pricing. All these procedures are variations on the same theme, since it can be shown that they are amenable to a similar algebraic core. The simplest of these variants is mark-up pricing. This we presented as:

$$p = (1+\theta)AVC \qquad (3.11)$$

$AVC$ is average variable cost. In the present context, the only kind of variable costs are the wage costs incurred by the wages paid to blue-collar workers. The average variable costs are the cost of variable labour divided by the level of output. Making use of equation (5.2), we may rewrite equation (3.11) as:

$$p = (1+\theta)wL_v/q$$
or
$$p = (1+\theta)w/y_v \qquad (5.30)$$

The fixed costs of firms, considering for the moment the interest costs on capital as part of the profits, are restricted to the wage costs of overhead labour. The total average costs are then the sum of the wages paid to fixed and variable labour, divided by the level of output. Making use of equation (5.29), total average costs, or what we also called $UC$, for unit costs, in Chapter 3, can be written as:

$$UC = wL/q = w(1+f/u)/y_v \qquad (5.31)$$

We have now expressed unit costs as a function of the rate of utilization of capacity. Naturally, as can be seen from equation (5.31), the higher the rate of utilization, the lower are unit costs. These unit costs fall until the rate of utilization reaches 100 per cent, at which point unit costs become equal to $w(1+f)/y_v$. For a firm to make net profits, net profits being here defined as the excess of the value of sales over total labour costs, the price must exceed the unit cost. In the present instance, the rate of utilization must be above $f/\theta$. All these relations are shown in Figure 5.13, which replicates Figure 3.8, but this time with the appropriate algebraic numbers. It is also shown on the graph that the share of variable costs in

*Figure 5.13* Share of gross profits, unit costs and share of net profits according to the rate of utilization of capacity

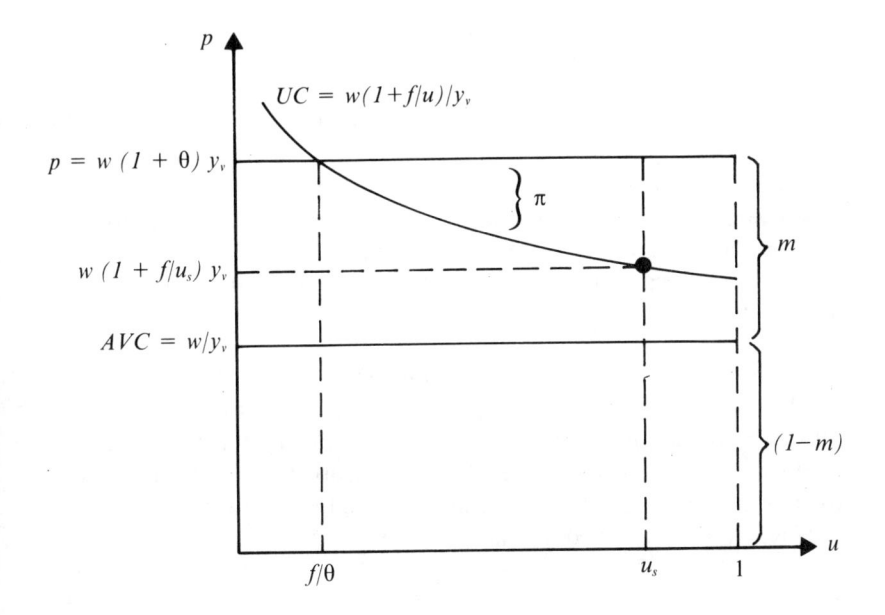

the value of output is equal to $(1-m)$, while that of the sum of fixed costs and profits is equal to $m$. This $m$ is the share of gross profits, or the degree of monopoly in Kalecki's terminology. To see this, recall from equation (3.12) that $m$ is defined as $\theta/(1+\theta)$ and that $p = (wL_v/q) + \theta(wL_v/q)$. The share of variable labour is then $1/(1+\theta)$, and the share of gross profits is: $1 - (wL_v/pq) = 1 - 1/(1+\theta) = \theta/(1+\theta)$. The share of net profits is also indicated in Figure 5.13. It is represented by the letter $\pi$, and it obviously changes, in contrast to the share of gross profits, with the rate of utilization of capacity. If capacity were to fall to $f/\theta$, net profits would be down to zero. We shall later see how that can occur.

A similar graph could have been constructed had we assumed a pricing procedure based on normal cost pricing; that is, one based on the calculation of full costs at a standard level of utilization of capacity. This requires the imputation of a mark-up on standard unit costs. The full cost principle, shown previously as equation (3.13), becomes:

$$p = (1+\theta')UC = (1+\theta')(1+f/u_s)w/y_v \qquad (5.32)$$

where $u_s$ is the standard rate of utilization of capacity. It is easy to find the mark-up on average variable costs which will yield the same price as the full cost principle (Rowthorn, 1981, p. 36). By equating the prices of equations (5.30) and (5.32), we see that, given a mark-up of $\theta'$ on unit costs, the same price would be obtained from a mark-up on prime costs only if the mark-up were equal to:

$$\theta = (1+\theta')(1+f/u_s) - 1 \qquad (5.33)$$

It is also possible to derive the same equivalence in the case of target-return pricing. When the mark-up is set in such a way as to obtain a standard rate of return $r_s$ on investment, $v$ being the capital/capacity ratio, the value of the mark-up $\theta'$ on unit costs, as was shown in Chapter 3, must be equal to:

$$\theta' = r_s v/(u_s - r_s v). \qquad (3.15)$$

By combining equations (3.15) and (5.33), we see that, to arrive at an identical price, given the value of the mark-up $\theta'$ on unit labour costs arising from the target-return pricing decision, the mark-up $\theta$ on marginal costs would have to be equal to:

$$\theta = (r_s v + f)/(u_s - r_s v) \qquad (5.34)$$

We may now write the price equation relating unit prime costs to price, when the pricing procedure is of the target-return type. In the notations of our simple macroeconomic model, equation (3.16) becomes:

$$p = \left(\frac{u_s + f}{u_s - r_s v}\right)\frac{w}{y_v} \qquad (5.35)$$

Note that the price is positive provided the denominator is also positive. For the formula to be meaningful, the standard rate of utilization of capacity must be greater than the product of the capital/capacity ratio and the standard rate of return. We need:

$$u_s > r_s v \qquad (5.36)$$

We have now obtained a very simple expression relating prices to unit prime costs $w/y_v$, although the assumed pricing behaviour of firms is of the sophisticated target-return pricing type. The advantage of equation (5.35) is that it shows that target-return pricing can be rewritten as a function of average variable costs, which are constant whatever the level of output beneath full capacity. Moreover deriving the price equations of the full cost and of the target-return models is important, because it shows that using the more simple mark-up model is appropriate, even if firms make use of more complex accounting and pricing procedures, as long as there is no change in the ratio of overhead to variable labour, the capital/capacity ratio, the standard rate of utilization of capacity and the target rate of return.

As one would expect, the higher the ratio of overhead to variable labour at full capacity, the higher the price relative to unit prime costs. Similarly the higher the target rate of profit, the higher prices relative to costs. Finally it can be verified, again as one would expect, that there is a negative relation between the standard rate of utilization of capacity incorporated into the pricing decision and the ratio of prices relative to direct costs. Taking the derivative of equation (5.35) with respect to the standard rate of utilization, one gets a negative expression:

$$dp/du_s = -(f+r_s v)/(u_s - r_s v)^2 < 0 \qquad (5.37)$$

In what follows, we will focus on the simplest of the price equations, that is equation (5.30) of mark-up pricing, but we will occasionally make use of the more complex target return version of cost-plus pricing.

**Mark-up Pricing and Effective Demand**

In the previous sections of this chapter, the principle of effective demand was seen through the employment function. Changing the real wage rate, or other parameters, we examined the consequences for the level of employment and derived an upward sloping demand curve for labour. In the coming sections, we explore the principle of effective demand through its impact on the rate of utilization of capacity. In particular, to illustrate the principle of effective demand, we shall make use of the graph depicting the cost curves of the representative firm. This will clearly demonstrate that post-Keynesian economics can claim, as much as neoclassical economics does, that there are microeconomic foundations to its macroeconomics.

Naturally our previous analysis is closely linked to that of the determination of the degree of utilization of plant capacity. There is a simple relationship between the overall level of employment of the economy and the rate of utilization of capacity. Making use of equations (5.1) to (5.3), (5.7) and (5.28), total employment may be rewritten as:

$$L = (f+u)q_{fc}/y_v \qquad (5.38)$$

The higher the degree of utilization of capacity, everything else equal, the higher the level of employment. To find out about the determinants of the rate of utilization of capacity, let us start with the same basic assumptions that led to the construction of our simple macroeconomic model in section 3 of the present chapter. Notably all wages $wL$ are consumed, while there are autonomous expenditures in real terms, investment and consumption by rentiers. Our condition of equilibrium (equation 5.13) between aggregate sales and the aggregate value of output may be written as:

$$wL + ap = pq$$

Dividing by $q$ one obtains:

$$w(L/q) = p(1 - a/q)$$

Note that the left-hand side of the above equation is nothing other than the definition of unit costs, which is given in terms of the rate of utilization $u$ in equation (5.31). The left-hand side of the equation may thus be represented in Figure 5.13 by the unit cost curve. Replacing $p$ by its value in equation (5.30) of the mark-up pricing procedure, and noting that $q$ is the product of full capacity output $q_{fc}$ and the rate of utilization, the requirements of effective demand can be rewritten as:

$$w(1 + f/u)/y_v = [(1 + \theta)w/y_v][1 - a/uq_{fc}]$$

This expression can be further simplified, by getting rid of $w/y_v$, yielding:

$$(1 + f/u) = (1 + \theta)(1 - a/uq_{fc}) \tag{5.39}$$

While, as already pointed out, the left-hand side of the above equation may be represented by the unit cost curve, the right-hand side of the equation is illustrated by the upward-sloping curves appearing in Figure 5.14. The downward-sloping curve portrays the effect of non-autonomous expenditures, while the upward-sloping one depicts the effects of autonomous expenditures relative to total output, given the price conditions relative to costs; that is, given the mark-up $\theta$. The rate of utilization of capacity which is consistent with sales equating output is found at the intersection of these two curves. An increase in the mark-up from $\theta_1$ to $\theta_2$ shifts up the upward-sloping curve, as shown on the graph, and implies a higher price level and hence, given the nominal wage rate, a lower real wage rate. The consequences for the rate of utilization are shown on the

*Figure 5.14 Microeconomic representation of effective demand constraints and determination of the rate of utilization of capacity*

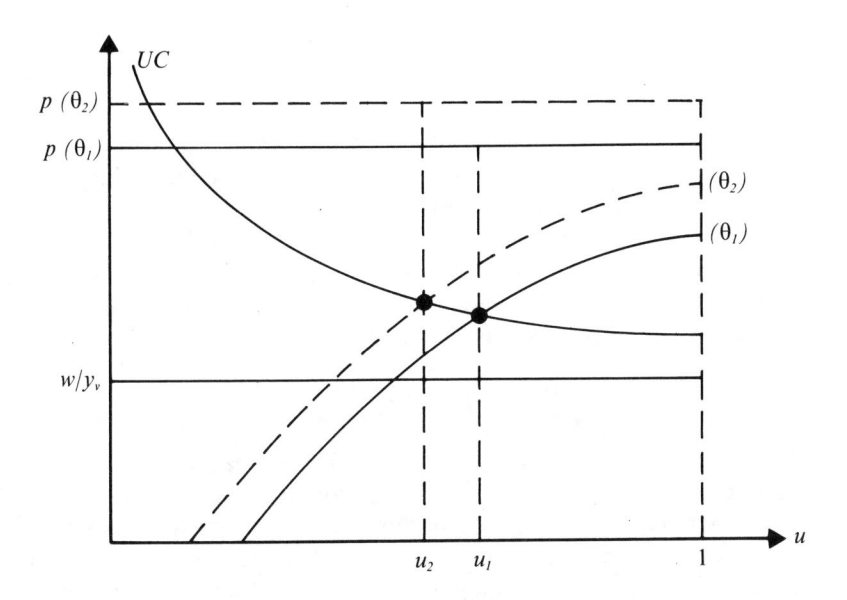

graph: the rate of utilization falls from $u_1$ to $u_2$. As we would expect, following our analysis of the employment function, the rate of utilization of capacity has an inverse relationship with the mark-up level.

This can be shown more formally by solving equation (5.39) for the rate of utilization. We obtain:

$$u = \frac{f}{\theta} + \frac{(1+\theta)}{\theta} \cdot \frac{a}{q_{fc}} \qquad (5.40)$$

The degree of use of capacity results from some special version of the multiplier. There are two exogenous sources of demand in the model. On the one hand, there is autonomous expenditures, the importance of which is reflected by the share of these autonomous expenditures relative to full capacity output. This share is multiplied by the inverse of the share of gross profits in national income, $\theta/(1+\theta)$. The larger the share of variable labour in national income, the larger the multiplier. This effect is further reinforced by the potential share of overhead labour in employment. It is obvious from equation (5.40) that any increase in the relative numbers of overhead labour $f$, or in autonomous demand $a$, leads to an increase in the rate of utilization of capacity. In the first case this is due to a shift upwards of the unit cost curve; in the second case it can be interpreted as a shift downwards of the upward-sloping curve. Naturally, when we derive equation (5.40) with respect to the mark-up, we find a negative expression.

$$du/d\theta = -[(a/q_{fc})+f)]/\theta^2 < 0 \qquad (5.41)$$

We now turn to the determination of the profit share in national income. A few preliminary remarks should first be made regarding some peculiar characteristics of our simplified model. It should be noted that profits in real terms are given once we assume the realization of sales expectations. From the demand side, nominal profits are simply the difference between aggregate demand and the costs of producing output. The nominal amount of profits, then, is equal to:

$$p\Pi^d = (ap+wL)-wL = ap \qquad (5.42)$$

Looking at things from the demand side, the nominal amount of profits is thus equal to the nominal amount of autonomous expenditures. It follows that the real amount of profits is equal to the real amount of autonomous expenditures, $a$, which is assumed to be given and fixed at the start of the period. The real amount of profits is thus also a given, fixed as soon as the level of real autonomous expenditures is set. Of course we could have proceeded otherwise, but any other assumption would not have changed drastically the behaviour of the model, or the way profits are determined at the macroeconomic level. We could have assumed, for instance, that only real investment expenditures $I$ are autonomous, and that rentiers spend a constant proportion $s_p$ of their overall profit income. The demand for consumption goods would then include two sorts of induced expenditures and equation (5.42) would then have to be rewritten in the following way:

$$p\Pi^d = [wL+(1-s_p)p\Pi+pI]-wL = pI/s_p \qquad (5.43)$$

Equation (5.43) corresponds to the standard way in which the relation between profits and autonomous expenditures is presented by post-Keynesian economists. As long as there are no savings out of wages, it makes no difference to adopt one approach of rentier consumption or the other. In all of the previous equations we could have replaced autonomous expenditures $a$ by the expression $I/s_p$. An increase in investment expenditures, or a decrease in the propensity to save out of profits, implies an increase in variable $a$. An increase in real autonomous expenditures may thus also be interpreted as the outcome of a reduction in the propensity to save out of profits. In his own presentation, Kalecki (1971, p. 86) assumes that the real consumption of rentiers is in part a function of past real profits and in part a given real amount. This view is similar to that of Robinson (1956, p. 248), who argues that rentiers' consumption is not closely tied to their receipts for the period. Interpreting past profits as historically given, equation (5.42) would be the relevant one. Interpreting past profits as closely related to current profits, one would choose equation (5.43).

While the real amount of profits $\Pi$ may be considered as an exogenous variable in the short-period model, the share of profits in national income, as well as the share of net profits with regards to the value of output of the firm, is an endogenous variable. Let us call this share of profits $\pi$. Still looking at it from the demand point of view, we deduce from equation (5.42):

$$\pi^d = ap/pq = a/q = a/uq_{fc} \tag{5.44}$$

The above equation shows that, when the rate of utilization of capacity $u$ is higher, the given amount of real profits are spread over a larger output, and as a consequence the share of profits seen from the demand side diminishes with rising rates of utilization. This is only one part of the story, however. When expectations are realized, this share of profits must be equal to the share of profits determined from supply-side considerations. The latter results from the difference between the value of output and the total cost of producing that output. We have:

$$\pi^s = (pq - wL)/pq = 1 - (w/p)(L/q)$$

Making use of the simple mark-up pricing procedure (equation 5.30), as well as of equation (5.29), the share of profits from the supply side is:

$$\pi^s = (\theta - f/u)/(1 + \theta) \tag{5.45}$$

This equation tells us that, looking at the share of profits from the supply side, it increases as the rate of utilization rises. This is of course consistent with the cost curves drawn in Figure 5.13, and the remarks made therein. The above equation, as well as equation (5.44), are illustrated in Figure 5.15 by the curves $\pi^s$ and $\pi^d$ respectively. The intersection of the two curves yields the equilibrium rate of utilization of capacity. The same intersection yields the actual share of profits in national income, as well as the share of net profits in the value of output at the level of the representative firm

*Figure 5.15 Impact of increases in various parameters upon the rate of utilization of capacity and the net share of profits in national income*

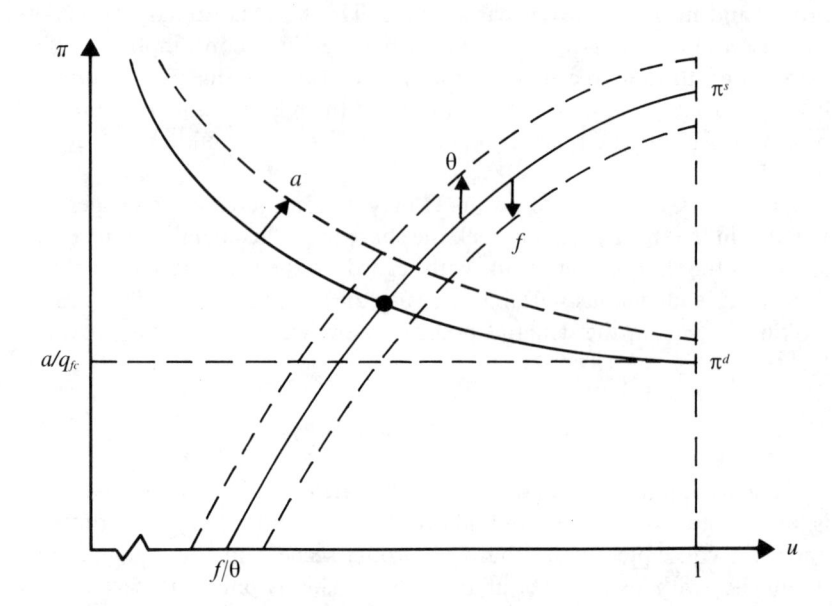

when the aggregate level of sales is equated to the aggregate value of output. The advantage of such a presentation in the present context is that each relevant parameter is only to be found in one of the two curves, so that only one curve shifts as one of the parameters changes.

It is obvious from equation (5.44) that, if the level of autonomous expenditures rises, for a given level of utilization of capacity, the share of profits from the demand point of view must rise. The curve $\pi^d$ would then shift up, as is shown by the dotted $\pi^d$ curve in Figure 5.15. At equilibrium, the rate of utilization and the share of profits would be higher, as shown by the new intersection of the two curves. We may now look at the factors affecting the $\pi^s$ curve, as shown by equation (5.45). A rise in the $f$ ratio, that is the ratio of fixed workers to the number of variable workers that would operate at full capacity output, leads to a downward shift of the $\pi^s$ curve, as shown by the lower dotted $\pi^s$ curve on Figure 5.15. The hiring of more overhead labour would thus induce a rise in the degree of utilization, but it would also cause a fall in the share of net profits. Finally an increase in the mark-up $\theta$, that is a decrease in the real wage rate relative to productivity, would provoke an upward shift of the $\pi^s$ curve. At the new equilibrium, the rate of utilization would be lower, but the share of profits in aggregate income, as well as the share of net profits in the sales value of the firm, would be higher. Capitalists are thus able in the short run to increase their share of profits by increasing the mark-up on costs, but they do so at the expense of the rate of utilization of capacity. Symmetrically, increased real wages relative to productivity lead to a higher degree of utilization of capacity and allow more workers to be employed, as we have seen in the previous sections. These higher wages, however, force down the share of profits. This inverse relationship is extensively used by authors close to the Marxist tradition, as we shall see in the next chapter.

The lesson to be drawn from the above exercise is that the share of profits varies according to various parameters, including the mark-up on direct unit costs and the level of autonomous expenditures. In particular it should be noted that a constant investment to output ratio does not deprive the model of its consistency. Indeed, by checking on equations (5.43) to (5.45), we see that the model determining the share of profits may be reinterpreted in terms of the investment to output ratio, $I/q$. Two statements can thus be made. The model is consistent, despite both a constant investment to output ratio and a constant mark-up; and, as was shown in Figure 5.15, the model determines simultaneously the share of profits and the level of output. The first statement contradicts the critique of post-Keynesian models made by Yellen (1980, p. 17), while the second statement contradicts Kaldor's earlier presumption that the theory of effective demand could not simultaneously determine employment and distribution (Kaldor, 1956, p. 94). Indeed it is this presumption which led Kaldor to assume full employment in his earlier models of growth and distribution. In his and other earlier post-Keynesian models, variations in the distribution of income following changes in the rate of investment were obtained by changing the mark-up, that is the profit margin, as the following quotation makes obvious.

In any given situation, with given productive capacity in existence, a higher rate of investment brings about a higher level of total gross income (through a higher level of employment of labour and utilization of plant) and a higher share of gross profit in gross income (by pushing up prices relatively to money-wage rates). Thus, within reason, investment generates the saving that it requires. (Robinson, 1975b, p. 177)

It should now be clear that Kaldor's and Robinson's earlier beliefs, as well as Yellen's critique with which they are associated, are incorrect when one takes overhead labour costs into account. This was recognized by Asimakopulos (1970) when he formalized remarks made by Joan Robinson. Her remarks were to the effect that, with target-return pricing, supernormal profits are made in a seller's market, 'through changes in output at constant prices, instead of through changes in prices, as must be supposed to occur under perfect competition' (Robinson, 1969, p. 260). This outcome is due, she said, to an element of quasi-fixed cost which is such that the 'average prime cost falls with output up to full capacity' (p. 261). Recalling that both Robinson (1956, p. 183) and Kaldor label as prime costs all the costs which are related to *running* a plant, rather than resting it, it is obvious that the average prime cost that Robinson is talking about is the average unit labour cost of the vertically integrated firm of our model. The presence of overhead labour costs allows for variations in the shares of wages and profits, although the investment to output ratio, the average direct costs and the mark-up on unit direct costs are all constant. Similarly an increase in the share of investment in output leads to an increase in the share of profits, although the mark-up is constant. Overhead labour costs thus play a major role which has been emphasized in the present chapter. Not surprisingly, as early as 1964, Kaldor recognized that he had been mistaken in assuming that the mechanism of effective demand could not simultaneously deal with the determination of the output level and that of the distribution of income. He attributed this earlier erroneous conception to the oversight of overhead labour costs. Without these, the share of profits could not go up when investment went up, unless the mark-up changed, and the mark-up could only change automatically in situations of full utilization of capacity.

The one important respect in which I would now amend the exposition of the [previous theory] . . . relates to the assumption of constant (short-period) prime costs. I did not realise then that this assumption – which makes a constant 'mark-up' equivalent to a constant *share* of profit in income – was not just a simplification, but was definitely misleading. In industry, short period labour costs per unit of output are not constant, but falling (mainly on account of the influence of 'overhead labour'); as a result of this, changes in the ratio of investment to output can elicit corresponding changes in the *share* of profits (and hence in the savings ratio) even if the 'mark-up' is constant; it follows from this that it is not *necessary* to assume full employment in order that the 'Keynesian' mechanism of adjusting the savings ratio to the investment coefficient should operate. (Kaldor, 1964b, p. xvi–xvii)

It is clear from the above that Kaldor had in mind all the ingredients that led to the construction of the present model of effective demand.

## Wage Differentials, Savings on Wages and Unemployment Benefits

We now enter some complications in our basic model of effective demand, releasing some of the simplifying assumptions which were made earlier. We shall see that these earlier simplifications did not alter in any way the

## Effective Demand and Employment

results at which one arrives in the more complete model. We shall deal with the unemployed, as well as a differentiated labour class.

Let us start with the latter. Let us assume that the wage rate offered to fixed labour is higher than that offered to variable labour. White-collar workers earn a salary equivalent to $w_f$, while blue-collar workers receive $w_v$. Let us also suppose that there is a salary scale, such that:

$$w_f = \sigma w_v \text{ with } \sigma > 1 \qquad (5.46)$$

The total labour costs faced by firms are now equal to $w_f L_f + w_v L_v$. Making use of equations (5.38) and (5.46), total labour costs may be rewritten as:

$$w_v(\sigma f + u) q_{fc}/y_v$$

Let us also assume that white-collar workers, in contrast to blue-collar workers, save part of their earned income, presumably because their overall income is so large that they cannot think of any way to spend it all. White-collar workers are thus part of the households who do not fully behave in accordance with the description of the post-Keynesian consumer, as presented at the end of Chapter 2. Call the propensity to save out of salary income received by white-collar workers $s_{wf}$. Consumption spending arising from salary and wage income is then inferior to total wages and equal to:

$$[w_v((1 - s_{wf})\sigma f + u)] q_{fc}/y_v$$

Considering spending to arise both from the above expression and from autonomous expenditures, and equating the value of production to the value of sales, we get:

$$pq = ap + [w_v((1 - s_{wf})\sigma f + u)] q_{fc}/y_v \qquad (5.47)$$

Assuming that prices are set according to the simple mark-up procedure of equation (5.30), we get an expression very similar to that of equation (5.40) as we solve for $u$:

$$u = (1 - s_{wf})\sigma \frac{f}{\theta} + \frac{(1+\theta)}{\theta} \cdot \frac{a}{q_{fc}} \qquad (5.48)$$

It could be seen, computing $du/d\sigma$, that an increase in the salaries of white-collar workers, given the real wage rate of blue-collar workers, has a favourable effect on the use of capacity, although part of the salaries is saved. Also, as one would expect, an increase in the propensity to save of salary earners would bring about a lower rate of utilization. As before, any increase in real autonomous expenditures or in the proportion of overhead labour at full capacity leads to an increase in the rate of utilization of capacity. Moreover an increase in the mark-up $\theta$ still leads to a reduction in the rate of utilization of capacity.

$$du/d\theta = -[\theta(a/q_{fc})+(1-s_{wf})\sigma f]/\theta^2 < 0 \qquad (5.49)$$

One may wonder whether the similarity of results extends to the determination of the profit share. Because there are now savings out of labour income, the overall amount of real profits is not given, as it was when only savings out of profits were allowed. Since profits vary, according to savings out of wages, it is clear that the implicit propensity to save out of profits is not constant any more, in contrast to what we observed with the help of equation (5.43). Nominal profits, seen from the demand side, are now equal to:

$$p\Pi^d = ap - s_{wf}w_f L_f \qquad (5.50)$$

From the above equation one can extract an expression of the share of profits, seen from the demand side:

$$\pi^d = \frac{a}{uq_{fc}} - \frac{s_{wf}\sigma f}{(1+\theta)u} \qquad (5.51)$$

We note that there are limits to the values that the various variables can take if we want aggregate profits to be positive. In particular savings on salaries and the premium of salaries over wages cannot be too high; $\pi^d$ is positive only as long as the following inequality is fulfilled:

$$(1+\theta)a/q_{fc} > s_{wf}\sigma f \qquad (5.52)$$

We can also rewrite equation (5.45), to get the profit equation from the supply side when one takes into account equation (5.46). One has:

$$\pi^s = (\theta - f\sigma/u)/(1+\theta) \qquad (5.53)$$

We may again interpret the impact on the actual share of profits of changes in its various determinants by making use of a graph, drawn in Figure 5.16, similar to that of Figure 5.15. There is a difference in the

*Figure 5.16* Impact of increases in various parameters upon the rate of utilization of capacity and the net share of profits in national income when white-collar workers are saving

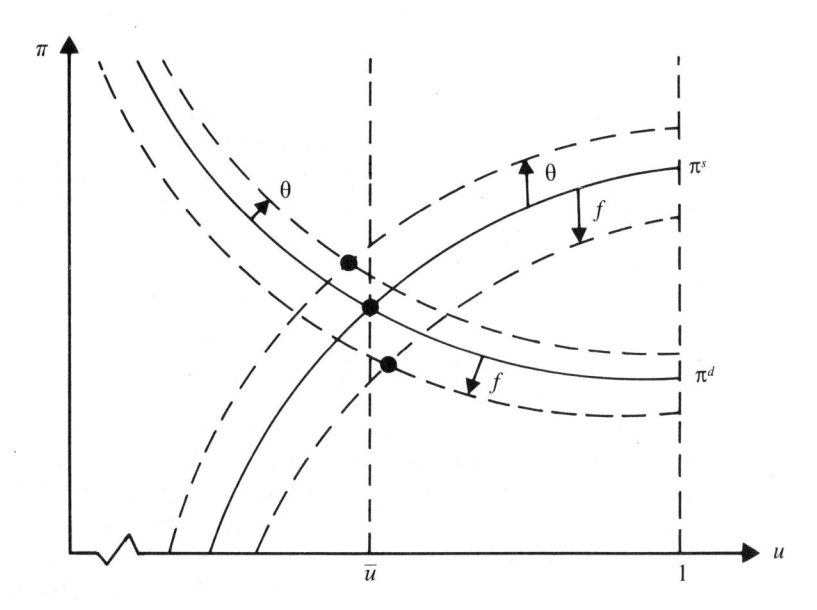

interpretation of the results. Whereas, in Figure 5.15, each parametric change only affected one of the two profit share equations, and hence only one curve at a time, Figure 5.16 shows instances where both curves shift as a result of a parametric change. As can be seen from equations (5.51) and (5.53), an increase in the mark-up of θ, as well as in the proportion $f$ of fixed labour and in the premium σ of salaries over wages, affect the share of profits from both the supply and the demand sides. One may thus wonder whether, under the new conditions, an increase in the mark-up still leads to an increase in the share of profits, and whether an increase in labour costs still leads to a fall in this share of profit. Starting with the mark-up, let us take the derivatives with respect to θ of both equations (5.51) and (5.53), to find out which of the $\pi^d$ or the $\pi^s$ curves shifts more, for a given rate of utilization. We find:

$$d\pi^s/d\theta = (1+f\sigma/u)/(1+\theta)^2 \tag{5.54}$$

$$d\pi^d/d\theta = (s_{wf}f\sigma/u)/(1+\theta)^2 \tag{5.55}$$

The value of (5.54) is necessarily larger than the value of (5.55) since $s_{wf}$ is always smaller than one. This means that at the given rate of utilization $\bar{u}$, the shift of the $\pi^s$ curve is necessarily larger than that of the $\pi^d$ curve. As can be seen in Figure 5.16, this implies that a larger mark-up $\theta$ leads to a higher profit share. The same exercise can be performed on the ratio $f$ of overhead to variable labour at full capacity. Note that the coefficient $\sigma$ plays a role identical to that of $f$. Overhead labour costs relative to variable cost at full capacity may augment either because more staff is required relative to workers operating machinery, or because white-collar workers increase their wage differential relative to blue-collar workers. Whatever we find about $f$ will also be true of $\sigma$. Let us take the derivatives of equations (5.51) and (5.53) with respect to $f$. We find:

$$d\pi^s/df = -\sigma/u(1+\theta) \tag{5.56}$$

$$d\pi^d/df = -s_{wf}\sigma/u(1+\theta) \tag{5.57}$$

Looking only at the absolute values, we see, for the same reasons as before, that the shift of the $\pi^s$ curve is more substantial than that of the $\pi^d$ curve, for a given rate of utilization $\bar{u}$. Checking on Figure 5.16, this implies that an increase in relative overhead costs leads to a fall in the share of profit, although there is an increase in the rate of utilization of capacity. The introduction of differential wage rates and the possibility of savings have not changed the main outcomes of the simple model.

One may also wish to introduce explicitly the presence of unemployed workers and of their unemployment benefits. Assuming, as does Nell (1978, p. 15), that the benefits received by the unemployed are deficit financed by the state, and that all welfare payments received are spent on consumption goods, unemployment benefits must be added to the components of aggregate demand. Let us call $L_{fe}$ the number of workers who are eligible to unemployment insurance, and $w_U$ the unemployment benefits received per period by those who are unemployed. Welfare payments on the grounds of unemployment insurance are thus equal to $w_U(L_{fe}-L)$. This amount must now be added to aggregate demand, as defined in equation (5.47). Taking explicitly unemployed workers into account, this equation becomes:

$$pq = ap + [w_v((1-s_{wf})\sigma f + u)](q_{fc}/y_v) + w_U(L_{fe}-L) \tag{5.58}$$

Calling $\upsilon$ the ratio $w_U/w_v$, and solving for the rate of utilization, one gets:

$$u = \frac{(1+\theta)a/q_{fc} + (1-s_{wf}\sigma f) + \upsilon(L_{fe}/L_{fc}-f)}{\theta - \upsilon} \tag{5.59}$$

Effective Demand and Employment   271

The reader may verify that all the standard results of the simplified model still hold. In particular an increase in the proportion of overhead labour leads to an increase in the rate of utilization of capacity, provided an employed white-collar worker spends more than an unemployed one: $w_f(1-s_{wf}) > w_U$. This sounds like a reasonable assumption to make. To conclude on this issue, all sorts of complications may be introduced, but they do not change the message which the basic model carries.

**Target-return Pricing**

One may wonder whether the results obtained depend on the pricing procedure which is adopted. Up to now, all of our attention has been devoted to the simpler mark-up pricing procedure. What if corporations use a variant of the full cost principle? It should be obvious that the pricing procedure has no impact on the effects of an increase in autonomous demand in this short-period model. One may doubt, however, that an increase in fixed labour costs still leads to an increase in the rate of utilization of capacity when pricing is done on the basis of unit costs rather than on the basis of prime costs.

We thus return to the condition required to equate sales to the value of output, when wage rate differentials and the saving propensity on salaries of fixed labour are taken into account; that is, when equations (5.46) and (5.47) are pertinent. We suppose this time that the relevant pricing equation is that of target-return pricing, that is equation (5.35). Because we assume that the salary of white-collar workers is superior to the wage paid to the blue-collar workers by a factor of $\sigma$, the basic target-return pricing equation must be slightly changed to incorporate this factor of wage differentials. Equation (5.35) becomes:

$$p = \left(\frac{u_s + \sigma f}{u_s - r_s v}\right) \frac{w}{y_v} \qquad (5.60)$$

With the price level determined by the target return procedure of equation (5.60), assuming that the level of activity is set by the aggregate equilibrium condition given by equation (5.47), and recalling that the level of output $q$ is equal to $uq_{fc}$, we can find the determinants of the rate of utilization of capacity in the case of target-return pricing.

$$u = \frac{(a/q_{fc})(u_s + \sigma f) + (1 - s_{wf})\sigma f(u_s - r_s v)}{(\sigma f + r_s v)} \qquad (5.61)$$

By inspecting equation (5.61), we can immediately see that $du/ds_{wf}$ and $du/$

$dr_s$ are necessarily negative. An increase in the rate of savings on salaries, or an increase in the target rate of return, induces a fall in the actual rate of utilization of capacity. It is also obvious that $du/da$ and $du/du_s$ are always positive. An increase in autonomous expenditures or an increase in the standard rate of utilization of capacity both lead to higher actual rates of utilization of capacity. The standard rate of profit and the standard rate of utilization thus play opposite roles. If we presume, as one is led to believe from equation (5.51) and as will become obvious later, that an increase in autonomous expenditures drives up both the rate of profit on existing capacity and the rate of utilization on capacity, these changes could induce further changes in the parameters determining the target-return price equation. If the target profit rate, and hence the mark-up on direct costs, are increased as a response to the higher rate of profit, this will have damping consequences on the actual rate of utilization. The movements of the target rate of return would thus appear to be stabilizing. On the other hand, if the standard rate of utilization is increased as a result of the higher actual rate of utilization, which corresponds to a lower mark-up on direct costs, the actual degree of plant utilization will rise further. The standard rate of utilization thus seems to play a destabilizing role in the short-period context.

We have so far found again all the results that the simpler mark-up pricing procedure had led us to. The particular attention brought to target-return pricing was, however, motivated by the questionable impact that an increase in overhead labour costs would impart on the rate of utilization of capacity when overheads contribute to the determination of the price level. As noted before, the effects of overhead costs can be ascertained by studying the impact of either $f$ or $\sigma$. Taking the derivative of equation (5.61) with respect to the ratio $f$ of overhead labour at full capacity, we get:

$$du/df = \frac{\sigma(u_s - r_s v)[(1 - s_{wf})r_s v - (a/q_{fc})]}{(f + r_s v)^2} \tag{5.62}$$

The sign that the above derivative takes is uncertain. Since the first term in parentheses is always positive, what matters for the derivative to be positive is the sign of the expression inside the square brackets. The positive relationship between $f$ and the rate of utilization that was found in the case of mark-up pricing is thus preserved under particular conditions.

$$du/df > 0 \text{ if } (1 - s_{wf})r_s v > (a/q_{fc}) \tag{5.63}$$

The same conditions apply in the case of an increase in the relative salary of overhead labour. An increase in overhead costs is more likely to have a positive impact on the rate of utilization the smaller the propensity to save on overhead salaries, the smaller the target rate of return (and hence the mark-up) and the larger the proportion of autonomous expenditures. One must thus conclude that the introduction of target-return pricing in our simple model of effective demand may modify one of the results at which we had previously arrived, namely, a rise in overhead costs may not lead to an increase in the rate of utilization when pricing decisions take overhead costs into account. With mark-up pricing, any increase in wage costs necessarily implied a higher level of activity.

One special case of effective demand and target-return pricing is of particular interest. Assume that there are no savings out of salary income. Then, recalling that $v = K/q_{fc}$, the inequality condition of (5.63) becomes:

$$du/df > 0 \text{ if } r_s K > a \tag{5.64}$$

Recalling that $a$ represents actual real profits when there is no saving out of earned income, the above inequality simply means that overhead costs have a positive effect on the degree of plant utilization when the amount of real profits which are being aimed at are larger than the amount of real profits that are actually realized. This will be the case when the actual rate of utilization of capacity is smaller than the standard rate of utilization of capacity upon which the pricing decision is made, as the reader can convince himself by looking back at Figure 3.8. This peculiar relationship can be further explored by checking the variations in the share of profit as labour overhead costs are changed. Let us again resort to the distinction between the share of profit from the demand side and the share of profit from the supply side. Since we assume no savings out of wage income, equation (5.44) is the proper one to represent $\pi^d$. As said above, the proportion of autonomous expenditures is the only determinant of real profits, and hence the only shifting factor of the $\pi^d$ curve. By contrast, the share of profit from the supply side is a more complex expression. With the proper substitutions, we get the following expression:

$$\pi^s = 1 - \frac{(\sigma f + u)(u_s - r_s v)}{u(u_s + \sigma f)} \tag{5.65}$$

To find out about the impact of overhead costs on the profit share, we take the derivative of equation (5.65) with respect to $f$, and get a rather simple expression:

$$d\pi^s/df = \frac{(u - u_s)(u_s - r_s v)}{u^2(u_s + \sigma f)^2} \tag{5.66}$$

*Figure 5.17 Impact of an increase in overhead costs upon the rate of utilization of capacity and the net share of profits in national income when target-return pricing procedures are in use*

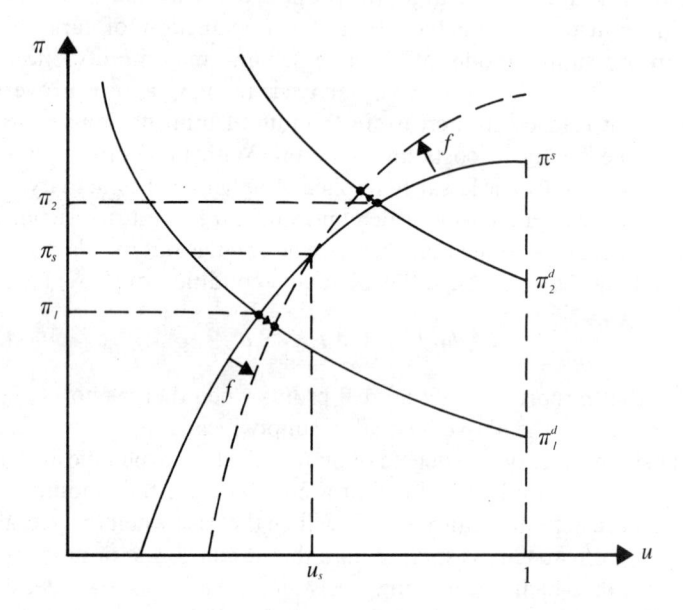

As we did with the previous figures, we can observe in Figure 5.17 the consequences of changing some of the determinants of the share of profits. As before, the $\pi^d$ curve is upward-sloping while the $\pi^s$ curve is downward-sloping. When overhead costs are increased, that is when $f$ is higher, the $\pi^s$ curve is being displaced. When the actual rate of utilization of capacity $u$ is smaller than the standard rate of utilization $u_s$, the $\pi^s$ curve shifts down, as can be read from equation (5.66). The consequences of that change is that the profit share is smaller and the rate of utilization of capacity is larger than in the initial position, as can be seen in Figure 5.17, when autonomous expenditures are such that the $\pi^d_1$ curve is the relevant one. This latter result confirms the inequality conditions given by (5.64). The actual share of profit, $\pi_1$, is indeed smaller than the share of profit $\pi_s$ which corresponds to the target rate of return. Reciprocally, if the actual rate of utilization of capacity $u$ is larger than the standard rate of utilization $u_s$, then the $\pi^s$ curve shifts up. This happens when, as can be seen from Figure 5.17, autonomous expenditures are such that the relevant curve is the $\pi^d_2$ curve, and when the actual share of profit $\pi_2$ is larger than the target share of profit $\pi_s$. The consequence of this shift is that, when overhead costs increase, the share of profit increases while the rate of utilization of capacity decreases.

The introduction of target-return pricing thus gives rise to interesting statics. Whereas the introduction of savings on wages, differential wage rates and explicit unemployment benefits did not modify any of the conclusions reached with the basic model of effective demand, the presence of target-return pricing procedures may lead to the disruption of previous results, namely those linked to the impact of overhead costs on the level of activity and on the share of profits.

## 5.5 TWO-SECTOR MODELS

So far the whole discussion has been in terms of a one-sector model. This was mainly because the introduction of a second sector would have complicated the analysis without adding much comprehension. It is now time to sketch the way in which the presence of two sectors changes the analysis presented above.

It should first be noted that two-sector models of all theories may exhibit behaviour which is not in accordance with the behaviour of the simplified one-sector model. A case in point is Samuelson's (1962) two-sector pseudo-production function, which turned out to demonstrate, once the assumption of proportional sectoral technical coefficients was dismissed, that the wage rate and the profit rate could not be used as indices of the scarcity of labour or of capital. The two-sector model showed that neoclassical substitution effects could not be relied upon, outside of the one-sector world. Neo-Ricardian models of growth and distribution, based on prices of production, have problems of their own within a two-sector framework. It has been shown that under some circumstances the rate of profit and the rate of growth may display an inverse relationship, in contrast to what one may expect (Spaventa, 1970). The direct relationship is preserved in all cases only if the propensity to save out of wage income is zero, or very close to zero. It has also been shown that the effect on the share of profits of a higher rate of saving out of profit income (Findlay, 1963, p. 4) or that of a higher rate of growth (Hagemann, 1991) may be positive or negative. On the other hand, a higher rate of saving out of wages is always associated with a higher share of profits, while a higher rate of growth is necessarily associated with a larger share of profits in the classical case. We may therefore suspect that some of the results obtained in our one-sector models of cost-plus pricing may not be necessarily valid in a more general context.

Let us then examine a two-sector model of mark-up pricing, to see to what extent the results obtained so far can be generalized when a distinction is made between the consumption and the investment sectors. To avoid complications, let us assume that the wage rate is the same for fixed and variable labour, and that there is no saving out of wages. Autonomous expenditures are still given in real terms, but we shall now distinguish between investment expenditures, called $a_i$, and autonomous consumption expenditures, called $a_c$. Let us call $p_i$ the price level in the sector producing capital goods and $p_c$ the price level in the consumption goods sector. Making use of the standard mark-up price equation, with the same variables as those enclosed in equation (5.30), but with the appropriate subscripts, we have two vertically-integrated sectors, the price equations of which are:

$$p_i = (1+\theta_i)w_i/y_{vi} \qquad (5.67)$$

$$p_c = (1+\theta_c)w_c/y_{vc} \qquad (5.68)$$

Now that we have two sectors, we may introduce a complication which is inherent to two-sector models: we may suppose that the workers in the investment sector have a different wage rate from that of the workers operating in the consumption sector. Their wage rate may be higher or lower. Let us call the ratio of the two $\beta$, so that:

$$w_i = \beta w_c \qquad (5.69)$$

One of the problems encountered by the neoclassical exponents of the distinction between Keynesian and classical unemployment is that the rate of investment in their static models is assumed to be given, despite changes in the real wage rate. As shown by Bhaduri (1983), this is inconsistent with neoclassical theory since fluctuations in the real wage rate should induce firms to modify their supply of investment goods. A neoclassical model based on the variations of the real wage rate cannot assume that the level of investment is fixed. In post-Keynesian models, the situation is different. Supply is determined by demand, as we have seen in the preceding sections of this chapter. Provided the aggregate post-Keynesian utilization function applies equally to the investment and the consumption sectors, the supply of investment goods as well as that of consumption goods results from the principle of effective demand. There is thus no incoherence, within post-Keynesian models, in assuming that the real wage rate is changing while supposing that the level of investment is fixed, determined by the autonomous demand for capital goods (Lavoie, 1986b, p. 227). Once we know the level of this autonomous demand for investment goods, we know what the level of utilization of capacity is in the investment sector. Again, with the previous notations and the appropriate subscripts, we have:

$$u_i = a_i/q_{fci} \tag{5.70}$$

The overall profits in the investment sector are given by:

$$\Pi_i = p_i a_i - w_i L_i \tag{5.71}$$

Making use of equations (5.29), (5.67) and (5.70), we see that the share of profits in the investment sector is given by:

$$\pi_i = (\theta_i - f_i/u_i)/(1 + \theta_i) \tag{5.72}$$

In the investment sector things are fairly simple: the actual share of profits depends directly on the rate of utilization of capacity, as one could directly observe from Figure 5.13, that is on the level of investment demand. It does not depend on the level of the real wage rate. Naturally things would be more complex if the investment level was not solely given in real terms, as firms producing investment goods would be effectively constrained in their ability to raise prices. Let us now turn to the sector producing consumption goods. In that sector there are three sources of demand: the wages which are being distributed in the consumption sector, the wages which have been distributed in the investment sector, and autonomous demand. All this must be equal to the value of the product in the consumption sector. Calling the output of the consumption sector $q_c$, we have:

$$p_c q_c = w_c L_c + w_i L_i + a_c p_c \tag{5.73}$$

We are now in a position to find the rate of utilization of capacity in the consumption sector. Let us denote as $\xi$ the ratio of variable labour that would be hired in the investment sector if it were operating at full capacity over the amount of variable labour that would be hired in the consumption sector if it were also operating at full capacity.

$$\xi = (q_{fci}/y_{vi})/(q_{fcc}/y_{vc}) \tag{5.74}$$

Calling the rate of utilization of capacity in the consumption sector $u_c$, and making use of equations (5.28), (5.38), (5.68), (5.69) and (5.74), we get:

$$u_c = [(1+\theta_c)(a_c/q_{fcc}) + f_c + \beta\xi(f_i + u_i)]/\theta_c \tag{5.75}$$

As one would expect, the rate of utilization of capacity in the consumption sector is higher the greater the level of autonomous consumption expenditures ($a_c$) and the higher the rate of utilization of capacity in the investment sector. Increments in the requirements of permanent staff also increase the rate of utilization. Moreover an increase in the wage rate of workers of the investment sector relative to that of the workers of the consumption sector, as evidenced by β, leads to higher rates of utilization in the consumption sector (Dixon, 1979–80, p. 188). As in the one-sector case, an increase in the mark-up $\theta_c$ leads to a decrease in the rate of utilization. Taking the derivative of equation (5.75) with respect to $\theta_c$ we find:

$$du_c/d\theta_c = -[(a_c/q_{fcc}) + f_c + \beta\xi(f_i + u_i)]/\theta_c^2 < 0 \qquad (5.76)$$

The conclusion that we can draw so far is that, looking at things from the point of view of the rate of utilization of capacity, the results that were drawn from the one-sector model appear to be equally valid in the two-sector model. To the extent that the rate of utilization can be defined in practice, a model based on the rate of utilization of capacity appears to be robust.

The existence of two sectors allows us to go into the details of the structure of employment and the operation of the employment multiplier. From equation (5.76), we can derive the relationship between the increases in the rates of utilization of capacity of the investment and of the consumption sectors.

$$du_c/du_i = \beta\xi/\theta_c \qquad (5.77)$$

We are now in a position to compare the direct and the indirect impacts of an increase in investment on employment; that is, the increase on the employment in the investment and consumption sectors respectively. Recall equation (5.38):

$$L = (f + u)\, q_{fc}/y_v \qquad (5.38)$$

Reinterpreting this equation within the two-sector framework, and using equation (5.74), the increases in the sectoral employment of labour are the following:

$$dL_i = (q_{fci}/y_{vi}) \cdot du_i \qquad (5.78)$$

$$dL_c = (\beta\xi/\theta_c)(q_{fcc}/y_{vc}) \cdot du_i = \beta(q_{fci}/y_{vi}) \cdot du_i \qquad (5.79)$$

We have found a simple relationship between the increase in the employment of the consumption sector and the increase in the employment of the investment sector following an increase in the level of investment. From the above two equations, we have:

$$dL_c = (\beta/\theta_c).dL_i \qquad (5.80)$$

If the ratio $\beta/\theta_c$ is larger than one, the indirect effects on employment resulting from an increase in the rate of investment are larger than its direct effects. The increase in the employment of workers of the consumption sector will be stronger, for a given increase in investment, the greater the wage differential in favour of the workers of the investment sector, and the smaller the mark-up in the consumption sector (Dixon, 1979–80, p. 186). Another way to make the latter statement is to say that the greater the real wage rate, overall and in the investment sector in particular, the larger the indirect effects of an increase in investment on employment. As can be seen from equation (5.80), the ratio of the sectoral increases in employment depends on purely distributive determinants, that is the real wage rate and the sectoral relative wage rate. By generally omitting distributive factors, neoclassical authors cannot pick up these sectoral effects.

To close this section, one might wish to find out whether an increase in the rate of investment would lead to an increase in the share of profits. From equation (5.72) we have already seen that higher investment generates a higher share of profits in the investment sector. What about the consumption sector? We can repeat the procedure which we have adopted on many occasions. Doing so, we find a share of profits which, seen from the supply side, is identical to that of equation (5.72), but with all the subscripts applying to the consumption sector. From the demand side, one should recall that the nominal profits of the consumption sector are:

$$\Pi^d_c = a_c p_c + w_i L_i \qquad (5.81)$$

This, with the appropriate substitutions, yields a share of profits of the consumption sector which, seen from the demand side, is equal to:

$$\pi^d_c = [(a_c/q_{fcc}) + \beta\xi(f_i + u_i)/(1+\theta_c)]/u_c \qquad (5.82)$$

It is obvious that an increase in the rate of investment, and hence in the rate of utilization of capacity in the investment sector, shifts up the $\pi^d_c$ curve. The result on the profit share of the consumption sector is the same as the one which can be observed in Figure 5.15. There is an increase in that share. Thus both sectoral shares of profits increase when investment increases. The question that remains to be solved is whether the overall share of profits also increases. The fact that it does not necessarily can be shown intuitively in the following way. Call $h_i$ and $h_c$ the shares of the values of output in the investment and the consumption sectors relative to the value of national product, the latter being $p_i a_i + p_c q_c$. The overall share of profits $\pi$ can then be written as the weighted average of the share of profits in each of the two sectors.

$$\pi = h_i \pi_i + h_c \pi_c \tag{5.83}$$

The change $d\pi$ in the overall share of profits, recalling that $h_c = 1 - h_i$ and hence that $dh_i = -dh_c$, may thus be written as:

$$d\pi = d\pi_i.h_i + d\pi_c.h_c + dh_i.(\pi_i - \pi_c) \tag{5.84}$$

Note that the last term of equation (5.84) could take on a negative value, because either of the two components of that term could take a negative value while the other component is positive. If the negative value of that last term is sufficiently large, it is conceivable that the overall share of profits decreases, although the first two terms of equation (5.84) are positive; that is, although both sectoral shares of profits increase. This could be precisely the case when investment expenditures increase. Indeed taking the derivative of the profit share $\pi$ with respect to the rate of utilization of capacity in the investment sector leads to a very complex expression, which may take either sign. Thus, as Asimakopulos (1975, p. 327) warns, 'it is possible that the over-all ratio of profit to output will fall, even if this ratio increases in each sector', although it is unlikely when changes in investment are small.

The lesson that must be drawn from this is that one cannot put much confidence in the results concerning the share of profits at which we arrived in the simple one-sector model. It would thus be a mistake to base a theory on the sign taken by the variations of the share of profits. Moreover, even at the sectoral level, that is without composition effects to reverse signs, there may be apparent paradoxical results when compared to the aggregate model. For instance, it could be shown that a higher mark-up in the consumption sector does not necessarily imply an increase in the share of profits of that sector, in contrast to what could be observed in the one-sector model. This is because of the fact that part of the demand for consumption goods which is autonomous, from the point of view of the consumption sector, is defined in nominal terms (the $w_i L_i$ part of equation (5.73)). An increase in the mark-up, and hence in consumption prices with given direct unit costs, diminishes this part of real autonomous demand for consumption goods.

It should be further observed that the variations of the overall share of profits do not necessarily follow those of the rate of profit. For instance, when there is an increase in investment expenditures, there is necessarily an increase in profits (see the sum of equations (5.71) and (5.81)). Since the prices of capital goods do not change unless there is a change in some other variable, the rate of profit must increase. A rise in the profit rate may thus be accompanied by a fall in the overall share of profits. The evolution of the aggregate share of profits may not be a relevant indicator of what is happening within each sector, or of how entrepreneurs perceive their situation to be. Indeed various paradoxes may arise when interdependent industries, rather than vertically integrated sectors, are taken into consideration (Steedman, 1992).

In contrast, we have had the opportunity to observe that the results obtained with regard to the rate of utilization of capacity turned out to be robust when set in a two-sector framework. This should be kept in mind when we deal with similar models in a growth context.

# 6. Accumulation and Capacity

## 6.1 HISTORICAL VERSUS LOGICAL TIME

As was said in the first chapter, one of the objectives of post-Keynesian theory is to combine the classical concerns for growth and distribution with the Keynesian principle of effective demand. Indeed this was Joan Robinson's explicit objective in her famous *Accumulation of Capital*, where she pointed out that her intention was to develop 'a generalisation of the *General Theory*, that is, an extension of Keynes's short-period analysis to long-run development' (1956, p. vi). Similarly the object of the present chapter is to extend to the long period the results of the previous chapter, which were obtained within the framework of the short period.

The method of analysis that will be employed to do so is that of comparative dynamics. Now post-classical authors of all persuasions usually become quite heated when they enter into discussions about the merits of historical rather than logical time, long-period versus short-period equilibrium or gravitation instead of steady-state analysis. Joan Robinson herself is responsible for much of the fury that has beset discussions about these methods of analysis, for, despite her insistence upon an analysis of disequilibrium set in historical time, she has herself never left the confines of comparative statics (or dynamics). This has somewhat bemused both her followers and those who were the target of her attacks, with a few notable exceptions.

One is Kregel (1980). His main point is that methods are usually general enough for several research programmes to fit in. The same point is made by Pasinetti (1977, p. 180) in his discussion of linear programming. Kregel's concern is comparative statics, a method of analysis which in his view can be successfully applied to both neoclassical and non-neoclassical models. Post-Keynesians need not, of necessity, avoid this method of analysis. This is an account which is quite coherent with the one Kregel (1976) presented earlier, when he discussed how expectations can be integrated into Keynes's models and the growth models of the post-Keynesians. Kregel argued that both Keynes and the post-Keynesians have a radically different approach to offer, although their method of analysis is based on the standard method of comparative statics.

Kregel believes that Joan Robinson's approach and that of the post-Keynesians is different from the method of the neoclassical research programme because it tames the real world differently. Whereas in neoclassical economics the taming is done through exchange economies and full information, post-Keynesians start with monetary production economies and uncertainty. It is ironic to note that, in defence of his long-period positions, Garegnani (1976) uses exactly the same strategies. For Garegnani, neoclassical economists compare long-period equilibria of supply and demand, assuming full employment. This is illegitimate and explains why neoclassical economists have reverted to temporary equilibria. But outside neoclassical economics, that is without its assumed full utilization of all factors, comparative statics within the long period is quite correct (Garegnani, 1989).

A further source of confusion emerged later. Subject to Robinson's critique, some neo-Ricardians have counter-attacked by reversing the critique (Committeri, 1986, p. 169; Ciccone, 1986, p. 22). Sraffians would be using the method of long-period positions, making no assumption of constant growth rates, reasserting Sraffa's claim of no constant returns to scale and assuming therefore a snapshot analysis at a constant level of output. On the other hand, post-Keynesians, who deal with formal models of accumulation of the Robinson/Kaldor/Pasinetti variety, would be making use of steady-state analysis, a sin according to some neo-Ricardians since steady states are associated with neoclassical theory.

As has been pointed out by Amadeo (1987, p. 77), it is a rather difficult task to find any significant differences between: (1) the notion of centre of gravitation associated with the long-period position; and (2), the concept of stability linked to comparative dynamics or steady-state growth models as applied by some post-Keynesians. Indeed one suspects that the main reason for which some neo-Ricardians make such a fuss of the notion of gravitation is that they do not accept the way the rate of profit is determined in the post-Keynesian growth models. The critique to the effect that growth models necessarily entail the proportionate growth of all industries does not hold, since Pasinetti (1981) has shown that growth models with vertically integrated sectors could be moulded from input–output accounts.

In my view, most of the discussions about steady states versus tranquility assumptions and versus centres of gravitation are a red herring. There may be good reasons to be suspicious of comparative dynamics or statics, reasons pointed out from very early on by Robinson (1953–4) when she criticized the notion of technical substitution in production functions.

However most post-classicals make use of comparative statics, some with classical prices of production, some with some simplified version of them, some with the overall state of capital as a given (the short period), others with capital as an endogenous variable (the long period). The debates which have surrounded production prices and long-period positions are due to the illegitimate exclusive association between a tool of analysis (comparative statics) and a school of thought (neoclassical economics) and to the desire by some neo-Ricardians to undermine a theory of the rate of profit – that of Robinson/Kaldor/Pasinetti – by criticizing the tools used (steady-state analysis). Once it is recognized that a tool of analysis should not be exclusively associated with a theory or with a research programme, much confusion should be cleared.

To conclude with the theme of historical time, it is likely that Joan Robinson herself was dissatisfied with the way she had attempted to introduce history. Other tools have now been brought to the fore by various post-classical authors to accommodate time and disequilibrium. Some are involved in chaotic economics; some deal with the traverse, without necessarily postulating full employment; some make use of limit cycles *à la* Goodwin; others have concentrated on the dynamic stability properties of post-classical models. It is in this sense, I presume, that post-classicals should have a 'Babylonian' pluralistic approach, as Dow (1985) would put it. What is more crucial is the economic theory and the hypotheses that drive the models supported by these various techniques.

As said above, the method adopted in this chapter is that of comparative dynamics. Issues and problems will generally be tackled one at a time, in order to fully understand their implications. This will be our way to temper the complexities of the real world in a manner amenable to readers of all backgrounds.

## 6.2 THE NEO-KEYNESIAN GROWTH MODEL: THE INFLATIONIST VERSION

Post-Keynesian economics is still mostly known for the models of growth and distribution that were developed by Robinson, Kaldor and Pasinetti in the late 1950s and early 1960s. For this reason it is important to distinguish between the models of growth that these authors constructed in those years and the models of growth which can be associated with the Kaleckian foundations which have been emphasized in the previous chapter. We shall call the former neo-Keynesian, while we shall term Kaleckian the later post-Keynesian models. There are two major related differences between the two groups of models of which one should take note. Firstly, the neo-Keynesian models, because they are still being inspired by the framework developed by Keynes, are basically set in a world of competition, whereas the post-Keynesian models of Kaleckian inspiration are part of an oligopolistic framework. The second difference between the two models is that the older neo-Keynesian model implicitly presumes that in the long period the rate of utilization of capacity is fixed at its normal level, whereas in the newer post-Keynesian model the rate of utilization of capacity is endogenous and is not assumed to be equal to a normal value, even in the long period. There are important consequences to the adoption of these differing assumptions, despite the other similarities of the two models.

**The Stability of the Model**

The most famous feature of the neo-Keynesian model of growth and distribution is that the rate of profit does not depend on microeconomic technical conditions or on relative physical endowments, but solely on macroeconomic variables, namely the rate of growth of the economy and some variable related to the propensity to save on profits. This is true either under the classical saving assumption, that is when assuming that all wages are consumed, or under the Pasinetti assumptions, that is assuming that wages can be saved while adding conditions regarding the rate of return on savings of different social classes, in which case it is the propensity to save on profits by the capitalist class which is the determinant of the rate of profit (Pasinetti, 1974, ch. 5). Turning to the classical saving assumption, the principle of effective demand requires that investment and savings be equal, the latter being only equal to savings on profits. This condition has already been presented under equation (5.43), which can now be rewritten as:

$$I = s_p \Pi \qquad (6.1)$$

The Cambridge equation is simply the dynamic version of this simple expression of the principle of effective demand. Dividing both sides of equation (6.1) by $K$, the stock of capital, and rearranging, one gets the overall rate of profit as a function of the overall rate of accumulation and of the propensity to save out of profit income:

$$r = g/s_p \qquad (6.2)$$

Although simple, the Cambridge equation gives rise to several controversial issues. In its standard interpretation by Kaldor, Pasinetti and

Robinson, it is the rate of growth which determines the rate of profit. This interpretation arises from the short-run Keynesian causal scheme, where investment is given and hence considered the exogenous variable. A natural development of this short-run causality is thus to suppose that the rate of growth of investment is the exogenous factor, while the rate of profit is the endogenous one. 'Thus, given conditions to save from each type of income (the thriftiness conditions) the rate of profit is determined by the rate of accumulation of capital' (Robinson, 1962, p. 12). Conversely, some neo-Radicals and the neo-Ricardians believe that an exogenous rate of profit determines the rate of growth. We shall see later that both variables may be seen as being endogenously determined. We could then just as well rewrite equation (6.2), denoting it as $g^s$ to indicate that it relates a given rate of growth to the supply of savings.

$$g^s = s_p r \qquad (6.3)$$

One simple way to have both variables endogenous, while preserving the one-way causality from output variables (the rate of investment) to price variables (the rate of profit), is to keep equation (6.2) while making the rate of growth decided by entrepreneurs a function of the expected rate of profit on future investment. This is precisely what Robinson (1962, pp. 47–8) proposes. She has a 'double-sided relationship between the rate of profit and the rate of accumulation', which gives rise to her famous banana-shaped diagram. On the one hand, the actual rate of profit is determined by the rate of accumulation decided by entrepreneurs and their firms. On the other hand, the rate of accumulation depends on the expected rate of profit, at a decreasing rate. Here we shall only present a linear version of this latter relationship, as does Amadeo (1986b, p. 86) for instance. Calling $r^e$ the expected rate of profit, and $\gamma$ the rate of growth if no profit was expected, we have the investment function in a growing mode, which we denote as $g^i$.

$$g^i = \gamma + g_r r^e \qquad (6.4)$$

Both of the coefficients $\gamma$ and $g_r$ may be said to reflect the intensity of the animal spirits of the entrepreneurs. In particular the $g_r$ parameter reflects the sensitivity of the rate of growth decided by entrepreneurs to changes in the expected rate of profit. The double-sided relationship between the rate of profit and the rate of accumulation is illustrated in Figure 6.1. It has been supposed that the slope of equation (6.3), the savings function so to speak, is steeper than that of equation (6.4), the investment function. This means that the sensitivity of investment decisions to changes in the

*Figure 6.1 Determination of the desired rate of accumulation when the model is stable: $g_r < s_p$*

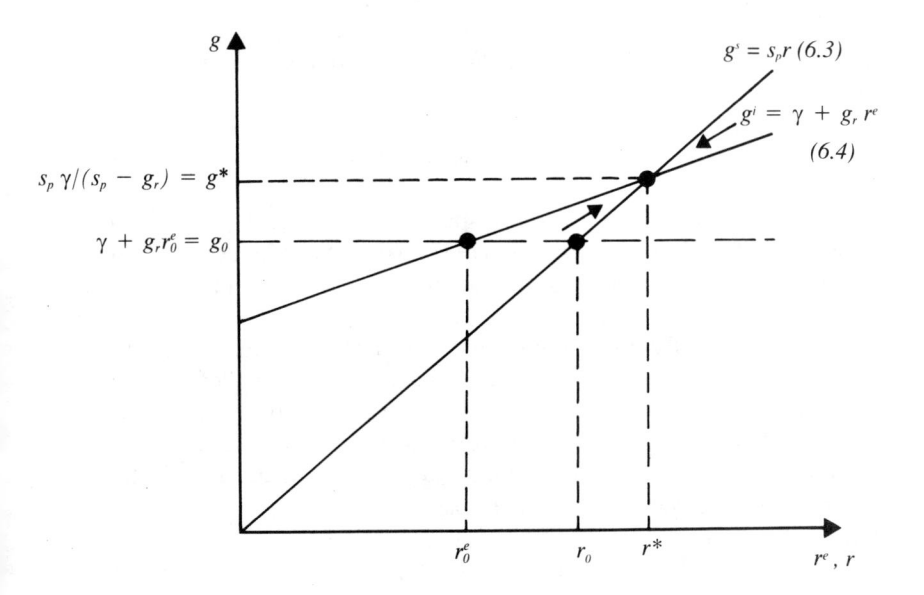

$$g^s = s_p r \quad (6.3)$$
$$g^i = \gamma + g_r r^e \quad (6.4)$$

$s_p \gamma / (s_p - g_r) = g^*$

$\gamma + g_r r_0^e = g_0$

Axis labels: $r_0^e$, $r_0$, $r^*$, $r^e, r$

expected rate of profit is less than the sensitivity of savings to changes in the actual rate of profit. We shall soon see the importance of this assumption.

To comprehend how the model functions, start out with an arbitrary expected rate of profit, say $r^e{}_0$, as in Figure 6.1. At that expected rate of profit, the rate of accumulation decided by the entrepreneurs will be $g_0$. Assume now that the rate of accumulation decided by the firms will be the one that will actually be realized; that is, assume that the economy is always at the point where saving equals investment, on the line given by equation (6.3). This is an assumption which is often made by post-Keynesians. Robinson (1962, p. 48) makes it in her original analysis, and this is why the curve $g^s$ of Figure 6.1 is often called the profit realization curve (Harris, 1978, p. 189). The supposition that the growth rate decided is the realized one is certainly a very strong one, which assumes away the questions posed by Harrod (1973), but one that needs to be made. If we do make it, then the actual rate of profit $r_0$ of the economy can be compared to the expected rate of profit $r^e{}_0$. We see on Figure 6.1 that the actual rate of profit is larger than the expected rate. Provided the new expected rate of profit responds positively to the actual rate of profit, the expected rate of profit will augment, eventually reaching the value $r^*$, at which point the expected rate of profit will turn out to be equal to the actual rate. For the model to be complete, we thus need one more equation which relates the expected rate of profit at time $t$ to the actual rate of profit at time $t-1$. Several formulations are possible. We may write this as some adaptative process:

$$r^e_t = \phi r^e_{t-1} + (1-\phi) r_{t-1} \text{ with } \phi < 1 \qquad (6.5)$$

When the actual rate of profit at period $t-1$ is equal to the expected rate of profit of the same period, there is no change in the expected rate of profit. We may then speak of an equilibrium rate of profit. The rate of growth $g^*$ which corresponds in Figure 6.1 to this value of the rate of profit is called by Robinson the desired rate of growth. This rate of growth is such that the expectations of the entrepreneurs are fulfilled. The equations (6.3) and (6.4) thus jointly determine an endogenous rate of accumulation and an endogenous rate of profit, assuming that in long-run equilibrium the expected and the realized rates of profit are identical. The desired rate of growth is thus equal to:

$$g^* = s_p \gamma / (s_p - g_r) \qquad (6.6)$$

It can be seen from equation (6.6) that, for the desired rate of accumulation to be positive, both the denominator and the numerator must be positive or both must be negative. Figure 6.1 corresponds to the case where both are positive. Let us now consider the case where $g_r > s_p$; that is, investment decisions are more sensitive than savings to changes in the rate of profit. This case is illustrated in Figure 6.2, with a value of $\gamma$ which is negative. There the slope of equation (6.3), the savings function given by $g^s$, is less steep than that of equation (6.4), the investment function given by $g^i$. Let us suppose, as we did in Figure 6.1, that the expected rate of profit $r^e_0$ is initially inferior to the equilibrium rate of profit $r^*$. Since firms expect a rate of profit of $r^e_0$, they set a rate of growth of $g_0$, which causes a realized rate of profit of $r_0$. As can be seen on the graph, the realized rate of profit is in this case smaller than the expected rate of profit. According to the adaptative process of equation (6.5), this should induce entrepreneurs to expect a smaller rate of profit in the next production period. The new growth rate decided by the entrepreneurs will be even further away from the equilibrium desired rate of growth. The model pictured by Figure 6.2 is unstable: once we are out of equilibrium, we are getting away from it, rather than converging on it. If the initial expected rate of profit had been higher than the equilibrium rate of profit, the realized rate of profit would

*Figure 6.2  Instability of growth model when investment is more responsive than savings to changes in profits: $g_r > s_p$*

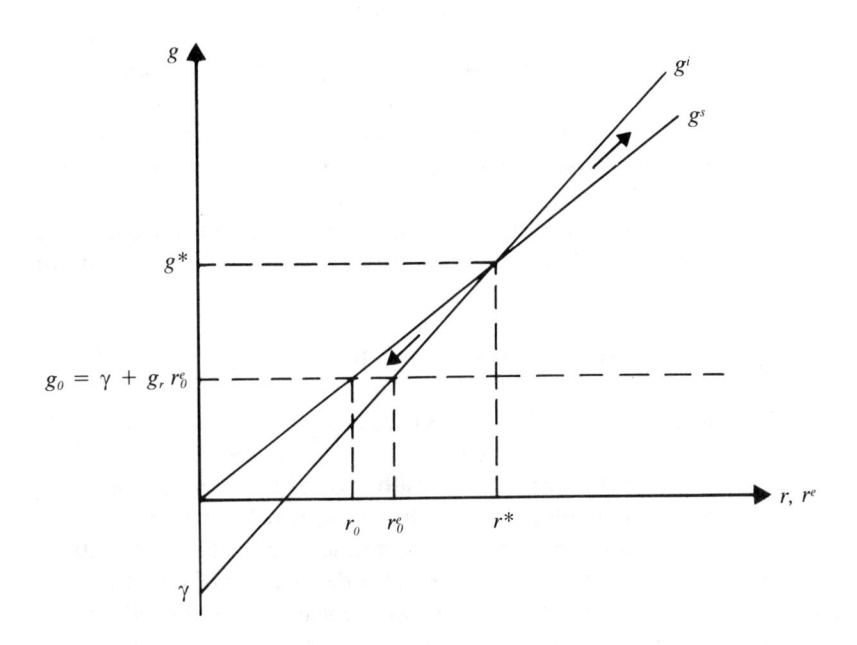

have been higher than the expected one, thus again leading the economy away from equilibrium. By contrast, when the rate of investment is less sensitive than saving to changes in the rate of profit, as can be seen in Figure 6.1, the model is stable. Expectations of rates of return that would be too optimistic, compared to the equilibrium rate of profit, would eventually lead firms to adopt the desired rate of growth. For the Robinsonian model of growth to be stable, we thus need the following inequality, which can be found in various forms in several post-Keynesian models, for instance Pasinetti (1974, p. 114):

$$g_r < s_p \tag{6.7}$$

The stability of the model requires the slope of the investment function, with respect to the rate of profit, to be smaller than the slope of the savings function. This does not necessarily mean that the above inequality is verified under all circumstances. One may presume that it is, since wide swings in economic activity are not often observed. It could be, however, that other phenomena, or other elements which have not been taken into consideration in the present very simple model, modify the requirements of stability, reversing the sign of the inequality (Skott, 1989). It may also be that structural crises, such as that of the 1929 crash, correspond to unstable systems. There would be accumulation regimes which are structurally unstable, and which precipitate the economic system into big depressions (Boyer, 1988). In the latter case the unstable model would correspond to a temporary situation. For our present purposes, however, we will suppose that the economy, and hence its model, is structurally stable, and will assume the realization of the inequality given by (6.7) or of other similar stability conditions. Let us then study further the implications of the model illustrated by Figure 6.1, taking into account the desired rate of accumulation and its corresponding equilibrium rate of profit.

**The Wage/Profit Frontier and the Inflation Barrier**

One of the major features of the neo-Keynesian model is that it transposes Keynes's paradox of thrift to the long period. As we saw in the previous chapter, any increase in the propensities to save leads to a reduction in the level of output or of employment. In the simple neo-Keynesian model of growth and distribution presented here, an increase in the propensity to save out of profits leads to a reduction in the desired rate of growth and in the equilibrium rate of profit. This can be easily seen by taking the derivative of equation (6.6) with respect to $s_p$, and recalling that the rate of profit is proportional to the rate of growth. We get:

$$dg^*/ds_p = -g_r/(s_p - g_r)^2 < 0 \qquad (6.8)$$

The paradox of thrift can be visualized on the right-hand side of Figure 6.3. Compared to Figure 6.1, the axes have been inverted, so that an increase in the propensity to save out of profits leads to a downward shift of the $g^s$ function, from $g^{s2}$ to $g^{s1}$. The desired rate of accumulation, following this increase in the rate of saving and assuming that the investment function is given by the curve $g^{i1}$, decreases from $g_2$ to $g_1$, while the equilibrium rate of profit also decreases, from $r_2$ to $r_1$. Keynes's paradox of thrift extends to the long period. Still, some authors have claimed that there exists a strong post-Keynesian tradition according to which higher thriftiness leads to faster accumulation (Asimakopulos, 1986, pp. 87–9). This tradition can be associated with Joan Robinson's inflation barrier, which turns upside down the causality associated with the Cambridge equation and introduces a Marxian view of accumulation and income distribution. A detour into the pricing determinants of the neo-Keynesian model is required to explain this inflation barrier.

It was mentioned at the beginning of this section that one ought to distinguish between the old neo-Keynesian models of growth and distribution, where the rate of utilization of capacity was assumed to be fixed in the long run, and the newer models of Kaleckian inspiration, where rates of utilization are endogenous. As pointed out in the preceding chapter, it seems that earlier post-Keynesians were initially convinced that there are two uses for the principle of effective demand. It could be put to work in the short period, to determine real income by 'varying the level of utilization of given capital equipment' (Robinson, 1962, p. 11); or it could be put to work in the long period, by modifying the level of prices relative to wages and hence changing the distribution of income and the share of savings relative to income (ibid., p. 12). These two uses of the multiplier and of the principle of effective demand were not seen as incompatible as long as 'one is conceived as a short-run theory and the other as a long-run theory' (Kaldor, 1956, p. 94). The cause of this dichotomy, as we argued earlier, is that earlier post-Keynesians considered the share of profits as the main regulator of the economy. They associated a higher share of profits with a higher share of investment, something that could not be achieved if one omitted overhead labour costs, unless one presumed that the mark-up automatically increased under these circumstances. This required that the economy operate beyond full capacity.

Both the earlier Kaldor and Robinson go to great lengths to ensure that in the long period firms have no excess capacity. Indeed both authors suppose that in the long period firms operate at full capacity (where the rate of utilization is equal to 100 per cent), something that Kaldor (1961, p. 199) calls full employment, and which Robinson calls normal capacity. In the case of the former author, a tentative proof, based on the instability of excess capacity situations when output is growing, is offered to sustain the belief that in the long run firms are necessarily operating at full capacity, and that consequently, changes in prices are the means by which savings are adjusted to investment decisions. In contrast, Robinson offers no proof. She relies upon the forces of competition to arrive at the same result, supposing that 'competition (in the short-period sense) is sufficiently keen to keep prices at the level at which normal capacity output can be sold' (Robinson, 1962, p. 46). The issue, then, is to find out what Robinson means by normal capacity. She says that the limit of the normal capacity of a plant is reached when 'any increase in the weekly rate of output would involve a rise in prime cost per unit of product' (Robinson, 1956, p. 184). This corresponds to what we have called, in Chapter 3, the practical capacity of a plant. Since Robinson generalizes this concept to the firm as a whole, normal capacity must be understood as the sum of all the practical capacities, that is the full capacity of a firm. It is the point at which there is a discontinuity in marginal costs and where they start rising, as in Figure 3.5. We may thus conclude, as Ciccone (1986, p. 22) does, that, 'although variations in the degree of utilization of capacity are admitted in the short period, Robinson excludes them as far as the long period is concerned'.

There are substantial consequences to the assumption that the rate of utilization of capacity in the long run is given (and here equal to unity). We shall underline two of them. The first is that changes in the distribution of income can only occur through changes in the price level relative to wages; that is, in the mark-up on unit costs. A higher level of demand, that is a higher rate of growth, is absorbed by higher prices. This is why the neo-Keynesian model is called an *inflationist* theory of growth (Rowthorn, 1981, p. 31). Note that the neo-Keynesian model is consistent with Eichner's view of the firm, according to which prices are set in response to investment financial needs. In the Eichnerian firm, a higher rate of investment requires higher profits and induces a higher mark-up, and hence higher prices relative to wage costs. This is a profit inflation theory of growth, which can be found in various guises among several other post-Keynesian authors (Seccareccia, 1984). The only difference between the Eichnerian model and the neo-Keynesian one is that in the latter competition prevails, changes in prices being induced by demand and the forces of competition, while in the former megacorps dominate oligopolistic markets, taking discretionary decisions when they change prices and income distribution to sustain their financial needs ensuing from accumulation.

The second consequence of assuming full capacity is that there is a necessary inverse relationship between the real wage rate and the rate of profit, as illustrated on the left-hand side of Figure 6.3. This is the wage/profit frontier, a well-known relation among neoclassical, Marxian and neo-Ricardian authors. The wage/profit frontier is usually shown using prices of production in two-sector or more complex models; however, it may also be shown from the national accounts within the context of a one-sector model (Amadeo 1986b). From a variant of equation (5.14), we know that the value of output is equal to the sum of the wage costs and the profits on capital:

$$pq = wL + rpK \tag{6.9}$$

This can be rewritten as:

$$p = w(L/q) + rp(K/q)$$

Within the framework imposed by Kaldor and Robinson to long period analysis, there is no overhead labour, so that output per unit of labour $q/L$ is a constant equal to $y$. Furthermore, for the earlier Kaldor and Robinson, the standard rate of utilization of capacity is unity, so that the capital output ratio $K/q$ is another constant, equal to $v$. In the context of the neo-Keynesian model, equation (6.9) may thus be rewritten as:

$$p = (w/y)/(1 - rv)$$

Rearranging the above equation, one gets the inverse relationship between the real wage rate and the rate of profit.

$$w/p = y(1 - rv) \qquad (6.10)$$

We are now ready to explain Robinson's inflation barrier. We know that a higher rate of growth causes a higher rate of profit, which itself induces a lower real wage rate because of equation (6.10), given the conditions imposed by the earlier post-Keynesians, that is given a rate of utilization which is fixed at full capacity. All this is illustrated in Figure 6.3 below. To the desired rate of growth $g_1$ corresponds a rate of profit $r_1$ and a real wage rate $(w/p)_1$. If the rate of growth were higher at $g_2$, the real wage rate would have to be lower at $(w/p)_2$. 'A higher rate of accumulation means a lower real-wage rate', as Robinson (1962, p. 58) said and as was initially shown by Findlay (1963, p. 5). Growth requires austerity measures imposed upon workers. High growth means low wages. It would seem that there is not much difference between the early post-Keynesians and some of the neoclassical Keynesians: both recognize that higher real wages increase the level of effective demand and hence the level of employment in the short run; but both would claim that an increase of the real wage rate would be detrimental to employment in the long run (Malinvaud, 1982, p. 9). There would thus be an inconsistency between the results obtained in the short run and those of long-period analysis.

The analysis of the inflation barrier further reinforces this inconsistency by reversing Keynes' paradox of thrift and by making savings the causal force behind investment. The inflation barrier rests upon the negative relationship between the real wage and the rate of growth. It also relies upon the reasonable hypothesis that workers refuse to have their real wages squeezed out by a higher rate of profit, induced by a higher rate of growth. There is then a minimum acceptable real wage rate (Kaldor, 1956, p. 98). If this minimum wage rate is reached, the neo-Keynesian model turns into a Marxian model, where the real wage rate is given and determines the other variables of the system (Marglin, 1984b). The conflict between the growth objectives of the firms and the minimum standards of living of the workers cannot be resolved, and inflation sets in. When this happens, says Robinson (1956, p. 238, 1962, p. 60), monetary authorities raise interest rates until the animal spirits of the entrepreneurs are dampened and investment is curtailed. At that point, inflation pressures are eliminated. The inflation barrier and its detrimental consequences on accumulation could have been avoided, however, if the propensity to save had been higher.

> In any given situation, the lower the level of expenditure on consumption by rentiers the further out the inflation barrier lies, and the higher the rate of accumulation that is possible. When entrepreneurs, taken as a whole, are aiming at a high rate of accumulation, and are held in check only by the inflation barrier, the more thrifty everyone is the better it suits them. (Robinson, 1956, pp. 53–4)

The standard Keynesian causal sequence is thus reversed. The rate of investment depends on the height of the acceptable real wage rate and on the degree of thriftiness. The higher the propensity to save, the higher the rate of accumulation. In a later work, Robinson (1962, p. 63) neatly summarizes her views of the inflation barrier: 'When it is the real wage which limits the rate of growth, greater thriftiness makes more investment possible in a perfectly straightforward and unambiguous sense.' This is consistent with Richard Kahn's claim that, in this situation, 'thrift can now be regarded as an influence on the rate of growth ... greater thriftiness means a higher rate of growth' (1972, p. 202).

The mechanism at work in the case of the inflation barrier may be interpreted graphically as in Figure 6.3. Suppose that initially the savings function is given by $g^{s2}$ while the investment function is given by $g^{i1}$. The equilibrium position, if there was no inflation barrier, would be given by the desired rate of growth $g_2$. This rate of growth would require a real wage rate equal to $(w/p)_2$. Suppose, however, that there is a minimum acceptable real wage rate, say $(w/p)_1$, which is superior to this required wage rate. To the minimum real wage rate $(w/p)_1$ corresponds a maximum attainable profit rate $r_1$. At this maximum rate of profit $r_1$, firms would be willing to accumulate at rate $g_1$, but they can only do so at rate $g_0$. Any attempt to grow at a rate above $g_0$ creates a conflict over the distribution of the surplus and generates inflation. Assuming that inflation brings about policies of restraint, the effect of these policies is to dampen animal spirits and to shift the investment curve from $g^{i1}$ to $g^{i2}$. The consequence of the inflation barrier is to bring down the desired rate of growth to $g_0$ and the actual rate of profit to $r_1$, by shifting the investment function and

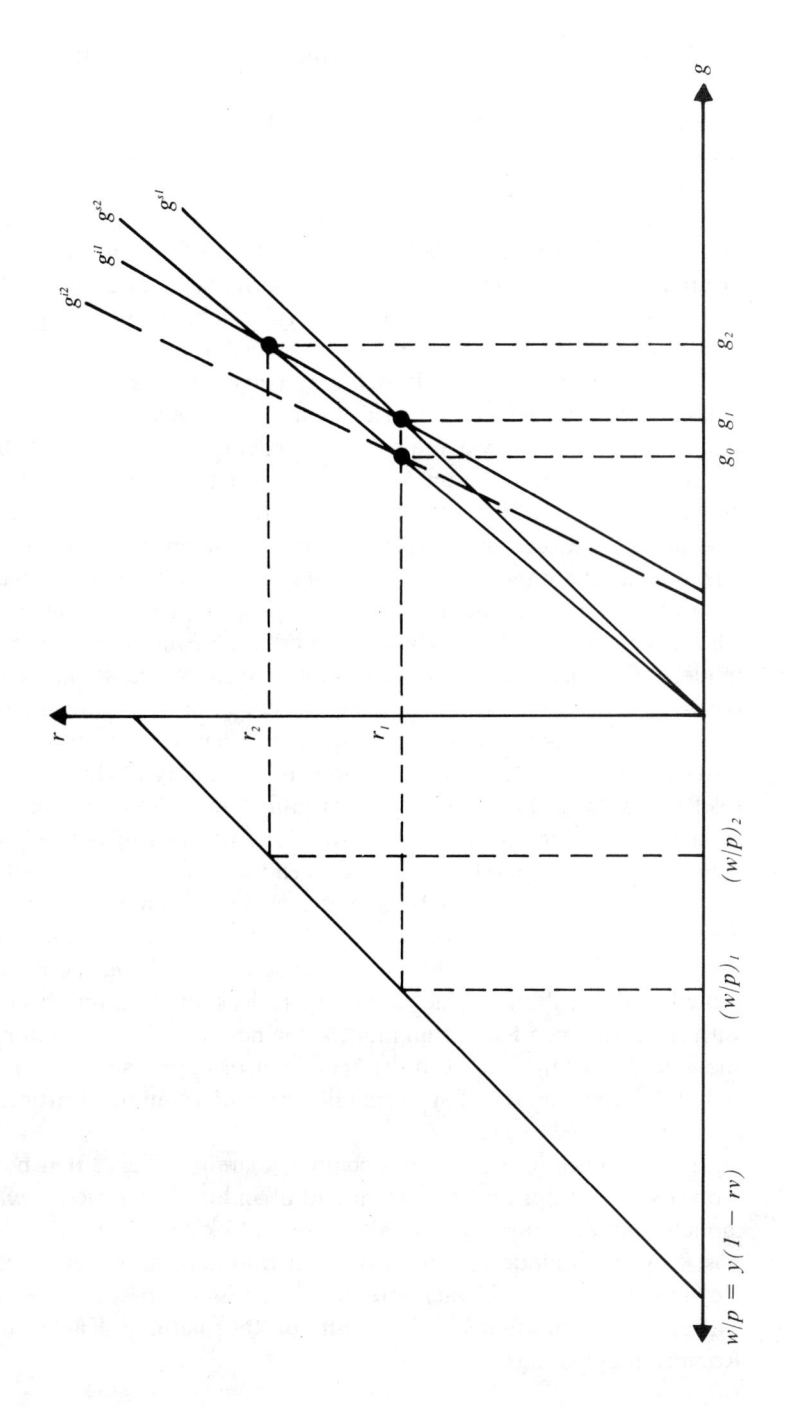

*Figure 6.3* The inflation barrier, or the demise of the paradox of thrift in neo-Keynesian models

making investment compatible with the savings rate and the given real wage rate.

What Kahn, Robinson and, more recently, Asimakopulos (1986) have been telling us is that, if instead the degree of thriftiness $s_p$ had been sufficiently higher, no such restraint would have been necessary. The savings equation would have shifted down from $g^{s2}$ to $g^{s1}$ and, with the initial animal spirits embodied in the investment function $g^{i1}$, the equilibrium desired rate of growth would have been higher, at $g_1$. When there is real wage resistance on the part of the workers, a higher propensity to save on profits is favourable to the economy since it allows a higher rate of growth at a given rate of profit, that is at a given real wage rate. When the inflation barrier has been reached, higher thriftiness generates a higher rate of accumulation by avoiding monetary restraints (Lavoie, 1990).

The case of the inflation barrier rests on the negative relationship between the real wage and the rate of growth. This is evidently true if one assumes that the economy always lies on the wage/profit frontier; that is, if one assumes that in long-run analysis the rate of utilization of capacity is fixed at its normal or full capacity level. In answer to Marglin (1984b), who was comparing the neoclassical, the Marxian and the neo-Keynesian models, all based on the hypothesis of a fixed degree of utilization of capacity, and thus reasserting the importance of the negative relationship between real wages and growth which is implicit to such an hypothesis, post-Keynesian authors have questioned the validity of this assumption (Nell, 1985; Dutt, 1987a). Once the variations in the rate of utilization of capacity are taken into account, in the long period and not only in the short run, the inverse relationship between the real wage rate and the rate of growth may not hold. There may then be no inflation barrier, and Keynes's paradox of thrift may then prevail in all circumstances in the long period. This is what we shall now see, by studying the models of growth and distribution which are in the Kaleckian tradition. By contrast with the earlier neo-Keynesian models, the newer post-Keynesian models show no discrepancy between the behaviour of the economy in the short run and in the long run. They generally leave no room for thriftiness and austerity policies.

As was argued in the previous chapter, there is evidence that both the more recent Kaldor and Robinson had abandoned their neo-Keynesian models and were turning towards more Kaleckian features. The newer post-Keynesian models in the Kaleckian tradition, rather than the neo-Keynesian ones, should therefore be viewed as the best representation, within one-sector models of growth, of the matured Kaldorian and Robinsonian heritage.

## 6.3 THE KALECKIAN GROWTH MODEL: THE STAGNATIONIST VERSION

The newer post-Keynesian model of growth and distribution is an extension of the short-run Kaleckian model that we developed in the preceding chapter. There is some irony in noting that this long-run model is an extension of the Kaleckian model presented by Asimakopulos (1975) and that it serves to destroy the contention that 'an increase in the propensity to save would ease financial constraints and allow higher investment', a claim made by Asimakopulos (1986, p. 89) himself.

It seems that the Kaleckian model of growth and distribution was originally developed independently by Bob Rowthorn and Amitava Dutt (Amadeo, 1987, p. 75), but the main results of their model were also arrived at by Del Monte (1975) in a paper published in Italian. The exact growth model to be presented here is closest to those displayed by Rowthorn (1981) and Kurz (1990b), another ironic fact since Rowthorn is usually considered to be a neo-Marxist author while Kurz is closest to the neo-Ricardian school. This goes to show how labels within the post-classical research programme are relative and it demonstrates that there is a substantial amount of interchange between the various schools of the post-classical tradition.

There are three crucial aspects according to which the forthcoming model may be unambiguously called a Kaleckian model of growth and distribution. First, there is the investment function, about which more will be said later. Second, prices relative to direct costs are assumed to be given, dependent on conventional forces instead of market forces. Prices are of the cost-plus type. Third, in contrast to the early Kaldorian hypotheses, the rate of utilization of capacity is assumed to be generally below unity, and labour is assumed not to be a constraint. This is an obvious Kaleckian feature, as the following quotation demonstrates.

A considerable proportion of capital equipment lies idle in the slump. Even on average the degree of utilization throughout the business cycle will be substantially below the maximum reached during the boom. Fluctuations in the utilization of labour parallel those in the utilization of equipment ... The reserve of capital equipment and the reserve army of the unemployed are typical features of capitalist economy at least throughout a considerable part of the cycle. (Kalecki, 1971, p. 137)

The Kaleckian assumption that the rate of capacity utilization may diverge from its normal or full-capacity rate even in the long run is questioned by some post-classical authors, as will be seen later in the chapter. This is an old controversy however. More than fifty years ago, Keynes objected to Kalecki precisely on those grounds: 'Is it not rather odd when dealing with "long-run problems" to start with the assumption that all firms are always working below capacity' (Keynes, 1973, pp. xii, 829).

**The Kaleckian Model with a Given Rate of Growth**

As we pointed out in Chapter 5, one of the most contentious issues in economics is the way investment decisions are determined. As a means of causing the main features of the Kaleckian growth model to stand out, we will first suppose that the rate of growth of the economy is a given, fixed for instance by the animal spirits of the entrepreneurs as many post-Keynesians would have it. Let us start then with the Cambridge relation, assuming that the rate of growth is an exogenous element:

$$r = g/s_p \tag{6.2}$$

Under the usual assumptions, equation (6.2) tells us that, if the rate of growth is given, so is the rate of profit. In symmetry with the terms that were used for the share of profits in Chapter 5, we may say that equation (6.2) determines the rate of profit seen from the demand side. We now need another equation to determine the rate of profit from the supply side, relating the rate of profit to the rate of utilization of capacity. This second equation is obtained by starting from the national accounts and adding to them the appropriate supply conditions. As seen before, the national accounts are:

$$pq = wL + rpK \tag{6.9}$$

Dividing the above equation by $pK$, the rate of profit is:

$$r = (q/K) - (wL/pK)$$

This can be rewritten as:

$$r = (q/K)[1 - (w/p)(L/q)] \tag{6.11}$$

Note that the term inside the square brackets is the complement of the share of wages, that is the share of profits. Making use of equation (5.29), we can rewrite the rate of profit as:

$$r = (q/K)[1 - (w/p)(1 + f/u)/y_v] \tag{6.12}$$

When the rate of utilization is endogenous, the capital/output ratio $K/q$

is not a constant, but rather a variable which depends on the value of the rate of utilization of capacity. Recall that we may write the capital/output ratio as:

$$K/q = (K/q_{fc})(q_{fc}/q) = v/u \qquad (6.13)$$

The true technical coefficient is thus the $v$ parameter, reflecting the capital to output ratio at full capacity, that is the capital to capacity ratio. Combining equations (6.12) and (6.13), we get what Steindl (1979, p. 3) and Rowthorn (1981, p. 8) call the profits function, and which we shall refer to as the profits cost curve.

$$r = \frac{u}{v}(1 - \frac{(w/p)}{y_v}) - \frac{f(w/p)}{vy_v} \qquad (6.14)$$

Equation (6.14) is a three-dimensional equation, which links the rate of profit to the real wage rate and to the rate of utilization of capacity. The parameters of the equation are the capital to capacity ratio $v$, the output per unit of variable labour $y_v$, and the ratio of fixed to variable labour at full capacity $f$. The relationship between the real wage rate and the rate of profit, for a given level of utilization of capacity, is illustrated on the left-hand side of Figure 6.4. The three oblique lines correspond to three different degrees of utilization of capacity. Naturally, for a given level of utilization, the negative relationship between the real wage rate and the rate of profit is preserved. The issue, however, is that the rate of utilization of capacity is not a given, but rather that it is an endogenous variable. This can be seen on the right-hand side of Figure 6.4. There is a positive relationship between the rate of profit and the rate of utilization of capacity, for a given level of the real wage rate.

We may now combine equations (6.2) and (6.14), that is the Cambridge equation with the profits cost curve. We see immediately that no relationship can be established between the rate of growth and the real wage rate. The same wage rate is compatible with different rates of accumulation. Let us assume, as is done in Figure 6.4, that the real wage rate is $(w/p)_0$. At a low rate of accumulation, say $g_1$, the profit rate induced by the Cambridge equation is $r_1$. At that rate of profit, the profits cost curve tells us that the rate of utilization of capacity is only $u_1$. At the higher rate of accumulation $g_3$, the induced rate of profit is $r_3$ and the rate of utilization is $u_3$. The higher rate of utilization shifts out the wage/profit frontier, as can be seen on the left side of the figure. The result is that a higher rate of growth can be achieved without the real wage rate being smaller. 'Differences in the rate of accumulation ... do not require changes in the real wage rate'

*Figure 6.4 The undetermined relation between real wages and the rate of accumulation, the latter being given and the rate of capacity utilization being endogenous*

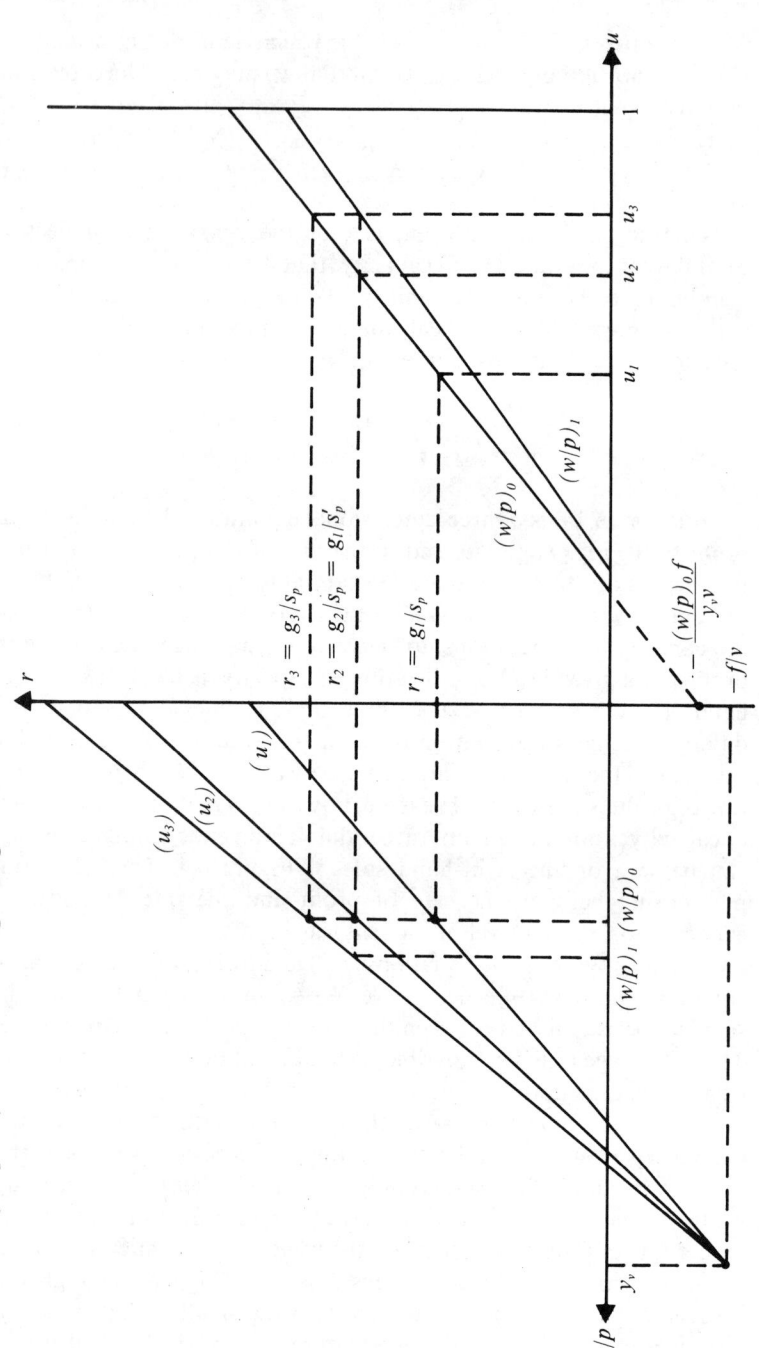

(Ciccone, 1986, p. 33). There is no iron law of accumulation any more. The disappearance of the negative relationship between the real wage rate and the actual rate of profit is due to the rate of utilization of capacity having become an endogenous variable. Note that the endogeneity of the degree of plant utilization has nothing to do with the rate of investment being a function of the rate of utilization; the rate of utilization is endogenous even if the rate of growth is a given of the analysis (Ciccone, 1987, p. 105). This can be seen more clearly, perhaps, if we solve equations (6.2) and (6.14) for the rate of utilization of capacity.

$$u = \frac{g(v/s_p) + f(w/p)/y_v}{1 - (w/p)/y_v} \qquad (6.15)$$

It now becomes clear that the rate of utilization of capacity is endogenous, depending on the given wage rate, the given rate of growth, the propensity to save and the various technical parameters defining the utilization function. It is also clear from equation (6.15) that overhead labour costs are not required to make the rate of utilization endogenous. If $f$ is set equal to zero, the above equation still makes sense. The profits curve would then rise from the origin. This is actually how Dutt (1984) and Amadeo (1986a), among many others, pursue their own analysis: there are no overhead costs. The major feature of their models, in contrast to that of Rowthorn, is that in the former the share of wages cannot change unless the mark-up on costs is modified, even when the rate of utilization of capacity is endogenously changing. The rest of their analysis is substantially similar to the one presented here. Once we accept that a higher rate of growth need not be associated with a higher share of profit, a simpler model with no overhead costs may then be constructed within the framework of an endogenous degree of plant utilization. This simplified model then allows us to make comparisons with similar models incorporating different closures or different price determinants. It also allows us to pursue more complex questions, for instance stability analysis in a two-sector model (Dutt, 1990a), something that will not be attempted in this book.

In the Kaleckian model of growth with overhead labour, however, the mark-up being given, the *share* of profit $\pi$ necessarily increases when the rate of growth is higher. This can be seen by looking at equation (6.12): the term inside the square brackets represents the share of profit. The share of profits changes with the variations in the rate of utilization of capacity $u$. Replacing this rate of utilization with its equilibrium value, from equation (6.15), we get the equilibrium share of profit as a function of the exogenous growth rate. Recalling the simple mark-up pricing procedure of equation (5.30), we also replace the ratio of the real wage rate to the marginal productivity of variable labour, the ratio $(w/p)/y_v$, with the expression $(1+\theta)$. One gets:

$$\pi = [\theta/(1+\theta)]\{1-f/[f+(1+\theta)gv/s_p]\} \qquad (6.16)$$

Taking the derivative of the above equation with respect to the growth rate, we find it to be positive. This shows, the mark-up being given, that there is a positive relationship between the rate of growth and the share of profits in a long-run model with overhead costs and an endogenous rate of utilization of capacity. This demonstrates the correctness of Kaldor's comment that was cited in Chapter 5, to the effect that 'changes in the ratio of investment to output can elicit corresponding changes in the share of profits . . . even if the mark up is constant'.

$$d\pi/dg = (\theta fv/s_p)/[f+(1+\theta)gv/s_p]^2 > 0 \qquad (6.17)$$

We may also note that a form of Keynes's paradox of thrift is a feature of the new post-Keynesian model of growth and distribution. Suppose, as is shown in Figure 6.4, that, starting from an original position characterized by a growth rate of $g_1$, there is a decrease in the propensity to save on profits from $s_p$ to $s_p'$. In the present model, the impact of such a reduction in thriftiness would be a higher rate of profit and a higher rate of utilization of capacity, in both cases a favourable effect for capitalist entrepreneurs. Naturally there would be no impact on growth or on the real wage, since they are both assumed to be given. One may guess, however, that, if accumulation depends positively on either of the two-above mentioned variables, a decrease in thriftiness would have a favourable impact on growth. This can be clearly seen by checking on equation (6.8). The paradox of thrift extends to the long period in a model of variable capacity utilization.

We may conclude this subsection by noting that the given rate of growth of Figure 6.4 could just as well have been the Robinsonian desired rate of accumulation that was identified in Figure 6.1 or in equation (6.6). If the investment function only depends on the rate of profit, actual or expected, then the rate of growth may still be considered as a given within the framework of the model of endogenous utilization of capacity. We then have a recursive determination of the rate of utilization of capacity. The rate of growth and the rate of profit are jointly determined, the former depending directly on the strength of animal spirits and inversely on the propensity to save on profits; the rate of growth then determines the rate of utilization of capacity, given the real wage rate and the technical parameters of the utilization function. Indeed the higher degree of capacity utilization is the mechanism which ensures that the higher rate of profit which is being expected is being realized (Bhaduri, 1986, p. 230). The endogenous rate of utilization of capacity replaces the flexible margins of profit of the neo-Keynesian competitive mechanism.

We may note further that, for a given rate of growth, there is a direct relationship between the real wage rate and the rate of utilization of capacity, as can be seen from Figure 6.4. If the wage rate is increased from $(w/p)_0$ to $(w/p)_1$, the rate of growth being given as $g_2$ (and for a given $s_p$), the rate of utilization of capacity must increase from $u_2$ to $u_3$ as a result of the profits cost curve shifting down. The direct relation between the real wage rate and the rate of capacity utilization can also be shown by taking the partial derivative of equation (6.15) with respect to the real wage rate.

$$\frac{du}{d(w/p)} = \frac{(f + gv/s_p)/y_v}{[1 - (w/p)/y_v]^2} > 0 \qquad (6.18)$$

We may now introduce a complication into the analysis by assuming that the investment function is endogenous with respect to the rate of utilization of capacity.

## Growth as a Function of the Rate of Utilization of Capacity

The standard Kaleckian model of growth and distribution assumes that the rate of investment in growth terms is a function of the rate of profit and of the rate of utilization of capacity. This is actually what Kaldor (1957, p. 601) informally proposes. It is also a simplification of the investment function advocated by Steindl (1952, pp. 127–9). For this reason in particular, Dutt (1990a) speaks of a Kalecki–Steindl closure. Steindl himself considers that several factors influence investment decisions, most of which are endogenous to the economic system. These factors are the retention ratio, the gearing ratio, the rate of profit and the rate of utilization of capacity. Steindl believes that none of these factors alone can explain investment by firms. Although they are interrelated, each factor plays an independent role. For instance, although Steindl knows that the rate of profit can be decomposed into the share of profit, the rate of utilization of capacity and the inverse of the capital to capacity ratio, as can be seen in the following equation, he still argues that the rate of utilization of capacity has an independent impact on the investment decision, besides that of the rate of profit.

$$r = \Pi/K = (\Pi/q)(q/q_{fc})(q_{fc}/K) = \pi u/v \qquad (6.19)$$

The exact form that an investment function should take will be discussed later. Enough has been said at this stage to justify the standard Kaleckian investment function used by Rowthorn (1981), Taylor (1983), Dutt (1984) and Agliardi (1988), which incorporates the rate of profit, as in the Robinsonian model, and the rate of utilization of capacity, which makes the rate of accumulation a truly endogenous variable. Their investment function can be written in linear form as:

$$g^i = \gamma + g_u u + g_r r \tag{6.20}$$

Since we have already shown that under the proper conditions the expected rate of profit would eventually become the realized one, we need not incorporate expected variables, as we did in the Robinsonian investment equation (equation (6.4)). In any case, with the new investment function, equation (6.20), we shall soon see under what conditions the model is stable. Combining the investment function with the savings function given by equation (6.3), we get what Rowthorn (1981, p. 12) calls the realization curve, which we may prefer to call the effective demand curve. This curve can be written in the same coordinates as the profits cost curve (equation (6.14)); that is, with the rate of profit expressed as a function of the rate of utilization of capacity.

$$r = \frac{g_u u + \gamma}{s_p - g_r} \tag{6.21}$$

Let us now turn our attention to the profits cost curve. Since the Kaleckian literature deals with Kalecki's degree of monopoly; that is, the gross profit margin or the share of gross profits (including overheads) in income, for comparison purposes we want to rewrite the profits cost curve of equation (6.14) in terms of the degree of monopoly. To be able to do so, let us assume that the pricing procedure is of the simple mark-up type, that is:

$$p = (1+\theta)w/y_v \tag{5.30}$$

Proceeding as we did to obtain equation (6.14), making use in particular of equation (5.45), we obtain a variant of the profits cost curve in terms of the mark-up θ, that is:

$$r = \frac{u\theta - f}{(1+\theta)v}$$

Recalling the relation between the mark-up and the gross profit margin, that is Kalecki's degree of monopoly given by equation (3.12), $m = \theta/(1+\theta)$, we may rewrite the above profits cost curve in the following standard way:

$$r = u(m/v) - (1-m)f/v \qquad (6.22)$$

We know from our previous analysis of the Robinsonian model that the propensity to save on profits must be larger than the sensitivity of investment growth to changes in the rate of profit (inequality (6.7)). The denominator of equation (6.21) is thus necessarily positive for the model to exhibit stability. Let us further assume, to ensure stability, as will soon be clear, that the slope of this effective demand curve with respect to the rate of utilization $u$ is smaller than the slope of the profits cost curve, given by equation (6.14). The stability condition is then:

$$g_u/(s_p - g_r) < m/v$$

which can be rewritten as:

$$s_p > g_r + g_u v/m \qquad (6.23)$$

The response of savings to an increase in the rate of profit must be larger than the total response of investment. This, incidentally, ensures that the slope of the effective demand curve given by equation (6.21) is positive. With these conditions in mind, which are more stringent than when investment only responded to the rate of profit (condition (6.7)), we may now present a visual representation of the solutions given by the interaction of the profits cost curve and the effective demand curve. This is done in Figure 6.5. On the right-hand side of the graph, the effective demand curve has been drawn with a smaller slope than that of the profits cost curves. Three of these have been drawn, each curve corresponding to a different wage rate. The curve most to the right, marked $(w/p)_3$, is the one with the highest real wage rate, that is the one with the lowest degree of monopoly $m$. It can be seen that the higher the real wage rate, the higher the resulting rate of utilization of capacity and the higher the rate of profit. Since the rate of profit is directly related to the rate of growth through the Cambridge equation, $g = rs_p$, this implies that the higher the real wage rate the higher the rate of accumulation.

The relationship between the real wage rate and the rate of growth implied by the Kaleckian model is thus a positive one, instead of a negative one as was the case in the earlier neo-Keynesian model of Robinson and Kaldor and as was implicit in the inflation barrier of the former.

*Figure 6.5* The positive relation between real wages and the rates of profit and of accumulation, when the rates of capacity utilization and of accumulation are endogenous

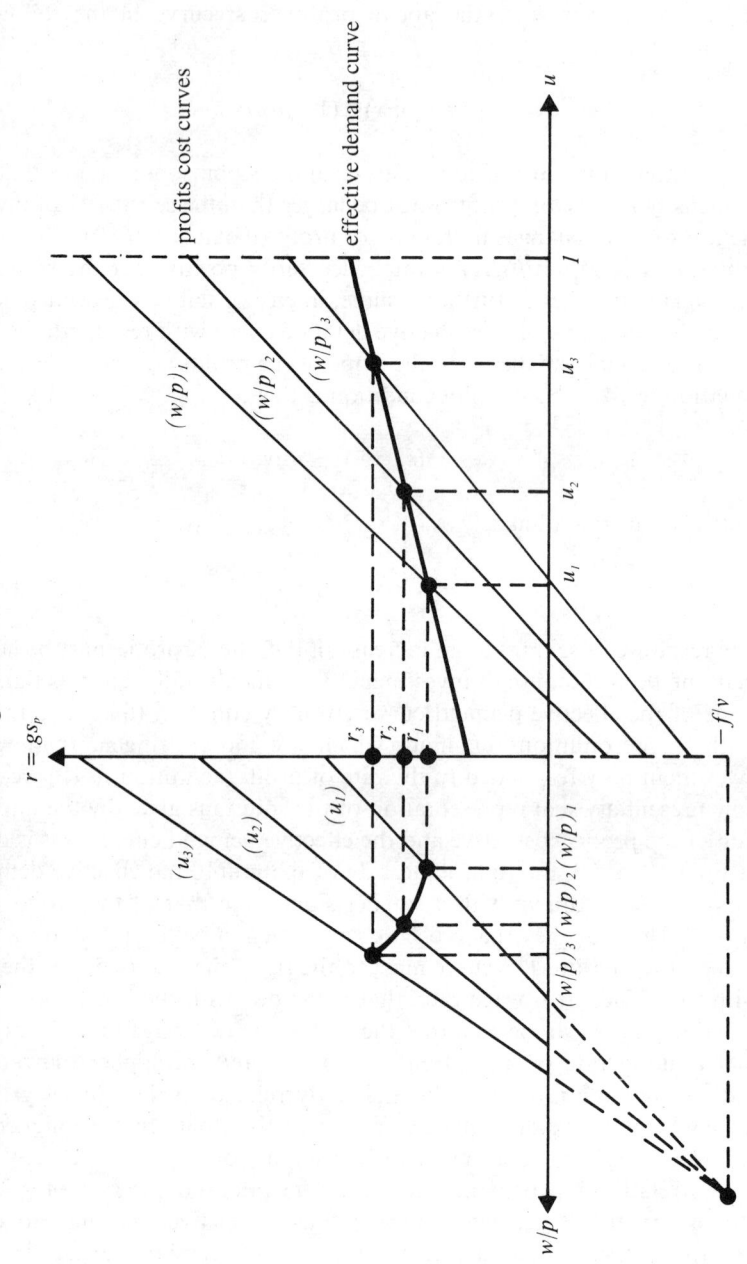

As the real wage rate is increased, so is the rate of utilization of capacity, with the effect of shifting the wage/profit frontier, and hence increasing the rate of profit and the rate of growth. The left-hand side of Figure 6.5 also shows that the downward-sloping wage/profit frontier at a fixed degree of plant utilization is replaced by a positive relation between the wage rate and the profit rate, when the rates of capacity utilization and of accumulation are endogenous. Rather than being downward-sloping, the relevant wage/profit curve is upward-sloping, as shown by the thick line on the graph.

The Kaleckian model of growth and distribution thus retrieves the results obtained in the case of the short period. Increases in the real wage rate have a positive effect on the rate of utilization of the economy in the long period as well. But, whereas in the short period an increase in wages could not lead to higher profits, it does so in the long period because of the presence of the rate of utilization of capacity as an argument of the investment function. We have here what Rowthorn (1981, p. 18) calls the paradox of costs. As is obvious from Figure 6.5, higher wage costs relative to productivity lead to a higher rate of profit, rather than to a lower one, as would be expected. As long as there is excess capacity, entrepreneurs and labour unions need not be in direct conflict over the macroeconomic distribution of income, since the overall size of national income can be increased, allowing both wage increases and a faster rate of accumulation of capital. As Del Monte (1975, p. 243) says, commenting on a similar model of his, the interesting feature of the Kaleckian model is that the degree of utilization is not unique. An increase in the degree of monopoly, far from leading to an increase in the rate of profit, leads to its decline because of the decrease in the rate of capacity utilization of the firms.

All the favourable results which can be associated with an increase in the real wage rate depend on the stability conditions which have been mentioned above, and formalized in the inequality (6.23). If the effective demand curve of Figure 6.5 had a larger slope than the profits cost curve (and a negative intercept), while still being positive, one would get precisely the opposite result: a higher real wage rate would be associated with a lower rate of utilization of capacity and a lower real wage rate. It is thus important to know which case is the more probable one and to discuss the issue of stability. There are many ways to approach the problem in the models of the type being discussed here (Committeri, 1986). The condition derived in (6.23) was based on the relative slopes of the profits cost and effective demand curves of Figure 6.5. Stability may also be discussed along the lines presented in the case of the Robinsonian model of growth; that is, by comparing the slopes of the investment and of the savings curves, incorporating in them the profits cost curve. Let us proceed, then, to the exercise that allowed us to understand the stability of the Robinsonian model. Let us suppose as before that entrepreneurs expect a certain rate of profit $r^e$, but that furthermore they expect a certain level of utilization of capacity, called $u^e$, adjusting their investment decisions accordingly. We then have a system of four equations:

$$g^i = \gamma + g_u u^e + g_r r^e \qquad (6.24)$$

$$g^s = r s_p \qquad (6.3)$$

$$r = u(m/v) - f(1-m)/v \qquad (6.22)$$

$$g^i = g^s \qquad (6.25)$$

To this system we can append a fifth equation, which determines the rate of utilization that would be expected in the next period, given the rate that was expected in the previous period and given the rate of utilization that has just been realized. This equation is similar to equation (6.5), which dealt with the expectations of the rate of profit. We have:

$$u^e_t = \phi u^e_{t-1} + (1-\phi) u_{t-1} \text{ with } \phi < 1 \qquad (6.26)$$

By replacing $r$ with its value in equation (6.22), the investment and the *realized* savings functions may now be written as:

$$g^i = (g_u + g_r m/v) u^e + \gamma - g_r f(1-m)/v \qquad (6.27)$$

$$g^s = s_p[u(m/v) - f(1-m)/v] \qquad (6.28)$$

The $g^i$ function depends on the expected rate of utilization of capacity, while the $g^s$ function depends on the actual rate of utilization. It is clear that both functions have a positive slope, although they may have a negative intercept with the $g$ axis. Two cases are possible, depending on the relative slopes of the two functions. These two cases are illustrated in Figure 6.6. If the slope of the savings function is steeper than that of the investment function, case (*a*), we get again the inequality of equation (6.23). Obviously it makes no difference here to look at the slopes of the profits cost curve and effective demand curve or to check on the slopes of the investment and *realized* savings curve. We may now use the same procedure as the one followed to verify the stability case of the Robinsonian model. Assume again that the rate of growth decided by firms on the basis of their beliefs about the rate of utilization is the actual rate of

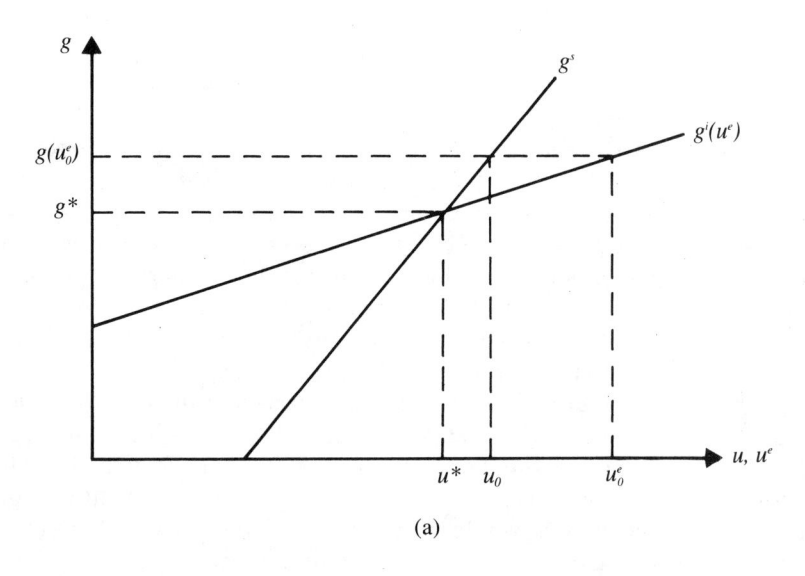

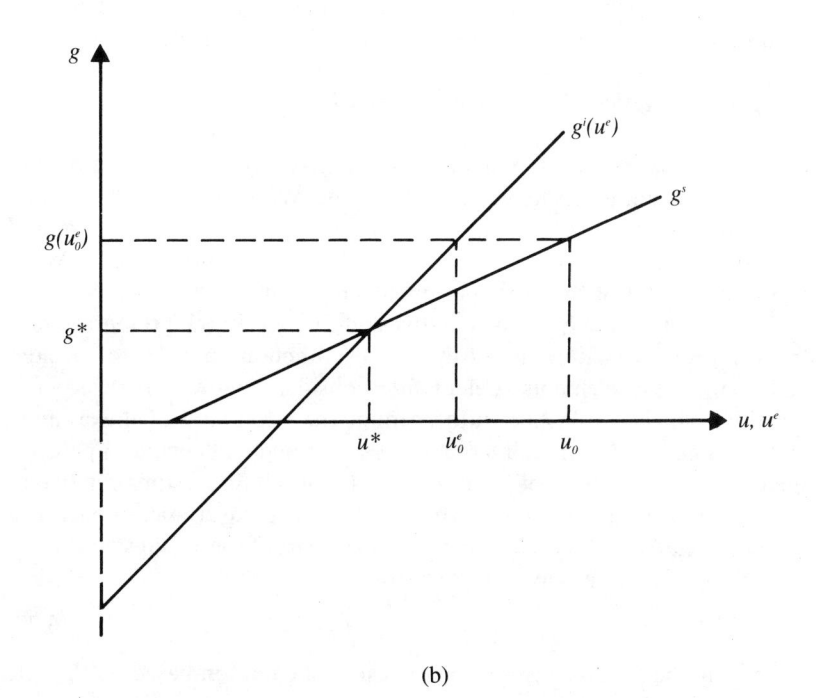

*Figure 6.6* The Kaleckian model of growth: (a) stable case; (b) unstable case

growth, and consequently assume, as does Amadeo (1987, p. 83), that the savings function is the realization curve *à la* Harris/Robinson, which is why we called it the *realized* savings curve. For a given rate of growth, given by the values of equation (6.27), including the expectations about the rate of utilization, the actual rate of utilization is given by the savings curve, equation (6.28).

The stable case is shown in Figure 6.6(a). For a given rate of growth $g(u^e_0)$, the actual rate of utilization of capacity $u_0$ is smaller than the expected one $u^e_0$. According to our mechanism of revision of expectations, this should induce firms to revise their expectations downwards, and hence choose a rate of growth which is closer to the equilibrium one; that is, the rate of growth for which the actual rate of utilization of capacity is equal to the one which is expected. Eventually the expected rate of utilization would be the equilibrium one, that is $u^*$. On the contrary, the equilibrium rate of growth would never be reached in the unstable case, illustrated by Figure 6.6(b), that is when condition (6.23) is not fulfilled. Suppose again that the initial rate of growth $g(u^e_0)$ decided by the firms is above the equilibrium one. We see on the graph that the actual rate of utilization of capacity $u_0$ would turn out to be larger than the expected one, $u^e_0$. This would induce firms to adopt a higher expected rate of utilization and hence a faster rate of investment, getting away from the solution of the model. Figure 6.6(b) thus depicts the unstable case.

**Comparative Statics of the Canonical Model**

Having dealt with the issue of stability, we may now extend the model to take into account issues temporarily left aside. We know that a higher real wage rate is conducive to a higher rate of utilization in the long run, and also to a higher rate of accumulation and a higher rate of profit. What about the impact of the other parameters of the model?

To deal with these questions, let us slightly modify the presentation of the profits cost function and of the savings function, in order to consider extra parametric elements. Let us first consider a more general savings function, which would take into account the possibility of government running a deficit. Let us call $b$ the government budget deficit as a percentage of the overall stock of capital. Let us omit all discussions relative to the payment of interest on government debt. The government deficit is a dissaving relative to the economy; it absorbs part of the savings on profits. The savings function may now be written as:

$$g^s = s_p r - b \qquad (6.29)$$

Keeping the standard Kaleckian investment equation based on the rate of profit and the rate of utilization, that is equation (6.20), the effective demand equation becomes:

$$r = (g_u u + \gamma + b)/(s_p - g_r) \qquad (6.30)$$

The reader may note that, if governments were running surpluses, the intercept with the $r$ axis of the curve described by equation (6.30) could be negative. Let us also explicitly introduce depreciation of capital into our model. Call $\delta$ the constant rate of depreciation of capital. We may further suppose, as we did in Chapter 5, that overhead labour is better paid than variable labour. Let us continue to call $\sigma$ the ratio of the salary paid to permanent staff to the wage rate paid to variable workers, and let us now define $w$ to be the wage rate paid to these variable workers. A rise in the wage rate will be equivalent to a rise in the overall wage rate as long as the $\sigma$ ratio stays constant. Using the same notations as in Chapter 5, profits net of depreciation may be written as:

$$p\Pi = pq - wL_v - \sigma w L_f - \delta p K \qquad (6.31)$$

Proceeding as we did to obtain equation (6.22), making use in particular of equation (5.53), we obtain a variant of the profits cost curve, net of depreciation:

$$r = u(m/v) - (1-m)f\sigma/v - \delta \qquad (6.32)$$

Our Kaleckian model of growth and distribution is now complete, incorporating the profits cost curve (equation 6.32) and the effective demand curve (equation 6.30). One of the neat features of the model is that each parameter only appears in one of the two equations. For this reason, we may call it the canonical model. This makes comparative statics much easier to perform, since we only need to know in which direction each curve is shifting to ascertain the impact of changes in the various parameters. We shall see later that there are circumstances under which this separability does not hold.

Let us first deal with the parameters of the effective demand curve. Let us start by reconsidering the paradox of thrift. This is illustrated in Figure 6.7. In the upper part of the graph, we see that an increase in the propensity to save on profits leads to a shift downwards of the profits cost curve, as well as to a flatter slope. The result is a lower rate of utilization of capacity and a lower rate of profit. In the lower part of the graph, which makes use of the $g^i$ and $g^s$ functions of equations (6.20) and (6.28), the latter being properly modified to accommodate equation (6.32), the $g^s$

312   Foundations of Post-Keynesian Economic Analysis

*Figure 6.7  The paradox of thrift: negative impact of an increase in the propensity to save on the rates of profit and of accumulation*

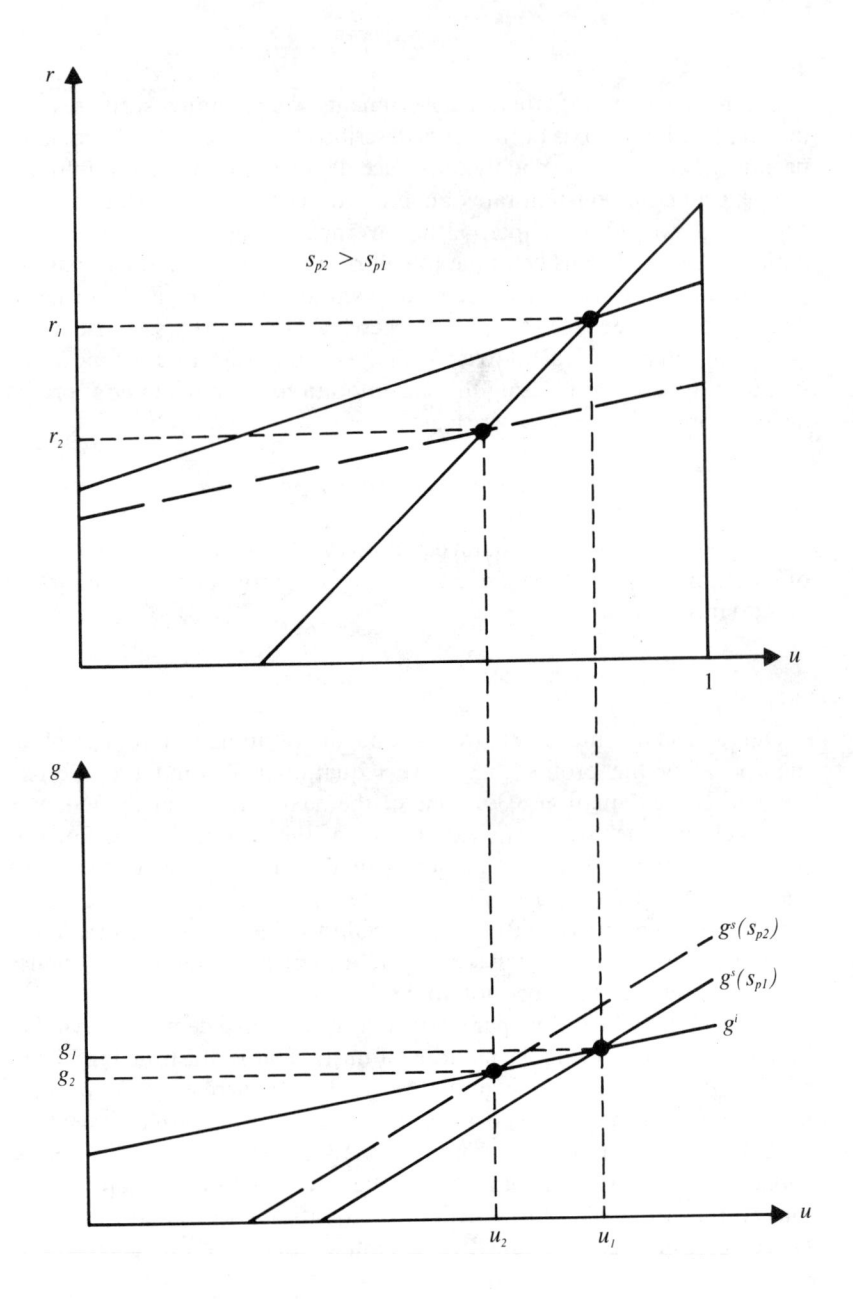

function shifts up. An increased propensity to save is thus also associated with a lower rate of growth. There is again proof, as one would have expected from the analysis already performed in the case of a given rate of growth, that the paradox of thrift extends to the long period.

Let us now consider an increase in the relative budget deficit, which enters the effective demand equation as one of the constant terms. This implies an upward parallel shift of the effective demand curve. The result, as one would expect in a Kaleckian type of model and as appears at the top of Figure 6.8, is an increase in the rate of utilization of capacity and in the rate of profit. We also see in the bottom part of the graph that an increase in the relative budget deficit induces a higher rate of growth. An increase in the autonomous growth component $\gamma$, which one can associate with more optimistic animal spirits or more favourable historical factors, would have led to exactly the same results.

Let us now deal with the effects of changes in the parameters of the profits cost curve. We already know from the previous subsection that an increase in the real wage rate, that is a decrease in the degree of monopoly $m$, leads to higher rates of growth, profit and utilization of capacity. Let us then deal with the other elements of costs. There are four other factors within equation (6.32) which would increase the cost of producing for firms. These are the requirements in machines, given by $v$; the rate of depreciation $\delta$; the salary premium $\sigma$ of overhead staff; and the relative numerical importance of overhead staff, defined by $f$. An increase in $v$ would shift down the profits cost curve. An increase in any of the other three factors leads to a parallel shift downwards of the profits cost curve. The consequences are shown in Figure 6.9. The new rate of utilization and rate of profit are higher, and hence so is the new rate of growth. We have another illustration of the paradox of costs. Higher costs, for a given productivity, lead to a more favourable position for the economy. Indeed, as is underlined by Rowthorn (1981, p. 18), 'under the assumed conditions, higher costs lead to higher profits'.

The paradox of costs brings to our attention a distinction that must be made between shifts in profits that are due to variations in the price–cost nexus from shifts in profits which result from changes in effective demand (Steindl, 1979, p. 3). The distinct profits cost curve and effective demand curve portray this distinction. In the example just given, an increase in overhead costs leads to a fall in profitability at given rates of capacity utilization. This is illustrated in Figure 6.9 by the shift downwards of the profits cost curve. *If the rate of utilization were to remain at its initial level*, here shown as $u_1$, the rise in costs would lead to a decline in the rate of profit from $r_1$ to $r_{u1}$. The higher overhead costs correspond, however, to additional revenues distributed to households. These higher revenues

*Figure 6.8 Positive impact on the rates of profit and of acculuation, following an increase in government deficit or an improvement in animal spirits*

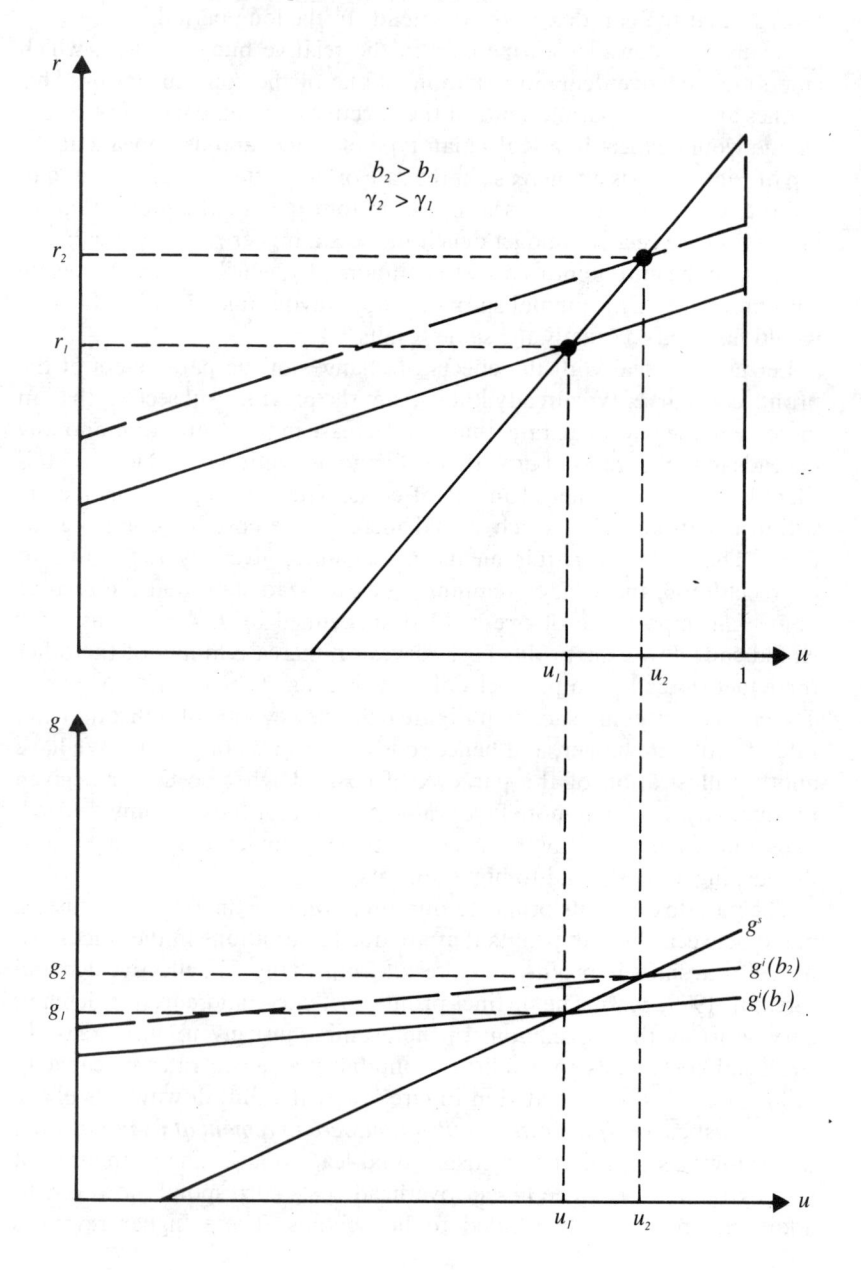

*Figure 6.9* *The paradox of costs: positive impact on the rate of profit of an increase in various components of costs*

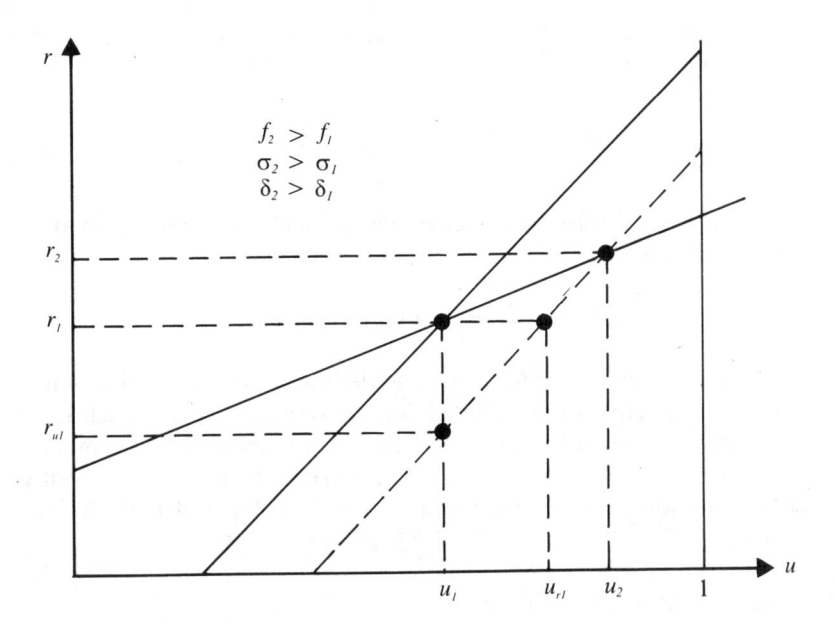

$f_2 > f_1$
$\sigma_2 > \sigma_1$
$\delta_2 > \delta_1$

generate additional demand, which induce a rise in the rate of utilization of capacity, from $u_1$ to $u_{r1}$ on the graph. So far there is no difference from the short-period story that was told in Chapter 5. Additional costs cannot increase overall profits even if we take effective demand into account. A divergence between the short-period analysis and the long-period one arises because we now assume that investment responds to changes in the rate of utilization of capacity. The higher rate of accumulation so induced augments the upward pressure on the rate of utilization of capacity and creates additional profits. The end result is a further increase in the rate of utilization, up to $u_2$, and above all an increase in profitability, the rate of profit increasing from $r_1$ to $r_2$. This is the mechanism which explains how higher costs lead to higher profits.

It should be pointed out, as indeed has been underlined in the various graphs used to illustrate the model, that the cost paradoxes are only valid provided the rate of utilization of capacity stays below unity. The other parameters being given, it requires that the real wage rate does not exceed a certain critical value. An increase in the real wage rate leads to an increase in the rate of growth, but this increase only occurs as long as the rate of capacity utilization is below unity. The range of relevance of the model is thus limited. There is an upper limit to the values which the real wage rate can take, or in other words there is a lower limit to the values that the margin of profit $m$ can take. Let us find some expression of these limits. From equations (6.30) and (6.32) we derive the equilibrium rate of capacity utilization.

$$u^* = \frac{(s_p - g_r)[(1-m)\sigma f + \delta v] + (b+\gamma)v}{(s_p - g_r)m - vg_u} \qquad (6.33)$$

For the rate of utilization to be smaller than one, we need the following inequality:

$$s_p > g_r + v(g_u + \gamma + b)/[m - (1-m)\sigma f - \delta v] \qquad (6.34)$$

When the sum of $\gamma$ and $b$ is positive, the above inequality is more stringent than equation (6.23) defining the stability of the model. In this case, whenever equation (6.34) is fulfilled, we know that the model is stable (Del Monte, 1975, p. 243). When the sum of $\gamma$ and $b$ is not positive, both conditions must be taken into account to know if the solution is relevant.

**Labour-saving Technical Progress**

We now explore the impact of technical progress. This will be done very superficially, as the issues involved are quite complex and difficult to model (Dosi, et al., 1988). The analysis will again rely on the work of Rowthorn (1981, pp. 22–30). In fact, in the previous subsection, we have already dealt with one kind of progress, that of the so-called capital saving technical progress. If, ceteris paribus, there is a decrease in the capital to capacity ratio $v$, equation (6.32) shows that the profits cost curve of Figure 6.9 will shift to the left, inducing a lower rate of growth and a lower rate of utilization of capacity. This contradicts, as mentioned by Rowthorn (1981, p. 27), the conventional Marxist view according to which an increase in the capital to capacity ratio – the organic composition of capital – would depress the economy.

Let us take for granted that there is no significant change in the capital to capacity ratio, one of the stylized Kaldorian facts (Kaldor 1961, p. 178). Let us consider then the so-called labour saving technical progress; that is, innovations that increase the marginal product $y_v$ of variable labour. From our discussion surrounding equation (5.28), we know that, as long as there is no change in the ratio of overhead labour to variable labour at full capacity, the $f$ parameter, any change in the $y_v$ variable induces a proportional change in the $y_f$ variable representing the productivity of overhead labour. Therefore we need concern ourselves only with the $y_v$ variable, noting that overall labour productivity $y$ grows at the same pace as the productivity of variable labour. Recollecting equation (5.29), that is $y = q/L$, and recalling that the growth rate of $q$ is $g$, we have

$$g_L = g - \lambda \qquad (6.35)$$

with $g_L$ the rate of growth of employment and $\lambda$ the rate of growth of labour productivity, or for short the rate of technical progress.

We may first note that, unless we add the necessary assumptions, the long-period rate of accumulation and the rate of utilization of capacity of the standard Kaleckian model do not depend on the rate of technical progress or on the value taken by the product to labour coefficient $y$ (Dutt, 1990a, p. 105). As long as technical progress does not have an impact on the degree of monopoly $m$, that is on the ratio of the real wage rate to labour productivity, it has no impact on the rate of accumulation. However, as is obvious from equation (6.35), unless technical progress induces faster accumulation by some mechanism, the fear in some quarters of the effects of technical progress are justified. Technical progress brings about a slower rate of growth $g_L$ of employment if the rate of accumulation $g$ is given, although real wages are assumed to grow at the same rate as labour productivity. We find again a result that had already been underlined for the short run. The often heard proposition that, when there are gains in productivity, no employment problems should appear if these gains are fully distributed to the workers, is shown again to be invalid. In the short period, we saw that an increase in autonomous expenditures was required to stop employment from falling off. In the long run, the only way for technical progress to have a favourable impact on employment, although real wages follow gains in productivity, is for technical progress to have induced effects on some of the variables of the model, in particular the rate of investment.

Technical progress may be incorporated in the standard Kaleckian model in a number of ways. The most obvious one is to include the rate of technical progress as one of the arguments of the investment function. This is a classical Schumpeterian proposition, the optimism of firms and that of their bankers riding on waves of innovation. One might add that it is also a Kaleckian proposition. Kalecki endorses such a view, arguing that 'capitalists investing "today" think to have an advantage over those having invested "yesterday" because of technical novelties that have reached them' (1971, p. 151). Furthermore Steindl (1979, p. 7) considers the pace of innovations to be a shift parameter of the Kaleckian investment function in his more recent work. Calling $g_\lambda$ the sensitivity of the investment function to the rate of technical growth, the investment function (equation 6.20) may be rewritten as:

$$g^i = \gamma + g_u u + g_r r + g_\lambda \lambda \qquad (6.36)$$

Another possible effect of technical progress is to make existing equipment obsolete. One would expect a faster pace of technical innovations to have a direct effect on the rate of depreciation. This variable would thus be endogenous, with $\delta_\lambda$ its sensitivity to the rate of technical progress (Rowthorn, 1981, p. 23). Equipment has to be replaced because it has become obsolete as a result of technological innovation. Along these lines, we could also suppose that the rate of depreciation depends on the rate of utilization of capacity. Obsolescence is not only technological, it also varies according to the state of business. There are two views on the matter. Some believe that the rate of depreciation is inversely related to the rate of utilization: 'High growth rate and high utilisation will tend to retard withdrawal of equipment ... A low growth rate and utilisation will lead to some premature withdrawal of equipment ...' (Steindl, 1979, p. 6). Others assume that the rate of depreciation is directly related to the rate of utilization, because of physical wear and tear (Kurz, 1990b, p. 214). As a result of these contradictory effects, we will omit the impact of the rate of capacity utilization on depreciation. The endogenous rate of depreciation is then simply equal to:

$$\delta = \delta_0 + \delta_\lambda \lambda \qquad (6.37)$$

Finally we may also consider the impact of technical change on the degree of monopoly $m$. Here we may use the framework put forward by the French regulationists, and consider two types of evolutionary regimes (Boyer, 1988). In the anti-Fordist regime, the indexation of real wages to productivity growth is low: there is a positive relation between the gross margin of profit and the rate of technical progress. In the Fordist regime, the indexation of real wages is high and the relation between the gross margin of profit and the rate of technical progress is negative. The degree of sensitivity of the margin of profit to changes of the pace of innovation is $m_\lambda$, and it may be positive or negative.

$$m = m_0 + m_\lambda \qquad (6.38)$$

The impact of technical progress on the rate of accumulation and on the rate of accumulation of the economy can now be assessed with the help of the effective demand equation and the profit cost function. The effective demand equation combines the savings equation (6.29) and the new investment equation (6.36). We have:

$$r = \frac{g_u u + \gamma + b + g_\lambda \lambda}{s_p - g_r} \tag{6.39}$$

On the other hand the new profits cost function combines elements of equations (6.32), (6.37) and (6.38). With the appropriate substitutions, it is written as:

$$r = \frac{u(m_0 + m_\lambda \lambda)}{v} - \frac{f\sigma[1 - (m_0 + m_\lambda \lambda)]}{v} - (\delta_0 + \delta_\lambda \lambda) \tag{6.40}$$

As a first step, let us see what happens when $m_\lambda$ is equal to zero. There are then only two additional effects due to the presence of technical progress, which are illustrated in Figure 6.10. The positive impact of faster technical progress on the investment function shifts up the effective demand curve (the partial derivative of equation (6.39) with respect to $\lambda$ is positive). This favourable impact on accumulation is reinforced by accelerated depreciation due to technological obsolescence, the $\delta_\lambda$ parameter. The faster the rate of technical progress, the more the profits cost curve shifts downwards to the right (the partial derivative of equation (6.40) with respect to $\lambda$ is negative). This is another instance of the paradox of costs. In this simplified version of the model, a faster pace of innovations does lead to higher rates of profit as well as to higher rates of capacity utilization, and hence, as shown on the left side of Figure 6.10, to a higher rate of accumulation.

The next question, then, is whether such an induced faster pace of accumulation is able to sustain a positive rate of growth of employment. This requires, as equation (6.35) shows, that the increase in the rate of accumulation $dg$ be greater than the inducing increase in the rate of technical progress $d\lambda$. To find the answer requires that the equilibrium value of the rate of growth be computed. This can be done by computing the equilibrium rate of utilization of capacity from equations (6.39) and (6.40) and substituting its value and that of $r$ in equation (6.36). Under the simplifying assumptions made in the paragraph above, the change in the equilibrium rate of growth, following an increase in the rate of technical change, is equal to:

$$\frac{dg^*}{d\lambda} = g_\lambda - g_r \delta_\lambda + \frac{u + g_r m/v[g_\lambda + (s_p - g_r)\delta_\lambda]}{(s_p - g_r)m/v - g_u} \tag{6.41}$$

*Figure 6.10 Positive impact on the rates of profit and of accumulation following an increase in the rate of technical progress*

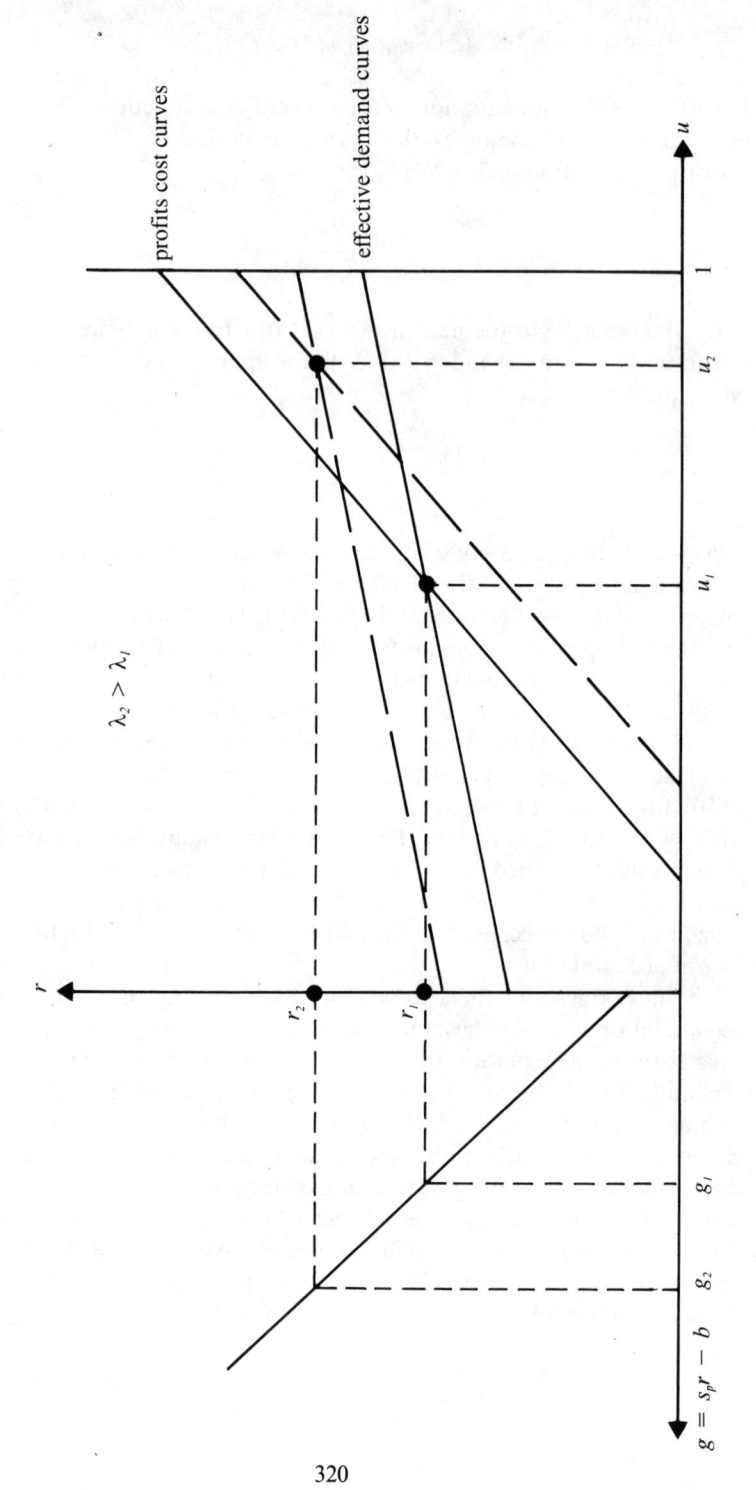

For this expression to be larger than unity, that is for the increase in the rate of accumulation to overcompensate the increase in labour productivity, so that the rate of growth of employment is positive, the following condition must be fulfilled:

$$s_p < \frac{g_r + g_u v/m}{1 - g_\lambda - g_u \delta_\lambda v/m} \qquad (6.42)$$

The above condition shows that thriftiness is detrimental to employment possibilities. As we would expect, the larger the response of depreciation to technical progress (the $\delta_\lambda$ parameter) and the larger the response to innovations of capacity enlarging investment (the $g_\lambda$ parameter), the higher the probability that technical progress will bring forth better employment possibilities. When condition (6.42) is fulfilled, the higher real wages brought about by technical progress are accompanied by higher employment. Under these circumstances everyone benefits from technical progress, not just workers with tenure or its equivalent. One may suspect that the present wave of innovations based on computer systems would not fulfil condition (6.42), because it does not require widespread scrapping of existing equipment and machines.

We may now consider the case that the French regulationists call the Fordist evolutionary regime. Let us suppose that technical innovations are accompanied by a decrease in margins of profit; that is, the $m_\lambda$ coefficient is negative. As can be seen from equation (6.40), the impact of such a regime would be to flatten and shift down the profits cost curve. Even in the absence of any other induced effects of technical progress, a faster pace of innovations in a Fordist regime would induce a higher rate of profit and a higher rate of capacity utilization, and hence a higher rate of accumulation. This is all shown in Figure 6.11. Technical progress thus has favourable effects in a Fordist wage/profit regime; it reinforces the effects which have been previously outlined.

When an anti-Fordist evolutionary regime is in place; that is, when technical progress has a positive impact on mark-ups, and when one also takes into account all the other effect of technical progress, just about anything can happen. The only impossible combination is a higher rate of capacity utilization and a lower rate of profit. The rate of profit, and hence the rate of accumulation, will be higher even in this unfavourable anti-Fordist case, provided the sensitivity of investment to the degree of utilization and to the rate of profit is small, while the propensity to save is large, given the other parameters. As can be seen, complex solutions quickly arise when more institutional content is given to the model.

322  Foundations of Post-Keynesian Economic Analysis

Figure 6.11  *Positive impact on the rate of profit of an increase in the rate of technical progress in the Fordist regime*

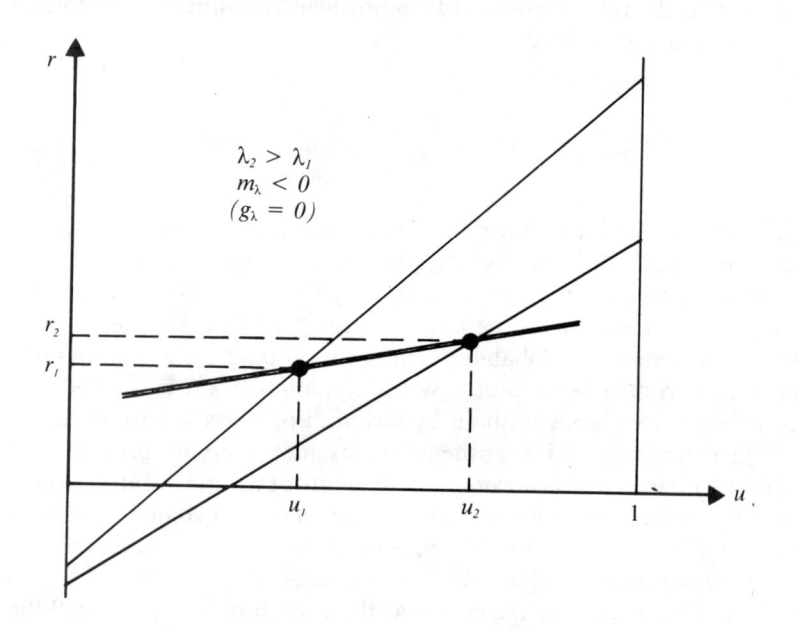

## Verdoon's Law and the Technical Progress Function

Hitherto the rate of technical progress has been assumed to be exogenous. This meant the assumption of a unidirectional causality, from the given rate of technical progress to the other variables of the model, in particular the rate of growth of the economy. Cumulative causation may also be introduced by assuming that the rate of technical progress is a function of the rate of growth of the economy. This is the well-known but somewhat controversial Verdoon's law, as reinterpreted by Kaldor (1978b). We may write it as follows:

$$\lambda = \lambda_0 + \lambda_g g \tag{6.43}$$

Although Kaldor himself nowhere links this version of Verdoon's law to his own previous work, it is clear that the above equation is close to Kaldor's technical progress function. The latter postulates a positive relation between the rate of technical progress and the rate of accumulation of capital per head, which we previously denoted by $\hat{k}$. The rationale of this relation is that innovations and improvements are more likely to be infused into the productive system when new investments are made and when entrepreneurs are more dynamic. Technical progress depends on the rate of progress of knowledge as well as on the speed with which innovations are introduced, that is with the pace of investment (Kaldor, 1961, p. 207). In its linear form, the technical progress function is:

$$\lambda = \lambda_0 + \lambda_k \hat{k} \qquad (6.44)$$

We see right away that there is no difference between Kaldor's linear technical progress function, the Cobb–Douglas function in its dynamic version with appropriate restrictions and the dynamic version of the national accounts. This can be seen by recalling that in our previous notations the rate of growth per unit of labour was $\hat{y}$, which is nothing other than the rate of technical progress $\lambda$ as we have just defined it. The dynamic expansion of the Cobb–Douglas function and of the national accounts identity yielded respectively:

$$\hat{y} = \mu + \alpha \hat{k} \qquad (1.3)$$

and

$$\hat{y} = \tau + \pi \hat{k} \qquad (1.7)$$

It is clear that all the above three equations are similar. Only their interpretation and that of their parameters are different. This shows again the weakness of instrumentalism. The same mathematical regressions may arise from different theories: prediction would be incapable of identifying the right one. The above also shows that one should beware of some of the successes of Verdoon's law for precisely the same reason as with those of the neoclassical production function. They may be an artefact.

We may combine the technical progress function with Verdoon's law: one gets what Michl (1985) calls the augmented technical progress function, which he shows to be similar to the dynamic expansion of a Cobb–Douglas function with returns to scale. When the $\lambda_g$ parameter is positive, there will be increasing returns to scale:

$$\lambda = \lambda_0 + \lambda_g g + \lambda_k \hat{k} \qquad (6.45)$$

The form of this equation again resembles that of the expanded national accounts, as can be seen by combining equations (1.6) and (1.8):

$$\hat{y} = \pi \hat{r} + (1 - \pi)\hat{\omega} + \pi \hat{k}$$

Michl also shows that both the $\lambda_g$ and the $\lambda_k$ parameters are significant when regressions are run on the augmented technical progress function. It is rather disconcerting to note that the value of the $\lambda_k$ coefficient is very close to the share of profits in manufacturing national accounts, between 0.38 and 0.40, exactly what one would expect if the augmented technical progress function turned out to be an artefact. Furthermore one would expect the rate of change of the rate of profit $\hat{r}$ to be close to zero, since there is usually no trend in the rate of profit. This is precisely what Michl gets: the $\lambda_0$ coefficient in his regressions is not significantly different from zero. However the regression, even if Verdoon's law depends on an algebraic fluke, would seem to add one piece of information. By comparing equations (6.45) and (1.6), we see that faster rates of growth of output $g$ are associated with faster rates of growth of real wages $\hat{\omega}$. The national accounts do not yield such a prediction. This relation between the rate of growth of real wages and the rate of growth of output, rather than the rate of growth of output per unit of labour as in equation (1.10) of the national accounts, is a peculiarity of Verdoon's law.

Assuming it is not an artefact, one would agree with Kaldor in believing that Verdoon's law is not just a measure of the economies of large-scale production. It is a dynamic relationship 'between the rates of change of productivity and of output, rather than between the *level* of productivity and the *scale* of output' (Kaldor, 1978b, p. 106). Having run semi-logarithmic regressions of Verdoon's law, McCombie (1982, p. 292) concludes that 'the Verdoon law (and the technical progress function, even in its linear form) should not be treated as being derived from the static Cobb–Douglas production function'. We may thus gather from this that, if Verdoon's law is not an artefact, it is not the result of Okun's law.

Let us then introduce Kaldor's version of Verdoon's law into our Kaleckian model of growth, by adding to it equation (6.43). This equation may be seen as equivalent to the technical progress function if we specify the latter as a function of the rate of accumulation, rather than accumulation per unit of labour, recalling that in steady growth the rate of accumulation of capital and the rate of growth of output are identical. Another possibility, put forward by Dixon and Thirlwall (1975, p. 209), is to assume that $\hat{k}$ is itself a function of the growth rate of output. The Kaleckian model of growth and distribution with induced technical progress combines equations (6.43), (6.29), (6.32), (6.36) and (6.37). From these equations we can compute the savings function and the investment function.

$$g^s = \frac{s_p(m/v)u - s_p[f\sigma(1-m)/v + \delta_0 + \delta_\lambda \lambda_0] - b}{1 + s_p \delta_\lambda \lambda_g} \qquad (6.46)$$

$$g^i = \frac{(g_u + g_r m/v)u - g_r[f\sigma(1-m)/v + \delta_0 + \delta_\lambda \lambda_0] + \gamma + g_\lambda \lambda_0}{1 + \lambda_g(\delta_\lambda g_r - g_\lambda)} \qquad (6.47)$$

The stability conditions of the model can be reassessed when there is cumulative causation. As usual, we want the slope (with respect to $u$) of the savings function to be steeper than that of the investment function. One should note that the slope of the investment function is not necessarily positive. Its slope could be negative if the denominator of equation (6.47) is negative. This will not happen provided the coefficient of induced investment due to technical progress is small enough; that is, if:

$$g_\lambda < 1/\lambda_g + g_r \delta_\lambda \qquad (6.48)$$

An investment function inversely related to the rate of capacity utilization would not make much sense, and we shall see soon that condition (6.48) is always fulfilled when stability conditions are respected. The stability condition of the model with cumulative causation is:

$$s_p > \frac{g_r + g_u v/m}{1 - \lambda_g(g_\lambda + g_u \delta_\lambda v/m)} \qquad (6.49)$$

This can be compared to the stability condition of the model without induced technical progress:

$$s_p > g_r + g_u v/m \qquad (6.23)$$

We see that the stability condition is more stringent when there is cumulative causation. The propensity to save on profits must be larger the greater the sensitivity of the rate of technical progress to the rate of growth of output; that is, the greater the Verdoon effect (the $\lambda_g$ coefficient). Cumulative causation makes things much more complicated. The presence of the stability condition imposes some restrictions on the values that the various parameters can take. In particular the propensity to save must by definition be inferior to one. This means that the left-hand side of equation (6.49) must be smaller than one. This restriction leads to the following inequality:

$$g_\lambda < 1/\lambda_g - [g_r + g_u(\delta_\lambda + v/m)]/\lambda_g \qquad (6.50)$$

From the comparison of conditions (6.50) and (6.48) it follows that, when the stability condition is fulfilled, the slope of the investment curve $g^i$, defined by equation (6.47), is necessarily positive. This of course makes good economic sense.

These stability issues having been cleared up, we may now examine whether the results that had been observed with the canonical Kaleckian model can be reproduced with the presence of cumulative causation. It can be seen immediately from equations (6.46) and (6.47) that an increase in government deficit $b$ leads to a downward shift of the $g^s$ curve, and hence to an increase in the rates of growth and of capacity utilization. A decrease in the propensity to save on profits $s_p$ leads to similar results. The paradox of thrift is preserved. Changes in most of the other variables involve the displacement of both curves.

This problem can be avoided by using the profits cost curve and the effective demand curve. Starting from the same equations as those that led to the above investment and savings curves, we get the equations of the effective demand and profits cost curves when induced technical progress is present.

$$r^{ED} = \frac{g_u u + \gamma + g_\lambda \lambda_0 + b(1 - g_\lambda \lambda_g)}{s_p(1 - g_\lambda \lambda_g) - g_r} \tag{6.51}$$

$$r^{PC} = \frac{(m/v)u - f\sigma(1-m)/v - \delta_0 - \delta_\lambda \lambda_0 + \lambda_g \delta_\lambda b}{1 + \lambda_g \delta_\lambda s_p} \tag{6.52}$$

One may note that the stability condition guarantees that the denominator of equation (6.51) is non-negative. Indeed a positive slope of the effective demand curve implies that

$$s_p > \frac{g_r}{1 - g_\lambda \lambda_g} \tag{6.53}$$

which is obviously implied by equation (6.49).

As in the canonical model, all the variables related to cost figure only in the profits cost curve. It is easily seen that any increase in costs, that is an increase in the $f$, $\sigma$ or $\delta_0$ parameters, or a decrease in the degree of monopoly $m$, leads to a downward shift of the profits cost curve. This implies, as could already be observed in Figures 6.5 and 6.9, that higher costs imply higher rates of utilization, higher rates of profit and hence higher rates of accumulation.

The paradox of costs thus brings to the fore a further paradox. Higher costs lead to higher rates of accumulation, which themselves lead to higher rates of technical progress. In a sense what we observe here is a dynamic reduced form of what we called the Webb effect in Chapter 5. Take the degree of monopoly, for instance. When there is a fall in $m$; that is, when real wages are increased relative to unit variable costs, the higher costs force some of the less productive firms to go under. This induces a rise in productivity. In dynamic terms we may say that higher costs eliminate those firms whose productivity increases the slowest and which are least likely to introduce technical innovations.

In growth analysis, higher real wages relative to unit costs, higher costs in general, and anything that would lead to faster accumulation induce faster rates of growth of productivity. This is the result of the Verdoon effect. It should also be recalled that a faster rate of technical progress is accompanied in the model by faster rates of increase in real wages. It follows that a fight now for higher real wages, that is a lower degree of monopoly, should lead to faster-growing real wages in the long run. There is no trade-off between gains in the short run and gains in the long run. Similarly government deficits and lower thriftiness, which increase the rate of accumulation, also lead to faster-growing productivity and faster-growing real wages. Policies of austerity which are usually based on long-run considerations, that is reduced government expenditures, reduced real wages or measures favouring savings rather than consumption, have no justification in the long period of a Kaleckian world.

## 6.4 DOCTRINAL ISSUES AROUND THE KALECKIAN MODEL

The results at which one arrives by using the Kaleckian model are particularly striking when one adds to it Verdoon's law. It is thus important to reconsider the crucial elements of the canonical Kaleckian model which allowed us to reproduce for the long run some of the key results, less subject to controversy, which were obtained for the short run. There are mainly two essential elements in the Kaleckian growth and distribution model. The first is the hypothesis that the rate of utilization of capacity can differ from its standard rate in the long run. The second is the exact form that the investment function should take. Savings by workers will also be considered.

### The Normal Rate of Utilization of Capacity

One can find three sorts of objection to the use of rates of utilization of capacity which diverge from the normal one, even in the long run. Some of these objections we shall discuss at length, others will be mentioned briefly. Of course, all of the objections centre around the notion and definition of normal rate of capacity utilization.

The first objection has to do with the optimality of excess capacity. It has been argued by Kurz (1986, 1990a) that the normal rate of utilization of capacity could not be something defined by conventions. 'The normal rates of utilization of the various items of plant and equipment are conceived to be in compliance with the principle of cost minimisation' (Kurz, 1986, p. 43). The normal rate of capacity utilization is defined in this view according to the optimal choice of technique. However this cannot be considered a valid objection to the approach taken here. The reader will recall that in Chapter 3 a distinction was made between the engineer-rated capacity of the segment of a plant and its theoretical capacity. The former was said to be the most efficient level of output per unit of time, given the existing and expected economic conditions at the time of the construction of the plant. Each segment of plant is thus operated at its most efficient rate, in compliance with the proper principles of cost minimization, the full capacity of a firm being the sum of all of its capacities so defined. What a rate of utilization of capacity below unity means is that some of the segments or some of the plants are not being utilized at all. It does not mean that plants are being run inefficiently, with inappropriate shifts. Cost minimization and excess capacities are not incompatible.

The rate of utilization being clearly defined over the set of all plants, rather than at the level of the plant segment, we may now deal with the other objections to the Kaleckian long-run approach. The second objection to the long-run inequality between the actual rate of capacity utilization and the normal one is based on the presumption that the normal rate is a target of the firms. This is a criticism of Kaleckian models that can be found in Auerbach and Skott (1988) and in Committeri (1986, 1987). In their view, the normal rate of capacity is an optimal rate of utilization that firms try to achieve, at least in the long run. Therefore entrepreneurs would not be content unless the rate of capacity utilization aimed at is realized. The only possible steady state is the one in which the actual rate of utilization is equal to its normal or desired level. This leads to the belief that the only rational steady-state analysis is one where those two rates are equal.

This is a most embarrassing objection to the Kaleckians. If the actual rate of capacity must eventually be equal to the normal rate, then the rate of utilization is not an endogenous variable in the long run any more. The objection is particularly valid since some Kaleckians have sometimes referred to the normal rate as the 'planned' degree of utilization of capacity (Steindl, 1952, p. 129; Amadeo, 1986b, p. 83), thus reinforcing the belief that the normal rate of capacity utilization is a target of firms which must be fulfilled in the long run. The complications arising from such an interpretation can be clearly spelled out by using an investment function

Figure 6.12 *Discrepancy between the actual and the expected rates of growth of sales when the actual and the normal rates of capacity utilization diverge, according to the neo-Ricardian interpretation*

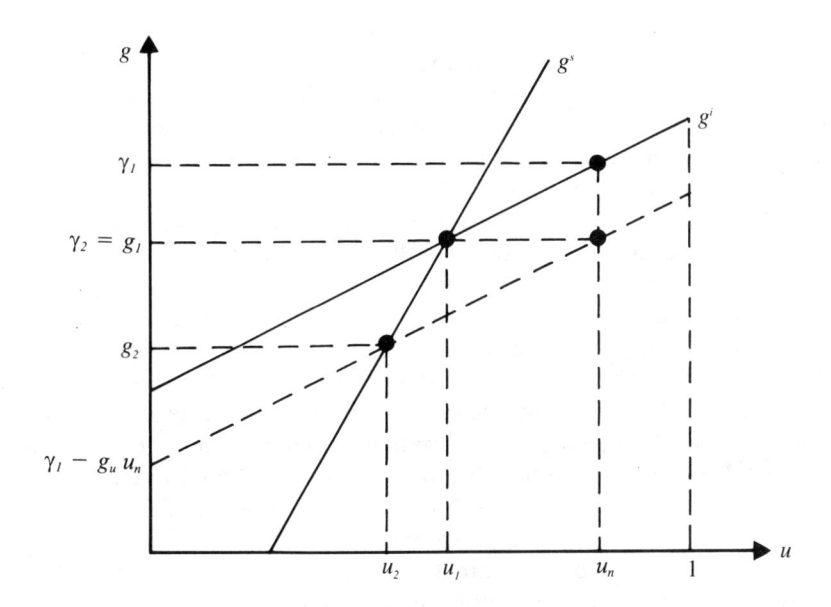

suggested by Steindl (1952, p. 128) and reintroduced by Amadeo (1986a, 1986b). This investment function is based on the distinction between the actual rate and the normal rate of capacity utilization, respectively denoted by $u$ and $u_n$.

$$g^i = \gamma + g_u(u - u_n) \tag{6.54}$$

The investment function is illustrated in Figure 6.12. If the actual rate of utilization turned out to be equal to the normal or desired one, the actual rate of growth would be equal to $\gamma$. As Committeri (1986, p. 173) points out, if firms are content about the degree of capacity utilization which is being achieved and do not desire to have it changed, one concludes that the rate of accumulation desired by the firms should be equal to the expected rate of growth of sales. It is clear from equation (6.54) that the exogenous parameter $\gamma$ then represents this expected rate of growth of sales. If, as is shown on the graph, it is assumed that the actual rate of capacity utilization $u_1$ is smaller than the planned rate $u_n$, the actual rate of growth $g_1$ must be smaller than the expected rate of growth of sales $\gamma_1$. Committeri argues that this cannot be a rational solution to a long-run growth model, since expectations of sales and of spare capacity are not realized. Furthermore there is an unstable process going on. If firms react to their unrealized sales expectations in the standard manner, the $\gamma$ coefficient should go down to $\gamma_2$, the investment curve $g^i$ should shift down, the actual rate of growth should drop to $g_2$, and the actual and normal rates of utilization of capacity should diverge even further. The conclusion of this exercise, if the normal rate of utilization of capacity is considered a target, is that the model is unstable. It must be *assumed* that the rate of utilization in the long run is always equal to its normal level.

Another problem, not yet mentioned, with the above interpretation, is that, if the normal rate of capacity utilization is a target rate, one should expect the target to change according to historical variations in the actual rate. The normal rate of utilization $u_n$ ceases to be an exogenous variable which helps to determine the actual utilization and accumulation rates. This was recognized early on by Amadeo (1986a, p. 155) and Ciccone (1986, p. 35). Of course it may be said that, if the normal rate of utilization tends towards the actual rate of utilization, the equilibrium rate of utilization is still endogenous, although in the long run the normal and the actual rates are necessarily equal. This, however, deprives the model of definite solutions, the more so if the expected rate of growth of sales $\gamma$ is also taken into consideration. To safeguard the Kaleckian model, one must thus deny that the normal rate of utilization of capacity is influenced by the rates of utilization which have been observed in the recent past. Ciccone (1986, p. 36), for instance, argues that this normal rate is determined by the average actual rate of utilization over very long periods of time, which include several business cycles. It then becomes obvious that the normal rate is not a target rate, but rather a convention, similar to the standard rate of utilization which is present in cost-plus pricing procedures. As we pointed out in Chapter 3, it is well known that the standard rate of utilization of capacity which is incorporated in the pricing formula used by GM underestimates the rate of utilization that was actually realized in most years by the company. This piece of information is confirmed by Clifton's (1983, p. 26) remark that cost-plus prices are based on standard volumes of utilization taken from historical data which cover several business cycles.

It has also been argued, both by Amadeo (1987, p. 79) and by Ciccone (1987, p. 97), that the main determinant of the normal rate of capacity utilization is not the past levels of capacity utilization, but rather the variance of demand which forces firms to hold excess capacity as a precautionary measure. Since the variance of demand may be considered to be a given, or at least may be considered to be independent of the other variables of the Kaleckian model, we may regard the normal rate of utilization of capacity to be also a given of the model. 'The fact that firms expect a higher or lower degree of utilization in the future, as compared with the precautionary degree, does not affect the latter, it only affects the firms' desired rate of growth of the stock of capital' (Amadeo, 1987, p. 79). This is entirely in line with Steindl's explanation of excess capacity. It led him to reject the intuitive belief that planned excess capacity equates actual long term excess capacity, and to conclude that 'the degree of utilization actually obtaining in the long run is no safe indication of the planned level of utilization' (1952, p. 12).

One must therefore make a distinction between the expected rate of utilization of capacity and the normal or standard rate of utilization. The former we defined in equations (6.24) and (6.26). It changes frequently in response to the actual values taken by the rate of utilization and it eventually comes to be realized if the model is stable (condition 6.23). By contrast, the normal rate of capacity utilization is not influenced by the other variables of the model, and it can never be achieved except by a fluke. Equation (6.54) must thus be reinterpreted as an investment equation depending on the expected rate of utilization, $u^e$ instead of $u$. As Amadeo (1987, p. 79) argues, 'if the expected degree of utilization is greater than the precautionary or normal degree it is only reasonable for firms to invest more'. It is ironic to note that, while Steindl proposed an investment function that relies on the distinction between planned and undesired capacity, he himself did not believe very much in the practical implications of such a distinction. To him, the essential idea was that investment activity is a function of the degree of utilization (1952, p. 13). To avoid confusion, it may then be a more prudent attitude to avoid reference to the normal rate of utilization of capacity in the investment function. One can rely instead on the simple argument that, other things equal, a higher rate of utilization of capacity induces more investment, as Dutt (1990a, p. 59) recommends.

We now come to the final two objections to the use of an endogenous rate of utilization in Kaleckian models of growth and distribution. Some neo-Ricardian authors argue that if the realized profit rate exceeds the normal profit rate, the latter will be revised upwards. As a consequence, the actual rate of capacity utilization would ultimately have to be equal to its normal rate and hence there would be no room for an endogenous rate of utilization. This argument, the third against the endogeneity of the rate of capacity utilization, will be dealt with in section 5 when target-return pricing is introduced into the Kaleckian growth model. We now consider the fourth and final objection to the Kaleckian model. Some authors recognize the possibility that the actual rate of utilization may diverge from the normal rate even in the long run, while at the same time denying its importance for the wage/profit frontier and economic analysis in general. We shall see that the analysis conducted by these critics resembles that pursued by those Marxists who are abandoning the hypothesis of a fixed rate of capacity utilization, while still adhering to the profit squeeze theory. The crucial aspect of both sets of authors is the form of their investment function.

## The Form of the Investment Function

One of the most striking results of the Kaleckian model is the positive relationship, even in the long run, between the real wage rate and the rate of accumulation, the same direct relation also holding between the real wage rate and the rate of profit. This contradicts one of the core elements of neo-Ricardian theory, the long-run inverse wage/profit frontier, from which the inflation barrier arises. It is no surprise that some neo-Ricardians would object to the Kaleckian positive wage/profit frontier.

Besides the rejection of mark-up prices as relevant long-run prices, the main neo-Ricardian response has been the denial that current profitability has any influence on expected profitability. This objection is related to the investment function. The view of both Ciccone (1986, p. 26) and Vianello (1989) is that new investment depends on expected profitability, computed at normal prices based on the normal rate of utilization of capacity. This means that the investment function depends on the (expected) normal rate of profit rather than on the actual rate of profit. The justification for this is that entrepreneurs cannot make future plans under the assumption that capacity will be perpetually overutilized. Plans must be made according to profitability at normal use of capacity. The rate of profit which represents 'the guiding light for investment and pricing decisions, cannot possibly be either an abnormally high or an abnormally low one' (Vianello, 1985, p. 84). Assuming as an extreme case that the actual rate of utilization has no impact on the investment function, the neo-Ricardian investment function can be written as follows, with $r_n$ denoting the (expected) normal rate of profit:

$$g^i = \gamma + g_r r_n \qquad (6.55)$$

Vianello's (1989) main argument is that Kaleckian authors fail to understand that expected profitability is hindered by a rise in real wages, even if actual profitability stays constant in the short and medium run. This fall in the expected normal rate of profit eventually leads to a fall in

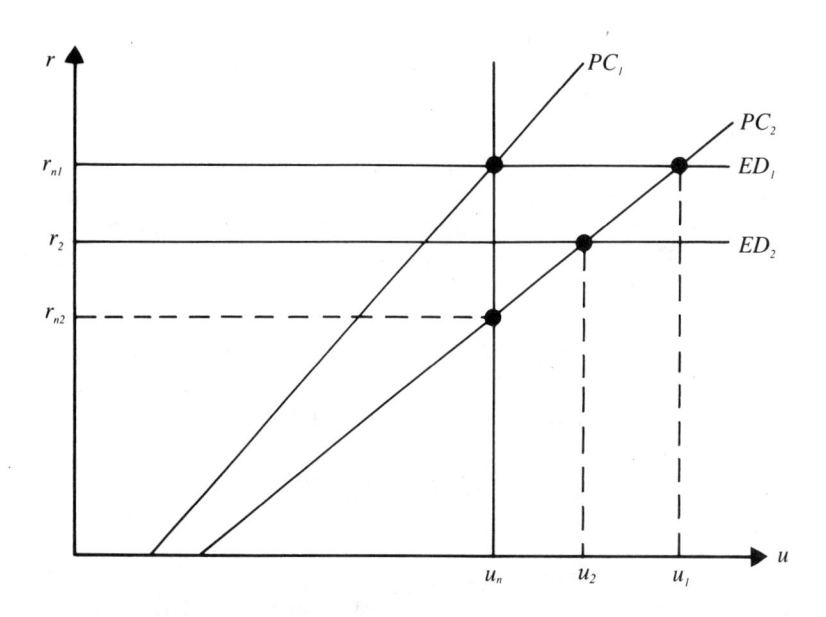

*Figure 6.13 Negative impact of an increase in real wages when investment only depends on the normal rate of profit*

investment activity, and hence to a fall in the actual rate of profit, thus justifying to some extent the pessimistic expectations. This reasoning is illustrated in Figure 6.13. Suppose we start from a fluke situation where the rate of utilization and the actual rate of profit happen to be at their normal rates, $u_n$ and $r_{n1}$. The initial profits cost curve is given by $PC_1$ and the effective demand curve must be $ED_1$. Now let us assume an increase in the real wage, with no change in the technical coefficients. This implies a downshift of the profits cost curve to $PC_2$. In the short or the medium run, with no change in the rate of accumulation, and hence no change in the actual rate of profit, the actual rate of utilization of capacity rises to $u_1$. It is this rise in the rate of utilization which allows actual profitability to stay constant, despite the rise in the real cost of wages.

According to Vianello, however, this situation will not last. Entrepreneurs will revise their view of the normal profit rate, taking into account the new real wage rate. The new normal profit rate $r_{n2}$ is given by the intersection of the new profits cost curve $PC_2$ and the normal rate of utilization $u_n$. The desired rate of accumulation, given by equations (6.55) and (6.29), falls, resulting in a downshift of the effective demand curve to $ED_2$. At the end of the process, the normal and the actual rates of utilization diverge, as may the actual and normal rates of profit. The actual rate of profit at the end of the process, that is $r_2$, is below the initial rate of profit $r_{n1}$, despite real wages having increased and despite the rate of capacity utilization being endogenous. Although the rate of utilization does not necessarily equal the normal rate of utilization or unity, the negative relation between the real wage rate and the rate of profit is preserved.

When one adopts the investment function of equation (6.55), the paradox of thrift prevails, but all the Kaleckian paradoxes of costs vanish. This can be seen by replacing the normal rate of profit with its value taken from equation (6.32). The investment function then appears under its explicit form.

$$g^i = \gamma + g_r[u_n m/v - (1-m)f\sigma/v - \delta] \tag{6.56}$$

while the effective demand constraint now reads as:

$$r = \frac{\gamma + b + g_r[u_n m/v - (1-m)f\sigma/v - \delta]}{s_p} \tag{6.57}$$

It then clearly appears that any increase in costs, that is an increase in the parameters $f$, $\sigma$ or $\delta$, leads to a downward shift of the investment function and hence of the effective demand function. The consequence of this shift is a drop in the rate of accumulation and in the rate of profit, as was the case for an increase in real wages in Figure 6.13. Higher costs are necessarily linked to lower rates of profit. The paradox of costs vanishes. This, however, as was pointed out above, partially depends on the extreme assumption that the actual rate of utilization of capacity has no induced effect on the investment function. This assumption need not be made. One may presume that firms take normal profitability into account while still responding to the actual rate of capacity utilization. The investment function of equation (6.56) would then become:

$$g^i = \gamma + g_u u + g_r[u_n m/v - (1-m)f\sigma/v - \delta] \tag{6.58}$$

This is precisely what Bhaduri and Marglin (1990) have done. They contend, as do Kurz (1990b), Blecker (1991) and Epstein (1990), that the investment function, if linear, should have the following form:

$$g^i = \gamma + g_u u + g_m m \tag{6.59}$$

As before, $m$ represents the gross margin of profit, derived from the mark-up on variable costs. The sensitivity of investment to changes in the margin of profit is $g_m$. In the model of Bhaduri and Marglin, there is no overhead labour and no depreciation of capital. Setting $f$ and $\delta$ equal to zero in equation (6.58), one gets:

$$g^i = \gamma + g_u u + grm(u_n/v) = \gamma + g_u u + g_r r_n \qquad (6.60)$$

It is clear that the investment function proposed by Bhaduri and Marglin as a replacement for the Kaleckian investment function is a variant of Vianello's case against the use of current profitability as an argument of the investment function. Like Vianello (1989, p. 183), Bhaduri and Marglin (1990, p. 388) argue that Kaleckians have omitted the depressing cost effects of higher wages on economic activity. Equation (6.60) makes it clear that the proponents of equation (6.59) suppose that the rate of profit to be taken into consideration should be calculated at a normal rate of utilization of capacity. If one argues, as Bhaduri and Marglin as well as many others do, that the margin of profit $m$ rather than the actual rate of profit $r$ should enter the investment function in addition to the rate of utilization of capacity, then one is in fact asserting that the normal rate of profit $r_n$ rather than the actual one should be included in the investment function in addition to the rate of utilization of capacity.

Although the arguments advanced by Vianello appear to be different from those put forward by Bhaduri and Marglin, they are fundamentally the same. The latter authors seem to argue that investment activity depends on a single variable, the actual rate of profit. That rate can, however, be decomposed into the rate of utilization of capacity and the share of profits in national income, as we have already seen:

$$r = \pi u/v \qquad (6.19)$$

In the special case where there is no overhead labour, the share of profits $\pi$ and the margin of profit $m$ are identical. Strictly speaking, an investment function based on the definition of the actual rate of profit, as shown by equation (6.19), should depend on the net share of profits $\pi$ rather than the margin of profit $m$. We shall nevertheless construct the rest of the argument around the normal rate of profit and the gross margin of profit. If we were to introduce instead the share of profits $\pi$ into the investment function, computations would be made more difficult without any of the qualitative arguments being changed.

Broadly speaking, an increase in the actual rate of profit may be due either to a rise in the actual rate of utilization of capacity or to a rise in the margin of profit, the latter case being roughly equivalent to a rise in the normal rate of profit. The proponents of equation (6.59) argue that, when investing, firms separate the effects on profits due to effective demand from those which follow from the firm's ability to cut its costs relative to prices. Bhaduri and Marglin (1990, p. 391) demonstrate that the canonical Kaleckian investment function, equation (6.20), when compared to equation (6.59), imposes restrictions on the relative response of investment to the two constituents of the profit rate. In their own equation, the rate of utilization plays no role in addition to that played as part of the actual rate of profit. This explains why in the end investment activity only depends on the rate of utilization and the normal rate of profit.

It will be explained in the next section why this type of investment function, despite its logical underpinnings, appears less satisfactory to the author than the canonical Kaleckian investment function. In the meantime, let us examine some of its consequences, in particular for the relation between the real wage rate and the profit rate. Let us combine equations (6.29) and (6.58), recalling that equation (6.59) is a simplified version of (6.58). One gets the effective demand curve:

$$r = \frac{g_u u + \gamma + b + g_r[u_n m/v - (1-m)f\sigma/v - \delta]}{s_p} \qquad (6.61)$$

The equation of the profits cost curve remains the same:

$$r = u(m/v) - (1-m)f\sigma/v - \delta \qquad (6.32)$$

The stability condition is:

$$g_u < s_p(m/v) \qquad (6.62)$$

Let us examine what happens when the real wage rate is lower, that is when the margin of profit $m$ is higher. If the new model is to retain the properties of the canonical Kaleckian model, the increase in the profit margin should lead to a fall in both the rate of utilization and the rate of profit. This will now happen under special conditions only. Taking the partial derivatives of the above two equations we get:

$$dr^{ED}/dm = g_r(u_n + f\sigma)/s_p v > 0 \qquad (6.63)$$

$$dr^{PC}/dm = (u + f\sigma)/v > 0 \qquad (6.64)$$

As can be seen in Figure 6.14, the rate of utilization falls if, for a fixed rate of utilization, given here by the $PC_1$ and $ED_1$ curves, the profits cost curve shifts more than the effective demand curve. This will happen if:

Figure 6.14  *The wage-led cooperative regime: possible negative impact of a decrease in real wages, although the investment function depends on the normal rate of profit or on the margin of profit*

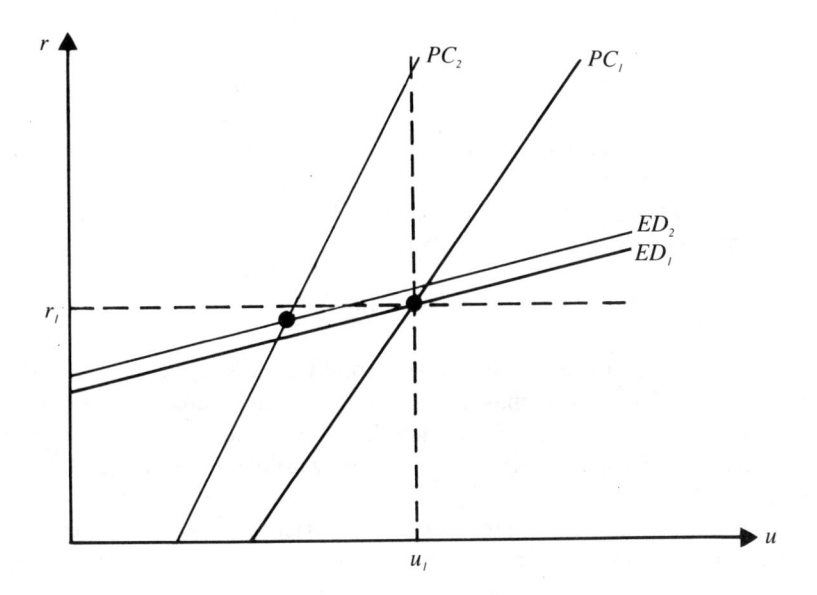

$$g_r < s_p(u+f\sigma)/(u_n+f\sigma) \quad (6.65)$$

To find out what happens to the rate of profit, equations (6.61) and (6.32) must be rewritten as a function of $r$. One has:

$$u^{ED} = \frac{s_p r - \gamma - b - g_r[u_n m/v - (1-m)f\sigma/v - \delta]}{g_u} \quad (6.66)$$

$$u^{PC} = \frac{rv + (1-m)f\sigma + \delta v}{m} \quad (6.67)$$

The partial derivatives give respectively:

$$du^{ED}/dm = -g_r(u_n+f\sigma)/vg_u \quad (6.68)$$

$$du^{PC}/dm = -(u+f\sigma)/m \quad (6.69)$$

It can be seen from Figure 6.14 that for the rate of profit to fall as a consequence of a drop in real wages, the profits cost curve must shift more than the effective demand curve at the given initial rate of utilization $u_1$. This implies that:

$$g_u > g_r(u_n+f\sigma)m/(u+f\sigma)v \qquad (6.70)$$

Combining the stability condition and the above condition, we have:

$$g_r(u_n+f\sigma)m/(u+f\sigma)v < g_u < s_p m/v \qquad (6.71)$$

Comparing the first and the last term of this inequality, the following condition emerges:

$$g_r < s_p(u+f\sigma)/(u_n+f\sigma)$$

Comparing the above condition with condition (6.65), we see that they are identical. This means that, if an increase in the degree of monopoly leads to a fall in the rate of profit, then there must also be a fall in the rate of utilization of capacity. This result becomes obvious when we inspect Figure 6.14.

We may conclude that there are strong restrictions upon the canonical Kaleckian case when an investment function incorporating the normal rate of profit or the margin of profit is introduced. A decrease in the real wage rate induces a fall in the rate of utilization if $g_r$, the sensitivity of investment to changes in the normal rate of profit, is small relative to the propensity to save. A decrease in the real wage rate also induces a fall in the rate of profit and the rate of growth if $g_u$, the sensitivity of investment to changes in the rate of utilization, is large relative to its sensitivity to changes in the normal rate of profit. The parameter $g_u$ cannot be too large, however, otherwise the stability condition cannot be fulfilled.

The advantage of the Bhaduri and Marglin investment function is that it enriches the post-Keynesian models of growth and distribution based on effective demand and endogenous rates of utilization of capacity. The canonical Kaleckian model then becomes one of three cases that arise from an investment function incorporating as an argument the normal rate of profit. The investment functions given by equations (6.59) or (6.60) may be considered as the answer of the neo-Ricardians and Marxians to the post-Keynesian critique of their models, in particular the objection that, if the rate of utilization is considered to be endogenous in the long run, increasing real wages may induce a higher rate of profit and of accumulation (Nell, 1985; Amadeo, 1986a; Dutt, 1987a). The investment function based on the normal rate of profit and the rate of utilization

Table 6.1  Growth regimes with an investment function dependent on normal profit

| | Regime | $dg/d(w/p)$; $dr/d(w/p)$ | | $du/d(w/p)$ | |
|---|---|---|---|---|---|
| 1 | Wage-led cooperative stagnationist Underconsumption | High $g_u$ | + | Low $g_r$ + | High $s_p$ |
| 2 | Profit squeeze stagnationist Over-accumulation | Low $g_u$ | − | Medium $g_r$ + | Medium $s_p$ |
| 3 | Exhilarationist Supply-side | Low $g_u$ | − | High $g_r$ − | Low $s_p$ |

introduces a variety of results, compatible with previous Marxian, post-Keynesian and even neoclassical models, although effective demand, rather than profit maximization or scarcity, is the major principle being invoked.

Particular *models* such as that of 'cooperative capitalism' enunciated by the left Keynesian social democrats, the Marxian model of 'profit squeeze' or even the conservative model relying on 'supply-side' stimulus through high profitability and a low real wage rate, fit into the more general Keynesian theoretical scheme. They become particular *variants* of the theoretical framework presented here. (Bhaduri and Marglin, 1990, p. 388)

The three variants mentioned are shown in Table 6.1. They depend on the values taken by the various variables and parameters, as indicated by the signs taken by conditions (6.65) and (6.70). The first of the three cases is what we have called the canonical Kaleckian model, or what Bhaduri and Marglin call the cooperative stagnationist model, which they associate with left-wing Keynesian policies and underconsumptionists. An increase in real wages is beneficial to the workers and to the capitalists earning profits. In the second case, an increase in the real wage leads to an increase in the rate of utilization of capacity but it induces a slowdown of accumulation. This is compatible with the Marxist profit squeeze view of stagnation, according to which high utilization rates of capacity are insufficient to compensate for the discouraging effect of high costs on expected profitability and investment activity. This is a conflict stagnationist model, since an increase in real wages induces a fall in the rate of profit. The wage/profit frontier is back. Looking at it the other way, Kurz (1990b) prefers to call such a regime of growth an over-accumulation regime, since lowering real wages encourages accumulation, but at ever lower rates of utilization of capacity. Finally there is the exhilarationist regime, so called because any reduction in demand caused by a fall in real wages is over-compensated by the enthusiastic response of entrepreneurs facing lower unit costs. This implies a high value of the $g_r$ or $g_m$ parameters, that is a high sensitivity of investment to changes in the normal rate of profit or in the margin of profit. This regime may also be called the supply-side growth regime since, as orthodox theory would have it, the supply-side effects overshadow those of demand. The fall in real wages would eventually restore full use of capacity and full employment.

The growth regimes of Table 6.1 could be further subdivided by considering the effects of other costs on the variables of the model. For instance, from equations (6.32) and (6.61) it can be shown that, while an increase in overhead or depreciation costs necessarily leads to a rise in the rate of utilization, it may induce either a rise or a fall in the rate of profit. The costs paradox of the Kaleckian model is thus under heavy fire when the standard Kaleckian investment function is abandoned, since, in the case of overhead costs, it requires the following inequality: $g_r(m/v) < g_u < s_p(m/v)$. Still, despite the multiplicity of growth regimes brought about by an investment function dependent on the rate of utilization of capacity and the normal rate of profit, several of the results obtained with the canonical Kaleckian model continue to prevail, whatever the growth regime which is in place. In particular the paradox of thrift remains, as does the positive relation between the deficit of government and the rate of accumulation. The paradox of thrift, within the context of the present model, thus appears as a robust result.

### Net Profit Shares and Changes in Real Wages

One of the reasons for which an investment function in terms of margins of profit has been proposed is that some authors do not believe that the canonical Kaleckian model and its main stagnationist view corresponds to some of the stylized facts of the last two decades. The following is a sample of this belief:

Recent trends in income distribution and economic growth in the OECD countries seem, at least at first sight, to cast doubt upon the stagnationist view. A number of studies have found that wage shares rose and profit shares fell in the United States and other western countries sometime after the mid-to-late 1960's. This distributional shift roughly coincides with the period of 'stagnation', or slower growth, accompanied by inflationary pressures. (Blecker, 1989, p. 395)

It should be noted that the post-Keynesian model that has been deve-

## Accumulation and Capacity

loped in the previous and present chapters is impervious to this critique. There is no inconsistency between low shares of profit and low growth rates or low rates of utilization in a Kaleckian model incorporating overhead costs. Indeed equation (6.17) has shown that in the Kaleckian model there is a necessary positive relationship between the net share of profits and the growth rate of the economy, for a given degree of monopoly. The question, however, is whether there can be a higher net share of profits accompanying a higher rate of growth when the latter is caused by a lower degree of monopoly. We now show that this is possible in a Kaleckian model with overhead costs.

Recall the definition of the rate of profit given by equation (6.19). The share of profits (net of fixed wage costs) is thus $\pi = rv/u$. Using this algebraic definition of the share of profits, we can substitute into it the effective demand function and the profits cost function, given by equations (6.30) and (6.32), to obtain the profit share as seen from the demand and supply sides respectively.

$$\pi^d = \frac{vg_u + v(\gamma + b)/u}{s_p - g_r} \qquad (6.72)$$

$$\pi^s = m - (1-m)\sigma f/u - \delta v/u \qquad (6.73)$$

It can be seen immediately that an increase in the degree of monopoly $m$ leads to a shift of the $\pi^s$ curve only, the shift being an upward one. As to the impact on the equilibrium share of profits, two cases arise, depending on the sign taken by $\gamma + b$ (Rowthorn, 1981, p. 21). When the sum is positive, the $\pi^d$ curve is downward-sloping, as illustrated in Figure 6.15. A fall in real wages, that is an increase in the degree of monopoly, leads to an increase in the share of net profits from $\pi_1^*$ to $\pi_2^*$. Under these conditions, it would thus appear that the movements of the share of profits are counter-cyclical. The share of profits increases when the rate of utilization and the rate of accumulation decrease as a result of the lower real wages. A specific instance of this case is the Dutt/Amadeo model without overhead costs, in which the $\gamma + b$ sum cannot be negative, and where the $\pi^s$ curve is horizontal. It can also be noted that this long-run result is fully consistent with the short-run result that was obtained when real wages were changed in Chapter 5. Indeed, Figures 6.15 and 5.15 are alike.

In the Rowthorn model with overhead costs, however, the $\gamma + b$ sum can be negative. Such a situation occurs if the government budget is in surplus or if positive profits are required for firms to invest. The $\pi^d$ curve then has a positive slope, as is shown in Figure 6.16. As in the previous case, an increase in the degree of monopoly shifts the $\pi^s$ curve upwards. This time,

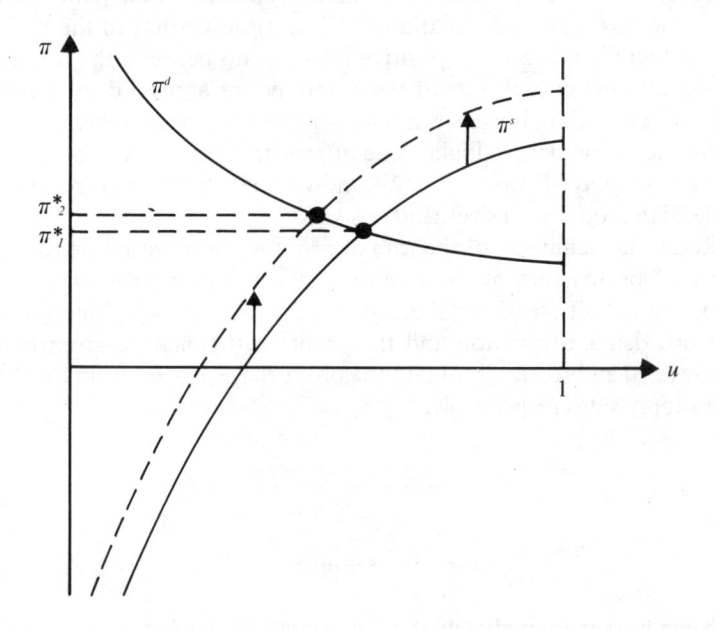

*Figure 6.15  Counter-cyclical changes in the net share of profits induced by falling real wages:* $b + \gamma > 0$

however, the share of profits falls from $\pi_1^*$ to $\pi_2^*$. The movements of the share of profits are thus procyclical. The share of profits decreases, as does the rate of capacity utilization, despite the increase in the margin of profit. In this case, which is just as likely as the other, the share of profits and the rate of accumulation increase together, just as they did in the earlier post-Keynesian models of Robinson and Kaldor.

The case described by Figure 6.16 shows that one need not go beyond the confines of a one-sector model to prove that the real wage rate and the wage share may move in opposite directions, as Steedman (1992) warns us, provided the effects of effective demand and variable rates of capacity utilization are taken into account. The reader may also verify for himself, in both Figures 6.15 and 6.16, that a variation in the demand parameters that induces an upward shift of the $\pi^d$ curve results in an increase of both the rate of utilization and the share of profits. This implies, as had been shown with equation (6.17), that for a given margin of profit the rate of accumulation and the share of profits increase together.

The stylized facts that have been observed in OECD countries are thus consistent with the stagnationist model: high mark-ups and low real wages may induce both slow growth and low net profit shares. High mark-ups

*Figure 6.16  Procyclical changes in the net share of profits induced by falling real wages:* $b + \gamma < 0$

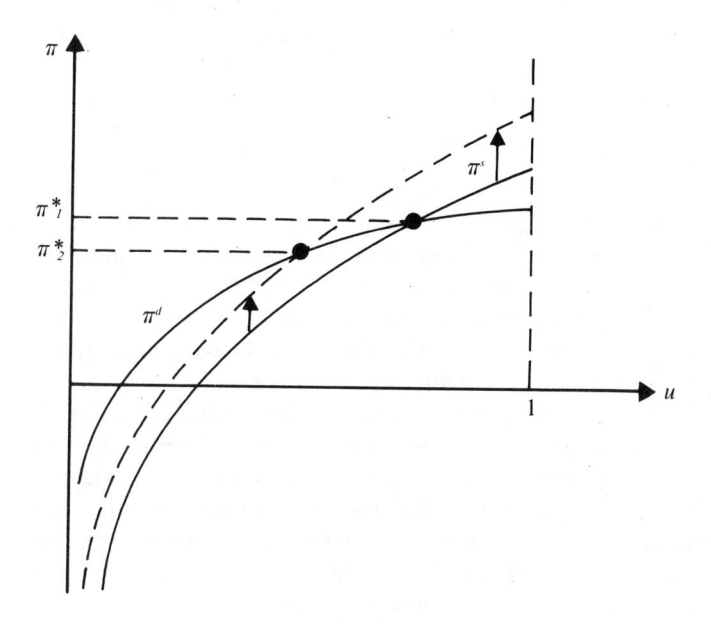

are not synonymous with high profit shares in Kaleckian models with overhead costs. As Weisskopf (1979, p. 354) warns: 'Because of the overhead labour phenomenon, a rise in the share of total wages (hourly wages plus salaries), and hence a decline in the share of profits may result from a decline in the rate of capacity utilisation as well as a rise in the strength of labour.' Indeed a close examination of Weisskopf's empirical assessment of the relative impact of these two factors on the actual rate of profit through the cycles shows that it is the fluctuations of the rate of capacity utilization which dominate, although profit squeeze may be associated with the slowdown of expansion (1979, p. 365).

Notwithstanding the above clarification, it seems that profit squeeze results are considered more compelling and are now mainly justified when associated with models of open economies (Bhaduri and Marglin, 1990, p. 385). Higher real wages may induce slower growth rates, not so much because the international competitiveness of the domestic firms would regress, but because the income elasticity of imports could eventually lead to a deterioration of the trade balance, eradicating the expansionary effects of higher wages (Blecker, 1989). While the conditions for a stagnationist growth regime are more stringent in an open economy, high real wages may still drive accumulation, especially if all the other countries adopt similar wage-led policies. The limits on growth imposed by an international environment have been neatly summarized by Thirlwall (1979, 1982), according to whom the maximum rate of growth of an open economy is equal to the ratio of the rate of growth of its exports to the income elasticity of its imports.

**Savings by Workers**

We have just seen that some of the standard Kaleckian results are sensitive to the exact form of the investment function. We now show that these same results also depend on the exact form of the savings function. Until now we have assumed that all savings originated from profits. This could be justified either by our analysis of household behaviour of Chapter 2 or by appealing to Pasinetti's famous theorem according to which the savings of workers in the very long run and under precise conditions have no impact on the overall saving propensity. Let us assume for the moment, as we did in some parts of Chapter 5 and in accordance with the analysis of Chapter 2, that the white-collar workers save on their salaries whereas blue-collar workers do not save on their wages. In our previous notations, this means that $s_{wf} > 0$ while $s_{wv} = 0$. We now have to assess the impact of overhead labour savings on the savings function.

Total nominal salaries of overhead labour are $\sigma w L_f$. Making use of equations (5.2), (5.7) and (5.28), total overhead salaries can be rewritten as $\sigma w f q / u y_v$. Savings on the salaries of overhead labour are then equal to $s_{wf}(\sigma w f q / u y_v)$. Dividing this expression yields savings as a percentage of nominal wealth. Making use of the mark-up equation (3.12) and of equation (3.13) allows us to get the new savings function, with staff savings included:

$$g^s = s_p r - b + s_{wf} f \sigma (1-m)/v \qquad (6.74)$$

Suppose the investment function is of the canonical Kaleckian form:

$$g^i = \gamma + g_u u + g_r r \qquad (6.20)$$

The effective demand curve, which combines the previous two equations, has the following equation:

$$r = \frac{g_u u + \gamma + b - s_{wf} f \sigma (1-m)/v}{s_p - g_r} \qquad (6.75)$$

The profits cost curve is still given by equation (6.32), while the stability condition is no different from the one arrived at without savings by overhead labour. Note that this stability condition implies that the denominator of the effective demand curve is necessarily positive.

$$s_p > g_r + g_u v/m \tag{6.23}$$

One of the reasons for which the propensity to save on all wages is usually assumed to be zero is that this hypothesis often generates simpler calculations and clear-cut results. This is particularly useful when models of different traditions are being compared. The introduction of savings on wages destroys the simplicity of the comparisons in general and of the canonical Kaleckian results in particular. This was established by Amadeo (1986b, p. 94) in the case of an economy without overhead costs and depreciation. In his model there is still a positive relation between real wages and accumulation, despite savings by workers, because his investment function only depends on the rate of utilization. He shows, however, that with savings on wages an increase in the real wage rate may not induce a higher rate of profit. The same occurs here in the case of savings by overhead labour. An increase in real wages, even with the canonical Kaleckian investment function, may lead to lower rates of profit, of capacity utilization and of accumulation. This can be shown using the same method as the one utilized in the previous subsection.

The partial derivatives of the profits cost and of the effective demand functions are respectively:

$$dr^{PC}/dm = (u + f\sigma)/v > 0 \tag{6.62}$$

$$dr^{ED}/dm = s_{wf} f\sigma/v(s_p - g_r) > 0 \tag{6.76}$$

An increase in the degree of monopoly $m$ shifts both curves upwards. The analysis is similar to the one presented in Figure 6.14, except that the shifting profits cost curves would now be parallel lines. There are again three possible growth regimes, depending on the values taken by the parameters and the variables, in conformity to the indications given in Table 6.1. Following a fall in the real wage rate, the rate of utilization will drop if the effective demand curve shifts less than the profits cost curve, for a given rate of profit. This will be the case when:

$$s_p > g_r + s_{wf} f\sigma/(u + f\sigma) \tag{6.77}$$

To find out about the effect of a wage decrease on the rate of profit, we rewrite equations (6.32) and (6.75) in terms of $r$. This yields equations (6.67) and (6.78) respectively.

$$u^{ED} = \frac{(s_p - g_r)r - \gamma - b + s_{wf} f\sigma(1-m)/v}{g_u} \qquad (6.78)$$

Taking the partial derivatives of equations (6.67) and (6.78), we get equations (6.69) and (6.79):

$$du^{ED}/dm = -s_{wf} f\sigma/v g_u \qquad (6.79)$$

For the rate of profit to fall following an increase in the degree of monopoly, the profits cost curve needs to shift more than the effective demand curve, as can be seen again in Figure 6.14. This requires that:

$$g_u v/m > s_{wf} f\sigma/(u + f\sigma) \qquad (6.80)$$

When there are positive savings by wage-earners, in this particular case by permanent staff only, the positive relation between real wages and rates of profits need not necessarily arise. As conditions (6.77) and (6.80) show, the canonical Kaleckian results require a high sensitivity of investment to changes in capacity utilization, a low sensitivity of investment to changes in the rate of profit, and low savings propensities on the part of permanent staff (cf. Taylor, 1990, p. 332). Also the smaller the share of permanent staff salaries, as measured by $f\sigma$, the higher the probability of an underconsumptionist growth regime. The latter conditions are intuitive: if the propensity to save on salaries was near zero, or if overhead salary costs were near zero, we would be back to the classical saving hypothesis and the canonical Kaleckian model.

The conditions ensuring the maintenance of the paradox of costs in the case of an increase in overhead costs, that is an increase in the rate of profit and in the rate of accumulation, are straightforward. They are:

$$s_p > g_r + s_{wf} \qquad (6.81)$$

$$g_u v/m > s_{wf} \qquad (6.82)$$

If condition (6.82) is fulfilled, (6.81) will also be met as a result of the stability requirements given by equation (6.23).

Finally it may be noted that the paradox of thrift applies to the savings of workers as well as to those on profits. As can be seen from equation (6.75), an increase in the propensity to save on salaries leads to a downward shift of the effective demand curve, and hence to lower rates of profit and of capacity utilization as well as slower growth. The impact of a fall in the propensity to save on salaries, from $s_{wf1}$ down to $s_{wf2}$, would be illustrated by Figure 6.8.

To sum up this subsection, a propensity to save on wages may jeopardize the results obtained with the canonical Kaleckian model. This is more likely to happen the higher the propensity to save of permanent staff and the larger their wage premium. A high sensibility of investment to the profit rate may also transform the economy into a profit squeeze or an exhilarationist regime. Nonetheless it should be pointed out that Pasinetti's famous theorem can be extended to a Kaleckian model. In that event, the very long-run rates of profit and of capacity utilization are not influenced by the propensity to save of workers. All the standard results of the canonical Kaleckian model are safeguarded, as demonstrated by Dutt (1990b). His demonstration relies on a model where firms have retained earnings, the financial rights of which are distributed to workers and capitalists in proportion to their share of equity capital, as suggested by O'Connel (1985).

Without dealing with that precise model, we now include explicitly the corporate firm into our Kaleckian model of growth and distribution, taking into consideration the question of finance.

## 6.5 FINANCE AND ACCUMULATION

### On the Absence of Finance in Growth Models

One of the surprising aspects of the evolution of Cambridge theory is that, starting from Keynes's *General Theory*, which described a monetary production economy, the Cambridge post-Keynesians have failed to incorporate money within their models of growth and distribution. As Kregel has pointed out, 'money plays no more than a perfunctory role in the Cambridge theories of growth, capital and distribution' (1985, p. 133). In this regard, Davidson's (1972) critique of Pasinetti's and Kaldor's neo-Pasinetti theorems is well known, Davidson's contention being that these theorems are misleading because they omit money.

For her part, although Robinson (1956, 1962) devotes several pages to rentiers, interest rates and finance constraints, she ends up adopting assumptions 'intended to reduce the importance of monetary policy in the operation of the model to a minimum, except as a stopper to inflation' (1962, p. 44). In her famous double-edged relationship between the rate of profit and the rate of growth, she indicates that the finance constraints appear among the general animal spirits of the entrepreneurs, symbolized by the expected rate of profit which comes in her investment function (1962, p. 43). But monetary factors do not enter, even implicitly, the second curve, that is the profit-realization curve.

Why post-Keynesians, with recent exceptions, have omitted explicitly to incorporate money and finance in their models of growth and distribution is difficult to say. One reason may be that both Robinson and Kaldor did not believe that variations in interest rates could have predictable consequences since, in their opinion, these variations were drowned by the independent fluctuations in animal spirits, which made the rate of accumulation an exogenous variable.

Our own attempt to integrate money and finance into models of growth and distribution is based on two sorts of considerations. First, the rate of interest is considered to be an exogenous variable, under the control of the central bank, as was discussed in Chapter 4. The rate of interest is a purely monetary and conventional phenomenon. The pace of accumulation has no feedback effect on the rate of interest: money is endogenous. This is in accordance with Robinson's main view of the role of money in growth models, since she argues that 'the banks allow their total lending (and therefore the supply of money) to increase gradually, at a constant rate of interest, as total wealth increases' (1962, p. 43). A different rate of interest corresponds to a different monetary regime. This is also how Sarantis (1990–1, p. 184) justifies and introduces monetary factors in his model of growth and distribution.

The second sort of considerations arises from the finance frontier of the firm which was discussed in Chapter 3 at the microeconomic level. The macroeconomic consequences now have to be brought to the fore. The discussion of the finance frontier led to three major points. First, firms need to make profits to be able to borrow. This financial constraint introduces an additional relation between the rate of profit, the rate of interest, the rate of accumulation and the leverage ratio which is deemed reasonable. Secondly, the retention rate of firms cannot be considered to be an exogenous variable once the interest payments and the variations in monetary policy are taken into account. Third, when pursuing target-return pricing, firms attempt to integrate the financial constraint within their pricing procedures. All three of these points will be incorporated within our Kaleckian model of growth and distribution. In addition the distributional consequences of changes in interest rate regimes will also be dealt with. It will be seen that money and finance have a crucial impact on all three major components of the Kaleckian model: the savings function, the investment function and the profits cost curve.

The Kaleckian model incorporating finance and interest rates that will be developed will also help to settle the controversy which has arisen between post-classical authors with regard to the causal link between the rate of interest and the rate of profit, on the one hand, and between the rate of interest and the rate of accumulation, on the other. Cambridge post-Keynesians, as is well known, claim that the determination of the rate of profit rests on the realized rate of growth modulated by the saving propensities on profits. The rate of interest, as was mentioned above, is left hanging in the air, independent of the rate of profit. 'The level of interest is ... not closely tethered to the level of profits and enjoys, so to say, a life of its own' (Robinson, 1956, p. 242). It has even recently been asserted by Nell that it is 'plausible to argue that the normal rate of profit determines the long-term rate of interest' (1988b, p. 267). Nell has further argued that 'Cambridge theories hold that aggregate demand tends to move inversely to interest rates' (1988b, p. 265), a claim which can also be found, under a more prudent formulation, in Kalecki's writings (1969, p. 15).

By contrast, most neo-Ricardians believe that lasting changes in interest rates have no predictable effect on investment expenditures (Pivetti, 1985, p. 99) and they have claimed that the rate of interest set by the monetary authorities determines the rate of profit (Sylos Labini, 1971, p. 270; Garegnani, 1979, p. 81; Vianello, 1985, p. 84; Pivetti, 1985, 1988). This causality is usually attributed to Sraffa's famous aside according to which the rate of profit is 'susceptible of being determined from outside the system of production, in particular by the level of the money rates of interest' (1960, #44). While some post-Keynesians have endorsed this view, arguing that 'sustained low interest will presumably in the long run reduce the normal rate of profit' (Harrod, 1973, p. 111), the causality from interest rates to profit rates proposed by the neo-Ricardians has generated several responses from irritated post-Keynesians (Pasinetti, 1988; Nell, 1988b; Wray, 1988). To some it is an 'inexplicable suggestion' (Bhaduri and Robinson, 1980, p. 103) which is 'excessively fanciful' (Robinson, 1979, p. 180).

We shall demonstrate in the rest of this section that these assessments are unjustified. The explanation proposed by Pivetti and endorsed by Roncaglia (1988b) can be fitted within our Kaleckian framework. Pivetti explicitly relies on a form of full-cost theory of prices, a theory to which post-Keynesians cannot object. The neo-Ricardian view is that the main determinant of profit margins is the overhead cost due to interest payments on borrowed capital and the opportunity costs on the firm's own capital. For neo-Ricardians, the level of the interest rate is the crucial determinant of profit margins. 'My analysis carries the view that the interest rate determines the mark-up over nominal wages' (Pivetti, 1988, p. 282). This is quite compatible with statements previously made by some post-Keynesians: 'Interest costs are passed on in higher prices in much the same way as wage costs' (Kaldor, 1982a, p. 63); 'Firms often have some standard rate of profit, which includes interest, that they add to the input costs' (Harrod, 1973, p. 44). The neo-Ricardian view is thus based on a theory of full-cost pricing, rather than the simple mark-up theory which we have been emphasizing in this chapter so far. To fully incorporate the impact of interest rates on distribution and growth, and to understand the neo-Ricardian contribution to that neglected part of post-Keynesian theory, one needs to go back to full-cost pricing procedures, more specifically the target-return pricing model.

**Target-return Pricing**

It was pointed out in Chapter 3 that mark-up pricing and target-return pricing are part of the same theoretical framework, that of cost-plus pricing procedures. Firms which have more sophisticated accounting procedures use target-return pricing or some form of full cost pricing, while the others rely on the more primitive mark-up procedure. In economic models, mark-up pricing is particularly useful, because of its simplicity. Having understood the mechanics of the Kaleckian growth model, we may now venture to introduce target-return pricing and the components of its target rate of return.

Our objective in bringing up target-return pricing is to consider the impact of interest rates and the finance frontier on what we have called the profits cost curve. Before we actually do so, we must make a detour and study the impact of the standard rate of return on the profits curve. To simplify the analysis, let us assume away depreciation and let us suppose that all workers earn the same wage rate ($\sigma = 1$). As was the case at the very beginning of the chapter, total profits are then equal to:

$$r = (q/k)[1 - (w/p)(1 + f/u)/y_v] \tag{6.12}$$

The price variable $p$ was previously determined by the mark-up equation (5.30). Let us now replace this $p$ with the target-return pricing formula that was defined in Chapter 5 in the case of overhead labour.

$$p = \left(\frac{u_s + f}{u_s - r_s v}\right)\frac{w}{y_v} \tag{5.35}$$

Making use of this formula and of equations (6.12) and (6.13), after some manipulations the profits cost function can be written as:

$$r = \frac{(f + r_s v)u - (u_s - r_s v)f}{v(u_s + f)} \tag{6.83}$$

We can compare this formula to the standard profits cost equation:

$$r = \frac{mu - (1-m)f}{v} \tag{6.22}$$

From the comparison, it follows right away that:

$$m = (f + r_s v)/(u_s + f) \tag{6.84}$$

The fundamental difference between the two profits functions given by equations (6.22) and (6.83) is that the former has a gross margin of profit $m$ which is truly exogenous, whereas the latter has a gross margin of profit which depends on other parameters. Changes in these parameters induce a shift of the profits cost curve and hence a change in the equilibrium values of the rate of profit and the rate of capacity utilization of the model. In particular, changes in the standard rate of return $r_s$, the value of which is itself dependent on the finance frontier, will have an impact on the profits cost function.

Before we examine the impact of changes in the standard rates, we should note that, if the actual rate of utilization of capacity $u$ turns out to be equal to the standard rate of utilization of capacity $u_s$, similar to the neo-Ricardian normal rate of capacity $u_n$, the actual rate of profit $r$ is then equal to the standard rate of return $r_s$ embodied in the margin of profit of the pricing procedure. This can be seen by rewriting equation (6.83) in the form of equation (6.85). There are thus strong family ties between this standard or target rate of return and the neo-Ricardian normal rate of profit.

$$r = \frac{(u - u_s)f + r_s v(u + f)}{v(u_s + f)} \tag{6.85}$$

Let us start by examining the impact of an increase in the ratio of overhead labour, as shown by $f$. First it should be noted that such an increase in a model based on full cost procedures leads to an increase in the margin of profit.

$$dm/df = (u_s - r_s v)/(u_s + f)^2 > 0 \tag{6.86}$$

The positive sign of the derivative is due to the fact that the numerator needs always to be positive for the price equation (5.35) to make economic sense. The increase in the margin of profit need not, however, push down the profits cost curve. This can be seen by taking the derivative of equation (6.86) with respect to $f$, which yields:

$$dr/df = (u_s - r_s v)(u - u_s)/v(u_s + f)^2 > 0 \text{ if } u > u_s \tag{6.87}$$

The partial derivative is positive whenever the actual rate of utilization of capacity is above the standard rate. This result is similar to the one that had

352     Foundations of Post-Keynesian Economic Analysis

*Figure 6.17*   *Impact of an increase in overhead costs on the rates of profit and of capacity utilization when target-return pricing is in use*

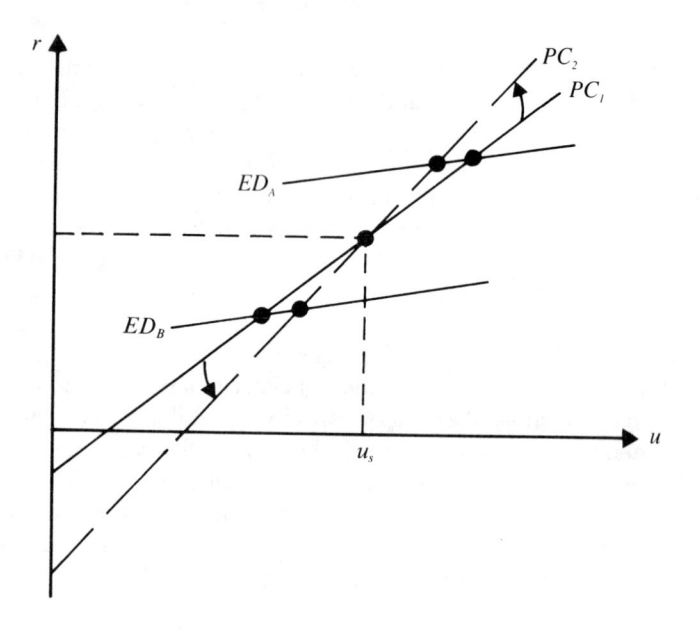

been observed in the static framework of Chapter 5, when the impact of an increase of overhead costs on the profit share was being assessed. Equation (6.87) shows that, when there is an increase in overhead costs in a model in which firms practise target-return pricing, the profits cost curve spins around the fixed point determined by the standard rates of profit and of capacity utilization. This is shown in Figure 6.17. To the initial overhead costs correspond the $PC_1$ curve, while the higher overhead costs correspond to the $PC_2$ curve. The impact of the rise of overhead costs on the rates of profit and of capacity utilization depends on the standard rate of capacity utilization compared to the actual one, which depends on the position of the effective demand curve, $ED_A$ or $ED_B$. It should be noted that a rise in overhead costs always brings the actual rates of profit and of utilization closer to their standard levels. It can also be noted that increases in overhead costs had a similar impact on the rate of utilization in the static case illustrated by Figure 5.17.

Let us now deal with a change in the standard rate of utilization of capacity which figures in the pricing formula. An increase of this standard rate is equivalent to a reduction of the margin of profit, as can be seen from equation (6.84). Taking the derivative one gets:

Figure 6.18 *Destabilizing impact of entrepreneurs revising their view of the standard rate of capacity utilization according to the values taken by the actual rate*

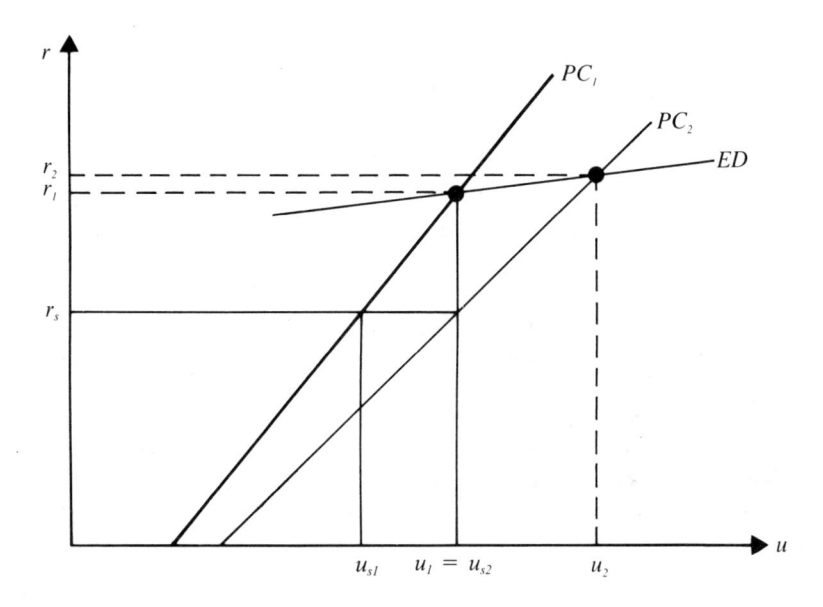

$$dm/du_s = -(f+r_sv)/(u_s+f)^2 < 0 \qquad (6.88)$$

It follows that an increase of the standard rate of utilization of capacity must be associated with a downward shift of the profits cost curve. This is illustrated in Figure 6.18. The initial profits cost curve is $PC_1$, to which corresponds a standard rate of utilization of capacity $u_{s1}$ and a standard rate of profit $r_s$. The effective demand curve being assumed fixed, the actual rates of utilization and of profit of the initial situation are $u_1$ and $r_1$ respectively. In the situation drawn, the actual rate of utilization exceeds its standard level, and hence so does the actual rate of profit. Let us suppose that firms react to this discrepancy by changing the standard rate of utilization which is utilized in the target-return pricing formula. What is to be shown is that tampering with the standard rate of utilization of capacity brings as much instability as meddling with the normal rate of utilization in the investment function.

Suppose, to simplify the graph, that the pricing formula incorporates a new rate of utilization of capacity which is equal to the actual one of the previous period; that is, $u_{s2} = u_1$. Let us further assume that the standard rate of profit is left unchanged. It can be seen in Figure 6.18 that the new actual rate of utilization $u_2$ will be even larger than in the previous period, while the discrepancy between the actual rate of profit and its standard rate has grown larger still, to $r_2 - r_s$. Letting the standard rate of utilization of capacity respond to the fluctuations in the current rate thus exacerbates the over-use or the lack of use of capacity. This result is valid both in the long run and in the short run, as the reader will recall from the discussion of target return pricing in the static framework of Chapter 5. Furthermore it will be recalled that instability was also observed when an investment function incorporating a normal (or standard) degree of capacity utilization, equation (6.54), was associated with the hypothesis that current values affected this normal rate. One is tempted to claim that the standard rate of utilization of capacity, or the normal rate, is a purely conventional parameter, because it cannot be otherwise for structural macroeconomic reasons. If entrepreneurs were to revise their view of the standard rate of capacity utilization according to the values taken by the actual rate, the economy would be highly unstable.

Let us now deal with changes in the standard rate of return. It is clear from equation (6.84) that an increase in the standard rate of profit leads to a rise in the profit margin $m$, as one would expect. Taking the derivative, one gets:

$$dm/dr_s = v/(u_s + f) > 0 \qquad (6.89)$$

It is equally clear from equation (6.85) that the profits cost curve shifts up when the standard rate of profit $r_s$ is increased in the target-return pricing formula. It is at this juncture, it seems, that the arguments in favour of long-term positions limited to normal or standard rates of utilization are the strongest. If firms respond to the over-utilization or to the under-utilization of capacity in the manner described by orthodox theory, that is by lowering prices in the latter case and by raising them in the former, the possible range of the actual rate of utilization in the long run should be smaller than if the gross margin of profit is truly exogenous. If firms diminish the standard rate of return whenever the actual rate of profit exceeds the standard rate, the possibilities of the actual rate of capacity utilization would be diminished to the point of uniqueness: the actual rate of capacity utilization could only be equal to its standard rate. This possibility corresponds to what was called in section 4 the third objection against the endogeneity of the rate of capacity utilization. The following quotation is representative of this neo-Ricardian objection. Assume that the normal rate of profit mentioned below is no different from the standard rate of profit used in target-return pricing, and that the normal rate of capacity utilization is the same concept as the standard rate of capacity utilization.

## Accumulation and Capacity

> ... The possibility of capacity utilization being different from its planned degree in the long run would have an important implication for theories of distribution and accumulation ... The *realized* rate of profit emerging from the interplay between distribution and effective demand may not be inversely related to the real wage, even in situations that the authors seem not to think limited to the short period; another way to say this is that the ... normal rate of profit $r_n$ (i.e. the rate of profit technically obtainable at the normal utilization degree with [the real wage rate] taken at its current level) may diverge from its realized rate, even for long periods of time. Now, we do not wish to quarrel with this reasonable proposition: the *observed* rate of profit is very unlikely to coincide with $r_n$, even in terms of averages covering long periods of time, although we might suspect that after all, there must exist *some* connection between the two rates. The model, however, contains no element for the exploration of this connection, as it implies a persistent and systematic divergence between [the actual and the normal degree of capacity utilization]. (Committeri, 1986, pp. 170–71)

Let us then suppose that firms react to a discrepancy between the actual and the standard rate of profit, and set the standard rate of profit (in the very long run) in the following manner:

$$r_{s(t)} = \phi r_{s(t-1)} + (1-\phi) r_{(t-1)} \quad \phi < 1 \tag{6.90}$$

Combining equations (6.89) and (6.90), we see that, whenever the rate of profit exceeds the standard rate of return, firms react by increasing the standard rate of return and the margin of profit. What happens is illustrated in Figure 6.19. The effective demand curve and the standard rate of utilization of capacity are assumed to be given. Let us start from a situation where the profits cost curve is $PC_1$, corresponding to a low standard rate of return $r_{s1}$. Under this situation, both the actual rate of profit and the actual rate of utilization are high, at $r_1$ and $u_1$. Because of equation (6.90), this situation will not last as firms revise the target rate of return, moving it up from $r_{s1}$ to $r_{s2}$. The profits cost curve shifts to $PC_2$, yielding a rate of profit which is still higher than the target rate. This process will go on until the standard rate of return is set at a level of $r_{s3}$, at which point the actual rate of profit will be equal to it, while the rate of utilization will be equal to its standard rate $u_s$. Note that changes in the standard rate of profit induced by the actual levels of the rate of profit tend to stabilize the model. An increase in the standard rate of profit, brought about by an excess of the actual rate of profit over the standard rate, pulls down both the actual rate of profit and the actual rate of utilization. This result is independent of the shape taken by the investment function.

The rate of utilization can only be an endogenous variable in the long run if the adjustment of the standard rate of return to the actual conditions is sluggish, and preferably non-existent. This is all too evident in equation (6.85), where it is obvious that the standard and actual rates of utilization

356   Foundations of Post-Keynesian Economic Analysis

Figure 6.19   The actual rate of capacity utilization ends up equating the standard rate of utilization when entrepreneurs revise their view of the standard rate of return according to the values taken by the actual rate of profit

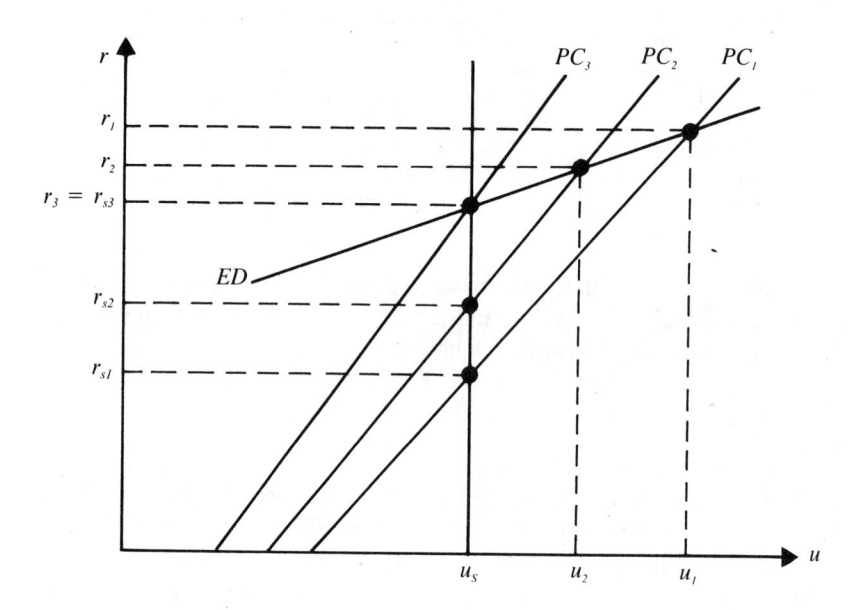

are equal if the standard and actual rates of profit are equated. If there exists a process ensuring this latter equality, the actual rate of utilization at the end of the adjustment process becomes a predetermined variable, equal to the conventional standard rate. The various cost and reaction parameters being given, the standard rate of utilization of capacity thus determines the rate of profit that is consistent with it, through the effective demand function of equation (6.21) for instance. This determines, then, the real wage rate and the rate of growth. The inverse relation between the rate of growth and the real wage which characterized earlier post-Keynesian models has been brought back. Because the rate of utilization is given, an increase in the exogenous determinants of the rate of growth induces an increase in the rate of profit and a fall in the real wage. This is represented in Figure 6.20 by an initial upward shift of the effective demand curve, from $ED_1$ to $ED_2$, which is followed by an induced upward shift of the profits cost curve, from $PC_1$ to $PC_2$, corresponding to an increase in the margin of profit. At the end of the process the rate of growth and the rate of profit have risen, but the real wage rate has fallen.

*Figure 6.20* The extreme Eichnerian model: the return of the downward-sloping wage/profit frontier when a mechanism equating the actual and the standard rates of capacity utilization is assumed

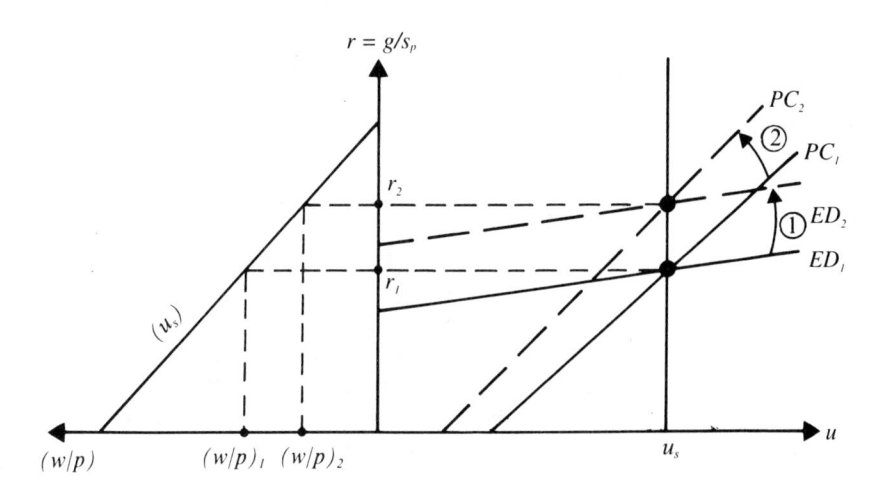

This antinomic variant of the Kaleckian model is symmetric to the Ciccone model that was developed in section 3. There the rate of utilization was endogenous while the rate of growth was exogenous. The level of the real wage rate determined the rate of utilization, for a given rate of growth. Here the rate of utilization is exogenous while the rate of growth is endogenous. The level of the real wage rate is determined by the standard rate of utilization of capacity and the determinants of the rate of growth. We shall see however, in Chapter 7, that the rate of utilization need not reach its standard rate, despite the actual rate of profit and the standard rate of return having equated each other by the process described above.

It should be noted that the results arrived at with the help of equation (6.90) are very similar to the story provided by Eichner and other post-Keynesians who have put much emphasis on the financial needs of investment growth and its effect on the margin of profit of corporations. In their models, a faster pace of investment induces firms to increase their margin of profit in search of additional funds to finance this investment. In the Eichnerian model, as in the *inflationist* model of the earlier Kaldor and

Robinson, increased investment is associated with higher prices relative to wage costs. Effective demand and growth rates have an impact on margins of profit. For these authors, while in the short run the actual and the standard rates of capacity utilization may diverge, this is not so in the long run. The reason for this is that they *assume* that the standard rate of profit will be adjusted to the actual trend of the rate of growth, and hence to the actual rate of profit, as in Figure 6.20. This leads Wood (1975, p. 129), for instance, to say that his model is a 'long run model of the determination of the share of profits at normal full capacity use'.

In this extreme version of the Eichnerian model, as in the earlier Cambridge models, there is thus an assumed mechanism which equates in the long run the actual rate of utilization of capacity to the standard level of utilization. The rate of accumulation depends on the secular expected rate of growth of sales, while the rate of utilization is the standard rate. In the Eichnerian scheme of causality, an increase in the expected secular rate of growth of sales would induce an increase in the rate of capital accumulation. An increase in the secular expected rate of growth is incorporated into the pricing formula, inducing a rise in the standard rate of profit which equates it to the actual rate of profit. Eventually the actual rate of utilization comes back to its normal level, as shown in Figure 6.20. This implies, however, that faster accumulation is inexorably linked to lower real wages and disposable income (Eichner, 1976, p. 279). The relation between real wages and the accumulation rate is thus reversed in the extreme Eichnerian model when compared to that of the Kaleckian model (Agliardi, 1988).

**Pricing and the Finance Frontier**

The discussion of the Eichnerian model has brought to the fore one of the essential determinants of the standard rate of return. These must now be examined. As we do so, four streams of post-classical theory are to be compared within the same framework: the Kaleckian school, the neo-Ricardian school, a less extreme version of the Eichnerian model, and a possible model reminiscent of the works of Minsky.

To uncover the possible determinants of the standard rate of return, one must go back to the finance frontier that was introduced in Chapter 3. We found that there is a three-way connection between the rate of interest $i$, the rate of profit $r$ and the rate of growth $g$ of a corporation, given the proxy $\rho$ for the leverage ratio. With appropriate simplifications, this relationship could be written as:

$$r = i + g/(1+\rho) \tag{3.5}$$

In Chapter 3, which dealt with the microeconomics of the firm, the other constraint was the expansion frontier of the firm. This constraint, combined with the finance frontier, allowed us to determine simultaneously the rate of profit and the rate of growth of the firm. From the standpoint of macroeconomics, the role of the expansion frontier is broadly played by the effective demand constraint inherent to the savings function. At this stage, two theoretical positions may be taken with regard to the impact of the finance frontier at the macroeconomic level. One position is to argue that the finance frontier is a strict constraint which replaces the investment function. The long-run rate of profit and the rate of accumulation are determined by the interaction between this strict finance frontier and the savings function. This is the position adopted by Wood (1975) and endorsed by Dougherty (1980, ch. 11). The second position is to consider that within the macroeconomic setting the finance frontier is only a loose constraint, which has compelling consequences for both the pricing formula and the investment function, without, however, replacing the latter. This is the position which will be mostly developed here. Nevertheless we start with the implications of the first position, that of Wood.

In Wood's model, there is no investment function of the sort described in the present chapter. Despite this, the rate of accumulation is not exogenous. It is determined, as indicated above, by the intersection of the savings curve (equation 6.3) and the finance frontier. That the latter replaces the investment function is more evident if we rewrite equation (3.5) as:

$$g^i = (r-i)(1+\rho) \tag{6.91}$$

In this version it appears that investment is strictly constrained by current or past profits, net of interest and dividend payments, given the proxy $\rho$ of the permissible leverage ratio. This constraint, joined to the savings function, gives the long-run rate of profit.

$$r = \frac{i(1+\rho)}{1+\rho-s_p} \tag{6.92}$$

This result appears rather weird: the rate of profit, and hence the rate of accumulation, are positively related to the rate of interest and to the propensity to save on profits. The paradox of thrift is gone! Wood's model proper is not based on an investment function given by equation (6.91), but rather on a slight variation of it, given by equation (3.9). However this changes nothing in the fact that models of determination of the rate of profit based on a strict interpretation of the finance frontier are unstable. The slope of the investment function incorporating the finance frontier, $1+\rho$, is necessarily greater than that of the savings function, $s_p$, since $s_p$ is always smaller than one. The model is unstable, a fact which explains its weird results. Wood's model, combining equations (6.3) and (6.91), can be illustrated graphically by Figure 6.2, which is an earlier instance of instability. Suppose in Figure 6.2 that firms decide to accumulate at a rate $g_0$, below the equilibrium rate $g^*$. The actual rate of profit $r_0$ that will then be realized will be below the rate of profit $r^c{}_0$ that is required to fulfil the criteria of the finance frontier. There will be an inducement to grow at an ever slower rate. One must thus conclude that the Wood model is unstable (Bortis, 1982; Lavoie, 1987, p. 162). The finance frontier cannot generally act as a strict constraint on investment.

Therefore it appears that interpreting the finance frontier as a strict constraint leads us to an unstable model and a dead end. We must thus revert to a loose interpretation of the finance frontier; that is, we must incorporate within the investment function and the pricing formula, but in a loose way, the possible constraining impact of finance. We deal first with the consequences for the pricing formula. Considering the importance of finance, the standard rate of profit may be written as a loose function of three variables or parameters:

$$r_s = r_s(i, g, \rho) \qquad (6.93)$$

Depending on the impact, or lack thereof, which is being emphasized, four positions can be developed by post-classical authors. The first position is the canonical Kaleckian model, in which the margin of profit is immune from the variations that could affect the finance frontier. Changes in the rate of interest or in the rate of growth of the economy do not modify the standard rate of return, or the margin of profit. It is assumed either that overhead costs do not enter into the mark-up decision, or that the standard rate of return is truly conventional, unaffected by the needs of financing accumulation. The margin of profit is truly exogenous.

The second position is a less extreme version of the Eichnerian model, where the standard rate of profit could be influenced by the actual rate of accumulation, without ever being equal, except by a fluke, to the actual rate of profit. This implies that the actual and the standard degrees of utilization of capacity usually diverge in the long run, although effective demand, as believed by the earlier neo-Keynesians, has a positive feedback impact on profit margins. What happens is that the price equation, as determined by the standard rate of profit, acts as a stabilizer, reducing the fluctuations of the rate of utilization of capacity. Prices relative to wage costs increase when the pace of accumulation picks up, while relative prices drop when there is a slowdown. For Eichner (1987a, p. 355), the rate of interest has no impact on the margin of profit which is required to fulfil the financial obligations of the firm. In his view, the standard rate of profit is fully determined by the secular rate of growth of the corporation. In its simplest form, this Eichnerian relationship can be written as:

$$m = m_0 + m_g g \qquad (6.94)$$

With this type of model, linked to a Kaleckian investment function, it may still be possible for real wages to go up while accumulation accelerates. This type of model quickly becomes complicated. For this reason, because it has been studied elsewhere (Lavoie, 1992b), and also because we shall see a variant of it when we tackle inflation in Chapter 7, we shall not discuss it any further. We are thus left with the impact that the interest rate and the leverage proxy could have on the margin of profit.

The third position corresponds to a model in which one would emphasize the changes in the normal leverage ratios, as proxied by ρ. This would correspond to some of the factors of financial risk underlined by post-Keynesians such as Minsky (1976). When the financial system is more prudent, refusing to lend to highly leveraged companies, there is a fall in the ρ parameter. This forces firms to generate their own sources of finance and induces an upward shift in the profits cost curve. In the (unlikely) absence of any effect on the investment function, which in any case would only reinforce the cost-induced effects, it would lead to a fall in the rates of profit and of capacity utilization. Prudent behaviour imposed by the banks does not restore realized profit margins in a Kaleckian type of model; it cuts them down. To be able to study this type of model fully, one would have to compare the evolution of the actual leverage ratio with its standard level. Several post-Keynesians are now working on this topic (Semmler, 1989).

Finally we come to the fourth position, that of the neo-Ricardians, developed in particular by Pivetti. Here the standard rate of profit, or the normal rate of profit as the neo-Ricardians call it, responds to changes in the rate of interest. As in the Kaleckian version, profit margins are not responsive to changes in effective demand. The neo-Ricardian view assumes that, in the long period, at a given rate of utilization of capacity, the rate of profit is the sum of two *independent* and exogenous elements: the rate of money interest and the normal profit of the entrepreneur (Pivetti, 1985, p. 87). Any lasting change in the money rate of interest is fully incorporated into the standard rate of profit, as it should be according to the finance frontier. Pivetti writes the relationship between the rate of interest and the standard rate of profit in the following way:

$$r_s = i + npe \qquad (6.95)$$

Here *npe* is the *normal profit of enterprise*. This, according to Pivetti, is the remuneration for the risk and trouble of employing capital productively. This premium may change from industry to industry. Pivetti makes clear that equation (6.95) determines a normal or standard rate of profit, not the actual one. This part of the neo-Ricardian view is thus concerned exclusively with the determinants of the profits cost curve, not the effective demand curve. 'The analysis concerns the explanation of the *normal* rate of profit, in the meaning that this term has always had in economic theory, and never refers to the actual rate of profit and actual profits which are of course acted upon by demand' (Pivetti, 1988, p. 281). In our notations, the impact of the rate of interest is on the rate of profit defined by the profits cost curve: a rise in the permanent rate of interest leads to a shift upwards of the profits cost curve. Assuming that the so-called normal profit of enterprise, which Pivetti believes to be objective, depends on the other (given) elements of the finance frontier, the neo-Ricardian view may be expressed by the following linear equation:

$$m = m_0 + m_i i \qquad (6.96)$$

The assumption of linearity is easily justified. When the above equation is differentiated, one gets the constant parameter $m_i$, which may be interpreted as the reduced expression of the right-hand side of equation (6.89), when the standard rate of profit is considered exogenous. In the rest of this section, our attention will be focused on this version of target-return pricing.

**Interest Rates and the Components of Effective Demand**

The impact of interest payments on effective demand is particularly interesting. As was recalled earlier in this section, neoclassical economists and post-Keynesians alike tend to attribute a damping role to high interest rates. This role will be preserved in the investment side of our effective demand constraint. However interest rates also have complex distribution consequences, which have derived effects on effective demand, through the savings function. The resulting effect of interest rates on realized profit rates and growth rates, even when associated with the impact of interest rates on the profit margin, may not be the conventional one.

Let us start with the investment function. In section 3 of this chapter, I asserted that the canonical Kaleckian investment function given by equation (6.20), which includes both the rate of utilization of capacity and the realized rate of profit, is preferable to an investment function that would only include the rate of utilization and the normal rate of profit (or the share of profit). This is so even though the investment function *à la* Bhaduri and Marglin appears to be based on more solid logical grounds, since the rate of utilization is not entered twice, as in the canonical Kaleckian investment function. It is now time to back the contention that I made earlier.

One may hesitate to incorporate the share of profit as one of the determinants of the investment function in a macroeconomic model, for five different reasons. First, changes in the share of profits may reflect changes in the composition of output rather than changes in the actual margin of profit that each industrial sector is able to maintain. This problem was underlined at the end of Chapter 5. The second reason, which militates against the inclusion of the share of profit, is related to what has just been discussed in the previous subsection. When finance requirements are taken into consideration, it is clear that an increase in the margin of profit that corporations try to impose at the standard degree of capacity may not necessarily imply better profitability. For instance, an increase in the margin of profit following an increase in the perceived permanent rate of interest does not entail good news for the entrepreneurs. Similarly an increase in the margin of profit induced by a drop in the permissible leverage ratio would not induce expectations of higher future profitability. Only an increase in the margin of profit induced by a higher secular rate of growth would have a positive effect on investment.

Thirdly, as has been argued by Dutt (1990a, p. 223), firms may be looking at the overall economy, rather than at their own situation, to judge the expected profitability of their investment plans. If this is so, firms would not be in a position to assess the current normal rate of profit; the available information would only allow them to estimate the actual rate of profit. As a consequence the rate of profit rather than the margin of profit would have to be the variable entering the investment function. The fourth argument, supporting the inclusion of the rate of profit in the investment function, is linked to the definition of the normal rate of utilization. A number of economists, in particular Sylos Labini (1971, p. 247), argue that excess capacity acts as a deterrent to entry. One may thus argue, as does Skott (1989, p. 54), that the normal (or standard) rate of capacity utilization is endogenous and depends inversely on the current rate of profit. The higher the rate of profit, the more likely to enter are rivals and competitors from abroad. A lower normal degree of capacity utilization is then called for to compensate for the stronger incentives to compete offered by the high rates of profit. Calling the normal rate of utilization which entered Amadeo's investment function of equation (6.54) $u_n$, we have:

$$u_n = u_{n0} - u_{nr}r \qquad (6.97)$$

where $u_{n0}$ and $u_{nr}$ are parameters.

Substituting the value of the normal rate of capacity utilization into equation (6.54), one gets:

$$g^i = \gamma + g_u(u - u_n) = \gamma + g_u u - g_u(u_{n0} - u_{nr}r) = \gamma' + g_u u + g_r r$$

Having started from an investment function which only depends on the rate of utilization, we end up with the canonical Kaleckian investment function. The final and crucial justification of this Kaleckian investment function, however, is the finance frontier (Agliardi, 1988, p. 284). Unless investment expenditures are entirely financed by retained earnings, firms can only invest as long as they can convince banks that they are worthy borrowers. Retained earnings are thus an important element of the investment function, independently of any effect which a high rate of capacity utilization may have on the desire to invest. The normal rate of profit or the margin of profit may be a good indicator of the profitability of investment to be expected for the future; but the realized rate of profit is also a good indicator of the borrowing possibilities of firms, a factor underlined not only by Kalecki (1971, p. 111) but also by Robinson:

Profit influences investment not only in providing the motive for it but also through providing the means. An important part of gross investment of firms is financed by gross retained profits. Moreoever, the amount that a firm puts up of its own finance influences the amount that it can borrow from outside. (Robinson, 1962, p. 86)

The independent influence of the rate of utilization over investment has been verified empirically by Fazzari and Mott (1986–7): in a time series study they show that sales and retained earnings of firms each have a positive impact on investment expenditures, while their flow of interest payments has a negative influence on investment. Similarly Chamberlain and Gordon (1989) show that capacity utilization and profitability net of interest payments are significant determinants of investment. These findings are entirely compatible with the investment function proposed by Kaleckians in general and Steindl in particular. They highlight the importance of the rate of utilization, independently of its effect on the realized rate of profit. They also show that, in a model in which interest payments are taken into consideration, the rate of profit net of dividend and interest payments should be part of the investment function. Steindl (1952, p. 128) himself goes so far as to argue that the rate of profit may have an influence on investment which goes beyond that of retained earnings. We will limit ourselves to the independent effects of the rate of utilization and of retained earnings, writing the investment function under a form suggested by Taylor (1985, p. 387) and picked up by many authors since.

$$g^i = \gamma + g_u u + g_r(r - i) \tag{6.98}$$

This is the function which we will use in our assessment of the impact of interest rates on effective demand. The last term of the equation represents the effect of retained earnings on the investment function; that is, the rate of profit net of the dividend and interest payments. This is based on the equations that were developed in Chapter 3, when discussing the finance frontier of the firm. It is assumed that the dividend pay-out rate to share-owners is identical to the interest rate on borrowed capital. The retained earnings of firms will thus be equal to $\Pi - iK$, as was the case for the individual firm in equation (3.2). Dividing this by $K$, we obtain the retained earnings of firms per unit of capital, $(r-i)$.

We are now ready to handle the savings function. The savings of the firm are their retained earnings. On the household side, let us continue to assume the classical case of no savings on wages. Let us suppose, however, that households save on their property income, that is on the dividends and interest payments which they receive. Let us call $s_h$ this propensity to save out of property income by households. Their savings per unit of capital are then $s_h i$. The new savings function is thus made up of two components: one related to corporate retained earnings and the other to household savings on their share of profit.

$$g^s = (r-i) + s_h i = r - (1-s_h)i \qquad (6.99)$$

This new savings function is different from the standard Cambridge relation in two ways. It incorporates the distributional impact of interest payments in its simplest form, and distinguishes between firms and households. The latter characteristic of the present savings function is worthy of praise, according to Robinson, since she claimed that 'the most important distinction between types of income is that between firms and households' (1962, p. 38). As to the role of the interest rate, it must be said that, while several authors have incorporated the rate of interest into the investment function, it has generally been omitted from the savings function, with the exception of Skott (1989), Dutt and Amadeo (1989) and Dutt (1992c). It can be seen from equation (6.99) that the rate of growth of savings is reduced whenever the interest rate is higher. Higher interest rates redistribute income from firms to households, whose propensity to save is lower than that of firms. Higher interest rates thus induce more consumption spending, not less, as the neoclassical authors would say on the basis of a naive model of the individual. Taking into account income classes and the distinction between households and firms leads to radically different conclusions. Note that the positive relation between interest rates and consumption had already been recorded by Joan Robinson.

A permanent fall in the level of interest rates relatively to the rate of profit has reduced the rentiers' share in profits (assuming that dividends have not been raised correspondingly), and this is likely to have a more important effect in reducing the proportion of consumption to profits than any effect there may be of lower interest in increasing the ratio of consumption to rentier income. (Robinson, 1956, p. 253)

Capital gains are omitted from the model, but including them would not change the general form of the savings function in any substantive way. This is shown by Skott (1989, p. 57) in a model which challenges Davidson's critique of the neo-Pasinetti theorem, introducing banking deposits with exogenous rates of interest alongside Kaldor's securities market with its endogenous valuation ratio. Money and interest rates thus do have a role to play in a theory of growth and distribution, even when an adjusting mechanism based on an endogenous valuation ratio is at work, as is the case in the models proposed by Kaldor (1966) and Skott.

One may wonder why the usual Cambridge savings function, $g = s_p r$, or some variation of it, has not been kept. The reason is that $s_p$ cannot be considered an exogenous parameter any more, since its major component, the retention ratio, is now endogenous. As was shown by equation (3.6), the retention ratio is dependent on the interest rate, a factor which is not under the control of the firm. It would thus be a mistake to assume that the retention ratio is constant, unless one only dealt with states that did not differ in their monetary policy.

## The Impact of Interest Rates on Profit and Capacity Utilization

We are now in a position to assess the impact of interest rates on the rate of profit, the rate of accumulation and the rate of capacity utilization, taking into account the effect of interest rates on both the profits cost function and effective demand. The former function is obtained by combining equations (6.22) and (6.96).

$$r = (m_0 + m_i i)u/v - (1 - m_0 - m_i i)f/v \qquad (6.100)$$

As to the effective demand constraint, it results from the combination of our two new investment and savings function, equations (6.98) and (6.99).

$$r = \frac{g_u u + (1 - s_h - g_r)i + \gamma}{1 - g_r} \qquad (6.101)$$

Taking into account the profits cost function in the investment and savings function, one finds the stability condition of the model:

$$g_r < 1 - g_u v/(m_0 + m_i i) \qquad (6.102)$$

The sensitivity of investment to changes in the rate of profit net of interest payments must be smaller than one. This implies that the denominator of the effective demand constraint in equation (6.101) is always positive. The profits cost curve and the effective demand curve thus have the usual shape. All the usual results regarding changes in overhead costs, the propensity to save and the margin of profit, except those provoked by changes in the interest rate, remain as they were in the canonical Kaleckian model. In particular, an increase in $m_0$, that is a fall in the real wage rate, would induce a lower rate of profit and a lower rate of capacity utilization.

The interesting question is to find out what will happen when interest rates go up. Let us take the derivatives, with respect to the interest rate, of equations (6.100) and (6.101). We get:

$$dr^{PC}/di = (u+f)m_i/v \qquad (6.103)$$

$$dr^{ED}/di = (1-s_h-g_r)/(1-g_r) \qquad (6.104)$$

Equation (6.103) shows that the profits cost curve always shifts upwards when the rate of interest is increased. With respect to the effective demand curve, two cases must be distinguished depending on the sum of the values taken by $s_h$ and $g_r$, the propensity to save out of property income of households and the sensitivity of investment to profits net of interest. When this sum is above unity, that is $s_h + g_r > 1$, the derivative given by equation (6.104) is always negative, implying that an increase in the rate of interest shifts the effective demand curve downwards. This first case is unambiguous and can be illustrated graphically by the right-hand side of Figure 6.10 (except that the two profits cost curves would not be parallel). A fall in the rate of interest would bring up the degree of capacity utilization from $u_1$ to $u_2$ and the rate of profit from $r_1$ to $r_2$. As a consequence, the rate of accumulation would also be higher.

In the second case, defined by the fact that $s_h + g_r < 1$, three possibilities arise, depending on the precise values taken by the various parameters. This multiplicity of subcases occurs because the effective demand curve shifts upwards, rather than downwards, when the rate of interest is higher. These three subcases are illustrated in Figure 6.21, with the original situation set at $u_1$ and $r_1$. Following an increase in the rate of interest, the rate of utilization increases if the effective demand curve shifts more than the profits cost curve at a given rate of utilization. Manipulating equations (6.103) and (6.104), it requires that:

$$s_h + g_r < 1 - \Gamma$$

where $\Gamma = (u+f)(1-g_r)m_i/v \qquad (6.105)$

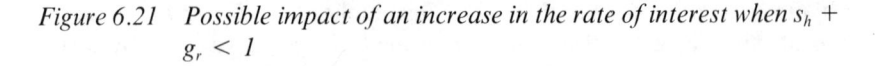

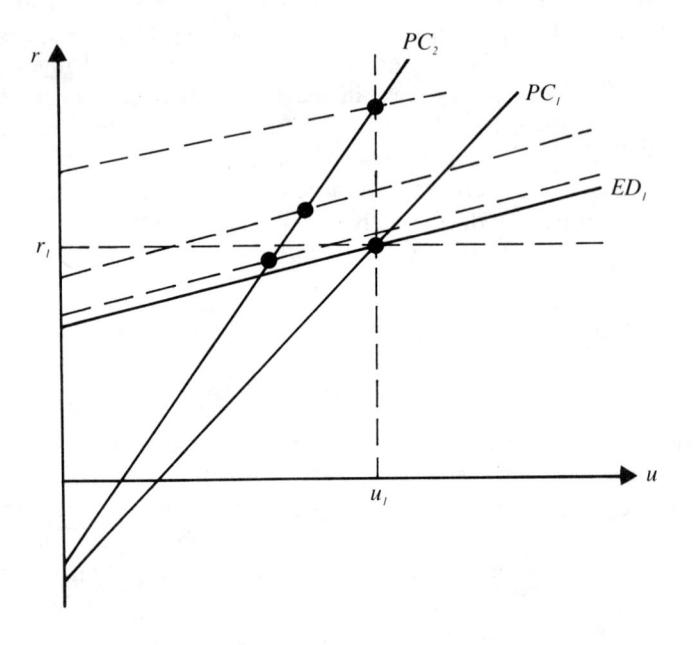

Figure 6.21 *Possible impact of an increase in the rate of interest when $s_h + g_r < 1$*

To know under which conditions the rate of profit increases when the rate of interest is higher, one has to find out whether the effective demand curve shifts more than the profits cost curve, but this time for a given rate of profit. To do so, the profits cost and effective demand functions have to be rewritten in terms of $u$:

$$u^{PC} = \frac{rv + (1 - m_0 - m_i i)f}{m_0 + m_i i} \tag{6.106}$$

$$u^{ED} = \frac{(1 - g_r)r - i(1 - s_h - g_r) - \gamma}{g_u} \tag{6.107}$$

The derivatives yield:

$$du^{PC}/di = -m_i (u + f)/(m_0 + m_i i) \tag{6.108}$$

$$du^{ED}/di = -(1 - s_h - g_r)/g_u \tag{6.109}$$

Following an increase in the rate of interest, the rate of profit will increase if:

$$s_h + g_r < 1 - \Lambda$$

where $\Lambda = m_i(u+f)g_u/(m_0+m_i i)$ (6.110)

It can be seen from the stability condition given by equation (6.102) that $\Lambda$ is always smaller than $\Gamma$. Similar operations can be performed to find out what happens to the rate of accumulation. Before we do so, note however that when $s_p + g_r = 1 + \Gamma$, that is when the increase in the rate of interest induces no change in the rate of capacity utilization, the induced increase in the rate of profit is always smaller than the exogenous change in the rate of interest, as is obvious from equation (6.104). This means that retained earnings expressed as a percentage of capital, $r - i$, decrease under these circumstances. Going back to the investment equation (6.98), it implies that the rate of accumulation decreases although the profit rate $r$ has increased. Still, provided $m_i$, $g_r$ and $s_h$ are sufficiently small, while $g_u$ is sufficiently large, there are circumstances under which the rate of accumulation will rise as a result of an increase in the rate of interest. This can be seen by rewriting equations (6.106) and (6.107) in terms of $g$, by making use of equation (6.99). One gets:

$$u^{PC} = [gv + i(1-s_h)v + (1-m_0-m_i i)f]/(m_0+m_i i) \quad (6.111)$$

$$u^{ED} = [(1-g_r)(g+i(1-s_h)) - i(1-s_h-g_r) - \gamma]/g_u \quad (6.112)$$

The derivatives yield:

$$du^{PC}/di = [(1-s_h)v - (u+f)m_i]/(m_0+m_i i) \quad (6.113)$$

$$du^{ED}/di = s_h g_r/g_u > 0 \quad (6.114)$$

The rate of accumulation increases as a result of a rise in the rate of interest whenever the first derivative is larger than the second. This implies the following inequality:

$$g_r < (g_u/s_h)[(1-s_h)v - (u+f)m_i]/(m_0+m_i i) \quad (6.115)$$

We may then construct Table 6.2, which summarizes the impact of the interest rate on the three main variables of our model under different conditions. One can see that the larger the sensitivity of investment to changes in the rate of capacity utilization, while the smaller the propensity to save out of property income, the sensitivity of investment to profit net of interest payments and the sensitivity of the margin of profit to interest costs,

Table 6.2  *Impact of the interest rate on the main variables, according to the values taken by the $s_h$ and $g_r$ parameters*

| $s_h + g_r$ | 0 | $1 - \Gamma$ | $1 - \Lambda$ | 1 | $1 + s_h$ |
|---|---|---|---|---|---|
| $du/di$ | + | − | − | | − |
| $dr/di$ | + | + | − | | − |
| $dg/di$ | + or − | − | − | | − |

the higher the probability that an increase in interest rates induces counter-intuitive favourable effects on the economy.

In the present model, when interest rates are changed, various effects come into play. A higher interest rate initially leads to a redistribution from the firm towards the household rentiers, which creates an increase in consumption. Higher interest costs, however, are partially or fully passed on to consumers, through higher mark-ups, which implies lower real wages and hence less consumption. This negative secondary effect may be further reinforced by the investment function, a smaller spread between profit and interest rates leading to less confident bankers and entrepreneurs, and hence to a lower desired rate of accumulation. A higher exogenous rate of interest thus induces a lower overall propensity to save, and may imply a higher rate of profit and a higher rate of growth of output. This surprising outcome is obtained by Dutt and Amadeo (1989) in a similar framework and by Skott (1989, pp. 58, 64, 68) in his revamped neo-Pasinetti model, although Skott does not seem to be aware of his result or does not believe the result to be worthy of mention.

Broadly speaking, in a manner which resembles but simplifies the classification proposed by Epstein (1990), we may differentiate between three regimes: one in which the class interests of the entrepreneurs and those of the rentiers coincide while being opposed to those of the workers; one where the labour class would be split against a united front of rentiers and entrepreneurs; and finally one in which entrepreneurs and workers should collude against rentiers. In the first regime, the rate of profit and the rate of interest both increase, while the rate of accumulation decreases, leading to a worsening of the employment situation at lower real wages. In the second regime, the rate of interest, the rate of profit and the rate of accumulation all move in sympathy, leading to an improvement of the employment situation, but at lower real wages. In the third regime, lower interest rates, and hence higher real wages, lead to higher profit rates and a faster rate of accumulation, a result more akin to Keynesian theory. We can thus concur with Pivetti's presumptions when he says that:

> Changes in interest rates *will* tend to be associated with changes in aggregate demand, but by a different route from the one traditionally envisaged. Both the propensity to consume and the inducement to invest, it will be acknowledged, are most likely to be affected by changes in the normal distribution of income between profits and wages. Indeed *this* is the route by which we envisage the rate of interest to influence the level of output and its composition. The direction of such influence, however, cannot be predicted on the basis of some apriori functional link ... The point, of course, is the significance of income distribution for effective demand: if money plays an important role in determining income distribution, it will also play an important role in the determination of the level and composition of output. (Pivetti, 1985, pp. 99–100)

The analysis conducted in this section illustrates the contention recently made by Dutt and Amadeo (1990, p. 80) that there is room for monetary theory within the neo-Ricardian research programme. Within this programme, output levels and income distribution are not independent from monetary factors: there is no classical dichotomy between real and monetary forces (Garegnani, 1990, p. 124). Neo-Ricardians have brought to our attention the impact of changes of monetary interest rates on income distribution and on effective demand, a consideration that had generally been omitted in mark-up models or savings functions, even by those post-Keynesians who claimed to be concerned with monetary production. However, the situation has recently evolved. Some authors now discern two components within the capitalist class, the rentiers on the one hand and the firms or their owners on the other, while taking into account the impact of money interest rates on investment, prices and real wages. Money now plays a role in post-classical models of growth and distribution.

# 7. Inflation

## 7.1 A TYPOLOGY OF INFLATION

**The Quantity Equation versus the Wage-cost Mark-up Relation**

In orthodox neoclassical economics, the so-called aggregate price level is determined by the level of the money stock. Furthermore inflation is ultimately the consequence of the excessive growth of the money supply. The Quantity Theory of money reigns, in its various incarnations and with the appropriate subtleties and restrictions. Except for short-run shocks, the economy is always at full employment, that is at its natural rate of unemployment. Output or its rate of growth being given in the Quantity equation, while the velocity of money is assumed to be stable in relation to certain key variables, prices and their rate of growth are determined by the level of the money stock and by its rate of growth. Inflation is a demand-led phenomenon. There is excess demand in the market for goods as well as an excess demand for labour. The cause of this is the excess of the growth rate of the money supply over the growth rate of real output. Some of the more eclectic neoclassical authors would go so far as to admit that this excessive growth rate of money is only the proximate cause of inflation, while sociological factors are the fundamental underlying cause (Addison *et al.*, 1980).

In post-Keynesian theory, the level of the money supply does not determine the level of prices, nor does the rate of growth of the money supply determine the rate of inflation. Excess money is not even a proximate cause of inflation. The major justification for this rejection of the Quantity Theory of money, as we have seen in Chapter 4, is that the supply of money is endogenous in the post-Keynesian framework. There cannot be an excess supply of money which would drive forward the inflationary forces. The supply of money only responds to the demand for money. There is no exogenous flow of money that would fuel inflation. In other words, if the money stock grows, it is for reasons which logically precede this growth.

Neoclassical authors strongly reject the notion of an endogenous stock of money. The main reason for this rejection is that, without an exogenous supply-led stock of money, orthodox authors are left without an explanation of the price level; it becomes indeterminate, a major flaw in neoclassical theory. By contrast, the endogeneity of money is not a source of embarrassment for post-Keynesian authors, for they have an alternative theory of the determination of the price level. Post-Keynesians argue that the 'economy is primarily a money-wage system' (Weintraub, 1978, p. 66). This is so, firstly because money enters the circuit when firms distribute wages and salaries to their employees, the stock of money resulting basically from this influx of money wages not having yet flowed back to firms and been repaid to the banks. Secondly, the economy is a money-wage system because, in a vertically-integrated system, costs are the determinant of the general price level, the main element of cost being the wage rate. Within the post-Keynesian framework, the money-wage rate is the exogenous factor explaining the price level which the orthodox authors have sought. Departing on this issue from the Quantity Theory, Keynes wrote that 'the long run stability or instability of prices will depend on the strength of the upward trend of the wage-unit (or, more precisely, of the cost-unit) compared with the rate of increase in the efficiency of the productive system' (1973, vii, p. 309). That wages are the main determinant of prices does not necessarily imply that wage increases are the main cause of price inflation. Most post-Keynesians view inflation as a conflict over the distribution of income. Two of these conflicts appear to be crucial: that between different groups of workers on the one hand, and that between labour taken overall and the non-labour constituents of the firm on the other. With the first distributional conflict is associated the wage–wage spiral, and with the second conflict is associated the wage–price spiral. These two spirals are the inflationary phenomena that will be discussed in the present chapter. Before we do so, however, we ought to establish a typology of the various sorts of inflation. This will allow us to put conflicting-claims inflation into perspective. Such a typology can be put forward with the help of what is perhaps one of the most well-known post-Keynesian relations, Weintraub's wage-cost mark-up relation. His macroeconomic equation (Weintraub, 1978, p. 45) may be written as:

$$p = \kappa' w/y \qquad (7.1)$$

where $p$ is the price level, $w$ the money wage rate, $y$ the output per unit of labour, and $\kappa'$ the average mark-up of prices over unit labour costs.

Equation (7.1) is a macroeconomic identity; $w/y$ are *actual* unit labour costs, rather than standard unit costs. Equation (7.1) is equivalent to the *old* full-cost variant of cost-plus pricing, given by equation (3.14). Full-cost pricing, using the symbols noted above and defined in equations (5.29) and (5.31), can be written as:

$$p = (1+\theta')w/y \qquad (7.2)$$

It is thus clear that equations (7.1) and (7.2) are identical, the mark-up factor $(1+\theta')$ here being equal to $\kappa'$. It should also be noted that, unless the rate of capacity utilization is constant, the $y$ parameter cannot be constant with overhead labour costs.

While equation (7.1) has been very popular with a number of post-Keynesians, a slight variation of it has been proposed by some Radical economists (Kotz, 1987). They start from the national accounts identity, to arrive at the price level expressed as a function of the share of profits in national income.

$$pq = wL + p\Pi \qquad (5.14)$$

Dividing by the level of output, we have:

$$p = wL/q + p\Pi/q$$

The term $\Pi/q$ is the share of real profits in terms of real output, or what we have previously called $\pi$; $q/L$ is simply $y$, that is output per unit of labour. Rearranging, we get the neo-Marxian equivalent of Weintraub's wage-cost mark-up equation, with $(1-\pi)$ equal to $1/\kappa'$:

$$p = w/y(1-\pi) \qquad (7.3)$$

It should now be even clearer that, if equations (7.1) and (7.3) are equivalent ways of expressing the same identity, neither of these equations can *explain* inflation. This is because we know from Chapters 5 and 6 that the share of profits $\pi$ is an endogenous variable, both in the short run and in the long run. Both equations are a truism; that is, an identity which, like the Quantity equation of the Monetarists, is an interesting way to put things but one that requires to be backed by a theory. We may, however, use either equation to derive an *ex post* assessment of the proximate sources of inflation. Calling $\hat{p}$ the rate of growth of prices, that is the rate of price inflation, and denoting the rate of growth of the other variables by a caret, ^, equation (7.1) yields:

$$\hat{p} = \hat{w} - \hat{y} + \hat{\kappa}' \qquad (7.4)$$

Of course we could also have arrived at a similar inflation accounting equation had we started from the standard simple mark-up equation which we used in preceding chapters:

$$p = (1+\theta)w/y_v \tag{5.30}$$

With $(1+\theta)$ equal to $\kappa$, the revised Weintraubian relation of inflation accounting becomes:

$$\hat{p} = \hat{w} - \hat{y}_v + \hat{\kappa} \tag{7.5}$$

It is clear that, in the long run, as Keynes had it, the rate of inflation hinges on the differential between the first two terms of equations (7.4) or (7.5), since one would not expect the share of profit to increase forever. 'The proximate determinant of inflation is then the rate at which nominal money wages rise in excess of the growth of average labor productivity' (Moore, 1979, p. 133). What are the fundamental causes of the variations given by equation (7.4) or (7.5)?

## A Conflict View of Inflation

Going back to equation (7.5), to each of the three terms of the equation one can attribute a different sort and a different cause of price inflation (Davidson, 1972, p. 341), each sort having been identified by Keynes in his three-stage description of the inflationary process which can be found in the *General Theory*.

In this work, but less so afterwards, Keynes believed that an increase in activity leads to an increase in prices because of diminishing productivity. This can be interpreted as a negative value of the rate of growth of labour productivity $\hat{y}$ in equation (7.4). In our post-Keynesian model of the firm and also because of our utilization function, such a possibility is ruled out. It is clear, however, that there may be some sectors of the economy that face diminishing returns, when demand for their products is expanding too quickly. This would be the case of raw materials. Since this can only be a temporary and local phenomenon, and since our Kaleckian model is not designed to take it into consideration, we shall ignore it from now on. Demand-determined prices are therefore excluded. As a consequence, and because issues related to open economies are not being discussed, the possibility of inflation being fuelled by a world-wide scarcity of raw materials will not be dealt with (Kaldor, 1976).

The next inflationary stage, according to Keynes, before full employment is reached, comes from an upward wage drift which we can associate with the $\hat{w}$ term in equation (7.5). Keynes called it semi-inflation, because it was not to be confused with absolute inflation, which occurred as a consequence of an excess demand. In the semi-inflation, wages and prices rise without either full employment or full capacity having been reached. To some extent the initial cause of the upward wage drift is the price increase due to the diminishing returns of the previous stage. Semi-inflations, according to Keynes (1973, vii, p. 302), have 'a good deal of historical importance', but they 'do not readily lend themselves to theoretical generalisations'. This is the sort of inflation upon which we shall focus our attention in the following sections.

Finally Keynes considered absolute or true inflation which, as was said above, he related to excess demand and monetary expansion (1973, vii, p. 303). While we may readily eliminate monetary expansion as a cause of inflation, several post-Keynesian authors have considered excess demand as a factor of inflation. Several post-Keynesian models of the Kaleckian type include an excess demand term in their inflation function (Taylor, 1985, 1991; Sarantis, 1990–1). This may be a matter of tradition, since, as was seen at the beginning of Chapter 6, earlier post-Keynesian models of growth and distribution were prone to the so-called inflation barrier. When firms raise the share of investment in national income, the margin and the share of profit are pushed up, either by competitive demand forces, as in the earlier Robinson and Kaldor models, or by the oligopolistic firms themselves, as in the Eichnerian models. In terms of equation (7.5), this implies a positive rate of growth of the mark-up $\hat{\kappa}$ which, presumably, induces rising wages. This is what Davidson (1972, p. 343) calls profits inflation, following Keynes's *Treatise on Money*. Others call it structural inflation (Seccareccia, 1984). When the increase in the mark-up, and hence the decrease in real wages, exceeds what the workers can take, the economy hits the inflation barrier.

One should note that profits inflation need not, of necessity, be related to excess demand. Two such cases may be considered. First, firms may decide to raise their mark-up in an attempt to adjust the standard rate of return to the historically observed rate of profit, which may have been high in the past because of high rates of growth. Profits inflation in this case is indirectly caused by high demand, but not by excess demand, since the recently observed rates of utilization of capacity may still be much below unity. It cannot be denied that demand can have an impact on inflation, even within a Kaleckian model, but the impact of demand is only of an indirect sort, acting through the mark-up desired by firms. Second, profits inflation may arise without demand being involved. It may be that firms have decided to increase their margins of profit for reasons which are unrelated to demand, for instance as a result of higher interest costs or because of changes in the perception of competitive pressures from abroad.

Profits inflation and the inflation barrier bring to the fore the conflict causes of inflation. It may be that the mark-up is almost a constant, while prices and nominal wages are quickly rising. This does not mean, however, that firms exercise no upward pressure on prices and that labour unions are entirely responsible for the state of chronic inflation. The conflicting forces may be such that the pressures being exercised on the mark-up are compensating each other, so that wages and prices are rising without the mark-up being changed. The conflict view of inflation combines the profits inflation theory, in which firms try to increase their share of income claims, with the semi-inflation theory, where groups of workers or workers overall also attempt to increase their share of real income.

Such a view of inflation is difficult to formalize or even to test empirically. As in the case of investment, it seems that the rate of increase of nominal wages depends on animal spirits, this time those of the leaders of the labour unions, of their members and of their employers, and it also depends on the attitude of government and of the public. This is why a number of post-Keynesians consider that the level of the money wage rate is an exogenous datum, given by historical and sociological circumstances which are almost outside the realm of economics. 'Post-Keynesian theory accepts Keynes's view that the nominal wage is for the most part exogenously determined' (Eichner and Kregel, 1975, p. 1305). The nominal wage rate is the exogenous element which supports the general price level and which mainstream authors have been looking for. 'In our model, as in reality, the level of the money-wage rate obtaining at any particular moment is an historical accident' (Robinson, 1962, p. 70).

The key difference, then, between the neoclassical and the post-Keynesian views of inflation is that for the former inflation is an excess demand phenomenon, whereas for the latter it is basically a supply-side issue. In neoclassical economics there is excess demand either on the market for goods or on the labour market, or on both. This is why neoclassical authors attach very little importance to cost-push and demand-pull distinctions. For them all inflations are the result of scarcity, either of goods or of labour. In the post-Keynesian view, while price or wage inflation may accompany increased activity, excess demand is generally not the cause of continually rising prices. Inflation is not the result of an objective scarcity; it arises from conflicting views about the proper distribution of income. The influence of demand is only an indirect one. This is consistent with the Kaleckian model that has been presented in the previous chapters. Since the rate of utilization of capacity is always below unity, there cannot be an inflation of the demand-pull type. There could be a wage inflation induced by a scarcity of labour, but this is considered to be a sectoral and temporary possibility rather than a generalized one. A reserve army of unemployed or underemployed people is always present, waiting in the peripheral sector of the economy to be hired by companies operating in the core, or such an idle manpower exists abroad and can be imported when required (Del Monte, 1975, p. 255; Eichner, 1987a, p. 886). Inflation is cost-led. 'Excess demand provides at most only a minor component of a comprehensive explanation' (Cripps, 1977, p. 110).

The different interpretations of the well-known Phillips curve exemplifies the divergences between the neoclassical and post-Keynesian approaches to inflation. For neoclassical authors, the Phillips curve is an example of the impact of scarcity and market forces: as labour becomes more and more scarce, because of higher levels of activity, the pressures on money wage demands expand. For post-Keynesian authors, higher levels of activity which give rise to lower rates of unemployment give labour more bargaining strength. Workers have more bargaining strength because firms make more profits and are more likely to yield to the wage demands of labour when times are good (Kaldor, 1959, p. 293). This was also recognized by Keynes, when he claimed that wage increases were discontinuously related to increased activity, the discontinuities being 'determined by the psychology of the workers and by the policies of employers and trade unions' (1973, vii, p. 302). While the impact of low unemployment on wage inflation is the same in both the neoclassical and the post-Keynesian view, the underlying theoretical explanations of this relationship are quite different. One is based on the universal principle of scarcity; the other relies on distributional conflicts.

The main feature of the post-Keynesian theory of inflation, then, is that it is based on a conflict view of income distribution. As Davidson (1972, p. 347) says, 'The distribution of income is both a cause and a consequence of inflationary processes.' This conflict view of inflation is underlined by Eichner and Kregel (1975, p. 1308): 'At the heart of the inflationary process is the question of relative income distribution'. There are aspiration gaps between what is expected and necessary on the one hand, and what is actually being obtained on the other. This conflict between fair pay and actual pay arises at two junctures of the economy: first there is a conflict between the resources that the firms wish to devote to their workers and that the latter wish to control through their wages; second there is a conflict over what each individual group of workers wishes to receive compared to what other groups are perceived to get. The first type of conflict is known under the term of wage–price spiral, or under the expression of real wage resistance. The second type of conflict is known under the expression of relative wage resistance or, simply, the wage–wage spiral.

It will be shown in the next section that these are the two main sources of inflation that have been emphasized by most post-Keynesian authors. Although wage–wage and wage–price inflations can be conceptually distinguished, they will both be considered here as arising from the same fundamental causes, which we shall divide, perhaps somewhat arbitrarily, into inductive and permissive reasons for inflation.

## 7.2 INDUCTIVE REASONS FOR INFLATION

There are two major inductive reasons for inflation: equity requirements and the diffusion of information. We shall treat each of these in turn.

### Fairness

One of the main distinguishing features between mainstream and non-orthodox theories of pay and of inflation is that the latter attach much importance to the notion of equity and justice, whereas the former do not (Wood, 1978, p. 7). Another way to put this distinction is to say that non-orthodox theories of pay emphasize customary rules whereas orthodox theories focus on market forces (Piore, 1979, p. 138). In the neoclassical theory of inflation, the focus of the analysis rests on what was called, at the beginning of Chapter 5, the anomic forces of competition. These are peripheral to the post-Keynesian explanation of inflation. At the core of non-orthodox theories of inflation are the normative pressures of fairness. In post-Keynesian theory, inflation is explained by normative values, that is pay norms, customs, equity and justice. These norms have an impact on the perception of what is a fair relative wage, a fair real wage, and a fair profit share. They do have an impact on both the wage–price spiral and the wage–wage spiral. The rational consumer presented in Chapter 2, concerned about his rank in the consumption hierarchy and about upholding his earnings to make ends meet, reappears under the guise of a rational worker, who is concerned about his status in the workforce, both in real terms and relatively to other workers (Baxter, 1988a, 1988b, pp. 211–50).

Fair real wages are difficult to define. Fair real wages depend to a large extent on historical experience. Fairness, both in absolute and in relative terms, is often established by history and custom (Hicks, 1974, p. 65). It is sometimes customary to associate fair increases in real wages with increases in productivity, but such an association is also sometimes refuted. It is then argued that fair real wages are unrelated to sectoral productivity but rather to the overall productivity of the economic system. Past experience plays an important role in determining the fairness of a wage offer. Rising real wages may have seemed unfair in the 1970s, because their rate of growth was lower than in the 1960s. In the early 1990s, stagnating real wages may seem quite just. It all depends on what is expected. The ultimate instance of a fair real wage is the real wage resistance which is put up by workers in the case of the inflation barrier.

The wage-earner's test for fair wages is not simply a comparison with other people's earnings; it is also a matter of comparison with his own experience, his own experience in the past. It is this which makes him resist a reduction in his money wage; but it also makes him resist a reduction in the purchasing power of his wage, and even a reduction in the growth of that purchasing power to which he has become accustomed. Thus there is a backlash of prices on wages – a Real Wage Resistance, it may be called. (Hicks, 1975, p. 5)

Nonetheless, however difficult it is to formalize or to test models based on fair wages, fairness is an essential and necessary feature of the labour market. As we saw in Chapter 5, the efficiency of a firm relies on the perception by the workers that they are treated fairly. Wage demands are based on what the workers perceive to be a just remuneration, both relative to what the firm can offer and relative to what other workers get or are expected to get. That workers are concerned with the fairness of their wage rate relative to that of other workers was recognized from very early on in the post-Keynesian literature. It is well known that Keynes himself underlined the importance of relative wages for the behaviour of workers and of their unions.

Any individual or group of individuals, who consent to a reduction of money-wages relatively to others, will suffer a *relative* reduction in real wages, which is a sufficient justification for them to resist it . . . In other words, the struggle about money-wages primarily affects the *distribution* of the aggregate real wage between different labour-groups . . . The effect of combination on the part of a group of workers is to protect their *relative* real wage. (Keynes, 1973, vii, p. 14)

Since each group of workers will gain, *cet. par.*, by a rise in its own wages, there is naturally for all groups a pressure in this direction, which entrepreneurs will be more ready to meet when they are doing better business. (Keynes, 1973, vii, p. 301)

While Robinson mainly focused her attention on the inflation barrier, she also recognized the importance of relative wages when she wrote that 'the causes of movements in money-wages are bound up with the competition of different groups of workers to maintain or improve their relative positions' (1962, p. 70) Similarly it seems that Kaldor initially only attached marginal importance to the wage–wage spiral, considering 'the outcome of the struggle of wage-earners in different industries and occupations to secure an improvement, or to prevent a deterioration, of their earnings relative to the wages paid in other occupations' as only a minor possible explanation of price inflation (1964, p. 143). The clearest and earliest exponent of wage–wage inflation, then, was Richard Kahn. In his memorandum to the Radcliffe Committee in 1958, he argues that, apart from periods of marked shortage of labour, the main cause of inflation is 'the competitive struggle between trade unions and different sections of labour, exacerbated by the absence of an agreement about relative wages (Kahn, 1972, p. 143). Like Keynes before him, Kahn says that 'restraint displayed by any one section of labour taken in isolation operates at the expense of their real wages, which are reduced as a result of wage increases secured elsewhere' (ibid., p. 142).

It is interesting to note that, in later papers on inflation, Hicks and Kaldor arrive at a consensus on the causes of inflation and wage rises. Besides the standard inflationary forces, Kaldor (1982b) and Hicks (1975, pp. 4–5) underline the same three sets of forces. Two of these causes have been discussed above, while the third cause has been mentioned when discussing the Phillips curve. These three causes are: (1) the normative pressures of relative fair wages and the need to preserve one's status within the pecking order of labour's hierarchy; (2) the normative pressures of fair real wages, both authors referring to real wage resistance; and (3) the normative pressures induced by high profits or rising profits, the latter inducing unions to demand higher wages in an attempt to share the affluence of their employers, while also encouraging firms to grant what seems to be a fair rise. The first set of forces relate to wage–wage inflation; the last two relate to wage–price inflation and the conflict over the appropriate share of profits. All three of these aspects will be formalized in the simple model of inflation that will be developed in the next section. They constitute the core of a post-Keynesian explanation of price and wage inflation based on the notion of equity.

The reader may wonder how a theory of inflation based on conflict between workers and entrepreneurs can be arrived at. Was it not demonstrated that real wages and profits could be simultaneously increased? The causes of the conflict are the following. First, as just mentioned above, higher profits should encourage workers to ask for even higher real wages. If there were no limits to this process, full capacity would be reached and the inflation barrier underlined by the Marxists and the earlier post-Keynesian models of growth and distribution would become pertinent. Second, and this is the mechanism that will be emphasized in the inflation model to be presented, the real wage that is being sought by the workers is in conflict with the margin of profit which is the target of firms. One may wonder, then, why firms aim at a margin of profit rather than a rate of profit. The fact is that firms may set a target rate profit, as in the target-return pricing formula, but this target profit rate is translated into a target profit margin based on the standard rate of utilization of capacity. The real wage targets of the workers and the mark-up targets of the firms may thus clash, even though real wages and the actual rate of profit rise together. This will be better understood at the very end of the chapter, when target-return pricing will be explicitly introduced into a conflicting-claims model of inflation.

There is an additional reason for which entrepreneurs and workers may be in conflict over the distribution of income. Rentiers also make claims over part of the profits which are realized by firms. It was seen at the end of the previous chapter that higher real rates of interest may induce entrepreneurs to raise the mark-up, and hence decrease the real wage rate. There is then the possibility of a conflict between entrepreneurs and rentiers over the distribution of profits, and the possibility of an indirect conflict between the rentiers and the workers. In previous work, the conflict between workers and rentiers has mainly been seen as a force that would induce the state to take measures to slow down the economy and the rate of inflation, rentiers exhorting the state to protect their fixed incomes from the erosion of rising prices (Kalecki, 1971, ch. 12; Rowthorn, 1977). This need not necessarily be the case in a world of price indexation. The indirect conflict between rentiers and workers may instead exacerbate the problem of inflation.

Finally it has been underlined by some post-Keynesians that the state and the private sector may be in conflict over the distribution of income (Hotson, 1976). Rising tax rates may intensify inflationary forces, either directly, as in the case of sales taxes which are passed on to the consumers, as one would expect in an oligopolistic environment, or indirectly, as in the case of income taxes, in which case there will be resistance over falling after-tax income.

**Information**

With the notion of fairness being the first of our two inductive reasons for inflation, the transmission of information is the second. Since fairness is, to a large extent, a relative notion, comparisons are required. These comparisons, in turn, require information about the profits of the firm, their margins of profit, the profits of the industry, the structure of wages, the deals negotiated elsewhere, the value of marginal benefits obtained elsewhere, the recent trend in earnings and so on. Some post-Keynesians have recognized the importance of the diffusion of information in the inflationary process. Davidson (1972, p. 344) writes that 'the increasingly readily available information on the earnings of others ... has created pressures which make wage-price inflation the most dangerous of current economic problems'. Similarly Wiles (1973, p. 378) claims that 'the communications revolution ... making everyone instantly aware of everything, has sharply increased the amount of envy and imitation in the world'.

One may suspect, assuming available information is correct, that the larger the set of information the larger is the potential for inflation. The positive relationship is explained by the fact that, if wages within a group are compared to those of a larger set of labour unions, there is a higher probability of a group finding its wages unfair relative to another group (Wood, 1978, p. 23). The larger the reference group the larger the absolute differentials in rates of productivity increases, and hence the larger the potential differential between wage increases and productivity increases in a given industry. On the other hand, when information is generally incorrect, better information may decrease rather than increase inflation pressures. For instance, the information to which the ordinary person or the ordinary union member has access is usually biased. The media have a tendency to publicize only the most spectacular and most outrageous wage deals, contributing somewhat to the inflationary forces by providing a biased informational content of wage spillovers. In any case, even if information could be accurate and comprehensive, only part of it can be processed by the union leaders and the members of the opposing negotiating team. Because there are limits to the information that can be processed in a world dominated by procedural rationality, only the base rates of a subset of occupations and of industries are taken into consideration when bargaining takes place. This explains why the wage increases arrived at in some key industries often have such an impact on all sectors of the economy.

The post-Keynesian view of the way wage increases are transmitted from one part of the labour market to another is borrowed from the Institutional analysis of wage inflation (see Burton and Addison, 1977, and Piore, 1979). Whereas neoclassical authors consider market forces to be the determinants of pay structure, customs being frictions to the market mechanisms, Institutionalists believe that the wage structure is fundamentally determined by historical norms, the competitive pressures of demand and supply exercising frictions on the customary system. In contrast to the neoclassical framework, where wage transmission can only occur through market forces and price expectations, Institutionalist labour economists believe that there are wage spillover mechanisms whereby wage increases are transmitted to markets which experience very different economic conditions.

Broadly speaking, two variants of the spillover mechanism may be presented. In the first variant, the generalized spillover hypothesis, the wage bargain in an industry depends on past wage bargains of all industries, in particular the rate of wage increase struck at the bargaining table. There is then a substantial amount of interdependence between all sectors of the labour market. This interdependence is justified by the desire of each labour group to keep its place within the wage-earners' hierarchy. Any pressure at any point in the wage matrix is likely to be felt throughout. In a tuned-down version of the generalized spillover hypothesis, only the labour groups which have the same contour enter within the spillover matrix. These labour groups have similar characteristics, defined either by the type of product which is being made or by the size of the firm to which they belong. Labour unions keep track of their relative position in the hierarchy by making comparisons with the other groups of the wage contour. One of the interesting characteristics of the generalized spillover hypothesis is that there is no inherent tendency for the general rate of wage inflation to incline towards that of the most inflationary sector (Chowdhury, 1983, p. 654).

The other major variant of the spillover mechanism, perhaps a more realistic one, is that of the wage leadership industry. This mechanism asserts that one industry, or just a few of them, enter the spillover matrix. All other wage bargains are struck in reference to a select group of key leading sectors. This is the counterpart, for the labour market, of the price leadership hypothesis of the product market. It may surprise no one that this type of transmission mechanism is very popular among post-Keynesians. As in the case of price leaders, wage leaders may be chosen for various reasons. Sometimes the most economically important industries will be chosen, as a kind of demonstration effect: if the strongest firms in the country yield to the demands of the labour unions, why should less powerful corporations refuse to grant identical wage increases? Eichner (1976, p. 159) calls these the bell-wether industries. At other times, in the hope of obtaining greater benefits, the designated wage leader is in an industry which is in a most favourable position: sales and profits are high, and productivity increases have been rapid (Kaldor, 1959, p. 294; 1976, p. 708).

The wage increase negotiated by the wage leader becomes the national standard of what constitutes a fair and equitable percentage increase in wage compensation. Because of the publicity and media attention which is devoted to the wage bargain struck in the key leading sectors, it may become impossible for employers in other sectors to deny similar increases. The apparent inequity of such a refusal might provoke strikes, the resentment of union officials and of workers whose place in the pecking order would fall, and it might even lead to the sabotage of production. One of the interesting consequences of the wage leadership hypothesis is that the average rate of wage inflation should gravitate around that obtained by the wage leader. Furthermore, if this process has been going on for some time, one can assert that the wage leader sets the standard with regard to the fair real wage rate. If there is a wage leader, and if other labour unions attempt to keep their place in the wage-earners' hierarchy, variations in the average real wage rate prevailing among the employees of the wage leader will induce similar variations in the fair or desired real wage rate at other labour unions.

Whatever the exact form of the spillover mechanisms, a major feature of the various wage bargains is their *imitative* character (Kaldor, 1976, p. 709). This is a well documented fact. It cannot be attributed to the greater competitiveness of labour markets compared to those of goods, since it appears that industries which are quickly expanding see their wages increase just as fast as industries with high proportions of laid-off workers (Scitovsky, 1978, p. 226). Furthermore, because of their imitative character, wage settlements appear to be independent of productivity increases across industries. This has led to the productivity inflation view. Unless they are a response to wage increases, productivity increases, far from diminishing price increases as would appear from equation (7.4), exacerbate inflation forces. Indeed, it has been shown that the national standards of wage increases are based on the rate of growth of labour productivity of the sectors with the highest such rates, implying that these sectors are the designated wage leaders (Eatwell, *et al.*, 1974). As long as the wage leaders are able to claim a share of these productivity gains there must be a general rise in prices, since workers in sectors without productivity gains get the same proportional increases in their nominal wages. The mystery, then, is why productivity gains in the bell-wether industries are transformed into wage increases instead of price reductions. We must now turn to the permissive reasons for inflation, recalling that the notion of fairness and the diffusion of information were the inductive reasons for inflation, and the cause of the imitative character of wage settlements.

## 7.3 PERMISSIVE REASONS FOR INFLATION

The permissive reasons for inflation may be divided into three groups, each related to a different actor in the economy. These three sets of reasons are grouped under the following headings: administered pricing, free collective bargaining and full-employment policy. According to several analysts (Bénassy et al., 1979; Scitovsky, 1978), it is the combined evolution of these three facets of the real world which explains why chronic inflation has been so prevalent since the Second World War, while before, except for war years, it was almost absent from most industrial countries.

**Administered Prices**

The existence of administered prices, instead of market prices, is often held responsible for the breakdown of price stability. With market prices, the general level of prices may increase or decrease. Recessions induce a downward price spiral. With administered prices, prices may only increase, except in sectors facing abnormal productivity improvements. With administered pricing, it is said that firms have the power to resist price cuts when demand for their products is falling.

The modern predominance of administered prices is often attributed to a generalization of industrial concentration to all sectors of economic activity (Bénassy et al., 1979, p. 426). It is said that oligopolistic structures now prevail over competitive ones. This may or may not be true. In any case, the importance of administered prices is not essentially based on the growth of oligopolies *per se*. It is based on the greater power of firms over consumers, or what neoclassical authors would call an increased asymmetry of information.

Firms now have more power over consumers because of the growing complexity of products (Scitovsky, 1978, p. 222; Slawson, 1981, p. 56). Consumers are generally in no position to assess correctly the quality of goods. Their ability to estimate the quality to cost ratio of a product, taking into account future repair costs, is usually lacking. The inability of the consumer to assess a product correctly is due to a number of factors. Individuals are now more specialized, ignoring all but the requirements of their trade; technologial advances have led to products which are beyond the comprehension of most consumers; the multiplicity of available products and the wide range of alternatives for a given kind of good have put enlightened consumer choice beyond the computational abilities of most households. All of these factors have led to a secular increase in the market superiority of sellers over consumers in product markets. The great variety of goods within the same sort of product has led to the development of brand control by manufacturers (Kaldor, 1982b). This has reinforced the imposition of administered pricing. It has also encouraged the development of brand loyalty on the part of consumers, as a procedural and rational response to their over-extended computational capabilities.

Brand loyalty and the growing complexity of products have also modified the means of competition. Because of information asymmetry, low prices may be associated with cheap products. A price lower than that offered by competitors may discourage rather than encourage consumption. Some executives boast that they never had to engage in price competition during their tenure as sales vice-president. Price competition becomes a strategy of last resort, when everything else has failed. We now understand why. Unless the firms of all sectors cut prices, consumers will hardly be any richer. They will not increase their expenditures in the sectors which have decided to cut back on their prices. Rather they will spend their increased real incomes on the goods which are next on their priority list. The change in relative prices will be of little influence.

Non-price competition prevails. Advertising becomes an important feature of competition because brand loyalty is developed by advertising. Brand loyalty erects barriers to entry which a newcomer has to overcome by massive and costly advertising expenditures when entering the market. Similarly product innovation may induce customers to buy the new line of products or to stay loyal to the brand previously chosen. Technical progress is introduced by improving the quality, the appearance or the performances of the new product, rather than by lowering the price of an existing good. Product innovation and quality enhancement are thus other powerful forms of non-price competition. Whereas a lower price can be matched overnight, a clever advertising campaign or the introduction of a successful innovation may take months or even years before competitors can find a parry and organize a riposte.

All of the above tends to show that there is an inflationary bias when prices are administered and non-price competition prevails. Prices will generally not be brought down when demand falters, while competition will not prevent prices from rising when costs increase. This is particularly clear in the case of prices administered by government.

## Free Collective Bargaining

In most popular discussions as well as in academic circles, and even in some left-wing circles, chronic inflation is often blamed on increasingly powerful labour unions. While in the recent past, in the 1970s for instance, it was possible to quantify the growing relative importance of trade unions among workers, the 1980s saw the demise of the labour union movement, reflected by the dwindling numbers of its membership. Still, taking a long view, no one can deny that the labour movement is now better organized than it was in the first half of the century.

The better organization of the labour movement is reflected in several ways. First, labour unions are financially more powerful. In some countries they control the pension fund of their members and can use it as a weapon when negotiating. Besides pensions, unions have access to large financial resources which they can use to support their striking members or to publicize their action and influence public opinion. A major cause of this improved financial situation is that laws in several countries have made it compulsory for all the workers covered by a particular collective agreement to pay union dues, whether or not they are members of the trade union. This is the Rand formula. Labour organizations do not have to collect dues: the employer collects them directly from the payroll. There cannot be free-riders. The ultimate threat for a labour union is for government to repeal the laws making the payment of dues compulsory and automatic.

Much of the improved situation of labour unions, then, arises from their improved legal status. Whereas unions used to be banned, the creation of trade union units is now regulated by law, with rules that both the employees and their employers must abide by. Although the certification of a new unit is still no easy matter, it is certainly much easier now for a labour union to be recognized than it was a few decades ago. Labour unions are also acknowledged by the state as a full-fledged economic partner. Their representatives are on the tripartite boards of national economic advisory institutes. They sometimes have direct access to the legislators.

One would have thought that the increased power of the labour unions would have been a good match for the already existing monopsonistic power of the firms, each countervailing the other. This would probably have been true if firms did not have a power of their own over product markets. In a world of administered pricing where, as explained above, firms dominate consumers, the conjunction of the power of the trade unions in labour markets and that of the firms in product markets produces an inflationary bias. Labour unions have all to lose from unsuccessful bargaining, for their relative position can change by the full amount of the wage increase which has been bypassed. On the other hand, by raising prices on product markets, firms are in a position to recuperate in profits a substantial part of the wage increase which has been granted. 'In the real world of oligopolistic firms and of collective bargaining, firms and workers have some power to change prices and wages. Dissatisfaction with existing wages and prices may then lead to increases in those wages and prices' (Sawyer, 1989, p. 363).

As we shall soon see, the power of the firms and of labour over their respective markets is limited by threats to general affluence. The market may punish unreasonable behaviour, giving rise in particular to unemployment. A new phenomenon has arisen, however: that of the unionization of workers and of professionals in the public sector. In many countries, changes in legislation have allowed civil servants and other employees paid by the state to join labour unions. Furthermore sectors which were under private control, such as education and health, have become state-financed and have quickly grown. From being a strictly private-sector institution, trade unions have become heavily involved with the public sector. As is well known, the so-called laws of the market do not apply to the public sector and to their workers, or at least they do not apply to the same extent. There is no obvious potential penalty for excessive wage claims. As a consequence of this change in the composition of the unionized labour force, the dynamics of wage negotiations have changed. In many instances, the key wage bargain occurs in the sectors under public control and without market sanctions. This, many observers claim, has also helped to produce an inflationary bias, at least in the 1960s and 1970s. In our present age of austerity policies, wage decrees in the public sector have set norms to be followed by the businesses of the private sector.

**Full Employment Policy**

A government policy of full employment is the third permissive reason for inflation. As was said in the above paragraph, unreasonable claims and wage concessions are less likely to be made when economic punishment is a threat. This means unemployment for the workers and bankruptcy for the firms. If, however, the state has a commitment to a high employment policy, the threats lose force. Corporate executives know that, provided their company has a large enough labour force, government will come to the rescue and bail out their debt-ridden enterprise. Similarly labour unions at large know that government will maintain monetary and fiscal policies that are conducive to high employment, no matter what the rate of wage inflation. At the level of the individual, the social safety nets provide the necessary economic security.

It is often claimed by neoclassical authors that earlier Keynesians were unaware of the difficulties of holding back price and wage inflation at or near full employment. The Phillips curve in its various incarnations has been acclaimed as a great achievement, since it underscored the difficulties of achieving stable prices and high employment policies. While the Phillips curve may have been a great revelation to some over-enthusiastic Keynesians, the dangers for price stability of a full employment policy were not unknown to all. Keynes himself was quite aware of the difficulties involved.

> Some people argue that a capitalist country is doomed to failure because it will be found impossible in conditions of full employment to prevent a progressive increase in wages. According to this view severe slumps and recurrent periods of unemployment have been hitherto the only effective means of holding efficiency wages within a reasonably stable range. Whether this is so remains to be seen. (Keynes, 1973, xxvi, p. 33)

> If money wages rise faster than efficiency, this aggravates the difficulty of maintaining full employment, and, so far from being a condition for full employment, it is one of the main obstacles which a full employment policy has to overcome ... some people over here are accustomed to argue that the fear of unemployment and the recurrent experience of it are the only means by which, in past practice, trade unions have been prevented from over-doing their wage-raising pressure. I hope this is not true. (Keynes, ibid., pp. 37–8)

Keynes was thus aware that the implementation of policies of full employment would bring with them substantial structural transformations, which had to be dealt with by modifying the political and economic institutions. This was done only occasionally, in some countries or in some time periods. As a result, the predictions that Keynes hoped would not come true did materialize. After some time, union leaders started to realize that firms would in the end abide by whatever wage claims they made. The firms would take their revenge by raising prices. The wage and price increases would be endorsed by a monetary policy subordinated to the full employment requirements. This could not go on forever.

As Kalecki (1971, ch. 12) had predicted as early as 1943, corporations and big rentiers got particularly 'boom tired' in the 1970s. The 'sack' had ceased to play its disciplinary function, because of the full employment policy and because of the social security net, while real interest rates had fallen below zero, causing both the employers and the rentiers to call for anti-inflation policies. Since then, that is over the past decade, most governments have been content with fighting inflation rather than promoting full employment. Security nets have been loosened, real interest rates have risen, minimum wage legislation has lagged behind the cost of living index. Recessions have been planned to create unemployment in an attempt to eradicate inflation.

We may thus say that one of the three permissive reasons for inflation is no longer present, in contrast to the situation that still prevailed a dozen years ago. Price and wage *administrators* now know that full-employment policies have been replaced by anti-inflation policies. The latter are a credible threat to affluence. They can be both severe and prolonged. With the current demise of planning and the present exaltation over the merits of free market capitalism, it seems that unemployment and other threats to affluence are the only wage and price policies that most industrial countries are ready to try at this stage. The belief, associated with several post-Keynesians (Galbraith, 1952; Eichner, 1976; Cornwall, 1983), that a sustained full-employment policy must be associated with a permanent incomes and price policy seems to have fallen into oblivion. Events in Eastern Europe and turnarounds of public opinion may, however, change that too.

## 7.4 A SIMPLE CONFLICTING-CLAIMS MODEL OF INFLATION

The intent of the rest of the chapter is to present a model of inflation based on the inconsistent income claims of firms and workers; that is, based on what has often been called 'real wage resistance' by some and 'aspiration gap' by others. In standard terminology, the focus of the analysis is on the wage–price spiral. As a first approximation, wage–wage inflation and other income conflicts will be omitted, as will be feedback effects from the real economy. This will allow us to understand the essentials of the conflicting-claims model of inflation. In the subsections to follow, some of these complications will be taken up.

**The Basic Conflicting-claims Model**

The basic post-Keynesian model of inflation based on conflicting claims has some affinity with Kalecki's last article, entitled 'Class struggle and distribution of national income' (1971, ch. 14). Whereas before he took the degree of monopoly to be an exogenous variable, Kalecki argues in this article that trade unions have the power to achieve reductions in the mark-up by demanding and achieving large increases in money wage rates. As was briefly discussed in Chapter 3, it is Kalecki's view that firms are able to shift to consumers a large part of the increase in wage costs, but that some redistribution in favour of workers occurs when trade unions have sufficient bargaining power, at least in a world with excess capacity. This view has been summarized by Rowthorn (1977, p. 179) as follows: 'The working class can shift distribution in its favour by fighting more vigorously for higher wages, although the cost of such militancy is a faster rate of inflation, as capitalists try, with only partial success, to protect themselves by raising prices.' Some authors have verified empirically that pressures from trade unions which result in large increases in money wage rates do have a constraining effect on mark-ups (Sylos Labini, 1979; Reynolds, 1987b).

As Dalziel (1990) recalls, several post-Keynesian, neo-Radical and even mainstream authors have constructed conflict models of inflation. In all these models, the rate of inflation is a function of the size of the inconsistency between the mark-up that firms wish to aim for and the real wage rate which the leading key labour bargaining units consider to be fair. Indeed the determination of the inflation rate in several British macroeconometric models is or was based on the discrepancy between actual and target real wages, as in the model of the Cambridge Economic Policy Group. As is clear from the mark-up pricing equation, $p = (1+\theta)w/y_v$, a target set in terms of real wages can always be made equivalent to a target set in terms of a mark-up. Provided there is no change in productivity, it is thus immaterial whether we assume that both firms and workers set real wage targets, or that they both set mark-up targets. In our model, real wage targets will be assumed and to simplify notations we shall call $\omega$ the real wage rate $w/p$. The adopted representation follows Dutt (1987a). Several other authors in the Kaleckian tradition partially or fully adopt the same depiction, among them Taylor (1985) and Sarantis (1990–1), who both call it core inflation.

The basic conflicting-claims model of inflation is based on two equations. It is assumed first that the rate of growth of money wages which labour unions manage to negotiate is a function of the discrepancy between their real wage target and the actual real wage rate. This seems like a reasonable assumption to make. Let us call $\omega_w$ the real wage sought by the labour unions and the workers. Suppose that the actual real wage rate of the previous period was $\omega_{t-1}$. If the new actual real wage rate is to be equal to the real wage rate aimed at by the workers, the rate of increase of the real wage rate, denoted by $\hat{w}$, needs to be:

$$\hat{w} = (\omega_w - \omega_{t-1})/\omega_{t-1} \qquad (7.6)$$

For the new actual real wage to be equal to the target real wage, given that prices are expected to increase at the rate of $\hat{p}^e$, the rate of increase in the money wage rate, denoted by $\hat{w}$, must then be equal to:

$$\hat{w} = \hat{\omega} + \hat{p}^e \qquad (7.7)$$

In general the new actual real wage rate will not be equal to what has been sought by workers. Wages may not be fully indexed and workers may not manage to obtain what they consider to be their fair real wages. Taking the time subscripts out, we may thus formalize this by writing the following equation determining the rate of wage inflation:

$$\hat{w} = \Omega_1(\omega_w - \omega) + \Omega_2 \hat{p}^e \qquad (7.8)$$

The $\Omega_1$ parameter indicates to what extent labour unions react to a discrepancy between the actual and the desired real wage rate. $\Omega_1$ may thus be considered as the bargaining power of the workers. This has to be distinguished from the fair wage which the labour unions feel they should obtain. Workers may feel that the real wage is much too low compared to what they consider to be the just rate, but they may have little means of implementing their beliefs. The $\Omega_2$ parameter is the rate of price 'indexation'. It is equal to one in the case of full indexation, and is generally less than unity. Since the analysis is barely modified by the introduction of the indexation parameter, the equation determining the rate of wage inflation can be rewritten in its simplest form as:

$$\hat{w} = \Omega_1(\omega_w - \omega) \qquad (7.9)$$

We may proceed in a similar way with the equation determining the rate of price inflation. It may be assumed that firms increase prices when the actual mark-up is below the mark-up which they would ideally desire to set, and that the larger the differential between those two mark-ups the higher the rate of price inflation. This may be formalized in terms of target real wage rates, which for the firm we may denote as $\omega_f$. When firms aim at lower real wage rates, given the actual real wage rate, they will speed up the rate of price inflation, depending on their bargaining power over both the labour and the product markets. It may also be supposed that, if firms expect a faster rate of wage inflation, which we may denote by $\hat{w}^e$, they will increase prices faster. With $\psi_1$ and $\psi_2$ adjustment parameters playing a role symmetric to the $\Omega$ parameters, the rate of price inflation is given by:

$$\hat{p} = \psi_1(\omega - \omega_f) + \psi_2 \hat{w}^e \qquad (7.10)$$

As was the case of the wage inflation equation, a simplified version of the price inflation equation can very well represent conflict price inflation without losing much substance. Omitting wage indexation, equation (7.10) becomes:

$$\hat{p} = \psi_1(\omega - \omega_f) \qquad (7.11)$$

At this stage the reader might be somewhat puzzled. In a world dominated by aggressive trade unions and large oligopolies, it is usually believed that workers have the power to impose the wage increases of their choice while firms exact the price increases of their liking. How is it possible for firms not to reach their mark-up or real wage rate targets if they have ultimate control over prices? As Tarling and Wilkinson (1985, p. 179) put it, 'why should distributional shares change in a system where wages are determined unilaterally by capitalists and where in the time sequence prices follow wages?' One must conclude that, in historical time, prices do not always follow wages, or that firms face constraints on prices that have not been discussed yet. In the latter case, foreign competition would be a good example. In the former case, one may think of firms having to publish price lists in advance, before wage bargaining is over. There would generally be a lag between the increase in costs and the increase in prices.

Different situations will thus arise, depending on the bargaining positions of firms and of unions, and depending on the time lags or reverse time lags between wage bargaining and price setting. We may consider that there is a long-run equilibrium in a model without technical progress when the actual real wage rate is a constant; that is, when the rate of wage inflation is equal to the rate of price inflation. In such an equilibrium, that is with $\hat{w}$ and $\hat{p}$ equal to each other, the margin of profit is a constant; that is, the $\hat{\kappa}$ variable in equations (7.4) and (7.5) is equal to zero. In inflation accounting terms, it would seem that there is no profits inflation, but it is clear from equations (7.8) and (7.10) that firms and labour unions are equally responsible for the rise in prices. They both use their bargaining power or their possibilities of indexation to obtain what they consider to be their fair share of income. Assuming that the expected price and wage inflations are correctly anticipated, the solution of equations (7.8) and (7.10) when they are equated is given by:

$$\hat{w} = \hat{p} = \mathbf{\Omega}_1(\omega_w - \omega)/(1 - \mathbf{\Omega}_2) = \psi_1(\omega - \omega_f)/(1 - \psi_2) \qquad (7.12)$$

Calling $\mathbf{\Omega}$ the ratio $\mathbf{\Omega}_1/(1-\mathbf{\Omega}_2)$, and calling $\psi$ the ratio $\psi_1/(1-\psi_2)$, the actual real wage rate of such an equilibrium price and wage inflation would be equal to:

$$\omega^* = (\mathbf{\Omega}\omega_w + \psi\omega_f)/(\mathbf{\Omega} + \psi) \qquad (7.13)$$

The real wage rate thus depends on the relative bargaining position of the labour class, a theoretical stance akin to that of the classical authors (Garegnani, 1990, p. 118). As Dalziel (1990) notes, at least three cases can be derived from the above equilibrium relation, two of which are in fact extreme cases. In the first case, firms have either an infinite bargaining power – $\psi_1$ tends to infinity – or they are able to index fully any wage increase, when $\psi_2$ is equal to unity. In either situation, the actual real wage

*Figure 7.1 Conflicting-claims inflation when the firms have absolute bargaining power over the real wage rate*

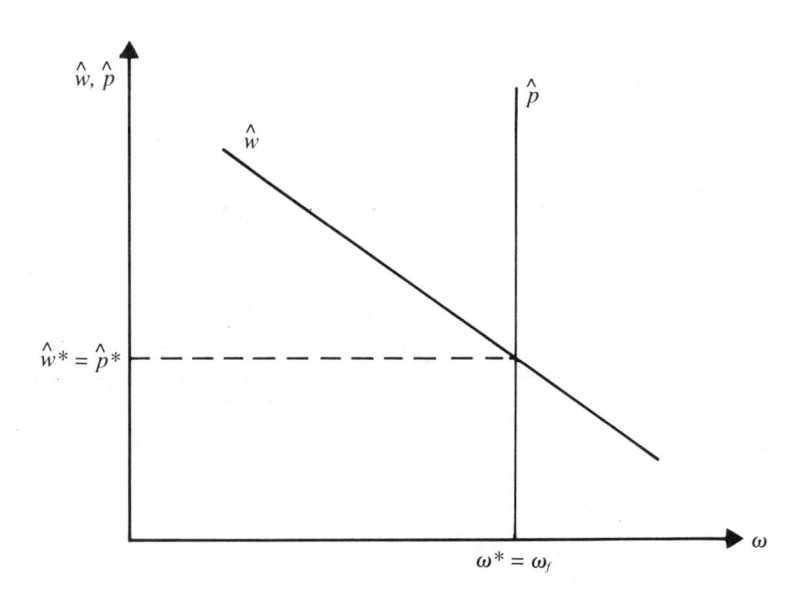

rate, as defined by equation (7.13), will tend towards $\omega_f$, the target real wage rate of firms. Firms do not let the margin of profit fall below its target level and they are able to respond immediately to any increase in their wage costs. This situation corresponds to the one that has been implicitly assumed previously in the book. It is also, I believe, the way mark-up pricing is viewed by most economists. The case of the infinite power of firms over the real wage rate is illustrated in Figure 7.1. A vertical line illustrates the fact that the actual real wage rate can be no different from the target real wage rate of firms, $\omega_f$. The rate of inflation depends on the bargaining power of trade unions, as well as on the discrepancy between the real wage sought by firms and the real wage sought by unions.

The other extreme case arises when labour unions have an absolute power over the real wage rate. This can happen either because they have infinite bargaining power, or because they are able to index fully nominal wages to nominal prices. In either situation, the actual real wage rate gets infinitely close to the real wage rate sought by the labour unions. To this case would seem to correspond the inflation barrier, where 'organised labour has the power to oppose any fall in the real-wage rate' (Robinson,

Figure 7.2 *Conflicting-claims inflation when labour unions have absolute bargaining power over the real wage rate*

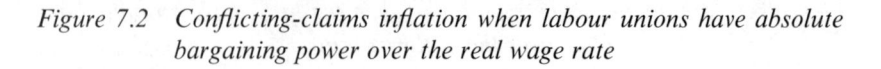

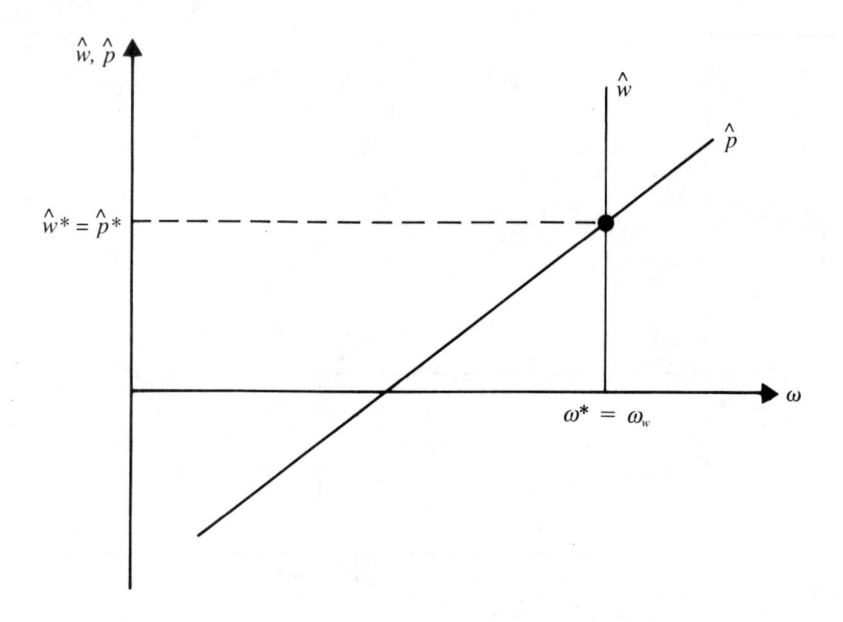

1962, p. 58). Firms are absolutely unable to raise the mark-up and hence decrease the real wage rate. The situation is shown graphically in Figure 7.2. The vertical line illustrates the ability of the trade unions to set the actual real wage rate at the level which they consider to be the fair one. In symmetry to the other extreme case, the rate of inflation is determined by the bargaining power of the firms and the discrepancy between the actual real wage rate and the real wage rate sought by the firms. A mixture of the above two extreme cases would be the South American case of structural inflation, where both the $\Omega_2$ and the $\psi_2$ parameters of indexation are very close to unity, and where there is runaway inflation.

Finally, there is the general case, in which the actual real wage is somewhere in between the targets fixed by the firms and the trade unions. The general case arises when neither group has absolute bargaining power or the ability to index fully wage or price increases. The inconsistent wage claims are made good by inflation and a compromise in the actual real wage rate. This situation is particularly easy to illustrate when there is no indexation, that is when equations (7.9) and (7.11) are the relevant ones. This is shown in Figure 7.3. The upward-sloping curve denoted $\hat{p}$ represents the rate of price inflation at different actual real wages. If the actual

*Figure 7.3* Conflicting-claims inflation when neither the firms nor the labour unions have absolute bargaining power over the real wage rate

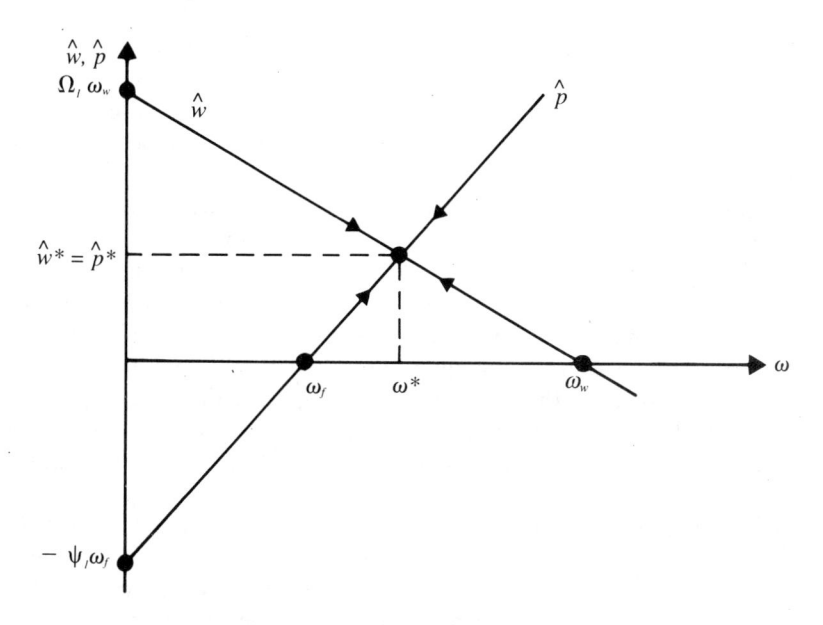

real wage was equal to the target real wage of the firm, the rate of inflation would be zero. The downward-sloping curve marked $\hat{w}$ represents the rate of wage inflation at various actual real wages. The rate of wage inflation would be zero if the actual and the target real wage of the trade unions were equal. This never occurs in the general case, unless the targets of the firms and of labour unions coincide.

The rate of price inflation $\hat{p}$ is at its steady-state level when it is equal to the rate of wage inflation $\hat{w}$, that is where the two curves intersect. This occurs at the intersection of the two lines drawn on the graph, the upward-sloping one representing the rate of price inflation as given by equation (7.11) while the downward-sloping curve represents the rate of wage inflation given by equation (7.9). At this intersection one also finds the real wage rate $\omega^*$ which equates the two inflation rates. It is easily found that $\omega^*$ is a stable equilibrium. If the actual wage rate were to be in excess of $\omega^*$, for instance, that is to the right of $\omega^*$ on the graph, it can be seen that the rate of price inflation would be higher than the rate of wage inflation. It follows that the real wage rate would eventually fall back to its steady-state value $\omega^*$.

### Impact of Changes in Bargaining Positions

In the basic model of inflation which has been presented above, the rate of inflation only depends on the bargaining strength of firms and labour unions and on the discrepancy between their respective target real wages. The rest of the economy, the rate of growth for instance, is assumed not to have any impact on the rate of inflation. Although this is an extreme assumption, which will be relaxed in the next section, it should be noted that Robinson adopts a similar stance in her growth analysis. Referring to Kalecki, she argues that money wages 'follow their own history more or less independently of what is happening to the equilibrium position in real terms', and that the rate of increase of money wages 'can react upon the real position by changing the distribution of real income' (1962, p. 17). We shall follow her intuitions on this issue and examine the impact of changes in bargaining positions on the distribution of income, and hence on the real rate of growth of the economy. To do so, we shall rely on equations (7.9) and (7.11) as we did in Figure 7.3, since these two equations are simpler to represent graphically and since indexation changes little in the analysis.

Let us first examine changes in the bargaining position of workers. The top part of Figure 7.4 illustrates an increase in the target real wage rate of workers, from $\omega_{w1}$ to $\omega_{w2}$. This is represented by a parallel upward shift of the $\hat{w}$ curve. It can be seen that an increase in the real wage sought by labour unions would lead in the end to a higher rate of price and wage inflation, shown on the graph by $\hat{p}_2^*$. Furthermore the new actual real wage rate, given by $\omega_2^*$, would be higher than before the change in the bargaining position of trade unions. None of these results is very surprising. They correspond to what one would expect from a more militant workforce. The analysis of an increase in the bargaining power of the workers would lead to similar results, except that the new upward-shifted $\hat{w}$ curve would not be parallel to the old one, as both curves would originate from the same point on the $\omega$ axis.

It is interesting to examine the effect that a more militant workforce would exert on the real economy. Accompanying the higher rate of inflation, there is then a redistribution in favour of the workers, since the real wage rate is now higher than it was before the change in their bargaining position. According to what was called the canonical Kaleckian model of growth and distribution in Chapter 6, the increase in the real wage rate leads to a higher rate of utilization of capacity and to a higher rate of growth of the economy. This positive relationship is illustrated in the bottom part of Figure 7.4. The exact form of the positive relation between the real wage rate and the real rate of growth depends on the

*Inflation* 399

*Figure 7.4 Higher rate of wage and price inflation and higher rate of accumulation resulting from an increase in the real wage rate sought by labour unions*

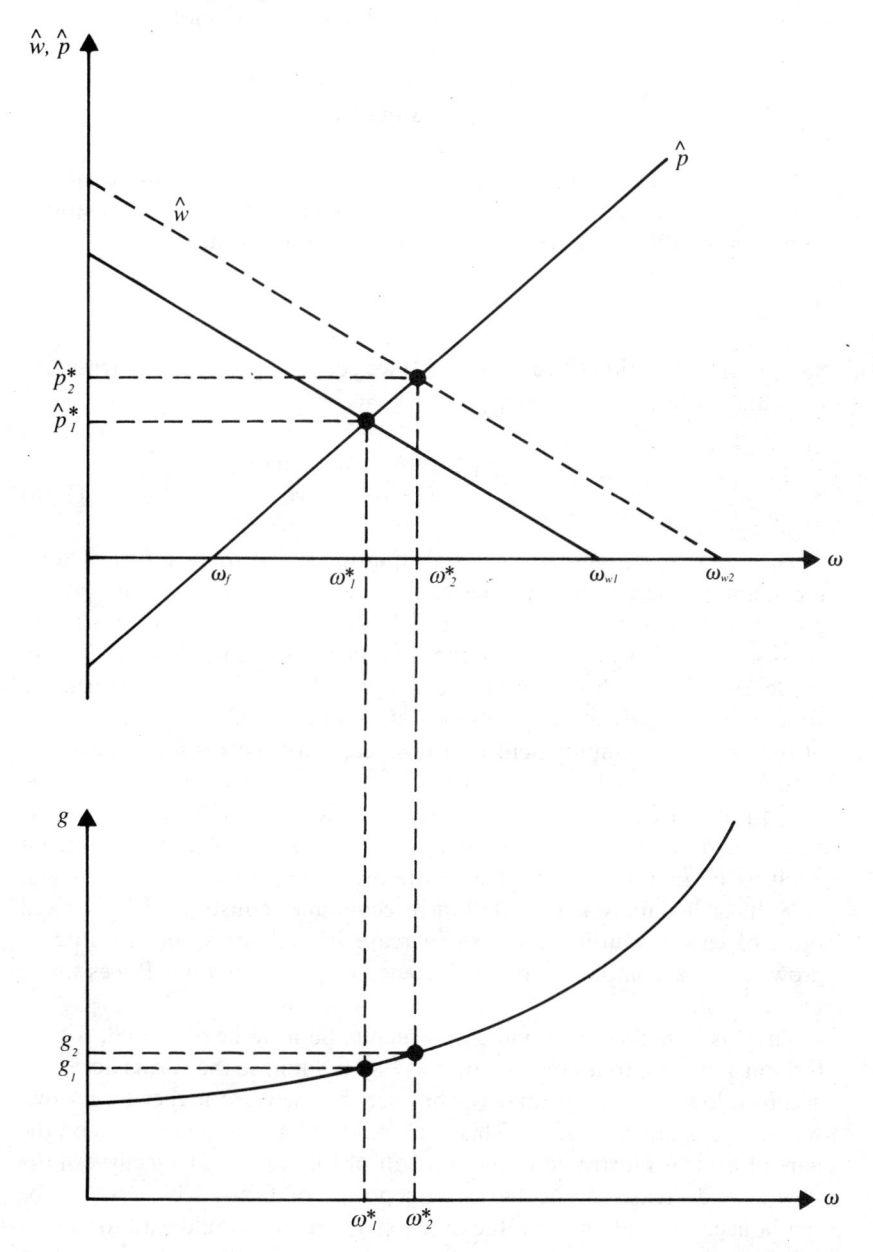

derivatives of the equilibrium growth rate. This equilibrium growth rate can be found by making use of the steady-state rate of capacity utilization (equation 6.33) and of equation (6.20). Supposing as a simplification that $g_r$ equals zero, we obtain in terms of the degree of monopoly $m$:

$$g^* = \gamma + \frac{g_u[s_p(1-m)f + (s_p\delta + b + \gamma)v]}{s_p m - v g_u} \qquad (7.14)$$

The above relation may be rewritten in terms of the real wage rate $\omega$. Making use of equations (5.30) and (3.13), we have the following relationship between the real wage rate and the margin of profit:

$$m = 1 - \omega/y_v \qquad (7.15)$$

Substituting equation (7.15) into (7.14) we get the equilibrium growth rate in terms of the real wage rate:

$$g^* = \gamma + \frac{g_u[(s_p\delta + b + \gamma)v + s_p f \omega/y_v]}{s_p(1 - \omega/y_v) - v g_u} \qquad (7.16)$$

The first and second derivatives of equation (7.16) are positive, yielding the shape of the relationship between the real wage rate and the rate of growth which is shown in Figure 7.4. Provided the first derivative is positive, as is always the case in the canonical growth model, our conflict model of inflation shows that there is a positive relationship between the strength of the bargaining position of the workers and the rate of growth of output and of employment up to full capacity. This is fully consistent with Kalecki's belief that 'a wage rise showing an increase in the trade union power leads ... to an increase in employment' (1971, p. 163). The model also seems to be consistent with the results of the mainstream analysis of inflation, as well as with the results obtained by Marglin (1984b) in his analysis of inflation in economies constrained by a fixed ratio of capacity utilization. An increase in activity – here its rate of growth – is accompanied by an increase in price inflation. Prices move procyclically.

There is, however, a second case which remains to be discussed, that of a change in the bargaining position of firms. Suppose that firms decide to accept a lower mark-up; that is, they set themselves a higher target real wage rate, $\omega_{f2}$, instead of $\omega_{f1}$. This more relaxed bargaining position on the part of firms is illustrated in the top half of Figure 7.5. The $\hat{p}$ curve shifts down. A decrease in the bargaining power of firms, which would be symbolized by a fall in the value of the $\psi$ parameter, would lead to similar

*Figure 7.5 Lower rate of wage and price inflation and higher rate of accumulation resulting from a decrease in the margin of profit sought by firms*

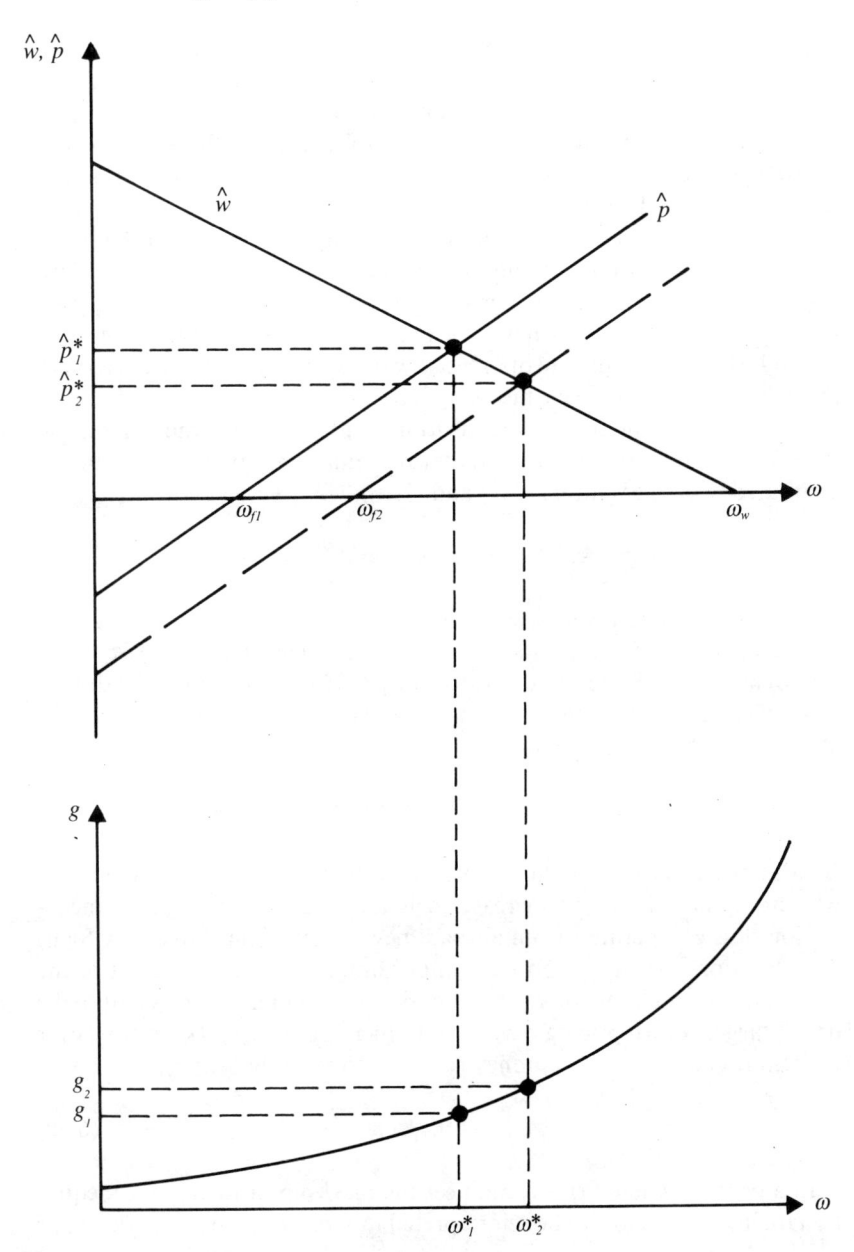

results, except that the new $\hat{p}$ curve would not be parallel to the old one. Weaker monopoly power or more relaxed bargaining on the part of firms leads to higher actual real wage rates ($\omega_2^*$ instead of $\omega_1^*$) and to lower rates of price and wage inflation ($\hat{p}_2^*$ instead of $\hat{p}_1^*$). Looking now at the bottom half of Figure 7.5, we see that lower rates of inflation accompany higher rates of growth. Inflation is counter-cyclical (Dutt, 1987a, p. 81). The mainstream view finds no support in this case.

This surprising result is due to the complementary effects of two key post-Keynesian propositions: a redistribution of income claims in favour of workers speeds up growth; less conflict over income slows down inflation. If firms accept a reduction in their target mark-up, both of these effects should occur until full utilization of capacity is reached. Naturally a rise in the target mark-up of firms, that is a decrease in the real wage rate aimed at by firms, would have the opposite effects: the rate of growth would be lower and the rate of inflation would be higher. The transition to this new situation may be called stagflation.

The impact of the bargaining position of firms and of trade unions on the steady-state rate of price and wage inflation can be algebraically computed. Using equations (7.9) and (7.13), we have:

$$\hat{p}^* = \hat{w}^* = \Omega_1 \psi_1 (\omega_w - \omega_f)/(\Omega_1 + \psi_1) \qquad (7.17)$$

It is obvious that any increase in the discrepancy between the wage offer of firms and the target of labour unions would lead to an increase in the rate of inflation. Since the derivative of $\hat{p}^*$ with respect to $\Omega_1$ and $\psi_1$ is positive, an increase in the bargaining power of firms or of labour unions also leads to higher inflation.

### Conflicting-claims Inflation and the Money Rate of Interest

Besides endogenous economic conditions, there are many reasons as to why firms may decide to increase their target mark-up: higher concentration, less competition from abroad, new social climate. We now focus our attention on another possibly important external determinant of the mark-up, which has already been discussed in Chapter 6. Firms that make use of target-return pricing may want to increase their mark-up whenever the real rate of interest on money rises. This we wrote as:

$$m = m_0 + m_i i \qquad (6.96)$$

In a context where firms cannot set the mark-up of their choice, equation (6.96) would have to be reinterpreted in terms of a target mark-up, or

## Inflation

in terms of a target real wage rate. Let us suppose that the central bank is able to set a real rate of interest, which is simply defined as the difference between the nominal rate of interest on money and the actual rate of price inflation. The real wage sought by firms, as it appears in equation (7.11), would then be equal to:

$$\omega_f = \omega_{f0} - \psi_i i \tag{7.18}$$

This is similar to the formulation adopted by Dutt and Amadeo (1989). The steady-state real wage rate arising from the bargaining process between firms and labour unions, when firms take into account the level of the real rate of money interest, would then be the result of the combination of equations (7.18), (7.11) and (7.9). It would be equal to:

$$\omega^* = (\Omega_1 \omega_w + \psi_1 \omega_{f0} - \psi_i i)/(\Omega_1 + \psi_1) \tag{7.19}$$

As one would expect, the higher the real rate of interest the lower the bargained real wage rate. The introduction of conflict inflation does not change the analysis that was made in Chapter 6 about the impact of the rate of interest on growth and capacity utilization. The analysis was conducted with the help of equation (6.96). We now know that, when firms do not have full control over the mark-up, the actual real wage rate is determined by equation (7.19). Expressing the real wage rate in terms of the degree of monopoly with the help of equation (7.15), this implies that the parameters $m_0$ and $m_i$ of equation (6.91) must be reinterpreted as being equal to:

$$m_0 = 1 - (\Omega_1 \omega_w + \psi_1 \omega_{f0})/y_v(\Omega_1 + \psi_1) \tag{7.20}$$

$$m_i = \psi_i/y_v(\Omega_1 + \psi_1) \tag{7.21}$$

The above two equations shows that all the results that were previously obtained with respect to interest rates, notably those of Table 6.2, need not be modified. The upshot of the present analysis is that, whereas before the $m_0$ and $m_i$ parameters were exogenous, they are now endogenous, determined by other parameters.

It should be noted that an increase in the real rate of interest, if it is passed on to consumers, leads to an increase in the rate of price inflation. This can be seen in the upper part of Figure 7.5, by supposing that an increase in the real rate of interest shifts the real wage rate sought by firms from $\omega_{f2}$ to $\omega_{f1}$. The rate of price inflation would then rise from $\hat{p}_2^*$ to $\hat{p}_1^*$. Since several post-Keynesian authors have argued that interest costs, like wage costs, are passed on through higher prices, it is not surprising to find that some post-Keynesians have underlined the possibility of a positive relationship between real rates of interest and price inflation (Hotson, 1976, pp. 103, 144). At best, a policy of higher interest rates may induce higher real growth, as shown in Table 6.2, accompanied by higher inflation rates. When real interest rates have a negative impact on real growth, austere monetary policies bring about the worst of all possible worlds: lower real growth and higher inflation rates. Stagflation in this sense can only be remedied by structural change: the values of the parameters representing the bargaining positions of both the firms and the trade unions must be weakened. One needs a feedback relation from the endogenous variables of the economy to the desired real wage rates.

Before we examine such feedback relations, let us briefly consider some implications of a feedback effect of the rate of inflation on the real variables of the model. It could be that fiscal policy is sensitive to the rate of inflation. Governments would decide to reduce their budgetary deficit when the rate of inflation rises. There would be a reaction function of budgetary policies with respect to the rate of inflation. Recalling that $b$ is the government deficit per unit of capital, one could imagine a feedback relation of the type:

$$b = b_0 - b_{\hat{p}}\hat{p} \tag{7.22}$$

The rate of inflation being given by equation (7.16), this equation can be rewritten as:

$$b = b_0 + b_{\hat{p}}'(\omega_f - \omega_w) \tag{7.23}$$

Recalling that any rise in $\omega_w$ and $\omega_f$ increases the actual real wage rate, while any increase in the real wage rate and in government deficit leads to a higher rate of output growth in the canonical Kaleckian model, it is clear that a higher real wage sought by firms can only have favourable effects on the economy. By contrast, if the $b_{\hat{p}}'$ coefficient is sufficiently strong, an increase in the real wage rate sought by workers could provoke a slowdown of the economy. The higher inflation induced by the more militant demands of the workers could induce such a restrictive fiscal stance that its negative effects on accumulation could overwhelm the direct favourable effects of a higher negotiated real wage rate. If governments are concerned with inflation, and if they take strong fiscal measures to combat inflation, a more militant workforce may thus have detrimental effects on the economy.

## 7.5 VARIANTS OF THE CONFLICTING-CLAIMS MODEL OF INFLATION

We now study some of the specific variants of the conflicting-claims model of inflation, taking into account endogenous targets, wage–wage inflation, technical progress, and target-return pricing.

**Endogenous Real Wage Targets of Workers**

It has been assumed up to now that the real wage targets set by the trade unions and the firms are not influenced by the pressures or the absence of pressures from demand. In view of the standard Phillips curve, this appears to be a somewhat extreme assumption. It may be interesting to see to what extent the conflict model of inflation is modified when demand considerations enter into it. In his own presentation of conflict inflation, Rowthorn (1977, p. 219) considers that the real wage sought by workers is reduced when surplus labour rises; similarly, the mark-up sought by firms is reduced when there is surplus capacity. We will here assume that the real wage sought by workers is proportional to the rate of growth of the economy and that the real wage rate sought by firms is inversely related to the rate of utilization of capacity. It could also have been assumed that the bargaining power of labour unions and firms, as reflected by the $\Omega$ and $\psi$ parameters, varies with the rate of growth and the rate of capacity utilization, but it would not change the analysis.

Let us first deal with the target set by trade unions. In its traditional version, the Phillips curve asserts that there is a negative relation between the rate of wage inflation and the rate of unemployment. Introducing this typical Phillips curve into the present model requires the use of a complex dynamic model. Indeed the rate of unemployment $U$, or its complement the rate of employment $E$, cannot be constant unless the rate of growth of the economy turns out to be exactly equal to the natural rate of growth. This can be shown in the following way. Recall that $L$ and $L_{fc}$ are the employed labour force and the labour force that would be employed at full employment. The rate of employment is then equal to:

$$E = 1 - U = L/L_{fc} \tag{7.24}$$

In dynamic terms, the rate of growth of the employment rate is equal to the difference between the rate of growth of employment and the rate of growth $n$ of the employable labour force. If there is neutral technical progress, the rate of growth of employment is equal to the real rate of growth of the economy minus the rate of technical progress. This can be seen from the combination of equations (6.35) and (7.24).

$$\hat{E} = g_L - n = g - \lambda - n \tag{7.25}$$

For the rate of employment or the rate of unemployment to be constant, the rate of growth of the economy needs to be exactly equal to the natural rate of growth, $n+\lambda$. This would unduly restrict the model to a single possible growth rate. One would be back to the neoclassical model. This is why post-Keynesian models of growth are not based on the assumption of a given rate of unemployment. However, if the target real wage rate of workers is made a function of the rate of employment, as is done by some post-Keynesian authors (Skott, 1989; Dutt, 1991), complex interactions with limit cycles and the like arise. In the present chapter we will simply suppose that the real wage rate sought by workers is a function of the *rate of growth* of unemployment, rather than the *level* of unemployment. As a further simplification, we will suppose that the target real wage rate is a linear function of the rate of change of the employment rate $\hat{E}$. It follows from equation (7.25) that the real wage rate sought by workers is a function of the real rate of growth of the economy. We have:

$$\omega_w = \omega_{w0} + \Omega_g g \tag{7.26}$$

Wage inflation is thus determined in the following way:

$$\hat{w} = \Omega_1(\omega_{w0} + \Omega_g g - \omega) \tag{7.27}$$

We may call equation (7.27) a quasi-Phillips curve. The foundations which underlie this particular version of the Phillips curve are more reasonable than they would first appear to someone accustomed to intermediate mainsteam macroeconomics. From very early on in the history of the Phillips curve it was empirically shown that the rate of wage inflation is significantly influenced by *the rate of change* of unemployment (Bowen and Berry, 1963). The same claim has been recently reasserted in the mainstream literature (Gordon, 1989). The main justification for equations (7.26) and (7.27) is that, as was discussed in the previous section, only the threat to affluence may slow down inflationary forces. If the rate of unemployment is constant, those still having a job do not feel that their job or their income is being threatened. Employed workers, who generally constitute the majority of workers, have little reasons to fear the possibility of unemployment. There will be little pressure on trade union leaders to sacrifice wage increases for the hope of a better employment outlook, even if the rate of unemployment is high. By contrast, workers may fear the possibility of losing their jobs if the rate of unemployment is rising. The faster it is rising, the more threatened workers feel, and the more likely they are to waive real wage objectives. 'The mechanism of the reserve army, in other words, requires not only the existence of unemployment but a *threat* to those still employed' (Boddy and Crotty, 1975, p. 10). It must be recognized, however, that the rate of unemployment cannot rise forever. The economy is in a leaden age (Robinson, 1962, p. 54). At some point there will be a structural break in the economy; that is, the values of the parameters will have to change.

We now examine how the endogeneity of the real wage rate sought by workers affects the analysis of conflict inflation. Figure 7.6 illustrates this slightly more complex variant. The top part of Figure 7.6 represents the two components of equation (7.27). The ω component is shown by the straight line while the sum of the constant term and of the $g$ term is represented by the upward sloping curve. We know the shape of this curve from equation (7.16) and the bottom part of Figure 7.4; that is, the canonical post-Keynesian model of growth and distribution is assumed to be valid. The distance between the curve and the straight line is in proportion to the rate of increase of wages. The $\hat{w}$ curve so derived is reproduced in the bottom part of Figure 7.6.

In the present case, the quasi-Phillips curve $\hat{w}$ is non-linear. Because of the curvature of the relationship between real wages and output growth, there are two levels of real wages that would correspond to the target real wage rate set by the labour unions. Let us call them $\omega_l$ and $\omega_h$. If firms had real wage targets of either $\omega_l$ or $\omega_h$, accumulation could proceed without price and wage inflation. At the lower of these two wage rates, $\omega_l$, the rate of growth is slow. At the higher wage rate, $\omega_h$, accumulation proceeds at a rapid pace. There are two possible rates of growth and hence two possible rates of growth of unemployment at which accumulation could proceed without inflation. Indeed to any rate of inflation corresponds two possible rates of accumulation.

The $\hat{p}$ curves in Figure 7.6 have been drawn in such a way that all intersections with the $\hat{w}$ curve are stable equilibria. If the $\hat{p}$ curves had been drawn flatter, however, that is, if it had been assumed that firms have little bargaining power, all points on the rising portion of the $\hat{w}$ curve would have been unstable candidates for equilibrium. Only the falling portion of the $\hat{w}$ curve would have been relevant and one would be back to the analysis pursued previously in Figure 7.5, when the complications of an endogenous real wage target were being ignored. If the rising portion of the $\hat{w}$ curve is pertinent, as it is in Figure 7.6, it should be noted that a fall in the real wage rate sought by the firms may lead to a reduction in the rate of wage and price inflation. A shift of the $\hat{p}$ curve from $\hat{p}_1$ to $\hat{p}_2$ would bring down the rate of price and wage inflation. This is because the impact on the real wage sought by labour unions of the fall in the rate of output growth overwhelms the impact of the fall in the actual real wage rate.

In this context, the analysis of an increase in the real rate of money

408   *Foundations of Post-Keynesian Economic Analysis*

*Figure 7.6   The wage inflation curve when labour unions respond to changes in the rate of unemployment and when the wage-led underconsumptionist regime prevails*

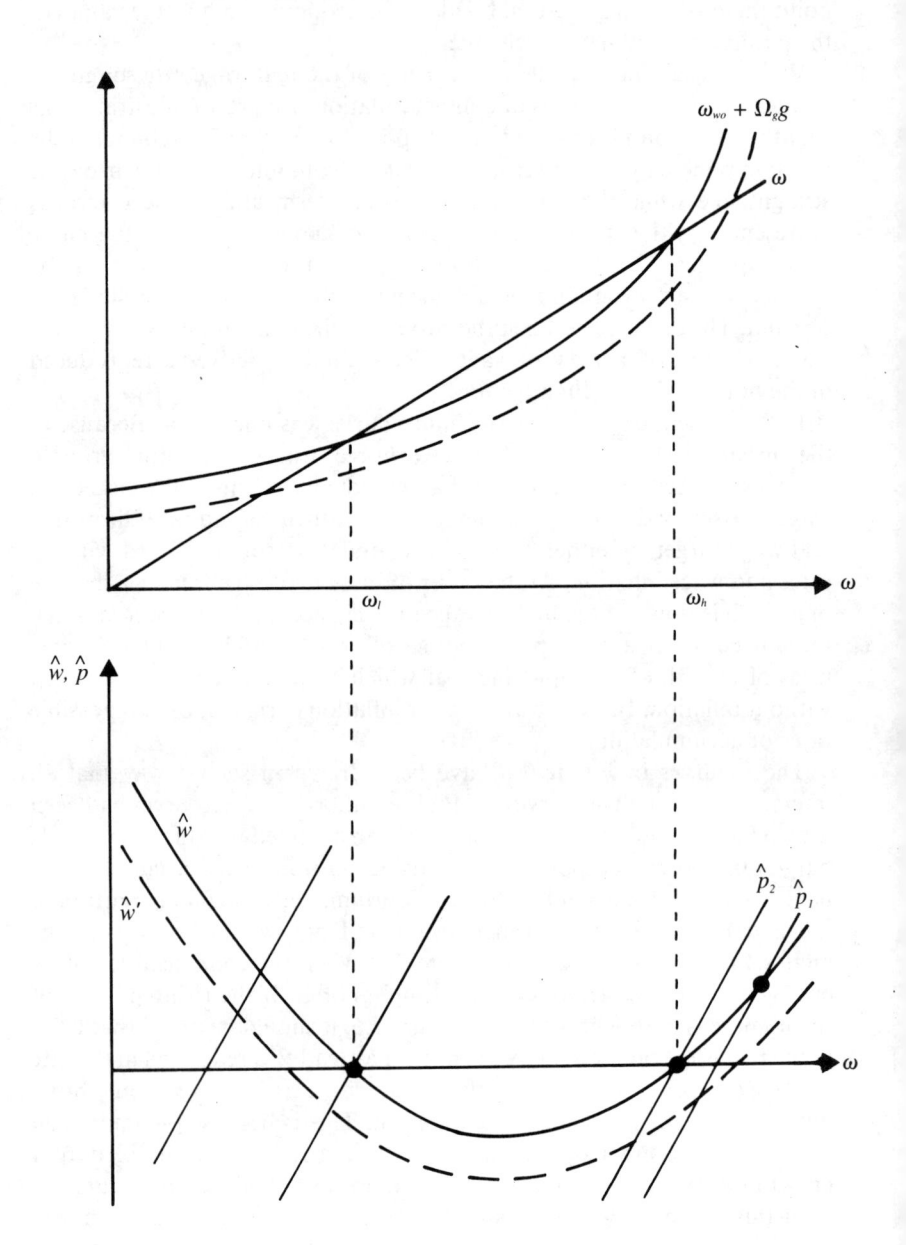

interest is particularly interesting. Consider that the shifts of the $\hat{p}$ curve are solely due to the exogenous variations in the real rate of interest. The modifications in the real wage rate will then be solely caused by the changes in interest rates. Let us suppose that the overall effects on the rate of accumulation of these variations in the real rate of interest lead to a curve in the ($\omega$, $g$) space which has a shape similar to that of the curve drawn in the bottom part of Figure 7.5. It could then be concluded that a rise in the real rate of money interest would be able to bring the rate of inflation down, provided the economy is on the upward-sloping portion of the $\hat{w}$ curve. For instance, increases in real interest rates that would shift the $\hat{p}$ curve from $\hat{p}_1$ to $\hat{p}_2$ would simultaneously bring down the rate of inflation and the rate of accumulation.

If firms do not adopt a target-return pricing procedure, but rather a simple mark-up procedure that does not take changes in interest rates into consideration, there will be an inverse relationship between real interest rates and inflation provided there exists an inverse relation between real interest rates and accumulation. When these two conditions hold, an increase in the real rate of interest does not shift the $\hat{p}$ curve, but it shifts down the whole $\hat{w}$ curve, leading to a fall in the rate of wage and price inflation. What happens is that the rise in the rate of interest shifts down the curve in the ($\omega,g$) plane, which is drawn under the *ceteris paribus* clause. This is illustrated in the top part of Figure 7.6 by the shift from the unbroken curve to the dotted one. The fall in the rate of output growth, given the actual real wage rate, leads to a fall in the real wage being sought by the workers. The implications of this shift are shown in the bottom part of Figure 7.6: there is a shift of the wage inflation curve from $\hat{w}$ to $\hat{w}'$. For a given target of firms, that is a given $\hat{p}$ curve, the actual real wage rate and the steady-state rate of inflation fall. In addition to the slower rate of output growth, the final results of the restrictive policies of the monetary authorities are thus a lower real wage rate and a lower rate of inflation. Therefore, even when firms do not pass on interest costs by increasing their profit margins, there is some justification in claiming that austere monetary policies are restrictive real wage policies in disguise.

On the other hand, if higher real interest rates lead to higher rates of accumulation, and they could, as we have seen in Table 6.2, increased interest rates would induce higher real wages and higher inflation. In Figure 7.6 there would be a shift from the $\hat{w}'$ curve to the $\hat{w}$ curve.

## Endogenous Real Wage Targets of Firms

Let us now deal with the question of an endogenous real wage rate sought by firms. In their conflict models of inflation, most authors assume that the target set by firms is influenced by the rate of utilization of capacity (Rowthorn, 1977; Dutt, 1991b). Such an assumption is based on the notion that, as firms approach full utilization of capacity, the laws of demand and supply begin to supplant cost-plus pricing procedures. Being near full capacity encourages businesses to take advantage of high demand conditions and to increase margins of profit. It makes no difference to the analysis to assume that this effect is generalized to all levels of the rate of utilization, and that the target mark-up generally increases with the rate of utilization of capacity. The target real wage rate, as seen by the firm, is then equal to:

$$\omega_f = \omega_{f0} - \psi_u u \qquad (7.28)$$

Price inflation, given by equation (7.11), is now equal to:

$$\hat{p} = \psi_1(\omega - \omega_{f0} + \psi_u u) \qquad (7.29)$$

It should be noted that very little difference to the analysis would occur if it was assumed instead that the mark-up sought by firms is a function of the rate of growth of the economy. We have seen in Chapter 6 that many post-Keynesians (Eichner, 1976; Harcourt and Kenyon, 1976) believe that faster accumulation induces firms to set higher mark-ups, the firms attempting in this way to meet their greater requirements of financial funds from internal sources. This led us to consider a tuned-down version of what we called the Eichnerian model, which we wrote as:

$$m = m_0 + m_g g \qquad (6.94)$$

In a model with conflicting income claims and powerful labour unions, firms cannot set the mark-up as they wish. As in the case of interest costs, the costs of growth have an impact on the actual real wage rate through their impact on the real wage rate sought by the firms when they bargain with the trade unions. One would have:

$$\omega_f = \omega_{f0} - \psi_g g \qquad (7.30)$$

In general, using equation (7.30) rather than equation (7.28) will make no difference to the qualitative results of the analysis. In particular, in the canonical Kaleckian model of growth and distribution, output growth and the rate of capacity utilization move in an almost identical manner, as can be seen from equations (6.33) and (7.14).

The $\hat{p}$ curve as defined by equation (7.30), the rate of accumulation $g$

*Figure 7.7* The wage inflation and the price inflation curves when the wage-led underconsumptionist regime prevails and when both labour unions and firms respond to economic conditions when they set their real wage targets

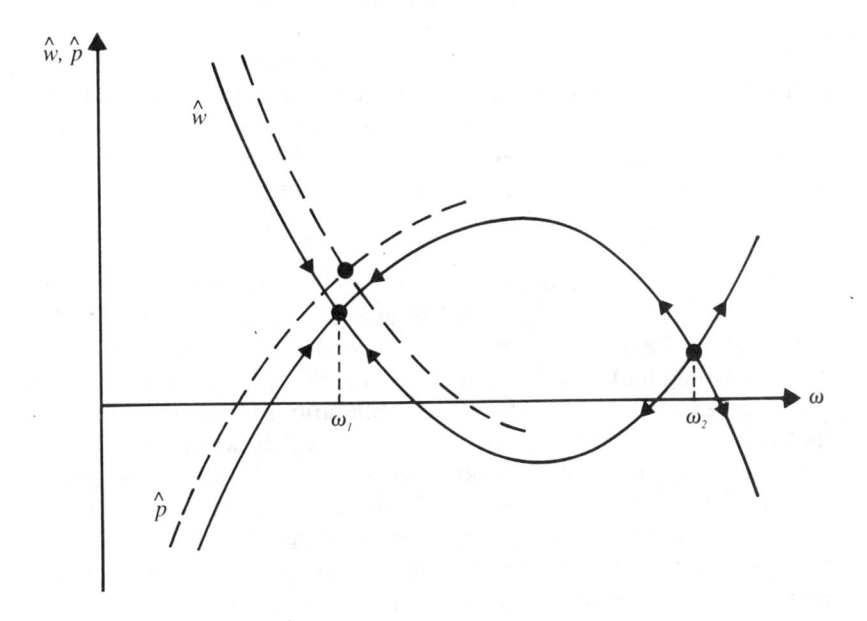

being given by equation (7.14), is illustrated in Figure 7.7. Its shape can be derived in a manner which is similar to the one used to obtain the $\hat{w}$ curve in Figure 7.6. The $\hat{p}$ curve, like the $\hat{w}$ curve, is non-linear. As a result, there are two possible equilibria, that is two wage rates for which the rate of price inflation is equal to the rate of wage inflation. These two real wage rates are denoted by $\omega_1$ and $\omega_2$. It is immediately apparent that the $\omega_1$ position is stable whereas the $\omega_2$ position is not. If the real wage rate turned out to be slightly inferior to $\omega_1$, the rate of wage inflation would exceed that of price inflation, and the real wage rate would return to $\omega_1$. The $\omega_1$ equilibrium is thus stable. By contrast, if the real wage rate were slightly below $\omega_2$, price inflation would exceed wage inflation until finally the real wage rate had fallen to $\omega_1$. The $\omega_2$ equilibrium is unstable.

The analysis of Figure 7.7 therefore shows that, if we assume the target real wage rate of both workers and firms to be endogenously determined, we can ignore the second equilibrium and proceed as if the $\hat{p}$ and $\hat{w}$ curves had the expected linear shapes. Introducing endogenous real wage targets does not change the basic conflicting-claims analysis of inflation that was pursued with the help of Figures 7.4 and 7.5. We might as well assume away the rising portion of the $\hat{w}$ curve and the falling portion of the $\hat{p}$ curve. In particular, it should be pointed out that any exogenous change that leads to an increase in the rate of growth would induce higher wage and price inflation. This would be the case, for instance, when there are more favourable entrepreneurial animal spirits (a higher $\gamma$ parameter). Such a possibility is illustrated in Figure 7.7, both curves shifting to their dotted lines. Indeed it is enough for one of the two curves to be sensitive to the rate of growth of the economy for this effect to occur. In particular, when firms increase their profit margins as the rate of accumulation increases, steady-state wage and price inflation rises. The Eichnerian model is prone to this effect, an outcome which we previously called profits inflation or structural inflation.

All of the above analysis has been conducted on the basis of the results obtained with the canonical model of growth and distribution that was presented in Chapter 6. The reader may wonder whether this analysis of inflation would look any different if the canonical model was replaced by the so-called over-accumulation and exhilarationist regimes. Figure 7.8 illustrates the case of the over-accumulation regime when the real wage rate sought by firms depends on either the growth rate or the rate of capacity utilization. As one may recall from Table 6.1, the former variable is inversely related to the actual real wage while the latter is directly related to the real wage. This explains the different sign of the slopes of the two curves shown in the upper part of Figure 7.8. It can be seen that, outside the canonical model, the $\hat{p}$ curve incorporating an endogenous target mark-up is always upward-sloping. Introducing the various growth regimes of Table 6.1 would accordingly leave unchanged the conflicting-claims analysis of inflation that was pursued with exogenous real wage targets. The same reasoning applies to the $\hat{w}$ curve: in over-accumulation and exhilarationist regimes, the $\hat{w}$ curve is always downward-sloping.

One must thus conclude that the introduction of endogenous real wage targets, at least in the manner in which they were introduced here, does not change substantially the basic analysis of real wage targets. An exogenous strengthening of the bargaining position of the trade unions leads to higher real wages and higher inflation; an exogenous weakening of the bargaining position of the firms also leads to higher real wages but to lower inflation. The impact of these exogenous changes on the rate of accumulation and the rate of growth of unemployment depends on the growth regime to which the economy is subjected. This is shown in Table 7.1. It can be seen that stagflation, that is a combination of slower output growth and higher inflation rates, can occur in all regimes, without having to resort to mistaken expectations.

*Figure 7.8 The price inflation curve when firms respond to economic conditions and when the over-accumulation regime prevails*

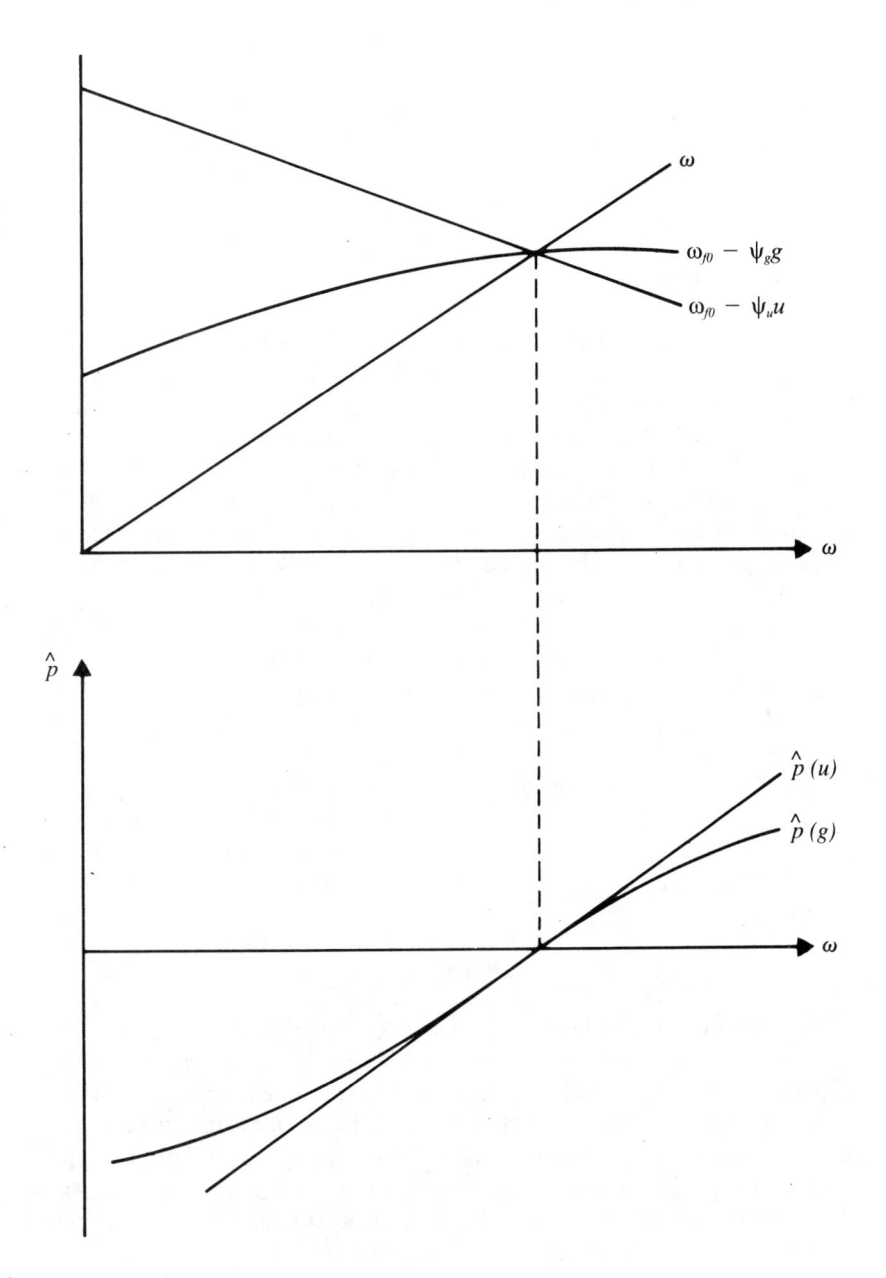

*Table 7.1 Growth regimes and exogenous changes in bargaining positions*

| Growth regime | Stronger trade unions | Stronger firms |
|---|---|---|
| Underconsumptionist | Faster accumulation<br>Higher inflation | Slower accumulation<br>Higher inflation |
| Over-accumulation and exhilarationist | Slower accumulation<br>Higher inflation | Faster accumulation<br>Higher inflation |

**Wage–wage Inflation**

Up to now, the rate of inflation has been solely explained in terms of a conflict between wage-earners on one side and firms and rentiers on the other. No attention was paid to the conflicts within the labour class, arising because of the importance of retaining one's position in the socio-economic hierarchy. While simple models of wage–wage inflation based on a reaction matrix have been provided elsewhere (Chowdhury, 1983), the intent of the present subsection is to accommodate the presence of wage–wage inflation in the conflicting-claims model of inflation. As we do so, technical progress will also be discussed.

The major characteristic of wage–wage inflation is that inflation would continue even if firms and trade unions in general agreed on a real wage target. Past attempts at catching up create a backlog of recriminations, some groups of workers believing that they have been left behind in the previous round of negotiations. The attempt by each group of workers to re-establish what they consider to be their rightful place in the social hierarchy leads to a trend of rising wages. The wage inflation curve, previously written in its basic form under equation (7.9), thus needs an additional constant term, reflecting the wage–wage inflation trend, here called $\Omega_{ww}$.

$$\hat{w} = \Omega_1(\omega_w - \omega) + \Omega_{ww} \tag{7.31}$$

As is obvious from Figure 7.9, once wage–wage inflation is taken into account, it is impossible for the rate of inflation to reach zero unless the real wage sought by firms is smaller than the real wage sought by workers. It can be seen from the graph that, when workers and firms agree on the same real wage target $\omega_w$, the rate of wage and price inflation is $\hat{p}_1{}^*$, whereas there is no inflation when firms set a real wage target of $\omega_f > \omega_w$. This inequality would seem to be a rather peculiar situation, which would arise very rarely indeed. Yet, before the Second World war, it was not

*Figure 7.9 Adding wage–wage inflation to a conflict model of inflation: the rate of inflation is positive although firms and labour unions agree on their real wage targets*

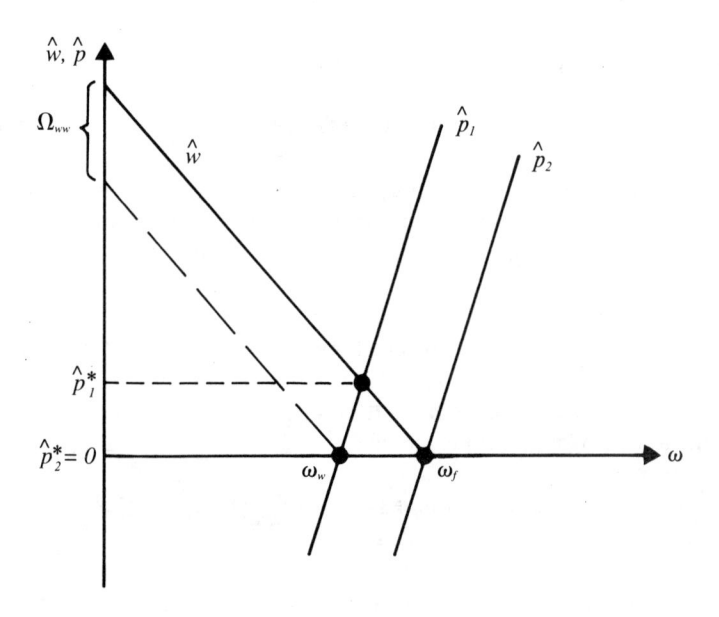

uncommon to observe long periods of stable prices. Since it is very unlikely that firms would set target real wage rates in excess of those fixed by trade unions for a long period of time, one must either conclude that the hypothesis of wage–wage inflation is incorrect or that some omitted factor must also be added to our basic inflation model. Increases in productivity are perhaps the required additional element in favour of the wage–wage inflation hypothesis, as we shall now see.

Technical progress can be added to the basic model of inflation in at least two ways. First, it could be argued that the higher the rate of technical progress the higher the wage inflation induced by wage–wage conflict, that is the higher $\Omega_{ww}$. This would be caused by the large nominal wage increases that would be demanded in sectors with large productivity increases. Sectors with low increases in productivity would ask for similar increases in wages, based on those obtained in sectors with high rates of technical progress. This is what some authors have called productivity-led inflation (Hicks, 1955). It is tightly linked to wage–wage inflation. A second possible impact of the rate of technical progress has been proposed by Rowthorn (1977, p. 238): 'Workers may be prepared to trade a lower share of output in return for a faster rise in real wages.' The target real wage rate of workers would thus be inversely related to the rate of technical progress. We shall ignore for now this second possible effect. Let $\lambda$ denote as before the rate of technical progress. Also, from now on, let $\omega$ denote the level of efficient wages; that is, $\omega = (w/p)/y_v$, to take into account changes in productivity. The $\hat{w}$ curve can be rewritten as:

$$\hat{w} = \Omega_1(\omega_w - \omega) + \Omega_{ww0} + \Omega_\lambda \lambda \qquad (7.32)$$

On the side of the firms, one may suppose that productivity increases are partially or fully passed on to consumers. If a proportion $\psi_\lambda$ of the productivity gains are passed on in the form of lower prices, the $\hat{p}$ equation can be rewritten as:

$$\hat{p} = \psi_1(\omega - \omega_f) - \psi_\lambda \lambda \qquad (7.33)$$

With technical progress, a constant $\omega$ requires that $\hat{w} = \hat{p} + \lambda$. Solving for $\omega$, the above two equations yield:

$$\omega^* = \frac{\Omega_1 \omega_w + \psi_1 \omega_f + \Omega_{ww0} + [\Omega_\lambda - (1 - \psi_\lambda)]\lambda}{\Omega_1 + \psi_1} \qquad (7.34)$$

The elements in the square brackets of equation (7.34) show that an increase in productivity would have no impact on the actual efficient real wage rate whenever the share of productivity gains $(1 - \psi_\lambda)$ that firms decline to pass on to consumers is equal to the share $\Omega_\lambda$ of these gains that workers wish to translate into nominal wage increases. When the $\Omega_\lambda$ parameter is relatively excessive, the economy is in the Fordist regime discussed in Chapter 6: there is a positive relation between efficient wages and technical progress. When the $\Omega_\lambda$ parameter is weak, the economy is in an anti-Fordist regime: the relation between efficient real wages and technical progress is negative. When workers are prepared to trade lower efficient wages for a faster rise in real wages, as suggested by Rowthorn, the economy is also in an anti-Fordist regime.

When there is technical progress and wage–wage inflation, a zero rate of price inflation does not require the equality of the profit margin targets set by labour unions and firms; that is, the efficient wage rates sought by unions and firms do not have to be equal. Figure 7.10 offers one of the many possibilities arising when there is no price inflation. The level of efficient wages $\omega^*$ which ensures a constant profit margin is given by the intersection of the $\hat{w}$ curve and the curve marked $\hat{p} + \lambda$. This yields the steady-state rate of wage inflation $\hat{w}^*$. The vertical projection on the $\hat{p}$

*Figure 7.10* Wage–wage inflation and technical progress combined in a conflict model of inflation: a divergence between wage inflation and price inflation

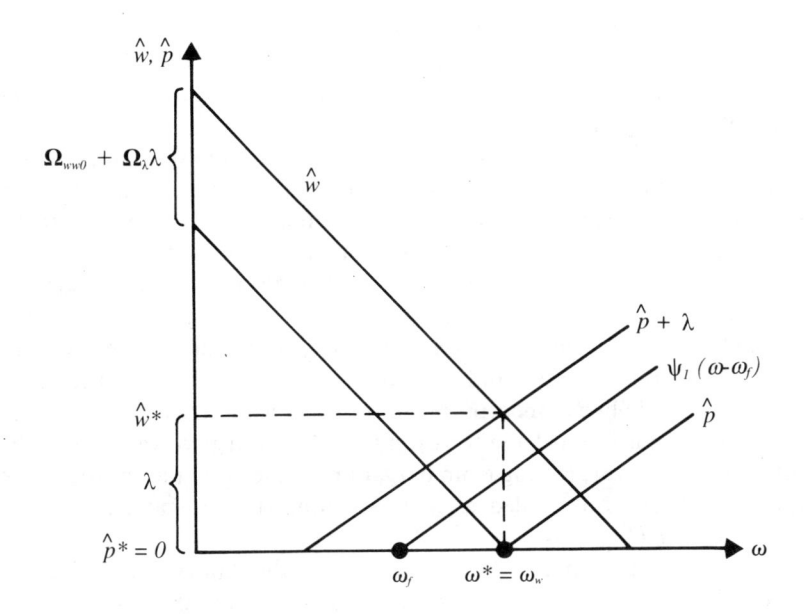

curve yields the steady-state rate of price inflation $\hat{p}^*$, here zero. Because of the presence of technical progress and of wage–wage inflation, situations that would seem impossible in the basic inflation model may arise. Here wage and price curves have been so constructed that there is no price inflation, despite the fact that the actual efficient wage rate is above the rate sought by firms ($\omega^* > \omega_f$). On the other hand, there is wage inflation despite the actual efficient wage rate being equal to the rate sought by labour unions ($\omega^* = \omega_w$).

## Target-return Pricing and Bargaining

We close our discussion of inflation by returning to endogenous real wage targets and target-return pricing procedures. While endogenous real wage targets may not modify the basic analysis of conflict inflation, it helps to solve a puzzle that was encountered in Chapter 6. The puzzle arose in the discussion of the implications of target-return pricing. The reader may recall that, if firms adjust the standard rate of return to the actual rate of profit, along the lines given by equations (6.89) and (6.90), the rate of capacity utilization of the economy eventually comes to rest at precisely its standard rate, which is predetermined by convention. In this antinomic variant of the Kaleckian model of growth and distribution, the trade-off between real wages and the rate of growth reappears. The rate of utilization becomes exogenous, as in neoclassical, neo-Marxian and early post-Keynesian models. To save the Kaleckian features of the model, it had to be assumed that the adjustment of the standard rate of return is non-existent or sluggish.

We are now in a position to give an explanation as to why the standard rate of return may fully adjust to the actual rate of profit, *without* the rate of utilization of capacity becoming exogenous. To do so, it has to be recognized once again that firms are not in a position to set the exact mark-up of their choice. One must thus distinguish between two sorts of margins of profit: the actual margin of profit, which arises from the bargaining process, and the target margin of profit, which corresponds to the standard rate of return and the standard rate of utilization of capacity that firms would like to incorporate into their pricing strategy. In terms of wage rates, one would have to distinguish between two wage rates: the actual real wage rate arising from bargaining, called $\omega^*$, and the real wage rate sought by firms, called $\omega_f$, corresponding to the standard rate of return *assessed* by firms.

Let us assume, then, that firms slowly adjust the standard rate of return according to the actual rate of profit, as is shown in the expression below:

$$r_{s(t)} = \phi r_{s(t-1)} + (1-\phi)r_{(t-1)} \quad \phi < 1 \qquad (6.90)$$

A long-run steady-state position is reached when the standard rate of return is the same in two successive periods; that is, when the standard rate of return and the actual rate of return are equal. In a world where trade unions have some bargaining power, the standard rate of return does not correspond to the actual real wage rate but rather to the real wage rate sought by firms. The process described by equation (6.90) may thus come to an end without the steady-state standard rate of return being actually incorporated in prices. This means that the rate of capacity utilization emerging from the adjustment process of the standard rate of return is not necessarily the standard rate of utilization, and that as a consequence the rate of utilization is endogenous despite the existence of this adjustment process. Going back to the formula defining target-return pricing, that is equation (5.35), we can make the following distinction. The real wage sought by firms is equal to:

$$\omega_f = y_v(u_s - r_s v)/(u_s + f) \qquad (7.35)$$

while the real wage which arises from the bargaining process is equal to:

$$\omega^* = y_v(u_s - r_s^* v)/(u_s + f) \tag{7.36}$$

where $r_s^*$ is the standard rate of return which is actually incorporated into the pricing formula.

The adjustment process, when the actual rate of profit is initially larger than the standard rate of return, is illustrated in Figure 7.11. Let us start from a situation in which the real wage rates desired by firms and by workers coincide, as shown on the left-hand side of the graph. There the $\hat{p}_1$ and the $\hat{w}$ curves intersect the $\omega$ axis at the same point, the real wage rate $\omega_w$. We have the triple equality: $\omega_w = \omega_{f1} = \omega_1^*$. This implies, as is obvious from equations (7.35) and (7.36), that the standard rate of return initially assessed by firms, called $r_{s1}$, and the standard rate of return incorporated in the pricing formula, called $r_{s1}^*$, are equal. We can draw the profits cost curve corresponding to this situation, shown on the right-hand side of the graph as $PC(\omega_w)$. For the given effective demand conditions, illustrated by the $ED$ curve, the actual rate of utilization of capacity is $u_1$, and the actual rate of profit is $r_1$. The actual rate of profit $r_1$ is thus much superior to the standard rate of return $r_{s1}$. As a result, firms will slowly revise upwards the standard rate of return $r_s$, along the lines of equation (6.90), as was illustrated in Figure 6.19. The real wage rate $\omega_f$ aimed at by firms, as defined by equation (7.35), would thus start to fall.

Two phenomena will now arise. First, as firms revise their estimate of what the standard rate of return is, a discrepancy arises between the real wage rate sought by firms and the real wage rate sought by workers. As a consequence the actual real wage rate becomes different from the real wage sought by firms, and hence a similar discrepancy arises between the standard rate of return *assessed by firms* and the standard rate of return *incorporated into prices*. Second, as real wages diminish, the actual rate of profit falls. There is thus a convergence between the rate of profit which falls and the standard rate of return which rises.

The end result is shown in Figure 7.11. Firms are seeking a real wage rate of $\omega_{f2}$, and hence a standard rate of return of $r_{s2}$. Because of the bargaining power of labour, inflation occurs at a rate of $\hat{p}_2^*$ while the actual real wage rate is $\omega_2^*$. At that rate, the new profits cost curve $PC(\omega_2^*)$ is such that the actual rate of profit, $r_2$ and the standard rate of return *assessed by firms*, $r_{s2}$, are equated. The adjustment process of the standard rate of return has led to a new rate of utilization of capacity, $u_2$, which is different from the standard rate, $u_s$. The rate of utilization in the very long run is thus still endogenous, despite the presence of an adjustment mechanism.

Figure 7.11 *Because of conflicting targets, the actual rate of capacity utilization does not end up equating the standard rate of utilization, despite entrepreneurs revising their view of the standard rate of return according to the values taken by the actual rate of profit*

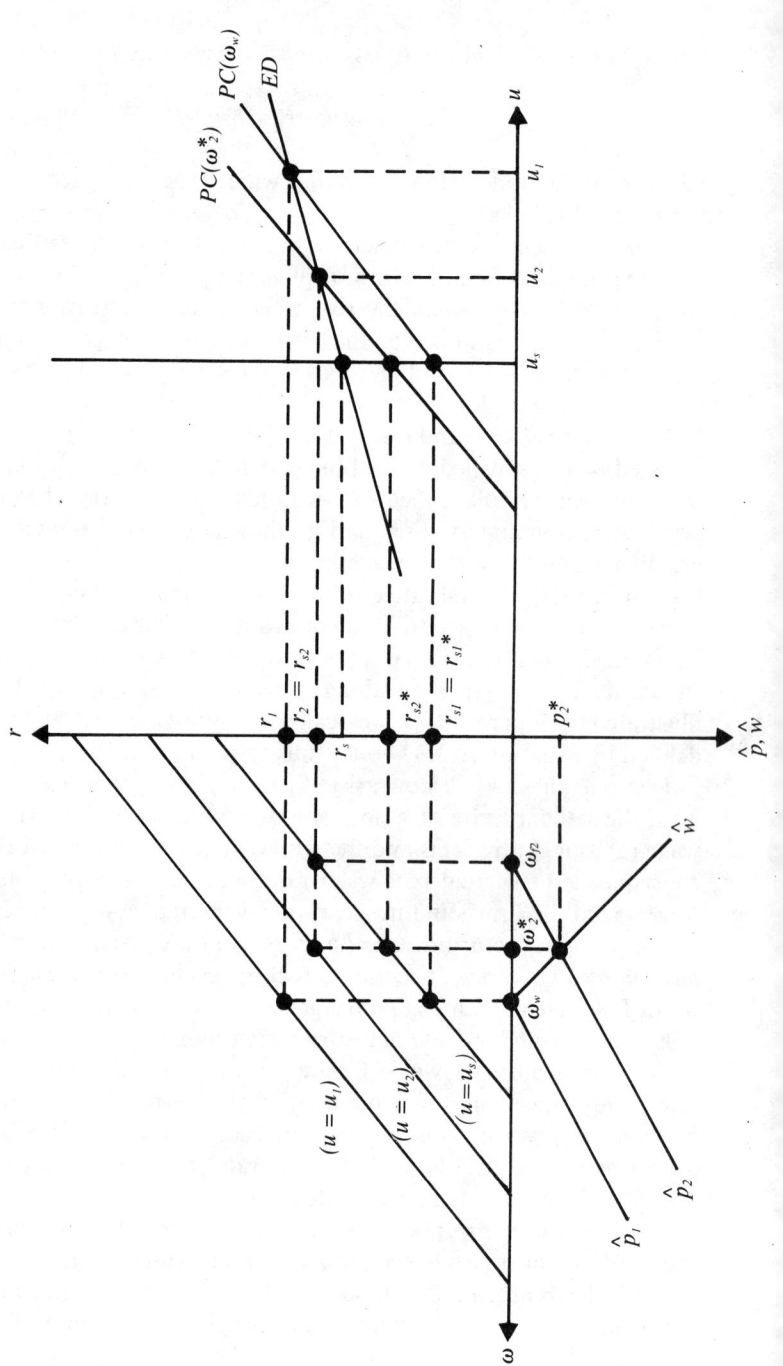

Real wage resistance in this example brings in inflation, but it also preserves the distinctive features of the Kaleckian model when this model is associated with an adaptative standard rate of return. The presence of bargaining power on the part of the workers allows us to respond to a criticism of the Kaleckian model of growth and distribution, the criticism being that there cannot be a true long-run steady state unless the standard rate of return and the rate of profit are equated (Committeri, 1986, p. 171). In the above model, the two rates are equated; that is, the actual rate of profit and the standard rate of return assessed by firms become equal. Despite this, the rate of utilization of capacity is still free to vary from its standard or normal value. The key characteristic of the Kaleckian model, that is the endogeneity of the rate of utilization of capacity, in the short run as well as in the long run, is thus preserved.

Even though we have assumed the most favourable conditions for pure prices of production to actually occur, in the longest of long runs actual prices are not equal to normal prices, in contrast to what neo-Ricardians believe they should be (Ciccone, 1987, p. 110). Demand conditions being given, say by the curve $ED$, neo-Ricardians maintain that normal prices should be set according to the standard rate of return $r_s$ of Figure 7.11 and that prices on this basis will be the centre of gravitation of prices. In our model, assuming that firms initially did set prices on the basis of a standard rate of return of $r_{s1}$, it will eventually be the case that a standard rate of return of $r_s$ will be assessed by firms. This target rate of return, however, is not a centre of gravitation. The standard rate of return assessed by firms will continue to rise until it equates the actual rate of profit, that is until $r_{s2}$ equates $r_2$. At that point the standard rate of return incorporated into prices, $r_{s2}*$, will be different from the standard rate of return $r_s$ that would correspond to the neo-Ricardian normal prices. Going back to the debate over the significance of production prices that was introduced at the end of Chapter 3, we may now reassert the opinion that pure production prices must be seen as the notional version of the more realist cost-plus prices. Prices which are actually set by firms are based on costs of production, but generally they are not normal prices in the classical sense, even when an adjustment mechanism prevails. Dutt (1990a, p. 130) concludes in a similar fashion when he studies the possible convergence of the sectoral rates of profit in a Kaleckian two-sector model.

# 8. Concluding Remarks

At the beginning of the book I pointed out that the economics of Kalecki provides better foundations for a post-Keynesian or post-classical research programme than does the economics of Keynes. The reader should be convinced by now that this is indeed the case. Keynes had great intuitions, notably on the question of relative wages, but on many issues his writings have led the non-orthodox astray. Kalecki's innovative theoretical views now seem to constitute the cement that pulls together the various schools of the post-classical research programme. Where Kalecki's writings appear to be particularly terse, the insights developed by Kaldor and Robinson fill many of the gaps.

In the course of the book, the irrelevance or the second-order relevance of crucial neoclassical concepts such as substitution or real balance effects has been demonstrated. In their place, income effects and the importance of income distribution have been emphasized, both for production and consumption activities. In particular it has been shown that higher real wages may lead to higher employment levels, higher rates of accumulation and also higher rates of profit. Under some circumstances it may even be that higher real wages bring about a faster pace of productivity growth. We need not sacrifice the present in the hope of a better future, as the paradox of thrift also demonstrates. These results have substantial implications for the conduct of economic policy.

I hope to have shown in the book that post-Keynesian economics, with its other associates from the post-classical tradition, is a progressive research programme. Post-Keynesian economists are not externally dwelling on the past writings of Keynes or other founders; they are forging ahead, improving on past deficiencies, building bridges towards the other non-orthodox schools. Whereas neoclassical economics appears to be fragmenting, post-classical economists seem to be developing common concerns. In the field with which I am most familiar, a clear example of the above is the recent introduction of money and interest rates into models of growth and distribution, taking into account the views of neo-Ricardian economists.

Several other factors show that the post-classical research programme, and the post-Keynesian school within it, are progressive. There is now a great profusion of books written in that tradition. Several journals devoted to post-Keynesian economics or to the post-classical tradition at large have been created over the past 15 years, many of them very recently. Post-Keynesian journals have also diversified. Empirical work in post-Keynesian economics is now more prevalent than ever. Post-Keynesian economists seem to have gone beyond the criticizing stage. Full-fledged models of the economy have been built, by D. M. Gordon, Eichner and Arestis, for instance.

Furthermore there is now a better balance between the literary bent and the mathematical tools. Whereas before, with a few exceptions, only the neo-Ricardians seemed to have any interest in mathematics, neo-Marxians and post-Keynesians alike now indulge in mathematical formalization. This has led to many interesting depictions of the real world, not covered in the present book, based in particular on an analysis of limit cycles. Students who like formalizing need not do neoclassical constrained optimization. The development of non-linear mathematics and non-linear models, to which Kaldor is not foreign, has made many post-Keynesian concepts and insights easier to justify and more amenable to formalization.

In the end, the eclectic nature of post-Keynesianism should prevail over the intolerance of neoclassical economics.

# References

Addison, J. T., Burton, J. and Torrance, T. S. (1980), 'On the causation of inflation', *Manchester School of Economics and Social Studies*, **48** (2), June, 140–56.

Agliardi, E. (1988), 'Microeconomic foundations of macroeconomics in the post-Keynesian approach', *Metroeconomica*, **39** (3), October, 275–97.

Ahmad, S. (1991), *Capital in Economic Theory: Neo-classical, Cambridge and Chaos,* Aldershot: Edward Elgar.

Akerlof, G. A. (1982), 'Labor contracts as partial gift exchange', *Quarterly Journal of Economics*, **97** (4), November, 543–69.

Alessie, R. and Kapteyn, A. (1991), 'Habit formation, interdependent preferences and demographic effects in the almost ideal demand system', *Economic Journal*, **101**, May, 404–19.

Amadeo, E. J. (1986a), 'The role of capacity utilization in long-period analysis', *Political Economy*, **2** (2), 147–85.

Amadeo, E. J. (1986b), 'Notes on capacity utilization, distribution and accumulation', *Contributions to Political Economy*, **5**, 83–94.

Amadeo, E. J. (1987), 'Expectations in a steady-state model of capacity utilization', *Political Economy*, **3** (1), 75–89.

Anand, P. (1991), 'The nature of rational choice and *The Foundations of Statistics*', *Oxford Economic Papers*, **43** (2), April, 199–216.

Andrews, P. W. S. (1949), *Manufacturing Business*, London: Macmillan.

Appelbaum, E. (1979), 'The Labor Market' in A. S. Eichner (ed.), *A Guide to Post-Keynesian Economics*, White Plains (NY): M. E. Sharpe, 100–19.

Arena, R. (1987), 'L'école internationale d'été de (1981–85): Vers une synthèse classico-keynésienne?', *Économie et Sociétés*, **21** (3), March, 205–38.

Arestis, P. and Eichner, A. S. (1988), 'The post-Keynesian and institutionalist theory of money and credit', *Journal of Economic Issues*, **22** (4), December, 1003–21.

Arnon, A. (1991), *Thomas Tooke: Pioneer of Monetary Theory,* Aldershot: Edward Elgar.

Arrous, J. (1978), *Imperfection de l'information, incertitude et concurrence,* doctoral dissertation, Université de Strasbourg et Université des Sciences Sociales de Grenoble.

Arrow, K. (1951), 'Alternative approaches to the theory of choice in risk-taking situations', *Econometrica*, **18** (4), October, 404–37.

Asimakopulos, A. (1970), 'A Robinsonian growth model in one sector notation – an amendment', *Australian Economic Papers*, **9**, December, 171–6.

Asimakopulos, A. (1971), 'The determination of investment in Keynes's model', *Canadian Journal of Economics*, **4** (3), August, 382–8.

Asimakopulos, A. (1975), 'A Kaleckian theory of income distribution', *Canadian Journal of Economics*, **8** (3), August, 313–33.
Asimakopulos, A. (1986), 'Finance, liquidity, saving, and investment', *Journal of Post Keynesian Economics*, **9** (1), Fall, 79–90.
Attali, J. and Guillaume, M. (1974), *L'anti-économique*, Paris: Presses Universitaires de France.
Auerbach, P. and Skott, P. (1988), 'Concentration, competition and distribution', *International Review of Applied Economics*, **2** (1), January, 42–61.
Baran, P. A. and Sweezy, P. M. (1968), *Monopoly Capital*, London: Penguin, first published 1966.
Baranzini, A. and Scazzieri, R. (1986), 'Knowledge in Economics: A Framework', in M. Baranzini and R. Scazzieri (eds), *Foundations of Economics: Structures of Inquiry and Economic Theory*, Oxford: Basil Blackwell.
Barrère, A. (1981), *La crise n'est pas ce que l'on croit*, Paris: Economica.
Baudrillard, J. (1972), *Pour une critique de l'économie politique du signe*, Paris: Gallimard.
Baumol, W. J. (1982), 'Contestable markets: an uprising in the theory of industry structure', *American Economic Review*, **72** (1), March, 178–83.
Baumol, W. J., Blinder, A. S. and Scarth, W. M. (1988), *Economics: Principles and Policy*, 2nd Canadian edn, Toronto: Harcourt, Brace, Jovanovitch.
Baxter, J. L (1988a), 'Intervening Variables in Economics: An Explanation of Wage Behavior', in P. Earl (ed.), *Psychological Economics*, Boston: Kluwer Academic, 125–46.
Baxter, J. L. (1988b), *Social and Psychological Foundations of Economic Analysis*, London: Harvester-Wheatsheaf.
Bénassy, J.-P., Boyer, R. and Gelpi, R.-M. (1979), 'Régulation des économies capitalistes et inflation', *Revue Economique*, **30** (3), May, 397–441.
Berger, P. (1972), 'Rapports entre l'évolution de la balance des paiements et l'évolution de la liquidité interne', in A. de Lattre and P. Berger (eds), *Monnaie et balance des paiements*, Paris: Armand Colin, 89–110.
Berger, P. (1975), 'Emission monétaire et multiplicateur de crédit', in *Essais en l'honneur de Jean Marchal*, vol. 2, Paris: Cujas.
Berle, A. A. (1959), *Power Without Property*, New York: Harcourt, Brace and World.
Berle, A. A. and Means, G. C. (1933), *The Modern Corporation and Private Property*, New York: Harcourt, Brace and World.
Bhaduri, A. (1983), 'Multimarket classification of unemployment: a sceptical note', *Cambridge Journal of Economics*, **7** (3), September, 235–41.
Bhaduri, A. (1986), *Macro-Economics: The Dynamics of Commodity Production*, Armonk: M. E. Sharpe.
Bhaduri, A. (1991), 'Keynesian and classical unemployment: a false distinction', *Economie Appliquée*, **44** (1), 43–9.
Bhaduri, A. and Marglin, S. (1990), 'Unemployment and the real wage: the economic basis for contesting political ideologies', *Cambridge Journal of Economics*, **14** (4), December, 375–93.
Bhaduri, A. and Robinson, J. (1980), 'Accumulation and exploitation: an analysis in the tradition of Marx, Sraffa and Kalecki', *Cambridge Journal of Economics*, **4** (2), June, 103–15.
Bianchi, M. (1990), 'The unsatisfactoriness of satisficing: from bounded rationality to innovative rationality', *Review of Political Economy*, **2** (2), 149–67.

Bils, M. J. (1985), 'Real wages over the business cycle: evidence from panel data', *Journal of Political Economy*, **93** (4), August, 666–89.

Birner, J. (1990), *Strategies and Programmes in Capital Theory: A Contribution to the Methodology of Theory Development*, doctoral dissertation, Amsterdam: University of Amsterdam.

Blatt, J. (1982), *Dynamic Economic Systems*, Armonk (NY): M. E. Sharpe.

Blaug, M. (1980a), *The Methodology of Economics*, Cambridge: Cambridge University Press.

Blaug, M. (1980b) 'Economic methodology in one easy lesson', *British Review of Economic Issues*, **2** (6), May, 1–16.

Blecker, R. A. (1989), 'International competition, income distribution and economic growth', *Cambridge Journal of Economics*, **13** (3), September, 395–412.

Blecker, R. A. (1991), 'Profitability and saving–spending behavior in the U.S. economy: a test of the exhilarationist hypothesis', conference on new directions in analytical political economy, University of Notre-Dame, Southbend.

Boddy, R. and Crotty, J. (1975), 'Class conflict and macro-policy: the political business cycle', *Review of Radical and Political Economics*, **7** (1), Spring, 1–19.

Boland, L. A. (1982) *The Foundations of Economic Method*, London: Allen and Unwin.

Bootle, R. (1984), 'Origins of the monetarist fallacy – The legacy of gold', *Lloyds Bank Review*, July, 16–37.

Bortis, H. (1982), 'Dr Wood on Profits and Growth: A Note' in M. Baranzini (ed.), *Advances in Economic Theory*, Oxford: Basil Blackwell, 262–70.

Bosworth, B., Burtless, G. and Sabelhaus, J. (1991), 'The decline in saving: evidence from household surveys', *Brookings Papers on Economic Activity*, (1), 183–227.

Bowen, W. G. and Berry, R. A. (1963), 'Unemployment and movements of the money wage level', *Review of Economics and Statistics*, **45** (2), May, 163–72.

Boyer, R. (1988), 'Formalizing Growth Regimes', in G. Dosi *et al.* (eds), *Technical Change and Economic Theory*, 608–30.

Brunner, E. (1967), 'Prix concurrentiels, prix normaux et stabilité de la branche', *Revue d'Economie Politique*, **77** (1), January–February, 32–50.

Burton, J. and Addison, J. (1977), 'The Institutionalist analysis of wage inflation: a critical appraisal', *Research in Labour Economics*, **1** (1), 333–76.

Caldwell, B. J. (1982), *Beyond Positivism: Economic Methodology in the Twentieth Century*, London: George Allen & Unwin.

Caldwell, B. J. (1989), 'Post-Keynesian methodology: an assessment', *Review of Political Economy*, **1** (1), March, 43–64.

Canterbury, E. R. and Burkhardt, R. J. (1983), 'What Do We Mean by Asking Whether Economics is a Science?', in A. S. Eichner (ed.), *Why Economics is not yet a Science*, Armonk (NY): M. E. Sharpe.

Carabelli, A. (1988), *On Keynes' Method*, London: Macmillan.

Carson, J. (1990), 'Kalecki's pricing theory revisited', *Journal of Post Keynesian Economics*, **13** (1), Fall, 146–52.

Chamberlain, T. W. and Gordon, M. J. (1989), 'Liquidity, profitability, and long-run survival: theory and evidence on business investment', *Journal of Post Keynesian Economics*, **11** (4), Summer, 589–610.

Chandler, A. D. (1977), *The Visible Hand: The Managerial Revolution in American Business*, Cambridge (Mass.): Harvard University Press.

Chick, V. (1977), *The Theory of Monetary Policy*, Oxford: Parkgate Books.

Chick, V. (1986), 'The evolution of the banking system and the theory of saving, investment and interest', *Economies et Sociétés*, **20** (8–9), August, 111–26.
Chowdhury, A. (1983), 'The decentralized labor market and the nonmarket consideration of wage inflation', *Journal of Post Keynesian Economics* **5** (4), Summer, 648–63.
Ciccone, R. (1986), 'Accumulation and capacity utilization: some critical considerations on Joan Robinson's theory of distribution', *Political Economy*, **2** (1), 17–36.
Ciccone, R. (1987), 'Accumulation, capacity utilization and distribution: a reply', *Political Economy*, **3** (1), 97–111.
Clarke, Y. and Soutar, G. N. (1981–2), 'Consumer acquisition patterns for durable goods: Australian evidence', *Journal of Consumer Research*, **8** (4), March 456–60.
Clifton, J. A. (1977), 'Competition and the evolution of the capitalist mode of production', *Cambridge Journal of Economics*, **1** (2), June, 137–51.
Clifton, J. A. (1983), 'Administered prices in the context of capitalist development', *Contributions to Political Economy*, **2**, March, 23–38.
Coddington, A. (1976), 'Keynesian economics: the search for first principles', *Journal of Economic Literature*, **14** (4), December, 1258–73.
Coddington, A. (1982), 'Deficient foresight: a troublesome theme in Keynesian economics', *American Economic Review*, **72** (3), June, 480–7.
Coghlan, R. (1978), 'A new view of money', *Lloyds Bank Review*, July, 12–27.
Colander, D. (1990), 'Workmanship, Incentives, and Cynicism', in A. Klamer and D. Colander, *The Making of an Economist*, 187–200.
Committeri, M. (1986), 'Some comments on recent contributions on capital accumulation, income distribution and capacity utilization', *Political Economy*, **2** (2), 161–86.
Committeri, M. (1987), 'Capacity utilization, distribution and accumulation: a rejoinder to Amadeo', *Political Economy*, **3** (1), 91–5.
Cornwall, J. (1983), *The Conditions for Economic Recovery*, Oxford: Martin Robertson.
Courbis, B., Froment, E. and Servet, J. M. (1991), 'Enrichir l'économie politique de la monnaie par l'histoire', *Revue Economique*, **42** (2), March, 315–38.
Coutts, K., Godley, W. and Nordhaus, W. (1978), *Industrial Pricing in the United Kingdom*, Cambridge: Cambridge University Press.
Cramp, A. B. (1971), 'Monetary Policy: Strong or Weak?', in N. Kaldor (ed.), *Conflicts in Policy Objectives*, Oxford: Basil Blackwell, 62–74.
Cripps, F. (1977), 'The money supply, wages and inflation', *Cambridge Journal of Economics*, **1** (1), March, 101–12.
Cyert, R. M. and Simon, H. A. (1983), 'The behavioral approach: with emphasis on economics', *Behavioral Science*, **28** (1), 95–108.
Dalziel, P. C. (1990), 'Market power, inflation, and incomes policy', *Journal of Post Keynesian Economics*, **12** (3), Spring, 424–38.
Darnell, A. and Evans, J. (1990), *The Limits of Econometrics*, Aldershot: Edward Elgar.
Davidson, P. (1960), *Theories of Aggregate Income Distribution*, New Brunswick (NJ): Rutgers University Press.
Davidson, P. (1962), 'Income and employment multipliers and price level', *American Economic Review*, **52** (4), September, 738–52.
Davidson, P. (1972), *Money and the Real World*, London: Macmillan.

Davidson, P. (1980), 'The dual-faceted Keynesian revolution: money and money wages in unemployment and production flow prices', *Journal of Post Keynesian Economics* **2** (3), Spring, 291–307.

Davidson, P. (1982–3), 'Rational expectations: a fallacious foundation for studying crucial decision-making processes', *Journal of Post Keynesian Economics*, **5** (2), Winter, 182–98.

Davidson, P. (1984), 'Reviving Keynes's revolution', *Journal of Post Keynesian Economics*, **6** (4), Summer, 561–75.

Davidson, P. (1986), 'Finance, funding, saving and investment', *Journal of Post Keynesian Economics*, **9** (1), Fall, 101–10.

Davidson, P. (1987), 'Sensible expectations and the long-run non-neutrality of money', *Journal of Post Keynesian Economics*, **10** (1), Fall, 146–53.

Davidson, P. (1988a), 'A technical definition of uncertainty and the long-run non-neutrality of money', *Cambridge Journal of Economics*, **12** (3), September, 329–37.

Davidson, P. (1988b), 'Endogenous money, the production process, and inflation analysis', *Economie Appliquée*, **41** (1), 151–69.

Davies, J. E. and Lee, F. S. (1988), 'A post-Keynesian appraisal of the contestability criterion', *Journal of Post Keynesian Economics*, **11** (1), Fall, 3–24.

Davis, R. G. (1976), 'Implementing Open Market Policy with Monetary Aggregate Objectives', in T. M. Havrilesky and J. T. Boorman (eds), *Current Issues in Monetary Theory and Policy*, Arlington Heights (IL): AHM Publishing, 446–65.

Deaton, A. and Muellbauer, J. (1980), *Economics and Consumer Behaviour*, Cambridge: Cambridge University Press.

De La Genière, R. (1981), 'Les fondements de la politique monétaire', *Banque*, March, 269–79.

Del Monte, A. (1975), 'Grado di monopolio e sviluppo economico', *Rivista Internazionale di Scienze Sociali*, **83** (3), May–June, 231–63.

Denton, F. T. (1988), 'The Significance of Significance: Rhetorical Aspects of Statistical Hypothesis Testing in Economics', in A. Klamer, D. N. McCloskey and R. Solow (eds), *The Consequences of Rhetoric*, Cambridge: Cambridge University Press, 163–83.

Deprez, J. (1988), "Mark-up pricing in a monetary economy: an extension of Eichner's megacorp", *Review of Radical Political Economics*, **20** (2–3), Summer & Fall, 127–132.

Deprez, J. (1990), "Vertical integration and the problem of fixed capital", *Journal of Post Keynesian Economics*, **13** (1), Fall, 47–64.

Desai, M. (1981), *Testing Monetarism*, London: Frances Pinter; New York: St Martin's Press (1982).

De Vroey, M. (1975), 'The transition from classical to neoclassical economics: a scientific revolution', *Journal of Economic Issues*, **9** (3), September, 415–39.

Dixon, R. (1979–80), 'Relative wages and employment theory', *Journal of Post Keynesian Economics*, **2** (2), Winter, 181–92.

Dixon, R. (1986), 'Uncertainty, unobstructedness, and power', *Journal of Post Keynesian Economics*, **8** (4), Summer, 585–90.

Dixon, R. and Thirlwall, A. P. (1975), 'A model of regional growth rate differences on Kaldorian lines', *Oxford Economic Papers*, **27** (2), July, 201–14.

Doeringer, P. B. and Piore, M. J. (1971), *Internal Labor Markets and Manpower Analysis*, Lexington (Mass): D. C. Heath.

Domowitz, I., Hubbard, R. G. and Petersen, B. C. (1986), 'Business cycles and the relationship between concentration and the price-cost margin', *Rand Journal of Economics*, **17** (1), Spring, 1–17.

Dosi, G., Freeman, C., Nelson, R., Silverberg, F. and Soete, L. (eds) (1988), *Technical Change and Economic Theory*, London and New York: Pinter.

Dostaler, G. (1988), 'La théorie post-keynésienne, la "Théorie Générale" et Kalecki', *Cahiers d'Economie Politique*, **14–15**, 123–42.

Dougherty, C. (1980), *Interest and Profit*, New York: Columbia University Press.

Dow, S. C. (1985), *Macroeconomic Thought: A Methodological Approach*, Oxford: Basil Blackwell.

Dow, S. C. (1988), 'Post Keynesian economics: conceptual underpinnings', *British Review of Economic Issues*, **10** (23), Autumn, 1–18.

Dow, S. C. (1990), 'Post-Keynesianism as politial economy: a methodological discussion' *Review of Political Economy*, **2** (3), 345–58.

Dow, A. C. and Dow, S. C. (1989), 'Endogenous Money Creation and Idle Balances', in J. Pheby (ed.), *New Directions in Post-Keynesian Economics*, Aldershot: Edward Elgar, 147–64.

Downey, E. H. (1987), 'The Futility of Marginal Utility', in R. Albelda, C. Gunn and W. Waller (eds), *Alternatives to Economic Orthodoxy*, Armonk: M. E. Sharpe, 48–59, first published in *Journal of Political Economy*, 1910.

Duesenberry, J. (1949), *Income, Saving and the Theory of Consumer Behavior*, Cambridge (Mass.): Harvard University Press.

Duménil, G. and Lévy, D. (1987), 'The dynamics of competition: a restoration of the classical analysis', *Cambridge Journal of Economics*, **11** (2), June, 133–64.

Dumouchel, P. and Dupuy, J.-P. (1979), *L'enfer des choses: René Girard et la logique de l'économie*, Paris: Editions du Seuil.

Dutt, A. K. (1984), 'Stagnation, income distribution and monopoly power', *Cambridge Journal of Economics*, **8** (1), March, 25–40.

Dutt, A. K. (1986–7), 'Wage rigidity and unemployment: the simple diagrammatics of two views', *Journal of Post Keynesian Economics*, **9** (2), Winter, 279–90.

Dutt, A. K. (1987a), 'Alternative closures again: a comment on growth, distribution and inflation', *Cambridge Journal of Economics*, **11** (1), March, 75–82.

Dutt, A. K. (1987b), 'Competition, monopoly power and the uniform rate of profit', *Review of Radical Political Economics*, **19** (4), Winter, 55–72.

Dutt, A. K. (1990a), *Growth, Distribution and Uneven Development*, Cambridge: Cambridge University Press.

Dutt, A. K. (1990b), 'Growth, Distribution and Capital Ownership: Kalecki and Pasinetti Revisited', in B. Datta, S. Gangopadhyay, D. Mookherjer and D. Roy (eds), *Economic Theory and Policy*, Bombay: Oxford University Press.

Dutt, A. K. (1991), 'Conflict inflation, distribution, cyclical accumulation and crises', *European Journal of Political Economy*, (forthcoming).

Dutt, A. K. (1991–2), 'Expectations and equilibrium: implications for Keynes, the neo-Ricardian Keynesians, and the Post Keynesians', *Journal of Post Keynesian Economics*, **14** (2), Winter, 205–24.

Dutt, A. K. (1992), 'Rentiers in Post Keynesian Models', in P. Arestis and V. Chick (eds), *Recent Developments in Post-Keynesian Economics*, Aldershot: Edward Elgar.

Dutt, A. K. and Amadeo, E. J. (1989), 'A Post Keynesian theory of growth, interest and money', working paper, for a Festschrift for L. L. Pasinetti.

Dutt, A. K. and Amadeo, E. J. (1990), *Keynes's Third Alternative: The Neo-Ricardians and the Post Keynesians*, Aldershot: Edward Elgar.

Earl, P. E. (1983a), *The Economic Imagination: Towards a Behavioural Analysis of Choice*, Armonk (NY): M. E. Sharpe; Brighton: Wheatsheaf Books.

Earl, P. E. (1983b), 'A Behavioral Theory of Economists' Behavior", in A. S. Eichner (ed.), *Why Economics is not yet a Science*, Armonk (NY): M. E. Sharpe, 90–125.

Earl, P. E. (1986), *Lifestyle Economics: Consumer Behaviour in a Turbulent World*, Brighton: Wheatsheaf Books.

Eatwell, J. (1983a), 'Theories of Value, Output and Employment', in Eatwell and Milgate, *Keynes's Economics*, 93–128.

Eatwell, J. (1983b), 'The long-period theory of employment', *Cambridge Journal of Economics*, **7** (4), December, 269–85.

Eatwell, J. and Milgate, M. (eds), (1983a), *Keynes's Economics and the Theory of Value and Distribution*, Oxford: Oxford University Press.

Eatwell, J. and Milgate, M. (1983b), 'Introduction', in Eatwell and Milgate, *Keynes's Economics*, 1–17.

Eatwell, J., Llewellyn, J. and Tarling, R. (1974), 'Money wage inflation in industrial countries', *Review of Economic Studies*, **41** (4), October, 515–23.

Eichner, A. S. (1976), *The Megacorp and Oligopoly: Micro Foundations of Macro Dynamics*, Cambridge: Cambridge University Press.

Eichner, A. S. (ed.) (1979), *A Guide to Post-Keynesian Economics*, White Plains (NY): M. E. Sharpe.

Eichner, A. S. (1983), 'Why economics is not yet a science', *Journal of Economic Issues*, **17** (2), June, 507–20.

Eichner, A. S. (1986a), *Toward a New Economics: Essays in Post-Keynesian and Institutionalist Theory*, London: Macmillan, Armonk (NY): M. E. Sharpe (1985).

Eichner, A. S. (1986b), 'A comment on a Post Keynesian view of average direct costs', *Journal of Post Keynesian Economics*, **8** (3), Spring, 425–6.

Eichner, A. S. (1987a), *The Macrodynamics of Advanced Market Economies*, Armonk (NY): M. E. Sharpe.

Eichner, A. S. (1987b), 'Prices and pricing', *Journal of Economic Issues*, **21** (4), December, 1555–84.

Eichner, A. S. and Kregel, J. A. (1975), 'An essay on post-Keynesian theory: a new paradigm in economics', *Journal of Economic Literature*, **13** (4), December, 1293–1311.

Encarnación, J. (1964), 'A note on lexicographic preferences', *Econometrica*, **32** (1–2), January–April, 215–17.

Epstein, G. (1990), 'A political economy model of comparative central banking', working paper 1990–3, University of Massachusetts, Amherst.

Fazzari, S. M. and Caskey, J. (1989), 'Debt Commitments and Aggregate Demand: A Critique of the Neoclassical Synthesis and Policy', in W. Semmler (ed.), *Financial Dynamics and Business Cycles: New Perspectives*, Armonk (NY): M. E. Sharpe, 188–99.

Fazzari, S. M. and Mott, T. L. (1986–7), 'The investment theories of Kalecki and Keynes: an empirical study of firm data, 1970–1982', *Journal of Post Keynesian Economics*, **9** (2), Winter, 171–87.

Findlay, R. (1963), 'The Robinsonian model of accumulation', *Economica*, **30** (1), February, 1–12.

Fisher, F. M. (1971), 'Aggregate production functions and the explanation of wages', *Review of Economics and Statistics,* **53** (4), November, 305–25.

Fog, B. (1956), 'A study of cost curves in industry', *Weltwirtshaftliches Archiv,* **77**, 44–53.

Freedman, C. (1983), 'Financial innovation in Canada: causes and consequences', *American Economic Review,* **73** (2), May, 101–6.

Friedman, M. (1953), 'The Methodology of Positive Economics', in *Essays in Positive Economics,* Chicago: University of Chicago Press, 3–43.

Friedman, M. (1970), 'A comment', *Lloyds Bank Review,* October, pp. 52–5.

Fujimoto, T. and Leslie, D. (1983), 'A two-class model of Keynesian unemployment', *Metroeconomica,* **35** (1–2), February–June, 54–71.

Galbraith, J. K. (1952), *A Theory of Price Control,* Cambridge (Mass.): Cambridge University Press.

Galbraith, J. K. (1962), *The Affluent Society,* Harmondsworth: Penguin, first published 1958.

Galbraith, J. K. (1972), *The New Industrial State,* 2nd edn, New York: New American Library, first published 1967.

Galbraith, J. K. (1975), *Economics and the Public Purpose,* Harmondsworth: Penguin, first published 1973.

Garegnani, P. (1976), 'On a Change in the Notion of Equilibrium in Recent Works on Value and Distribution', in M. Brown, K. Sato and P. Zarembka (eds), *Essays in Modern Capital Theory,* Amsterdam: North-Holland, 25–45.

Garegnani, P. (1978), 'Notes on consumption, investment and effective demand: I', *Cambridge Journal of Economics,* **2** (4), December, 335–53.

Garegnani, P. (1979), 'Notes on consumption, investment and effective demand: II', *Cambridge Journal of Economics,* **3** (1), March, 63–82.

Garegnani, P. (1983), 'Two Routes to Effective Demand', in J. A. Kregel (ed.), *Distribution, Effective Demand and International Economic Relations,* London: Macmillan, 69–80.

Garegnani, P. (1989), 'Some Notes on Capital, Expectations and the Analysis of Changes', in G. R. Feiwel (ed.), *Joan Robinson and Modern Economic Theory,* London: Macmillan, vol. 1, 344–67.

Garegnani, P. (1990), 'Sraffa: Classical versus Marginalist Analysis', in K. Bharadwaj and B. Schefold (eds), *Essays on Piero Sraffa: Critical Perspectives on the Revival of Classical Theory,* London: Unwin Hyman, 112–58.

Gedeon, S. J. (1985), 'A comment on and extension of Lavoie's "The endogenous flow of credit and the post Keynesian theory of money"' *Journal of Economic Issues,* **19** (3), September, 837–42.

Gedeon, S. J. (1985–6), 'The post Keynesian theory of money: a summary and an Eastern European example', *Journal of Post Keynesian Economics,* **8** (2), Winter, 208–21.

Georgescu-Roegen, N. (1954), 'Choice, expectations and measurability', *Quarterly Journal of Economics,* **48** (4), November, 503–34.

Georgescu-Roegen, N. (1966), 'The Nature of Expectations and Uncertainty', in *Analytical Economics,* Cambridge (Mass.): Harvard University Press, 241–75.

Gimble, D. E. (1991), 'Labor market theory and the Veblenian dichotomy', *Journal of Economic Issues,* **25** (3), September, 625–48.

Godley, W. and Cripps, F. (1983), *Macroeconomics,* London: Fontana Paperbacks.

Goodhart, C. A. E. (1984), *Monetary Theory and Policy: The UK Experience*, London: Macmillan.

Goodhart, C. (1989a), 'Has Moore become too horizontal?', *Journal of Post Keynesian Economics*, **12** (1), Fall, 29–34.

Goodhart, C. (1989b), 'The conduct of monetary policy', *Economic Journal*, **99**, June, 293–346.

Gordon, R. J. (1989), 'Hysteresis in history: was there ever a Phillips curve?', *American Economic Review*, **79** (2), May, 220–5.

Granger, C. W. J. and Newbold, P. (1974), 'Spurious regressions in econometrics', *Journal of Econometrics*, **2** (2), July, 111–20.

Graziani, A. (1984), 'The debate on Keynes's finance motive', *Economic Notes*, (1), 5–33.

Graziani, A. (1990), 'The theory of the monetary circuit', *Economies et Sociétés*, **24** (7), July, 7–36.

Green, F. (1984), 'A critique of the neo-Fisherian consumption function', *Review of Radical Political Economics*, **16** (2–3), Summer and Fall, 95–114.

Green, F. (1991), 'Institutional and other unconventional theories of saving', *Journal of Economic Issues*, **25** (1), March, 93–113.

Grellet, G. (1976), 'Le principe des avances et la théorie keynésienne de l'emploi', in A. Barrère (ed.), *Controverses sur le système keynésien*, Paris: Economica, 194–203.

Guerrien, B. (1989), *Concurrence, flexibilité et stabilité*, Paris: Economica.

Hagemann, H. (1991), 'A Kaldorian Saving Function in a Two-sectoral Linear Growth Model', in E. J. Nell and W. Semmler (eds), *Nicholas Kaldor and Mainstream Economics*, London: Macmillan, 449–68.

Hahn, F. H. (1972), *The Share of Wages in National Income*, London: Weidenfeld & Nicolson.

Hahn, F. H. (1975), 'Revival of political economy: the wrong issues and the wrong arguments', *Economic Record*, **51**, September, 360–4.

Hahn, F. (1982), 'The neo-Ricardians', *Cambridge Journal of Economics*, **6** (4), December, 353–74.

Haines, W. M. (1982), 'The psychoeconomics of human needs: Maslow's hierarchy and Marshall's organic growth', *Journal of Behavioral Economics*, **9**, Winter, 97–121.

Hall, R. L. and Hitch, C. J. (1939), 'Price Theory and Business Behaviour', *Oxford Economic Papers*, **1** (2), May, 12–45.

Hamermesh, D. S. (1986), 'The Demand for Labor in the Long Run", in O. Ashenfelter and R. Layard (eds), *Handbook of Labor Economics*, Amsterdam: North Holland, vol. 1, 429–71.

Hamouda, O. F. and Harcourt, G. C. (1988), 'Post Keynesianism: from criticism to coherence?' *Bulletin of Economic Research*, **40** (1), January, 1–33.

Harcourt, G. C. (1972), *Some Cambridge Controversies in the Theory of Capital*, Cambridge: Cambridge University Press.

Harcourt, G. C. and Kenyon, P. (1976), 'Pricing and the investment decision', *Kyklos*, **29** (3), 449–77.

Harrington, R. L. (1983), 'Monetarisms: real and imaginary: a review article', *The Manchester School of Economic and Social Studies*, **51** (1), March, 63–71.

Harris, D. J. (1974), 'The price policy of firms, the level of employment and distribution of income in the short run' *Australian Economic Papers*, **13**, June, 144–51.

Harris, D. J. (1978), *Capital Accumulation and Income Distribution*, Stanford: Stanford University Press.
Harrod, R. F. (1952), *Economic Essays*, London: Macmillan.
Harrod, R. F. (1972), 'Imperfect competition, aggregate demand and inflation', *Economic Journal*, **82**, March, 392–401.
Harrod, R. F. (1973), *Economic Dynamics*, London: Macmillan.
Harrod, R. F. (1976), 'Economic Dynamics and Economic Policy', in K. Dopfer (ed.), *Economics of the Future*, London: Macmillan, 69–81.
Haynes, W. W. (1964), 'Pricing practices in small firms', *Southern Economic Journal*, **30** (4), April, 315–24.
Heijdra, B. J. and Lowenberg, A. D. (1988), 'The Neoclassical economic research program: some Lakatosian and other considerations', *Australian Economic Papers*, **27**, December, 272–84.
Heiner, R. A. (1983), 'The origin of predictable behavior', *American Economic Review*, **73** (4), September, 560–95.
Heinsohn, G. and Steiger, O. (1983), 'Private property, debts and interest or the origin of money and the rise and fall of monetary economies', *Studi Economici*, (21), 3–55.
Hendry, D. F. (1980), 'Econometrics–alchemy or science?', *Economica*, **47**, November, 387–406.
Hendry, D. F. and Ericsson, N. R. (1991), 'An econometric analysis of U.K. money demand in monetary trends in the United States and the United Kingdom by Milton Friedman and Anna Schwartz', *American Economic Review*, **81** (1), March, 8–38.
Henry, J. (1982), 'Les méthodes "post-keynésiennes" et l'approche post-classique', *Actualité Economique*, **58** (1–2), January–June, 17–60.
Henry, J. and Seccareccia, M. (1982), 'Introduction: la théorie post-keynésienne: contributions et essais de synthèse', *Actualité Economique*, **58** (1–2), January–June, 5–16.
Herendeen, J. B. (1975), *The Economics of the Corporate Economy*, New York: Dunellen.
Hey, J. D. (1982), 'Search for rules for search', *Journal of Economic Behavior and Organization*, **3** (1), March, 65–81.
Hey, J. D. (1983), 'Whither uncertainty?', *Economic Journal*, **93**, Supplement, 129–38.
Hicks, J. R. (1937), 'Mr. Keynes and the Classics', *Econometrica*, **5**, 147–59.
Hicks, J. R. (1955), 'The economic foundations of wage policy', *Economic Journal*, **65**, September, 389–404.
Hicks, J. (1974), *The Crisis in Keynesian Economics*, Oxford: Basil Blackwell.
Hicks, J. R. (1975), 'What is wrong with Monetarism?', *Lloyds Bank Review*, October, 1–13.
Hicks, J. R. (1976a), 'Revolutions in Economics', in S. J. Latsis (ed.), *Methods and Appraisal in Economics*, Cambridge: Cambridge University Press, 207–18.
Hicks, J. R. (1976b), 'Must stimulating demand stimulate inflation?', *Economic Record*, **52**, December, 409–22.
Hicks, J. (1982), *Money, Interest and Wages*, Cambridge (Mass.): Harvard University Press.
High, J. (1983–4), 'Knowledge, maximizing and conjecture: a critical analysis of search theory', *Journal of Post Keynesian Economics*, **6** (2), Winter, 252–64.

Hodgson, G. M. (1982), 'Theoretical and policy implications of variable productivity', *Cambridge Journal of Economics,* **6** (3), September, 213–26.

Hodgson, G. M. (1988), *Economics and Institution: A Manifesto for a Modern Institutional Economics,* Cambridge: Polity Press.

Hodgson, G. M. (1989), 'Post-Keynesianism and Institutionalism: the Missing Link', in J. Pheby (ed.), *New Directions in Post-Keynesian Economics,* Aldershot: Edward Elgar.

Hoogduin, L. (1987), 'On the difference between the Keynesian, Knightian and the classical analysis of uncertainty and the development of a more general monetary theory', *De Economist,* (1), 52–65.

Hoogduin, L. (1991), *Some Aspects of Uncertainty and the Theory of a Monetary Economy,* doctoral dissertation, Groningen: Rijksuniversiteit.

Hotson, J. H. (1976), *Stagflation and the Bastard Keynesians,* Waterloo: University of Waterloo Press.

Houthakker, H. S. and Taylor, L. D. (1970), *Consumer Demand in the United states: Analyses and Projections,* 2nd edn, Cambridge (Mass.): Harvard University Press.

Ingrao, B. and Israel, G. (1990), *The Invisible Hand,* Cambridge (Mass.) and London: MIT Press.

Ironmonger, D. S. (1972), *New Commodities and Consumer Behaviour,* Cambridge: Cambridge University Press.

Isenberg, D. L. (1988), 'Is there a case for Minsky's financial fragility hypothesis in the 1920's?', *Journal of Economic Issues* **22** (4), December, 1045–69.

Jarsulic, M. (1989), 'Endogenous credit and endogenous business cycles', *Journal of Post Keynesian Economics,* **12** (1), Fall, 35–48.

Johnston, J. (1960), *Statistical Cost Analysis,* London: McGraw-Hill.

Jossa, B. (1989), 'Class Struggle and Income Distribution in Kaleckian Theory', in M. Sebastiani (ed.), *Kalecki's Relevance Today,* New York; St Martin's Press, 142–59.

Kagel, J. H., R. C. Battalio, H. Rachlin, R. L. Bassmann, L. Green and W. R. Klemm (1975), 'Experimental studies of consumer demand behavior using laboratory animals', *Economic Inquiry,* **13** (1), March, 22–38.

Kahn, R. F. (1972), *Selected Essays on Employment and Growth,* Cambridge: Cambridge University Press.

Kahn, R. F. (1983), 'Malinvaud on Keynes', in J. Eatwell and M. Milgate, *Keynes's Economics,* 214–28.

Kaldor, N. (1934), 'The equilibrium of the firm', *Economic Journal,* **44**, March, 60–76.

Kaldor, N. (1939), 'Speculation and economic stability', *Review of Economic Studies,* **7**, October, 1–27.

Kaldor, N. (1956), 'Alternative theories of distribution', *Review of Economic Studies* **23**, March, 83–100.

Kaldor, N. (1957), 'A model of economic growth', *Economic Journal,* **67**, December, 591–624.

Kaldor, N. (1959), 'Economic growth and the problem of inflation: Part 2', *Economica,* **26** (4), November, 287–98.

Kaldor, N. (1961), 'Capital Accumulation and Economic Growth', in F. A. Lutz and D. C. Hague (eds), *The Theory of Capital,* New York: St Martin's Press, 177–228.

Kaldor, N. (1962), 'Comment', *Review of Economic Studies,* **29**, 246–50.

Kaldor, N. (1964a), 'Monetary Policy, Economic Stability and Growth', in *Essays on Economic Policy*, vol. 1, London: Duckworth.

Kaldor, N. (1964b), 'Introduction', in *Essays on Economic Policy*, vol. 1, London: Duckworth.

Kaldor, N. (1966), 'Marginal productivity and the macro-economic theories of distribution', *Review of Economic Studies*, **33**, October, 309–19.

Kaldor, N. (1970a), 'Some fallacies in the interpretation of Kaldor', *Review of Economic Studies*, **37**, January, 1–7.

Kaldor, N. (1970b), 'The new monetarism', *Lloyds Bank Review*, July, 1–17.

Kaldor, N. (1972), 'The irrelevance of equilibrium economics', *Economic Journal*, **82**, December, 1237–52.

Kaldor, N. (1976), 'Inflation and recession in the world economy', *Economic Journal*, **86**, December, 703–14.

Kaldor, N. (1978a), 'Introduction', in *Further Essays on Economic Theory*, London: Duckworth, 7–24.

Kaldor, N. (1978b), 'Causes of the Slow Rate of Economic Growth in the United Kingdom', in *Further Essays on Economic Theory*, London: Duckworth, 100–38.

Kaldor, N. (1981), *Origins of the New Monetarism*, Cardiff: University College Cardiff Press.

Kaldor, N. (1982a), *The Scourge of Monetarism*, Oxford: Oxford University Press.

Kaldor, N. (1982b), 'Inflation – An Endemic Problem of the Twentieth Century', mimeo, Lecture at the Goethe University of Frankfurt, June.

Kaldor, N. (1983a), 'Keynesian Economics After Fifty Years', in D. Worswick and J. Trevithick (eds), *Keynes and the Modern World*, Cambridge: Cambridge University Press, 1–28.

Kaldor, N. (1983b), *Limitations of the 'General Theory'*, London: The British Academy.

Kaldor, N. (1985a), *Economics Without Equilibrium*, Armonk (NY): M. E. Sharpe.

Kaldor, N. (1985b), 'Lessons of the Monetarist Experiment' in C. van Ewijk and J. J. Klant (eds), *Monetary Conditions for Economic Recovery*, Dordrecht: Martinus Nijhoff, 243–62.

Kaldor, N. (1986) 'Limits on growth', *Oxford Economic Papers*, **38** (2), July, 187–98.

Kalecki, M. (1935), 'Essai d'une théorie du mouvement cyclique des affaires', *Rèvue d'Economie Politique*, **49**, 285–305.

Kalecki, M. (1937), 'The principle of increasing risk', *Economica*, **4** (76), November, 441–7.

Kalecki, M. (1939–40), 'The supply curve of an industry under imperfect competition', *Review of Economic Studies*, **7**, 91–112.

Kalecki, M. (1944), 'Professor Pigou on the classical stationary state: a comment', *Economic Journal*, **54**, April, 131–2.

Kalecki, M. (1969), *Studies in the Theory of Business Cycles 1933–1939*, Oxford: Basil Blackwell.

Kalecki, M. (1971), *Selected Essays in the Dynamics of the Capitalist Economy*, Cambridge: Cambridge University Press.

Kania, J. J. and McKean, J. R. (1976), 'Ownership, control, and the contemporary corporation: a general behavior analysis', *Kyklos*, **29** (2), 272–91.

Katouzian, H. (1980), *Ideology and Method in Economics*, New York: New York University Press.

Kelsey, D. (1988), 'The economics of chaos or the chaos of economics', *Oxford Economic Papers,* **40** (1), March, 1–31.
Kenyon, P. (1979), 'Pricing', in A. S. Eichner (ed.), *A Guide to Post-Keynesian Economics,* White Plains (NY): M. E. Sharpe.
Keynes, J. M. (1973), *The Collected Writings of John Maynard Keynes,* London: Macmillan, St Martin's Press and Cambridge University Press.
v:  *A Treatise on Money, 1 The Pure Theory of Money* (1930);
vi:  *A Treatise on Money, 2 The Applied Theory of Money* (1930);
vii:  *The General Theory* (1936);
viii:  *Treatise on Probability* (1921);
ix:  *Essays in Persuasion* (1931);
xii:  *Economic Articles and Correspondence: Investment and Editorial;*
xiv:  *The General Theory and After: Part II, Defence and Development;*
xx:  *Activities 1929–31: Rethinking Employment and Unemployment Policies;*
xxvi:  *Activities 1943–6: Shaping the Post-War World: Bretton Woods and Reparations.*
Kirman, A. (1989), 'The intrinsic limits of modern economic theory: the emperor has no clothes', *Economic Journal,* **99**, Supplement, 126–39.
Klamer, A. and Colander, D. (1990), *The Making of an Economist,* Boulder (Col.): Westview Press.
Knight, F. (1940), *Risk, Uncertainty and Profit,* London: The London School of Economics and Political Science, first published 1921.
Kohli, M. (1988), 'Wages, work effort, and productivity', *Review of Radical Political Economics,* **20** (2&3), 190–5.
Kotz, D. M. (1987), 'Radical Theories of Inflation', in *The Imperiled Economy,* book 1, New York: Union for Radical Political Economy, 83–92.
Koutsoyiannis, A. (1975), *Modern Microeconomics,* London: Macmillan.
Kregel, J. A. (1973), *The Reconstruction of Political Economy: An Introduction to Post-Keynesian Economics,* London: Macmillan.
Kregel, J. A. (1976), 'Economic methodology in the face of uncertainty: the modelling methods of Keynes and the post-Keynesians', *Economic Journal,* **86**, June, 209–25.
Kregel, J. A. (1980), 'The theoretical consequences of economic methodology: Samuelson's foundations', *Metroeconomica,* **32** (1), February, 25–38.
Kregel, J. A. (1984–5), 'Constraints on the expansion of output and employment: real or monetary?', *Journal of Post Keynesian Economics,* **7** (2), Winter, 139–52.
Kregel, J. A. (1985), 'Hamlet without the prince: Cambridge macroeconomics without money', *American Economic Review,* **75** (2), May, 133–9.
Kurz, H. D. (1985), 'Effective demand in a classical model of value and distribution: the multiplier in a Sraffian framework', *Manchester School of Economic and Social Studies,* **53** (2), June, 121–37.
Kurz, H. D. (1986), 'Normal positions and capital utilization', *Political Economy,* **2** (1), 37–54.
Kurz, H. D. (1990a), 'Effective demand, employment and capital utilisation in the short run', *Cambridge Journal of Economics,* **14** (2), June, 205–17.
Kurz, H. D. (1990b), 'Technical Change, Growth and Distribution: A Steady-State Approach to Unsteady Growth', in *Capital, Distribution and Effective Demand: Studies in the 'Classical Approach to Economic Theory,* Cambridge: Polity Press, 210–39.

Lachmann, L. M. (1977), *Capital, Expectations and the Market Process*, Kansas City: Sheed, Andrews and McMeel.

Lancaster, K. (1971), *Consumer Demand: A New Approach*, New York: Columbia University Press.

Lanzillotti, R. F. (1958), 'Pricing objectives in large companies', *American Economic Review*, **48** (5), December, 921–40.

Lavoie, M. (1982), 'Structures financières, endettement et profits', *Economie Appliquée*, **35** (3), 269–300.

Lavoie, M. (1984a), 'The endogenous flow of credit and the Post Keynesian theory of money', *Journal of Economic Issues*, **18** (3), September, 771–97.

Lavoie, M. (1984b), 'Un modèle post-keynésien d'économie monétaire fondé sur la théorie du circuit', *Economies et Sociétés*, **18** (2), 493–518.

Lavoie, M. (1985a), 'La distinction entre l'incertitude keynésienne et le risque néoclassique', *Economie Appliquée*, **38** (2), 493–518.

Lavoie, M. (1985b), 'Credit and Money: The Dynamic Circuit, Overdraft Economics, and Post-Keynesian Economics', in M. Jarsulic (ed.), *Money and Macro Policy*, Boston: Kluwer-Nijhoff, 63–84.

Lavoie, M. (1985c), 'The Post Keynesian theory of endogenous money: a reply', *Journal of Economic Issues*, **19** (3), September, 843–8.

Lavoie, M. (1986a), 'Minsky's Law or the theorem of systemic financial fragility', *Studi Economici*, (29), 3–28.

Lavoie, M. (1986b), 'Chômage classique et chômage keynésien: un prétexte aux politiques d'austérité', *Economie Appliquée*, **39** (2), 203–38.

Lavoie, M. (1987), *Macroéconomie: Théorie et controverses post-keynésiennes*, Paris: Dunod.

Lavoie, M. (1990), 'Thriftiness, growth and the post-Keynesian tradition', *Economies et Sociétés*, **24** (7), July, 123–34.

Lavoie, M. (1991), 'Noyau, demi-noyau et heuristique du programme de recherche néoclassique', *Economie Appliquée*, **44** (1), 51–69.

Lavoie, Marc (1992a), 'Towards a new research programme for post-Keynesianism and neo-Ricardianism', *Review of Political Economy*, **4** (1), 1992.

Lavoie, M. (1992b), 'A Post-Classical View of Money, Interest, Growth and Distribution' in G. Mongiovi and C. Rühl (eds.), *Macroeconomic Theory: Diversity and Convergence*, Aldershot: Edward Elgar.

Lawson, K. (1985), 'Uncertainty and economic analysis', *Economic Journal*, **95**, December, 909–27.

Lawson, T. (1988), 'Probability and uncertainty in economic analysis', *Journal of Post Keynesian Economics*, **11** (1), Fall, 38–65.

Lawson, T. (1989), 'Abstraction, tendencies and stylised facts: a realist approach to economic analysis', *Cambridge Journal of Economics*, **13** (1), March, 59–78.

Lea, S. E. G., Tarpy, R. M. and Webley, P. (1987), *The Individual in the Economy: A Survey of Economic Psychology*, Cambridge: Cambridge University Press.

Leathers, C. G. and Evans, J. S. (1973), 'Thorstein Veblen and the New Industrial State', *History of Political Economy*, **5** (2), Fall, 420–37.

Le Bourva, J. (1959), 'La théorie de l'inflation, le rapport des experts et l'opérattion de décembre 1958', *Revue Economique*, **10** (5), September, 713–54.

Le Bourva, J. (1962), 'Création de la monnaie et multiplicateur du crédit', *Revue Economique*, **13** (1), January, 29–56.

Lee, F. S. (1984a), 'Full cost pricing: a new wine in a new bottle', *Australian Economic Papers*, **23**, June, 151–65.

Lee, F. S. (1984b), 'The marginalist controversy and the demise of full cost pricing', *Journal of Economic Issues*, **18** (4), December, 1107–32.
Lee, F. S. (1985), 'Full cost prices, classical price theory, and long period method analysis: a critical evaluation', *Metroeconomica*, **37** (2), June, 199–219.
Lee, F. S. (1986), 'Post Keynesian view of average direct costs: a critical evaluation of the theory and the empirical evidence', *Journal of Post Keynesian Economics*, **8** (3), Spring, 400–24.
Lee, F. S. (1988), 'Costs, increasing costs, and technical progress: response to the critics', *Journal of Post Keynesian Economics*, **10** (3), Spring, 489–91.
Lee, F. S. (1990), 'The modern corporation and Means's critique of neoclassical economics', *Journal of Economic Issues*, **24** (3), September, 673–94.
Le Héron, E. (1986), 'Généralisation de la préférence pour la liquidité et financement de l'investissement', *Economies et Sociétés*, **20** (8–9), 67–93.
Leibenstein, H. (1950), 'Bandwagon, Snob and Veblen effects in the theory of consumer's demand', *Quarterly Journal of Economics*, **64** (1), February, 183–207.
Leibenstein, H. (1978), *General X-Efficiency Theory and Economic Development*, London: Oxford University Press.
Leijonhufvud, A. (1973), 'Life among the econ', *Western Economic Journal*, **11** (3), September, 327–37.
Leijonhufvud, A. (1976), 'Schools, Revolutions and Research Programmes in Economic Theory, in S. Latsis (ed.), *Method and Appraisal in Economics*, Cambridge: Cambridge University Press, 65–108.
Levine, A. L. (1988), 'Sraffa, Okun, and the theory of the imperfectly competitive firm', *Journal of Economic Behavior and Organization*, **9** (1), January, 101–5.
Levy-Garboua, L. and Levy-Garboua, V. (1972), 'Le comportement bancaire, le diviseur de crédit et l'efficacité du contrôle monétaire', *Revue Economique*, **23** (2), March, 243–82.
Lipsey, R. G., Purvis, D. D. and Steiner, P. O. (1988), *Economics*, 6th edn, New York: Harper & Row.
Loasby, B. J. (1976), *Choice, Complexity and Ignorance*, Cambridge: Cambridge University Press.
Lubrano, M., Pierse, R. G., and Richard, J. F. (1986), 'Stability of a U.K. money demand equation: a Bayesian approach to testing exogeneity', *Review of Economic Studies*, **53**, August, 603–34.
Lucas, R. (1981), *Studies in Business Cycle Theory*, Cambridge, Mass: MIT Press.
Lutz, M. A. and Lux, K. (1979), *The Challenge of Humanistic Economics*, Menlo Park: Benjamin/Cummings.
Machina, M. J. (1987), 'Choice under uncertainty: problems solved and unsolved', *Economic Perspectives*, **1** (1), Summer, 121–54.
Mainwaring, L. (1977), 'Monopoly power, income distribution and price determination', *Kyklos*, **30** (4), 674–90.
Malinvaud, E. (1953), 'Capital accumulation and efficient allocation of resources', *Econometrica*, **21** (2), April, 233–68.
Malinvaud, E. (1977), *The Theory of Unemployment Reconsidered*, Oxford: Basil Blackwell.
Malinvaud, E. (1982), 'Wages and unemployment', *Economic Journal*, **92** (1), March, 1–12.
Mansfield, E. (1991), *Microeconomics: Theory and Applications*, 7th edn, New York: W. W. Norton.

March, J. G. (1978), 'Bounded rationality, ambiguity, and the engineering of choice', *Bell Journal of Economics*, **4** (2), Autumn, 587–610.
Marchal, J. (1951), 'The construction of a new theory of profit', *American Economic Review*, **41** (4), September, 549–65.
Marglin, S. A. (1975), 'What do bosses do? Part II', *Review of Radical and Political Economics*, **7** (1), Spring, 20–37.
Marglin, S. A. (1984a), *Growth, Distribution and Prices*, Cambridge (Mass.): Harvard University Press.
Marglin, S. A. (1984b), 'Growth, distribution, and inflation: a centennial synthesis', *Cambridge Journal of Economics*, **8** (2), June, 115–44.
Marris, R. (1964a), *The Economic Theory of Managerial Capitalism*, New York: Free Press of Glencoe.
Marris, R. (1964b), *The Economics of Capital Utilisation*, Cambridge: Cambridge University Press.
McCombie, J. S. L. (1982), 'Economic growth, Kaldor's laws and the static–dynamic Verdoorn law paradox', *Applied Economics*, **14** (3), June, 279–94.
McCombie, J. S. L. and Dixon, R. (1991), 'Estimating technical change in aggregate production functions: a critique', *International Review of Applied Economics*, **5** (1), 24–46.
McKenna, E. J. and Zannoni, D. C. (1990), 'The relation between the rate of interest and investment in post-Keynesian and neo-Ricardian analysis', *Eastern Economic Journal*, **16** (2), April–June, 133–43.
McKenzie, R. B. and Tullock, G. (1978), *The New World of Economics: Explorations in the Human Experience*, revised edn, Homewood (IL): Richard D. Irwin.
Means, G. C. (1936), 'Notes on inflexible prices', *American Economic Review*, **26** (1), March, Supplement, 23–35.
Messori, M. (1991), 'Financing in Kalecki's theory', *Cambridge Journal of Economics*, **15** (3), September, 301–13.
Meulendyke, A.-M. (1988), 'Can the Federal Reserve influence whether the money supply is endogenous? A comment on Moore', *Journal of Post Keynesian Economics*, **10** (3), Spring, 390–7.
Michl, T. R. (1985), 'International comparisons of productivity growth: Verdoorn's law revisited', *Journal of Post Keynesian Economics*, **7** (4), Summer, 474–92.
Milgate, M. (1982), *Capital and Employment*, London: Academic Press.
Milgate, M. and Eatwell, J. (1983), 'Unemployment and the Market Mechanism', in Eatwell and Milgate, *Keynes's Economics*, 260–79.
Minsky, H. P. (1957), 'Central banking and money market changes', *Quarterly Journal of Economics*, **71** (2), May, 171–87.
Minsky, H. P. (1976), *John Maynard Keynes*, London: Macmillan; New York: Columbia University Press (1975).
Minsky, H. P. (1980), 'Capitalist financial processes and the instability of capitalism', *Journal of Economic Issues*, **14** (2), June, 505–23.
Minsky, H. P. (1986), *Stabilizing an Unstable Economy*, New Haven (NJ): Yale University Press.
Mirowski, P. (1990), *More Heat than Light*, New York: Cambridge University Press.
Mongin, P. (1986), 'La controverse sur l'entreprise (1940–1950) et la formation de l'irréalisme méthodologique', *Economies et Sociétés*, **20** (3), March, 95–151.

Mongiovi, G. (1991), 'Keynes, Sraffa and the labour market', *Review of Political Economy,* **3** (1), 25–42.
Moore, B. J. (1973), 'Some macroeconomic consequences of corporate equities', *Canadian Journal of Economics,* **6** (4), November, 529–44.
Moore, B. J. (1979), 'Monetary Factors', in A. S. Eichner (ed.), *A Guide to Post-Keynesian Economics,* White Plains (NY): M. E. Sharpe, 120–38.
Moore, B. J. (1988a), *Horizontalists and Verticalists: The Macroeconomics of Credit Money,* Cambridge: Cambridge University Press.
Moore, B. J. (1988b), 'The endogenous money supply', *Journal of Post Keynesian Economics,* **10** (3), Spring, 372–85.
Moore, B. J. (1989), 'On the endogeneity of money once more', *Journal of Post Keynesian Economics,* **11** (3), Spring, 479–87.
Moss, S. J. (1978), 'The post-Keynesian theory of income distribution in the corporate economy', *Australian Economic Papers,* **17**, December, 303–22.
Moss, S. J. (1980), 'The End of Orthodox Capital Theory', in E. J. Nell (ed.), *Growth, Profits & Property: Essays in the Revival of Political Economy,* Cambridge: Cambridge University Press, 64–79.
Mott, T. (1985–6), 'Towards a post-Keynesian formulation of liquidity preference', *Journal of Post Keynesian Economics,* **8** (2), Winter, 222–32.
Musella, M. and Panico, C. (1992), 'Kaldor on Endogenous Money and Interest Rate', in G. Mongiovi and C. Rühl (eds), *Macroeconomic Theory: Diversity and Convergence,* Aldershot: Edward Elgar.
Myatt, A. (1986), 'On the non-existence of a natural rate of unemployment and Kaleckian micro underpinnings to the Phillips curve', *Journal of Post Keynesian Economics,* **8** (3), Spring, 447–62.
Naples, M. I. (1987), 'Cyclical and Secular Productivity Slowdown', in *The Imperiled Economy,* book 1, New York: Union for Radical Political Economics, 159–70.
Nell, E. J. (1967a), 'Theories of growth and theories of value', *Economic Development and Cultural Change,* **16** (1), October, 15–26.
Nell, E. J. (1967b), 'Wicksell's theory of circulation', *Journal of Political Economy,* **75** (4), August, 386–94.
Nell, E. J. (1978), 'The simple theory of effective demand', *Intermountain Economic Review,* Fall, 1–32.
Nell, E. J. (1984), 'Effective Demand, Real Wages and Employment', in H. Hagemann and H. D. Kurz, *Beschäftgung, Verteilung und Konjunktur: Festschrift für Adolph Lowe,* Bremen: Bremen University, 132–59.
Nell, E. J. (1985), 'Jean Baptiste Marglin: a comment on growth, distribution and inflation', *Cambridge Journal of Economics,* **9** (2), June, 173–8.
Nell, E. J. (1986), 'On monetary circulation and the rate of exploitation', *Thames Papers in Political Economy,* Summer, 1–35.
Nell, E. J. (1988a), *Prosperity and Public Spending: Transformational Growth and the Role of Government,* Boston: Unwin Hyman.
Nell, E. J. (1988b), 'Does the rate of interest determine the rate of profit?', *Political Economy,* **4** (2), 263–7.
Nell, E. J. (1992), 'Demand, Pricing and Investment', in *Transformational Growth and Effective Demand,* New York: New York University Press, 377–446.
Niehans, J. (1983), 'Financial innovation, multinational banking, and monetary policy', *Journal of Banking and Finance,* **7** (4), December, 537–51.

Niehans, J. (1984), *International Monetary Economics*, Baltimore and London: John Hopkins University Press.
Niggle, C. J. (1989), 'The Cyclical Behavior of Corporate Financial Ratios and Minsky's Financial Instability Hypothesis', in W. Semmler (ed.), *Financial Dynamics and Business Cycles: New Perspectives*, Armonk (NY): M. E. Sharpe, 203–20.
Niggle, C. J. (1991), 'The endogenous money supply theory: an institutionalist appraisal', *Journal of Economic Issues*, **25** (1), March, 137–51.
O'Connel, J. (1985), 'Undistributed profits and the Pasinetti and dual theorems', *Journal of Macroeconomics*, **7** (1), Winter, 115–19.
O'Donnell, R. M. (1989), *Keynes: Philosophy, Economics and Politics*, London: Macmillan.
O'Donnell, R. M. (1990), 'An overview of probability, expectations, uncertainty and rationality in Keynes's conceptual framework', *Review of Political Economy*, **2** (3), 253–66.
Okun, A. M. (1981), *Prices and Quantities*. Washington (DC): The Brookings Institution.
Orléan, A. (1987), 'Anticipations et conventions en situation d'incertitude', *Cahiers d'Economie Politique*, **13**, 153–72.
Panico, C. (1988), *Interest and Profit in the Theories of Value and Distribution*, London: Macmillan.
Parguez, A. (1980), 'Profit, épargne, investissement; éléments pour une théorie monétaire du profit', *Economie Appliqueé*, **33** (2), 425–55.
Parguez, A. (1988), 'Hayek et Keynes face à l'austérité', in G. Dostaler and D. Ethier (eds), *Friedrich Hayek: Philosophie, économie et politique*, Montréal ACFAS; Paris: Economica (1989), 143–60.
Parkin, M. and Bade, R. (1985), *Modern Macroeconomics*, 2nd edn, Scarborough: Prentice-Hall.
Paroush, J. (1965), 'The order of acquisition of durable goods', *Econometrica*, **33** (1), January, 225–35.
Parrinello, S. (1982), 'Flexibility of choice and the theory of consumption', *Metroeconomica*, **34** (1–3), February–October, 1–10.
Pasinetti, L. L. (1974), *Growth and Income Distribution: Essays in Economic Theory*, Cambridge: Cambridge University Press.
Pasinetti, L. L. (1977), *Lectures in the Theory of Production*, New York: Columbia University Press.
Pasinetti, L. L. (1980–1), 'The rate of interest and the distribution of income in a pure labor economy', *Journal of Post Keynesian Economics*, **3** (2), Winter, 170–82.
Pasinetti, L. L. (1981), *Structural Change and Economic Growth*, Cambridge: Cambridge University Press.
Pasinetti, L. L. (1988), 'Sraffa on income distribution' *Cambridge Journal of Economics*, **12** (1), March, 135–8.
Pasinetti, L. L. (1990), 'A la mémoire de Piero Sraffa, économiste italien à Cambridge', in R. Arena and J.-L. Ravix (eds), *Sraffa Trente Ans Après*, Paris: Presses Universitaires de France et C.N.R.S., 3–18.
Patinkin, D. (1965), *Money, Interest and Prices*, 2nd edn, New York: Harper & Row.
Pencavel, J. (1986), 'Labor Supply of Men: A Survey', in O. Ashenfelter and R.

Layard (eds), *Handbook of Labor Economics*, Amsterdam: North Holland, Vol. 1, 3–102.

Penrose, E. T. (1959), *The Theory of the Growth of the Firm*, Oxford: Basil Blackwell.

Pesek, B. P. (1979), 'A note on the theory of permanent income', *Journal of Post Keynesian Economics*, **1** (4), Summer, 64–9.

Petri, F. (1992), 'Notes on Recent Theories of Aggregate Investment as a Decreasing Function of the Interest Rate' in G. Mongiovi and C. Ruhl (eds), *Macroeconomic Theory: Diversity and Convergence*, Aldershot: Edward Elgar.

Piore, M. (ed.) (1979), *Unemployment and Inflation: Institutionalist and Structuralist Views*, White Plains (NY): M. E. Sharpe.

Pivetti, M. (1985), 'On the monetary explanation of distribution', *Political Economy*, **1** (2), 73–103.

Pivetti, M. (1988), 'On the monetary explanation of distribution: a rejoinder to Nell and Wray', *Political Economy*, **4** (2), 275–83.

Podolski, T. M. (1986), *Financial Innovation and the Money Supply*, Oxford: Basil Blackwell.

Polemarchakis, H. M. (1983), 'Expectations, demand, and observability', *Econometrica*, **51** (3), May, 565–74.

Pollin, R. (1991), 'Two theories of money supply endogeneity: some empirical evidence' *Journal of Post Keynesian Economics*, **13** (3), Spring, 366–96.

Poole, W. (1982), 'Federal Reserve operating procedures' *Journal of Money, Credit, and Banking*, **14** (2), November (part 2), 575–95.

Reich, M. (1984), 'Segmented labour: time-series hypothesis and evidence', *Cambridge Journal of Economics*, **8** (1), March, 63–81.

Remenyi, J. V. (1979), 'Core demi-core interaction: toward a general theory of disciplinary and subdisciplinary growth', *History of Political Economy*, **11** (1), 30–63.

Reynolds, P. J. (1987a), *Political Economy: A Synthesis of Kaleckian and Post Keynesian Economics*, Brighton: Wheatsheaf Books.

Reynolds, P. J. (1987b), 'Wage rises and income distribution – a note', *Manchester School of Economic and Social Studies*, **55** (1), March, 77–87.

Rima, I. (1984a), 'Whatever happened to the concept of involuntary unemployment?', *International Journal of Social Economics*, **11** (3–4), 62–71.

Rima, I. (1984b), 'Involuntary unemployment and the respecified labor supply curve', *Journal of Post Keynesian Economics*, **6** (4), Summer, 540–50.

Robbins, L. (1932), *An Essay on the Nature and Significance of Economic Science*, London: Macmillan.

Robinson, J. (1952), *The Rate of Interest and Other Essays*, London: Macmillan.

Robinson, J. (1953–4), 'The production function and the theory of capital', *Review of Economic Studies*, **21**, 81–106.

Robinson, J. (1956), *The Accumulation of Capital*, London: Macmillan.

Robinson, J. (1962), *Essays in the Theory of Economic Growth*, London: Macmillan.

Robinson, J. (1964), 'Pre-Keynesian theory after Keynes', *Australian Economic Papers*, **3** (1–2), June–December, 25–35.

Robinson, J. (1966), *An Essay on Marxian Economics*, 2nd edn, London: Macmillan, 1st edn 1942.

Robinson, J. (1969), 'A further note', *Review of Economic Studies*, **36**, April, 260–2.

Robinson, J. (1971), *Economic Heresies: Some Old-fashioned Questions in Economic Theory*, London: Macmillan.
Robinson, J. (1973), *Collected Economic Papers IV*, Oxford: Basil Blackwell.
Robinson, J. (1975a), 'The unimportance of reswitching', *Quarterly Journal of Economics*, **89** (1), February, 32–9.
Robinson, J. (1975b), *Collected Economic Papers, III*, 2nd edn, Oxford: Basil Blackwell.
Robinson, J. (1977), 'Michal Kalecki on the economics of capitalism', *Oxford Bulletin of Economics and Statistics*, **39** (1), February, 7–17.
Robinson, J. (1978), 'Keynes and Ricardo', *Journal of Post Keynesian Economics*, **1** (1), Fall, 12–18.
Robinson, J. (1979), 'Garegnani on effective demand', *Cambridge Journal of Economics*, **3** (1), March, 179–80.
Robinson, J. and Eatwell, J. (1973), *An Introduction to Modern Economics*, London: McGraw-Hill.
Rogers, C. (1983), 'Neo-Walrasian macroeconomics, microfoundations and pseudo-production models', *Australian Economic Papers*, **22**, June, 201–20.
Rogers, C. (1985), 'The monetary control system of the South African reserve bank: Monetarist or Post Keynesian?', *South African Journal of Economics*, **53** (3), September, 241–7.
Rogers, C. (1989), *Money, Interest and Capital: A Study in the Foundations of Monetary Theory*, Cambridge: Cambridge University Press.
Roncaglia, A. (1978), *Sraffa and the Theory of Prices*, New York: John Wiley.
Roncaglia, A. (1988a), 'Wage Costs and Employment: The Sraffian View', in J. A. Kregel, E. Matzner and A. Roncaglia (eds), *Barriers to Full Employment*, London: Macmillan, 9–23.
Roncaglia, A. (1988b), 'The Neo-Ricardian Approach and the Distribution of Income', in A. Asimakopulos (ed.), *Theories of Income Distribution*, Boston: Kluwer, 159–80.
Rousseas, S. (1986), *Post Keynesian Monetary Economics*, Armonk (NY): M. E. Sharpe.
Rousseas, S. (1989), 'On the endogeneity of money once more', *Journal of Post Keynesian Economics*, **11** (3), Spring, 474–8.
Rowley, R. and Renuka, J. (1986), 'Sims on causality: an illustration of soft econometrics', *Scottish Journal of Political Economy*, **33** (2), May, 171–81.
Rowthorn, R. E. (1977), 'Conflict, inflation and money' *Cambridge Journal of Economics*, **1** (3), September, 215–39.
Rowthorn, R. (1981), 'Demand, real wages and economic growth', *Thames Papers in Political Economy*, Autumn, 1–39, reprinted in *Studi Economici*, (18), 1982, 3–54, and also in M. C. Sawyer (ed.), *Post-Keynesian Economics*, Aldershot: Edward Elgar.
Roy, R. (1943), 'La hiérarchie des besoins et la notion de groupes dans l'économie de choix', *Econometrica*, **11** (1), January, 13–24.
Runde, J. (1990), 'Keynesian uncertainty and the weight of arguments', *Economics and Philosophy*, **6** (2), October, 275–92.
Rymes, T. K. (1971), *On Concepts of Capital and Technical Change*, Cambridge: Cambridge University Press.
Salant, W. S. (1985), 'Keynes and the modern world: a review article', *Journal of Economic Literature*, **23** (3), September, 1176–85.

Samuelson, P. (1962), 'Parable and realism in capital theory: the surrogate production function', *Review of Economic Studies*, **29**, June, 193–206.

Sarantis, N. (1990–1), 'Distribution and terms of trade dynamics, inflation, and growth', *Journal of Post Keynesian Economics*, **13** (2), Winter, 175–98.

Sato, K. (1974), 'The neoclassical postulate and the technology frontier in capital theory', *Quarterly Journal of Economics*, **88** (3), August, 353–84.

Sawyer, M. C. (1989), *The Challenge of Radical Political Economy*, London: Harvester Wheatsheaf.

Sawyer, M. C., Aaronovitch, S. and Samson, P. (1982), 'The influence of cost and demand changes on the rate of change of prices', *Applied Economics*, **14** (2), April, 195–209.

Sayer, A. (1984), *Method in Social Science: A Realist Approach*, London: Hutchinson.

Schefold, B. (1983), 'Kahn on Malinvaud' in J. Eatwell and M. Milgate, *Keynes's Economics*, 229–46.

Schefold, B. (1984), 'Sraffa and Applied Economics: Are There Classical Supply Curves?' Centro Di Studi Economice Avanzati, Conference on Streams of Economic Thought, Trieste-Udine.

Schefold, B. (1985), 'On Changes in the Composition of Output', *Political Economy*, **1** (2), 105–42.

Scherer, F. M. (1970), *Industrial Market Structure and Economic Performance*, Chicago: Rand McNally.

Schlesinger, H. (1979), 'Problems of Monetary Policy in Germany: Some Basic Issues', in E. Wadsworth and L. de Juvigny (eds), *New Approaches in Monetary Policy*, Alphen aan den Rijn: Sijthoff & Noordhoff, 3–12.

Schmitt, B. (1966), *Monnaie, salaires et profits*, Paris: Presses Universitaires de France.

Schor, J. (1985), 'Changes in the cyclical pattern of real wages: evidence from nine countries, 1955–1980', *Economic Journal*, **95** (2), June, 452–68.

Schor, J. (1987), 'Class Struggle and the Macroeconomy: The Cost of Job Loss', in *The Imperiled Economy*, book 1, New York: Union for Radical Political Economics, 171–82.

Scitovsky, T. (1976), *The Joyless Economy*, Oxford: Oxford University Press.

Scitovsky, T. (1978), 'Market power and inflation', *Economica*, **45**, August, 221–33.

Seccareccia, M. (1984), 'The fundamental macroeconomic link between investment activity, the structure of employment and price changes: a theoretical and empirical analysis', *Economies et Sociétés*, **18** (4), April, 165–219.

Seccareccia, M. (1988), 'Systemic viability and credit crunches: an examination of recent Canadian cyclical fluctuations', *Journal of Economic Issues*, **22** (1), March, 49–77.

Seccareccia, M. (1991a), 'An alternative to labour-market orthodoxy: the post-Keynesian/Institutionalist policy view', *Review of Political Economy*, **3** (1), 43–61.

Seccareccia, M. (1991b), 'Salaire minimum, emploi et productivité dans une perspective post-keynésienne', *Actualité Economique*, **67** (2), June, 166–91.

Seccareccia, M. (1991c), 'Post-Keynesian Fundism and Monetary Circulation', in G. Deleplace and E. J. Nell (eds), *Money in Motion: The Circulation and Post-Keynesian Approaches*, London: Macmillan (forthcoming).

Semmler, W. (1984), *Competition, Monopoly and Differential Profit Rates*, New York: Columbia University Press.

Semmler, W. (ed.) (1989), *Financial Dynamics and Business Cycles: New Perspectives*, Armonk (NY): M. E. Sharpe.

Shackle, G. L. S. (1971), *Expectations, Enterprise and Profit*, London: Allen & Unwin.

Shackle, G. L. S. (1972), *Epistemics and Economics*, Cambridge: Cambridge University Press.

Shackle, G. L. S. (1984), 'Comment on the papers by Randall Bausor and Malcolm Rutherford', *Journal of Post Keynesian Economics*, **6** (3), Spring, 388–93.

Shaikh, A. (1974), 'Laws of production and laws of algebra. The humbug production function', *Review of Economics and Statistics*, **56** (1), February, 115–20.

Shaikh, A. (1980), 'Laws of Production and Laws of Algebra: Humbug II', in J. Nell (ed.), *Growth, Profits & Property: Essays in the Revival of Political Economy*, Cambridge: Cambridge University Press, 80–95.

Shapiro, C. and Stiglitz, J. E. (1984), 'Equilibrium unemployment as a worker discipline device', *American Economic Review*, **74** (3), June, 433–44.

Shapiro, N. (1981), 'Pricing and the growth of the firm', *Journal of Post Keynesian Economics*, **4** (1), Fall, 85–100.

Shipley, D. D. (1981), 'Pricing objectives in British manufacturing industry', *Journal of Industrial Economics*, **29** (4), June, 429–43.

Simon, H. A. (1976), 'From Substantive to Procedural Rationality', in S. J. Latsis (ed.), *Method and Appraisal in Economics*, Cambridge: Cambridge University Press, 129–48.

Simon, H. A. (1979), 'On parsimonious explanations of production relations', *Scandinavian Journal of Economics*, **81** (4), 459–74.

Simon, H. A. (1986), 'Interview: the failure of armchair economics', *Challenge*, **29** (5), November–December, 18–25.

Sinn, H.-V. (1983), *Economic Decisions under Uncertainty*, New York: North Holland.

Skott, P. (1989), *Conflict and Effective Demand in Economic Growth*, Cambridge: Cambridge University Press.

Slawson, N. D. (1981), *The New Inflation: The Collapse of Free Markets*, Princeton: Princeton University Press.

Spaventa, L. (1970), 'Rate of profit, rate of growth and capital intensity in a simple production model', *Oxford Economic Papers*, **22** (2), July, 129–47.

Sraffa, P. (1960), *Production of Commodities by Means of Commodities: Prelude to a Critique of Economic Theory*, Cambridge: Cambridge University Press.

Steedman, I. (1980), 'Heterogeneous labour and classical theory', *Metroeconomica*, **32** (1), February, 39–50.

Steedman, I. (1985), 'On input demand curves', *Cambridge Journal of Economics*, **9** (2), June, 165–72.

Steedman, I. (1988), 'Sraffian interdependence and partial equilibrium analysis', *Cambridge Journal of Economics*, **12** (1), March, 85–95.

Steedman, I. (1992), 'Questions for Kaleckians', *Review of Political Economy*, **4** (2).

Steedman, I. and Krause, U. (1986), 'Goethe's *Faust*, Arrow's Possibility Theorem and the Individual Decision-taker', in J. Elster (ed.), *The Multiple Self*, Cambridge: Cambridge University Press, 197–231.

Steindl, J. (1952), *Maturity and Stagnation in American Capitalism*, Oxford: Basil Blackwell.
Steindl, J. (1979), 'Stagnation theory and stagnation policy', *Cambridge Journal of Economics*, **3** (1), March, 1–14.
Steindl, J. (1982), 'The role of household saving in the modern household', *Banca Nazionale del Lavoro Quarterly Review*, March, 69–88.
Strauss, J. H. (1944), 'The entrepreneur: the firm' *Journal of Political Economy*, **52** (2), June 112–27.
Sylos Labini, P. (1949), 'The Keynesians', *Banca Nazionale del Lavoro Quarterly Review*, November, 238–42.
Sylos Labini, P. (1971), 'La théorie des prix en régime d'oligopole et la théorie du développement', *Revue d'Economie Politique*, **81** (2), March–April, 244–72.
Sylos Labini, P. (1979), 'Prices and income distribution in manufacturing industry', *Journal of Post Keynesian Economics*, **2** (1), Fall, 3–25.
Tarling, R. and Wilkinson, F. (1985), 'Mark-up pricing, inflation and distributional shares: a note', *Cambridge Journal of Economics*, **9** (2), June, 179–85.
Tarshis, L. (1980), 'Post-Keynesian economics: a promise that bounced?', *American Economic Review*, **70** (2), May, 10–14.
Tatom, J. A. (1980), 'The problem of procyclical real wages and productivity' *Journal of Political Economy*, **88** (2), April, 385–94.
Taylor, L. (1983), *Structuralist Macroeconomics: Applicable Models for the Third World*, New York: Basic Books.
Taylor, L. (1985), 'A stagnationist model of economic growth', *Cambridge Journal of Economics*, **9** (4), December, 381–403.
Taylor, L. (1990), 'Real and money wages, output and inflation in the semi-industrialized world', *Economica*, **57**, August, 329–53.
Taylor, L. (1991), *Income Distribution, Inflation and Growth: Lectures on Structuralist Macroeconomic Theory*, Cambridge (Mass.): MIT Press.
Temin, P. (1976), *Did Monetary Forces Cause the Great Depression?*, New York: W. W. Norton.
Thirlwall, A. P. (1979), 'The balance of payments constraint as an explanation of international growth rate differences', *Banca Nazionale del Lavoro Quarterly Review*, **32**, March, 45–53.
Thirlwall, A. P. (1982), 'The Harrod trade multiplier and the importance of export-led growth', *Pakistan Journal of Applied Economics*, **1** (1), 1–21.
Thomas, J. G. (1981), 'Illusion monétaire et illusions monétaristes', *Revue d'Economie Politique*, **91** (6), November–December, 947–65.
Thurow, L. C. (1983), *Dangerous Currents: The State of Economics*, Oxford: Oxford University Press.
Tobin, J. (1975), 'Keynesian models of recession and depression', *American Economic Review*, **65** (2), May, 195–202.
Townshend, H. (1937), 'Liquidity-premium and the theory of value', *Economic Journal*, **47**, March, 157–69.
Tversky, A., Slovic, P. and Kahneman, D. (1990), 'The causes of preference reversal', *American Economic Review*, **80** (1), March, 204–27.
Veblen, T. (1899), *The Theory of the Leisure Class*, New York: Modern Library (1931).
Veenhoven, R. (1989), 'National Wealth and Individual Happiness', in K. G. Grunert and F. Ölander (eds), *Understanding Economic Behaviour*, Dordrecht: Kluwer Academic, 9–32.

Vianello, F. (1985), 'The pace of accumulation', *Political Economy*, **1** (1), 69–87.
Vianello, F. (1989), 'Effective Demand and the Rate of Profit: Some Thoughts on Marx, Kalecki and Sraffa', in M. Sebastiani (ed.), *Kalecki's Relevance Today*, New York: St Martin's Press, 164–90.
Walsh, V. C. and Gram, H. (1980), *Classical and Neoclassical Theories of General Equilibrium, Historical Origins and Mathematical Structures*, New York: Oxford University Press.
Walters, A. A. (1963), 'Production and costs: an econometric survey', *Econometrica*, **31** (1–2), January–April, 1–66.
Watts, M. J. and Gaston, N. G. (1982–3), 'The "reswitching" of consumption bundles: a parallel to the capital controversies?', *Journal of Post Keynesian Economics*, **5** (2), Winter, 281–8.
Webb, S. (1912), 'The economic theory of a legal minimum wage', *Journal of Political Economy*, **20**, December, 973–98.
Weintraub, E. R. (1975), 'Uncertainty and the Keynesian Revolution', *History of Political Economy*, **7** (4), Winter, 530–48.
Weintraub, E. R. (1985), *General Equilibrium Analysis: Studies in Appraisal*, Cambridge: Cambridge University Press.
Weintraub, S. (1958), *An Approach to the Theory of Income Distribution*, Philadelphia: Clifton.
Weintraub, S. (1978), *Capitalism's Inflation and Unemployment Crisis*, Reading (Mass.): Addison-Wesley.
Weiss, L. W. (1980), 'Quantitative Studies of Industrial Organisations', in M. Intriligator (ed.), *Frontiers of Quantitative Economics*, Amsterdam: North Holland, vol. 1, 362–403.
Weisskopf, T. E. (1979), 'Marxian crisis theory and the rate of profit in the postwar U.S. economy', *Cambridge Journal of Economics*, **3** (4), December, 341–79.
Weisskopf, T. E., Bowles, S. and Gordon, D. M. (1983), 'Hearts and minds: a social model of U.S. productivity growth', *Brookings Papers on Economic Activity*, (2), 381–441.
Wells, P. (1983), 'A Post Keynesian view of liquidity preference and the demand for money', *Journal of Post Keynesian Economics*, **5** (4), Summer, 523–36.
Whittaker, J. and Theunissen, A. J. (1987), 'Why does the reserve bank set the interest rate?', *South African Journal of Economics*, **55** (1), March, 16–33.
Wiles, P. (1973), 'Cost inflation and the state of economic theory', *Economic Journal*, **83**, June, 377–98.
Winslow, E. G. (1989), 'Organic interdependence, uncertainty and economic analysis', *Economic Journal*, **99**, December, 1173–82.
Wojnilower, A. M. (1980), 'The central role of credit crunches in recent financial history', *Brookings Papers on Economic Activity*, (2), 277–326.
Wood, A. (1975), *A Theory of Profits*, Cambridge: Cambridge University Press.
Wood, A. (1978), *A Theory of Pay*, Cambridge: Cambridge University Press.
Wray, L. R. (1988), 'The monetary explanation of distribution: a critique of Pivetti', *Political Economy*, **4** (2), 269–73.
Wray, L. R. (1989), 'Two reviews of Basil Moore', *Journal of Economic Issues*, **23** (4), December, 1185–9.
Wray, L. R. (1990), *Money and Credit in Capitalist Economies: The Endogenous Money Approach*, Aldershot: Edward Elgar.

Wray, L. R. (1991), 'Bouldings's balloons: a contribution to monetary theory', *Journal of Economic Issues,* **25** (1), March, 1–20.

Wulwick, N. (1988), 'Okun's Law: policy, proofs and predictions', History of Economics Society Meeting, working paper.

Yellen, J. L. (1980), 'On Keynesian economics and the economics of the post-Keynesians', *American Economic Review,* **70** (2), May, 15–19.

Yordon, W. J. (1987), 'Evidence against diminishing returns in manufacturing and comments on short-run models of price–output behavior', *Journal of Post Keynesian Economics,* **9** (4), Summer, 593–603.

# Name Index

Aaronovitch, S. 142
Addison, J.T. 372, 383
Agliardi, E. 304, 358, 364
Ahmad, S. 26
Akerlof, G.A. 249
Alessie, R. 73
Amadeo, E.J. 283, 286, 292, 297, 301, 310, 328, 329, 330–31, 338, 341, 345, 365, 370, 403
Anand, P. 45
Andrews, P.W.S. 64, 95, 123
Appelbaum, E. 217, 220, 222
Arena, R. 148
Arestis, P. 174, 178, 192, 423
Arnon, A. 149
Arrous, J. 78, 81
Arrow, K. 39, 49
Asimakopulos, A. 127, 135, 226, 230–31, 265, 280, 290, 296–7
Attali, J. 77
Auerbach, P. 328

Bade, R. 249
Baran, P.A. 95, 102, 140
Baranzini, A. 7, 13
Barrère, A. 57
Baudrillard, J. 75
Baumol, W.J. 94, 96
Baxter, J.L. 62, 76, 223, 379
Bénassy, J.P. 386
Berger, P. 183, 190
Berle, A.A. 101, 108
Berry, R.A. 406
Bhaduri, A. 2, 131, 245, 276, 303, 334–5, 338, 343, 349, 362
Bianchi, M. 58
Bils, M.J. 240
Birner, J. 26
Blatt, J. 49

Blaug, M. 9, 12, 20
Blecker, R.A. 334, 340, 343
Boddy, R. 407
Boland, L.A. 10
Bootle, R. 171
Bortis, H. 360
Bosworth, B. 91
Bowen, W.G. 406
Bowles, S. 250
Boyer, R. 290, 318
Brunner, E. 95, 123, 127, 131, 136
Burkhardt, R.J. 15, 21
Burton, J. 383

Caldwell, B.J. 8, 9, 11, 21
Canterbery, E.R. 15, 21
Carabelli, A. 45
Caskey, J. 244
Carson, J. 136
Chamberlain, T.W. 364
Chandler, A.D. 103
Chick, V. 162, 182, 212
Chowdhury, A. 384, 414
Ciccone, R. 283, 291, 301, 330, 332, 421
Clarke, Y. 68
Clifton, J.A. 96, 105, 330
Coddington, A. 42, 50
Coghlan, R. 212
Colander, D. 15, 17, 19
Committeri, M. 283, 307, 328–30 355, 421
Cornwall, J. 391
Courbis, B. 150
Cournot, A.A. 18
Coutts, K. 142–3
Cramp, A.B. 186
Cripps, F. 151, 170, 378
Crotty, J. 407

Cyert, R.M. 51–2, 55, 95, 123

Darnell, A. 22, 24
Dalziel, P.C. 392, 394
Davidson, P. 39, 42, 48, 50, 110, 123, 128, 153, 155, 157, 159, 170, 182, 232, 347, 366, 375–6, 378, 382
Davies, J.E. 96, 100
Davis, R.G. 180, 184
Deaton, A. 86
Debreu, G. 39
De La Genière, R. 179
Del Monte, A. 297, 307, 316, 378
Denton, F.T. 22
Deprez, J. 147
Desai, M. 23
De Vroey, M. 17
Dixon, R. 36, 100, 278–9, 324
Dobb, M. 1
Doeringer, P.B. 218
Domowitz, I. 142
Dosi, G. 316
Dostaler, G. 2
Dougherty, C. 359
Dow, A.C. 192
Dow, S.C. 8, 11, 192, 284
Downey, E.H. 62
Duesenberry, J. 75
Duménil, G. 148
Dumouchel, P. 76
Dupuy, J.-P. 76
Dutt, A.K. 9, 135, 140, 232, 244, 296–7, 301, 303–4, 317, 331, 338, 341, 347, 363, 365, 370, 371, 392, 402–3, 406, 410, 421

Earl, P.E. 15, 16, 60, 62–3, 68–9, 72, 78, 144
Eatwell, J. 12, 13, 26, 30, 123, 193, 385
Eichner, A.S. 1–3, 8, 15, 63–4, 73–4, 82, 85, 95–6, 98, 101, 103, 104, 107–8, 119–20, 122–3, 128, 133, 136, 142, 145, 147, 161, 171, 174, 178, 184, 192–4, 202, 217, 224, 357–8, 360, 377–8, 384, 391, 410, 423
Encarnación, J. 71
Epstein, G. 334, 370
Ericsson, N.R. 170, 216
Evans, J. 22, 24

Evans, J.S. 101

Fazzari, S.M. 114, 244, 364
Findlay, R. 275, 293
Fisher, F.M. 32, 33, 35
Fog, B. 123, 127
Freedman, C. 185, 205, 207
Friedman, M. 7, 24, 215–16
Fujimoto, T. 234

Galbraith, J.K. 75, 89, 95, 99–104, 107, 134, 391
Garegnani, P. 30, 36, 88, 161, 193, 283, 349, 371, 394
Gaston, N.G. 79
Gedeon, S.J. 150, 177
Georgescu-Roegen, N. 45, 47, 50, 62, 71, 78–9, 84
Gimble, D.E. 218
Girard, R. 76
Godley, W. 142, 151, 170
Goodhart, C.A.E. 169, 179–81, 185–7, 190, 205, 210, 212–13
Goodwin, R.M. 284
Gordon, D.M. 250, 423
Gordon, M.J. 364
Gordon, R.J. 406
Gram, H. 13, 145
Granger, C.W.J. 22
Graziani, A. 151, 159–60
Green, F. 25, 58, 89–90
Grellet, G. 232
Guerrien, B. 37, 40
Guillaume, M. 77

Hagemann, H. 275
Hahn, F.H. 28, 36–7
Haines, W.M. 65
Hall, R.L. 95–6, 131
Hamermesh, D.S. 36, 219
Hamouda, O.F. 3
Harcourt, G.C. 3, 26, 107, 137, 232, 410
Harrington, R.L. 186
Harris, D.J. 26, 123, 226, 287, 310
Harrod, R.F. 14, 27, 95, 120, 131, 134, 194, 287, 349
Hayek, F. 14
Haynes, W.W. 132, 134
Heijdra, B.J. 6

Heiner, R.A. 13, 54, 60
Heinsohn, G. 150
Hendry, D.F. 23, 170, 216
Henry, J. 2, 13
Herendeen, J.B. 108, 110
Hey, J.D. 52, 56
Hicks, J.R. 3, 13, 97, 185, 194, 202, 379–81, 414
High, J. 49
Hitch, C.J. 95–6, 131
Hodgson, G. 11, 52, 55, 146, 248
Hoogduin, L. 42, 45
Hotson, J.H. 382, 404
Houthakker, H.S. 86
Hubbard, R.G. 142

Ingrao, B. 39
Ironmonger, D.S. 79
Isenberg, D.L. 199
Israel, G. 39

Jarsulic, M. 202
Johnston, J. 115, 122, 123
Jossa, B. 140

Kagel, J.H. 66
Kahn, R.F. 1, 98, 155, 187, 294, 296, 381
Kaldor, N. 1–4, 8, 14, 25, 27, 89–90, 95–6, 98, 103, 112–14, 123–4, 126–8, 134, 136, 138, 161, 170–71, 183–4, 186–7, 193–4, 201–2, 204, 210, 216, 230, 266, 283–5, 291, 293, 296, 302–3, 305, 316–17, 322, 324, 342, 348, 349, 357, 366, 375–6, 378, 381, 384–6, 422–3
Kalecki, M. 1, 2, 4, 27, 92, 95, 97–8, 109–11, 114, 123, 127, 129, 135–6, 140, 142–3, 157, 159, 176, 199, 201, 225, 231–2, 247, 263, 297, 303–5, 317, 348, 364, 382, 390–92, 398, 422
Kania, J.J. 102
Kapteyn, A. 73
Katouzian, H. 15
Kay, N.M. 64
Kelsey, D. 24
Kenyon, P. 106, 107, 137, 410
Keynes, J.M. 1–3, 12, 43–9, 54, 56–7, 59–60, 152–4, 157, 159–60, 175–6,
194, 200–201, 230, 232, 238, 247, 282, 290, 293, 297–8, 302, 347, 373, 375–8, 380–81, 390, 422
Kirman, A. 37, 40
Klamer, A. 15, 19
Knight, F. 12, 45–9
Kohli, M. 250
Kotz, D.M. 374
Koutsoyiannis, A. 99, 119, 122, 136
Krause, U. 72
Kregel, J.A. 3, 8, 123, 161, 193, 196, 282, 377–8
Kuhn, T. 4
Kurz, H.D. 232, 297, 318, 328, 334, 339

Lachmann, L.M. 43
Lakatos, I. 4
Lancaster, K. 78, 79, 80, 81, 84
Lanzillotti, R.F. 95, 131–2, 134, 139
Laudan, L. 4
Lavoie, M. 5, 7, 43, 113, 149, 151, 160, 170, 174, 178, 238, 276, 296, 360–61
Lawson, K. 8, 9, 44–5, 51, 57
Lea, S.E.G. 66, 78
Leathers, C.G. 101
Le Bourva, J. 152–3, 165, 171, 177, 184, 190–91, 201
Lee, F.S. 95–6, 100, 122, 126, 128, 131, 135–7, 143, 147
Le Héron, E. 193
Leibenstein, H. 75–6, 116, 250
Leijonhufvud, A. 5, 18
Leslie, D. 234
Levine, A.L. 144
Lévy, D. 148
Levy-Garboua, L. and V. 174
Lipsey, R.G. 20
Loasby, B.J. 43
Lowenberg, A.D. 6
Lubrano, M. 185
Lucas, R. 24, 48, 50
Lutz, M.A. 65–7, 78
Lux, K. 65–7, 78

Machina, M.J. 56
Mainwaring, L. 144
Malinvaud, E. 27, 98, 238, 293
Mansfield, E. 123

March, J.G. 51, 95
Marchal, J. 100, 101
Marglin, S.A. 18, 25, 58, 90–92, 293, 296, 334–5, 338, 343, 362
Marris, R. 76, 103–4, 111, 113–14, 116, 125
Marshall, A. 65
Marx, K. 3, 17–18, 103, 149
Maslow, A. 65, 78, 82
McCombie, J.S.L. 36, 324
McKean, J.R. 102
McKenna, E.J. 231
McKenzie, R.B. 67
Means, G.C. 95–7, 101
Menger, K. 65
Messori, M. 151
Meulendyke, A.-M. 185
Michl, T.R. 323–4
Milgate, M. 9, 13, 26, 30, 193
Minsky, H.P. 42, 46, 178, 184, 197, 199, 204, 207, 247, 358, 361
Mirowski, P. 18
Modigliani, F. 25
Mongin, P. 136
Mongiovi, G. 36, 222, 235
Moore, B.J. 116, 136, 161, 170–71, 174–7, 180–82, 187, 192–4, 201–2, 213, 216, 375
Moss, S.J. 26, 112
Mott, T. 114, 193, 196, 364
Muellbauer, J. 86
Musella, M. 177
Myatt, A. 245

Naples, M.I. 249
Nell, E.J. 12, 73, 76, 78, 151, 222, 225, 234–5, 238, 243, 247, 250, 270, 296, 338, 349
Newbold, P. 22
Niehans, J. 150, 214
Niggle, C.J. 162, 199, 201
Nordhaus, W. 142

O'Connel, J. 347
O'Donnell, R.M. 12, 45, 59
Okun, A.M. 96, 129, 134, 135, 229
Orléan, A. 57

Panico, C. 177, 194
Parguez, A. 14, 151

Parkin, M. 249
Paroush, J. 68
Parrinello, S. 52
Pasinetti, L.L. 2, 14, 17, 27, 58, 64, 75, 78, 90, 125, 145, 147, 193–4, 282–5, 289, 344, 347, 349
Patinkin, D. 246
Pencavel, J. 25, 220–21
Penrose, E.T. 103, 108, 115
Pesek, B.P. 25
Petersen, B.C. 142
Petri, F. 30, 231
Piore, M. 218, 379, 383
Pivetti, M. 194, 197, 231, 349, 361–2, 371
Podolski, T.M. 205, 212
Polemarchakis, H.M. 39
Pollin, R. 197, 203
Poole, W. 185

Read, L. 27
Reich, M. 219
Remenyi, J.V. 4, 5
Renuka, J. 24
Reynolds, P.J. 146, 392
Ricardo, D. 14, 18, 87
Richardson, G.B. 64
Rima, I. 222–3
Robbins, L. 13
Robinson, J. 1, 4, 9, 14–15, 26–7, 64, 83, 90, 95, 99, 103, 105, 108–9, 123–4, 127, 131, 138–9, 153, 175–7, 197, 199, 203, 225, 232, 263, 265–6, 282–4, 290–94, 296, 305, 308, 310, 342, 347–9, 358, 365–6, 376–7, 380, 385, 398, 407, 422
Rogers, C. 8, 13, 30, 36, 174, 178, 195
Roncaglia, A. 9, 12–13, 30, 87, 146–7
Rousseas, S. 182, 201, 204
Rowley, R. 24
Rowthorn, R.E. 120, 131, 226, 255, 258, 292, 297, 299, 304, 307, 313, 316, 318, 341, 382, 391, 405, 410, 414
Roy, R. 63, 87
Runciman, W.G. 76
Runde, J. 46
Rymes, T.K. 14, 27

Salant, W.S. 215

# Name Index

Samson, P. 142
Samuelson, P. 3, 27, 275
Sarantis, N. 348, 376, 392
Sato, K. 32
Sawyer, M.C. 2, 7, 142, 388
Sayer, A. 9
Scazzieri, R. 7, 13
Schefold, B. 26, 64, 86, 148, 234–5
Scherer, F.M. 132–3
Schlesinger, H. 179
Schmitt, B. 151
Schor, J. 238, 249
Schumpeter, J.A. 149
Schwartz, A. 216
Scitovsky, T. 223, 385–6
Seccareccia, M. 13, 155, 201, 217–18, 252, 292, 376
Semmler, W. 145, 361
Shackle, G.L.S. 12, 43, 48, 50, 62
Shaikh, A. 33, 35–6
Shapiro, C. 248
Shapiro, N. 118, 137
Shipley, D.D. 99, 132, 134
Simon, H.A. 9, 12, 35–6, 51–2, 55, 56, 123
Sinn, H-V. 49
Skott, P. 107, 126, 290, 328, 363, 365, 366, 370, 406
Slawson, N.D. 386
Smith, A. 148
Solow, R. 27, 35
Soutar, G.N. 68
Sonnenschein, H. 26, 37, 40
Spaventa, L. 275
Sraffa, P. 1, 3, 27, 87, 348
Steedman, I. 32, 87, 281, 342
Steiger, O. 150
Steindl, J. 95, 119–20, 124–5, 127, 136, 140, 160, 299, 303, 313, 317–18, 328, 329, 331, 364
Stiglitz, J.E. 248
Strauss, J.H. 102
Sweezy, P.M. 95, 102, 140
Sylos Labini, P. 97, 107, 110, 124–5, 131, 147, 149, 201, 348, 363, 392

Tarling, R. 394
Tarshis, L. 136

Tatom, J.A. 240
Taylor, L. 135, 304, 364, 376, 392
Taylor, L.D. 86
Temin, P. 183
Theunissen, A.J. 164
Thirlwall, A.P. 324, 343
Thomas, J.G. 180
Thurow, L.C. 22
Tobin, J. 247
Tooke, T. 149
Townshend, H. 194
Tullock, G. 67
Tversky, A. 56

Veblen, T. 75, 89, 105
Veenhoven, R. 77
Vianello, F. 332–4, 348

Walsh, V.C. 13, 145
Walters, A.A. 8, 122–3
Watts, M.J. 79
Webb, S. 250
Weintraub, E.R. 4, 43
Weintraub, S. 43, 135, 182, 373
Weiss, L.W. 140
Weisskopf, T.E. 250, 343
Wells, P. 195
Whittaker, J. 164
Wicksell, K. 149
Wiles, P. 145, 383
Wilkinson, F. 394
Winslow, E.G. 10, 12, 57
Wojnilower, A.M. 189
Wood, A. 104, 108–9, 112, 114, 116, 118, 131, 137, 218, 358–60, 379, 383
Wray, L.R. 149, 151, 192, 198, 200–201, 349
Wulwick, N. 229

Yellen, J.L. 220, 235, 265
Yordon, W.J. 127–8
Young, A. 103

Zannoni, D.C. 231

# Subject Index

accumulation
  desired rate of 287–8
  and the expected rate of growth of sales 329
  model of Eichnerian 293, 357–8, 360, 410
  model of endogenous Kaleckian 303–16, 398–402, 414
  model of given Kaleckian 298–303
  model of neo-Keynesian 284–96, 356–7
  model of profit squeeze 339, 413–14
  stability or instability of 288–90, 308–10, 324–5, 329, 353–4, 360
animal spirits
  definition of 232
  and investment 231–2, 348
  monetary policies to dampen 294–6
  and uncertainty 47, 49
  of union leaders 377
asymmetries 9, 87, 387
auxiliary hypotheses 8, 18

Banking School 149
behaviouralism 64, 95
borrowing norms *see* leverage ratios; liquidity ratios
bounded rationality *see* procedural rationality

Cambridge
  capital controversies 3, 26–36, 275
  economists 1–2
  equation 262, 285, 305, 366
capacity
  actual rate of utilization of 227, 260–73, 301, 305–16
  endogenous rates of utilization of 285, 291, 298, 302–3, 354–6, 418–21
  full 120, 266, 315–16
  optimal rate of utilization of 328
  planned excess 124–6, 330
  practical 119, 328
  standard rate of utilization of 131–2, 146, 257–9, 272, 351
  theoretical 119
capital to capacity ratio 132, 299
causality
  and the Cambridge equation 285–6
  cumulative 321
  and investment 160–61
  and post-Keynesian economics 7, 9, 296
  and temporal ordering 9, 24
central banks
  accomodating and non-accommodating 182, 205–6, 210–11
  initiatives of 181–9
  in the monetary circuit 161–9
chaos 24, 284
circuit theory 5, 151–69
class analysis
  and accumulation 370–71
  and consumer behaviour 78, 88
  and organicism 7, 10
classical economics
  and the definition of consumer goods 86–7
  and gravitation 148, 182–3, 421
  and the post-classical synthesis 4, 14
consumer
  bandwagon effect 75
  choice, post-Keynesian principles of 62–5
  envy and relative deprivation 76–7

goods and their characteristics 78–85
goods and groups of goods 80–81
hierarchy 73, 75–8, 222–3
snob and Veblen effects 76
conventions
   and banking practices 177
   and cost accounting 134–6
   and hours of work 223–4
   and the standard rate of utilization of capacity 330
   and technical coefficients 119
   *see also* fairness; rules of thumb
constant marginal costs
   below full capacity 120–23
   and empirical evidence 122–3, 126–8
   at the industry level 128, 230
   and stylised facts 8
   and upward drift 120–21, 126–8
cost-plus pricing
   determinants of 137–41
   and stylised facts 8
   variants of 129, 256–9
   and variations of demand 141–4
crowding out 167

data mining 22
debt ratios *see* leverage ratios; liquidity ratios
degree of monopoly 129, 257, 304, 391
depreciation 311, 318
diminishing returns 5, 8, 94, 226, 229, 375
direct costs *see* constant marginal costs
dividends *see* retention rate
divorce of management and ownership 101–5

economics
   and ideology 17–18
   and mathematics 18–19, 284, 423
   and the sociology of its profession 15–16
effective demand
   curve and accumulation 304
   and employment 233–9
   and expectations 232
   and income distribution 265–6, 291
   and stability 237–8
   and unemployment benefits 270–71
   and wage differentials 266–70
   *see also* accumulation
employment
   curve *see* labour
   and distribution 265
   and technical progress 319, 321
Engel curves, 74, 85
eurobanks 214–15
Evolutionarists 5, 58
exchange models 13–14
expansion frontier 115–16

fairness
   and interest rates 194
   and prices 134
   and real wages 379–80
falsification 8, 20–21, 24
finance, initial and final 159–60
finance frontier
   of the firm 109–14
   at the macroeconomic level 358–9
financial fragility hypothesis 199
financial innovation 203–15
full-cost pricing
   compared to mark-up pricing 130, 135–6
   definition of 129, 131, 256
   and procedural rationality 55

government deficits
   and accumulation 310, 313–14
   and the creation of money 165–8, 216
   and inflation 404
gross substitutability, axiom of 39, 67

habits 12, 55, 61, 90
   *see also* conventions; rules of thumb
historical time 9, 128, 147, 157, 282–4, 394
humanistic economics 64–5

impossibility theorem 26, 36–40
income distribution *see* accumulation; effective demand, and income distribution; inflation, barrier; inflation, distributional conflict view of; inflation, radical view of; interest rates, as a distributive

variable; interest rates, and the standard rate of profit
income effects
  and household choice 64, 73, 83–5
  in macroeconomics 88, 93
  and perverse effects in general equilibrium models 39
  and the supply of labour 220–22
increasing risk, Kalecki's principle of
  earlier version (1937) 176, 199
  later version (1971) 109–10, 176, 363–4
individualism 10–11, 40, 58
inflation
  and accumulation 398–421
  barrier 290–96, 376–7, 380–81, 395–6, 412
  distributional conflict view of 377, 381–2, 391–402
  and endogenous money 216, 372–3
  and excess demand 372, 375–6
  and indexation 392–4
  and interest rates 194, 402–3
  Radical view of 374
  a rainfall theory of 23
  and the wage–cost mark-up relation 373–5
  wage–wage 380–81, 414–17
  see also technical progress and inflation
information
  and corporate power 100
  and inflation 382–5
  overload of see procedural rationality, and computational requirements
Institutionalists 2, 5, 9, 12, 58, 218, 383
instrumentalism 7–9, 12, 20, 128
interest rates
  and the actual rate of profit 348, 366–70
  and bond rates 166
  and the demand for money 185–6
  and the discount rate 163, 195–6
  as a distributive variable 193–4
  as an exogenous variable 150, 193–4, 347
  and the finance frontier 110–13, 358–9
  as an indicator of monetary policy 186, 189, 409
  and investment 188, 231
  and liquidity preference 192–203
  and the monetary circuit 156–7
  and rising activity 197–203
  and the standard rate of profit 349, 360–62, 402–4
investment as a function of
  the expected rate of profit 286
  the normal rate of profit 332–4
  the normal rate of utilization 328
  the rate of profit net of interest 365
  the rate of utilization 304, 331, 362–3
  the share of profit 334, 362
  technical progress 317
  see also animal spirits; interest rates
Keynes effect 243, 248
labour
  demand and productivity 240–43
  demand and real wages 235–40
  hierarchy 381, 384–5
  overheads 127, 226, 266, 272–4, 343, 351–2
  power 248
  productivity 227–9, 255
  supply 220–24
leverage ratios
  and accumulation 360–61, 363–4
  and procedural rationality 55, 61
  and the supply curve of money 197–200
lexicographic ordering
  and characteristics 78–85
  and needs 64
  and wants 68–72
liability management 162–3, 212–14
life-cycle hypothesis see savings, and the permanent income hypothesis
liquidity preference see interest rates
liquidity ratios
  and the behaviour of banks 197–202
  and procedural rationality 55, 106
long period
  and full employment 36
  and the neo-Ricardians 196, 283
  and short period 3
managerial school 103

markets
  contestable 96
  imperfect 95–8
mark-up pricing
  definition of 129, 256
  and effective demand 259–66
  and marginalist pricing 136–7
  and net share of profits 265–6, 302
  and procedural rationality 55, 61
  and stylised facts 8
Marxists *see* Radicals
maximization
  of growth rate 103–5, 107, 117–18
  of profits 8, 9, 99, 107, 117–18, 136–7, 234
  of utility 5
  *see also* optimization
measurement without testing 25, 219
megacorp
  and its characteristics 95
  and diversification 117
  and permanence 100
monetarism 22, 182, 205, 215
money
  and accumulation 347, 371
  broad 207–8
  and credit 153, 175–6
  and credit control 188–9
  and the credit divisor 174, 207–10
  and effective demand 161
  and the finance motive 153
  high-powered 161, 171–4
  and monetary policy 185, 189, 210–11
  in an open economy 189–92
  and reverse causation 171–4, 204–5
  and the standard post-Keynesian endogenous view 170–78, 347
  and stylised facts 8
  supply as a rising curve 197–203
  velocity of 203–11
  *see also* central banks; interest rates; liability management; overdraft economies

needs
  and characteristics 80–84
  defined against wants 65–7
  overlapping 64, 82–3
neoclassical
  aggregate economics 5, 28–32, 41
  economics and aggregate demand 244–7
  economics and empirical work 20–26, 32–36
  economics and its essentials 6–14
  economics and household choice 61–2
  economics and money 150, 373
  economics and its standard definition 13
  general equilibrium theory 4, 9–10, 36–41
  synthesis 3
neo-Ricardian economics
  and the classical analysis of consumer goods 86–8
  and cost-plus prices 144–8, 349, 361, 421
  and interest rates 194, 196
  and the rate of accumulation 286, 332–4, 354–6, 370
  and regularities 9, 12, 196
  in relation to the synthesis 2, 5, 371, 422
  and uncertainty 12–13
non-compensatory filtering rules 69–72
normal-cost pricing 131
  *see also* target-return pricing
normal rate of profit *see* profits, standard rate of
normal rate of capacity utilization *see* capacity, optimal rate of utilization of; capacity, standard rate of utilization of
norms *see* conventions; rules of thumb

Okun's law 229–30
ophelimity 75
opportunity
  cost 66
  frontier *see* expansion frontier
optimization 13, 15, 51, 61, 327–8
organicism 10–12, 57
overdraft economies
  definition of 161–2
  imperfect or impure 178–9, 183–4, 191
  and overdrafts of firms 175

overheads *see* full-cost pricing; labour, overheads

paradox
  of costs 307, 312–15, 319, 326–7, 333–4, 339
  macroeconomic 11
  of profit share changes 280–81, 340–43
  of thrift 290, 292, 302, 311–12, 327, 333, 339–40, 346, 422
Pasinetti's theorem 285, 344, 347
Penrose effect 116–17
Phillips curve 389, 405–7
Pigou effects *see* real balance effects
post-classical research programme
  definition of 4–5, 422
  essentials of 6–14
  and money 150
post-Keynesian economics
  and the aggregate demand curve 244–7
  and the aggregate supply curve 244
  definition of 1–4
  and the IS curve 235–6
  synthesis of 1–4
power
  and firms 99–103, 393, 395
  and growth 103–5
  and labour unions 387–9, 395–6
price leaders 96, 134, 137, 384
prices
  administered 95–8, 148, 386–7
  fair 134
  natural and market 148
  non-clearing 95, 133, 146
  production 144–8, 421
pricing *see* cost-plus pricing; mark-up pricing; target-return pricing
prime costs *see* constant marginal costs
procedural rationality
  and computational requirements 52–4
  definition of 51–2
  and household choice 63
  and presuppositions 11–13
  rules of 55–8
production functions
  and accounting identities 35–6, 323

  aggregate 5, 41
  CES 33–6
  Cobb-Douglas 27, 32–6, 323–4
  with fixed coefficients 8, 27, 119
  shifts and movements of 27
production models 13–14
profits
  actual rate of 146, 305–16, 332–4, 354–5
  cost curve 299, 305
  inflation theory *see* inflation barrier
  margin of 129, 137–8, 257, 304
  as a mean to grow 105–6, 117
  microeconomic share of 144–5
  in the monetary circuit 157–60, 167–8
  net share of 257, 262–70, 274, 279–80, 301–2, 340–43
  possible convergence between the actual and the normal rate of 331, 354–7, 418–21
  propensity to save out of 231, 262
  realization curve 287, 304, 308
  standard rate of 132–3, 146, 257–9, 272, 332–4, 353–5
  *see also* maximization, of profits

Quantity Theory 3, 204, 372–4

Radicals 2, 5, 218, 248, 286, 296, 338, 375
rationality *see* procedural rationality; substantive rationality
real balance effects 91, 216, 243–8, 422
real wage resistance 380–81
realism 7–9, 12, 21, 61, 148, 421
regulation school 5, 321
rentiers
  and accumulation 347, 370–71
  and inflation 382
  and luxury goods 87
reproducibility
  and constant marginal costs 97
  and cost-plus prices 137, 145
  and post-classical synthesis 7, 14, 27
retained earnings
  and the availability of finance 105–14
  and profits in the monetary circuit 158–9

retention rate 108, 113, 348, 365
returns to scale
  constant 115, 283
  increasing 103–4, 324
risk
  definition of 43
  and procedural rationality 55
rules of thumb 10–12, 55–61, 67–8
  *see also* conventions

savings
  and the classical hypothesis 91–2, 231, 364
  and the disequilibrium hypothesis 89–90
  and interest and dividend income 365, 370
  and the monetary circuit 155
  and the permanent income hypothesis 24–5, 90–91
  and profits in the circuit 160
  and the relative income hypothesis 75
  and salaries of managers 92, 267–70, 344–7
  *see also* Cambridge, equation
scarcity 7, 13–14, 39, 145, 150, 377
Socioeconomists 5
Sonnenschein–Mantel–Debreu theorem *see* impossibility theorem
stagflation 402
standard rate of return *see* profits, standard rate of
storytelling 9
Structuralists 5
stylised facts 8
substantive rationality
  and computational requirements 52
  definition of 51
  and presuppositions 11–13
substitution effects
  and consmer theory 64, 67, 73, 80–81, 85–8, 93, 422
  and the firm 119, 283, 422
  and general equilibrium models 39, 41
  and money 150
  and the supply of labour 220–22
supply and demand analysis 5, 9, 30, 41, 148

target-return pricing
  and accumulation 350–58
  and bargaining 417–21
  definition of 131–3
  and effective demand 271–5
  and the interest rate 360–61
  and procedural rationality 61
  in vertically integrated economy 257–9
technical progress
  and accumulation 316–27
  and depreciation 318
  and effective demand 240–43
  and employment 319–21
  function 322–4
  and inflation 383, 385, 415–16
  and interest rates 194
  and the margin of profit 318–20
  and marginal costs 128
  and its proper measurement 27

uncertainty
  definition of 43–4
  and ergodicity 48
  gap 54
  and money 42
  and neoclassical objections to it 47–50
  and nihilism 50
  and procedural rationality 55–8
  and realism 44, 53
  and stability 11, 13, 59–61
  and the weight of an argument 45–7
unemployment
  benefits *see* effective demand
  involuntary 8, 248, 253–4
  Keynesian 237–8
  planned 389–90
  rate of change of 406–8
  and wealth effects 243–8
utilization function 225

Verdoon's law 322–7
verificationism 24

wage differentials
  between classes of workers 266–70
  between sectors 277–9
wage efficiency effects *see* Webb effects
wage and price policies 391, 409
wage/profit

frontier 292, 295–6, 356
positive relation 305–7
Walrasian economics *see* neoclassical, general equilibrium theory

wealth effects *see* real balance effects
Webb effects 248–55

X-inefficiency effects 116, 250